Special Edition Using Linux

Fifth Edition

Jack Tackett, Jr.

Steve Burnett

Rob Napier

Jeff Tranter

QUE®

A Division of Macmillan Publishing USA
201 W. 103rd Street
Indianapolis, Indiana 46290

Contents at a Glance

Special Edition Using Linux, Fifth Edition

International Standard Book Number: 0-7897-2180-5

Library of Congress Catalog Card Number: 99-63851

Printed in the United States of America

First Printing: October 1999

01 00 99 4 3 2 1

Trademarks

This publication was produced using the Advent **3B2** Publishing System.

Warning and Disclaimer

Publisher
Dean Miller

Executive Editor
Jeff Koch

Acquisitions Editor
Gretchen Ganser

Development Editor
Maureen A. McDaniel

Managing Editor
Lisa Wilson

Senior Editor
Susan Ross Moore

Copy Editor
Chuck Hutchinson

Indexer
Erika Millen

Proofreaders
Christina Smith
Megan Wade

Technical Editor
John Scroggins

Team Coordinator
Cindy Teeters

Software Development Specialist
Michael Hunter

Interior Designers
Louisa Klucznik
Ruth Lewis

Cover Designer
Dan Armstrong

Copy Writer
Eric Borgert

3B2 Design
Daniela Raderstorf

3B2 Layout
Susan Geiselman
Daniela Raderstorf

CONTENTS

About the Authors

Jack Tackett, Jr. is the Senior System and Network Administrator for Railinc's Netredi E-Commerce project, serving over 16 million transactions a month to North America's rail industry. He oversees the daily administration for the site's servers and network conntections across North America. He has been a system administrator for a variety of other operating systems—from Unisys Mainframes to UNIX and Windows NT. Jack's books include the bestselling *Special Edition Using Linux* (Editions 1-4), *Red Hat Unleashed*, *Using Visual C++*, and *The Visual C++ Construction Kit*. Jack has been quoted in various news media including the *Wall Street Journal*, *PC Magazine*, and *The LA Times*. He invites your comments at `tackett@usinglinux.com`.

Steve Burnett is an information technology consultant in Research Triangle Park, NC. His most recent degree was a M.S. in Technical Communication. His professional interests have centered around systems administration, integration, and interoperability. Any comments may be sent to him at `burnett@netwharf.com`.

Rob Napier (`rnapier@employees.org`) is an engineer with Cisco Systems in Research Triangle Park, NC. He has been working with Linux since 1995 and is currently an officer for the Triangle Linux Users Group (`www.trilug.org`). He is the author of the "Finding the Answers in Linux" mini-HOWTO (`http://www.employees.org/~rnapier/linuxanswers.html`).

Jeff Tranter started using Linux in 1992. He is the author of the book *Linux Multimedia Guide*, co-author of *Tcl/Tk in a Nutshell*, maintains the Linux CD-ROM and Sound HOWTO documents, and has written some small Linux utilities and a number of magazine articles. In spite of all that, he still considers playing with Linux a hobby and works by day as a software developer for a large telecommunications company. He lives in Kanata, Ontario, sometimes called Canada's Silicon Valley North, with his wife and two teenagers.

Dedication

To Peggy, Mary Louise, and Carolyn—Love always...

—Jack

To Merrie.

—Steve

Acknowledgments

From Jack Tackett:

First, I want to thank all the readers of the first four editions of this book for their patronage and for their helpful and insightful comments. Your comments are important and make a difference, please keep them coming. You have made this a better project!

I want to say thank you for the tremendous efforts put forth by the Linux developers scattered across the globe. I also want to acknowledge the fine contributions begun by Linus Torvalds and continued by so many others around the world—thanks for creating Linux and breathing life into such a monumental effort! Also, thanks to Matt Welsh, et al., for the work on the Linux Documentation project.

Next, I want to express my regards for the people at the Que Continuum. I especially want to thank Gretchen, Maureen, Chuck, Susan, Jeff, and John for their help in getting this project off the ground and finished.

To Steve Burnett for once again lending his immense talents to getting this project completed. Also thanks to Paul Barrett for his initial help with the research that eventually led to this book.

To David Fugate of Waterside, the greatest agent in the world. Thanks for all your help, David!

To my friends Paul Barrett, Keith E. Bugg, Gregg and Beckie Field, Dave and Lola Gunter, Israel Janovich, Dianna Smith, Kell and Joy Wilson, Dennis and Carolyn Golden, Adrian Polimico, Mark and Jennifer Shaw, and Joe Williams: Thanks for the memories! Thanks to my combined family—the Tacketts and the Martins—for their support in all my endeavors. Also, a big thank you to the best cousins in the world—Bill and Hope Tackett, Jr.

I'd like to thank Dr. Joe Daugherty of the University of North Carolina-Asheville for all his support. Also thanks to Myrtice Trent of the Blue Ridge Technical Community College. Thanks for the help and encouragement you both provided.

Next a great big thank you to my co-workers at Railinc—thanks to everyone!

Finally, to my wife Peggy, who has yet again put up with me spending endless hours at the computer writing yet another computer book. Thanks, sweetheart, and I love you!

From Steve Burnett:

To the Linux development community at large: your continued efforts have made enormous improvements to the usage and capabilities of the operating system and applications. In the short time since Jack and I wrote the previous edition of this book, Linux has grown so much we felt a new edition was necessary.

Locally, the members of the recently formed Triangle Linux User Group have collectively been of great help with their activity and enthusiasm. For more specific thanks: Jack, nice to work together again. My thanks to Rob Napier for contributing on this edition, and to David Fugate for his usual coordination. Of course, thanks to Merrie for tolerating my extra work.

INTRODUCTION

Linux is no longer a "not ready for prime time" operating system! That's what we wrote in the beginning of the fourth edition of this book, and a few months later Linux exploded onto the mainstream consciousness. Major news media from the *Wall Street Journal* to CNN seemed to discover Linux overnight (probably not as a complete result of the fourth edition though <g>). Today Linux is a viable alternative to the high-priced, closed-ended operating systems of the past. Linux is one of two operating systems gaining market share, and it's gaining share more quickly than the other one, Windows NT.

Many commercial uses of Linux abound, ranging from being used to create many of the fantastic special effects for James Cameron's Oscar-winning mega hit *Titanic;* to being used as the operating system for new network computers; to being used to create inexpensive, massively parallel supercomputers as in the Beowulf project. Many large-scale IS departments are no longer afraid to adopt Linux into their operations, even though many had Linux systems clandestinely running services before the media attention! As Linux evolves, you have to keep up with the changes; that's why you will find plenty of new material in this fifth edition of Que's popular *Special Edition Using Linux*.

Many chapters have been rewritten to highlight the most available distributions—Red Hat, Caldera, and Debian. In addition, the book contains updated and expanded coverage of X Windows and two of the more popular window managers, KDE and GNOME. We've rearranged several chapters to provide a better flow and ease of use in finding information when you need it. Also, we've considered your suggestions and have revamped the installation chapters and provided more troubleshooting tips throughout the book.

If you're just tuning in, though, you might want to know just what the heck Linux is. In 1991, Linus Torvalds, then a 23-year-old college student, began a personal project to expand the Minix operating system into a full-fledged clone of the UNIX operating system that was so popular on college campuses. The project is still evolving: Linux is continuously updated and expanded by literally hundreds of people around the world.

Therefore, Linux is a unique animal in the computer (r)evolution. It isn't a commercial product backed by a huge corporation; rather, it's an operating system born of frustration and built by a ragtag team of computer enthusiasts around the world. This team used Internet resources to communicate and build the operating system named Linux.

But don't think Linux is just a hobby for hackers around the world—it's not! Plenty of commercial products are being written specifically for Linux. In fact, several companies are porting their UNIX-based applications, such as Corel's WordPerfect, to Linux. As a matter of fact, Corel has adopted the Debian distribution of Linux for its new Network Computer and has released the resulting software to the development community. Companies such as IBM, Oracle, and Dell are actively supporting Linux and the Open Source community.

Note

Although estimating the total number of Linux users or installations in the world is difficult, a working estimate shows between 5,000,000 and 10,500,000 active Linux users worldwide. For more information, check out the following URL:

```
http://www.redhat.com/redhat/linuxmarket.html
```

If you don't understand what a *uniform resource locator (URL)* is or how to use it, don't despair! This book will help you learn how to make your way around the Internet using Linux.

→ See "Understanding URLs," p. 703

Many Fortune 500 companies use Linux for internal projects and mission-critical applications. And recently, large companies such as IBM, Oracle, and Corel began to embrace the concept of open solutions by releasing their own software into the development community, just as Linus Torvalds and others released their software to the world.

Plenty of free applications and utilities are also available for Linux. Since the inception of Linux, almost the entire GNU library of utilities has been ported to Linux, and the X Windows GUI system—so popular on UNIX-type workstations—also has been ported. GNU (a recursive acronym for *GNU's Not UNIX*) is a project started by one man to make software available to anyone who wants access. The GNU General Public License in Appendix C describes the philosophy under which Linux and many other fine software packages are distributed. The accompanying CD-ROMs contain many of these packages.

This book provides you with enough information to use and enjoy Linux. The accompanying CD-ROMs contain the Red Hat 6.0, Caldera OpenLinux 2.2 Lite, and Debian 2.1 distributions, each of which uses the 2.2 Linux kernel.

At this point, the first order of business is to help you pronounce the word *Linux*. To most Americans, the pronunciation is *LEN-nucks*, with the short *i* sound. The official pronunciation is *LIH-nucks*.

ON THE WEB

You can hear Linus pronounce *Linux* in English at the following URL:

`ftp://ftp.linux.org/pub/kernel/SillySounds/english.au`

WHO SHOULD USE THIS BOOK?

Anyone interested in the Linux phenomenon can use this book as a guide to installing, configuring, and using Linux. Linux is often called a UNIX clone, but it's actually a POSIX-compliant multiuser, multitasking operating system for Intel 386 and later processors. (POSIX is an international standard for operating systems and software detailing interoperability standards.) Linux doesn't require MS-DOS or Windows to operate; in fact, Linux can replace those programs on your computer.

Because Linux is still evolving, it's imperative that you understand the possibility of losing existing data on your system. *Do not install Linux without first backing up your system.* You might need to repartition your hard drive to make room for this new operating system, although you can install Linux on top of MS-DOS or repartition your hard drive without losing data. If you take the proper precautions, you can easily install and enjoy Linux.

Note

The most current version of Linux is always available on the Internet from the sources listed in Appendix A, "Sources of Information." The accompanying CD-ROMs contain the latest possible versions of Linux, but due to the rapid development of this popular operating system and the chaotic process in which it's developed, providing the latest and greatest versions on a CD-ROM is impossible. In fact, although all efforts are made to keep the book and CD-ROMs in sync, that also is nearly impossible. Unlike commercial software, which changes infrequently and under controlled conditions, Linux and related software are perpetually dynamic.

Because Linux is similar to UNIX, many of the operations and procedures necessary for using Linux also apply to many UNIX systems. By learning to use Linux, you also learn how to use most UNIX systems.

UNIX has evolved over the years to become the premier operating system used by hundreds of thousands of people throughout the world. This isn't an accident. Earlier versions of UNIX were harder to manipulate than other operating systems, but despite this fact, UNIX managed to amass a distinguished following in academic and scientific circles. These professionals realized not only what a powerful, flexible, and manageable operating system UNIX is, but also its potential to be the best operating system ever. Their efforts have culminated in the UNIX of today with its marvelous utilities bundled with the newest communications capabilities and graphical user interfaces (GUIs).

The UNIX of today promises again to revolutionize the personal computer industry and perhaps redirect the industry's growth. UNIX has evolved from a minicomputer operating system to one that crosses all hardware platforms. We have no reason to think that this evolution will stop. UNIX may well become the standard for what most users dream of—complete standardization and compatibility of all computer systems, regardless of size or power.

UNIX comes in several flavors from a variety of vendors, including versions for the Intel PC platforms, but most of these versions cost big bucks. Linux provides a relatively inexpensive—free if you have access to the Internet—solution to learning about UNIX-type procedures and commands, understanding the X Windows GUI, and accessing the Internet via Linux.

Who Should Not Use This Book?

If you are a Linux kernel hacker or a UNIX guru, this book may not be your cup of tea. This book is a great resource if you want to know more about Linux and UNIX but have never been involved with either operating system.

However, if you know how to install Linux and maneuver around in UNIX, you might still find this book of use, particularly if you are only a UNIX user and have never had the chance to perform system administration tasks. Several sections of the book explain the finer points of system administration and how to maintain a Linux/UNIX system. Typically, a normal UNIX user is never allowed to perform these system administration tasks, but with Linux, you become king of the hill and ruler of the system, free to do whatever you want to do!

Now, if you don't have a clue what MS-DOS is or what a floppy disk looks like, you might want to brush up on some computer basics before tackling Linux. Linux isn't for the faint of heart; you must have some understanding of how a computer works. If the thought of repartitioning or reformatting your hard drive sends shivers down your spine, you probably should put off learning Linux for a while until you become more comfortable with your computer system.

Hardware Needed to Use This Book

Most of Linux has been written across the Internet by computer *hackers*(not *crackers*, but people who truly enjoy writing software that accomplishes something). Thus, the hardware supported by Linux is the hardware owned by the various hackers.

Many hardware manufacturers are accepting Linux as a valid market and are beginning to write drivers for their hardware. They are also providing hardware specifications to the world so that Linux developers can write software to work with the hardware. Many companies are also farming out work to Linux developers specifically to write drivers for their hardware. These companies then release the code into the community under GNU guidelines. This is a dramatic change from a few years ago when many manufacturers withheld information for proprietary and competitive reasons.

Table I.1 provides a brief list of the supported hardware. If you don't have the correct hardware, it's unlikely that you'll be able to boot Linux and productively use the system.

Forewarned is forearmed! If you are unsure about your hardware, then you can check out the Linux Hardware Database on the Web at the following site:

`http://ldh.datapower.com.`

Red Hat also maintains a list of supported hardware at the following site:

`http://www.redhat.com/corp/support/hardware/intel/60/rh6.0-hcl-i.ld.html`

Our Linux Environment

We feel it's only fair to let you know what types of systems we used to create this book. The test machine was a Pentium II 233-based system with 64MB of RAM and an Adaptec SCSI controller, a 6 gigabyte Segate SCSI drive, an NE2000 PCI Ethernet card, a 24x ATAPI CD-ROM, and a Matrox Mystique video card. The name server used in our network is a no-name 486dx100 system with IDE drives and 32MB of memory running Red Hat Linux. This machine is also the main sendmail server for the site. The main Web server is a Digital Equipment Alpha (multia) also running Red Hat Linux. The entire site is connected to the Internet via an ISDN line using an Ascend Pipeline 75 router.

TABLE I.1 A BRIEF LIST OF HARDWARE SUPPORTED BY LINUX

Item	Description
CPU	Intel 386 and later (and compatibles), DEC Alpha, Sun Sparcs, and PowerMacs.
Bus	ISA, EISA, VESA local bus, and PCI; the MicroChannel bus isn't fully supported yet.
RAM	Minimum of 2MB of RAM; 4MB is recommended.
Hard drive controller	AT standard hard drive controller; Linux supports MFM, RLL, ESDI, and IDE controllers. Linux also supports several popular SCSI drive and CD-ROM drive controllers.
Disk space	Minimum of 20MB; 80MB is recommended.
Monitor	Linux supports Hercules, CGA, EGA, VGA, and SVGA video cards and systems; X Windows has other requirements detailed in Chapter 24, "Installing the X Windows System."
Mouse	Any standard serial mouse (for example, Logitech, Microsoft, or Mouse Systems) or bus mouse from Microsoft, Logitech, or ATIXL.
CD-ROM drive	Any CD-ROM drive that uses a true SCSI interface works; some proprietary CD-ROM drives such as the SoundBlaster series are also supported. CD-ROM drives known to work with Linux include NEC CDR-74, Sony CDU-45, Sony CDU-31a, Mitsumi CD-ROMs, and Texel DM-3042.
Tape drive	Any SCSI tape drive works; other drives hosted from a floppy controller may also be supported. Now, the Colorado Jumbo 120 and 250 using the QIC 80 format are supported.
Printer	If you can access your parallel printer from MS-DOS, you should be able to access it from Linux; some fancy features might not be accessible.

TABLE I.1 A BRIEF LIST OF HARDWARE SUPPORTED BY LINUX

Item	Description
Ethernet card	If you have access to an Ethernet network, Linux supports several standard Ethernet cards for accessing your network. Cards supported include 3Com's 3C503, 3C509, and 3C503/16; Novell's NE1000 and NE2000; and Western Digital's WD8003 and WD8013.

ON THE WEB

The following Web site provides more information on MicroChannel bus support:

`http://glycerine.itsmm.uni.edu/mca/`

HOW TO USE THIS BOOK

You might prefer to read this book from cover to cover. The information progresses from simple to complex as you read through the various sections and their chapters. Because the information is separated into seven parts and five appendixes, each with its own particular emphasis, you can choose to read only those parts that appeal to your immediate needs. Don't, however, let your immediate needs deter you from eventually giving attention to each chapter. Whenever you have the time, you can find a wealth of information in them all!

PART I: INSTALLING LINUX

Part I, "Installing Linux," provides a detailed overview of the Linux system as well as instructions to get Linux up and running. It consists of seven chapters:

- Chapter 1, "Understanding Linux," introduces the Linux operating system and provides a general overview of the various components that make up the Linux system and various distributions.
- Chapter 2, "Linux Installation Overview," provides a general overview of installing various Linux distributions, with specific emphasis on supported hardware and potential problems and their resolutions.
- Chapter 3, "Installing Red Hat Linux," gives detailed instructions for installing the version of Red Hat provided on the accompanying Red Hat CD-ROM.
- Chapter 4, "Installing Caldera OpenLinux," gives detailed instructions for installing the version of OpenLinux provided on the accompanying CD-ROM.
- Chapter 5, "Installing Debian Linux," provides a basic introduction to installing the version of GNU/Debian Linux provided on the accompanying CD-ROM.

- Chapter 6, "Adding Sound Cards and Other Hardware," provides instructions on adding sound to your Linux system as well as other hardware.
- Chapter 7, "Upgrading and Installing Software," provides you with the information needed to install new software using the Red Hat Package Management system (RPM) and the Debian Package Management system. The chapter also covers installing software from the Internet and tells you how to patch existing programs.

PART II: SYSTEM ADMINISTRATION

Part II, "System Administration," provides basic information on configuring and managing a typical Linux installation. The following eight chapters cover this topic:

- Chapter 8, "Understanding System Administration," provides a brief background of the processes and procedures needed to configure and maintain a Linux system.
- Chapter 9, "Using the vi Editor," instructs you how to use UNIX's visual editor. Although vi isn't the most productive editor in the world, every Linux/UNIX system has it, and sometimes it's the only editor available for use.
- Chapter 10, "Booting and Shutting Down," details the various actions that happen when you boot up or shut down a Linux system, and it explains why you can't simply switch off the power supply. This chapter contains a complete description of the files Linux uses to boot.
- Chapter 11, "Managing User Accounts," shows you how to add, delete, and manage user accounts on your machine.
- Chapter 12, "Backing Up Data," explains the necessity of backing up your data, as well as the procedures needed to back up your Linux system.
- Chapter 13, "Improving System Security," gives you a brief overview of system security on Linux systems and then explains the procedures needed to maintain a reasonably secure system.
- Chapter 14, "Configuring the Linux Kernel," illustrates how to configure a kernel, no matter what distribution you are using, for your hardware.
- Chapter 15, "Working with the Linux PPC Kernel," illustrates how to configure a kernel for the Power PC chip found in a variety of computers such as Apple Macintosh systems.

PART III: WORKING WITH LINUX

Part III, "Working with Linux," increases your skill at working with the Linux command-line tools and utilities. This section also provides detailed knowledge of how to be more productive with various Linux features. Everything you learn in these eight chapters can be transferred easily to other UNIX-type systems:

- Chapter 16, "Understanding Linux Shells," introduces you to the magical world of Linux shells, the powerful capabilities that exist through the use of shell scripting, and the different shells you might encounter with different versions of Linux.
- Chapter 17, "Managing Multiple Processes," explores the capabilities of Linux when you run more than one process at a time. You learn how to initiate and manage multiple processes, as well as how to control and stop them.
- Chapter 18, "Printing," covers all the printing basics, from issuing print commands and checking printer status to canceling print jobs and dealing with common printing problems.
- Chapter 19, "Understanding the File and Directory System," provides an overview of file permissions, users, and file types.
- Chapter 20, "Managing File Systems," provides an overview of creating, mounting, and using a file system under Linux.
- Chapter 21, "Managing NFS and the Automounter," provides a detailed explanation of Network File System (NFS) services and how to configure Linux to use NFS with other systems.
- Chapter 22, "Managing NIS and LDAP," provides an overview of Network Information Services (NIS) and how to configure Linux to use NIS with other systems in your network.
- Chapter 23, "Using Samba," provides a detailed explanation of Samba and how to configure Linux to use Samba with other Linux systems, as well as with NT systems.

Part IV: Using X Windows

Part IV, "Using X Windows," provides a greater understanding of the procedures and processes necessary to install, configure, and use the X Windows system on Linux. This section also provides an overview of the top two window managers for X KDE and GNOME.

- Chapter 24, "Installing the X Windows System," provides you with the necessary information to get the X Windows system up and running under Linux. Under Linux, the X Windows system is called XFree86 and is similar to other GUI environments such as Microsoft Windows or the OS/2 Workplace Shell.
- Chapter 25, "Using X Windows," provides you with information necessary to use the X Windows system under Linux.
- Chapter 26, "Working with KDE," provides you with information necessary to use the KDE window manager with X under Linux. KDE is typically the default window manager for Debian Distributions.
- Chapter 27, "Working with GNOME," provides you with information necessary to use the GNOME window manager with X under Linux. GNOME is installed by default on Linux distributions based on Red Hat.

Part V: Network Administration

Part V, "Network Administration," provides a greater understanding of the procedures and processes necessary to administer a robust Linux system.

- Chapter 28, "Understanding the TCP/IP Protocol Suite," provides an overview of the network transport protocol suite in use today on the Internet.
- Chapter 29, "Configuring a TCP/IP Network," shows you how to set up and configure TCP/IP on Linux.
- Chapter 30, "Configuring IP Masquerade," gives you the basics of IP masquerade. This chapter covers compiling, installing, and configuring the necessary files to create a firewall and basic administration of the system.
- Chapter 31, "Connecting to the Internet," illustrates how to configure and use Point-to-Point Protocol (PPP) lines to connect with the Internet.

Part VI: Using the Internet

The four chapters in Part VI, "Using the Internet," provide a basic overview of the Internet.

- Chapter 32, "Accessing the Network with `telnet`, `ftp`, and the `r-` Commands," provides you with information on how to use various programs such as Telnet and FTP to access information around the world.
- Chapter 33, "Surfing the Internet with the World Wide Web," gives you an overview of using various Linux utilities to search for and retrieve information from the Internet, with emphasis on the Web.
- Chapter 34, "Using Electronic Mail," gives you an overview of electronic mail (email) and how to use it in Linux.
- Chapter 35, "Surviving Usenet News," provides you with an explanation of Usenet newsgroups, as well as instructions for accessing this global community of newsgroups.

Part VII: Setting Up Linux Internet Servers

Part VII, "Setting Up Linux Internet Servers," provides detailed information on setting up and running various Internet servers on Linux. Five chapters make up this part:

- Chapter 36, "Getting Started with Apache," gives you the basics to get started with Apache. It covers compiling and installing Apache, and it gives you the basic configuration options.
- Chapter 37, "Configuring an FTP Server," discusses the major configuration options for creating an anonymous FTP server.
- Chapter 38, "Configuring Domain Name Service (DNS)," provides you with the necessary information to get your system up and running with Domain Name Service (DNS).

- Chapter 39, "Configuring Email," provides you with the necessary information to get your email system up and running with sendmail.
- Chapter 40, "Configuring a Usenet News Service," provides you with the necessary information to set up Usenet news on your system.

PART VIII: APPENDIXES

The appendixes provide supplementary information on installing and using Linux, as well as licensing information for using Linux. The book contains the following five appendixes:

- Appendix A, "Sources of Information," provides you with a detailed listing of books, magazines, Usenet newsgroups, and FTP sites dealing with Linux. Also, you get a brief glimpse of the myriad resources available to you as a Linux user.
- Appendix B, "The Linux How-To Index," provides a list of all the main and mini-How-Tos available. How-Tos provide information on *how to* accomplish a specific task with Linux. This How-To comes directly from the Internet.
- Appendix C, "The GNU General Public License," is the verbatim license for using GNU applications. It describes your responsibilities when modifying, distributing, or using GNU programs.
- Appendix D, "The Open Source Definition," is the verbatim definition of the Open Source Movement as defined at `www.opensource.org`.
- Appendix E, "What's on the CD-ROM?" discusses the contents of the three CD-ROMs included with this book.

CONVENTIONS USED IN THIS BOOK

This book uses several special conventions that you need to become familiar with. These conventions are listed here for your reference:

- Linux is a *case-sensitive*operating system; that means when this book instructs you to type something at a command or shell prompt, you must type exactly what appears in the book, exactly as it is capitalized.
- This book uses a `monospaced typeface` for Linux commands to set them off from standard text.
- If you're instructed to type something, what you are to type also appears in `monospace text`. For example, if the book gives the instruction

  Enter `cat`

  you must press the letters *c*, *a*, and *t* and then press the Enter key.

- Keys are sometimes pressed in combination; when this is the case, the keys are presented like this:

  Ctrl+h

  This example implies that you must press and hold the Ctrl key, press the *h* key, and then release both keys.

Note This book uses a convention for key names that may vary from what you are accustomed to. To avoid confusion in the case-sensitive UNIX environment, this book uses lowercase letters to refer to keys when uppercase letters may be the norm. For example, this book uses the form Ctrl+c instead of the form Ctrl+C (the latter form may make some readers wonder whether they should press Ctrl and Shift and *c*).

- Some sample listings show a portion of the screen after you type a specific command. These listings show the command prompt or shell prompt—usually a dollar sign ($)—followed by what you type in **`bold monospace`**. Don't type the dollar sign when you follow the example on your own system. Consider this example:

  ```
  $ lp report.txt &
  3146
  $
  ```

  You should type only what appears in **`bold`** on the first line (that is, type `lp report.txt &` and then press Enter). The rest of the listing shows Linux's response to the command.

- When discussing the syntax of a Linux command, this book uses some special formatting to distinguish between the required portions and the variable portions. Consider the following example:

  ```
  lp filename
  ```

  In this syntax, the *`filename`* portion of the command is a variable; that is, it changes depending on what file you actually want the `lp` command to work with. The `lp` is required because it's the actual command name. Variable information is presented in *`italic monospace`*; information that must be typed exactly is not in italic.

- In some cases, command information is optional; that is, it's not required for the command to work. Square brackets (`[]`) enclose optional parts of the command syntax. Consider the following example:

  ```
  lp filename [device1] [abc]
  ```

  Here, `lp` is the command name and is neither optional nor variable. The *`device1`* parameter is both variable and optional (it is in italic and enclosed in square brackets); this means that you can type any device name in place of *`device1`* (without the brackets), or you can type nothing at all for that parameter. The `abc` parameter is optional (you don't have to use it if you don't want to), but it's not variable; if you use it, you must type it exactly as it appears in the book—again, without the brackets.

- Tips, notes, and cautions appear throughout the book in special formats to make the information they contain easy to locate. Longer discussions not integral to the flow of the chapter are set aside as sidebars with their own headings.
- The book also contains many cross-references to appropriate topics throughout the book. A typical cross-reference appears as follows:

→ See "Using X Windows," p. xxx

PART I

INSTALLING LINUX

CHAPTER 1

UNDERSTANDING LINUX

In this chapter

by Jack Tackett, Jr.

WHAT IS LINUX?

To understand Linux, you must first understand the question, "What is UNIX?" UNIX is arguably the most versatile and popular operating system found today on scientific and high-end workstations.

Linux is a project initiated to create a working version of UNIX on Intel-based machines, more commonly referred to as IBM PC-compatible computers that most people are familiar with.

The Linux operating system has been designed and built by hundreds of programmers scattered around the world. The goal has been to create a UNIX clone, free of any commercially copyrighted software, which the entire world can use.

Actually, Linux started out as a hobby of Linus Torvalds while he was a student at the University of Helsinki in Finland. He wanted to create a replacement for the Minix operating system, a UNIX-like operating system available for Intel-based PCs.

Note

Many of the terms used within the chapter are discussed later, so don't worry if some of them are unfamiliar to you now.

Linux is basically a UNIX clone, which means that with Linux you get many of the advantages of UNIX. Linux multitasking is fully *preemptive*, meaning that you can run multiple programs at the same time, and each program seems to process continuously. Other systems, such as Microsoft Windows 3.1, allow you to run multiple programs, but when you switch from one program to another, the first program typically stops running. Microsoft's Windows 98 and Windows NT are more like Linux because they allow preemptive multitasking. Linux allows you to start a file transfer, print a document, copy a floppy, use a CD-ROM, and play a game—all at the same time.

Linux is fully multiuser capable, which means that more than one person can log in to and use the system at the same time. Although the multiuser feature may not be very useful at home, it gives many people in a corporate or university setting access to the same resources at the same time yet eliminates the need to duplicate expensive machines. Even at home, you'll find the capability to log in to separate accounts on what are called *virtual terminals* very useful. Also from home, you could provide your own personal online service by using Linux and several modems.

→ See "Managing Users," p. 47

Linux is free—or nearly so. In fact, for the price of this book, you've received three fully functioning distributions of Linux (Red Hat Linux, Caldera OpenLinux, and Debian) on the accompanying CD-ROMs. Everything you need to get Linux up and running is provided on the CD-ROMs, including hundreds of applications.

Linux provides a learning opportunity unparalleled today. Here, you have a complete working operating system, including source code, with which to play and learn what makes it tick. Learning what makes Linux tick is something you can't do in a typical UNIX environment, and it's definitely something you can't do with a commercial operating system because no vendor is willing to give away the source code.

Finally, Linux gives you a chance to relive—or perhaps experience for the first time—the chaos of the early PC revolution. In the mid-1970s, computers were the provinces of large organizations, such as government, big business, and universities. The ordinary person had no access to these marvels. But with the introduction of the microprocessor and the first personal computers, things changed. At first, PCs were the province of the *hackers*—dedicated computer enthusiasts—who hacked the early systems because those systems could do very little in the way of productive work. But as the hackers experimented and became entrepreneurs, and as the capabilities of PCs increased, PCs became commonplace.

Note

The term *hacker* has unfortunately taken on a negative connotation in today's society. See the section "Hackers" later in this chapter for more details on hackers versus crackers.

The same is true today of system software (that is, operating systems). Linux represents a breakaway from a system controlled by large organizations that stifle creativity and enhancements in the name of market share.

WHY USE LINUX?

You'll want to use Linux because it's the only operating system today that's freely available to provide multitasking and multiprocessing capabilities for multiple users on IBM PC-compatible hardware platforms. No other operating system gives you these same features with the power that Linux enjoys. Linux also separates you from the marketing whims of the various commercial providers. You aren't locked into upgrading every few years and paying outrageous sums to update all your applications. Many applications for Linux are freely available on the Internet, just as the source code to Linux itself is available on the Internet. Thus, you have access to the source code to modify and expand the operating system to your needs—something you can't do with commercial operating systems such as Windows NT, Windows 98, MS-DOS, and OS/2.

Freedom from commercial vendors is also a potential downside to using Linux. Because no single commercial vendor supports Linux, getting help isn't just a phone call away. Linux can be finicky and may or may not run properly on a wide range of hardware. The potential to damage or delete data files residing on your system also exists because Linux is constantly changing and doesn't go through a rigorous testing process before it's released.

Linux isn't a toy; it's a system designed to give users the feeling of tinkering with a new project, just like in the beginning of the PC revolution. However, Linux is relatively stable on many systems and presents you with an inexpensive opportunity to learn and use one of the most popular operating systems in the world today—UNIX. Many CD-ROM vendors and software companies, such as Red Hat and Caldera, now support the Linux operating system. Linux is an alternative to other UNIX systems and can be used in place of those sometimes-expensive systems. If you program on UNIX systems at work, for example, you might want a UNIX-like system at home. Are you a system administrator of a UNIX system at work? If so, you can perform some of your duties from home by using Linux. Or do you not have a clue as to what UNIX is? Well, then, Linux provides a low-cost introduction to UNIX.

Linux also provides you with easy access to the Internet and the rest of the information superhighway.

Linux Distributions

Linux is distributed by many different organizations, each of which provides a unique collection of programs along with the core group of files that constitute a Linux release. The current release of Linux on the accompanying CD-ROMs is kernel version 2.2.5-15. This distribution may also contain experimental kernels with drivers for unique hardware. Under Red Hat, the kernels are part of the Red Hat Package Management (RPM) system and are installed as part of the system. Caldera's OpenLinux follows the same scheme because it is based on the Red Hat distribution.

Luckily for you, by having bought this book, you've made the decision of which distribution to use rather easy. The three CDs accompanying this book offer complete versions of Red Hat's, Debian's, and Caldera's distributions (the companies' Internet versions, not the ones sold commercially). The following lists many distributions that are available on the Net and from various CD-ROM vendors:

- MCC Interim Linux
- Linux Mandrake
- LinuxPPC
- LinuxWare
- Slackware Linux
- S.u.S.E. Linux
- TurboLinux
- Debian Linux
- Yggdrasil Plug-and-Play Linux CD-ROM and the Linux Bible

- Caldera (this vendor uses Red Hat's distribution as the base for its distribution, then adds additional features such as Novell and Windows support along with customer support)
- Red Hat

The "Distribution How-To" also provides an exhaustive list of Linux distributions. You'll learn later in this chapter how to access the various How-Tos that accompany each Linux release.

Tip #1 from *Jack*

After installing Linux, you can find the distribution How-To in the directory `/usr/doc/HOW_TO/`.

Before installation, you can find the file in the following directories:

- **Red Hat:** `<cdrom-drive letter>:doc/HOWTO/other-formats/html/Distribution-HOWTO.html`
- **Caldera:** `<cdrom-drive letter>:col/doc/HOWTO/other-formats/html/Distribution-HOWTO.html`
- **Debian: not available from the CD-ROM.**
- **On the web at** `http://www.linux.org/help/howto.html`.

ADVANTAGES OF USING LINUX

Using Linux has many advantages. Of the many operating systems available today, Linux is the most popular free system that's widely available. For the IBM PC, Linux provides a complete system with built-in multiuser and multitasking capabilities that take advantage of the entire processing power of your 386 and higher computer systems.

Linux comes with a complete implementation of the TCP/IP networking protocol. With Linux, you can connect to the Internet and the vast wealth of information it contains. Linux also provides a complete email system to send messages back and forth through cyberspace.

Linux also has a complete graphical user interface (GUI), XFree86, that's based on the popular X Window System. XFree86 is a complete implementation of the X Window System that can be distributed free of charge with Linux. XFree86 provides the common GUI elements you find on other commercial GUI platforms, such as Windows and OS/2.

Today, all these features are available for Linux and are basically free. All you have to pay is the price for acquiring the programs from the Internet or via mail order (available from several different vendors). Of course, because you've purchased this book, you already have the entire Linux system on the accompanying CD-ROMs.

OPEN SYSTEMS PORTABILITY

In the never-ending quest for standardization, many organizations have taken a renewed interest in the direction in which operating systems are developing. UNIX hasn't gone unnoticed. The drive to standardize UNIX stems from the many UNIX variants now available. You'll learn more about how those variants were developed in the following section.

Efforts have been made to combine, collate, and otherwise absorb all versions of UNIX into a single all-encompassing version of the operating system. Initially, the effort met with guarded enthusiasm, and some effort was expended on coming to terms with blending the different versions. As with many noble efforts, this one was doomed to failure because developers weren't willing to sacrifice part of what they had already invested in their particular versions. (Sadly enough, many developers still feel that way.)

However, the continued existence of UNIX varieties isn't necessarily cause for alarm. Despite the different varieties, all are still inherently superior to all other operating systems available today because each contains the same elements described in the preceding pages.

Portability is merely the capability to transport an operating system from one platform to another so that it still performs the way it should. UNIX is indeed a portable operating system. Initially, UNIX could operate on only one specific platform—the DEC PDP-7 minicomputer. Today, the many UNIX variants can operate in any environment and on any platform, from laptops to mainframes.

Portability provides the means for different computer platforms running UNIX to communicate accurately and effectively with any of the other platforms. These systems can communicate without the addition of special high-priced after-market communications interfaces. No other operating system in existence can make this claim.

APPLICATIONS

Although using an operating system is sometimes fun in and of itself, it isn't the reason most people use a computer. Most people need to do productive work with their computers. Linux has literally thousands of applications available today, including programs for spreadsheets, databases, word processing, application development in a variety of computer languages, and telecommunications packages to get you online. Linux also comes with a wide range of games, both text- and graphics-based. When you need a break from the drudgery of the daily grind, Linux can provide a few minutes (or hours) of relaxation.

ADVANTAGES FOR COMPUTER PROFESSIONALS

If you're a computer professional, Linux provides a wealth of tools for program development. It includes compilers for many of the top computer programming languages today, such as C, C++, and Smalltalk. If you don't like those languages, Linux provides you with tools, such as Flex and Bison, that you can use to build your own computer languages. These tools come with the CD-ROMs accompanying this book, but their commercial counterparts can cost several hundred dollars each. If you want to learn one of the aforementioned languages but don't want to spend hundreds of dollars for another compiler, Linux and its development tools are for you.

Linux also allows you to communicate with your company's office systems. And if you're a UNIX system administrator, Linux can help you perform your duties from home. Although working from home is booming as more companies realize the productivity increases and savings to overhead, perhaps some day you too can use Linux to do your job at home and then only occasionally visit the office for personal meetings.

Two of the industry's buzzwords are *open systems* and *interoperability*, both of which refer to the capability of many different systems to communicate with one another. Most open systems specifications require Portable Operating System Interface (POSIX) compliance, which means some form of UNIX. Linux meets those standards today. In fact, Linux was designed for source-code portability, so if you have a corporate program running on one version of UNIX, you should be able to port that system relatively quickly to a system running Linux.

Corporations are insisting on these types of open systems so that they aren't locked into using any one vendor. Remember the old adage "Don't put all your eggs in one basket"? Corporations today are becoming leery of systems controlled by single companies because those in control can dictate how the software behaves and what hardware systems the software supports. If that company chooses a direction that's not good for your corporation, tough luck. You're stuck with that company's decision whether you like it or not. With UNIX/ Linux and open systems, however, you're in control of your own destiny, and many of today's top companies—IBM, Dell, and Nortel—are embracing this new technology. Why? Because if the operating system doesn't have a feature they need, they can find plenty of consultants who can make the necessary changes, which is possible because you have the source code to your operating system.

EDUCATION

Students, note that Linux provides you with editors to write your assignments and spell checkers to proof those assignments. With Linux, you should be able to log in to your school's computer network. Of course, with access to the Internet, you also have an instant tap into the limitless wealth of information there. You also have access to thousands of experts in a wide variety of subjects who can answer your questions. Linux can be useful, even if your major isn't computer science.

Linux provides such advantages for so little because of the spirit and philosophy of the community that built and continues to build it. Linux is a great experiment that took on a life of its own. Literally hundreds of computer hackers from around the world contributed to its development. Linus Torvalds first developed what became Linux for himself and later released his brainchild to the world under the GNU copyleft (as opposed to a *copyright*).

→ See "The GNU General Public License," p. 861

HACKERS

At the basic level, Linux is a system built by and for hackers. The popular definition of *hacker* has a negative connotation in today's society, but computer hackers aren't criminals by their definition of the word. Their definition deals with how they approach any activity in life—not just when dealing with computers. Hackers feel a certain depth of commitment and an enhanced level of excitement at hacking a system. *Hacking* basically means learning all there is to know about a system, becoming immersed in the system to the point of distraction, and being able to fix the system if it breaks.

Hackers basically want to know how a system they find interesting works. Most are not interested in making money or seeking revenge, although certain hackers do cross that line to become what the hacker community calls *crackers*. Computer hackers become outraged when they're compared with these vandals and criminals the popular media now call *hackers* (instead of *crackers*). We hope that Linux gives you a feeling of what it's like to be a hacker, and ideally, you will avoid becoming a cracker.

If you're simply the curious type and want to learn more about UNIX, Linux is for you. In it, you'll find a fully functional version of UNIX to which you have free, unrestricted access—something you seldom find in the real world. Most UNIX users are given accounts on UNIX machines that grant them only limited rights and privileges, and in such cases, normal users can't use or experiment with certain UNIX/Linux commands. But this environment isn't conducive to learning all about UNIX. With Linux, however, you have complete run of the place and can do what you want whenever you want. Of course, with this great power comes great responsibility: You must learn how to manage a real UNIX system, which can be fun in and of itself.

DISADVANTAGES OF USING LINUX

Linux has many advantages, and disadvantages. No operating system can meet the needs of everyone, including Linux. The following section outlines some of those disadvantages.

LACK OF TECHNICAL SUPPORT

Perhaps the biggest disadvantage of using Linux is the fact that no single corporate entity is in charge of its development. If something goes wrong or you have a problem, no toll-free technical support numbers are available for you to call for help. But when you really think about it, do such numbers provide real support for current commercial systems? How often are you referred elsewhere—providing you get through to tech support—to have your question answered? How many times are you asked to post a question on an online service to get help? Well, with Linux, although no tech support number is available, literally thousands of users in the online communities can help answer your questions. (See Appendix A, "Sources of Information," for places to go for help.) Also, many providers, particularly Red Hat and Global Knowledge, now offer certifications in installing and maintaining Linux systems.

In the past, having no source of technical support was a problem with Linux, no doubt about it. The same was true of Linux applications. Although a few commercial programs are available for Linux, most programs are developed by small groups and then posted to the world via the Internet. Many developers, however, do help out with questions. Today, most of the major software application vendors are rushing to port their products to Linux—among them Oracle, Corel, and SAS.

Note

Many commercial companies are now building Linux applications that they sell. For people to use their applications, though, these companies typically provide a free copy of a Linux distribution along with their product and thus supply technical support for that version of Linux.

HARDWARE PROBLEMS

Other disadvantages are that Linux can be hard to install, and it doesn't work on all hardware platforms. Unlike in a commercial program development operation, for which a cohesive group spends months building and testing a program against a variety of conditions and hardware, Linux developers are scattered across the globe. No formal quality-assurance program exists. Developers release their programs when they feel like releasing them. Also, the hardware supported by Linux depends on the hardware each developer owns while writing that portion of the code. Thus, Linux doesn't work with all the hardware available for PCs today.

Of course as many software vendors rush to support Linux, so too have hardware vendors. IBM is the biggest proponent of Linux. It goes out of its way to ensure hardware from various vendors will work on Linux (and other Unix OS) in their Netfinity server line. In fact IBM adopted Apache as its Web server.

Caution

If your system doesn't have the hardware supported by Linux, you'll have problems installing and running the system. Chapter 3, "Installing Red Hat Linux," Chapter 4, "Installing Caldera OpenLinux," and Chapter 5, "Installing Debian Linux," provide details on the hardware you need to use Linux. You can also search the Linux Hardware database online at `http://lhd.datapower.com`.

If you have the hardware that's supported, chances are you'll have no problem installing and using Linux. If you don't have the necessary hardware—well—Linux developers expect you to fix it. After all, it is a hacker's system.

INABILITY TO USE CURRENT SOFTWARE

Another disadvantage is that your current applications for such operating systems as DOS and OS/2 more than likely won't work under Linux. Fortunately, those other systems can *coexist*with Linux, overview of; thus, although you can't use both operating systems at the same time, you can leave Linux and boot the other operating system to use your applications there.

Work is in progress on Linux emulators that run DOS and Windows programs, as well as the Executor project to run Macintosh programs under Linux. Red Hat and Caldera both support 16-bit DOS programs. The WINE emulator is still under development.

Tip #2 from
Jack

To use DOS under Red Hat Linux, simply type the command `dos`:

```
[root@test]#dos
```

You can then run any available 16-bit DOS programs.

Also, Caldera, Inc. has ported Sun's Windows Applications Binary Interface (WABI) product to Linux. WABI allows Windows 3.1 applications to run under X on Linux. Caldera sells this product, unlike many Linux applications, along with several other Linux applications. However, Caldera provides the Red Hat distribution of Linux free of charge to run the applications the company sells.

To install Linux, you typically have to repartition your hard drive—although repartitioning is not always necessary. *Repartitioning* means erasing part of your drive, which wipes out your programs and data on that drive. Currently, you cannot install Linux safely without repartitioning. If you plan to install Linux, you should back up your disk first (making two or three backups is safest). Also, you might not have enough hard disk space to install Linux and keep your other software on the same disk, in which case you have to decide what goes and what stays. No matter what, you have to back up your system, repartition the drive, restore your old software, and then install Linux, which can be a time-consuming and error-prone process.

Note

Some alternatives to repartitioning your hard drive do exist. You can share space with Linux and DOS, or you can use a program that repartitions your drive without erasing files. These alternatives do work, but you still face the possibility of losing data while installing the system. Also, by repartitioning, you gain improved performance and better control over the amount of disk space used for Linux.

The amount of disk space you need to run Linux depends on the various applications you plan to install. You should have at least 700MB free on the drive where you want to install Linux, in addition to the programs and data you want to keep from your other operating systems. If you have 1.6GB free, you should have more than enough space for a full installation of Linux.

Lack of Experience

Finally, unless already a UNIX guru, you must learn how to manage a Linux system. Unlike DOS, Windows, and OS/2, Linux and UNIX need to be managed. The manager, usually called the *system administrator*, or *sys admin*, is responsible for maintaining the system. The system administrator is responsible for performing such duties as adding and deleting user accounts, backing up the system on a regular basis, installing new software, configuring the system, and fixing things when they go wrong (which happens even on commercial versions of UNIX in use every day). Because UNIX doesn't run perfectly 100 percent of the time, the system administrator must maintain the system. This need for maintenance presents a great opportunity for you to learn how to be a system administrator on a UNIX system.

Tip #3 from *Jack*

There are many training programs now available, so if your company is leery of using Linux, just show them support and training is available (and that you of course would be the perfect person to attend the training).

See the following Web sites for more information:

```
http://www.redhat.com/products/training.html
http://db.globalknowledge.com/catalog/course.asp?course=6900
```

→ See "Understanding Centralized-Processing Systems," p. 186

Overcoming the Disadvantages

At first, you might think that using Linux puts you all alone in the world, making you survive by yourself. This notion is partially true because Linux started life as a hacker's system, and hackers like to tinker and fix systems themselves. But today, because the popularity of Linux has grown, many sources of help are available.

Thousands of pages of documentation are provided with most distributions of Linux. You can find this information in the `/doc` directory on the accompanying CD-ROM.

In addition, several magazines are devoted to Linux, and you can find plenty of online sources of information and online users willing to help with your questions. If you work for a commercial entity and need a professional contractor, these contractors also are available. After you install Linux, you can also find a wealth of online help providing information on almost every Linux command and program available. Check out Appendix A, "Sources of Information," to see that you're not alone.

DISAPPEARING DISADVANTAGES

Although all the disadvantages discussed in the preceding sections still exist, many are slowly disappearing as new companies come into existence to build on Linux and offer new solutions. Two such companies are Red Hat and Caldera. We chose Red Hat as the primary distribution for this book because of its ease of use and installation. Caldera also uses the Red Hat package management system for installation and its own programs, LISA and Lizard, to install the distribution. Both Red Hat and Caldera provide online, fax, and email-based technical support for their products and their versions of Linux.

THE COMMERCIAL SIDE OF LINUX

Linux has become an enterprise-ready operating system. Many companies use Linux as an inexpensive Web server for their intranets. Linux is also used for various network applications (such as DNS), for routing, and as firewalls. Also, many Internet service providers (ISPs) use Linux as their main operating system.

Many commercial programs are also available for Linux, overview of; you can check them out in the "Commercial How-To." Other organizations, such as NASA and Digital Domain, use Linux to render various images, including high-resolution planetary images (NASA) or realistic special effects for movies such as *Titanic* (Digital Domain).

Tip #4 from Jack

After installing Linux, you can find the commercial How-To in the directory `/usr/doc/HOW_TO/`.

Before installation, you can find the file in the following directories:

- Red Hat: `<cdrom-drive letter>:doc/HOWTO/other-formats/html/Commercial-HOWTO.html`
- Caldera: `<cdrom-drive letter>:col/doc/HOWTO/other-formats/html/Commercial-HOWTO.html`
- Debian: not available from the CD-ROM.
- On the Web at `http://www.linux.org/help/howto.html`.

COMMERCIAL PROGRAMS FROM RED HAT

Although Red Hat released one of the most popular distributions of Linux, the company also has produced several commercial programs. Red Hat has also created a Linux package manager, called RPM (Red Hat Package Manager), which it released under the General Public License (GPL) for other distributions to use.

Along with its GPL versions of Linux and RPM, Red Hat also provides an application framework called Applixware, which contains a word processor, a spreadsheet program, a presentation graphics program, a mail tool, and various development tools. Red Hat also provides a commercial version of Motif for developing and running X under Linux.

Commercial Programs from Caldera

Caldera originally provided a networking-based distribution based on Red Hat and technology from Novell, where many of Caldera's principals previously worked. Their second-generation product, Caldera OpenLinux Base, is a low-cost UNIX-like operating system based on the Linux 2.2 kernel and the OpenLinux distribution from Caldera. It includes a graphical user interface capable of managing system and networked resources, including client and server interaction with the Internet and all major networking systems. The menu-driven installation is provided in multiple languages. Caldera OpenLinux Base is a non-dedicated gateway and includes all Internet client, server, and router protocols and services. OpenLinux Base also includes a commercial X server from MetroLink and a fully licensed Linux version of the Netscape Navigator.

Caldera also provides Corel's WordPerfect for Linux, as well as an Internet office suite containing a bundle of complete business applications. These commercial programs, as well as dozens more, are available from Caldera.

Caldera also licensed and ported Sunsoft's WABI technology to allow end users to run the most popular Windows 3.1 applications on Linux-based system software.

Commercial Programs from Debian

As for Debian, Corel recently selected the Debian distribution for their upcoming KDE/WordPerfect offering.

A Brief History of Linux

The history of Linux is tied to the history of UNIX and, to a lesser extent, a program called Minix. Minix was an operating system tutorial written by the well-known and respected computer scientist Andrew Tannebaum. This operating system became popular on several PC platforms, including MS-DOS-based PCs. But more on Minix later—first, a brief history of UNIX.

Although AT&T created the UNIX operating system, many other companies and individuals have tried to improve the basic idea over the years. The following sections examine a few of the leading variants in use today.

AT&T

Ken Thompson (a computer programmer for AT&T Bell Laboratories) and a group of people working under Ken's direction developed an operating system that was flexible and completely compatible with programmers' varied needs. Legend tells that Ken, who had been using the MULTICS operating system, dubbed this new product UNIX as he joked with others on his development team. He was lampooning the MULTICS multiuser operating system: UNIX was derived from *uni*, meaning *one* or *single*, followed by the homophone X. Perhaps the greater joke in this bit of folklore lies in the fact that MULTICS is remembered by few users today as a viable multiuser operating system, whereas UNIX has become the de facto industry standard for multiuser multitasking operating systems.

BSD

Berkeley Software Distribution (BSD), University of California at Berkeley, released its first version of UNIX, based on AT&T's Version 7, in 1978. BSD UNIX, as it's known throughout the industry, contained enhancements developed by the academic community at Berkeley that were designed to make UNIX more user-friendly. The user-friendly "improvements" in BSD UNIX were an attempt to make UNIX appeal to casual users in addition to the advanced programmers who liked its flexibility in conforming to their changing demands. Despite being less than 100 percent compatible with AT&T's original UNIX, BSD UNIX did accomplish its goals: The added features enticed casual users to use UNIX.

BSD has become the academic UNIX standard. The original creators of BSD have since released a version for the Intel platform called, appropriately enough, BSD. This version too has a limited distribution on the Internet and via CD-ROM vendors. The authors also wrote several articles a few years ago in the computer magazine *Dr. Dobb's Journal*, detailing the design and implementation of BSD386 or FreeBSD. Today, BSDI, the commercial version of FreeBSD, is another popular operating system similar to Linux.

USL

UNIX System Laboratories (USL) was an AT&T spin-off company that had been developing the UNIX operating system since the early 1980s. Before Novell purchased it in 1993, USL produced the source code for all UNIX System V derivatives in the industry. However, USL itself didn't sell a shrink-wrapped product at that time.

USL's last release of UNIX was UNIX System V Release 4.2 (SVR4.2). SVR4.2 marked USL's first entry into the off-the-shelf UNIX marketplace. In a joint venture with Novell, which temporarily created a company called Univel, USL produced a shrink-wrapped version of SVR4.2 called UnixWare. With Novell's purchase of USL, Novell shifted the focus of USL from source-code producer to UnixWare producer. Novell has now sold its version of UNIX to the Santa Cruz Operation (SCO).

Recently, SCO made a free single-user license available to the public for using SCO UNIX. The program costs $19 for the distribution media, not unlike Linux. However, whereas SCO provides a copy of its operating system, it doesn't provide the source code. Some in the Linux community suspect Linux is giving the UNIX community—or at least the SCO community—some stiff competition.

XENIX, SunOS, and AIX

Microsoft developed its UNIX version, XENIX, in the late 1970s and early 1980s, during the peak of the PC revolution. Processing power available in PCs began to rival that of existing minicomputers. With the advent of Intel's 80386 microprocessor, it soon became evident that XENIX, which had been developed specifically for PCs, was no longer necessary. Microsoft and AT&T merged XENIX and UNIX into a single operating system called System V/386 Release 3.2, which can operate on practically any common hardware configuration. XENIX is still available today from Santa Cruz Operation (SCO), a co-developer with Microsoft, whose efforts to promote XENIX in the PC market have made this version of UNIX one of the most commercially successful.

Sun Microsystems has contributed greatly to UNIX marketability by promoting SunOS and its associated workstations. Sun's work with UNIX produced a version based on BSD. Interestingly enough, AT&T's SVR4 is compatible with BSD, too—no doubt an offshoot of AT&T and Sun Microsystems' collaboration in UNIX System V Release 4.0.

IBM's venture into the world of UNIX yielded a product called Advanced Interactive Executive (AIX). Although AIX isn't as well known as some other UNIX versions, AIX performs well and has no problem holding its share of the operating system market. It's perhaps the old belief that any UNIX version is an unfriendly, unforgiving operating system that has kept AIX from gaining a better market reception.

Linux

As you learned earlier in this chapter, Linux is the brainchild of a computer science student named Linus Torvalds. Linux began life as a hobby project in 1991 for Linus, who was then 23. He hoped to create a more robust version of UNIX for Minix users. Minix, as mentioned earlier, is a program developed by computer science professor Andrew Tannebaum.

The Minix system was written to demonstrate several computer science concepts found in operating systems. Torvalds incorporated these concepts into a standalone system that mimics UNIX. The program was widely available to computer science students all over the world and soon generated a wide following, including its own Usenet newsgroups. Linus Torvalds set out to provide his fellow Minix users with a better platform that could run on the widely available IBM PC. Linus targeted the emerging 386-based computers because of the task-switching properties of the 80386 protected-mode interface.

What follows are some of the statements Linus made when announcing his Linux program:

> "After that it was plain sailing: hairy coding still, but I had some devices, and debugging was easier. I started using C at this stage, and it certainly speeds up development. This is also when I started to get serious about my megalomaniac ideas to make 'a better Minix than Minix.' I was hoping I'd be able to recompile gcc under Linux some day...
>
> "Two months for basic setup, but then only slightly longer until I had a disk driver (seriously buggy, but it happened to work on my machine) and a small file system.

> That was about when I made 0.01 available [around late August of 1991]: it wasn't pretty, it had no floppy driver, and it couldn't do much [of] anything. I don't think anybody ever compiled that version. But by then I was hooked, and didn't want to stop until I could chuck out Minix."

Note

These announcements are from the "Linux Installation and Getting Started Guide," by Matt Welsh (copyright 1992-94 by Matt Welsh, 205 Gray Street NE, Wilson, NC 27893, `mdw@sunsite.unc.edu`). They're used subject to section 3 of Matt's copyright.

You can obtain the complete "Linux Installation and Getting Started Guide" from the Linux Documentation Project's various archives sites. You can find this book on `metalab.unc.edu` in the directory `/pub/Linux/docs/LDP/install-guide`. For information on how to access archives and download files, refer to Chapter 33, "Surfing the Internet with the World Wide Web."

In a later announcement, made in the `comp.os.minix` user group on October 5, 1991, Linus introduced to the world Linux version 0.02, the first official version of Linux:

> "Do you pine for the nice days of Minix 1.1, when men were men and wrote their own device drivers? Are you without a nice project and just dying to cut your teeth on an OS you can try to modify for your needs? Are you finding it frustrating when everything works on Minix? No more all-nighters to get a nifty program working? Then this post might be just for you."
>
> "As I mentioned a month ago, I'm working on a free version of a Minix look-alike for AT-386 computers. It has finally reached the stage where it's even usable (though [it] may not be depending on what you want), and I am willing to put out the sources for wider distribution. It's just version 0.02, but I've successfully run `bash`, `gcc`, `gnu-make`, `gnu-sed`, `compress`, and so forth under it."

WHO OWNS LINUX?

IBM owns the rights to OS/2, and Microsoft owns the rights to MS-DOS and MS Windows, but who owns the rights to Linux? First and foremost, Linux isn't public domain software; various components of Linux are copyrighted by many people. Linus Torvalds holds the copyright to the basic Linux kernel. Red Hat, Inc. owns the rights to the Red Hat distribution version. Caldera holds the rights to the Caldera OpenLinux product. The Debian distribution is a creature of the Open Systems movement with Richard Stallman's group embacing it as the first of many kernels as part of the GNU Hurd project, but single corporation controls Debian. Many Linux utilities are under the GNU General Public License (GPL). In fact, Linus and most Linux contributors have also placed their work under the protection of the GNU GPL. You can find the license on each of the accompanying CD-ROMs in the root directory in the file named `copying`.

This license is sometimes referred to as the *GNU copyleft* (a play on the word *copyright*). This license covers all the software produced by GNU (itself a play on words—GNU's Not UNIX) and the Free Software Foundation. The license allows programmers to create software for everyone. The basic premise behind GNU is that software should be available to everyone, and that if someone wants to modify the program to his or her own ends, that should be possible. The only caveat is that the modified code can't be restricted; others must also have the right to the new code.

→ See "How to Apply These Terms to Your New Programs," p. 868

The GNU copyleft, or GPL, allows a program's creators to keep their legal copyright but allows others to take, modify, and sell the resulting new program. However, in doing so, the original programmers can't restrict any of these same rights to modify the program from the people buying the software. If you sell the program as is or in a modified form, you must provide the source code. That's why Linux comes with the complete License source code.

CHAPTER 2

Linux Installation Overview

In this chapter

by *Jack Tackett, Jr.*

UNDERSTANDING LINUX'S HARDWARE REQUIREMENTS

This chapter gives you a basic overview of the information you need to install, configure, and use almost any Linux distribution.

Note

This book assumes that you have a working knowledge of DOS and of such tasks as formatting your hard drive, working with partition tables, and determining sector sizes. If this information sounds like a foreign language, check out *Using MS-DOS 6.2, Special Edition,* or ask a computer guru buddy to help you through this information.

You're about to make major changes to your system, so be careful. It's a good idea to have paper and pen nearby to take notes just in case something does go wrong; besides, you'll need to jot down some numbers along the way.

To be able to install Linux successfully, you need supported hardware. Choosing the right level of hardware for your Linux system depends on such factors as the number of users to be supported and the types of applications to be run. All this information translates into requirements for working memory, hard disk storage space, the types of terminals needed, and so forth.

ON THE WEB

For current information on supported hardware, see the following Web sites.

For the Red Hat distribution, see

`http://www.redhat.com/corp/support/hardware/intel/60/rh6.0-hcl-i.ld-1.html`

For Caldera, see

`http://www.calderasystems.com/products/openlinux/hardware.html`

For Debian, see

`http://www.debian.org/releases/slink/i386/ch-hardware-req.en.html#s-hardware-supported`

Most Linux systems today consist of PCs. These Linux installations are often for only a single user, although they may also be tied into larger Linux or UNIX systems.

Caution

Linux is a constantly evolving system, and hardware support is sporadically updated. The distributions on the accompanying CD-ROMs are relatively stable, but new hardware support may have been provided by the time this book is printed and the CD-ROM is created. Although many hardware components have clones or compatible replacements, not all may work with Linux. If you do have the hardware described in this chapter, the odds are excellent that Linux installs, boots, and operates properly. If

you don't have the equipment listed, Linux may or may not operate properly, but the odds are against you getting a system up and running.

If you're using a version of Linux in a single-user configuration (the most likely configuration), you're the system administrator, also known as the superuser. It's your responsibility to understand the system well enough to perform the administrative duties required to keep it operating at an optimum level. These duties include keeping enough space on the hard drive, backing up regularly, ensuring that all devices attached to the system have the proper software drivers, installing and configuring software, and so forth.

Tip #5 from Jack

As the system administrator, or superuser, you wield immense power on your system. It is best if you log in as a regular user for your day-to-day work and log in as the superuser, whose login name is root, only when you need to administer the system.

The level of hardware you need depends heavily on the hardware used by the myriad people who programmed the Linux system. Unlike commercial software developers who can afford to test their systems on many different hardware configurations, Linux developers typically have access only to their personal computers. Luckily, because so many Linux developers exist, most of the standard hardware found in the PC world is supported.

The System's CPU

A basic system requires an IBM-compatible PC with an Intel 80386 or later CPU in any of the various CPU types and Intel's various Pentium processors. Other CPU clones, such as the 80686 clone chips made by Cyrix and Advanced Micro Devices (AMD), are also compatible with Linux.

The Linux kernel has also been ported to other processors. Among those now supported are the DEC Alpha, the PowerPC (Macintoshes), Sun Sparcs, and even embedded systems processors such as those used in Corel's Network PC running the Debian distribution.

The System's Bus

The type of bus used to communicate with the peripherals is also important. Linux works with only the ISA, EISA, and PCI buses. The MicroChannel Architecture (MCA) bus used on IBM's PS/2 isn't supported, although a port is in process. Some newer systems use a faster bus, called the *local bus*, for disk access and video displays, for example. Linux does support the VESA Local Bus but might not support a non-VESA Local Bus architecture.

Memory Needs

Linux requires surprisingly little RAM to run, especially when compared to comparable operating systems such as OS/2 and Windows NT. Linux requires at least 16MB of RAM, although 64MB is highly recommended. If you have less than 32MB of RAM, you need to use what's called a *swap file*. The basic rule of thumb is that the more memory your system contains, the faster your system runs.

The next memory consideration for Linux is the use of the X Window System clone called XFree86. XFree86 is a version of the X Window System that can be freely distributed and is included with Linux for that reason. XFree86 is a GUI similar to Microsoft Windows.

→ See "Installing the XFree86 System," p. 508

Disk Drives and Space Requirements

Although you can run Linux from a floppy-drive-only system, running Linux from your system's floppy drive isn't recommended.

Note

You can boot Linux from a floppy drive. *Booting a system* refers to the process of starting a computer system and loading the operating system into memory to start the system. The term is derived from the phrase *bootstrapping*.

For a home-based system, you no longer need a floppy drive if you have a bootable CD-ROM (check your BIOS to be sure).

For better system performance, you should install Linux on a hard drive. Linux supports all IDE-enhanced drives. Linux also supports a wide range of SCSI hard-drive controllers. If your controller is a true SCSI controller—that is, not a proprietary version of SCSI—Linux can use your controller. Linux now supports SCSI controllers from Adaptec, Future Domain, Seagate, UltraStor, the SCSI adapter on the ProAudio Spectrum 16 card, and Western Digital. The following card types are supported:

Adaptec 152x/1542/1740/274x/284x/294X
Buslogic
EATA-DMA (DPT, NEC, AT&T)
Seagate ST-02
Future Domain TMC-8xx, 16xx
Generic NCR5380
NCR 53c7, 8xx
Always IN2000
Pro Audio Spectrum 16
Qlogic
Trantor T128/T128F/T228
UltraStor
7000FASST

If you have the proper drive controller, you must worry about disk space requirements. Linux supports multiple hard drives and can be installed across drives. Unlike other operating systems, Linux doesn't need to be installed on the same hard drive; pieces can be installed on different drives.

Caution

Unless you're installing Linux onto a brand-new hard drive, you need to repartition and reformat the drive. This process destroys all information currently stored on that portion of the drive. Thus, backing up your files–twice–before installing Linux is imperative. If space permits, you can split a single hard drive into multiple partitions and copy your files back to one of the partitions.

The amount of disk space required depends on the software you install and the amount of data you expect that software will generate. Linux requires less disk space than most implementations of UNIX systems. You can run a completely functional Linux system, without X Window System support, in 600MB. For a complete installation of everything in the distribution, more than 1.6 GBs (gigabytes) is recommended.

Swap Space

Finally, as mentioned earlier in the section "Memory Needs," if you have limited RAM, you need swap space. Whereas systems such as Microsoft Windows create a swap file that resides on your hard drive as any other file, Linux allows the swap file to reside on a separate swap partition. Most Linux installations use partitions rather than files. Because you can place multiple partitions on the same physical hard drive, you can place the swap partition on the same drive as Linux, but for better performance, you should place the swap partition on a separate drive.

Linux allows up to eight swap partitions that can be no larger than 16MB. A rule of thumb is to set the swap file size to twice the amount of physical RAM contained on your system. Thus, if you have 8MB of physical RAM, your swap partition should be 16MB in size.

Tip #6 from *Jack*

Use the `df` command to see how much swap space, or amount of any disk space, you have available. For example, to display the amount of space available in megabytes use:

```
df -m
```

Monitor Requirements

For text-based terminals, Linux supports all standard Hercules, CGA, EGA, VGA, and SuperVGA video cards and monitors. To take advantage of the color-coding directory listings available with Linux, you need a color monitor. So for text-based operation, any video/controller combination should work.

The big problems occur when you run the X Window System distributed with Linux. To use XFree86, you need a video adapter that uses one of the chipsets listed in Table 2.1. *Chipsets* are a group of integrated circuits, or computer chips, used to take information from the computer and convert the data into a form that can be displayed on a video monitor. To find the chipset used by your video adapter, you can check the documentation included with your card to determine whether it has any problems using XFree86.

TABLE 2.1 VIDEO CHIPSETS SUPPORTED BY LINUX

Manufacturer	Chipset(s)
Tseng	ET3000, ET40000AX, ET4000/W32
Western Digital	WD90C00, WD90C10, WD90C11, WD90C24, WD90C30, WD90C31
Trident	TVGA8800CS, TVGA8900B, TVGA8900C, TVGA8900CL, TVGA9000, TVGA9000i, TVGA9100B, TVGA9200CX, TVGA9320, TVGA9400CX, TVGA9420
ATI	28800-4, 28800-5, 28800-a
NCR	77C22, 77C22E, 77C22E+
Cirrus Logic	CLGD5420, CLGD5422, CLGD5424, CLGD5426, CLGD5428, CLGD6205, CLGD6215, CLGD6225, CLGD6235
OAK	OTI067, OTI077
S3	86C911, 86C924, 86C801, 86C805, 86C805i, 86C928
Compaq	AVGA
Western Digital/ Paradise	PVGA1

Note

The release notes for the current version of XFree86 distributed with Linux should contain a more recent list of supported and nonsupported chipsets.

Some problems encountered by the XFree86 developers are caused by adapter manufacturers who don't provide the necessary information on programming the cards to display information. Without this information, developers can't support the X Window System on those adapters. Also, some manufacturers provide this information but require either royalty payments or nondisclosure agreements for others to use the information. These types of restrictions make it impossible to support these adapters on a freely distributed system like the XFree86 system for Linux.

CD-ROMs

To install the Linux system included on the accompanying CD-ROMs, you must have a CD-ROM drive supported by Linux. Because most CD-ROMs use a SCSI interface controller, any SCSI controller listed earlier in the section "Disk Drives and Space Requirements" should also work with a CD-ROM attached to the controller. Linux also now supports many of the new EIDE and ATAPI CD-ROMs available on the market.

Many of the CD-ROMs included with multimedia packages may or may not work with Linux, depending on whether the controller is a true SCSI adapter or a proprietary adapter. Proprietary adapters for the most part don't work. However, Linux does specifically support the Creative Labs SoundBlaster line of CD-ROMs and provides a specific installation configuration for those CD-ROMs. Other CD-ROMs known to work with Linux include the following:

NEC CDR-74	Okano
Sony CDU-541	Wearnes CD with interface card
Sony CDU-31a or 33a	
Plextor DM-3024	Most IDE/ATAPI CD-ROMs
Aztech	Mitsumi CD-ROMs
Orchid	SoundBlaster, Panasonic Kotobuki, Matsushita, TEAC-55a, or Lasermate

Network Access

You can connect a Linux system to the world in several ways, but the two most popular (and supported) methods are via network controller cards and modems. Network controller cards include Token Ring, FDDI, TAXI, and Ethernet cards. Most common business networks use an Ethernet controller card. Table 2.2 lists several of the Ethernet adapters supported.

TABLE 2.2 ETHERNET CONTROLLER CARDS SUPPORTED BY LINUX

Manufacturer	Interface Card
3Com	3c503, 3c503/16, 3c509
Novell	NE1000, NE2000
Western Digital	WD8003, WD8013
Hewlett-Packard	HP27245, HP27247, HP27250

At home, you'll more than likely connect to the outside world via a modem and a communications protocol such as SLIP or PPP. Linux supports almost every type of modem on the market, internal and external. If you can access the modem from MS-DOS, you'll have no problem accessing the modem from Linux.

→ See "Understanding the Requirements for SLIP and PPP," p. 664

MISCELLANEOUS HARDWARE

The following sections list miscellaneous hardware supported by Linux, such as mouse devices, tape drives, and printers. Although such hardware makes Linux easier to use and more robust, it isn't required.

MOUSE DEVICES

Using text-based Linux doesn't require a mouse. Unlike many UNIX implementations, however, Linux does allow you to cut text from any area of the screen and paste it to the command line by using a mouse. If you intend to use the X Window System clone, XFree86, you must use a mouse.

Linux supports most serial mouse devices, including the following:

- Logitech
- MM series
- Mouseman
- Microsoft
- Mouse Systems

Linux also supports the Microsoft, Logitech, ATIXL, and PS/2 bus mouse devices. In fact, any pointing devices, such as trackballs and touch screens, that emulate the previously listed mouse devices should work with Linux.

TAPE DRIVES

Tape drives provide a great deal of storage space for backing up your computer system. Linux supports several SCSI-based tape systems, as shown in Table 2.3. Linux also supports the popular Colorado Memory Systems tape drives (120 and 250 versions), which are plugged into a system's floppy-disk controller. The versions that plug into the printer port aren't now supported. Most drives supporting QIC-02 should also work with Linux.

TABLE 2.3 TAPE-BACKUP DRIVES SUPPORTED BY LINUX

Manufacturer	Model
Exabyte	All SCSI models
Sanko	CP150SE
Tandberg	3600
Wangtek	5525ES, 5150ES, 5099EN

PRINTERS

Linux supports the complete range of parallel printers. Configuring Linux to support serial printers is tedious and error-prone. Serial printer support isn't well documented or supported by the basic Linux installation programs. If you have a serial printer, you might have problems using it under Linux. If you have a parallel printer, your biggest problem is most likely the *stair-step effect*, illustrated here:

```
This is line one.
                 This is line two.
                                  This is line three.
```

How UNIX and Linux treat carriage returns and linefeeds produces the stair-step effect. Under most UNIX systems, the command to move the paper down one line (linefeed) and then position the print head at the beginning of the line (carriage return) is represented by one control character. Under systems such as MS-DOS and Windows, however, each command is represented by a different control character. When you print a UNIX file under a printer configured for MS-DOS systems, you see the stair-step effect because the file contains only the linefeed control character and not the carriage-return control character.

→ See "Knowing What You Need to Configure Printers," p. 392

Compiling Necessary Information

Before starting the installation, you need the following information about your system:

- The type of video card, chipset, and monitor used
- The serial port used by your mouse
- The serial port used by your modem
- The network information for your computer, if it's connected to a network (items such as its IP address, gateway, and domain name)
- The type of hard drive and CD-ROM drive in your system and their controller types
- The name you intend to call your system
- A password for the system administrator's root account

If you're connecting to the Internet, you can get most of this information from either your network administrator or your Internet service provider (ISP).

Starting the Installation Process

After compiling the information, you need to decide on the media you intend to use to install Linux. Traditionally, you would use a program called rawrite to create boot and root floppies. Today, if your system supports bootable CD-ROMs, you can boot from the CD. Caldera allows you to install from the CD while you're running Windows (but you need the unpartitioned space to do so). You can also install via a network connection using File Transfer Protocol (FTP), Hypertext Transfer Protocol (HTTP), and Network File System (NFS). The subsequent chapters guide you through each process.

Note You can also run part of the Linux file system from the CD-ROM without installing all the software. You can choose to do so during installation.

UNDERSTANDING THE VARIOUS INSTALLATION METHODS

If you're reading this book, you will probably install Red Hat Linux from the accompanying CD-ROM. However, you can use one of the following four methods to install Red Hat: from CD-ROM, via NFS, via FTP, or from a hard drive.

To install Linux directly from a CD-ROM, you need access to DOS. From the DOS prompt, execute the command

```
[cdrom-drive]:\dosutils\autoboot
```

where [*cdrom-drive*] is the drive letter for your system's CD-ROM.

Caution This method erases your hard drive. Be sure to back up any files you fear losing.

If you have another partition available, you can install Linux to coexist with your system without erasing what's already there. To do so, you need the CD-ROM, an empty partition, and a boot disk. You'll learn later in this chapter how to create the boot disk, as well as how to repartition your hard drive.

NFS (Network File System) provides a way to install Red Hat across a network. First, you must mount the CD-ROM drive on a machine supporting the ISO-9660 file system with RockRidge extensions and then export the file system via NFS. You need to know the path to the exported file system and the IP number or, if DNS is configured, the name of the system.

FTP (File Transfer Protocol) is a method for transferring files across the Internet. (Chapter 32, "Accessing the Network with `telnet`, `ftp`, and the `r-` Commands," explains FTP in more detail.) To install via FTP requires a boot disk and the supplemental disk described later in this chapter.

Installing Red Hat from a hard drive requires the same boot and supplemental disks used for an FTP installation. First, you create a directory named `RedHat`. Then you copy the corresponding directory from the CD-ROM, and all the subdirectories there, to the `RedHat` directory. You can use the following DOS commands to do so:

```
cd \RedHat
xcopy /s e:\RedHat
```

The `cd` command assumes that you're already on the installation hard drive; the `xcopy` command assumes that your CD-ROM drive is drive E.

No matter which method you use, you need at least the boot disk to proceed with installation. But first, you should gather the information described earlier in this chapter.

You can install Caldera's OpenLinux directly from the CD-ROM, even if you're running Windows. The OpenLinux CD provides a multimedia-based setup program. You simply double-click the Setup icon, shown in Figure 2.1, in the `winsetup` folder on the CD-ROM.

Figure 2.1 You can use Caldera's impressive multimedia installation program from Windows.

Debian installs much like Red Hat: You either can boot from the CD-ROM or use installation diskettes you create.

If you intend to use other operating systems on the same computer (such as Windows 95, Windows 98, Windows NT, or OS/2), you need to create the necessary partitions for these operating systems. Typically, you need to use the operating system's partitioning software because Linux can't handle these other partition types.

ON THE WEB

A product named System Commander, from V Communications, lets you install and switch between 32 different operating systems. You can find more information about this product at the following site:

`http://www.v-com.com/`

Next, you should check for any last-minute changes to your favorite distribution. The reasons for checking are many, but the two major reasons are that Linux is constantly updated, and this chapter is being written at least a month before the CD-ROM is cut. In the interim, new material or bug fixes may have been released.

ON THE WEB

You can also check for updated material on the Web at these sites:

`http://www.redhat.com/errata`

`http://www.calderasystems.com/doc/openlinux/errata.html`

`http://www.debian.org/releases/slink/#errata`

Table 2.4 lists the currently available update packages that fix known problems in the Red Hat 6.0 distribution.

→ See "Installing Packages with RPM," p. 169

TABLE 2.4 RED HAT ERRATA LISTING

Date Released	Package
29-Jul-1999	squid
29-Jul-1999	gnome
29-Jul-1999	samba
23-Jul-1999	enlightenment
23-Jul-1999	gnumeric
09-Jul-1999	rdist
07-Jul-1999	rpm
07-Jul-1999	netkit-base, traceroute
24-Jun-1999	net-tools
24-Jun-1999	talk
21-Jun-1999	KDE
21-Jun-1999	mod_php3
17-Jun-1999	XFree86
16-Jun-1999	dev, rxvt, screen
10-Jun-1999	wu-ftpd
10-Jun-1999	utempter
03-Jun-1999	kernel update
29-May-1999	New Boot Images
27-May-1999	Sparc kernel and egcs
25-May-1999	Netscape
22-May-1999	INN
14-May-1999	Applications

TABLE 2.4 RED HAT ERRATA LISTING

Date Released	Package
13-May-1999	apmd
12-May-1999	pump
11-May-1999	xscreensaver

For information on Caldera, see the file `/pub/OpenLinux/updates/README` at `ftp://ftp.caldera.com/pub/OpenLinux/updates/`.

These directories contain various updated boot disk images and update packages in RPM format for the releases of Caldera OpenLinux 1.3:

```
kdelibs-1.1-2.i386.rpm
kdelibs-devel-1.1-2.i386.rpm
kdelibs-1.1-2.src.rpm
dosemu-0.98.5-1.i386.rpm
dosemu-0.98.5-1.src.rpm
opendos-hdimage-7.02-4.i386.rpm
opendos-hdimage-7.02-4.src.rpm
```

If you're not installing directly from the CD-ROM, you next need to repartition your current hard drive to make room for Linux. This step may cause problems because repartitioning a hard drive destroys any data contained on the affected partitions. After making room for Linux, you need to boot the Linux system and create its new partitions and file systems. Typically, Linux systems need a primary partition to store the files on and a swap file partition, especially if you have a machine used in text mode with 8MB or less of memory.

Note

A *file system* is basically a section of your hard drive specially formatted to hold certain types of files. UNIX and Linux use file systems to represent entire sections of the directory tree. This use is in contrast to MS-DOS, which places subdirectories in the directory tree on the same logical drive. UNIX systems use the directory tree format because placing subdirectories on different drives is safer. If one drive malfunctions, only the information on that drive needs to be replaced or fixed.

→ See "Understanding File Systems," p. 440

After creating the file systems, you then can install the Linux operating system, its support files, and various application packages distributed with the system. To install Linux, you must first boot a stripped-down version of the operating system. You do so by creating a boot disk and a supplemental disk set containing the stripped-down operating system.

CREATING THE BOOT AND SUPPLEMENTAL DISKS

You create the boot and supplemental disks by using the rawrite program. You can find this program on the accompanying CD-ROM in the `/dosutils` subdirectory. For this step, you need two formatted floppies: one labeled *boot* and the other labeled *supp*. Place the boot disk in drive A and enter the following:

```
E:\dosutils>rawrite

Enter disk image source file name: e:\images\boot.img
Enter target diskette drive: A:
Please insert a formatted diskette into drive A: and press -ENTER-
```

If you want to abort the process, simply press Ctrl+c to stop. If rawrite fails, try a new formatted disk. If the problem persists, you should have your hardware checked for possible problems.

PARTITIONING YOUR HARD DRIVE

After you back up your system and make the necessary boot and supplemental disks, you must prepare your system's hard drive for Linux.

Caution

This process is the most dangerous because maximum data loss is assured. If you haven't backed up your system, do so now. Although you can use an experimental program called FIPS and commercial programs such as Partition Magic to do nondestructive repartitioning, a full backup is recommended, just in case problems occur.

Red Hat provides a program called Disk Druid to partition your hard drive. For Caldera and Debian, you use a program called fdisk (Debian also provides a program called cfdisk). Just like its DOS counterpart, fdisk allows you to create partitions on your hard drive.

You should plan your disk partitions now and also plan on how much disk space you want to allocate to each partition because this portion of the installation provides the greatest source of problems, especially if you run out of disk space. The following partitions and sizes are a good starting point:

`swap`	64MB
`/`	128+MB
`boot`	16MB
`usr`	600+MB (if you install everything!)
`var`	256MB
`home`	All available space

INSTALLING THE SYSTEM

After you create the appropriate partitions, each distribution requires you to select which components to install. If you program for a living, you should install the programming components. Linux provides compilers and interpreters for a variety of languages, such as C, C++, Java, Perl, and FORTRAN. If you like games, you should install the X Window System and games components. After you select the components, the install program proceeds with copying the necessary files from the source media (typically the CD-ROM or the network) to your system. This process can take some time—even when you're installing from the CD-ROM—so plan to wait awhile.

Tip #7 from *Jack*

During installation, you can monitor what the system does via virtual terminals.

MANEUVERING THROUGH LINUX

After installing Linux and rebooting, you're faced with a system prompt based on the name you gave your system during installation. Under Red Hat, the prompt looks similar to the following:

```
Red Hat Linux release 6.0 (Hedwig)
Kernel 2.2.5-15 on an I686
web login:
```

The prompt might indicate a different version of Linux, however, depending on the kernel version, machine name, and distribution.

You must now supply a username and a password. A username identifies you to the operating system because Linux can support many different users, both at different times and concurrently. An account also provides each user with a default directory, called the *home directory*. Many accounts are also set up to restrict users to certain directories on the system and to prevent them from using certain commands, primarily to protect the files of one user from the prying eyes of another.

ENTERING COMMANDS

You enter commands in Linux much as you do in DOS and other command-line-oriented operating systems. Linux, like UNIX, is case sensitive; if Linux doesn't know a command, make sure that you've spelled it correctly and that you've entered it in the proper case. Most commands are executed after you press Enter.

RECALLING COMMAND HISTORY

Linux also provides a history function to recall previous commands. This history is kept across sessions, too. You can press the ↑ key to recall previous commands and then press

Return to activate that command. To get a complete listing of all the prior commands you've entered, use the `history` command, as shown here:

```
[tackett@web~]$ history
1 clear
2 adduser
3 history
```

When you have the preceding history list, you can repeat the command by using the ↑ key and cycling through the commands until the proper one appears on the command line. Alternatively, you can press ! (the *bang* character) and enter the number of the command you want to re-execute. For example, if you want to repeat the `adduser` command in the preceding list, you enter the following:

```
[tackett@web~]$ !2
```

The number of entries in the history list is user-defined in the user account's `.profile` configuration file. See Chapter 16, "Understanding Linux Shells," for more information on the `.profile` configuration file.

Tip #8 from Jack

> Linux provides many different command shells, some of which don't provide the history functions. To switch to a different shell, simply invoke the command for that shell, for example
>
> `sh` invokes the default shell—typically bash for Linux installations.
>
> `csh` invokes the c shell and `tcsh` invokes the t shell.
> `ksh`, or `pdksh`, invokes the korn shell.

Making Selections

If you have a mouse with your system, and you have installed the selection program, you can also use your mouse to copy text from other areas of your screen to the command line. To select the text, simply move the mouse cursor (which appears as soon as you click the left mouse button) by holding down the left mouse button as you drag the cursor across the desired text, and then press the right mouse button to copy the text to the command line. This technique is useful if you need to enter a long filename on the command line.

Completing Commands

Linux also offers another nice feature when you're entering commands. You can start to type a filename and then press Tab. Linux searches the directory for a file beginning with the same letters you've typed and completes the filename it finds. If Linux can't find a unique filename, it beeps and completes the filename to the last common character. For example, if you want to copy a file called `todo_monday` to `todo_today`, you type `cp to` at the prompt and then press Tab. Linux beeps and fills out the command line like this:

```
[tackett@web~]$ cp todo_
```

If you now type an `m` and press Tab, Linux places the entire `todo_monday` filename on the command line.

MANAGING USERS

On many systems, the person responsible for maintaining the user accounts is referred to asthe *system administrator*. The system administrator sets up user accounts and performs other duties. For more information on the various aspects of system administration, check out the chapters in Part II, "System Administration." On your Linux system, you're the system administrator, so it's your responsibility to set up accounts for yourself, family, and friends.

To add an account for yourself, you must create that account as the system administrator. System administrators are also sometimes referred to as *superusers* because they have so much control over the system. To begin your trek through Linux, you must first log in as the superuser via the root account.

→ See "Using the `adduser` Command," p.251

LOGGING IN AND OUT

To log in as root, you enter `root` at the login prompt. Linux then asks for a password.

By using a password, you prevent unauthorized users from logging in to any account. Linux wants to make sure that the username is, in fact, the correct user. You shouldn't share your passwords with just anyone. Linux protects the password you type by not *echoing*—that is, not displaying—the letters onscreen, so make sure that you enter the correct password.

If you enter an invalid username or password, Linux gives the following error message and starts the process over:

```
web login: jack
Password: password
Login incorrect

web login:
```

Once logged in you can enter Linux commands. You enter most commands in the same way you enter them in DOS: You type the command with any needed parameters and press Return.

Tip #9 from
Jack

If you want to switch to another user account you can do so in a variety of ways. You can enter the command login, which logs you out of the current account and prompts you for a new username and password. You can use the `su` command to switch users, as in

```
su tackett
```

You are prompted for the password (unless you are currently the superuser) and allowed to execute commands as that user. When done enter the exit command and Linux returns you to the previous user account.

To log out, you enter `logout`. This command returns you to the login prompt. If this command doesn't work, try the `exit` command.

USING BASIC COMMANDS

You need to know some basic commands to get around the system. The following sections provide some of the commands you need to use your Linux system. Many of the "commands" presented in the following sections are actually utility programs that Linux uses to extend its command set. These programs are found in the `/bin`, `/sbin`, and `/usr/bin` directories.

GETTING HELP FOR COMMANDS WITH MAN

To get online help for each of the various Linux commands, you can type `man`. Linux then displays, a screen at a time, any information it has on the command. If you aren't sure of what command to use, you can try the `-k` parameter and enter a simple keyword that represents the topic of interest. `man` then searches through its help files (called man, or manual, pages) for a topic that contains the keyword. Linux also provides an alias for this command, called `apropos`.

If you enter the command `man ls`, Linux provides help on the `ls` command, including all its parameters. The command `man -k cls` provides a listing of commands that have the word `cls` in the help file; the command `apropos cls` is the same as `man -k cls`.

USING DIRECTORY-MANIPULATION COMMANDS

Linux provides many commands to work with directories. Like other operating systems you may have used, Linux allows you to create, delete, and move directories, as well as display information about the directory.

CHANGING THE CURRENT WORKING DIRECTORY WITH cd

Linux, like DOS and other operating systems, stores files in a tree structure called a *directory*. You can specify a file via a path from the root directory, specified with the `/` character, to the file itself. Thus, the configuration file for Emacs for the user `jack` can be exactly specified as follows:

```
/home/jack/.emacs
```

If you're familiar with the DOS limits of eight characters for a filename and three characters for an extension, you'll be pleasantly surprised to learn that Linux has no such limit on filenames.

→ See "Understanding Filenames and Pathnames," p. 408

Linux also uses the concept of a home directory, which is specified when an account is added to the system. A user's home directory is usually specified with the ~ (tilde) character. You can use the tilde in place of the directory name, where the user wants to copy a file from the current directory `\usr\home\jack` to his or her home directory:

```
cp .emacs ~
```

To move around the Linux directory structure, you use the change directory command, `cd`. If you enter `cd` without any parameters, Linux immediately returns you to your home directory. To move from one directory to another directory, you use the `cd` command much as you do in DOS—that is, `cd` *`new-directory`*. Linux also uses the `.` (single dot) to represent the current directory and the `..` (double dot) to represent the parent directory. In fact, it's DOS that emulates UNIX, not UNIX/Linux emulating DOS.

Note

Be careful how you specify the directory separator. DOS uses as its directory separator the `\` (backslash) character, which Linux uses as the character for continuing a command on another line. To separate directory names in Linux, you must use the `/` (forward slash) character.

Also, although DOS doesn't mind if you fail to use spaces when specifying the `.` and `..` parameters, Linux does. Linux doesn't understand `cd..`, but it understands `cd ..`. Linux needs the space separating the command and the parameter.

Displaying Information About Files and Directories with `ls`

`ls` stands for *list* and is used by Linux to display a list of files. This command is the counterpart to the DOS `DIR` command. (Linux also accepts the `dir` command to list files in a directory.) Under Linux, the `ls` command displays all the main files in a directory in color. By default, blue indicates directories, and green indicates executable programs. You can change the default colors by modifying the file `/etc/DIR_COLORS`.

→ See "Listing Files," p. 420

`ls` takes many parameters to specify not only how to display a file but also what files to display. The most common parameter is `-la`, which tells `ls` to display information in a long format for every file in a directory.

The command `ls -la` lists all information about every file in the current directory. The command `ls .emacs` lists the file `.emacs`, whereas `ls -l .emacs` lists all information about the file `.emacs`.

The command options `-ltar`—that is, `ls -ltar`—list the same information as the preceding `ls` command, except that the file listings are displayed in order from oldest to most recent.

CREATING NEW DIRECTORIES WITH `mkdir`

Because Linux's file system is based on directories, Linux provides the `mkdir` command so that users can create new ones. Unlike DOS, which has an alias for the `mkdir` command called `MD`, Linux requires that the full `mkdir` command be spelled out. You must specify a name for each new directory, as shown in the following example:

```
mkdir backup
```

Tip #10 from *Jack*

Linux does provide a way, via the command shell, to make aliases for command names; thus, if you simply can't live without the DOS `MD` command and hate typing `mkdir`, you can alias `MD` to the `mkdir` command.

To create a new command called `mk`, use the following command:

```
alias mk=mkdir
```

→ See "Aliasing Commands," p. 347

DELETING DIRECTORIES WITH `rmdir`

The `rmdir` command deletes Linux directories. The command takes the name of the directory to delete. This directory must be empty; otherwise, Linux can't remove it.

For example, if the `/backup` directory has two directories within it, the command `rmdir /backup` fails. The command `rmdir/backup/jack/*` removes all files in the `/backup/jack` directory, and then `rmdir /backup/jack` removes the now-empty `/backup/jack` directory.

Caution

You can't delete a directory that contains files by using the `rmdir` command. Instead, you can use the `-r` flag to the `rm` command. For example,

```
rm -r *
```

deletes everything from the current directory and every directory below the current directory. Be very careful using this command because the moment you delete a directory, you can't recover the directory or the files that were located in the directory. Make backups.

USING FILE-MANIPULATION COMMANDS

Because Linux treats directories and files similarly, it provides similar commands for manipulation.

Copying Files with cp

The `cp` command is similar to the DOS `COPY` command. You use this command to copy one or more files from one directory to another directory. The syntax of `cp` is as follows:

```
cp from-filenameto-filename
```

You must supply both the *from-filename* and *to-filename* parameters for the files to be copied. If you want to preserve the filename, you can use the dot (.) as a placeholder for the *to-filename* parameter. This use is in contrast to DOS, where you can leave off the *to-filename*.

The command `cp fred1 fred1.old` copies the file `fred1` to a backup file named `fred1.old`, whereas the command `cp ~fred1.old/backup/jack` copies the file `fred1.old` from the home directory to the `/backup/jack` directory. (The ~ character represents the user's home directory.)

Moving Files with mv

The `mv` command, which is similar to the DOS `MOVE` command, allows you to move files from one directory to another directory. Moving a file has the same effect as copying the file to a new directory and then deleting the file in the old directory. `mv` doesn't make a copy of the file.

The syntax of the `mv` command is identical to the `cp` command:

```
mv from-filenameto-filename
```

The command `mv fred1 fred1.old` copies the file `fred1` to a backup file named `fred1.old` and deletes the old `fred1` file, whereas the command `mv ~fred1.old /backup/jack` moves the `fred1.old` file from the home directory to the `/backup/jack` directory.

Deleting Files with rm

To delete files under Linux, you use the `rm` command. The `rm` command is dangerous because as soon as a file is deleted, you can never recover it. For safety reasons, you should use the following form of the `rm` command:

```
rm -i filename
```

The `-i` parameter tells the command to query, or inquire, you to see whether that's the file you really want to remove. For example, the command `rmfred1` removes the file named `fred1`, whereas the command `rm-ifred1` deletes the `fred1` file after asking whether you really want to remove this file.

Caution

As soon as you delete a file under Linux, that file is gone. You can't undelete a file or directory under Linux like you can with DOS. If you delete a file, your only hope is a backup copy.

Displaying File Contents with `more`

The `more` command displays a screen of a text file. You can look through a text file without invoking an editor, printing the file, or trying to pause the terminal as it displays the file. To display the contents of your Emacs configuration file, for example, you can type the following:

```
more .emacs
```

Tip #11 from

Jack

> **If you try to pass a binary data file to `more`, you could have some unpleasant effects; for example, your terminal can lock up. If your terminal does lock up, try pressing Ctrl+q or Ctrl+s.**
>
> **Use the `strings` command if you want to see any text a binary file contains. `strings` displays to the screen any printable ASCII characters contained in the binary file.**

A disadvantage of using `more` is that you can't back up to see a screen of information after it passes. The command described in the following section overcomes that problem, though.

Using `less`—A Better `more`

`less` displays information one screen at a time on your terminal. The program's name is a play on words for the program it's meant to replace—`more`. Like `more`, `less` can display a screen of information in a text file, but unlike `more`, `less` allows you to page back and forth within the file. You can use the following command, for example, to browse through the `README` file located in the `info` directory:

```
less /info/readme
```

Clearing the Screen with `clear`

Sometimes after filling your terminal screen with information, you want a blank screen while you sit and contemplate your next action. Under DOS, you can use the `cls` command, but under Linux, you must use the `clear` command.

Dealing with DOS Files Under Linux

During installation, you are given the chance to make any DOS partitions you have available visible to Linux. These partitions are then placed in a directory you specify during configuration—for example, `/dosc`.

If you want to copy these files to a floppy, using the `cp` command might cause problems because UNIX and Linux treat text files a little differently than DOS, especially when dealing with carriage returns and linefeeds. To help you overcome this problem, developers created a group of programs to help deal with MS-DOS files under a UNIX environment. These programs are the `m-` commands, which include such commands as `mcopy` and `mdir`. `mcopy` works just like the DOS `COPY` command, and `mdir` provides a directory listing. As you may notice, they resemble their DOS counterparts, except that they begin with the letter *m*, hence the name "`m-` commands." The `m-` commands are part of the `mtools` package, which is a collection of public-domain programs that allows UNIX to interact with DOS files much more easily.

These commands also make copying files to floppy disks much easier because you can use the DOS designation, like `A`, rather than the Linux designation `/dev/fd0`. For more information on the `m-` commands, enter the following:

```
man mtools
```

Table 2.5 provides a brief listing of the various `m-` commands.

TABLE 2.5 THE m- COMMANDS

Command	Description
`mattrib`	Displays the file attributes for the specified file(s)
`mcd`	Changes the directory to the specified path
`mcopy`	Copies the files specified to the new path
`mdel`	Deletes the specified files
`mdir`	Provides a directory listing
`mformat`	Formats a floppy
`mlabel`	Labels the DOS file system
`mmd`	Makes a directory
`mrd`	Removes a directory (must be empty, just as in DOS)
`mren`	Renames an existing DOS file
`mtype`	Displays the text contents of a DOS file

Note

Although you can view a DOS file with Linux and even do some editing on text files in DOS partitions that Linux can see, you can't execute DOS or Windows programs under Linux. However, projects are under way across the Internet to supply such emulation for Linux. Although the prospects look very good for such emulators in the future, at this time DOS and Windows emulation isn't fully available.

SHUTTING DOWN LINUX

When you're finished using a DOS machine, you can typically just turn off the power and walk away. You could also do the same under Windows, although you're likely to cause file damage. Under Linux, simply turning off the power presents even more chances for damaging your system, both to hardware and file systems. You must shut down Linux in an orderly fashion, or you might corrupt the operating system to the point where it can't boot the next time you try.

Linux keeps a lot of information about itself and files in memory, in areas called *buffers*, before writing the information to disk. This process helps improve system performance and control access to the hardware—something a multitasking operating systems needs to maintain so that one user doesn't try to use a hardware device that another user is using. If you turn off the power, this information is lost, and you can corrupt your file system.

→ See "Shutting Down Linux," p. 243

Because Linux is a multiuser and multitasking operating system, it must make sure that every user stops processing gracefully and saves any work in progress before shutting down the system to prevent data loss and file damage. This shutdown process also gives each user logged in to the system time to log out. To shut down Linux in an orderly fashion, you must use the `shutdown` command. The `shutdown` command syntax is as follows:

`shutdown [-r]` *`time-to-shutdown`* `[`*`message`*`]`

Tip #12 from *Jack*

For a quick restart you can use the `reboot` command. Also most Linux distributions for Intel PCs also trap the Ctrl+Alt+Delete three-finger salute and perform a reboot.

If you want to halt the system, you can specify the `-h` flag to `shutdown` or use the `halt` command.

`reboot` and `halt` can be dangerous since they do not perform a full shutdown sequence as does `shutdown`. When using `reboot` or `halt` you may want to use the `sync` command to flush all data cached in your system to the drives, just to be safe. For example:

```
sync; reboot
```

or

```
sync; halt
```

the semicolons allow you to specify multiple commands on the same command line.

The optional `-r` flag indicates that Linux should immediately reboot after it shuts down. This option is useful if you want to quit Linux and boot to another operating system.

`time-to-shutdown` indicates when the system should shut down. The time is specified on a 24-hour clock, so you can tell the machine to shut down at 11 p.m. by entering the following:

```
shutdown 23:00
```

The *message* parameter is a message sent to each user logged in to the system. This message is displayed on their terminals. You can use this message to tell users why you're shutting down the system. For example, if you need to do weekly backups, you can use the following message to make sure that everyone logs out of the system:

```
shutdown -r 23:00 Shutting down at 11:00pm for maintenance
```

Remember, don't simply turn off the computer or press the reset button to exit Linux.

Caution

On some systems, Linux traps the Ctrl+Alt+Del reboot keystroke and executes an orderly shutdown as though the user had typed the `shutdown` command. However, on some systems, Linux can't detect this keystroke combination and reboots immediately.

If you do accidentally turn off your system and damage the file structure, you can use the `fsck` command to try to repair the file system.

→ See "Using the `fsck` Command," p. 449

TROUBLESHOOTING

After your machine reboots, the LILO prompt should appear. Make sure that you can boot to your old operating system if you left it on the hard drive. If that system was DOS, press Shift and then type the short word you used to identify the DOS partition when you installed LILO. If you enter an invalid word, press Tab to get a list of valid operating system types. If you're having problems at that point, place your DOS boot disk in the boot drive and reboot.

You should be able to boot from your boot disk. When your system is up and running under DOS, try the Linux boot disk you created during installation—not the ones you created to originally install the entire system. If that boot disk doesn't work, you may have to reinstall Linux. Potential problems to check initially are the kernels and your hardware. Before starting over, make sure that you have the appropriate hardware. If you made notes during the installation process, check which kernel you installed against what hardware you have. Make sure your hardware is supported by Linux.

Below are some answers to common problems listed on Red Hat's Web site. These troubleshooting tips are used under the provisions of GNU's GPL.

Q: Can I use a hard drive that has more than 1023 cylinders?

A:The infamous 1023 cylinder question. Yes, but not to boot Linux. You can install Linux on partitions above the 1023 cylinder, but to boot Linux, the `root` directory and specifically the `/boot` directory must be installed on the first hard drive below 1024.

Q: How do I add arguments for LILO at the prompt?

A:Some hardware requires that extra parameters be fed to the kernel before the kernel will recognize the hardware. You can accommodate this by editing the `/etc/lilo.conf` file to provide the necessary parameters, or you can provide them manually during boot up. See the LILO HOW-TO for more examples of LILO parameters.

Q: Why does LILO hang on LI?

A:This is a symptom of the 1023 cylinder problem addressed previously. If you have installed the boot system above 1023, LILO will not be able to boot the system. You can try to boot from a floppy using the rescue disk you made during installation, or you can repartition your hard drive and reinstall Linux.

Q: The installation will not find the SCSI card.

A:To remedy this, you need to add a boot-time argument such as the following:

```
LILO: linux qlogicfas=0x230,11,5
```

This option can be made permanent so you don't have to re-enter it. See the LILO configuration option `append` in the lilo.conf man page.

Q: How do I uninstall LILO?

A:If you want touninstall LILO and reinstall the original boot record, try using this command

```
lilo -u /dev/hda
```

which represents the boot record of the first IDE drive. Parameters may vary for your machine, for example, if your first hard drive is a SCSI drive, you would use `/dev/sda`.

Q: Can I use LILO and Win98 on one installation?

A:Yes, install Windows 98 first and then install Linux. During the installation, tell Linux to place LILO in the MBR. You can also use a commercial program such as System Commander.

Q: How do I mount a CD-ROM?

A:Installing Red Hat 6.0 should place the proper entries in your `/etc/fstab` file, as shown in the following listing:

```
#
# /etc/fstab
#
# You should be using fstool (control-panel) to edit this!
#
# <device>   <mountpoint>   <filesystemtype> <options>   <dump>   <fsckorder>
/dev/sda1               /                       ext2      defaults 1 1
/dev/sda5               /home                   ext2      defaults 1 2
/dev/cdrom              /mnt/cdrom              iso9660   noauto,ro 0 0
/dev/fd0                /mnt/floppy             ext2      noauto 0 0
/dev/sda6               /var                    ext2      defaults 1 2
/dev/sda2               none                    ignore          0 0 0
```

```
none                    /proc                   proc        defaults
/dev/sda7               none                    swap        sw
```

Note the use of `noauto` for the `cdrom` entry. Without this setting, Linux will try to automount the CD-ROM when it boots, which isn't really a problem unless there's no CD in the drive.

If there is not an entry in your `fstab` file, you can either edit `/etc/fstab` or use the X Window Control Panel tool to add the appropriate mount information. Also, make sure the mount point `/mnt/cdrom` does indeed exist. If the entry is correct, you can `cd` to the mount point and issue the following commands:

```
cd /mnt
mount cdrom
```

Q: I have Red Hat 5.0 and have upgraded to the `ld.so` *RPM package listed in the errata, but my* `libc5` *applications still create a seg fault. What is wrong?*

A:The problem with crashing `libc5` applications can be caused by several things.

Before or after the upgrade, another version of `libc` might have been installed that was not obsoleted by the upgrade process, or the `libc5` libraries might have been placed in a location that causes conflict.

To find out if this is the case, run this command:

```
rpm -qa ¦ grep libc
```

It should produce the following output:

```
glibc-devel-2.0.5c-12
libc-5.3.12-24
glibc-debug-2.0.5c-12
rpm-2.4.10-1glibc
rpm-devel-2.4.10-1glibc
glibc-profile-2.0.5c-12
glibc-2.0.5c-12
```

If you see items like `libc-debug-5.3.12-18` or `libc-5.4.44-2`, you will need to remove these packages (with the command `rpm -e libc-debug`) and run `ldconfig Dv`.

Your `/etc/ld.so.conf` file has been changed from an optimal setting. For optimal loading, set your `/etc/ld.so.conf file` in the following order:

```
/usr/i486-linuxaout/lib
/usr/i486-linux-libc5/lib
/usr/openwin/lib
/usr/X11R6/lib
```

Q: Some of my older applications get the incorrect time.

A:Some `libc5` apps want `/usr/lib/zone` info. You can either recompile them for `libc6`, or you can provide a symlink with the following command so things will work.

```
ln -s ../share/zoneinfo /usr/lib/zoneinfo
```

Q: I have all the latest updates installed, but my programs still get the incorrect time.

A:If you have installed all the latest updates and your programs still get the incorrect time, try checking the settings in `/etc/sysconfig/clock`. They probably look something like this:

```
UTC=true
ARC=false
```

This means that Linux will assume your BIOS clock is set to the UTC or GMT time zone. More than likely, the clock is set to your local time zone, and you need to change the UTC line to the following:

```
UTC=false
```

Q: When the system boots up, I see a message that says I have unknown PCI hardware. What does this mean?

A:The error "unknown PCI device" can occur for several reasons. The first and most harmless one is that PCI isn't responding to Linux's queries in a way it understands, but Linux is able to keep going. The more common occurrence is that the system hangs on, querying PCI bus cards, and cannot get any further.

Because this is a hardware problem in the kernel, there is not much that Red Hat can do except point you to the maintainer of that section of the kernel. That person might be able to let you know what is going on and might want to look at what hardware you do have in your system so she can better handle it in the future. The maintainer can be reached at:

`linux-pcisupport@cck.uni-kl.de`

Include the following information

`/proc/pci`

which is your exact hardware description. Try to find out which device is unknown. It may be your main board chipset, your PCI-CPU bridge, or your PCI-ISA bridge. If you can't find the actual information in your hardware booklet, try to read the references of the chip on the board.

Q: Linux isn't detecting my NE2000 compatible network card.

A:It has been found that some NE2000s that worked with earlier kernels do not work with the later 2.0.x kernels. For some, the following workaround will enable them to work.

You can try to get the card to work by entering the following settings:

```
insmod 8390

insmod ne io=0XXXX irq=Y
```

Note

Replace `XXXX`and `Y` with your IO address and IRQ. Most common values for the IO address are 0x300 and 0x310. The IRQ can be anything.

After this, use `ifconfig` or `netcfg` to configure the card. Sometimes, even though the card is recognized, it fails to transfer TCP/IP packets. This is being looked into.

If the previous settings work, add them to `/etc/conf.modules`. It should look something like this:

```
alias eth0 8390
alias eth0 ne
options eth0 io=0xXXX irq=Y
```

Q: I have installed Linux, and it seems to initially start booting. However, when it gets down to something called sendmail, the machine seems to hang. What is happening, and what should I do?

A:If after the install the machine seems to hang when it reaches certain processes like sendmail, apache, or SMB, there is probably a network problem. The most common cause is that Linux cannot look up the name of the machine you have called the box (if you set up networking to have a machine name). The machine is currently paused waiting for the network timeout of DNS lookups and will eventually bring up the login prompt. When you get the prompt, log in as root and check the usual culprits for a problem.

If you are directly on a network with a DNS server, make sure that the `/etc/resolv.conf` file has the correct values for your machine's DNS server. Check with your systems administrator for the correct values.

If you are using Linux on a network without a DNS server (or if this box is going to be the DNS server), you will need to edit the `/etc/hosts` file to have the hostname and IP address so that the lookups will occur correctly. The format of the `/etc/hosts` file is like the following example

```
127.0.0.1          localhost localhost.localdomain
192.168.200.1      mymachine mymachine.mynetwork.net
```

where the example machine is called `mymachine`.

CHAPTER 3

INSTALLING RED HAT LINUX

In this chapter

by Jack Tackett, Jr.

Starting the Installation Process

This chapter gives you the information you need to install the Red Hat distribution of Linux. Although this book leads the way, you might find the need to use the resources, such as the various How-Tos, provided on the Red Hat CD-ROM. However, Red Hat is one of the easiest distributions to install, so take heart!

First, you need to decide how to install the product. Table 3.1 describes the various methods available for installing Red Hat 6.0. No matter what medium you select, you need either one or two blank floppy disks, depending on your selected installation method. If you have a PC capable of booting from a CD-ROM, and you do not need PC card (PCMCIA) support, then you need just the Red Hat CD-ROM and no floppy disks.

Table 3.1 Installation Methods

Method	Description	Pros/Cons
Floppy/CD-ROM	You can use this traditional method to install most Linux distributions.	A floppy boot disk is used, and then installation continues from the CD-ROM. This installation method is the most likely to succeed on the first try.
CD-ROM	You can boot and install directly from CD-ROM by using autoboot.	This method is fast, but you must have a PC that can boot from a CD-ROM. Most older systems do not have this capability.
Hard Drive	You can copy CD-ROM contents to an unused hard drive or partition and install from the copy.	This method is fast, but you need the free space for the copy and free space for the installation.
HTTP	You can install from a remote location viathe Web.	You must have a supported network card and a network connection. Transfers may be slow, depending on your connection speed. In fact, you should attempt an HTTP install only if you have a cable modem or xDSL connection.
FTP	This method is the same as for HTTP, but it uses a remote FTP server.	This method poses the same problems as an http installation—slow connections and possible hardware incompatibilities.

TABLE 3.1 INSTALLATION METHODS

Method	Description	Pros/Cons
NFS	You can install from a Network File System server.	This method is typically used in local area networks (LANs) to install many Linux systems from a single site. Network problems and bandwidth may cause problems.

If you're doing a full installation and not upgrading a previous version of Red Hat Linux, you need to decide on what class of installation after you decide on the method. Red Hat provides for three types of installations: workstation, server, and custom.

Caution

Installing Red Hat Linux over another distribution, such as Caldera, Debian, Slackware, or SuSE, may destroy important configuration files, data, and program files. Red Hat does not save information from those distributions as it does when upgrading from prior Red Hat distributions. If possible, you should put your home directories on a separate drive so that upgrades can go smoothly from one system to another. You should also save your `/etc` directory and `/var` directory. If you have installed local software, such as programs from `/usr/local`, then you should save that information, too.

- **Workstation**—Select workstation if you intend to use Linux for your day-to-day tasks. Be careful, though, because selecting Workstation erases all prior Linux partitions along with all the data selected. You need approximately 600MB for a typical workstation installation.
- **Server**—Select server if you want to have a complete Linux Internet server and a capable workstation system, too. A server installation also destroys data and requires more disk space. You need over 1.7GB of disk space for a complete server installation.
- **Custom**—This type of installation is typical of previous versions of Red Hat. With this selection, you can pick and choose your partition sizes and installation packages.

INSTALLING FROM FLOPPIES OR CD-ROM

To start the installation process, you need one or two (depending on the installation method) 3 1/2-inch 1.44MB formatted floppy disks. You will use these disks to create a boot disk for the Linux installation. You should also have an extra disk available to create a rescue disk.

Next, you should make sure that you have enough hard disk space to install Linux. Everything on the CD-ROM, if installed, requires about 1.7GB of disk space, but you can get by with less, especially if you don't install the X Window System. To decide on the amount of space, you should decide how much space you want for user accounts—that is, the space you want to provide to your users. On a single-user system, 500MB is adequate.

Next, you need to decide how much swap space your machine needs. You can figure on at least 64MB. Finally, you can figure about 256MB for your root directory. It is the main directory from which all other directories under Linux are accessed.

→ See "Linux Standard Directories," p. 418

Tip #13 from Jack

You can also run part of the Linux file system from the CD-ROM without installing all the software, but at a great decrease in system performance. You can choose to do so during installation.

If you decide to install and configure the X Window System (highly recommended), you should also write down what type of chipset your video card uses. If you have a serial mouse and modem, write down the serial port that each is using. You need this information later during the configuration process.

→ See "Installing the XFree86 System," p. 508

UNDERSTANDING THE VARIOUS INSTALLATION METHODS

If you're reading this book, you will probably install Red Hat Linux from the accompanying CD-ROM. However, you can use one of the following five methods to install Red Hat: from CD-ROM, via Network File System (NFS), via File Transfer Protocol (FTP), via a Session Message Block (SMB) image on a shared drive, or from a hard drive.

To install Linux directly from a CD-ROM, you need access to DOS. From the DOS prompt, execute the command

```
[cdrom-drive]:\dosutils\autoboot
```

where [*cdrom-drive*] is the drive letter for your system's CD-ROM.

Caution

This method erases your hard drive. Be sure to back up any files you fear losing.

If you have another partition available, you can install Linux to coexist with your system without erasing what's already there. To do so, you need the CD-ROM, an empty partition, and a boot disk. You'll learn later in this chapter how to create the boot disk, as well as how to repartition your hard drive.

For those of you who have systems that can boot from a CD-ROM (check your BIOS settings), you can boot and install from the Red Hat CD-ROM.

NFS (Network File System) provides a way to install Red Hat across a network. First, you must mount the CD-ROM drive on a machine supporting the ISO-9660 file system with RockRidge extensions and then export the file system via NFS. You need to know the path to the exported file system and the IP number or, if Domain Name Service (DNS) is configured, the name of the system.

FTP (File Transfer Protocol) is a method for transferring files across the Internet. (Chapter 32, "Accessing the Network with `telnet`, `ftp`, and the `r-` Commands," explains FTP in more detail.)

Installing Red Hat from a hard drive requires the same boot disk used for an FTP installation. First, you create a directory named `RedHat`. Then you copy the corresponding directory from the CD-ROM, and all the subdirectories there, to the `RedHat` directory. You can use the following DOS commands to do so:


```
cd \RedHat
xcopy /s e:\RedHat
```

The `cd` command assumes that you're already on the installation hard drive; the `xcopy` command assumes that your CD-ROM drive is drive E.

No matter which method you use, you'll need to gather some information.

COMPILING NECESSARY INFORMATION

Before starting the installation, you need the following information about your system:

- The type of video card, chipset, and monitor used
- The serial port used by your mouse
- The serial port used by your modem
- The network information for your computer, if it's connected to a network (items such as its IP address, gateway, and domain name)
- The type of hard drive and CD-ROM drive in your system and their controller types
- The directory structure you want to use on your system, such as placing `/home` on a separate hard drive and `/var` on a separate partition from your swap file
- The name you intend to call your system (the hostname)

If you're connecting to the Internet, you can get most of this information from either your network administrator or your Internet service provider (ISP).

If you intend to use other operating systems on the same computer (such as Windows 95/98, Windows NT, or OS/2), you need to create the necessary partitions for these operating systems. Typically, you need to use the operating system's partitioning software because Linux can't handle these other partition types.

ON THE WEB

A product named System Commander, from V Communications, lets you install and switch between 32 different operating systems. You can find more information about this product at the following site:

`http://www.v-com.com/`

Next, you should check for any last-minute changes to the Red Hat distribution. The reasons for checking are many, but the two major reasons are that Linux is constantly updated, and this chapter is being written at least a month before the CD-ROM is cut. In the interim, new material or bug fixes may have been released.

ON THE WEB

You can also check for updated material on the Web at the following site:

`http://www.redhat.com/errata`

If you're not installing directly from the CD-ROM, you next need to repartition your current hard drive to make room for Linux. This step may cause problems because repartitioning a hard drive destroys any data contained on the affected partitions. After making room for Linux, you need to boot the Linux system and create its new partitions and file systems. Typically, Linux systems need a primary partition to store the files on and a swap file partition, especially if you have a machine with 8MB or less of memory.

Note

A *file system* is basically a section of your hard drive specially formatted to hold certain types of files. UNIX and Linux use file systems to represent entire sections of the directory tree. This use is in contrast to MS-DOS, which places subdirectories in the directory tree on the same logical drive. UNIX systems use the directory tree format because placing subdirectories on different drives is safer. If one drive malfunctions, only the information on that drive needs to be replaced or fixed.

→ See "Understanding File Systems," p. 440

After creating the file systems, you then can install the Linux operating system, its support files, and various application packages distributed with the system. To install Linux, you must first boot a stripped-down version of the operating system. You do so by creating a boot disk containing the stripped-down operating system.

CREATING THE BOOT, SUPPLEMENTAL, AND RESCUE DISKS

You create the boot and supplemental disks by using the rawrite program. You can find this program on the accompanying CD-ROM in the `/dosutils` subdirectory. For this step, you need two formatted floppies: one labeled *boot* and the other labeled *rescue*. Place the boot disk in drive A and enter the following:

```
E:\dosutils>rawrite

Enter disk image source file name: e:\images\boot.img
Enter target diskette drive: A:
Please insert a formatted diskette into drive A: and press -ENTER-
```

If you want to abort the process, simply press Ctrl+c to stop. If rawrite fails, try a new formatted disk. If the problem persists, you should have your hardware checked for possible problems.

Next, you should create a rescue disk. Unlike previous releases of Red Hat, with 6.0, you cannot use the installation disk to boot the system in case of problems. To provide for better problem resolution, Red Hat has introduced a rescue disk image (`rescue.img`). To create the rescue disk, you can use `rescue.img` as the source file in the preceding `rawrite` commands.

INSTALLING THE LINUX SYSTEM

To start the Linux installation, you place the boot disk you created into your disk drive and reset your computer. After your system does its hardware and BIOS checks, you should see the following boot messages on your system:

```
Welcome to Red Hat Linux
To install or upgrade a system running Red Hat 2.0 or later, press the
<ENTER> key.
To enable expert mode, type expert <ENTER>. Press <F3> for more information
about expert mode.
This disk can no longer be used as a rescue disk. Press <F4> for more
information on the new rescue disk.
Use the Function Keys listed below for more information
[F1-Main] [F2-General] [F3-Expert] [F4-Rescue] [F5-Kickstart] [F6-Kernel]
boot:
```

Table 3.2 provides information on the various function keys and their uses. Typically, you only need to press Enter to continue installation.

TABLE 3.2 INSTALLATION FUNCTION KEYS

Function Key	Description
F1	Displays the main screen shown earlier in this section. Pressing F1 always returns you to this screen.
F2	Provides general information on the installation process.
F3	Explains expert mode. Basically, the Linux installation process autoprobes the hardware trying to determine what is installed. This probing can hang a system. If your system hangs, you must enter expert mode and specify your system's hardware during installation.
F4	Provides instructions on creating and using the rescue disk.
F5	Allows you to perform an unattended installation using a configuration file in Red Hat 6.0. This screen provides information on performing such an installation.

TABLE 3.2 INSTALLATION FUNCTION KEYS

Function Key	Description
F6	Tells you how to pass some extra parameters to the kernel during boot-up if Linux can't boot properly.

Tip #14 from *Jack*

For more information on passing boot parameters, see the "Linux BootPrompt How-To" on the CD-ROM at `/doc/HOWTO/BootPrompt-HOWTO`. You can use either WordPad or a word processor such as Microsoft Word to read this file; however, the file is too large to use Notepad.

The system displays the following prompt and then begins initializing the system:

```
Loading initrd.img....
loading vmlinuz....
```

After booting, your system displays the Welcome screen (see Figure 3.1).

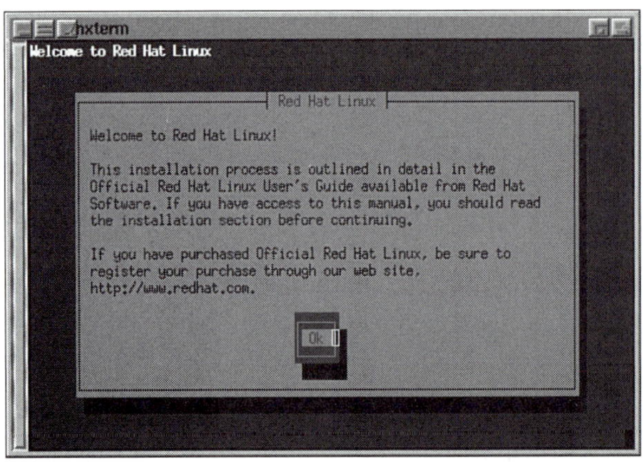

Figure 3.1 The Red Hat Linux Welcome screen greets you at the beginning of your adventure.

Press Enter to continue. The next screen asks you which language to use during installation.

Note

Moving around in the dialog boxes is easy, and the installation program provides reminders at the bottom of most screens. To move from element to element (field), you can press Tab or Alt+Tab. You use the spacebar if you need to select an item from a list or check a check box. To choose a button (typically OK or Cancel), you press Enter. To scroll through a list of selections, you use the arrow keys.

The next dialog box asks you to select the type of keyboard used by your system (see Figure 3.2).

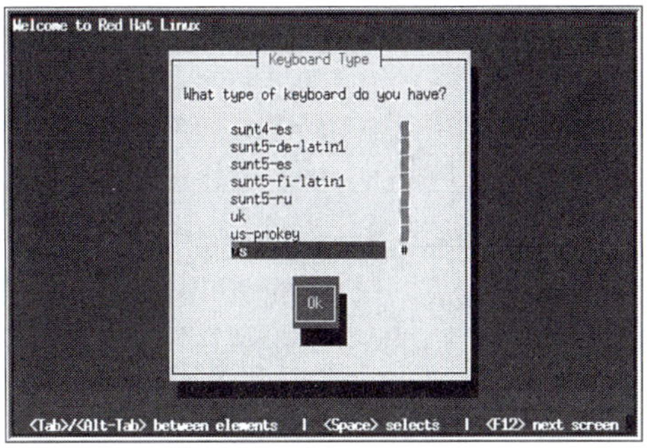

Figure 3.2
Linux uses the selections you make about your keyboard during installation and when you boot your system in the future.

Tip #15 from Jack

You can use `/usr/sbin/kbdconfig` to change your keyboard selection in the future.

The next screen asks whether you need PCMCIA (PC Card) support for your system (see Figure 3.3). Select the appropriate answer by using the Tab key, and press Enter.

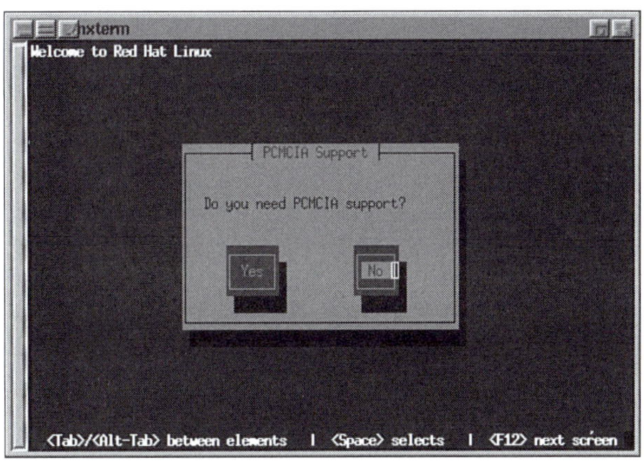

Figure 3.3
Red Hat Linux provides optional support for PCMCIA cards.

Next, you need to select the installation method. After you select your installation method, press Enter. The installation program prompts you to insert the Red Hat CD-ROM into the CD-ROM drive. When you're done, simply press Enter to continue.

Note

The rest of this chapter assumes that you're installing from the local CD-ROM drive. If you select another method of installation, see the appropriate help topics or Red Hat's Web site at `http://www.redhat.com`.

Next, the installation program attempts to autoprobe the system's CD-ROM type. If the program determines the CD-ROM correctly, installation continues; if not, you must select the type from the following selections:

SCSI	Use this selection for true SCSI devices
Other CDROM	Use this selection for non-IDE or soundcard-compatible CD-ROMs

If you select Other, the installation program displays the selection dialog box shown in Figure 3.4. Select the appropriate drive type and press Enter to continue installation.

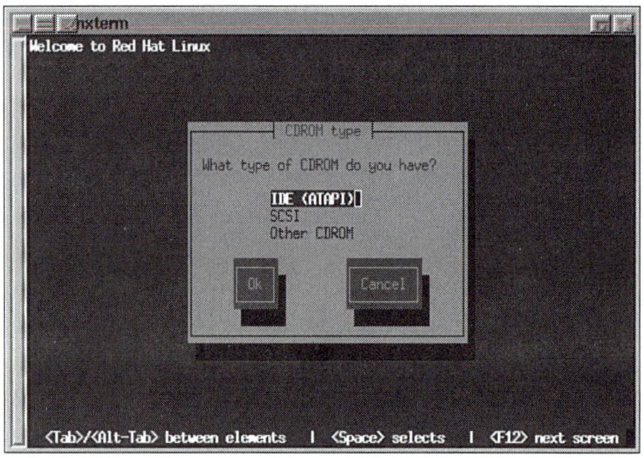

Figure 3.4
The Red Hat Linux installation program needs to know what type of CD-ROM is used in your system.

The Other CDROM category includes such drives as those sold by Creative Labs (SoundBlaster) and other multimedia kit-based CD-ROMs, as well as the following:

Aztech CD	Sanyo
Goldstar R420	Sony CDU-31A
Mitsumi	Sony CDU-5xx
Optics Storage 8000	SoundBlaster/Panasonic
Phillips CM206/CM260	

Depending on your selection, the installation program may ask for some parameters, such as IRQs or DMA addresses. Or the program may try to determine these values automatically by probing your hardware. It's best to let the program autoprobe first before providing parameters.

Tip #16 from *Jack*

Any time the installation program probes the system's hardware, the system may hang. If that happens, you must reboot and redo the installation. Be sure to try to collect the needed information, such as IRQs and DMA addresses, before attempting to reinstall.

After detecting your CD-ROM type, the system starts its installation from the CD-ROM drive. First, it asks you whether you're installing a new system or upgrading an existing Red Hat system. Red Hat 6.0 easily upgrades over versions 2.0 or greater, but no Linux distribution easily upgrades over a different distribution version. So if you have a prior distribution version, such as Slackware, you would be wise to just perform a new installation and blow away your prior system—after backing up important data files, of course. If you're upgrading from a previous version of Red Hat, the installation program saves any current configuration files with the `.rpmsave` extension.

→ See "Updating Packages with RPM," p. 171

All actions performed by the installation program are also saved in the file `/tmp/upgrade.log`.

Tip #17 from *Jack*

> To see what the installation program is doing, you can press Alt+F3 to change to the virtual terminal that displays every action taken.

Next, the installation program probes for any SCSI devices. The program may ask you to select a SCSI controller and display the Configuration dialog box, where you tell the system whether you have any SCSI adapters in your system. Choose the appropriate button and continue.

If you have a SCSI adapter, the program displays the Load Module dialog box from which you can select from the following SCSI drivers:

Adaptec 152x	Iomega PPA3 (Parallel port Zip)
Adaptec 1542	NCR 5380
Adaptec 1740	NCR 53c406a
Adaptec 2740, 2840, 2940	NCR 53C810/53C820 PCI
AdvanSys Adapters	Pro Audio Spectrum/Studio 16
Always IN200	Qlogic FAS
Buslogic Adapters	Qlogic ISP
DTC 3180/3280	Seagate ST01/02
EATA DMA Adapters	Trantor T128/T128F/T228
EATA PIO Adapters	UltraStor 14F/34F
Future Domain TMC-885, TMC-950	UltraStor 14F/24F/34F
Future Domain TMC-16x0	Western Digital wd7000

ON THE WEB

For current information on hardware that Red Hat 6.0 does and doesn't support, see Red Hat's Web site at the following address:

`http://www.redhat.com/corp/support/hardware/intel/60/rh6.0-hcl-i.ld.html`

Next, you must partition your disks—or at least select the partitions you've already created. The installation program displays the Disk Setup dialog box shown in Figure 3.5. You can use the command-line fdisk program or the GUI-based Disk Druid program. If you want to use fdisk, move to the fdisk button and press Enter. When you press this button, you drop into the fdisk program to partition the selected hard drive. If you want to use the Disk Druid program, skip forward to the section "Using Disk Druid."

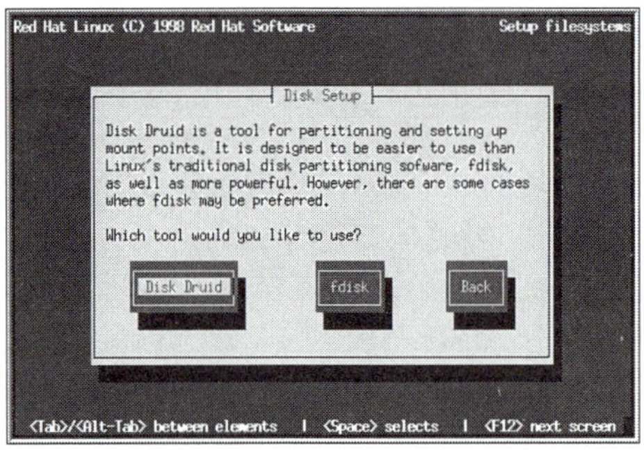

Figure 3.5 You have to prepare your hard drives for installation. You can use the GUI program Disk Druid or the command-line fdisk program.

USING THE LINUX FDISK PROGRAM

At the fdisk prompt, type `m` for a list of commands. Table 3.3 lists the available commands.

Caution

You use the fdisk program native to Linux for these actions. Be careful because this program is different from the fdisk programs included with other operating systems such as MS-DOS, Windows 95/98, and OS/2. You cannot use these programs interchangeably! For example, you cannot use Linux's fdisk to rearrange a partition for a DOS partition. Although you can use any fdisk to create partitions, you must use the appropriate operating system's version of fdisk to perform such actions as setting file types.

TABLE 3.3 THE LINUX FDISK COMMANDS

Command	Description
`a`	Toggles a bootable flag
`c`	Toggles the DOS compatibility flag
`d`	Deletes a partition
`l`	Lists known partition types

TABLE 3.3 THE LINUX FDISK COMMANDS

Command	Description
m	Displays this menu
n	Adds a new partition
p	Displays the partition table
q	Quits without saving changes
t	Changes a partition's system ID
u	Changes display/entry units
v	Verifies the partition table
w	Writes the table to disk and exits
x	Provides extra functionality for experts only

To begin the partitioning, select the p command (press p and then Enter) to display the current partition table, which should reflect the drive you partitioned earlier with the DOS FDISK program. Listing 3.1 shows a possible listing from the p command.

LISTING 3.1 EXAMPLE OF A CURRENT PARTITION TABLE

```
Disk/dev/hda: 15 heads, 17 sectors, 1024 cylinders
Units = cylinders of 255 * 512 bytes
Device       Boot        Begin        Start       End       Blocks       Id       System
dev/hda1                   1        1          41      5219      1     Novell?
```

Note

Your screen might appear different than what's shown in Listing 3.1 because the values are different for each drive type and the partitions already defined on that drive.

Listing 3.1 indicates the various partitions already defined that it can detect, the starting and ending locations of the partition, and how big it is in blocks. The listing also indicates the partition type. Table 3.4 shows all the different types of partitions you can define by using the Linux fdisk program. The primary partition types used here are 83-Linux Native and 82-Linux Swap. You can get a similar listing by using the l command.

TABLE 3.4 PARTITION CODES AND TYPES IN LINUX FDISK

Hex Code	Partition Type
0	Empty
1	DOS 12-bit FAT
2	XENIX root

TABLE 3.4 PARTITION CODES AND TYPES IN LINUX FDISK

Hex Code	Partition Type
3	XENIX usr
4	DOS 16-bit < 32MB
5	Extended
6	DOS 16-bit >= 32MB
7	OS/2 HPFS
8	AIX
9	AIX bootable
a	OS/2 Boot Manager
40	Venix 80286
51	Novell?
52	Microport
63	GNU HURD
64	Novell
75	PC/IX
80	Old MINIX
81	MINIX/Linux
82	Linux Swap
83	Linux Native
93	Amoeba
94	Amoeba BBT
a5	BSD/386
b7	BSDI fs
b8	BSDI swap
c7	Syrinx
db	CP/M
e1	DOS access
e3	DOS R/O
f2	DOS secondary
ff	BBT

In Listing 3.1, Linux prints a note about the different physical and logical endings at the bottom of the screen. The difference exists because on the system used to write this chapter, a prior partition containing the DOS D drive was left intact, whereas the C drive was repartitioned to a smaller C drive to make room for Linux. Thus, space exists between the C drive and the D drive. The necessary partitions required by Linux will be created here.

The begin, start, and end numbers from Listing 3.1 are very important, so you should write them down. You'll need them in a later step to specify the necessary sizes of the partitions you'll add.

Tip #18 from *Jack*

While the numbers are very important, you can specify the disk space using +xxxM bytes rather than cylinder numbers. Cylinder numbers are much more accurate though.

ADDING THE NECESSARY PARTITION

Because you've repartitioned the drive for DOS, you shouldn't have to delete any partitions for Linux. You should only have to add partitions. To add a partition, you issue the `n` command, which displays the following:

```
Command Action
e extended
p primary(1-4)
```

Now, you can press p and then Enter. When fdisk asks for the partition number, enter your selection and press Enter. If you indicate a partition number already in use, fdisk reports this fact and asks you to delete the partition before trying to add it to the partition table. For this example, enter `3` to add a third primary partition that's referred to as `/dev/hda3`.

Next, fdisk asks for the location of the first cylinder. This is usually the first available cylinder; in fact, fdisk displays a default range for your selection, as shown in this example:

```
First cylinder (42-1024) :
```

Notice that the first partition ends at cylinder 41 and that the next partition begins at cylinder 1024. Thus, the range supplied by fdisk here allows you to start the next partition anywhere in the range of 42-1024. It's a very good idea not to place partitions just anywhere throughout the disk; instead, choose the next available location, which in this case is cylinder 42. Enter `42` and press Enter.

Note

Linux can have trouble booting from partitions defined to start at cylinders above 1024. If you can create a Linux partition only in this range, you might have to boot Linux from a floppy. If the `/boot` directory is located within the first 1024 cylinders, the system boots fine. Otherwise you'll learn how to create a boot floppy (different from the boot floppy used for installation) later in this chapter. The only downside is that booting Linux from a floppy takes a little longer than booting it from the hard drive.

Now fdisk wants you to specify how much space to allocate for this partition. You can express this size in number of cylinders or by the number of bytes (`+size`), kilobytes (`+sizeK`), or megabytes (`+sizeM`). Because you should already know the approximate size you need for the swap file, you can define this partition first and then leave the rest of the disk space for the Linux program partitions. Thus, for this example, your machine has 8MB of RAM, so you need to specify a 16MB partition size by replying as follows:

```
Last cylinder or +size or +sizeM or +sizeK (42-1023): +16M
```

You should then use the `p` command to look at the new partition table you've defined. In this example, the new partition table looks like this:

```
Disk /dev/hda: 15 heads, 17 sectors, 1024 cylinders
Units = cylinders of 255 * 512 bytes
Device      Boot    Begin    Start    End    Blocks    Id    System
/dev/hda1  *         1        1        41     5219 1    DOS   12-bit FAT
/dev/hda2           1024     1024     4040   384667+ 51        Novell?
Partition 2 has different physical/logical endings:
phys=(967, 14, 17) Logical=(4039, 14.17)
/dev/hda3          42       42     170     16447+    83    Linux native
```

By default, fdisk makes the new partition a Linux Native type. To change this type to a swap partition, you need to use the `t` command. To do so, enter `t`, and then enter the partition number you want to change; in this example, enter `3`. fdisk then requests that you enter the hexadecimal value of the desired partition type from Table 3.4 (if you don't have the table handy, you can type `l` to get the list of codes). Because you want a swap partition in this case, enter `82` at the prompt.

As you can see, fdisk reports the new partition type, but you can also use the `p` command to double-check that partition 3 is now a Linux swap partition.

Now you can add your Linux partitions. For this example, add only one partition, but if you want to have multiple partitions for various reasons, you can also do so at this time. To add a partition, enter `n`, specify `p` for another primary partition, and then specify the number for this partition (`4`). To keep from fragmenting different partitions across the drive, start the last partition where the other left off, at cylinder 171. Because you want to use the rest of the space for the Linux system, you can specify the last cylinder instead of an exact byte count. Thus, enter `1023`, as shown here:

```
Command (m for help): n
Command action
e extended
p primary partition (1-4)
p
Partition number (1-4): 4
First cylinder (171-1024): 171
Last cylinder or +size or +sizeM or +sizeK (171-1023): 1023
```

Now use the `p` command to verify the new partitions. If you need to make any changes, you can do so now.

When you're satisfied with the layout of your partitions, you can use the `w` command to write the partition table information to the hard disk. None of your changes are permanent until you use the `w` command; thus, if you feel you've made some changes in error, you can use the `q` command to exit without altering the partition table. If you use the `w` command, Linux tells you the partition table has been altered and then resynchronizes the disks to match the new partition table. If your Linux system hangs at this point, you can reboot with the installation boot and root disks until you're back at the `#` prompt.

Caution

Don't use the Linux fdisk program to create or modify partitions for other operating systems. Doing so could leave the hard drive in a useless state for both operating systems.

CREATING THE SWAP PARTITION

Most current distributions of Linux provide automatic creation and activation of the swap file during installation, so you don't have to worry about creating the swap file. However, if you're using a distribution that does not create the swap file, you might need to create and activate the swap file before continuing with the installation.

Note

If you get an "out-of-memory" type error during the installation procedures that follow, you should increase the size of your swap file. If you already have the maximum of 16MB, you need to create and activate another swap partition by following these instructions. Remember that the Red Hat installation program allows only one swap partition.

Next, you need to activate the swap system by using the `swapon` command, as follows:

```
# swapon /dev/hda3
```

Again, if you're using the accompanying Red Hat CD-ROM, you shouldn't have to worry about activating the swap system as long as you create the partition for one. During installation, the installation program detects the swap partition and automatically starts the system for installation.

After you create your partitions on the various hard drives and return to the Partitioning Disks dialog box, choose the Done button to continue with the installation.

Next, the system asks you to select the active swap space, which should be the partition you created and marked as type Linux Swap (82) in the preceding section. Select this partition and choose OK. The program then initializes the swap space.

After creating the swap space, the program displays the Select Root Partition dialog box. The *root partition* is your main file system for Linux where all the boot files are located. Select the device (hard drive) for your root partition from the list box and press Enter. Now you can mount the other partitions, if any, from the Partition Disk dialog box. From here, you also can mount any DOS or OS/2 file systems so that you can access them from Linux. Select the partition to edit from the list box and press Enter. From the Edit Mount Point dialog box, you can specify a mount point—that is, a directory—to which you want this partition mounted.

→ See "Mounting and Unmounting File Systems," p. 444

After you select the root and mount points for your various partitions, the program formats those you selected. You select the partitions to format from the Format Partition dialog box.

USING DISK DRUID

Selecting the Disk Druid button on the Disk Setup dialog box (refer to Figure 3.5) displays the Disk Druid main screen shown in Figure 3.6.

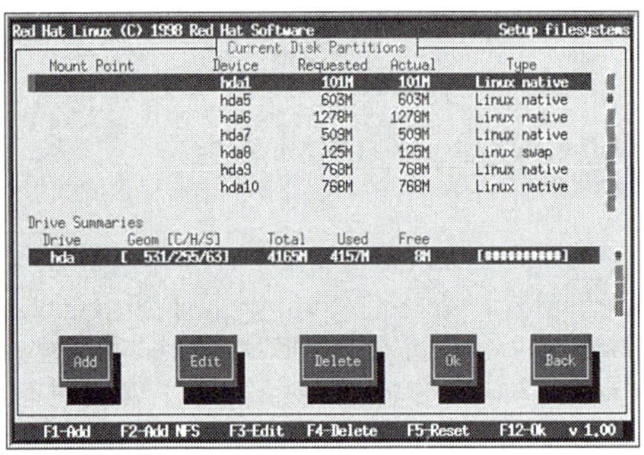

Figure 3.6 Disk Druid makes partitioning disks and creating mount points a snap.

Using Disk Druid, you can create partitions, set mount points on specified devices, set sizes of partitions, and specify file system types. Disk Druid provides information on these attributes. Table 3.5 lists the various fields and buttons on the Disk Druid main screen and describes what task each field or button performs.

→ See "Understanding File Systems," p. 439

TABLE 3.5 DISK DRUID FIELDS

Field/Button	Description
Mount Point	*Mount point* is another term for a directory. This field lists the location in which the specified directory and all subdirectories will be placed.
Device	This field indicates the physical hard drive and partition to which this mount point belongs.
Requested Size	In this field, you can specify either a default size for a partition or an initial size that can be allowed to grow.
Actual Size	This field indicates the actual size allocated for the partition.

TABLE 3.5 DISK DRUID FIELDS

Field/Button	Description
Type	This field indicates the file system type of the partition.
Drive Summaries	This portion of Disk Druid's main screen provides information on the specified device (hard drive/patron) including such information as the amount of space available. Remember, a hard drive device can have several partitions.
Add	This button adds a new partition.
Edit	This button edits the selected mount point.
Delete	This button deletes the selected mount point.
Ok	This button commits the specified changes to your system and continues with the installation program.
Back	This button returns to the previous dialog box in the installation program and aborts all changes you have specified.

To add a new partition, you can click the Add button or press the F2 function key to display the Edit New Partition dialog box shown in Figure 3.7.

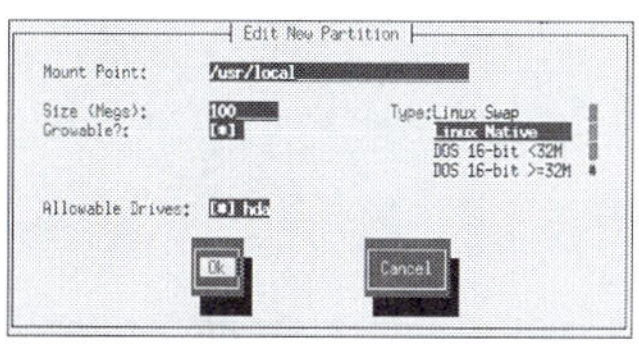

Figure 3.7
You don't need to remember all those different file system types. The Edit New Partition dialog box presents them all in a list box.

Here, you can enter the mount point for this new partition in the Mount Point field. Examples are the root partition (`/`) or the var partition (`/var`). Next, you can specify the size of the partition in megabytes and indicate whether you want the partition to grow in size as necessary when you add and delete other partitions. Next, you must select from the Type list box what type of file system you want on the partition. Finally, you can select which physical hard drive to place the partition on by selecting the appropriate hard drives from the list of Allowable Drives.

Note

If you specify a size that's too big for the space available on the indicated device, Disk Druid tells you and prompts you to reduce the amount of requested space. Disk Druid also warns you of other potential problems and provides you with possible solutions.

INSTALLING THE SOFTWARE COMPONENTS

Congratulations! Your system is now prepped for Linux, but you're only halfway finished. Now you must select the various software components to install and then configure them.

The installation program displays the Components to Install dialog box, from which you can select the various packages. Table 3.6 describes each package.

TABLE 3.6 THE INSTALLATION COMPONENTS

Component	Description
Printer Support	Allows you to print from your Linux system.
X Window System	Provides the GUI for all UNIX—hence, Linux—-workstations; the X Window System is a powerful GUI like Windows 95/98 and OS/2.
Mail/WWW/News tools	Provides programs to use email, surf the World Wide Web, and read and post Usenet news.
DOS/Windows Connectivity	Allows you to access DOS files, run DOS programs, and run some Windows programs (with limited success).
File Managers	Provides tools such as Midnight Commander to manipulate your file systems.
BRU Backup Util	Provides a single-user version of the popular tape backup program.
BRU X11 Front End	Provides a GUI interface under the X Window System to BRU.
Real Media Client	Allows you to access Real Media programs on the Internet.
Real Media Server	Allows your Linux server to provide Real Media content to the Internet.
Graphics Manipulation	Provides programs to work with graphic images such as xv and the popular The GIMP.
X Games	Provides popular strategic and arcade type games that run under the X Window System.
Console Games	Provides games that run on a text console.
X Multimedia Support	Provides multimedia support for the X Window System.
Console Multimedia Support	Provides multimedia support for text consoles.
Print Server	Allows your Linux box to act as a print server on your network.
Networked Workstation	Provides networking applications and Simple Network Management Protocol (SNMP) support.
Dialup Workstation	Allows you access to the Internet via dial-up lines—that is, via a modem.

Table 3.6 The Installation Components

Component	Description
News Server	Allows your system to act as a news server (if you can get a news feed), thus providing news to your users.
NFS Server	Allows your system to export and attach to other file systems on your network.
SMB (Samba) Connectivity	Provides SMB services, both client and server.
IPX/NetWare Connectivity	Provides access to Novell NetWare networks.
Anonymous FTP/Gopher Server	Allows you to set up your system so that others can access it via anonymous FTP.
Web Server	Includes the most-used Web server software today, Apache.
DNS Name Server	Provides the software needed to run your own Domain Name Server on your Linux system.
PostGres (SQL) Server	Allows you to run the PostGres SQL database system.
Network Management Workstation	Provides utilities and tools to help troubleshoot and monitor your network, including SNMP services.
TeX Document Formatting	Provides a series of programs used to add formatting codes to documents.
Emacs	Installs the ubiquitous editor for Linux (you can do anything with Emacs, or so the Emacs gurus say).
Emacs with X Window System	Provides an X Window System front end to the powerful Emacs editor.
C Development	Provides the GNU `gcc` compiler and tools.
Development Libraries	Provides various libraries needed by the various development tools, such as `gcc` and `g++`.
C++ Development	Installs the GNU C++ compiler, `gcc`.
X Development	Provides the tools, libraries, and miscellaneous items (such as fonts) needed to develop X Window System applications.
Extra Documentation	Provides the Linux documentation project containing the important How-Tos, along with other helpful information.
Everything	Installs everything on the CD-ROM. You need about 350MB available, not counting free space for your data files.

Note You can select individual packages by checking the appropriate check box in the dialog box, or you can install everything by selecting that list option. To select a package to install, simply move to the desired component and press the spacebar. After you select all your components, tab to the OK button and press Enter.

Tip #19 from
Jack

You can use the RPM program described in Chapter 7, "Upgrading and Installing Software," to install any package in the future.

The next dialog box after the installation informs you that you can see the files installed by viewing the file `/tmp/install.log`. Press Enter to continue with the installation.

Now comes the hard part—waiting. Transferring and decompressing upward of 1600MB of programs can take awhile. Setup firsts installs a file system on your indicated partitions and then starts installing software. In the Install Status dialog box, the system informs you of its progress as it installs the various files you selected. Installation time varies depending on what you're installing and how fast your machine can process the information. Relax and order a pizza!

Configuring Your System

After installing the software, the installation program begins to configure your system. It first configures your mouse by displaying the Configure Mouse dialog box. Here, you can simply select the mouse type that best describes your mouse from the list box. Remember, many mouse devices can emulate the Microsoft serial mouse if they have to. The Emulate 3 Buttons check box is there because many PC mouse devices have only two buttons, and the X Window System usually uses three buttons to maneuver and make program selections. If you check this box, the system makes clicking both mouse buttons at the same time the same as pressing the middle button on a three-button mouse. After you make your selection, choose OK.

Tip #20 from
Jack

You can use the command `/usr/sbin/mouseconfig` to reconfigure your mouse at any time in the future.

Next, you must specify the serial port that your mouse connects to. After you make the selection from the list box, tab to the OK button and press Enter. The program then prompts you to select the type of video card in your system.

Caution

Try to select the correct video card because of all things software-based, the only subsystem that software can easily destroy is your video card and monitor. If you make the wrong decision, you might fry your monitor! Although this outcome is highly unlikely, there's still the slight possibility, so choose wisely, young Linux Walker.

The system now tries to install the proper XFree86 server for your hardware.

→ See "Installing the XFree86 System," p. 508

Next, you must select your monitor. Again, you should be as specific as possible. After you select your monitor, the program asks for the amount of video memory your card contains. Make the appropriate selection and choose OK to continue.

Remember all those warnings about frying your monitor? Well, now you really have a chance to toast it, so be careful. The next screen prompts you to select the clockchips located on your video card. These chips are used to drive the video signals through your card and into your monitor. If they're way out of synchronization, the signals can—you guessed it—fry your monitor (few actually explode, most just fizzle and smoke). Please be careful! If you have no clue as to what clockchips your card is using, take the default selection, No Clockchip Setting, and choose OK.

After you select your clockchips (or lack thereof), the system can autoprobe and try to configure the X Window System. The autoprobe might hang your system, but as long as nothing is seriously wrong (for example, you selected outrageous clock speeds for your card), you can simply reboot and continue with the installation. You do have the option to skip the autoprobe and continue with the installation.

Note

I have installed Red Hat many times, and Red Hat 6.0 is the first distribution to properly configure my X Window System. You may have worse luck than me, especially when dealing with laptops, but don't worry if your X installation fails. You can configure X after installation by using the various configuration programs available.

→ See "Configuring XFree86," p. 514

If the autoprobe succeeds, the system displays an information screen on selecting the resolutions you want to use with your system. You can select more than one, as long as your video card and monitor can handle the resolutions. Finally, the program tells you how to start and stop your X Window System.

CONFIGURING YOUR NETWORK

After configuring the X Window System, the installation program continues with your network. If your machine is or will be connected to the Internet and you installed the networking components, you should choose Yes and continue.

First, the system asks which Ethernet driver to use in the Load Module dialog box. Select the appropriate driver for your Ethernet card and choose OK.

Again, the installation program might try to autoprobe your hardware to determine certain values for the card. This probing can hang the system and force you to reboot. If this happens, hang in there. First, make sure that you selected the correct driver. Then see whether you need to pass any special parameters to the device, such as IRQ or DMA address settings. You can do so by selecting the Specify Parameter option instead of the autoprobe option.

Note

Ethernet is the most popular network interface for Linux today. Other technologies, such as Token Ring, ISDN, and ATM, have some support.

If the system can detect your network card, it leads you through setting up your TCP/IP network.

CONFIGURING THE TCP/IP NETWORK

The installation software uses the Configure TCP/IP dialog box to gather your system's TCP/IP information. Your network administrator or Internet service provider can provide the following information: your machine's IP number, netmask, network address, and broadcast address.

Next, the system must configure your network. It gathers information from the Configure Network dialog box. You must specify your network's domain name and your system's host name. The domain name is typically the last two parts of an Internet address. For example, if the name is `www.netwharf.com`, then `netwharf.com` is the domain name and `www` is the host name.

Next, your network administrator must give you the values for your system's default gateway and the primary name server. Your network may also have a secondary name server, too, so enter the value in the appropriate place.

Note

Be careful what you name your host because this name will appear on your default prompt line, in mail messages, and in log reports. Do you really want your boss to receive mail from `uradork.netwharf.com`**?**

Configuring the Clock

Next, you have to specify how your system will keep time and in what time zone it exists. You do so in the Configure Timezones dialog box. Check whether you want to use local time or Greenwich mean time (GMT), and then pick your time zone from the list box. After you make your selections, choose OK.

Selecting the Services to Start on Reboot

For the next step, you need to specify the services (programs and daemons) that your system will start automatically when it boots. You select from the list of services displayed in the Services dialog box, shown in Figure 3.8. Table 3.7 provides a list of the available services and a description of their uses. Those services marked with an asterisk (*) have been selected by Red Hat to start on reboot by default.

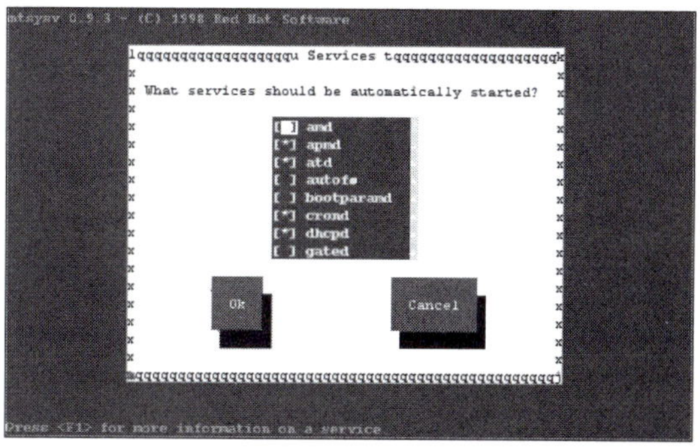

Figure 3.8 Linux gives you control of which programs to start at boot time, which is similar to the startup folder under Microsoft Windows.

→ See "Understanding the Boot Process," p. 234

Table 3.7 Startup Services

Service	Description
`amd`	Runs the automount daemon
`apmd*`	Monitors battery status and can shut down the system on low battery conditions
`atd*`	Runs `at` commands at their scheduled times
`autofs`	Automatically mounts file systems when you use them
`bootparamd`	Allows Sun servers to boot from a Linux box using `bootp`
`crond*`	Runs the `cron` daemon
`dhcpd*`	Provides Dynamic Host Configuration Protocol (DHCP) services
`gated`	Runs the `gate` daemon to provide routing services for Boarder Gateway Protocol (BGP) and other routing protocols
`gpm*`	Runs the program that provides mouse support to Linux

TABLE 3.7 STARTUP SERVICES

Service	Description
`httpd*`	Runs the Apache Web server
`Inet*`	Starts the `internet` super daemon (`inetd`) that provides all the sevices specified in `/etc/inet.conf`
`inmd`	Starts the Usenet news server `innd`
`kerneld*`	Starts the `kerneld` daemon, which loads and unloads kernel modules as they are needed
`keytable*`	Loads the appropriate keyboard map
`lpd*`	Provides printing services to Linux
`mars-new`	Loads the MArs NetWare file and print server daemon
`mcserv`	Provides midcommander remote file services
`named*`	Provides Domain Name Service (DNS) services
`network*`	Provides control of all the network interfaces
`nfs*`	Provides Network File System (NFS) server services
`nfsfs*`	Mounts and unmounts all NFS mount points specified in `/etc/exports`
`pcmcia`	Provides access to PCMCIA (PC Cards) services
`pnserver`	Starts the Real Media services
`portmap*`	Provides Remote Procedure Call (RPC) support for other protocols like Network File System (NFS)
`postgresql`	Runs the `postgres` database and provides Structured Query Language (SQL) services
`random*`	Saves and restores a random value to help generate better random numbers (which are used for various security systems)
`routed`	Provides for automatic router table updates using the Routing Information Protocol (RIP)
`rusersd`	Provides services that allow users to find one another over the network
`rwalld`	Enables users to use the `rwall` command to write messages on remote terminals
`rwhod`	Provides remote users with a list of all of the users logged into a machine by running the `rwho` daemon
`sendmail*`	Runs the `sendmail` daemon to provide email
`smb*`	Provides Session Message Block (SMB, or Samba) client/server services
`snmpd*`	Provides Simple Network Management Protocol (SNMP) support to Linux
`sound*`	Provides access to sound cards
`squid*`	Runs the `squid` proxy Web server
`syslog*`	Provides logging capability to your Linux system
`xntpd`	Starts the `NTPv3` daemon
`ypbind`	Binds YP/NIS clients to a yellow pages server

TABLE 3.7 STARTUP SERVICES

Service	Description
`yppasswd`	Allows users to change their passwords on systems running YP/NIS
`ypserv`	Provides NIS server functions

Tip #21 from
Jack

> Although you can manually change the services that run on startup by editing the appropriate `rc.d` files (see Chapter 10, "Booting and Shutting Down"), you can use the `/usr/sbin/ntsysv` command to go back to the Services dialog box and reconfigure the services with the GUI.

SELECTING YOUR ROOT PASSWORD

Now you must select your root password. This password is the ultimate key into your system, so you should take some care in choosing it. The superuser, or root, on a Linux/UNIX system can do great things—and can also wreak awesome damage. You should pick a secure password and be careful whom you give it to. In the Root Password dialog box shown in Figure 3.9, you enter the password twice to confirm what you've typed.

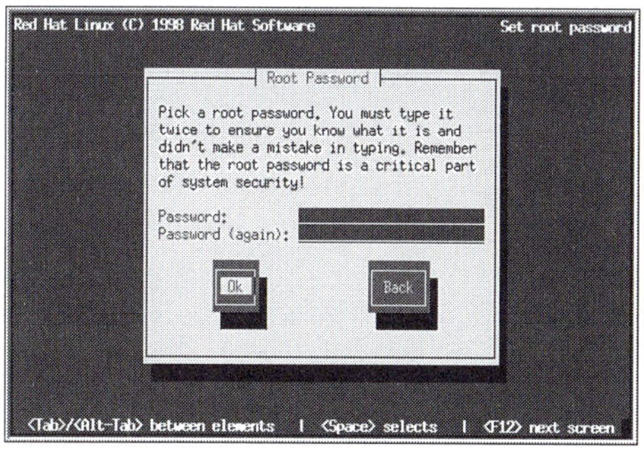

Figure 3.9 You must choose a root password wisely "young Linux Walker."

Although you can fix users' accounts when they forget their passwords, if you forget the root password, you might be forced to reinstall the system. However, booting from a floppy and editing the password file may allow a recovery.

→ See "Dealing with Password Security," p. 277

INSTALLING LILO

Next, you are asked to create a boot disk, as shown in the Bootdisk dialog box in Figure 3.10. We highly recommend you create a disk, just in case you cannot boot your computer in the future. A boot disk is your first tool for repair, followed by the rescue disk you created.

Figure 3.10
A boot disk can help you recover from a variety of system crashes or corrupted configuration files.

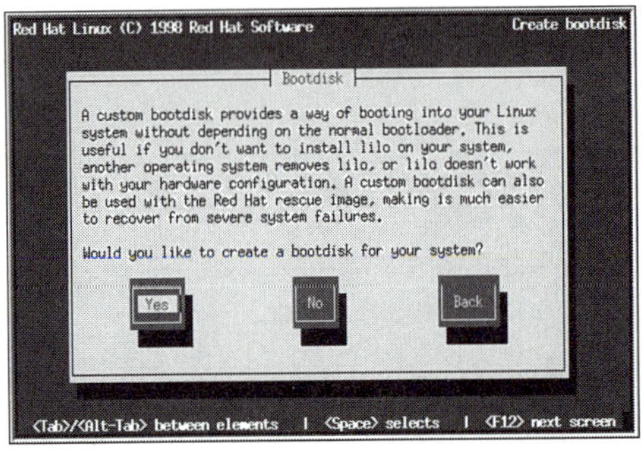

After creating the boot disk, you are asked to install LILO. *LILO* stands for *LInux LOader*. LILO, which is a program executed at system startup, lets you choose which operating system is used to boot the computer. You can use LILO to boot several different operating systems, such as Linux and MS-DOS. Press Tab to get a list of operating systems LILO can boot.

With LILO, you can specify a default operating system to boot and a default time limit before it boots that system. For example, if you have MS-DOS and Linux on your computer, you can configure LILO to boot either one. You could then tell LILO to boot MS-DOS if no one intervenes after 30 seconds. Before that 30 seconds is up, however, a user can specify another operating system to boot instead of the default. You can press the Ctrl, Alt, or Shift key to stop the timed process.

You specify all this information while configuring LILO. You can later directly edit the `lilo.conf` file located in the `/etc` directory. If you don't want to boot Linux automatically, you can select the Skip button to continue. Otherwise, select a hard drive to install LILO and press Enter to edit the entry.

Congratulations! After you load LILO, your system is up and running—and, let's hope, problem free.

TROUBLESHOOTING

After your machine reboots, the LILO prompt should appear. Make sure that you can boot to your old operating system if you left it on the hard drive. If that system was DOS, you can press Shift and then type the short word you used to identify the DOS partition when you installed LILO. If you enter an invalid word, you can press Tab to get a list of valid operating system types. If you're having problems at this point, place your DOS boot disk in the boot drive and reboot.

→ See "Troubleshooting," p. 55

You should be able to boot from your rescue disk. When your system is up and running under DOS, try the Linux rescue disk you created during installation. If that rescue disk doesn't work, you might have to reinstall Linux. Potential problems to check initially are the kernels and your hardware. Before starting over, make sure that you have the appropriate hardware. If you made notes during the installation process, check which kernel you installed against what hardware you have.

Going Back to the Beginning

After you complete the setup and configuration of your system, you should reboot the system so that all your setup and configurations can take effect.

Rebooting Linux is more involved than rebooting DOS; you can't just turn off the power and turn the system back on. If you do so in Linux, you can damage the file structures and systems. Linux tries to repair itself on boot-up. So, remember, don't turn off the power while you're running Linux.

→ See "Performing Backups and Restoring Files," p. 263

To exit Linux, you use the following command:

```
shutdown [-r] time
```

The optional `-r` indicates that the system should reboot after shutting down, and *`time`* indicates the time that the system should shut down. You can use `now` in place of *`time`* to indicate immediate shutdown. Linux also recognizes the warm boot keys used by DOS to reboot the machine, Ctrl+Alt+Delete, which Linux interprets as the command

```
shutdown -r now
```

When you shut down this way, make sure that you've removed the root disk from the drive, and reboot your new Linux machine.

Case Study: Installing Red Hat Linux on DEC Alphas

Unlike other distributions, Red Hat also provides Linux for Digital Equipment Corporation (DEC) Alphas. This distribution isn't included on the accompanying Red Hat CD-ROM, but it's available from Red Hat. For more information on getting this distribution, see Red Hat's Web site at `http://www.redhat.com/products/rhl-alpha.html`. When you have the correct distribution, you can use the following instructions to install Red Hat Linux on an Alpha.

Note

Red Hat also has a distribution for Sun's line of Sun Sparc processors. See Red Hat's Web site for more information.

Before installing the distribution on an Alpha, you should read the installation instructions in the first part of this chapter because many of the steps are the same. You also need access to a computer capable of reading and writing MS-DOS disks because you must create an installation floppy.

USING SUPPORTED ALPHA HARDWARE

Red Hat supports various Alpha hardware from both Digital Equipment Corporation (DEC) and other vendors. The following hardware is supported:

- AlphaPC64 (Cabriolet, Aspen Telluride)
- AxpPCI133 (Noname)
- EB64+ (Aspen Alpine)
- EB66 (NekoTek Mach 1)
- EB66+
- Jensen (DEC PC 150, 2000 model 300, Cullean)
- Universal Desktop Box (UDB, a.k.a. Multia)
- AlphaStation 200, 250, 255, 400 (Avanti machines)
- EB164 (Aspen Avalanche, Timerline, Summit)
- Kinetic's Platform 2000 machines
- PC164 (Durango)
- Alcor AlphaStations 500, 600 (Maverick, Brett)
- Alpha-XL
- Alpha-XLT (XL 300, XL 366)
- Mikasa AlphaServer 1000—the 1000A is NOT supported

All these systems have SCSI systems supported by Red Hat Linux. The video systems should work, too, although S3 support for the Jensen systems isn't included by default. To run the X Window System with a Jensen system, you need to download the X server from `ftp://ftp.azstarnet.com/pub/linux/axp/jensen`. Finally, all Ethernet solutions for these systems are supported, and the kernels for these machines also support Token-Ring adapters.

The hardware list changes frequently, so you should check the up-to-date list on Red Hat's Web site at `http://www.redhat.com`.

CREATING THE BOOT AND ROOT DISKS

You need to create a boot and root floppy for an Alpha installation. The boot disk contains a program image allowing you to boot the system. The root floppy provides an image of the Linux kernel for the system to use during installation. Just as for Intel machines, you use the rawrite program to create these disk images.

The boot disk image depends on the type of Alpha used. These images are located in the `/images` directory with a `README` file that provides more information on each image described in Table 3.8.

Table 3.8 Boot Images Available for DEC Alphas

Image	Description
`cab.img`	AlphaPC64, Cabriolet
`noname.img`	AxpPCI33, Noname, Universal Desktop Box (Multias)
`eb64p.img`	EB64+, Aspen Timberlines
`eb66.img`	EB66
`eb66p.img`	EB66+
`jensen.img`	Jensens
`avanti.img`	AlphaStation 200, 250, and 400
`xl.img`	Alpha XL
`xlt.img`	Alpha XLT
`eb164.img`	EB164-based machines
`p2000.img`	Platform 2000
`alcor.img`	Alcor-based machines
`mikasa.img`	Mikasa-based machines

To create a boot image for a Universal Desktop Box, you use the command

```
E:\dosutils\rawrite -f E:\images\noname.img -d a: -n
```

where `E:` represents the drive letter of your CD-ROM. After creating the boot disk, you must create the root disk, which contains the RAM disk image of the Linux kernel. You can create the root disk by using the following command:

```
E:\dosutils\rawrite -f E:\images\ramdisk.img -d a: -n
```

Installing the Main Red Hat Distribution

After you have your boot media ready, you can install Linux. The installation procedure is very much like the one outlined earlier in the section "Installing the Linux System." The installation program guides you through the process, prompting you to make selections from a list of possible choices.

To begin, you place your boot disk into the floppy drive and restart your system. At the prompt, you enter the following command:

```
boot fd0:vmlinux.gz root=/dev/fd0 load_ramdisk=1
```

You might see several SCSI messages flash by onscreen. Don't worry about them unless you see a message such as `scsi0 : 1`, which indicates that you have a SCSI termination problem that needs to be fixed before continuing with the installation. If all goes well, you should see the message `VFS: Insert Root floppy to be loaded into ramdisk`. Insert the root disk you created and press Enter to continue the installation process.

CHAPTER 4

Installing Caldera OpenLinux

In this chapter

by Jack Tackett, Jr.

WHAT YOU NEED TO INSTALL OPENLINUX

This chapter gives you the information you need to install the Caldera OpenLinux distribution. Like Red Hat and Debian, OpenLinux is a complete distribution of a multiuser, multitasking operating system based on the Linux 2.2.5 kernel. The CD-ROM accompanying this book contains a noncommercial version of Caldera's OpenLinux distribution. The version on the CD-ROM is a subset of Caldera's commercial OpenLinux Base product and as such does not contain programs such as Partition Magic or technical support.

ON THE WEB

For more information on Caldera's product line, visit the company's Web site at the following URL:

`http://www.calderasystems.com`

Your system must have the following components to successfully install OpenLinux:

- An 80386 or higher Intel-based PC (Caldera doesn't support other processors at this time).
- A 3 1/2-inch floppy drive.
- At least 16MB of RAM (32MB or more recommended).
- About 250MB of disk space, but a minimal system without the X Window System requires only about 100MB. A full installation with everything installed requires almost 1300MB.
- A mouse and video card supported by XFree86.

To briefly summarize, you need to partition your hard drive, create the boot floppy, and then install and configure the system.

Caution

You're about to make major changes to your system, so be careful. If you intend to install OpenLinux on your current Windows machine, you should make a backup copy of your system first.

INSTALLATION METHODS

To get started with your installation, you first need a distribution of Caldera OpenLinux, which is supplied on the accompanying CD-ROM. To start the installation process, you need to decide on an installation method. OpenLinux allows you to boot and install from the CD-ROM if you have a drive capable of booting from CD-ROM. Caldera also enables you to create the installation disks from Windows 98 or Windows NT. Finally, you can install the system onto a Windows machine if you have enough disk space to create a proper installation partition.

Next, you must decide how you intend to boot Linux. You have two choices:

> **Note** *Booting a system* refers to starting up the system's operating system and is a reference to the phrase "pulling yourself up by your bootstraps."

- You can boot Linux from a floppy disk, in which case you need an extra formatted disk—for a total of three disks.
- You can use a program called LILO (the *Linux Loader*). LILO allows you to specify which operating system to boot. Such programs as OS/2, Windows 98, and Windows NT provide similar functionality.

Next, you should make sure that you have enough disk space to install Linux. Most people can get by with 1000MB devoted to Linux; however, you can get by with less space if you don't plan to use such applications as TeX and the X Window System.

Having paper and pen nearby is a good idea, so you can take notes just in case something goes wrong. Besides, you'll need to jot down some numbers along the way. For configuring XFree86, the X Window System program distributed with Linux, you should write down what type of chipset your video card uses. If you have a serial mouse and modem, you should write down the serial port that each uses. You'll need this information later during the configuration process. The information gathered here will be used later on to help configure your new system. The time that you spend listing all the information now will reduce any aggravation later.

Making the Preparations

If you have a brand new system, or if you have an existing system but don't care what happens to the data already stored on the computer, you can skip most of the following sections and go directly to "Creating the Install and Modules Disks." If, however, you're already using a system and you simply want to add Linux, you must do some planning because Linux is another operating system, not just a collection of programs.

First, you must decide whether you want to erase the current contents of your system or whether you want to consolidate space and install OpenLinux in the free space generated.

In general, when you install Linux—a new operating system—you must do the following if you cannot boot from the CD-ROM:

- **Create the Linux boot disks**—You must create two floppies because you need to bootstrap Linux onto the new system.

- **Repartition the hard drive to make room for Linux**—Repartitioning a hard drive may cause problems because it destroys any data stored on the affected partitions.
- **Boot Linux**—After making room for Linux, you need to boot the Linux system to gain access to the tools required to create its new partitions and file systems.
- **Create the Linux partitions**—Typically, Linux systems need a primary partition to store the files on and a swap file partition, especially if you have a machine with 32MB or less of memory.
- **Create the file systems**—A *file system* is basically a section of your hard drive specially formatted to hold files. UNIX and Linux use file systems to represent entire sections of the directory tree. This use is in contrast to MS-DOS, which places subdirectories in the directory tree on the same logical drive. UNIX systems use the file system structure because placing subdirectories on different drives is safer. If one drive malfunctions, only the information on that drive must be replaced or fixed.
- **Install the Linux system and software applications**—After creating the file systems, you install the Linux operating system, its support files, and various application packages distributed with the system, such as the games and networking support packages.

PREPARING THE INSTALLATION FLOPPIES

You must make an installation disk for your PC. To install Linux, you need to repartition your hard drive to make room for the new operating system. Unfortunately, you can't simply copy the files over to an MS-DOS, OS/2, or Windows file system.

If your system can boot a CD-ROM, or if you have free partitions on your current hard drive, or if you don't mind destroying your current file system, you can install directly from the CD-ROM and not bother with making the installation disk. Making the modules disk is recommended, however, because you might need one of the drivers found on that disk.

Tip #22 from Jack

If your system uses a Buslogic SCSI controller, you definitely need the modules disk.

Note

To launch an OpenLinux installation from the CD-ROM, change the directory to `d:/col/launch` (using the series of commands `d:`, `cd col`, and then `cd launch`) and proceed according to the instructions in that directory's `README.us.txt` file. Remember to create the modules disk discussed in the next section.

If you use floppies, you need to decide on an installation program. Caldera provides two: Lizard and LISA. The Lizard installation, which is a graphical user interface (GUI) program, provides a user-friendly installation process, if it works. Unfortunately, if you need to specify unique parameters to the installation program—for example, to use hardware drivers available only on the modules disk—then the Lizard installation program is not a viable option; you should use LISA instead. LISA, which stands for the *Linux Installation and System Administration* program, provides a text-based menu system to first install OpenLinux and then help administer the system.

CREATING THE INSTALLATION AND MODULES DISKS

For the next step, you need to create the installation disks for Linux. Two floppies are needed with OpenLinux: the installation and the modules floppies. You create these floppies in one of two ways:

- From the CD-ROM installation program
- With an MS-DOS program called `rawrite` that's provided with most Linux distributions

CREATING THE INSTALLATION DISKS FROM THE CD-ROM

To start the Windows Setup program (which is a very nice multimedia program) from the CD, simply double-click the setup icon in the `winsetup` folder. The main setup screen then appears, as shown in Figure 4.1.

Figure 4.1 Caldera offers a variety of multimedia presentations as well as a variety of installation options.

From the main menu screen, you can do the following:

- Install Products
- View Online Documentation
- View Our Web site (`www.calderasystems.com`)
- Multimedia Presentations
- Register Now (not supported on enclosed CD)

- Contact Us
- Support and Training

To install OpenLinux, select the first menu option, Install Products. This selection displays the installation screen shown in Figure 4.2.

Figure 4.2
Caldera allows you to create installation disks from Windows and to install under Windows.

The first selection, Launch Linux Install, must run in DOS mode so it closes all your running programs and starts the installation process. You must prepare your hard drive prior to selecting this option (See "Preparing the Hard Disks" later in this chapter.)

The next selection, Create Floppy Install Diskettes, provides you the choice of creating floppies to use either the text-based installation program LISA or the GUI Lizard installation program. LISA provides a more robust installation than Lizard if you need to specify specific hardware during installation. After you create the necessary disks on your PC, you can install the system at any time.

Tip #23 from *Jack*

The commercial version of OpenLinux provides several utilities to allow you to repartition and install Linux on a Windows PC. If you want to install the program on a PC running Windows, you should choose the Partition & Launch Linux Install selection. This option installs a version of Partition Magic on your PC. You then can repartition part of your hard drive to create enough space to install Linux (between 250MB and 1300MB).

Caution

Repartitioning your drive is a dangerous undertaking. Make sure you have backups of your system on zip disks, tape, or CDRs. An even better solution is to allocate an entire drive to Linux.

To create the installation disks from the Setup program, select Create Floppy Install Diskettes, which displays the screen shown in Figure 4.3.

Figure 4.3
OpenLinux provides graphical tools to create the Lizard and LISA installation disks directly from the CD-ROM.

You should make sure you have two blank floppies available to create the disks.

Creating the Installation Disks from DOS

To create the installation disks from DOS, you use rawrite, which writes the contents of a file directly to a floppy without regard to the format. You use rawrite to transfer the images to the appropriate floppies.

Note

The examples in this chapter assume that your CD-ROM is drive `D:`. If it is not, you need to substitute the appropriate drive letter for your CD-ROM.

To create the installation disk, you can issue the following command:

```
D:/col/launch/floppies/rawrite3.com
```

This command starts the rawrite program, and you can follow the prompts. When you're asked for the file, indicate the appropriate installation file. For 1.44MB floppies, use the `install.144` file (as in `D:/col/launch/floppies/install.144`). For 2.88MB installation floppies, use the `install.288` file.

Next, following the same instructions, you can create the modules disk. This disk can be placed on either a 1.44MB floppy or a 2.88MB floppy. Specify the filename `D:/col/launch/floppy/modules.144`.

INSTALLING LINUX

To use the disks you just created, you simply place the installation disk into the drive and reboot your system. If you are installing from a DOS system, you should read the instructions found in the file `d:/col/launch/dos/README.us`. No matter which way you boot the system, the installation program displays a splash screen and welcomes you to Caldera's OpenLinux product. You are then asked to boot the system.

If you have any parameters to pass to the kernel before it boots, you can enter them at the `boot:` prompt. (For information on these parameters, see the "BootPrompt How-To" in `/doc/HOWTO`.) If you don't need to pass on any parameters, press Return to continue the installation.

The system now goes through a series of probes trying to determine what type of equipment your system uses. Then the Linux Installation and System Administration (LISA) program begins. During the installation, you can maneuver around the various dialog boxes by using the cursor keys to select choices from list boxes. The Tab key moves you from one item to another in a dialog box, such as from list boxes to buttons. At any time, you can press the Escape key to cancel a selection. To enter your selections, press the Return key.

Tip #24 from *Jack*

During installation, you can use the key sequence Alt+F6 to see the progress of the installation.

On the first screen, you can select the language to be used during installation. You can choose from English, German, French, Italian, Spanish, or Portuguese. After you make a selection, LISA asks you to select a keyboard to use. The Linux system uses configuration information based on your selection to bind certain keys to certain language characters.

USING A PREVIOUS CONFIGURATION

Next, LISA asks whether you want to use a previously saved configuration. The Caldera distribution allows you to create several installation configurations and save them. If you want to reinstall at a later date, you can reuse this predefined configuration so that you don't have to go through the entire configuration process again. Because this is your first time installing the OpenLinux system, you can simply answer No.

CONFIGURING LISA

Next, you must configure LISA. Typically, the defaults shown on the Change LISA Setup dialog box are acceptable. If you need to make changes, you can select the following options and make the appropriate change:

- **Disable Plug-and-Play Cards**—This option turns off the BIOS setting that interacts with Plug-and-Play cards. During autoprobing and configuration, these cards can cause problems with Linux.
- **Automatic Network Configuration with** `bootp`—This option allows another computer to issue network configuration to the current machine via the `bootp` protocol. At least initially, you should configure your own network options instead of trying to use `bootp`.
- **Automatic Network Configuration with Netprobe**—This option provides for network setup using Netprobe. Netprobe is a Caldera product similar in function to a computer running `bootp`, which allows remote network configuration.
- **Use Selection and Continue**—This option tells the program to accept your selections and continue with the installation.

PROBING FOR HARDWARE

Next, the system autodetects all the hardware it can. If LISA does not locate all your hardware, you have to use the modules disk you created earlier to load the appropriate hardware drivers. First, the system probes for IDE and ATAPI equipment. You can review the hardware list displayed by the Hardware Found (IDE/ATAPI) dialog box to see whether all your hardware has been detected. When you click the Continue button, LISA asks whether all hardware has been detected. If not, select No and continue with the hardware probes.

If the probe still does not find all your hardware, LISA displays the Kernel Module Manager dialog box. This dialog box gives you the following options:

- Continue with Installation
- Analyze Kernel Modules
- Load Kernel Modules
- Remove Modules

During installation, your typical selections are to load and analyze kernel modules. How much hardware you have to add support for determines how many times you cycle through the various dialog boxes associated with the Kernel Module Manager.

ANALYZING KERNEL MODULES

You can select the Analyze Kernel Modules function if you want to see what hardware was detected. You can also use this function to see what modules you or LISA have added through the course of installation. You can also review any messages the system has generated during the boot process. Table 4.1 describes each function in the Analyze Kernel dialog box.

TABLE 4.1 THE ANALYZE KERNEL FUNCTIONS

Function	Description
Return to Previous Screen	Returns you to the Kernel Modules dialog box.
Show Hardware That Has Already Been Found	Displays all the hardware found so far in your system.
Show Loaded Kernel Modules	Displays all kernel modules currently installed on your system.
Verbose System Analysis	Provides more detailed information messages during installation.
Display Boot Process Messages	Lists all information generated during the boot process (similar to the information displayed by the Alt+F6 key sequence). This information includes the results of probing your system and installing various kernel modules.
Store Information on a DOS Floppy	Allows you to create a copy of all the information available from the Analyze Kernel Module functions.

LOADING AND REMOVING KERNEL MODULES

The Load Kernel Modules function allows you to load various device drivers into Linux to support your hardware. These drivers are on the modules disk you created earlier. Table 4.2 lists the various subfunctions available in the Load Kernel Modules dialog box.

TABLE 4.2 THE LOAD KERNEL MODULES FUNCTIONS

Function	Description
Return to Previous Menu	Returns you to the Kernel Modules dialog box
Load Driver for CD-ROM	Allows you to select a driver for your CD-ROM from the modules disk
Load Driver for SCSI Adapter	Allows you to load a driver for your system's SCSI adapter
Load Driver for Network Card	Allows you to select a driver for your Ethernet card

To load a driver not currently available in the installation program, you must remove the installation disk from the floppy drive and then insert the modules disk. For example, several SCSI controllers are available from the installation disk, including Adaptec 2940s. However, the default installation disk does not contain drivers for Buslogic adapters. Therefore, to support a Buslogic controller, you need the modules disk. You are led through a series of dialog boxes to select the desired driver and also to provide any additional configuration information for the device. LISA offers context-sensitive help throughout the process; you can simply press F1 at any time to get help.

You should work your way down the function list, first installing support for your CD-ROM, then for any SCSI devices, and then for your network card. If you find you have installed the wrong driver, or if LISA's autoprobe installed the wrong driver, you can select the Remove Kernel Module function and indicate which module is to be removed. Next you need to prepare a place on your hard drive to install Linux.

PREPARING THE HARD DISKS

MS-DOS refers to most partitions and hard drives with a letter such as C or D. Linux refers to them in a very different manner. Linux refers to everything—devices, files, and so on—in the same manner.

Linux and MS-DOS communicate with hardware via a series of programs called *device drivers*. Whereas MS-DOS device drivers usually have an `.SYS` extension and can reside anywhere on the system, Linux stores all such device drivers in the `/dev` directory.

Note What Microsoft and Windows folks call *device drivers* are usually called *modules* in Linux.

The drivers Linux uses in installation were specified using the Kernel Modules dialog box. The important point to remember, though, is that because the hard drive, floppy drives, and CD-ROM drives are hardware, Linux uses device drivers in the `/dev` directory to access the drives. Linux also references these drives by their subdirectory names instead of by letters. Table 4.3 displays a typical Linux device directory.

TABLE 4.3 LINUX DEVICES

Device	Filename
Floppy drive A	`/dev/fd0`
Floppy drive B	`/dev/fd1`
First hard drive	`/dev/hda`
First primary partition on hard drive A	`/dev/hda1`
Second primary partition on hard drive A	`/dev/hda2`
First logical partition on hard drive A	`/dev/hda4`
Second hard drive	`/dev/hdb`
First primary partition on hard drive B	`/dev/hdb1`
First SCSI hard drive	`/dev/sda`

Notice that the entire hard drive is referred to as `/hdletter`. The primary partitions are given the next set of four numbers, followed by the logical partitions. Thus, logical partitions always start at `/dev/hda4`. SCSI hard drives and CD-ROMs follow the same convention, except that the `hd` is replaced by `sd`.

REPARTITIONING YOUR DOS DRIVE

This section assumes that you need to repartition a DOS drive. First, you execute FDISK by typing `fdisk` at the DOS prompt. The FDISK Options screen appears (see Figure 4.4).

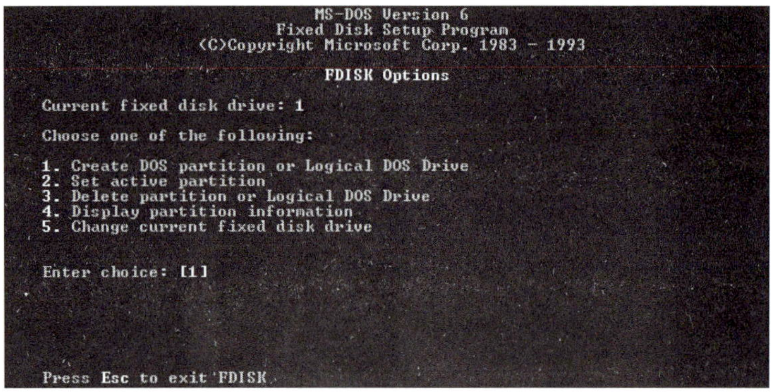

Figure 4.4
From the FDISK Options screen, you can look at current partitions, create new partitions, and delete old partitions.

The screen shown in Figure 4.4 might look different depending on which version of MS-DOS you're using. Pick menu option 4, Display partition information. The Display Partition Information screen appears (see Figure 4.5). Write down the information in this screen. You need the current partition table information if you decide to abort the Linux installation and put your system back the way it was before you started.

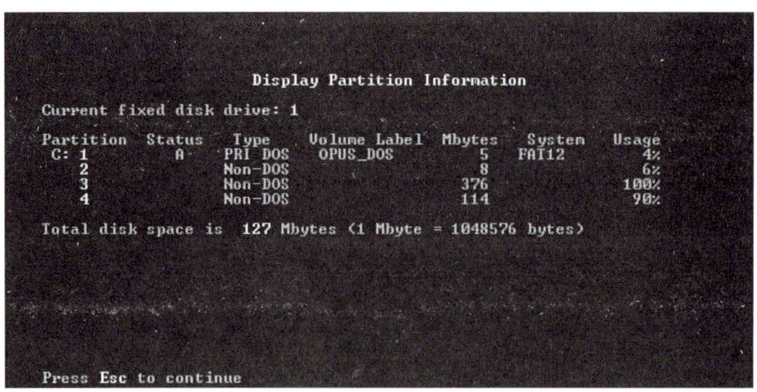

Figure 4.5
You can look at current partition information by using the Display Partition Information screen in MS-DOS 6.x.

An Alternative to Repartitioning Your Hard Drive

You may not need to repartition your hard drive, although it's thought that repartitioning offers the best introduction to Linux. You can use FIPS to non-destructively repartition your hard drive.

FIPS stands for *First non-destructive Interactive Partition Splitting*. A program developed by Arno Schaefer as a result of the Linux project, FIPS is used to move around DOS partitions to make room for Linux partitions.

You can find the complete instructions for using FIPS in the document `fips.doc` located on the accompanying Red Hat CD-ROM in the `/utils/fips` directory. This program can help only if you have enough free space left on your drive to install Linux; otherwise, you need to delete unneeded files or use the process described earlier to repartition your hard drive.

DELETING PARTITIONS

Unfortunately, FDISK doesn't allow you to simply resize a partition; you must first delete the partition and then add it back with the desired size. From the FDISK Options screen, choose menu option 3, Delete Partition or Logical DOS Drive, which deletes the necessary partitions. The Delete DOS Partition or Logical DOS Drive screen appears (see Figure 4.6).

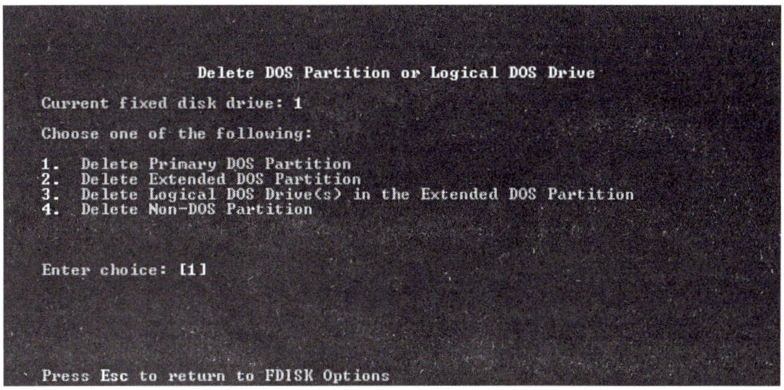

Figure 4.6
Use the Delete DOS Partition screen to delete a specific partition or logical drive.

Pick the appropriate menu option for the type of partition you're deleting, such as a primary DOS partition. For example, option 1, Delete Primary DOS Partition, allows you to delete primary DOS partitions.

Choose option 1 to display the Delete Primary DOS Partition screen (see Figure 4.7). The screen asks for a volume name of the partition and then a confirmation to see whether you really want to delete the partition. Because all information on the partition will be destroyed, FDISK wants to make absolutely sure that you want to delete the primary DOS partition.

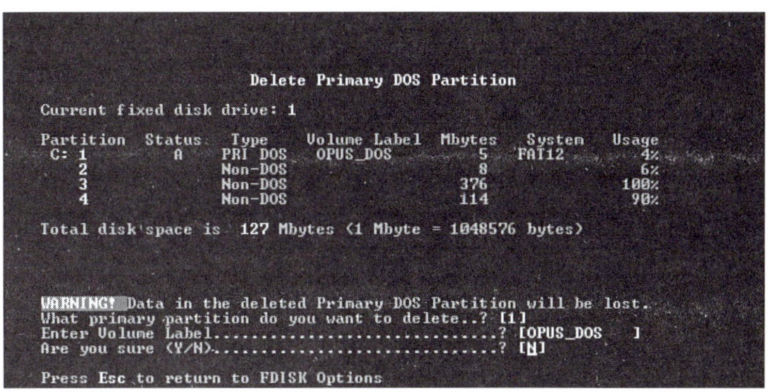

Figure 4.7
MS-DOS warns you when you try to delete a primary DOS partition.

ADDING PARTITIONS

After you delete all the necessary partitions, you must add the appropriate partitions for your DOS system by selecting the Create a DOS Partition menu item on the FDISK Options screen. Figure 4.8 shows the Create a DOS Partition or Logical DOS Drive screen.

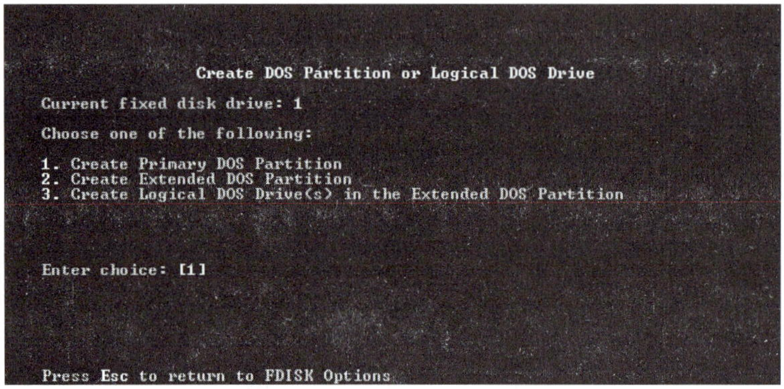

Figure 4.8
Most operating systems require a primary active partition to boot properly.

Note

You can't add the Linux or OS/2 partitions with the DOS FDISK program. Partitioning the hard drive for Linux is covered later in the section "Using the Linux `fdisk` Command."

Providing all the space available for the partition and making the partition the active partition are the FDISK defaults, as shown in Figure 4.9.

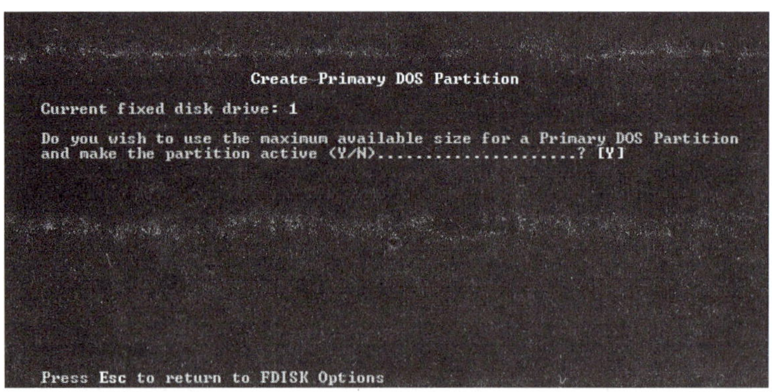

Figure 4.9
You can use all the disk space for one partition or spread out the free space across several partitions.

Active indicates that the partition is bootable. To boot DOS, you must specify the primary partition as active. Choose N (no) for this first selection so that you can specify the exact amount of disk space to provide to your DOS partition. Answering no to the question in Figure 4.9 displays the Specify Disk Space for the Partition screen. Specify the desired space for your DOS partition either in megabytes or in percentage of space available and press Return.

Next, you must set this partition as active. From the FDISK Options screen, choose menu option 2, Set Active Partition, and simply follow the instructions on the set active menu screen.

FORMATTING THE PARTITION

After you repartition your hard drive, you need to prepare the new partition for DOS and restore the appropriate files back to the DOS partition. Reboot your computer with the boot disk you made earlier. Then format the appropriate drive and transfer the system files by using the following DOS command:

```
format c: /s
```

When the partition is formatted, you can restore your backup to the new drive. Remember, if you reduced the size of the partition, not all the files will fit on the new drive. It might be necessary to place the files that don't fit on the new drive onto other DOS drives or partitions.

USING THE LINUX FDISK PROGRAM

At the `fdisk` prompt, you can enter `m` for a list of commands. Table 4.4 shows a list of available commands.

TABLE 4.4 THE LINUX *fdisk* COMMANDS

Command	Description
`a`	Toggles a bootable flag
`c`	Toggles the DOS compatibility flag
`d`	Deletes a partition
`l`	Lists known partition types
`m`	Displays this table
`n`	Adds a new partition
`p`	Prints the partition table
`q`	Quits without saving changes
`t`	Changes a partition's system ID
`u`	Changes display/entry units
`v`	Verifies the partition table
`w`	Writes the table to disk and exits
`x`	Provides extra functionality (experts only)

To begin the process of partitioning, you select the `p` command to display the current partition table, which should reflect the drive you partitioned earlier with the DOS FDISK program. Listing 4.1 shows a possible display from the `p` command.

LISTING 4.1 AN EXAMPLE OF A CURRENT PARTITION TABLE

```
Disk /dev/hda: 15 heads, 17 sectors, 1024 cylinders
Units = cylinders of 255 * 512 bytes

Device       Boot     Begin     Start     End      Blocks     Id     System
dev/hda2      1024      1024     4040     384667+     51     Novell?
Partition 2 has different physical/logical endings:
phys=(967, 14, 17) Logical=(4096, 14.17)
```

Note You might see different information than what's shown here because the values are different for each type of drive and the partitions are already defined on that drive.

The display in Listing 4.1 indicates the various partitions already defined, the starting and ending locations of the partitions, and how big each partition is in blocks. The display also indicates the partition type. Table 4.5 lists all the different partition types you can define by using the Linux `fdisk` command. The primary partitions used here are 83-Linux Native and 82-Linux Swap. You can get a similar listing by using the `l` command.

TABLE 4.5 THE KNOWN LINUX PARTITION TYPES

Reference Number	Type
0	Empty
1	DOS 12-bit FAT
2	XENIX root
3	XENIX usr
4	DOS 16-bit < 32MB
5	Extended
6	DOS 16-bit >=32MB
7	OS/2 HPFS
8	AIX
9	AIX bootable
a	OS/2 Boot Manager
40	Venix 80286
51	Novell?
52	Microport
63	GNU HURD
64	Novell
75	PC/IX
80	Old MINIX

TABLE 4.5 THE KNOWN LINUX PARTITION TYPES

Reference Number	Type
81	MINIX/Linux
82	Linux Swap
83	Linux Native
93	Amoeba
94	Amoeba BBT
a5	BSD/386
b7	BSDI fs
b8	BSDI swap
c7	Syrinx
db	CP/M
e1	DOS access
e3	DOS R/O
f2	DOS secondary
ff	BBT

Notice the note about the different physical and logical endings at the end of Listing 4.1. The difference exists because, on the system used to write this chapter, a prior partition containing the DOS D drive was left intact, whereas the C drive was repartitioned to a smaller C drive to make room for Linux. As a result, space exists between the C drive and D drive. The necessary partitions required by Linux will be created here.

The begin, start, and end numbers from the display are very important. You should write them down because you'll need them in a later step to specify the necessary sizes of the partitions you'll add.

ADDING THE NECESSARY PARTITIONS

Because you've repartitioned the drive for MS-DOS, you shouldn't have to delete any partitions for Linux. You should only have to add partitions. A standard set of partitions should include the following:

- A `/` (root) partition for the whole system
- A `swap` partition for the swap file
- A `/usr` partition for software
- A `/home` partition for user directories
- A `/var` partition for log files

To add a partition, issue the `n` command, which displays the following:

```
Command Action
```

```
e extended
p primary(1-4)
```

Now, you can press the p key and then Return. When fdisk asks for the partition number, enter your selection and press Return. If you indicate a partition number that's already in use, fdisk reports this fact and asks you to delete the partition before trying to add it to the partition table. For this example, enter `3` to add a third primary partition that's referred to as `/dev/hda3`.

Next, fdisk asks for the location of the first cylinder. This is usually the first available cylinder. In fact, fdisk displays a default range for your selection, such as the following:

```
First cylinder (42-1024) :
```

From the preceding example, you can infer that the first partition ends at cylinder 41, and the next partition begins at cylinder 1024. Thus, the range supplied by fdisk allows you to start the next partition anywhere in the range of 42 to 1024. It's a very good idea not to place partitions just anywhere throughout the disk, so choose the next available location—in this case, cylinder 42.

Note

Linux can have trouble booting from partitions defined to start at cylinders above 1024. If you create a Linux partition starting above 1024, you might have to boot Linux from a floppy. You'll learn how to create a boot floppy (which is different than the boot floppy used for installation) later in this chapter. The only downside is that booting Linux from a floppy takes a little longer than booting from the hard drive.

Now fdisk wants you to specify how much space to allocate for this partition. You can express this size in number of cylinders or by the number of bytes (`+size`), kilobytes (`+sizeK`), or megabytes (`+sizeM`). Because you should already know the approximate size you need for the swap file, you can define this partition first and then leave the rest of the disk space for the Linux program partitions. For this example, because your machine has 8MB of RAM, you need to specify a 16MB partition size by replying like this:

```
Last cylinder or +size or +sizeM or +sizeK (42-1023): +16M
```

You should then use the `p` command to look at the new partition table you've defined. In this example, the new partition table looks like this:

```
Disk /dev/hda: 15 heads, 17 sectors, 1024 cylinders
Units = cylinders of 255 * 512 bytes

Device       Boot    Begin    Start    End    Blocks     Id     System
/dev/hda1    *       1        1        41     5219 1     DOS   12-bit FAT
/dev/hda2            1024     1024     4040   384667+ 51       Novell?

Partition 2 has different physical/logical endings:
phys=(967, 14, 17) Logical=(4039, 14.17)
/dev/hda3           42      42     170    16447+    83     Linux native
```

By default, fdisk makes the new partition a Linux native type. To change this type to a swap partition, you need to use the `t` command. To do so, enter `t` and then enter the partition number you want to change; in this example, enter **3**. fdisk then requests that you enter the hexadecimal value of the desired partition type (refer to Table 4.5). If you don't have Table 4.5 handy, you can enter **l** to get the list of partition type codes. Because you want a swap partition in this case, enter **82** at the prompt.

As you can see, fdisk reports the new partition type, but you can also use the `p` command to verify that partition 3 is now a Linux swap partition.

Now you can add your Linux partitions. For this example, you will add only one partition. But if you want multiple partitions for various reasons, you can add them at this time. To add a partition, enter `n`, specify `p` for another primary partition, and then specify the number for this partition, which is **4**. To keep from fragmenting different partitions across the drive, start the last partition where the first left off, at cylinder 171. Because you want to use the rest of the space for the Linux system, you can specify the last cylinder instead of an exact byte count. Thus, enter **1023**, as in the following example:

```
Command (m for help): n
Command action
e extended
p primary partition (1-4)
p
Partition number (1-4): 4
First cylinder (171-1024): 171
Last cylinder or +size or +sizeM or +sizeK (171-1023): 1023
```

Now use the `p` command to verify the new partitions. If you need to make any changes, you can do so now.

When you're satisfied with the layout of your partitions, you can use the `w` command to write the partition table information to the hard disk. None of your changes are permanent until you use the `w` command; thus, if you feel you've made some changes in error, you can use the `q` command to exit without altering the partition table. When you issue the `w` command, Linux tells you that the partition table has been altered and then resynchronizes the disks to match the new partition table. If your Linux system hangs at this point, you can reboot with the installation disk.

CREATING THE SWAP PARTITION

After you partition your system as you see fit, LISA asks you to set up a swap partition. From the Configure Swap Space dialog box, select the partition you created for swap and select the Continue button. LISA then configures, formats, and activates the swap area.

INSTALLING THE LINUX SOFTWARE SYSTEM

Now that the system is partitioned for Linux, you can install the various software packages that form the OpenLinux system. LISA displays the Installation Source Selection dialog box.

From here, you can select the installation media: CD-ROM, hard disk, or Network File System (NFS).

Installing from the CD-ROM is a breeze with the enclosed CD package. However, you can copy the contents of the CD-ROM to a hard drive partition and access it from there. Also, if you have a working network connection, you can connect to another computer and install from that machine. You might want to perform such an installation if OpenLinux cannot recognize your CD-ROM.

After you make your selection, follow the instructions to begin software installation. (Remember that you can access help by pressing F1.) For example, if you choose to install from the CD-ROM, you are asked to select the appropriate hardware device. LISA typically already has this device selected.

You then need to select the root partition (`/`) to which all the software will be copied. After you select from the list of partitions, LISA formats and prepares the root partition for installation. During this time, you see a screen of numbers and hear lots of disk activity, but don't worry, this activity is normal.

After preparing the root partition, LISA asks whether you want to place other directories under the root onto their own partition. Be careful here: The default answer is No, but you do want to place the `/usr`, `/home`, and `/var` directories onto the partitions you created earlier. So answer Yes and repeat the process for each directory.

After creating the mount points for your file systems, LISA asks you what packages you want to install. A basic system requires about 100MB; a full installation requires around 1300MB. You can select from the following list:

Minimal System without the X Window System (94MB)

Minimal System with the X Window System (152MB)

Small Standard System (192MB)

Standard System (754MB)

All Packages (1300MB)

LISA generates a package listing after you select the installation size. LISA then begins the automated package installation. You can relax, sit back, and watch the installation.

CONFIGURING YOUR SYSTEM

After package installation, you need to configure your system. (Here you'll need the system and network information you gathered earlier in this chapter.) If you are connected to a network, you need the appropriate information from your service provider or network coordinator. You also need to select a root password. This password is important, so choose wisely and don't forget it.

Tip #25 from
Jack

For complete details on using LISA see http://www.calderasystems.com/doc/openlinux/english/install.html.

To begin, LISA asks for a host name. This is the name others on the network will call your machine. You also need to provide your domain name, which is typically something like `company.com`. The host name and domain name create the fully qualified domain name for your computer (such as `opus.netwharf.com`).

→ See "IP Addresses," p. 604

You need to provide the IP address of your computer, along with its netmask and the default gateway. After supplying this information, you need to specify your network's domain name server, or DNS machine.

After setting up your network, you need to configure your clock and time zone information. It is recommended that you use local time, even though most Internet servers use Greenwich mean time (GMT), because most PCs have their BIOS clocks set to local time, not GMT. Setting a PC to GMT may cause problems, especially if you use other operating systems on the machine. At this point, select local or GMT time, and then specify your time zone, such as EST.

Next, you must specify what type of mouse you are using. Most ATX systems use a PS/2 style mouse. If you are using a serial mouse, make sure you remember which serial port your mouse uses. The next step is to select the printer you intend to use with your system, if necessary.

→ See "Understanding Key Terms Used in This Chapter," p. 164

Now you must select a root password. This password, which is for the superuser's account, allows anyone to do anything he or she wants to your system. Do not give this password to just anyone! And do not forget the root password. If you do forget, more than likely you will have to reinstall the system.

Note

See Chapter 13, "Improving System Security," for password tips and rescue options.

After setting your root password, you need to create your first user account. LISA uses a default value of `col` (for Caldera OpenLinux), but you can specify any name you want—even your own. This first user account allows you to use the system as a regular user instead of as the superuser (root). Typically, you should not use the root account for day-to-day user tasks because of the potential for creating problems. After you specify the new account name, you can simply accept the default values for the other items requested. These fields, such as group, are explained in Chapter 11, "Managing User Accounts."

→ See "Adding a User" p. 250

Next, you indicate how you want your system to boot.

INSTALLING LILO

As mentioned earlier, LILO stands for the *Linux Loader*. LILO is a program executed at system startup; it lets you choose which operating system will be used to boot the computer. You can use LILO to boot several different operating systems, such as Linux and MS-DOS. With LILO, you also can specify a default operating system to boot and a default time limit the system should wait before it boots that system. For example, if you have MS-DOS and Linux on your computer, you can configure LILO to boot either one. You can tell LILO to boot MS-DOS if no one intervenes within 30 seconds. Before that 30 seconds is up, however, a user can specify another operating system to boot instead of the default. You can press the Ctrl, Alt, or Shift key to stop the timed process. You can press Tab to get a list of operating systems LILO can boot.

You specify all this information while configuring LILO. Although you can directly edit the `lilo.conf` file located in the `/etc` directory, the LILO installation screen provides a better interface for editing the file.

After you configure your system, Setup lets you install LILO with the option to configure LILO.

UNINSTALLING LILO

If you're running LILO version 0.14 or newer, you can uninstall LILO by using the following command:

```
opus:~# lilo -u
```

If you have a previous version, you must remove or disable LILO from its primary partition first. You can use the Linux fdisk or MS-DOS FDISK program to make another partition active.

If you placed LILO within the MBR (master boot record), you must replace it with another MBR from another operating system. With MS-DOS 5.0 or above, the command `c:\>fdisk /mbr` restores the MS-DOS MBR.

When LILO is removed from the active partition or the MBR, you're free to remove the files from `/etc/lilo`.

→ See "Removing Files or Directories," p. 426

GOING BACK TO THE BEGINNING

After you complete the setup and configuration of your system, the Setup program returns you to the main menu. From there, you can choose the Exit option to leave Setup. If you want to change options, you can do so here. (In case you don't change the options during installation, Chapter 7, "Upgrading and Installing Software," provides information on updating and installing software after your initial installation.) For now, choose Exit to leave the Setup program.

Choosing Exit returns you to the system prompt, indicated by the `#` sign. You're now in Linux and can issue simple commands, such as `ls` for a directory listing of files. At this time, though, you should reboot the system so that all your setup and configurations settings can take effect.

Rebooting Linux is more involved than rebooting DOS. You can't turn off the power and turn the system back on. If you do so in Linux, you can damage the file structures and systems. Linux tries to repair itself on bootup. You should not turn off the power while running Linux. To exit Linux, you use the following command:

```
shutdown [-r] time
```

The optional `-r` flag indicates that the system should reboot after shutting down. *`time`* indicates the time that the system should shut down; you can use `now` in place of `time` to indicate immediate shutdown. Linux also recognizes the warm-boot keys used by DOS (Ctrl+Alt+Delete) to reboot the machine, which Linux interprets as the command

```
shutdown -r now
```

→ See "Shutting Down Linux," p. 243

When you shut down this way, make sure you've removed all the floppy disks from the drive and reboot your new Linux machine.

TROUBLESHOOTING

After you reboot your machine, the LILO prompt should appear. If not, the following list of LILO messages may help deduce the problems:

LILO Prompt	Description
Nothing	Indicates the system can not find the LILO program.
L	Indicates a possible media error.
LI	LILO cannot find the kernel image.
LIL	Indicates a media error.
LIL-	Indicates a corrupted descriptor table.
LILO	Success! LILO susccessfully loaded and you can now boot your choice of operating systems.

If there are errors, check the hardware and your configuration in `/etc/lilo.conf`. After booting Linux you need to make sure that you can boot to your old operating system if you left it on the hard drive. If that system was DOS, press the Shift key, and then type the short word you used to identify the DOS partition when you installed LILO. If you enter an invalid word, you can press Tab to get a list of valid operating system types. If you're having problems at this point, you can place your DOS boot disk in the boot drive and reboot.

You should be able to boot from your boot disk. When your system is up and running under DOS, try the Linux boot disk you created during installation—not the ones you created to originally install the entire system. If that boot disk doesn't work, you may have to reinstall Linux. Potential problems to check initially are the kernels and your hardware. Before starting over, make sure that you have the appropriate hardware. If you made notes during the installation process, check which kernel you installed against what hardware you have. Make sure your hardware is supported by Linux.

Below are some answers to common problems.

Q: Can I use a hard drive that has more than 1023 cylinders?

A: The infamous 1023 cylinder question. Yes, but not to boot Linux. You can install Linux on partitions above the 1023 cylinder, but to boot Linux, the root directory and specifically the `/boot` directory must be installed on the first hard drive below 1024.

Q: How do I add arguments for LILO at the prompt?

A: Some hardware requires that extra parameters be fed to the kernel before the kernel will recognize the hardware. You can accommodate this by editing the `/etc/lilo.conf` file to provide the necessary parameters, or you can provide them manually during boot up. See the LILO HOWTO for more examples of LILO parameters.

Q: Why does LILO hang on LI?

A: This is a symptom of the 1023 cylinder problem addressed previously. If you have installed the boot system above 1023, LILO will not be able to boot the system. You can try to boot from a floppy using the rescue disk you made during installation, or you can repartition your hard drive and reinstall Linux.

Q: The installation will not find the SCSI card.

A: To remedy this, you need to add a boot-time argument such as the following:

```
LILO: linux qlogicfas=0x230,11,5
```

This option can be made permanent so you don't have to re-enter it. See the LILO configuration option `append` in the lilo.conf man page.

Q: How do I uninstall LILO?

A: If you want to uninstall LILO and reinstall the original boot record, try using this command

```
lilo -u /dev/hda
```

which represents the boot record of the first IDE drive. Parameters may vary for your machine; for example, if your first hard drive is a SCSI drive, you would use /dev/sda.

Q: Can I use LILO and Win98 on one installation?

A: Yes, install Windows 98 first and then install Linux. During the installation, tell Linux to place LILO in the MBR. You can also use a commercial program such as System Commander. The commercial version of Caldera OpenLinux provides utilities to both repartition your system and also manage booting multiple operating systems.

Q: How do I mount a CD-ROM?

A: Installing OpenLinux 2.3 places the proper entries in your /etc/fstab file, as follows:

```
#
# /etc/fstab
#
# You should be using fstool (control-panel) to edit this!
#
# <device>     <mountpoint>     <filesystemtype>     <options>   <dump>     <fsckor-
der>
/dev/sda1                 /                          ext2       defaults 1 1
/dev/sda5                 /home                      ext2       defaults 1 2
/dev/cdrom                /mnt/cdrom                 iso9660    noauto,ro 0 0
/dev/fd0                  /mnt/floppy                ext2       noauto 0 0
/dev/sda6                 /var                       ext2       defaults 1 2
/dev/da2                  none                       ignore     0 0 0
none                      /proc                      proc       defaults
/dev/sda7                 none                       swap       sw
```

Note the use of noauto for the cdrom entry. Without this setting, Linux will try to automount the CD-ROM when it boots, which isn't really a problem unless there's no CD in the drive.

If there is not an entry in your fstab file, you can either edit /etc/fstab or use the X Window Control Panel tool to add the appropriate mount information. Also, make sure the mount point /mnt/cdrom does indeed exist. If the entry is correct, you can cd to the mount point and issue the following commands:

```
cd /mnt
mount cdrom
```

Q: When the system boots up, I see a message that says I have unknown PCI hardware. What does this mean?

A: The error unknown PCI device can occur for several reasons. The first and most harmless one is that PCI isn't responding to Linux's queries in a way it understands, but Linux is able to keep going. The more common occurrence is that the system hangs on, querying PCI bus cards, and cannot get any further.

Q: I have installed Linux, and it seems to initially start booting. However, when it gets down to something called sendmail, the machine seems to hang. What is happening, and what should I do?

A: If, after the install, the machine seems to hang when it reaches certain processes like sendmail, Apache, NFS, or SMB, there is probably a network problem. The most common cause is that Linux cannot look up the name of the machine you have called the box (if you set up networking to have a machine name). The machine is currently paused waiting for the network timeout of DNS lookups and will eventually bring up the login prompt. When you get the prompt, log in as root and check the usual culprits for a problem.

If you are directly on a network with a DNS server, make sure that the `/etc/resolv.conf` file has the correct values for your machine's DNS server. Check with your systems administrator for the correct values.

If you are using Linux on a network without a DNS server (or if this box is going to be the DNS server), you will need to edit the `/etc/hosts` file to have the hostname and IP address so that the lookups will occur correctly. The format of the `/etc/hosts` file is like the following example:

```
127.0.0.1         localhost localhost.localdomain
192.168.200.1     mymachine mymachine.mynetwork.net
```

The example machine is called `mymachine`.

CHAPTER 5

Installing Debian Linux

In this chapter

by Jack Tackett, Jr.

About Debian

This chapter gives you the information you need to install the Debian distribution of Linux. Though this book leads the way, you might find the need to use the resources provided on the CD-ROM. First, you must determine whether you have the appropriate hardware. After you have determined that you have the necessary hardware, you must prepare for the installation. Following the steps provided in this chapter should ensure a smooth installation.

Debian GNU/Linux, the distribution's official title, is the Linux distribution supported by the GNU community and not by a company, such as Red Hat or Caldera. The community subscribes to a set of high-quality standards, as indicated on its Web site at `http://www.debian.org/doc/debian-policy/`.

The distribution is maintained by a group of volunteers started by Ian Murdock. Many Debian proponents feel the only pure GNU/Open Source Linux solution is Debian.

What You Need to Install Debian

When you're ready to install Debian, having paper and pen nearby is a good idea so that you can take notes just in case something does go wrong. Besides, you'll need to jot down some numbers and information before starting and along the way. To install Debian, you need the following:

- Your host name (be careful, you don't really want your boss to see email from studmuffin, do you?)
- Motherboard
- Video card
- Monitor
- Disk system (EIDE or SCSI)
- Mouse

If you plan to access the Internet or a local network, you need to know the following network information (most of which you can get from your local area network team at work or from your Internet service provider):

- The system on your network that you should use as a Domain Name Service (DNS) server
- Your domain name
- Your computer's IP address
- The IP address of your network
- The netmask to use with your network
- The broadcast address to use on your network

- The IP address of the default gateway system you should route to, if your network has a gateway
- Your network interface card, which is typically Ethernet but may be Token Ring

The general installation procedure is as follows:

1. Determine the hardware requirements, including disk space.
2. Determine the installation method, whether from floppies or from CD-ROM.
3. Install the system.
4. Configure the system.
5. Decide how to boot the system.

Debian supports the hardware supported by the Linux kernel, as indicated in the "Linux Hardware How-To."

Tip #26 from Jack

You can find the "Linux Hardware How-To" at the following address:

`http://metalab.unc.edu/LDP/HOWTO/Hardware-HOWTO.html`

You can boot the installation program from either a floppy or the CD-ROM. You need to create the rescue floppy to use a floppy drive, or you need to set your computer to boot from CD-ROM. No matter what media you use to boot, the system then runs the `dbootstrap` program to install and configure a base Debian system.

You also must decide how to boot Linux. You have two choices. You can boot Linux from a floppy disk, in which case you need an extra formatted disk. The other choice is to use a program called LILO, the Linux Loader. LILO is a program that allows you to specify which operating system to boot. OS/2 and Windows NT provide similar functionality.

Next, you should make sure you have enough disk space to install Linux. A minimal system requires at least 4MB of RAM and 35MB of free disk space, but this type of system is minimal—usable at best as a terminal. For a system running the X Window System and some usable software, you can figure on 300MB of disk space. For a robust system, you need around 800MB, and for a full installation, you need around 2000MB (2GB).

For configuring XFree86, you need to write what type of chipset your video card uses. If you have a serial mouse and modem, you should write down the serial port that each is using. You'll need this information later during the configuration process.

Preparing to Install Debian

If you have a brand-new system or a system on which you don't care what happens to the data already stored on the computer, you can skip most of the following sections and go directly to the section "Creating the Rescue and Driver Floppies." If, however, you're already using a system and simply want to add Linux, you must do some planning. The main reason is that Linux is another operating system, not just a collection of programs.

If you intend to install Debian on a system already in use, you should back up your essential files to a zip disk or CD-R system. Installing Debian can be a destructive process on your system. After making the necessary backups, you need to inventory your hardware as described previously. Debian makes no additional hardware restrictions other than those imposed by the Linux kernel. If you have a standard PC, you should have no problems.

Caution

If you have any Windows-specific hardware, such as a WinModem or printer, you will have a problem when installing Debian. These devices rely on Windows to do much of their processing, something Linux cannot do.

Tip #27 from *Jack*

For information on installing Debian or other Linux distributions on a laptop, see the following Web site:

`http://www.cs.utexas.edu/users/kharker/linux-laptop/`

Debian supports four architectures: Intel x86-based architectures; Motorola 680x0 machines such as Atari, Amiga, and Macintoshes; DEC Alpha machines; and Sun SPARC machines. They are referred to as i386, m68k, Alpha, and Sparc, respectively.

Debian does not run on 286 or below Intel processors but should run on nearly all other Intel x86 processors and nearly all clones.

Tip #28 from *Jack*

If you have problems installing Debian from your floppy drive *and* you have a Cyrix CPU, you need to disable the system's cache memory from the BIOS setup menu. Remember to re-enable the cache after installation. The symptoms seem to be problems with the floppy drive after a switch from 16-bit to 32-bit mode and more investigations continue to see if Debian can supply a workaround to this issue.

Debian supports most industry standard motherboards, including some multiprocessor boards, and all system buses.

Tip #29 from

Jack

To use multiple processors, called Symmetric Multiprocessing, or SMP, you need a specialized kernel to take advantage of those processors. Otherwise, your system uses only the first processor on the motherboard.

You need a VGA-compatible display interface for the console terminal. Older standards such CGA, MDA, or HGA should also work, assuming you do not require X11 support.

Note

Unlike some other distributions, Debian does not utilize a GUI environment during the installation process. This way, you are ensured a successful installation across a wide hardware base.

Debian's X Window System support, like the other distributions, is determined by the underlying support found in the XFree86's X Window System, which includes support for most of the newer AGP video cards.

→ See "Installing the XFree86 System," p. 508

Debian supports most storage devices such as floppies, IDE/EIDE/ATAPI, and SCSI devices. Debian does not support older style drives such as MFM or RLL hard disks, however. Support for other storage devices, such as parallel port zip drives, can be added later with a modified kernel, as described in Chapter 14, "Configuring the Linux Kernel." Debian does not support the following drive controllers:

- EATA-DMA protocol-compliant SCSI host adapters such as the SmartCache III/IV, SmartRAID controller families, and the DPT PM2011B and PM2012B controllers
- The 53c7 NCR family of SCSI controllers (but 53c8 and 5380 controllers are supported)

As shown in the "Linux Hardware How-To," Linux supports a myriad of hardware peripherals. Some items Debian does not support include sound cards, by default, but you can add sound support later. Debian also does not support the following network interface cards (NICs):

- AX.25 cards and protocols
- 3Com EtherLink Plus (3c505) and EtherLink16 (3c507)
- NI5210 cards
- Generic NE2100 cards
- NI6510 and NI16510 EtherBlaster cards
- SEEQ 8005 cards
- Schneider & Koch G16 cards

- Ansel Communications EISA 3200
- Zenith Z-Note built-in network card
- Microchannel (MCA) network cards

Tip #30 from Jack

The following Web site contains unofficial images to support Microchannel NICs:

`ftp://ns.gold-link.com/pub/LinuxMCA/`

Now that you know your hardware is supported by Debian, you need to decide how you intend to use the system—as a standalone workstation, a server, or a development machine. Table 5.1, based on the Debian documentation, provides an overview of each type of system and its requirements. During installation, you select which profile to install.

TABLE 5.1 SYSTEM PROFILES

Profile	Description
Server_std	A small server profile, useful for a stripped-down server that does not have a lot of niceties for shell users. It basically has an FTP server, a Web server, DNS, NIS, and POP. It takes up around 80MB. Of course, this is just the size of the software; any data you serve up would be additional.
Dialup	A standard desktop box, including the X Window System, graphics applications, sound, editors, and so on. The size of the package is around 500MB.
Work_std	A more stripped-down user machine, without the X Window System or X applications, possibly suitable for a laptop or mobile computer. The size is around 140MB. (Note that I have a pretty simple laptop setup including X11 in even less space—around 100MB.)
Devel_comp	A desktop setup with all the development packages, such as Perl, C, C++, and so on. The size is around 475MB. Assuming you are adding X11 and some additional packages for other uses, you should plan around 800MB for this type of machine.

PARTITIONING YOUR HARD DRIVE

Next, you need to partition your hard drive for installation. This process is the most dangerous because maximum data loss is assured. If you have not backed up your system, do so now. Although you can use an experimental program called FIPS or commercial programs such as Partition Magic that do nondestructive repartitioning, a full backup is recommended, just in case problems occur.

WHY USE PARTITIONS?

In the early days of PCs, hard drives were few and far between. Most computers used floppies to hold the operating system and programs and their data. IBM, with the introduction of the IBM PC XT, introduced a 10MB hard drive. Early operating systems such as DOS could access only a limited amount of space on hard drives. Then hard drive manufacturers kept expanding the space on their hard drives quicker than the operating system's capability to access the additional space. The operating system got around this problem by letting the user split the hard drive into sections, called *partitions*. These partitions can hold program files, other operating systems, or data.

Typical MS-DOS systems have one partition, which is referred to as drive C. If you split the drive into partitions, these partitions are typically referred to in alphabetical order as D, E, and so on. MS-DOS also allows you to install multiple hard drives, so the next drive in this chain might be referred to as F. UNIX and Linux do not use drive letters to refer to partitions; instead, they use directory names to refer to partitions. Also, as indicated earlier, Linux users can place different directories on different partitions and even on different drives. You can also place different operating systems on different partitions.

Debian needs at least one partition for itself. You can have a single partition containing the entire operating system, applications, and your personal files, but most people feel that the swap partition is also a necessity, although it's not strictly true. "Swap" is scratch space for an operating system, which allows the system to use cheap disk storage as "virtual memory." By putting the swap area on its own partition, Linux can make much more efficient use of it (it is possible to force Linux to use a regular file as swap, but doing so is not recommended).

In general, I recommend a minimum of three partitions: one for the operating system itself, one for all the home directories, and one for swap. As mentioned previously, for efficiency reasons you need swap on its own partition. For safety reasons, you should place your home directory on a separate partition, or better, on a separate drive so that problems on one partition do not destroy data on another partition. For ease of upgrades, you need to split system files across partitions. Thus, you can upgrade your operating system while protecting user files in their home directories.

NAMING PARTITIONS

Linux refers to disks and partitions in a different way than Windows and MS-DOS. Table 5.2 illustrates the naming conventions used by Linux.

→ See "Understanding File Systems," p. 440

TABLE 5.2 DISK AND PARTITION NAMING SCHEMES FOR LINUX

Device	Name
First floppy drive	`/dev/fd0`
Second floppy drive	`/dev/fd1`

TABLE 5.2 DISK AND PARTITION NAMING SCHEMES FOR LINUX

Device	Name
First SCSI disk (SCSI ID address-wise)	`/dev/sda`
First partition on SCSI disk	`/dev/sda1`
Second partition on first SCSI disk	`/dev/sda2`
Second SCSI disk	`/dev/sdb`
First partition on SCSI disk	`/dev/sdb1`
Second partition on second SCSI disk	`/dev/sda2`
First SCSI CD-ROM	`/dev/scd0` (sometimes `/dev/CD-ROM`)
Master IDE/primary controller	`/dev/hda`
Slave disk IDE/primary	`/dev/hdb`

Basically, you distinguish partitions on a drive by appending the next numeric value to the device name.

EXPLAINING PARTITIONS

Partitions are specified in a section of the hard drive referred to as the *boot record* in what is called a *partition table*. This table is used by the various operating systems to determine what operating system to boot and where their files can be found physically on the hard drive. The boot record is used to boot, or start up, the machine's operating system. LILO and other boot managers use this section of the hard drive, typically found on the first sectors of the drive, to control which operating system to start.

The partition table holds information about the locations and sizes of the various partitions on the hard drive. The three kinds of partitions are primary, extended, and logical. DOS and some other operating systems must boot from primary partitions. Hard drives can contain only four primary partitions. An extended partition does not contain data itself; instead, it allows the user to define other, logical partitions on the drive. Thus, to get around the four-limit primary partition number, you can define an extended partition and then define other logical partitions within the extended partition. Some operating systems such as MS-DOS and versions of OS/2 before version 2.0 require that they be installed in a primary partition, but they can access logical drives in extended partitions. This information is important to remember if you are going to have both a DOS system and a Linux system reside on the same drive. DOS must go in a primary partition.

USING FDISK

Partitions are created, destroyed, and managed by a program usually called FDISK. Each operating system has its own version of FDISK, so you must be sure to use the correct one. If you are currently using DOS or are planning to use DOS, you must first repartition the DOS drive using DOS's FDISK. You later use the Linux version of cfdisk to create the Linux partitions. If you are using OS/2, you also need to use the OS/2 version of FDISK to prepare the OS/2 partitions.

Partition Requirements

When you're ready to start partitioning your hard drive, you first should plan what partitions you need. DOS requires a primary partition. Linux and OS/2 can reside in other partitions. If you are using the OS/2 boot manager, which also works well with Linux, you must prepare for its use also. You must also be aware if you are shrinking a current DOS partition to make room for Linux that not all of your files can be restored to the new, smaller DOS partition. Note that you can access DOS partitions from Linux, moving, saving, and editing DOS files under Linux. However, you cannot execute DOS programs under Linux.

Note

Two experimental components of Linux allow you to emulate DOS under Linux and also install Linux under DOS. Both systems are still in the implementation stage and are, thus, more suited for Linux hackers. These topics are covered in Chapter 2, "Linux Installation Overview." You can also find plenty of information on these topics in the Linux world.

Next, you should jot down the number of partitions you need and how much disk space to provide for each.

DOS Requirements

If you want to boot DOS, it must go in a primary partition. A bootable version of DOS does not require much space—just enough for the system files, `COMMAND.COM`, `CONFIG.SYS`, and any driver files needed to start your system. For instance, I provide a 5MB DOS partition on my first drive to boot DOS. When DOS is loaded and running, you can access any of the other extended and logical drives on the system. Unfortunately, although Linux can access DOS files in a DOS partition, DOS cannot access Linux files in a Linux partition.

OS/2 Requirements

OS/2 versions 2.0 and later do not need a primary partition. The OS/2 system can install and boot from an extended partition. Thus, you can install DOS on a primary partition and create an extended partition area for OS/2 and Linux. The space required for OS/2 is version- and feature-dependent, so you should consult your OS/2 documentation for space requirements. You should also subtract 1MB from available space if you intend to use the OS/2 boot manager.

Linux Requirements

As explained earlier, Linux stores files on file systems, and these file systems can reside on different partitions, basically as safety precautions. Linux requires one partition for each file system. The next consideration is for a swap partition. Linux, like most operating systems that use disk space for memory (called a *virtual memory configuration*), needs a swap file or a swap partition to simulate physical memory using disk space. Linux typically uses a swap partition of at least 64MB.

Also, Linux limits the partitions per drive to 15 partitions for SCSI disks (3 usable primary partitions, 12 logical partitions) and 63 partitions on an IDE drive (3 usable primary partitions, 60 logical partitions).

REPARTITIONING

This section assumes you need to repartition a DOS drive. To do so, execute FDISK by typing `fdisk` at the DOS prompt. You then see the FDISK Options screen (see Figure 5.1).

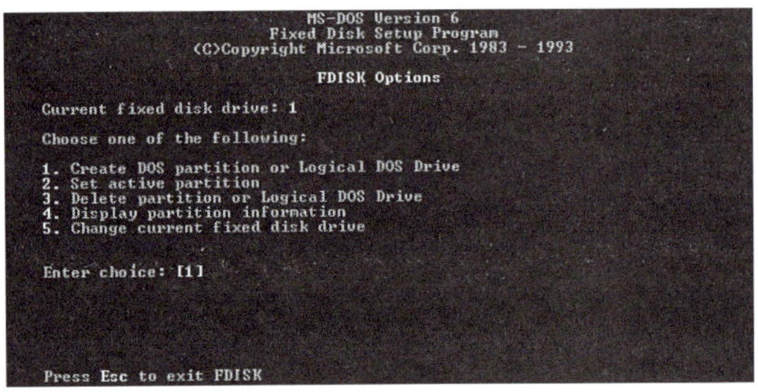

Figure 5.1
FDISK provides many options used to create, delete, and modify partitions.

The screen shown in Figure 5.1 might appear different depending on which version of MS-DOS you are using. Pick menu option 4, Display Partition Information. The Display Partition Information screen appears (see Figure 5.2).

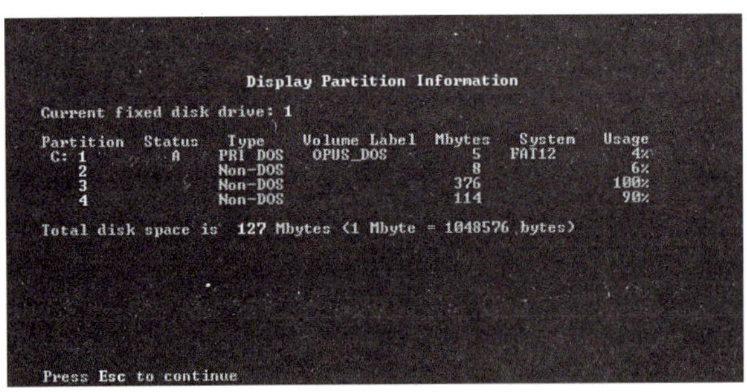

Figure 5.2
The Display Partition Information screen in MS-DOS 6.0.

You should write down this information. You need the current partition table information if you decide to abort the Linux installation and put your system back the way it was before you started.

> **Note**
>
> You might not need to repartition your hard drive, although it is thought that repartitioning offers the best introduction to Linux. You can use FIPS to nondestructively repartition your hard drive.

> FIPS stands for the First nondestructive Interactive Partition Splitting program. It is a program developed by Arno Schaefer as a result of the Linux project and is used to move around DOS partitions to make room for Linux partitions.
>
> You can find the complete instructions for using FIPS in the document `fips.doc` located on the enclosed CD-ROM in the `/tools/fips20` directory. This program can help only if you have enough free space left on your drive to install Linux; otherwise, you either need to delete unneeded files or use the process described earlier to repartition your hard drive.

Deleting Partitions

Unfortunately, FDISK does not allow you to simply resize a partition; you must first delete the partition and then add it back with the desired size. From the FDISK Options screen, choose menu option 3, Delete Partition or Logical DOS Drive, which deletes the necessary partitions. The Delete DOS Partition or Logical DOS Drive screen then appears (see Figure 5.3).

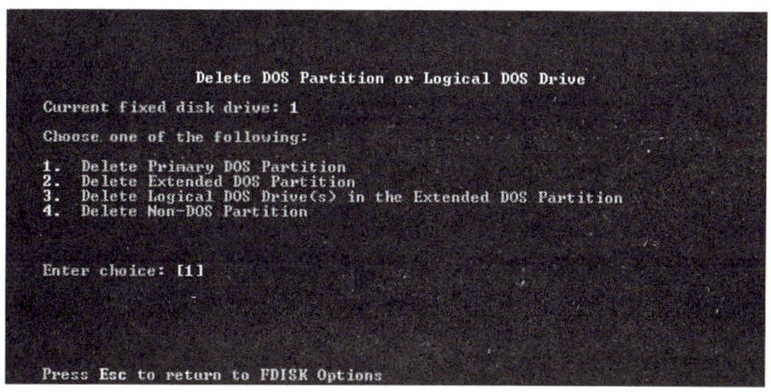

Figure 5.3
The Delete DOS Partition or Logical DOS Drive screen.

Here, you should pick the appropriate menu option for the type of partition you are deleting, such as a primary DOS partition. For example, option 1, Delete Primary DOS Partition, allows you to delete primary DOS partitions. Choosing option 1 displays the Delete Primary DOS Partition screen (see Figure 5.4).

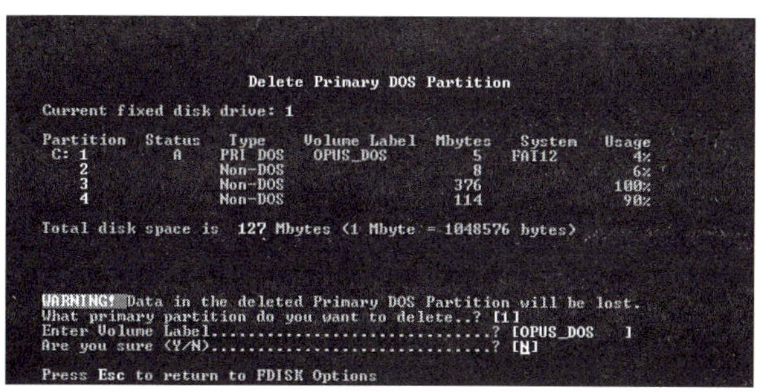

Figure 5.4
The Delete Primary DOS Partition screen.

This screen asks for a volume name of the partition and then a confirmation to see whether you really want to delete the partition. Because all information on the partition will be destroyed, FDISK wants to be absolutely sure that you want to delete the primary DOS partition.

ADDING PARTITIONS

After you have deleted all the necessary partitions, you must then add the appropriate partitions for your DOS system. You cannot add the Linux or OS/2 partitions with the DOS FDISK program. Partitioning the hard drive for Debian Linux is covered earlier in this chapter. Figure 5.5 shows the Create DOS Partition or Logical DOS Drive screen.

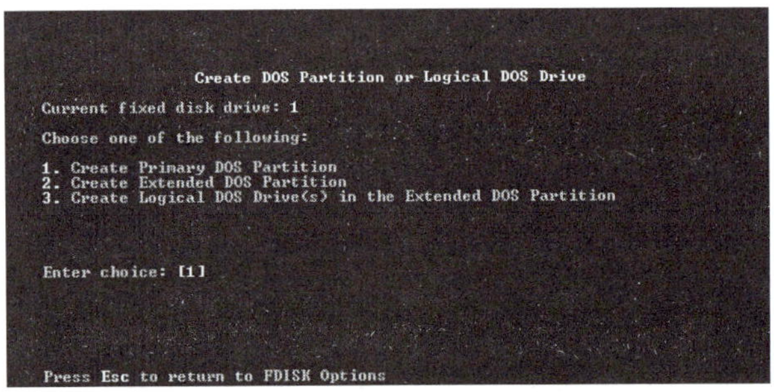

Figure 5.5
The Create DOS Partition or Logical DOS Drive screen.

Providing all the space available for the partition and making the partition the *active* partition are the FDISK defaults (see Figure 5.6).

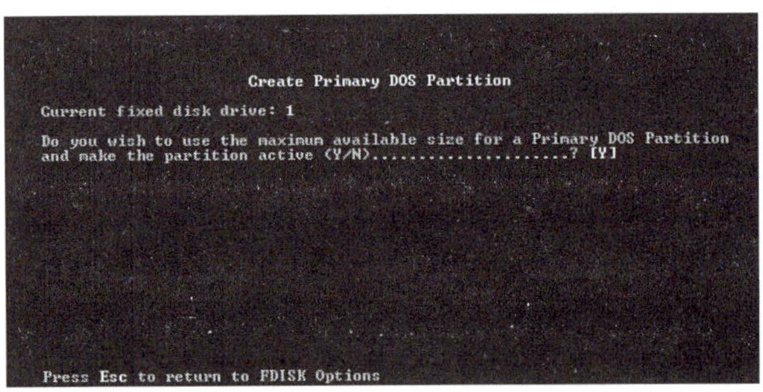

Figure 5.6
The Create Primary DOS Partition screen.

Active indicates that the partition is bootable. To boot DOS, you must specify the primary partition as active. Say No to this first selection so that you can specify the exact amount of disk space to provide to your DOS partition. Answering No to the question in Figure 5.6 displays the Specify Disk Space for the Partition screen. There, you can specify the desired space for your DOS partition either in megabytes or in percentage of space available and press Enter.

Next, you must set this partition active. From the FDISK Options screen, choose menu option 2, Set Active Partition, and simply follow the instructions on the Set Active menu screen.

INSTALLING DEBIAN

You can boot the installation system from floppies, bootable CD-ROM, or a non-Linux boot loader. You can install the entire system from floppies, but this approach is not recommended; it takes more than seven floppies and a lot of time to create and use them. The typical installation procedure is to create a boot floppy and then install from the CD-ROM. After you have booted the system, you can install from CD-ROM, a Network File System (NFS) server, FTP, HTTP, or from another hard drive. The easiest way to boot and install, if it works, is to boot directly from the CD-ROM.

INSTALLING FROM CD-ROM

If you have a bootable CD-ROM drive, you need to make sure it is selected in your BIOS settings as a boot device. Then you can place the CD-ROM that accompanies this book into the drive and reboot your computer.

If the system boots properly, you can continue installing system files, as described later in this chapter; otherwise, you need to create a bootable system for installation. If your hardware does not support bootable CD-ROMs, you should boot into DOS and execute the `boot.bat` file located in the `\boot` directory on your CD-ROM. Then you can skip down to "Installing the System Files." However you decide to boot, you can install the base Debian system from the CD-ROM. To do so, simply boot using one of the other installation techniques; when it is time to install the base system, and when you install the complete system, just point your installation system at the CD-ROM drive.

INSTALLING FROM DOS

Even though you can run DOS programs from Windows 98 and NT, you must be in DOS mode, not Windows, to perform this installation. To install from DOS, you need to copy the following files into a directory on the DOS drive:

- `resc1440.bin`
- `drv1440.bin`
- `base2_1.tgz`
- `root.bin`
- `linux`
- `install.bat`
- `loadlin.exe`

These files are located in the `install` folder on the CD-ROM.

Next, you must boot into pure DOS mode (that is, you must not have any drivers loaded). To enter DOS mode from Windows, go to the start, shutdown menu option and select Restart the Computer in MS-DOS Mode, as shown in Figure 5.7.

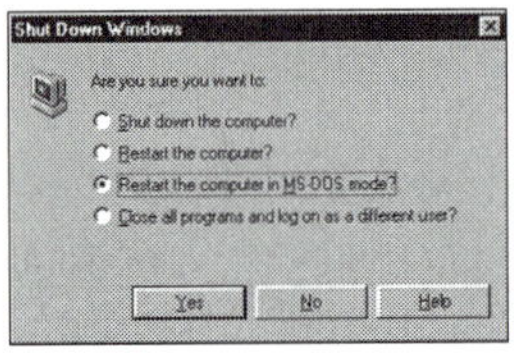

Figure 5.7
Installing Debian from DOS requires you to be in MS-DOS mode, not in a DOS compatibility window while running Windows.

At the DOS prompt, execute the install.bat program you copied. You can now continue installing the system as detailed in the section "Installing the System Files."

CREATING THE RESCUE AND DRIVER FLOPPIES

The Debian distribution of Linux included on the CD-ROM accompanying this book contains the disk images of two floppies needed with Debian: the rescue and driver floppies. Disk images are files containing the complete contents of a floppy disk in raw form. Disk images, such as `resc1440.bin`, cannot simply be copied to floppy drives. A special program is used to write the image files to floppy disk in raw mode. This program is required because these images are raw representations of the disk; it is required to do a sector copy of the data from the file onto the floppy. You create these floppies with an MS-DOS program called rawrite2, which is provided with most Linux distributions. You use rawrite2 to transfer the images to the appropriate floppies.

You use the rescue disk to start the Linux system for installation. It contains bare-bones device drivers and a basic version of the operating system. This rescue disk is specific to the hardware and type of floppy drive your system uses to boot (usually the A drive under MS-DOS). To create this disk, you issue the following command from the DOS prompt:

```
rawrite2 -f file -d drive
```

`file` is one of the floppy disk images described next. *`drive`* indicates which floppy drive to use, either `a:` or `b:`. You need to create the rescue and root disks at the minimum to install Debian.

The Debian documentation describes the following image files:

The files `resc1440.bin`, `resc1440tecra.bin`, and `resc1200.bin` are the Rescue Floppy disk images. The Rescue Floppy is used for initial setup and for emergencies, such as when your system doesn't boot for some reason. Therefore, it is recommended you write the disk image to the floppy even if you are not using floppies for installation. The tecra images are alternate kernels for people who have problems with the standard disks.

The files drv1440.bin, drv1440tecra.bin, and drv1200.bin are the Drivers Floppy disk images. They contain the kernel modules, or drivers, for all kinds of hardware not necessary for initial booting. You are prompted to choose the drivers you need during the installation process. If you used a special Rescue Floppy image, you need to use the corresponding Drivers Floppy image.

The following set of files make up the base system:

base2_1.tgz

base14-1.bin, base14-2.bin, base14-3.bin, base14-4.bin, base14-5.bin, base14-6.bin, base14-7.bin

base12-1.bin, base12-2.bin, base12-3.bin, base12-4.bin, base12-5.bin, base12-6.bin, base12-7.bin

These files contain the base system that will be installed on your Linux partition during the installation process. This set of files is the bare minimum necessary for you to be able to install the rest of the packages. The base2_1.tgz file is for installation from nonfloppy media—that is, CD-ROM, hard disk, or NFS.

The file root.bin is the Root image. This file contains an image of a temporary file system that gets loaded into memory when you boot. It is used for installations from hard disk and from CD-ROM.

The program rawrite2.exe is a DOS utility to write a floppy disk image to a floppy. You should not copy images to the floppy; instead, you should use this utility to copy them sector by sector.

The program loadlin.exe is the Linux boot loader. You need this boot loader if you are installing from a DOS partition or from a CD-ROM.

The file install.bat is a DOS batch file for starting Debian installation from DOS. This batch file is used in installations from hard disk or CD-ROM.

The file linux is very important; it is the kernel program, the core of the operating system. This file is the Linux kernel image to be used for hard disk and CD-ROM installations.

The files install.txt and install.html are in the Installation Manual in plain ASCII and HTML format, respectively.

The files fdisk.txt and cfdisk.txt are the instructions for using your available partitioning programs.

The file basecont.txt contains a list of the contents of the base system.

The file md5sum.txt lists the MD5 checksums for the binary files. If you have the md5sum program, you can ensure that your files are not corrupt by running the following:

```
md5sum -v -c md5sum.txt
```

You need to create only the rescue disk to install from the CD-ROM. To create it, use the following command:

```
rawrite2 -f resc1440.bin -d a:
```

Now you just place the resc1440 disk into the drive and reboot your computer.

INSTALLING THE SYSTEM FILES

After you reboot, the system displays startup messages, the welcome to Debian GNU/Linux 2.1, and then the following prompt:

```
boot:
```

You can press the F4 or F5 keys for more information or press Enter to continue the installation.

Tip #31 from *Jack*

Keep the rescue floppy because, as its name implies, you can use this floppy in the future should you have problems booting the system. At the `boot:` prompt, you can press F3 to get more information on the rescue disk.

Pressing Return starts the dbootstrap program, which is responsible for the initial system installation and configuration. The primary goal is to install and configure the core of the system so that you can continue with the full installation. dbootstrap is a text-based menu-driven program that leads you through the installation and configuration process. You use the up- and down-arrow keys to move between menu selections and then Return to accept a selection. If you make a mistake, you can return to a previous step via the menu selection to correct the error.

Tip #32 from *Jack*

Debian displays any error messages on the third virtual terminal. You reach this display by pressing Alt+F3 and return to the installation screen by pressing Alt+F1.

When the system has finished booting, you should see the Select Color or Monochrome Display dialog box. If your monitor can display only black and white, press Return to continue with the installation. Otherwise, you can use the arrow keys to move the cursor to the Color menu item and then press Return. The display should change from black and white to color. Then you can press Return again to continue with the installation.

Next, you configure the keyboard by selecting the appropriate entry from the Configure the Keyboard dialog box. After installation, you can select from a wider range of keyboards by running the kbdconfig program.

After selecting a keyboard, you need to partition your hard drives. If you prepped the drives previously, you can continue; otherwise, now you need to partition and format the drives using fdisk.

Tip #33 from *Jack*

You can also use the program cfdisk to partition your drives. You can find more information on cfdisk in the `tools` folder on the Debian CD-ROM.

USING THE LINUX FDISK PROGRAM

When you're ready to partition your drives, at the fdisk prompt, type `m` for a list of commands. Table 5.3 lists the available commands.

Caution

You use the fdisk program native to Linux for these actions. You should be careful because this program is different from the fdisk programs included with other operating systems such as MS-DOS, Windows 95/98, and OS/2. You cannot use these programs interchangeably! For example, you cannot use Linux's fdisk to rearrange a partition for a DOS partition. Although you can use any fdisk to create partitions, you must use the appropriate operating system's version of fdisk to perform such actions as setting file types.

TABLE 5.3 THE LINUX FDISK COMMANDS

Command	Description
`a`	Toggles a bootable flag
`c`	Toggles the DOS compatibility flag
`d`	Deletes a partition
`l`	Lists known partition types
`m`	Displays this menu
`n`	Adds a new partition
`p`	Displays the partition table
`q`	Quits without saving changes
`t`	Changes a partition's system ID
`u`	Changes display/entry units

TABLE 5.3 THE LINUX FDISK COMMANDS

Command	Description
v	Verifies the partition table
w	Writes the table to disk and exits
x	Provides extra functionality for experts only

To begin the partitioning, select the p command (press p and then Return) to display the current partition table, which should reflect the drive you partitioned earlier with the DOS FDISK program. Listing 5.1 shows a possible listing from the p command.

LISTING 5.1 EXAMPLE OF A CURRENT PARTITION TABLE

```
Disk /dev/hda: 15 heads, 17 sectors, 1024 cylinders
Units = cylinders of 255 * 512 bytes

Device          Boot      Begin       Start       End       Blocks  Id   System

dev/hda1                  1024        1024        4040      384667+ 51   Novell?
Partition 2 has different physical/logical endings:
phys=(967, 14, 17) Logical=(4096, 14.17)
```

Note

Your screen may appear different than what's shown in Listing 5.1 because the values are different for each drive type and the partitions already defined on that drive.

Listing 5.1 indicates the various partitions already defined that it can detect, the starting and ending locations of the partition, and how big each partition is in blocks. The listing also indicates the partition type. Table 5.4 shows all the different types of partitions you can define by using the Linux fdisk program. The primary partition types used here are 83-Linux Native and 82-Linux Swap. You can get a similar listing by using the l command.

TABLE 5.4 THE KNOWN LINUX PARTITION TYPES

Reference Number	Type
0	Empty
1	DOS 12-bit FAT
2	XENIX root
3	XENIX usr
4	DOS 16-bit < 32MB
5	Extended
6	DOS 16-bit >= 32MB

TABLE 5.4 THE KNOWN LINUX PARTITION TYPES

Reference Number	Type
7	OS/2 HPFS
8	AIX
9	AIX bootable
a	OS/2 Boot Manager
40	Venix 80286
51	Novell?
52	Microport
63	GNU HURD
64	Novell
75	PC/IX
80	Old MINIX
81	MINIX/Linux
82	Linux Swap
83	Linux Native
93	Amoeba
94	Amoeba BBT
a5	BSD/386
b7	BSDI fs
b8	BSDI swap
c7	Syrinx
db	CP/M
e1	DOS access
e3	DOS R/O
f2	DOS secondary
ff	BBT

In Listing 5.1, Linux prints a note about the different physical and logical endings at the bottom of the screen. The difference exists because, on the system used to write this chapter, a prior partition containing the DOS D drive was left intact, whereas the C drive was repartitioned to a smaller C drive to make room for Linux. Thus, space exists between the C drive and the D drive. The necessary partitions required by Linux will be created here.

The begin, start, and end numbers from Listing 5.1 are very important. You should write them down because you'll need them in a later step to specify the necessary sizes of the partitions you'll add.

ADDING THE NECESSARY PARTITIONS

Because you've repartitioned the drive for DOS, you shouldn't have to delete any partitions for Linux. You should only have to add partitions. To add a partition, you issue the `n` command, which displays the following:

```
Command Action
e extended
p primary(1-4)
```

Now, you can press p and then Return. When fdisk asks for the partition number, enter your selection and press Return. If you indicate a partition number already in use, fdisk reports this fact and asks you to delete the partition before trying to add it to the partition table. For this example, enter `3` to add a third primary partition that's referred to as `/dev/hda3`.

Next, fdisk asks for the location of the first cylinder. This is usually the first available cylinder. In fact, fdisk displays a default range for your selection, such as the following:

```
First cylinder (42-1024) :
```

Notice that the first partition ends at cylinder 41 and that the next partition begins at cylinder 1024. Thus, the range supplied by fdisk here allows you to start the next partition anywhere in the range of 42 to 1024. It's a very good idea not to place partitions just anywhere throughout the disk; instead, choose the next available location, which in this case is cylinder 42. Enter `42` and press Return.

Note

Linux can have trouble booting from partitions defined to start at cylinders above 1024. If you can create a Linux partition only in this range, you might have to boot Linux from a floppy. You'll learn how to create the Rescue floppy. The only downside is that booting Linux from a floppy takes a little longer than booting from the hard drive.

Now fdisk wants you to specify how much space to allocate for this partition. You can express this size in number of cylinders or by the number of bytes (`+size`), kilobytes (`+sizeK`), or megabytes (`+sizeM`). Because you should already know the approximate size you need for the swap file, you can define this partition first and then leave the rest of the disk space for the Linux program partitions. For this example, because your machine has 8MB of RAM, you need to specify a 16MB partition size by replying as follows:

```
Last cylinder or +size or +sizeM or +sizeK (42-1023): +16M
```

You should then use the `p` command to look at the new partition table you've defined. In this example, the new partition table looks like this:

```
Disk /dev/hda: 15 heads, 17 sectors, 1024 cylinders
Units = cylinders of 255 * 512 bytes
Device      Boot    Begin     Start     End     Blocks     Id      System
/dev/hda1 *         1         1          41     5219 1     DOS     12-bit FAT
/dev/hda2           1024      1024      4040    384667+    51       Novell?
```

```
Partition 2 has different physical/logical endings:
phys=(967, 14, 17) Logical=(4039, 14.17)
/dev/hda3            42       42   170  16447+     83      Linux native
```

By default, fdisk made the new partition a Linux native type. To change this type to a swap partition, you need to use the `t` command. To do so, enter `t` and then enter the partition number you want to change; in this example, enter `3`. fdisk then requests that you enter the hexadecimal value of the desired partition type from Table 5.4. (If you don't have the table handy, you can type `l` to get the list of partition type codes.) Because you want a swap partition in this case, enter `82` at the prompt.

As you can see, fdisk reports the new partition type, but you can also use the `p` command to double-check that partition 3 is now a Linux swap partition.

Now you can add your Linux partitions. For this example, you will add only one partition. But if you want to have multiple partitions for various reasons, you can add them at this time. To add a partition, enter `n`, specify `p` for another primary partition, and then specify the number for this partition, which is `4`. To keep from fragmenting different partitions across the drive, start the last partition where the first left off, at cylinder 171. Because you want to use the rest of the space for the Linux system, you can specify the last cylinder instead of an exact byte count. Thus, enter `1023`, as shown here:

```
Command (m for help): n
Command action
e extended
p primary partition (1-4)
p
Partition number (1-4): 4
First cylinder (171-1024): 171
Last cylinder or +size or +sizeM or +sizeK (171-1023): 1023
```

Now use the `p` command to verify the new partitions. If you need to make any changes, you can do so now.

When you're satisfied with the layout of your partitions, you can use the `w` command to write the partition table information to the hard disk. None of your changes are permanent until you use the `w` command; thus, if you feel you've made some changes in error, you can use the `q` command to exit without altering the partition table. When you issue the `w` command, Linux tells you the partition table has been altered and then resynchronizes the disks to match the new partition table. If your Linux system hangs at this point, you can reboot with the installation boot and root disks until you're back at the `#` prompt.

Caution

Don't use the Linux fdisk program to create or modify partitions for other operating systems. Doing so could leave the hard drive in a useless state for both operating systems.

CONFIGURING A SWAP PARTITION

After configuring your drives, the installation asks whether you want to initialize and activate a swap partition. This disk area is used as slow memory when the system runs out of RAM. A swap partition is strongly recommended if you have less than 32MB of RAM. Select the next menu item to continue the installation. If you do not want a swap partition, you can select the menu option Do Without a Swap Partition; otherwise, you should select the partition to activate as a swap partition and press Return.

After selecting the partition, you can scan the entire swap area for bad disk blocks and remove them from the pool of available blocks, thus averting a future problem. Select Yes from the `dbootstrap` menu to initialize the swap area.

Tip #34 from *Jack*

Most of today's disk drives do not suffer from bad blocks, so you can generally save the time and skip initializing the disk space. However, if you have older drives or well-used drives, initialization is a small price to pay for peace of mind.

INITIALIZING LINUX PARTITIONS

Next, `dbootstrap` displays the Initialize a Linux Partition dialog box. You can now initialize various Linux partitions for your system. Although you can have just one partition for everything, I recommend at least two: one for the operating system and one for users' home directories. Select Next to initialize and mount the `/` disk partition, called the *root*.

→ See "Linux Standard Directories," p. 418

You can use the arrow keys to continue to initialize and mount the various partitions you created, such as `/usr`, `/var`, and `/opt`. After initializing all the partitions, you can install the kernel.

CONFIGURING THE SYSTEM

Install Operating System Kernel and Modules is the next menu selection. `dbootstrap` presents you with a selection of drives from which you can install Debian, typically your CD-ROM. You can also select to install from another hard drive or via the network. Although you can specify several devices or locations from which to install Debian, for the typical installation from CD-ROM, you can simply press Return for the default selections.

After installing the kernel, you need to configure the various devices on your system, such as Ethernet cards. Using the Configure Device Driver Modules menu selection, you can install on your system the drivers needed for various devices to be made available on startup.

Tip #35 from *Jack*

You can reconfigure any module or device driver after installation by using the modconf program.

CONFIGURING THE NETWORK

After installing the various device drivers needed by your system, you need to configure the network, even if your system is not connected to a network. If you are not connected to a network, you just have to select a host name for your system and then answer No to the Is Your System Connected to a Network selection.

You need the information listed in the previous section What You Need to Install Debian to configure your system for connection to a network. However, if you will be connecting to the network via PPP, you should not configure the network at this time. To configure, you can simply answer the various questions asked by `dbootstrap` from the information you have. The primary network connection should be `eth0` if you are using Ethernet.

After configuring the base network, you can then proceed to install the base system.

INSTALLING THE BASE SYSTEM

When you're ready to install the base system, you are prompted to specify the path to the `base2_1.tgz` file. You can simply press Return and let `dbootstrap` find the file, or you can type the path at the prompt. At this point, you have a minimal Debian system, but now you must perform some configuration before the system will run.

`dbootstrap` next asks you to select your time zone. You can specify your time zone in many ways, but the suggested method is to go to the Directories: pane of the dialog box and select your country (or continent). That selection changes the listed time zones so that you can select your geographic location in the Timezones: dialog box.

Next, `dbootstrap` asks if your system clock is to be set to Greenwich Mean Time (GMT) or local time. Select GMT if you intend to run only Debian on your computer; otherwise, select local time.

Next, you need to decide whether to boot Linux from the master boot record (MBR) or from some other boot manager or floppy. `dbootstrap` asks you to make a selection. If you select to boot from the MBR, you cannot boot directly into any other operation system. If you do not select to boot from the MBR, you can later use either the `fdisk` command or the `activate` command to set the bootable partition.

Tip #36 from *Jack*

If you want to uninstall Debian booting from the MBR so that you can boot into DOS/ Windows, you can use the command `fdisk /mbr` to restore the DOS boot block.

`dbootstrap` next asks you to create a boot floppy, which is a very good idea. If your installation fails, or at some future time you have problems booting into Debian, the boot floppy can usually boot Debian so that you can troubleshoot the problems.

Finally, you need to select the Reboot the System menu item to reboot your system and continue with the rest of the installation.

CONFIGURING THE BASE SYSTEM

After rebooting, you are asked to set the password for the superuser account, called the *root account*. This username (root) is the most powerful account on any UNIX system, allowing the person logged in as root full access to everything while being bound to none of the security precautions other users must follow. The root account is meant to be used only for system administration, so you must not use the account for day-to-day activities.

Next, Debian asks you to create a normal user account to use for your day-to-day tasks. You can use almost any name, but your password should not be a word easily guessed by others. The same goes for the root password. Try to select a password of at least six characters, and use a number to help make the password harder to break.

→ See "Dealing with Password Security," p. 277

After you create the normal user account, Debian then requests you to enable shadow password support. Shadow passwords provide even more security to your system, not only for the root account but for all users. Without shadowed passwords, your password file (`/etc/passwd`) can be read by anyone on your system, and even though passwords are encrypted, crackers can easily break passwords using a variety of methods.

Note

Although unencrypting a password from the encrypted one is practically impossible, some programs can encrypt millions of words or character patterns and then compare them to password files. A UNIX system checks a password this way: You enter the password, the system encrypts the password, and then it compares the password just encrypted to the encrypted password stored in the password file. If they match, the user is allowed access to the system.

Enabling shadow password support allows the system to store the encrypted passwords in a file that can be accessed only by the superuser. Thus, crackers cannot gain access to even the encrypted passwords normally stored in `/etc/passwd`. I highly recommend that you enable shadow password support.

Tip #37 from
Jack

If you decide not to use shadow passwords in the beginning but decide later that you want to use them, you can use the `shadowconfig` command to reconfigure your system.

After you create the root and a user account, the system then asks you whether you want to use one of the preconfigured profiles, as described in Table 5.1, to install. Selecting the various packages to install can be time-consuming, considering over 2,000 packages are available. The canned selections provide for an easy choice. However, you can use the dselect program to individually select from the various packages available. You can run the `dselect` command at any point to install packages. After you have made your selections, either a profile or packages, the system then starts installing your selections.

Congratulations! After installing all the selected packages, your Debian system is ready to go.

CHAPTER 6

Adding Sound Cards and Other Multimedia Hardware

In this chapter

by Jeff Tranter

SOUND CARDS

Most PCs today are sold with sound cards. Compared with just a few years ago, current sound cards provide very high quality digital audio at an extremely affordable price. In contrast to the traditional use of UNIX systems for running multiuser text-based applications, Linux systems today make use of multimedia, including sound. Applications for multimedia are limitless, ranging from a single user running a graphical desktop environment that uses sound for feedback all the way to using Linux as the basis for a professional digital audio recording studio.

A LITTLE HISTORY

Actually, several different sound card drivers are available under Linux. A little history is in order to help you understand where they came from.

In the early days of Linux (prior to version 1.0), Hannu Savolainen of Finland developed a kernel driver for the Creative Labs SoundBlaster card. He and others extended the driver over time to support many other types of popular sound cards. While working on a part-time basis, Hannu could see that with more effort the sound drivers could be ported quite easily to other UNIX-compatible operating systems and extended to support more sound cards. To this end, the U.S. company 4Front Technologies hired Hannu to work full time on turning the sound card drivers into a commercial product. This product has come to be known as the Open Sound System (OSS). OSS now runs on a many different operating systems and is sold as a commercial product. A freely available sound driver derived from OSS, now usually called OSS/Lite, continues to be included with the Linux kernel.

Some time after Hannu developed the sound drivers, a group of people headed by Jaroslev Kysela were using Gravis UltraSound sound cards, one of the first affordable sound cards that supported wavetable synthesis technology. They were unhappy with the kernel sound card driver and started the Gravis UltraSound Project to develop their own. Eventually, the project expanded in scope to include support for more sound cards and became the Advanced Linux Sound Architecture (ALSA).

To make things somewhat more confusing, the OSS/Lite sound drivers in the 2.0 kernel were modified by Alan Cox under the sponsorship of Red Hat Software so that they were configured as separate kernel loadable modules, making it easier to configure sound when installing a Red Hat Linux system. Red Hat shipped these modified drivers with several versions of Red Hat Linux. With the release of Linux 2.2, these changes were included as part of the standard kernel distribution.

One other class of kernel sound driver is available, one that may become more common as hardware manufacturers realize the importance of supporting Linux. Some hardware vendors may choose to develop their own drivers and release them separately. For example, Creative Labs has developed Linux drivers for their SoundBlaster Live! card. Often these drivers are made available only as precompiled binaries. This approach allows hardware vendors to keep information about their card designs proprietary, presumably to make it harder for competitors to copy. The disadvantage is that, without source code, users cannot enhance the driver or fix bugs themselves, and the modules may work only with specific versions of the Linux kernel. Some people feel that this restriction goes against the Open Source spirit of Linux. Whether it is truly advantageous to the hardware vendor is a subject of debate in the Linux community.

Sound Drivers

In effect, kernel sound drivers come in four flavors, all of which are partially compatible but have subtle differences and their own advantages and disadvantages. Although this information is somewhat debatable, it is summarized in Table 6.1.

Table 6.1 Sound Driver Comparison

Driver	Advantages	Disadvantages
OSS/Lite	Freely available Included with Linux kernel Supports most sound cards	Not very actively developed anymore No direct support for plug-and-play
OSS	Supports many sound cards Easy installation Multiplatform Supports plug-and-play High compatibility with OSS/Lite Has additional features	Commercial product (costs $) No source code provided
ALSA	Freely available Mostly compatible with OSS/Lite Has additional features Is actively developed Supports plug-and-play	Currently supports only a few sound cards Not fully compatible with OSS/Lite
Vendor Supplied	May support sound cards that are not supported by any other driver	May be binary only May not be fully compatible with OSS/Lite

Looking ahead, the ALSA team plans to submit their code for inclusion into the standard kernel source sometime during the 2.3 kernel series, making it the "official" sound driver in 2.4. It is unclear if OSS/Lite will continue to be included as an alternative or will disappear entirely.

Having said all that, although much of the information in this section is applicable to all sound drivers, I will focus on the OSS/Lite drivers since they are shipped with most current Linux distributions. Depending on your needs, you might want to explore ALSA or OSS, in which case you should consult the documentation that comes with those products.

The information in this chapter is applicable to Linux on the Intel x86 platform, and to a lesser extent on systems that use ISA or PCI bus-based sound cards. On other Linux platforms where sound hardware is built in, the process is different, so you should consult documentation specific to that platform.

SOUND CARD TECHNOLOGY

The typical PC sound card consists of several different functional blocks.

A *digital-to-analog (D/A) converter*, sometimes inaccurately called a Digital Signal Processor (DSP), converts between the digital form that sound files are stored in a computer to the analog form required for playback to a loudspeaker.

In digital form, sound is represented as a sequence of discrete numbers, known as *samples*, representing the value of the sound pressure at specific points in time. The number of bits used to store each sample is known as the *sample size*. The greater the sample size, the more accurately the sound can be represented. The most common sound sample sizes are 8 and 16 bits (hence, the common classification of sound cards as 8- or 16-bit cards). The rate at which the sound samples are measured is known as the *sample rate*. The greater the sampling rate, the more accurately the sound card can be reproduced. A sampling rate of 8,000 samples per second with an 8-bit sample size provides telephone-quality sound. CD audio uses 44,100 16-bit samples per second. The trade-off with using large sample sizes and sample rates is that the amount of data storage required increases.

The complement to the D/A converter is the *analog-to-digital (A/D) converter* used for recording sound. It converts analog signals such as that from a microphone to digital form that can be stored in a computer. These two devices, the A/D and D/A converters, allow sound to be recorded, stored on a computer, and later played back. The sound can be speech, music, or anything else that can be captured by a microphone.

The first generation of sound cards used a simple and inexpensive technique called *FM synthesis* for generating sound. This type of sound generation requires very little effort on the part of the processor to produce sound but is generally limited to music and sound effects. The disadvantage of FM synthesis is that it is artificially created and therefore generally does a poor job of reproducing the sound of real musical instruments (and cannot handle human speech at all). Most sound cards today continue to provide an FM synthesis chip for backward compatibility.

Many modern sound cards use a technology called *wavetable synthesis* that is essentially a hybrid of the D/A converter and FM synthesis techniques. The sounds of real musical instruments, converted to digital format, can be stored in memory on the sound card itself and played back. Circuitry on the sound card allows this to be done mostly in hardware. This technology produces a much more realistic sound when producing computer music.

Tip #38 from *Jeff*

The `timidity` program performs wavetable synthesis in software using any sound card with a D/A converter. This provides sound quality comparable to that of wavetable cards at the expense of some processing power.

An essential component of all sound cards is a *mixer*. It is the circuit that controls volume levels of signals passing through the sound card, controls effects such as bass and treble, and selects the input sources when recording and playing back sounds. You could think of it as a set of volume and tone controls that can be adjusted in software.

Many sound cards include a MIDI bus interface. *MIDI*, an acronym for *musical instrument digital interface*, is a standardized protocol for connecting together and communicating with electronic musical instruments. Common MIDI devices include sound synthesizers, piano keyboards, and even computer-controlled lighting systems. MIDI is most commonly used by professional and serious amateur musicians.

Because sound cards are often used for games, many also include one or more joystick ports.

COLLECTING HARDWARE INFORMATION

Configuring sound cards under Linux can be a little tricky and unpredictable. It might be completely straightforward (particularly if you have one of the more common sound cards) or next to impossible (for example, the sound hardware built in to some laptop computers can be unique). Fortunately, you can postpone sound card support until after your basic Linux system is up and running. In addition, Linux distributions are continually being improved to make configuration simpler.

The first step in configuring your sound card is to collect as much information about your sound hardware as possible. If you've been reading this book in sequence, then you probably did that in Chapter 2, "Linux Installation Overview." If not, then it's time to collect that information now.

Although you can often successfully configure sound support with incomplete information, as much of the following information as you can get will be useful:

- The sound card manufacturer and model name
- Settings for IRQ number, DMA channels, and I/O ports
- The type of sound chip used (particularly for "no-name" cards)
- The type of bus used (for example, ISA, ISA plug-and-play, or PCI)

If necessary, you can open the PC and physically examine the card to determine these settings (for example, look at jumper switch settings).

It is also helpful if you can verify that the card was working under another operating system before Linux was installed. Using the same settings under Linux is not strictly necessary but is recommended.

Tip #39 from *Jeff*

Under Microsoft Windows 95 or 98 you can use the System Properties applet to display the resources used by sound cards and other devices.

Tip #40 from *Jeff*

A note on compatibility: Virtually all sound card manufacturers claim their products are "SoundBlaster compatible." Essentially, this claim means only that these products provide software drivers for MS-DOS and Windows that are compatible with the SoundBlaster card drivers. Under Linux, this software cannot be used, so the cards must be compatible at the hardware level with a card that is supported under Linux. Although few people have this luxury, the ideal situation is that you select the model of sound card being purchased to ensure that it is compatible with Linux. Fortunately, most popular sound cards do work under Linux, and some manufacturers are now indicating Linux compatibility in their product marketing literature.

CONFIGURATION METHODS

You can choose from three main methods of configuring sound support under Linux. They are covered here in order of preference, starting with the simpler methods that may not work in all cases and then the more complex methods that you might need to fall back on.

USING AN AUTOMATED CONFIGURATION PROGRAM

Some Linux distributions include a utility to configure sound support in an automated or semi-automated manner. It can be a standalone tool or part of a larger system administration utility. When this method works, using such a utility is the easiest way to configure sound and appears to be the way that Linux distributions are headed in the future—easy-to-use, often graphical, system administration tools as an alternative to (but not replacement for) the traditional configuration file-based system administration. Note that you generally need to be logged in as the system administrator (user root) to perform these functions.

Under Red Hat Linux, using the `sndconfig` program is the recommended way to configure sound. This utility first probes for plug-and-play sound cards and displays any cards found. If no plug-and-play cards are available, it presents you with a list to select from. You then select the settings for I/O port, IRQ number, and DMA channels. For plug-and-play cards, the program can optionally pick the settings automatically. The program then saves the card type in a file (`/etc/sysconfig/soundcard`) and for plug-and-play cards creates the appropriate configuration file (`/etc/isapnp.conf`) for the ISA plug-and-play utilities to configure the card on system startup. The file `/etc/conf.modules` is configured to load the appropriate kernel modules for the selected type of sound card. As a final check, it even plays a sound file of Linus Torvalds speaking to verify that the sound card is working.

Under Caldera OpenLinux, the COAS system administration tool provides a similar capability to configure sound cards.

Other Linux distributions may include sound configuration tools. If not, or if the automated tools fail for your system, you should use the manual method described in the next section.

If you are using the OSS or ALSA sound drivers, you should use the configuration tools that come with that software.

Tip #41 from *Jeff*

> You can obtain utilities such as `sndconfig` separately and install them on other Linux distributions even if they were not provided by your vendor. Make sure you install any other packages required by `sndconfig`.

Loading Kernel Modules

The second method is to manually perform the same steps that were described in the preceding section.

The first step is optional and applies only to ISA plug-and-play sound cards. Unless you're using a sound driver that directly supports plug-and-play devices (that is, OSS or ALSA), you need to use the `isapnp` tools to configure the sound card settings. Follow these steps:

1. Save a copy of the existing `/etc/isapnp.conf` file, if any.
2. Use the `pnpdump` tool to generate a new `/etc/isapnp.conf` file. This is typically done with the command `pnpdump >/etc/isapnp.conf`.
3. Edit the file (typically by uncommenting the appropriate lines) to select the desired device settings.
4. Run `isapnp` to configure the ISA plug-and-play cards in your system.

You can find more details on the ISA plug-and-play tools in the system manual pages for `ispnp`, `pnpdump`, and `isapnp.conf`.

The appropriate kernel sound driver modules are loaded by the `kerneld` daemon (or in newer kernels, the `kmod` thread in the kernel). The configuration file `/etc/conf.modules` needs to be configured to indicate the drivers to be loaded. Again, you can find the detailed documentation in the manual pages for `kerneld`. A typical portion of the configuration file for a SoundBlaster 16 card using the OSS/Lite drivers is shown in Listing 6.1.

Tip #42 from *Jeff*

> An advantage of using sound drivers built as kernel loadable modules is that `kerneld` (or `kmod`) will automatically unload them if they are not used, freeing up memory for other uses.

Listing 6.1 Typical `/etc/conf.modules` Entries for the OSS/Lite Sound Driver

```
# 2.2.0 OSS/Lite sound drivers
alias sound sb
alias synth0 midi
alias midi opl3
options opl3 io=0x388
options sb io=0x220 irq=10 dma=3 dma16=7 mpu_io=0x330
```

For the ALSA driver, the module names are different. An example is shown in Listing 6.2. You should consult the ALSA documentation to determine the correct options for your sound card.

LISTING 6.2 TYPICAL /etc/conf.modules ENTRIES FOR THE ALSA SOUND DRIVER

```
# 0.4.0 ALSA sound drivers with OSS emulation
alias char-major-116 snd
alias char-major-14 soundcore
alias snd-card-0 snd-sb16
alias snd-slot-0 snd-card-0
alias sound-service-0-0 snd-mixer-oss
alias sound-service-0-1 snd-seq-oss
alias sound-service-0-3 snd-pcm1-oss
alias sound-service-0-4 snd-pcm1-oss
options snd snd_cards_limit=1
# options for SB16
options snd-sb16 snd_port=0x220 snd_mpu_port=0x330 snd_irq=10 \
      snd_dma8=3 snd_dma16=7 snd_dma8_size=64 snd_dma16_size=128 \
      snd_mic_agc=1 snd_isapnp=0
# after loading, initialize mixer
post-install snd-sb16 alsactl restore
```

Under OSS, you generally use the `soundon` script to load and configure the drivers.

When the sound drivers are configured properly, they should be loaded automatically when an application opens a sound device. You can proceed now to the section on testing.

The presumption here is that the appropriate kernel sound modules were provided for you when the system was installed. Typically, they are located in the directory `/lib/modules/x.y.z/misc`, where *x.y.z* is the kernel version. If that is not the case, you need to create them as part of building a new kernel. This task is beyond the scope of this chapter and is covered in Chapter 14, "Configuring the Linux Kernel."

If you are new to Linux and are not yet comfortable with system administration tasks such as editing configuration files and rebooting the system, I recommend that you gain a basic familiarity with the system, such as is covered in Part II of this book, "System Administration," before attempting to set up kernel sound support.

BUILDING SOUND SUPPORT INTO THE KERNEL

The third and final method of setting up sound support is to compile the appropriate sound drivers into the kernel. With this method, you also have to configure plug-and-play cards, but because the drivers are linked into the kernel itself, you don't need to worry about the loading of modules.

Again, the process of configuring, building, and installing a new kernel is beyond the scope of this chapter and is the subject of Chapter 14.

Testing Your Sound Card

To verify that your sound card configuration is correct, answer these three questions:

- Can you load the sound drivers into the kernel?
- Did the drivers find the sound card?
- Do the sound devices work?

If configured properly, the kernel drivers should automatically be loaded if any sound devices are accessed. An easy way to access them is to run the command `cat /dev/sndstat`, which displays the contents of the sound status device. If all goes well, you should see a result that shows information about the loaded drivers. A typical output is shown in Listing 6.3.

Listing 6.3 Example of `/dev/sndstat` Output for the OSS/Lite Sound Driver

```
Sound Driver:3.5.4-960630 (Sat Jan 4 23:56:57 EST 1997 root,
Linux fizzbin 2.0.27 #48 Thu Dec 5 18:24:45 EST 1996 i586)
Kernel: Linux fizzbin 2.0.27 #48 Thu Dec 5 18:24:45 EST 1996 i586
Config options: 0

Installed drivers:
Type 1: OPL-2/OPL-3 FM
Type 2: Sound Blaster
Type 7: SB MPU-401

Card config:
Sound Blaster at 0x220 irq 5 drq 1,5
SB MPU-401 at 0x330 irq 5 drq 0
OPL-2/OPL-3 FM at 0x388 drq 0

Audio devices:
0: Sound Blaster 16 (4.13)

Synth devices:
0: Yamaha OPL-3

Midi devices:
0: Sound Blaster 16

Timers:
0: System clock

Mixers:
0: Sound Blaster
```

Keep in mind that this output is for OSS/Lite. For OSS, sample output is shown in Listing 6.4.

LISTING 6.4 EXAMPLE OF `/dev/sndstat` OUTPUT FOR THE OSS SOUND DRIVER

```
OSS/Linux 3.9.2p 4Front Technologies 1996-1999

License serial number: N12345678
Options: AWE APCI MIX
This copy of OSS is licensed to Jeff Tranter

Build: 2.2.10-UP

Card config:
Software mixing (audio)
Generic PnP support
SoundBlaster PnP at 0x220 irq 10 drq 3,7
SB MPU-401 at 0x330 irq 10

Audio devices:
0: Creative SB16 PnP (4.13) (DUPLEX)
1: SB secondary device (DUPLEX)
2: SoftOSS v1.2 CH #0
3: SoftOSS v1.2 CH #1
4: SoftOSS v1.2 CH #2
5: SoftOSS v1.2 CH #3
6: SoftOSS v1.2 CH #4
7: SoftOSS v1.2 CH #5
8: SoftOSS v1.2 CH #6
9: SoftOSS v1.2 CH #7

Synth devices:
0: SoftOSS v1.2

Midi devices:
0: Sound Blaster 16

Timers:
0: System clock
1: SoftOSS

Mixers:
0: Sound Blaster
1: SoftOSS
```

If reading `/dev/sndstat` produces an error such as `cat: /dev/sndstat: Operation not supported by device`, then your modules are not being loaded. Proceed to the "Troubleshooting" section at the end of this chapter.

The output of `/dev/sndstat` should indicate that the sound drivers were correctly detected at the correct addresses. If devices were not found, then check out the "Troubleshooting" section.

Note that if you are using the ALSA drivers, you don't have `/dev/sndstat`; the equivalent is the `/proc/asound` directory. Looking at the files in this directory should give you an indication of whether the drivers are loaded.

If the drivers are loaded, it's time to test the card. A good first test is to run a mixer program and verify that you can set the gain settings without any errors. Common mixer programs include `xmixer`, `aumix`, and `kmix`. Setting all levels to their maximums is a good idea for now; this way, you can make sure that if the card is working, you'll be able to hear it.

To test the D/A converter, you can use a sound player program such as `play` or `kmedia` to play a sound file. You likely have some sound files on your system; look for files with the extension `.wav` or `.au`. (Using the command `locate *.wav *.au` is a good way to find some.) You should hear the sound played through the speakers. Under Red Hat Linux, for example, the famous sound file of Linus Torvalds speaking can be found in `/usr/share/sndconfig/sample.au`.

To test the A/D converter, you need a microphone and some software for recording sound to a sound file. You might have to dig around on your machine or download some software to do your testing. Look for programs called `rec` or `vrec`.

To test the FM synthesizer on a sound card, you need a MIDI player application such as `playmidi`, `kmid`, and `kmidi` and some MIDI files (the file extension is usually `.mid`). Try playing a MIDI file with one of these applications. Because you're checking FM synthesis, you probably won't be very impressed by the sound quality.

Testing the MIDI bus interface on a sound card is outside the scope of this chapter. If you are fortunate enough to have MIDI devices, you are definitely in the ranks of the advanced users.

AUDIO CDs

If your sound card is working now, you've probably made it over the biggest hurdle. This section describes how to get your CD-ROM drive to work with the sound card to play music CDs.

Audio CD players and CD-ROM drives use the same basic technology. Most CD-ROM drives can play audio CDs. Listening to some music while programming is a great way to relax.

To use your CD-ROM drive, you need software to control it. Many CD player programs exist, ranging from simple command-line tools to complex graphical applications. Some of the more common programs include `cdplay`, `cdp`, `kscd`, and `xplaycd`.

Although most CD-ROM drives include a front panel headphone jack and volume control, most users connect the drive to their sound card and play it through speakers.

Tip #43 from *Jeff*

When you're playing audio CDs, the drive always runs at single speed. Your drive may make a noticeably different sound when playing audio. If you want to use a CD-ROM drive only to play music, then don't waste your money on an expensive high-speed drive. In fact, if you have an old drive lying around and a spare IDE device port in your machine, you might want to consider installing it as a second drive. That way, you can listen to music even when you're using the CD-ROM for data.

INSTALLATION

The first prerequisite for installation is to make sure that the CD-ROM drive is working properly for accessing data CDs. If you installed Linux from CD, then you should be in business; otherwise, go back and review the appropriate sections in Chapters 2 through 5.

Now you can insert a music CD, plug headphones into the front panel headphone jack, and run a CD player application. You should be able to listen to music without any involvement from your sound card. In fact, if you don't have a sound card, you can plug amplified speakers into the headphone jack and listen to CDs. If you don't get any sound from the front panel jack, look at the suggestions in the "Troubleshooting" section.

You may already hear sound from the speakers connected to your sound card. If not, fire up a sound mixer program and set the CD and master gain levels to suitable levels for listening.

One note on a point of possible confusion: If you have accessed a CD-ROM drive under Linux, you may know that you need to mount the drive. You don't mount audio CDs; doing so only produces error messages.

DOING MORE WITH CD AUDIO

Although audio CDs do not contain information on the artist or track names, they do have a unique signature made up of the number of tracks and lengths of each track. Many CD player programs can match this signature against a list of data for known discs and display the track information. You can enter the information yourself and save it so that the application will display it when the disc is played in the future. You can access databases of CD-ROM information on the Internet that some CD player applications can directly download when playing a CD, saving you the trouble of entering it.

Programs such as `cdparanoia` can "rip" digital audio from CDs and save it to a sound file. Because the data is stored entirely in digital format, no degradation of the quality occurs. At the high sampling rates and sample sizes used for CD audio, this format requires a lot of storage space. Using an MP3 audio encoder, you can compress this format down by a factor of approximately 10. You then can play the resulting file with an MP3 player program.

Tip #44 from *Jeff*

CDs can have both data tracks for storing software as well as audio tracks containing sound. Some games use audio tracks to play the music that accompanies the game. Even if the game does not run under Linux, you can listen to the audio tracks using a CD player program.

JOYSTICKS

Joysticks are most commonly used for playing games, and several Linux games can make use of them. They have other applications too, being a suitable input device whenever a continuously variable analog input is required. Other creative applications include using a joystick as a way to shut down or reboot a Linux system that lacks a keyboard.

In Linux 2.0 and earlier kernels, the joystick driver was a separate package that had to be obtained and compiled separately. With Linux 2.2 and later, the joystick drivers are included in the standard kernel distribution. Many improvements were made in the drivers in 2.2, including support for many more types of joysticks and those found on the non-Intel x86 versions of Linux.

At the time of this writing, at least 32 different models of joysticks are supported by 11 different kernel drivers. They include devices that connect through a joystick connector, parallel port, serial port, or (on some platforms) dedicated joystick interfaces built in to the computer. Joysticks using USB interfaces are not yet supported.

LOADING THE KERNEL JOYSTICK MODULES

Like most kernel drivers, the joystick drivers can be compiled into the kernel or built as kernel loadable modules. Using modules is preferred because this approach provides more flexibility and allows the drivers to be unloaded when not needed, freeing up more memory.

The presumption here is that the appropriate kernel joystick modules were provided for you when your Linux system was installed. Typically, they are located in the directory `/lib/modules/x.y.z/misc`, where `x.y.z` is the kernel version. If that is not the case, you need to create them as part of building a new kernel. This task is beyond the scope of this chapter and is covered in Chapter 14.

If the joystick drivers are built and installed, you should be able to manually load them. For a traditional PC analog joystick, you can load the driver by using the command `modprobe joystick-analog`. This command should result in a message either sent to the console or to the kernel message log (displayed using the command `dmesg`) such as this:

```
js: Version 1.2.13 using 166 MHz RDTSC timer.
js0: Analog 3-axis 2-button joystick at 0x201
```

With a properly configured `/etc/conf.modules` file, the kernel automatically loads the drivers when the joystick devices are accessed. The following is a typical entry for an analog joystick:

```
# joystick - 2 button, 3 axes
alias char-major-15 joy-analog
options joy-analog js_an=0x201,0x3f
```

A program called `jstestis` included with the joystick driver package; it verifies the operation of the driver with your joystick.

Joystick support is still being actively developed. For the most up-to-date documentation, you should consult the documentation on joysticks included with the kernel in `/usr/src/linux/Documentation`. You also might want to download the full package from the joystick driver author's Web site to pick up the latest changes and the test programs.

OTHER MULTIMEDIA DEVICES

As Linux matures, support for more unusual and interesting hardware devices increases. This support can sometimes be challenging if the hardware vendors do not provide much information on programming the devices. Some of the general categories of multimedia devices include the following:

- Full-motion video cards than can capture video for storage and later playback
- TV and radio tuner cards for turning your PC into a software-controlled radio or television
- Digital cameras for capturing images that can be displayed and manipulated
- Scanners for digitizing paper documents

Linux currently supports many CD-R, CD-RW, DVD-ROM, and DVD-RAM drives. DVD video support is still in the early stages at the time of this writing. USB support is coming but is very incomplete, mostly limited to the most common devices such as keyboards and mice.

This area is very dynamic, with support for new devices appearing almost daily. To find out the current status of these devices, you can check Internet Web sites related to Linux. Several sources are listed later in this chapter. You might need to run the latest development version of the kernel or even install special kernel patches.

If you have a hardware device and are uncertain whether it is supported under Linux, you can do a little research to dig up some information. Specialized hardware is most likely to work if it uses a standard interface such as a serial, SCSI, or parallel port. Specialized interface cards and protocols can be a problem.

If no driver exists, writing a kernel driver is not necessarily the daunting task that it may appear. If you have a good understanding of how to communicate with the hardware device and a knowledge of C programming, writing a kernel driver can be within the ability of a Linux hobbyist.

MULTIMEDIA APPLICATIONS

When your sound card or other multimedia hardware is up and running, many applications are available for you to make use of that hardware. Only a few of the major categories are listed here. Some of the resources listed in the next section can point you to specific programs. Popular multimedia applications include the following:

- Sound file playback and recording tools
- CD-player programs
- MP3 players
- MIDI file players, sequencers, and editors
- Sound mixers
- Video players (for file formats such as MPEG, QuickTime, and AVI)
- Graphics editing and manipulation tools
- Image rendering tools
- Toolkits for developing multimedia applications
- Games of all types

Trying Linux multimedia applications can be an interesting experience. The quality can range from a hack full of bugs written by a beginning programmer to a professional application that is as good as or better than commercial applications costing hundreds of dollars.

INFORMATION RESOURCES

You can find a plethora of information about Linux and multimedia, much of it available on the Internet.

Tip #45 from *Jeff*

The Linux Documentation Project (LDP) is an initiative to create freely available documentation for Linux. Out of this project has come the well-known Linux How-To documents and several book-length manuals. Often you can find LDP manuals in Linux systems in the `/usr/doc` directory or on the Internet at `http://www.linuxdoc.org` or `http://metalab.unc.edu/LDP`.

Most Linux commands have manual pages (also called *man pages*) that you can access by using the `man` command. GNU tools are documented using the info format that can be viewed using GNU Emacs or the `info` program. In addition, graphical environments such as KDE and GNOME typically provide graphical browsers for searching and accessing online documentation, including info and man pages.

The Linux kernel comes with some documentation. Although usually quite terse, these README files are often the only documentation for recent development in the kernel. They are conventionally located in the directory `/usr/src/linux/Documentation` if you have the kernel source code installed.

The Web is the primary information resource on the Internet. A few useful sites (subject to change) related to the topics in this chapter are listed in Table 6.2.

TABLE 6.2 WEB SITES FOR MULTIMEDIA ON LINUX

URL	Description
`http://www.alsa-project.org`	The ALSA Project
`http://www.opensound.com`	Open Sound System
`http://www.linuxdoc.org`	The Linux Documentation Project
`http://www.mostang.com/sane`	SANE (Scanner Access Now Easy)
`http://www.freshmeat.net`	Announcements of Linux Applications
`http://sound.condorow.net`	Linux MIDI and Sound Applications

For answers to specific questions, you can check out the many Linux-related Usenet newsgroups and mailing lists.

Finally, you might be able to find a local Linux user group in your area. Joining this user group can be a great way to get answers and find out what is happening locally. If you can't find a user group, why not consider starting one?

TROUBLESHOOTING

Symptom: Kernel modules don't load

You might have an incorrect `/etc/conf.modules` file. Edit the file and make sure that the correct drivers are specified. You can manually load the modules using the `insmod` or `modprobe` commands to experiment with the settings.

The `kerneld` daemon may not be running (or `kmod` support is not compiled into the kernel). Check if the kerneld process is running using the `ps` command. It should be started by one of the system startup scripts.

Also, the kernel sound modules may not have been installed in the correct directory, usually `/lib/modules/`*`x.y.z`*`/misc`. If you built the kernel, make sure that you ran the commands `make modules` and `make modules_install` to build and install the modules.

Symptom: Sound card not detected

You may have the wrong sound card drivers loaded. Try loading a different driver (for example, many cards listed as SoundBlaster compatible are really equivalent to the Windows Sound System).

The wrong I/O address may have been specified for the sound driver. Check if the settings used match the card jumpers or plug-and-play settings.

The plug-and-play settings may not have been configured correctly. Check the `/etc/isapnp.conf` file and verify that the selections there are correct.

Symptom: IRQ/DMA timeout

If this occurs when playing a sound file, you most likely selected the wrong IRQ number or DMA channel. Check that you used the setting that match the card jumpers or plug-and-play setting.

The plug-and-play settings may not have been configured correctly. Check the `/etc/isapnp.conf` file and verify that the selections there are correct.

Symptom: Device Conflicts

You have an IRQ, DMA, or I/O setting conflict between two devices. Note that conflicts can occur, even for plug-and-play devices. You need to ensure that resources do not conflict between cards. Find out what settings are possible for jumper settings and Plug and Play cards. If this becomes complex, I suggest drawing a table. Find a combination of settings that avoid conflicts and configure your cards accordingly.

Symptom: "kernel-module version" mismatch error

The sound modules may have been built with a different kernel from the one being run; you need to recompile using the current kernel version. You may have built a kernel but neglected to build the modules, install them, and update the dependencies file. Make sure you have run the commands `make modules`, `make modules_install`, and `depmod -a`.

Symptom: Sound works only for user root

You need to change the permissions on the device files to allow non-root users to read/write. For example, the command `chmod a+rw /dev/dsp` would grant all users access to the DSP device.

Symptom: No sound playback but no error messages

If this occurs, the most likely reason is that you are not setting the mixer gain levels. Use a mixer program to set the levels to a suitable value.

Symptom: Cannot record

This can be caused by not setting the mixer gain levels or not setting the mixer recording source. Use a mixer program to correct it. Another possibility is a microphone that is bad or plugged into the wrong input jack. Use a known good microphone and check where it is plugged in.

Symptom: "device busy" error

This can be due to a device conflict (described earlier). Another possibility is that another application has opened the audio device. Use the `ps` and `fuser` commands to check for a process which is using sound.

Symptom: No sound after a reboot

Make sure that the system startup scripts initialize plug-and-play devices. Verify that the sound drivers get automatically loaded on system startup. Set the mixer volume levels to an appropriate value using a mixer program.

Note: OSS uses the `soundon` script to load the drivers. This can be automated by adding a call to `soundon` in a system startup script such as `rc.local`.

Symptom: CD doesn't play through headphones

This indicates a problem that is not related to a sound card. First, make sure the drive works with data CDs. Use a known good audio CD. If it still fails, try another CD player program.

Symptom: Plays through headphones but no sound from sound card

This indicates a problem with the sound card. Make sure that there is an audio cable connected from the CD-ROM drive to the sound card. Check that the mixer volume and CD gain levels are correctly set using a mixer program. Make sure that the speakers are turned on and have power (if applicable), volume controls are turned up, and they are connected to the correct sound card jack.

It is possible that you have a sound card with a nonstandard mixer circuit that is not supported under Linux. A new kernel sound driver or alternative drivers such as OSS or ALSA may support the card. You may also be able to work around the problem by initializing it under another operating system and soft-booting into Linux.

Symptom: Sound skips

This can be caused by a dirty or scratched CD; replace with a known good one. The CD-ROM drive may also need cleaning or is simply defective.

Symptom: Only user root can play CDs

You need to set file permissions on the device file for the CD-ROM drive to allow users to read and write.

CHAPTER 7

Upgrading and Installing Software

In this chapter

by Jack Tackett, Jr.

UNDERSTANDING KEY TERMS USED IN THIS CHAPTER

The base Linux system initially contains only a core set of utilities and data files. The system administrator installs additional commands, user application programs, and various data files as required. Applications get updated frequently. System software changes as new features are added and bugs are fixed. The system administrator is responsible for adding, configuring, maintaining, and deleting software from the Linux system.

The word *installing* means copying the associated program files onto the system's hard disk and *configuring* the application (assigning resources) for proper operation on a specific system. The configuration of a program instructs it as to where parts of the application are to be installed and how it is to function within the system environment in general.

Both the Red Hat and Caldera distributions of Linux ease the pain of installing and upgrading software by including the Red Hat package management system accessed via the `rpm` command. However, you'll also find yourself installing software that isn't in `rpm` format. Many of the software packages available on the Internet are in compressed `tar` format.

On large systems, an administrator usually installs applications because most users don't have access to the tape or floppy drives. Administrative permission is also often needed to install components of the applications into system directories. Components may include shared libraries, utilities, and devices that need to go into directories that normal users can't access.

Table 7.1 lists some terms and definitions that you should become familiar with.

TABLE 7.1 TERMS RELATED TO APPLICATION INSTALLATION

Term	Definition
Superuser	The highest privileged user on the system. Also called the *root user*.
System administrator	The person in charge of keeping the Linux system optimized and properly running. The system administrator has superuser privileges and can install new software onto the system.
Dependencies	The reliance/requirement of various software components to each other. A given program may require a specific library or other daemon in order to work properly.
Installing applications	The initial installation or update of a program for a UNIX system. The process usually requires superuser privileges and access to the computer's tape or floppy disk drive.
Configuring	The act of setting up an application to work with your particular system. Configuring can include setting up the application for many users to use, putting it in accessible directories, or sharing it with the network.

UNDERSTANDING THE POLITICS OF UPGRADING

What software should you upgrade? How often should you upgrade? The answers to these questions are largely determined by the purpose of your system—personal or business—and the demands of your users. Software versions are changing all the time. Various parts of the Linux system are constantly being updated. You wouldn't have time to use your system if you tried to keep up with each and every upgrade that comes out.

Typically, you shouldn't have to reinstall the entire Linux system when you upgrade your system software. Usually, only a tiny portion of the system software changes with a new release. You might have to upgrade your kernel or upgrade your system libraries, but you probably won't have to do a full reinstallation. However, when you upgrade software packages, you quite often have to completely install a new version, especially if you're several versions behind when you upgrade.

Tip #46 from *Jack*

The Red Hat package manager used by Red Hat and Caldera provides a mechanism to install packages across the net via `ftp`:

```
rpm -u ftp://ftp.netwharf.com/pub/rpms/somepkg-1999.rpm
```

The Red Hat distribution also allows you to install over the network from an automated script called a kickstart installation. See `http://www.redhat.com/mirrors/LDP/HOWTO/KickStart-HOWTO.html` for more information.

Note

Making a current backup of your system before upgrading software is a good idea. That way, if something goes wrong, you can always get back to your original system.

→ See "Considering Backup Tips," p. 261

In general, you should upgrade your system if a new version of either system or application software fixes a serious problem or adds functionality that you need. It's up to you to determine what constitutes a serious problem. If a new release of a software package fixes something that has caused problems on your system, poses a serious security hole, or fixes a bug that could damage your system, installing it is probably worth your time.

Note

Don't try to keep up with every release of every piece of software; upgrading for the sake of upgrading takes too much time and effort. With a little research, you can keep your system working in good condition and update only the parts that need upgrading as you go along.

INSTALLING SOFTWARE

Installing a major program onto a Linux system is more complicated than installing a similar program on a single-task operating system, such as MS-DOS or Apple Macintosh System 7.6. The multiuser nature of Linux means that every application on the system sometimes receives simultaneous calls for access.

To further complicate installation, most application programs—with the exception of very simple ones—require configuration to your specific system before they can be used. It's up to the system administrator installing the software to identify items specific to the system's configuration when prompted during an application's configuration process.

For example, one user may have only an older character-based terminal, whereas another has a fancy new X Windows terminal. The superuser must make sure that the application responds correctly to the older terminal, sending only ASCII characters—that is, letters and numbers—and that the X Windows terminal receives full advantage of the application's colors and graphics. The system administrator manages the system and has the responsibility of keeping it optimized (all programs up to current versions, proper user accounts assigned, and so forth).

As already stated, loading a program onto a Linux system is more complicated than doing so on single-user operating systems. The system administrator who's installing an application might have to create new directories to house the files associated with a particular program. Some software packages call for the configuring or reconfiguring of system devices. Although the end user worries only about learning the new program's features and operating commands, the superuser must make sure that system resources are properly allocated, configured, and maintained for the program (while, of course, not messing up any already installed applications).

Installing software by using menus or commands is outwardly a relatively simple task; to the system itself, however, the task is complex. Applications for single-user operating systems, such as DOS programs, usually run only one copy of themselves at a time and have no competing programs. In even a simple Linux installation with only one user logged in, many processes can be running at the same time. Multiply this activity by several users all running programs—including some users who use the same application—and the complexity increases dramatically.

The Linux operating system excels at juggling a multitude of processes, programs, users, and peripherals simultaneously. To live in a Linux environment, an application must be properly loaded. An ill-behaving application, or one improperly installed, can cause a system *crash* (when a process or program goes wild and locks the CPU, causing it to lose control of all the currently running programs). The system shuts down, all users are kicked off, and their programs are interrupted. There's often much wailing and gnashing of teeth from frustrated persons in the midst of some complicated task.

As the one loading a new application, the system administrator or superuser is responsible for making sure that the application is compatible with the system and testing the application after it's installed. Understanding the loading of software onto a Linux system first requires a basic knowledge of the responsibilities and privileges of the system administrator.

UNDERSTANDING THE SYSTEM ADMINISTRATOR'S JOB

If you use Linux on a small system, you're probably your own system administrator. You install and run your applications. It's your responsibility to keep a current backup of files, maintain a proper amount of free space on the hard disk, make sure that the system runs optimally through memory management and other means, and do everything else required in the administration of an efficient and productive system. If you're a user in a larger system environment, a specific person probably handles system administration. The following list briefly summarizes what the system administrator does:

- Starts and stops the system, as needed.
- Makes sure that enough free disk space is available and that file systems are free of error.
- Tunes the system so that the maximum number of users have access to the system's hardware and software resources and so that the system operates as fast and as efficiently as possible.
- Protects the system from unauthorized entry and destructive actions.
- Sets up connections to other computer systems.
- Sets up or closes user accounts on the system.
- Works with software and hardware vendors and with those with training or other support contracts for the system.
- Installs, mounts, and troubleshoots terminals, printers, disk drives, and other pieces of system and peripheral hardware.
- Installs and maintains programs, including new application programs, operating system updates, and software-maintenance corrections.
- And nothing else. Too often system administrators log in as root and do everything from there, but doing so can cause a myriad of problems on your system. Use system administration tasks, and use your user account for day-to-day tasks!

USING THE RED HAT PACKAGE MANAGER

Both the Red Hat and the Caldera OpenLinux distributions make use of Red Hat Package Manager (RPM) packages (or RPMs) for managing software installation.

Note

The Debian distribution also uses packages but in a different package system format. Also, typically (although not required of either system), RPMs have an `.rpm` extension, whereas Debian packages have a `.deb` extension.

A package contains a complete, fully tested, and configured program. The package is typically built from a source code package so that developers and users know what they are getting. To manage these packages, Red Hat Software developed the Red Hat Package Manager and released it to the world.

The current version, RPM 3.0, is backward-compatible with previous versions of RPM; however, parts of the program were totally rewritten to improve the product. For more information, see the white paper on Red Hat's Web site at `http://www.redhat.com/knowledgebase/rpm3.0/`.

RPM has six modes of operation, five of which can be used from either the command line or the X Windows-based tool called Glint. The various modes are installing, uninstalling, updating, querying, verifying, and building. You can build an RPM package only in text mode from the command line.

Note For more information on building packages with RPM, see the book *Maximum RPM* (Sams Publishing) or Red Hat software's *Maximum RPM*.

You use RPM from the command line in the format

```
rpm [options] package_name
```

where *`options`*is one of many different flags used by RPM to manipulate packages, and *`package_name`* indicates the software package to be used. The package name usually looks like this: `quota-1.55-4.i386.rpm`. The package name follows this format:

Name	quota
Version	1.55
Release	4
Computer architecture	i386
Extension	`.rpm` (typically)

However, the package file can be any name because the information about the package itself is contained inside the file.

LOCATING PACKAGES

You can find most packages provided with your distribution on the CD-ROM under the directory `/RedHat/RPMS`. To mount the CD-ROM and list the various packages available, use the following commands:

```
cd /mnt
mount CD-ROM
cd CD-ROM/RedHat/RPMS
ls ¦ more
```

Most of these packages were installed during your installation of Linux. However, if you decided not to install certain packages, you can install them now from this collection of packages.

RPM also allows you to install packages located on other computers by using FTP, as you will see in the next section.

Installing Packages with RPM

To install a package from the command line, you use the `-i` option like this:

```
rpm -i quota-1.66-6.i386.rpm
```

This command installs the quota package on your system. The `-i` option instructs the `rpm` command to install the package `quota-1.66-6.i386.rpm` onto the local system. To run the installation, RPM goes through a series of steps:

- **Checks dependency**—Each package may depend on other software already being installed.
- **Checks conflicts**—RPM checks to see whether a component is already installed or that the component is not older than the one currently installed.
- **Processes configuration files**—RPM attempts to provide a proper configuration file, and if it finds a previous configuration file, it saves that file for future reference.
- **Installs files**—RPM unpacks the various components from the package and places them in the proper directories.
- **Performs post-installation processing**—After installing the various components, RPM performs any necessary tasks to properly configure the system.
- **Updates the database**—RPM keeps track of all its action via a database.

The command provides no feedback during this installation, but you can use the `-v` (verbose) option to get more information. Table 7.2 provides a list of other options you can use during installation.

Table 7.2 Installation Options

Option	Description
`-vv`	Provides very verbose information.
`-h`	Prints hash marks (#) periodically during installation. These marks allow you to see that RPM is actually doing something and is not just hung.
`-percent`	Prints the percent completed during installation instead of `#`.
`-test`	Does not install the package, but performs a dry run to test installation and reports any errors.
`-replacefiles`	Replaces files from other packages.
`-force`	Tells RPM to ignore certain conflict errors and install the package anyway.

To install a package located on another machine, you can use an FTP-type URL to designate the package:

```
rpm -i ftp://ftp.netwharf.com/pub/RPMS/quota-1.66-6.i386.rpm
```

Tip #47 from Jack

> **You can use the `vh` flags, eg**
>
> ```
> rpm -ivh ftp://ftp.netwharf.com/pub/RPMS/quota-1.66-6.i386.rpm
> ```
>
> **to provide verbose output and hash marks as the package is installed. The `-ivh` argument is preferred; the output and hash marks are helpful to eliminate confusion if the package does not install fully or the core dumps.**

This command assumes that the remote machine accepts anonymous FTP.

→ See "Using FTP with a Web Browser," p. 706

If you need to specify a username and password to install the file, you can use the following command:

```
rpm -i ftp://mark@ftp.netwharf.com/pub/RPMS/quota-1.66-6.i386.rpm
Password for mark@ftp.netwharf.com: <enter your password here>
```

Note

> **You can enter your username and password in the command at the same time, like this:**
>
> ```
> rpm -ivh ftp://mark:password@ftp.netwharf.com/pub/RPMS/
> quota-1.66-6.i386.rpm
> ```
>
> **However, this method for entering commands is not secure because someone could look over your shoulder or (more likely) recall the command from your history file.**

Uninstalling Packages with RPM

One of the benefits of using RPM is the ease of installing new programs. If you've heard about a new program on the Internet, you can install the package and test the new program. What happens, then, if you decide the software is not for you and you want to get rid of it? Fortunately, RPM makes uninstalling a package just as easy as installing one. To uninstall a package, you use the `-e` option:

```
rpm -e quota-1.66-6.i386.rpm
```

Tip #48 from
Jack

You can indicate the RPM package by name only such as `rpm -e quota` without the version indicators and it will work. The only exception is if you have more than one version of the package installed.

When erasing a package from your system, RPM goes through the following sequence of actions:

- **Checks dependencies**—RPM checks its database to see whether any other packages depend on this database. If so, RPM does not delete the package unless explicitly told to do so.
- **Executes scripts**—RPM executes a pre-uninstall script.
- **Checks configuration files**—RPM saves a copy of any modified configuration files.
- **Deletes files**—RPM deletes every file associated with the specified package.
- **Executes scripts**—RPM executes a post-uninstall script.
- **Updates the database**—RPM removes all references to the package from its database.

As with the `-i` option, you can use the `-v` and `-vv` options to get verbose information from the `erase` command. You can also use the `-test` option to see what problems might occur if you were to really remove the package. Finally, you can use the `-nodeps` option to tell RPM to ignore dependencies and go ahead and remove the package.

Tip #49 from
Jack

You can also use the `-nodeps` option to force an installation.

Caution

Be careful using the `-nodeps` option. If you remove a package on which another program depends, that program might not work correctly in the future.

UPDATING PACKAGES WITH RPM

After you install a package, you eventually will need to install upgrades either for bug fixes or for new features. RPM makes the typically horrendous task of upgrading a program effortless with the `-U` (note the uppercase) option. Say someone has added several new features to the quota program and released a new package called `quota-2.01-1.i386.rpm`. To upgrade to the new version, you would use the following command:

```
rpm -Uvh quota-2.01-1.i386.rpm
```

While upgrading, RPM installs the specified package and then erases all the older versions of the packages (if any exist). RPM also spends a great deal of time processing any configuration files associated with the package. Thus, while RPM is upgrading a package, you might see a message like the following, indicating that a configuration file is being saved to a new file:

```
Saving syslog.conf to syslog.conf.rpmsave
```

This message indicates that RPM has created a new configuration file that may be compatible with your system. After upgrading, you should compare the two configuration files and make any necessary modifications to the new file.

Querying Packages with RPM

To see what packages are installed on your system, you can use the following command:

```
rpm -qa
```

This command lists every package currently installed on your system. To get information on a specific package, just use the `-q` option. Table 7.3 provides the various options you can use with the `rpm -q` command to query RPM packages.

Table 7.3 RPM Query Options

Option	Description
`-q` *`name`*	Provides the package name, version, and release number
`-qa`	Lists all packages currently installed
`-qf` *`file`*	Queries the package associated with *`file`*
`-qp` *`package`*	Queries *`package`*
`-qi` *`package`*	Provides the name, description, release, size, build date, installation date, and other miscellaneous information about *`package`*
`-ql` *`package`*	Lists the files associated with *`package`*

Caution

The various `-q` options do not work well when specifying symbolically linked files. For the best results, use `cd` to change to the appropriate directory where the real file is located before using the `-q` options.

If you find a new package, for example, and want to know more information about it, you can use the following query command:

```
rpm -qip quota-1.66-6.i386.rpm
```

The command displays output similar to the following:

```
# rpm -qip quota-1.66-6.i386.rpm
Name        : quota                        Relocations: (not relocateable)
Version     : 1.66                              Vendor: Red Hat Software
Release     : 6                             Build Date: Tue Apr 13 11:05:47 1999
Install date: (not installed)               Build Host: porky.devel.redhat.com
Group       : System Environment/Base       Source RPM: quota-1.66-6.src.rpm
Size        : 79332                            License: BSD
Packager    : Red Hat Software <http://developer.redhat.com/bugzilla>
Summary     : System administration tools for monitoring users' disk usage.
Description :
The quota package contains system administration tools for
monitoring and limiting users' and or groups' disk usage, per
filesystem.
```

VERIFYING PACKAGES WITH RPM

The final RPM mode verifies a package. You might need to check the consistency of a file on your system at some point. Say you suspect that a file has been corrupted accidentally by an errant program or a user. You need to compare the current files against the originals you installed. RPM allows you to do so with the `-V` option (note the uppercase). Verifying a package compares the size, MD5 checksum, file permissions, file type, and file owner and group settings. To verify that a particular package's files have not been modified since they were installed, you can use `rpm -V` *`packagename`*. For example, to verify the quota package, you enter the following:

```
rpm -V quota
```

If nothing has changed, RPM does not display any output. If something has changed, RPM displays a string of eight characters indicating what has changed and the name of the file that has changed. You then need to inspect the various files in the package and determine whether you need to reinstall the damaged package. Table 7.4 lists the possible output codes.

TABLE 7.4 VERIFICATION FAILURE CODES

Code	Meaning
c	The file is a configuration file.
5	The file failed the MD5 checksum test.
S	The file size has changed since installation.
L	A problem exists with the symbolic links.
T	The file modification time does not match the original.
D	This code indicates a device attribute.
U	The user setting is different.
G	The group setting is different.
M	The mode differs, either in permission or file type.

Tip #50 from
Jack

The following command verifies all installed packages on your system:

```
rpm -Va
```

USING THE DEBIAN PACKAGE MANAGEMENT SYSTEM

A Debian package, like an RPM package, contains all the files necessary to install a program or suite of programs. A Debian package ends in a `.deb` extension, and you install the package using the `dpkg` tool. The naming convention used for Debian packages follows this format: `packagename-`*`version-debian-revision-number.deb`*, where version is the program version number and debian-revision-number refers to the version of Debian (currently 2.1) supported by the package. `dpkg` is analogous to RPM, in that you can install, remove, and upgrade programs. The command `dpkg -help`provides an extensive listing of instructions as does the man page.

To install a package, you use the `--install` flag and specify the name of the Debian archive package file (`.deb` extension). For example, to install the quota program you use the following command:

```
dpkg -install quota-1.6-2.1.deb
```

`dpkg` checks dependencies to make sure all required components are installed and installs them if need be. Then like RPM, it runs a pre install and then post install script.

To completely remove a package, use the `--purge` flag command as follows:

```
dpkg --purge quota
```

Tip #51 from
Jack

You do not need to use the entire package name as long as `dpkg` can distinguish between similar named packages.

If you need to keep the program's configuration files for future reference or use, use the `--remove` flag to remove only the executable components of the package.

If you need to find which package deals with a given program, use the `--search` option, for example:

```
dpkg --search quota
```

Debian maintains its package database in `/var/lib/dpkg/info/`.

INSTALLING NON-LINUX SOFTWARE

Unfortunately, most of the software programs you'll find aren't in RPM or Debian package formats. Typically, these pieces are downloaded via anonymous FTP from some archive site.

The process of installing software can range from extremely simple to almost impossible. The level of difficulty depends on how well the software authors wrote their installation scripts and how good their installation documentation is.

DECIPHERING SOFTWARE PACKAGE FORMATS

The software packages that you get via anonymous FTP are virtually all in the form of compressed tar files. These files can be created in a couple of different ways. Typically, a directory tree contains source files, libraries, documentation, executables, and other necessary files that are bundled into a tar file by using the tar program. This tar file is then usually compressed to save space.

The software package probably has an extension at the end of the filename that tells you what format it's in. If the file ends in `.gz`, it was compressed with the GNU gzip program. It is the most common file-compression format for Linux software packages. If the archive name ends with a `.Z`, it was compressed with the compress program. For example, the software package `foo.tar.gz` is a tar archive that has been compressed with `gzip`.

Note Sometimes, a tar file that has been compressed with gzip is written with the `.tgz` extension instead of `.tar.gz`.

→ See "Using tar," p. 265

INSTALLING THE SOFTWARE

After you figure out the package format, you need to figure out where you want to place the source files so that you can build the software package. Some software packages are fairly large, so placing them on a file system that has a good bit of free space is a good idea. Some people create a separate file system for sources and mount it under a directory, such as `/usr/local/src` or `/src`. Wherever you decide to build your software packages, make sure that you have enough disk space so that the software can be compiled successfully.

Now you can move the software package to the source tree that you've set up and then decompress it and expand the archive. If a file is compressed with gzip, you can decompress it by using the `gzip -d` command. For example, the command

```
gzip -d foo.tar.gz
```

expands the compressed file `foo.tar.gz` and replaces it with the tar archive named `foo.tar`. See Table 7.5 for `gzip` command-line flags.

Table 7.5 Flags for the gzip Command

Flag	Flag Name	Description
-a	ascii	ASCII text; converts end-of-line characters by using local conventions
-c	stdout	Writes on standard output; keeps original files unchanged
-d	decompress	Decompresses
-f	force	Forces overwrite of output file and compresses links
-h	help	Gives a help listing
-l	list	Lists compressed file contents
-L	license	Displays software license
-n	no-name	Doesn't save or restore the original name and time stamp
-N	name	Saves or restores the original name and time stamp
-q	quiet	Suppresses all warnings
-S suffix	suffix .suf	Uses `suffix .suf` on compressed files
-t	test	Tests compressed file integrity
-v	verbose	Changes to verbose mode
-V	version	Displays the version number
-1	fast	Compresses faster
-9	best	Compresses better (that is, the file is smaller)
file		Specifies file(s) to (de)compress; if none given, uses standard input

For files that have been compressed with the `compress` command, you can use the `uncompress` command to expand them. For example, the command

```
uncompress foo.tar.Z
```

expands the compressed file `foo.tar.Z` and replaces it with the tar archive named `foo.tar`.

After you expand the compressed file, you need to expand the `tar` file into a directory tree. You should put the source for each separate package in its own directory in your source tree. Before un- `tar`-ing the file, you should look at its tar listing to see whether it was created with a directory as the first entry. You can use the following command to see whether the first entry in the `tar` file is a directory:

```
tar -tvf tarfile-name | more
```

If so, the tar file creates the directory when it's expanded. If no directory entry is listed at the top level of the `tar` file, all the files at the top level are extracted into the current directory. In this case, you need to make a directory and move< the `tar` file into it before you expand it.

Note You should always check for a top-level directory before expanding a `tar` file. You might have quite a mess if the `tar` file expands and places a few hundred files in the current directory instead of in a subdirectory.

When you have the `tar` file where you want to expand it, you can use this command to expand the source tree in the `tar` file:

```
tar -xvf tarfile-name
```

The next step depends on how the software package that you're installing was written. Typically, you change directory to the top-level directory of the software sources and look for a file named something like `README.1ST`. The top-level source directory should contain a few documentation files that explain the installation process.

Note On most versions of Linux, you can decompress a `tar` file on-the-fly as you extract it. Simply add the `z` flag to the `tar` command, as in `tar -zxvf foo.tar.gz`.

The typical installation process involves editing the file named `Makefile` to edit the destination directories where the software places its compiled binaries. You then usually run `make` followed by `make install`.

The `make` process probably varies with each package that you install. For some packages, some sort of configuration shell script may ask you questions and then compile the software for you. Make sure that you read the documentation files that come with the package.

REVIEWING FILE PERMISSIONS

Permissions for a software package are usually set automatically during installation. The installation script that comes with your application usually installs each file with the proper ownership and permissions. Only when something goes wrong and a user who should be able to access the program can't do so are you required to find the directory the application was copied to and check the permissions.

Typically, the executable file that you run to start the application is installed with permissions that let any user run the file; however, only the superuser can delete or overwrite it. The application usually is installed in a directory with read and execute permissions, but no write permissions.

→ See "File Permissions," p. 414

SOLVING PROBLEMS

A well-written and well-supported application installs onto your system with minimal requests for information from you. It sets permissions properly so that all you have to do is test the program and inform your users—often through email—that the application is now available. But things can and do go wrong in the installation of programs and their subsequent operation (or nonoperation). If, for whatever reason, the program doesn't complete the loading process or fails to operate correctly after installation, it's your responsibility to determine why and to fix the problem.

If a program doesn't install completely, your troubleshooting efforts often require no more than reading the documentation and `README` files supplied with the application and looking for a list of exceptions or problems and their solutions. However, no one expects you to possess expertise and familiarity with the scores of software packages available for Linux. Occasionally, you might require outside help.

If you can't solve the problem by using the information that came with the package, you should try looking on Usenet news to see whether you can find any discussion of the package in question. A question posted in the appropriate Linux group on Usenet can solve a lot of problems. If you can't find help on the Net, you can try to contact the application developer, usually via email. Remember, Linux is free, and so are most of the software packages available for Linux. Don't expect shrink-wrapped manuals and 24-hour technical support lines. But if you weren't the adventurous type, you wouldn't be using Linux, right?

REMOVING APPLICATIONS

If an application is superseded by a better package or is no longer used by any user on the system, removing it is a good idea. Disk space is always precious; you certainly don't want old, unused programs to hog space required by new applications.

Like installation, removal of a program on a Linux system is more complicated than for single-user operating systems. Sometimes just erasing the application's files and removing its directory aren't enough. Drivers and other software connections must be disconnected to avoid future problems. By taking notes and capturing the installation messages to a log file, you can usually figure out what was changed when the software was installed. You can then deduce what files to remove and which files to change to successfully delete a package.

CASE STUDY: UPGRADING YOUR KERNEL

Along with upgrades for other software, new versions of the kernel sources are released regularly. These versions may fix bugs or add new functionality. Alternatively, you might decide to upgrade your kernel because you need to reconfigure it or add new device drivers. In any case, the process is fairly straightforward. You should make sure that you have a backup of your system software and a Linux boot floppy before you start so that you can recover if you should damage your system. For a complete description of how to rebuild the Linux kernel, see Chapter 14, "Configuring the Linux Kernel."

The process for upgrading your kernel is detailed in the "Kernel How-To" document, which is regularly posted to the Linux newsgroups on the Internet and is available on the various Linux FTP sites, including `metlab.unc.edu`. Be sure to get a copy of this How-To and read it thoroughly before you start your kernel upgrade.

The first step in the basic process of upgrading your kernel is getting the new kernel sources, which are available via anonymous FTP from the various Linux archive sites. When you have the sources, you need to preserve your current kernel sources. To do so, move your `/usr/src/linux` directory to another name, such as `/usr/src/linux.old`. Unpack the kernel sources in the `/usr/src` directory, which creates the `linux` subdirectory in the process. At that point, change to the `linux` directory and look at the documentation and the `README` files. Things may change as new kernels are released, so be sure to read the documentation.

From here, the process may vary a bit. Typically, you enter `make config`, which runs a configuration script and asks you questions about your system. If the configuration phase completes successfully, you then enter something similar to `make dep`. This command checks for all the file dependencies to make sure that the new kernel finds all the files it needs to compile. The basic building commands are as follows:

```
cd /usr/src/linux
make mrporper
make menuconfig
make dep
make zImage
make modules
make modules install
```

After the dependency check is complete, you typically enter `make mrproper` to delete any old object files that are left lying around in the kernel source directory. If everything goes okay up to this point, you can enter `make bzImage` or `zImange` to compile the new kernel. After it compiles, you can install it with the LILO boot manager, and off you go.

Again, be sure to read the "Kernel How-To" before trying to perform this operation. The How-To goes into detail on setting up your kernel and will probably save you hours of frustration. Also, it might keep you from trashing your current Linux system in the process.

PART II

SYSTEM ADMINISTRATION

CHAPTER 8

Understanding System Administration

In this chapter

by Jack Tackett, Jr.

UNDERSTANDING THE IMPORTANCE OF PROPER ADMINISTRATION

A Linux system should have at least one person designated as the system administrator to manage the system and oversee its performance. The system administrator is responsible for seeing that the system is functioning properly. He or she knows who to call if things can't be fixed locally and knows how to provide software and hardware facilities to current and new users.

A Linux system requires initial configuration and continuous attention to ensure that the system remains effective, trustworthy, and efficient for all users. The system administrator is the person responsible for attending to the Linux system's needs. As such, this person is responsible for many different tasks.

All UNIX systems are different in one way or another, and each is unique in the way it must be administered. Linux is no exception. Your administrative duties vary, based on such variables as the number of users you manage, the kinds of peripherals (printers, tape drives, and so on) attached to the computer, networking connections, and the level of security you require.

A system administrator, alone or with a support staff, must provide a secure, efficient, and reliable environment for system users. The administrator has the power and responsibility to establish and maintain a system that provides effective and dependable service. In a multiuser environment, a number of competing purposes and priorities exist. The administrator exercises the power and responsibility necessary to provide a well-functioning system.

Delegation of administrative responsibilities varies from system to system. On large systems, administrative tasks can be divided among several people. Conversely, some small systems don't even require a full-time administrator; such systems simply designate a certain user to act as system administrator. If you work in a networked environment, your system may be administered over the network by a network administrator.

Each Linux system has a single user who can perform virtually any operation on the computer. This user is called the *superuser* and has a special login name called *root*. The home directory for the root user, when logged in to the system, is typically `/` (the root directory of the file system) or a specific home directory, such as `/home/root`.

The system administrator logs in as the superuser to perform tasks that require special access privileges. For normal system work, the system administrator logs in as an ordinary user. The superuser's login name—root—is used only for limited special purposes. The number of users who can log in as root should be kept to a minimum (two or three at most). When any person logs in to the system as root, that person is a superuser and has absolute power on the system. With this privilege, the superuser can change the attributes of any file, stop the system, start the system, back up the system's data, and perform many other tasks.

The administrator must be aware of many of the technical aspects of the computer system. Also, the administrator must be aware of the users' needs, as well as the system's primary purpose. Any computer system is a finite resource, and therefore, policies regarding its use must be established and enforced. Thus, the administrator must play a policy-enforcing role as well as a technical role. That policy-enforcing role, combined with the power to perform virtually any possible action, requires a responsible, skillful, and diplomatic person in the role of administrator.

The precise job description of the system administrator often depends on the local organization. As system administrator, you might find yourself involved in a wide variety of activities, from setting policy to installing software to moving furniture. However, all system administrators have to perform or manage a number of tasks, such as the following:

- **Manage users**—Add users, delete users, and modify users' capabilities and privileges.
- **Configure devices**—Make available and share such devices as printers, terminals, modems, and tape drives.
- **Make backups**—Schedule, make, and store backups for possible restoration in case the system's files are lost or damaged.
- **Shut down the system**—Shut down the system in an orderly manner to avoid inconsistencies in the file system.
- **Train users**—Provide or obtain training for users so that they can use the system effectively and efficiently.
- **Secure the system**—Keep users from interfering with one another through accidental or deliberate actions.
- **Log system changes**—Keep a log book to record any significant activity concerning the system.
- **Advise users**—Act as the "local expert" to aid the system's ordinary users.

UNDERSTANDING MULTIUSER CONCEPTS

A multiuser system employs two main concepts: multitasking and multiuser services. Linux has the apparent capability to execute multiple tasks concurrently—though transparently to the user. For example, you can read your email while compiling a program.

Each task—whether it's a simple command entered on the command line or a complex application—starts one or more processes. Everything running on a Linux system is associated with a process. And because Linux can run many processes simultaneously, Linux is a multitasking operating system.

You can connect to a computer running UNIX (referred to as a *server*) in many ways. You can use a terminal or a computer; you can be located physically near the server and connected with a cable, or you can be on the other side of the planet connected with high-speed data lines or ordinary phone lines. Whether you're using a terminal or computer and how you're connected to the server determine whether the computer's resources are considered to be distributed or centralized.

A single-user computer operating system, such as DOS, is designed to be used by one person at a time. All the processing is done on one computer that has sole access to resources, such as printers, storage area, and processing.

Multiuser systems use the centralized-processing and distributed-processing models described here to accommodate many users simultaneously:

- In a *centralized-processing environment*, many users (large systems can have hundreds of users) access the resources of one computer; storage, printer, memory, and processing tasks are all performed by that one computer.
- In the *distributed-processing environment*, processing can occur on the user's own workstation, and the central processor is used to distribute applications and data. Printers and storage can be connected to the user's workstation or to the main server.

UNDERSTANDING CENTRALIZED-PROCESSING SYSTEMS

As technology during the 1950s and 1960s advanced, operating systems began to allow multiple users to share resources from separate terminals. By using a batch-processing sequence, two users could execute two sets of instructions while sharing a processor, storage, and output.

With the advent of a switched telephone network, computers began to use telephone resources to extend computer resources geographically. In this model, each processor used communications-processing resources to connect with remote terminals. This process created a need for computers and terminals to communicate in a better way. The result was the development of *front-end processing* for communications tasks and the centralized-processing model.

Until personal computers became inexpensive, powerful, and ubiquitous, most UNIX systems used the centralized-processing model. With centralized processing, mainframe computers handled all the processing. Users connected to the mainframe and shared its resources. This model is used less and less today, although it's still appropriate for computing sites where users are separated geographically.

For example, your bank may have one main processing center, yet all the bank's branches can access the data center regardless of their locations. On each user's desk is a terminal, including a keyboard, a monitor, and a direct connection to the mainframe so that the terminal can access the centralized resources: processing, printing, and storage (see Figure 8.1). The centralized-processing model is usually made up of many elements, such as the server, front-end processors, terminals, modems, and multiport adapters.

When a user requests data, the request is processed by the computer in the bank's main office. Results of the processing are then sent back to the terminal in the branch office. All data is processed and stored by the mainframe computer.

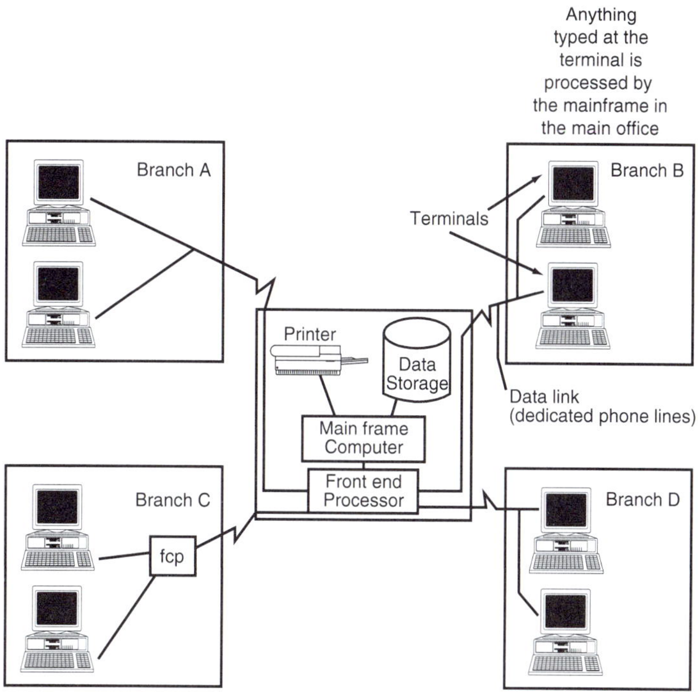

Figure 8.1
Big Iron refers to the centralized-processing model of a computing environment.

ELEMENTS OF THE CENTRALIZED-PROCESSING MODEL

To make the centralized-processing model work, you need many elements, including the server, front-end processors, terminals, modems, and multiport adapters.

A *server* can be defined as any computer set up to share its resources (processing power, storage, printers, and so on). For example, you can use an IBM-compatible PC as a server as long as it has enough hard disk space and RAM.

A *front-end processor* connects the communication channels and the server. It handles the details of communication so that the server is free to process its data.

Two popular types of terminals are used today: *dumb terminals* and *smart terminals*. Traditionally, UNIX is used with dumb terminals, which have keyboards and monitors but nothing else. The most important point to realize about dumb terminals is that they have no local processing power. The communications port on the terminal is connected—directly or through a modem—to the server. When you type at a dumb terminal, each keystroke is transmitted to the server, where it's processed. Smart terminals can complete minimal processing at the local site. Cash registers and other point-of-sale devices are examples of smart terminals, as are the familiar automated teller machines (ATMs). The local device stores the transaction request and then transmits the entire request instead of transmitting each keystroke as a dumb terminal does.

To connect your terminal to a telephone line, you use a *modem*. Modems translate the digital signals of terminals and computers into analog signals required by telephone lines. Modems are always used in pairs. The first one connects your terminal to the telephone line; the second connects the server to the telephone line. To make the connection, you dial out on the terminal. When the modem on the other end (the one connected to the server) answers, your terminal can communicate with the server.

To expand the number of available ports that users can connect to, you can install a *multiport adapter*. Typically, a PC has only two serial ports: COM1 and COM2. If you want to use a PC as a server for more than two users, however, you need more ports. The multiport adapter, in this case, consists of a card that you install inside the computer, a small box with eight or more connectors (locations to plug in eight or more serial cables), and a cable that connects the box and the card. Software is supplied with the adapter to permit the added connectors to function as additional serial ports.

UNDERSTANDING DISTRIBUTED-PROCESSING SYSTEMS

In distributed processing, the terminal is replaced by a workstation, which is itself a computer usually running DOS or UNIX. Programs can be located and run from the server or from your workstation. Similarly, files can be located on either system. If you process a file on your workstation, you store it on the server so that others can access it. You can print on local printers connected to your workstation or on printers connected to the server.

Because workstations are in common use, your bank probably uses a distributed-processing system instead of the centralized system described in the preceding section. Figure 8.2 shows the same bank with a distributed-processing system.

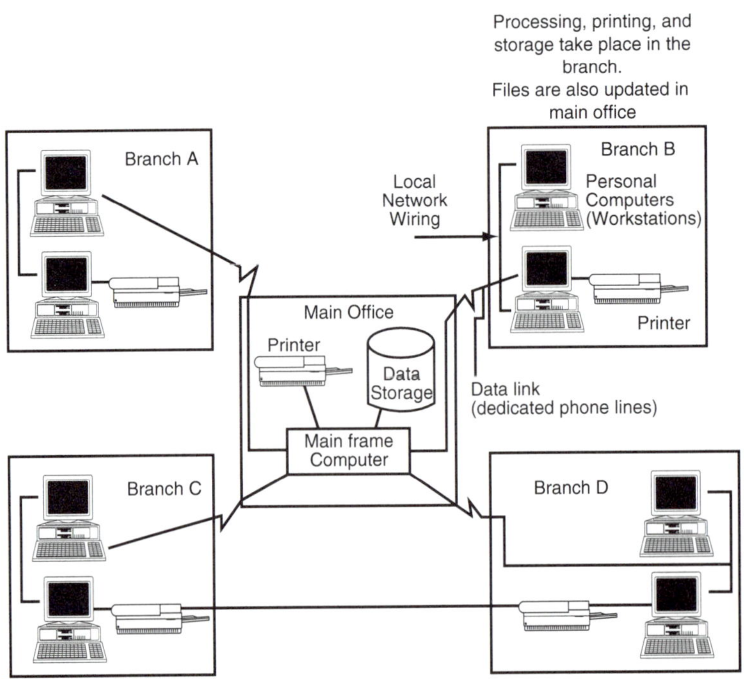

Figure 8.2
Web-centric or client-server typifies the distributed-processing model.

ELEMENTS OF THE DISTRIBUTED-PROCESSING MODEL

Distributed processing uses file servers, workstations, network interface cards, hubs, repeaters, bridges, routers, and gateways. The purpose of the *file server* is to distribute files and segments of programs to workstations, print from a central location, and control flow on the connection between workstations. More than 90 percent of processing occurs at the workstation level, leaving 5 to 10 percent of the load at the file server for administrative tasks.

In addition to using a personal computer as a file server, you can use it as a Linux *workstation*.

Note

A *workstation* is a computer used by one person for their own activites. A *server* is a computer used to provide services for many people. Linux can function as either. As a workstation Linux allows a single person to perform daily tasks such as reading email and writing reports. As a server, Linux can function as a Web server providing Web pages to many different users, or as a file server, allowing many people to store files on the Linux box rather than their workstation.

Linux was designed to run in a minimal hardware configuration. In fact, you can run Linux with a 386SX microprocessor and 4MB of RAM! Because most current systems are more powerful than Linux's minimum requirements, you should have no problem with computing power. The amount of disk space required depends on the software you install and the amount of data you expect that software will generate. Linux requires less disk space than most implementations of UNIX systems. You can run a completely functional Linux system, without X Windows support, in 600MB. For a complete installation of everything in the distribution, 1.6+ GBs (gigabyte) is recommended.

Generally, resources should be applied to the workstation level, where most of the processing occurs. The amount of additional resources depends on the types of tasks you plan to do. For example, word processors take minimal resources (hard drive, RAM, quality of monitor) compared with graphics-intensive tasks such as those you might perform in multimedia and computer-aided design (CAD) programs. For applications involving CAD, you need very large hard disks (4 gigabytes or more), a lot of RAM (64MB, or even 128+MB), and high-resolution monitors and video cards (1,280 × 1,024 or higher). You might even want a tape drive for backing up your system and a CD-ROM drive for loading large applications.

A *network interface card* (*NIC*) attaches to a slot on the motherboard and is the physical link between the computer and the cabling for the network. Network interface cards are generally available for coaxial or twisted-pair cabling.

The *hub* serves as a connecting point for network cables, such as 10BaseT Ethernet, and can be passive or active. A passive hub usually has four connectors. An active hub usually has at least eight ports and amplifies or relays the signal.

Repeaters amplify or regenerate the signal over the network so that you can extend the normal distance limitations of network cabling.

Use a *bridge* when you need to connect two different network types. For example, you use a bridge to connect ISDN to Ethernet, Ethernet to Token Ring, ATM to FDDI, etc.

Routers are used in large, complex networks that provide many paths for network signals to travel to the same destination. The router determines which is the most effective route and sends the signal along that route.

Use a *gateway* when you need to connect dissimilar network types, which use different protocols. The gateway performs the necessary protocol conversions so that the two networks can communicate. For example, an SNA network connected to a TCP/IP network would require a gateway.

TOPOLOGIES

The term *topology* refers to how workstations and file servers are connected in a network. The names of various topologies are derived from the pattern the cables make after you connect the various terminals, workstations, and file servers. The most common topologies are *star*, *bus*, and *ring*. When more than one topology is used in a network, it's referred to as a *hybrid network*.

STAR TOPOLOGY

With the star topology, all workstations are connected to a central file server or hub (see Figure 8.3). You can have passive or active hubs in this scheme.

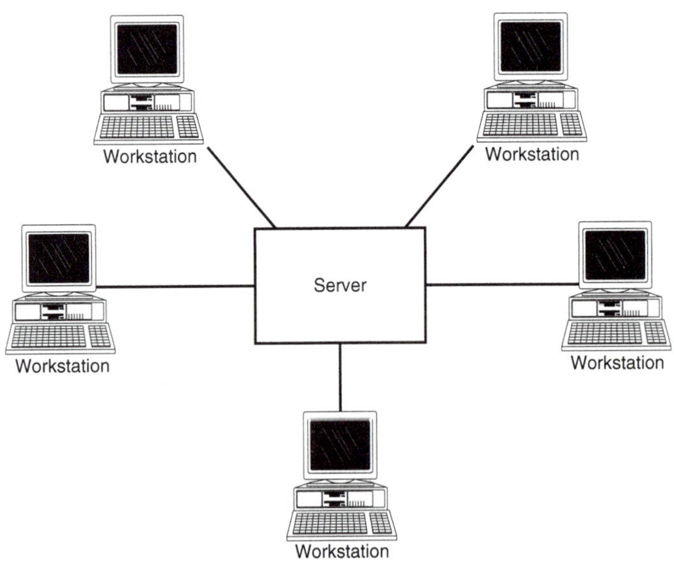

Figure 8.3 Information radiates out from a central server in a star topology.

A *passive* hub is simply a connecting point for the workstations. An *active* hub, called a switch, modifies the signals from workstations and offers amplification of the signal, among other functions. AT&T's StarLan is an example of a network using star topology.

Bus Topology

In a bus topology, all workstations and file servers share a common pathway (see Figure 8.4). They are, in fact, connected directly. The bus topology is the foundation for Ethernet and token bus.

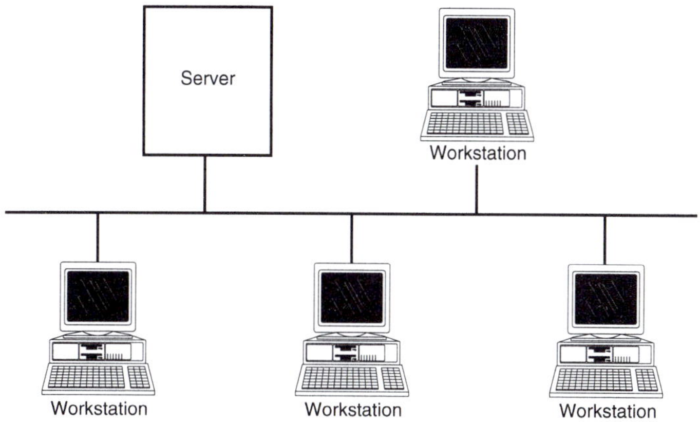

Figure 8.4
A bus topology distributes information to various workstations along a common pathway.

Ring Topology

A ring topology looks like a wagon wheel without the hub (see Figure 8.5). The server is connected to the workstations in bus fashion, except that the last items along the network are connected to make a closed loop. Ring topologies use a repeater, which IBM refers to as a Multistation Access Unit (MAU). The IBM Token-Ring Network is an example of a ring topology.

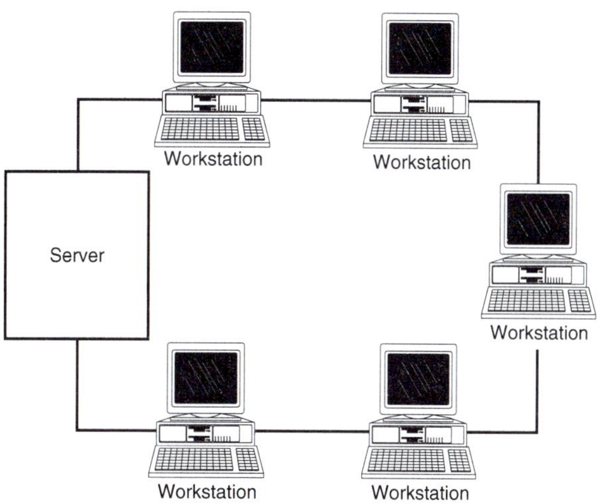

Figure 8.5
In a ring topology, data flows around a network from the server to the workstations in bus fashion, usually negotiating access with some form of token.

Hybrid Topology

In the 1970s and 1980s, firms with decentralized purchasing departments experienced the growth of different topologies on their networks. For example, the accounting department in a given company used a bus network; the purchasing department installed Token-Ring machines; manufacturing used an Ethernet bus; and administration relied on mainframe technology. This combination of networks planted the seeds for enterprise computing and hybrid wide area networks. The integration of these networks linked dissimilar topologies, such as rings, stars, and buses.

UNDERSTANDING THE CLIENT/SERVER MODEL

The result of the development of distributed processing is the *client/server model*. Today, Linux can be used in this model as the client, the server, or both.

To understand a client/server setup, assume that several Linux workstations (the clients) are connected in a bus topology to a server (a high-end PC with lots of disk space, also running Linux). The server has directories for each client where important files can be stored and backed up with the server's nightly backup. The server also has directories from which clients can share files. Connected to the server is a fast laser printer that everyone can access and a tape drive suitable for backing up the large hard disks. Also, several of the clients have their own slower, less-expensive laser printers connected locally.

Note

The server in this example is a PC running Linux—just like the clients' PCs, although the server is more powerful. There's no reason why the server can't act like a client at times and share resources from the clients. In other words, any Linux system can function as both a client and a server.

PERFORMING ADMINISTRATION IN A NETWORKED ENVIRONMENT

A UNIX network usually takes the form of many computers, large and small, tied together over directly connected wires or common telephone lines. Administering the network is usually the task of a person or persons located at one of the sites in the network.

Most people can learn Linux and administer a network. In a production environment, finding a qualified person right away would be nice; however, such people are somewhat rare—and usually well paid. In fact, the growth of the Linux market has exacerbated this fact. With practice and patience, even people with limited backgrounds in computers can learn to administer a corporate UNIX/Linux computer.

DEFINING THE ROLE OF THE NETWORK ADMINISTRATOR

Any time you have more than a few UNIX/Linux systems connected in a network, you should probably have a dedicated network administrator. Some expertise is needed to decide how systems are connected (local area networks or modems), the level of security needed, and how shared peripherals (printers, tape backups, and so on) are distributed. On a day-to-day basis, the administrator maintains lists of system names, network addresses, and user access and generally makes sure that the network is running properly.

Corporations with networks of hundreds of computers can afford to have several administrators with extensive training in selected topics. Having these administrators can be a necessity if you have complex printing needs, for example. Administering printers and printing can require extensive knowledge of specific printers and how to interface that equipment to Linux.

UNDERSTANDING HARDWARE AND SOFTWARE ISSUES

If, as system administrator, you're required to choose the networking software and hardware for the computers under your control, you should consider several factors. As with most things in life, you balance what you need with what you can afford.

If your systems are close together in the same building, a local area network (LAN) is a low-cost, high-speed means of networking your computers. You can put an Ethernet board in each Linux system and use TCP/IP as the networking protocol software. TCP/IP is a standard component of Linux distributions.

To connect over greater distances, you can use modems for lower-speed transmissions such as Point-to-Point Protocol (PPP) or Serial Line Internet Protocol (SLIP) to provide asynchronous TCP/IP connections. You also can use Unix to Unix CoPy (UUCP) software for email, news, and file transfers (although UUCP has limitations and is all but supplanted by TCP/IP in today's Internet). For higher speeds over long distances, you can use ISDN, cable modems, xDSL or get leased lines from the telephone company.

Don't buy just any old networking hardware. Although many off-the-shelf networking hardware products come with the drivers needed to make them work with DOS, the same isn't true with Linux. As a result, Linux systems have many standard networking drivers built in. Table 8.1 shows some of the Ethernet cards now supported by Linux. Check the "Ethernet How-To" for updates to this list.

Tip #52 from
Jack

You can find the HOW-TOs on your system in the `/usr/doc/HOWTO` directory. They are also available on the RedHat CD-ROM in the `/RedHat/doc/HOWTO` directory. If you mount the CD-ROM with the following command

```
mount /mnt/cdrom
```

then you can `cd` to the directory and read the various How-Tos with your favorite editor.

On the Web you can find the How-Tos at `http://www.linux.org/help/howto.html`.

→ See "The Linux How-To Index," p. 843

Table 8.1 Some Ethernet Cards Now Supported Under Linux

Manufacturer	Cards
3Com	3c503, 3c503/16, 3c509, 3c579, 3c590/3c595
SMC (Western Digital)	WD8003, WD8013, SMC Elite, SMC Elite Plus, SMC Elite 16 ULTRA
Novell Ethernet	NE1000, NE2000, NE1500, NE2100
D-Link	DE-600, DE-650, DE-100, DE-200, DE-220-T
Hewlett-Packard	27245A, 27247B, 27252A, 27247A, J2405A
Digital	DE200, DE210, DE202, DE100, DEPCA (rev. E), 21040
AMD	Pcnet-32 cards
Allied Telesis	AT1500, AT1700
Intel	Ethernet express
PureData	PDUC8028, PDI8023

Applications that aren't integrated with networking products can be used in a network environment. For example, you can install an application on a Linux system and have many users from other computers use the application by running the remote execution commands built into UNIX. Alternatively, you can share an application by remotely mounting the file system that contains the application and then running it from the local system.

Performing Common Networking Administrative Tasks

Administration of a network takes on several dimensions. Most networks don't just occur; typically, they evolve. In the ideal situation, the administrators are involved with the purchase of the computers and software so that they know what's expected of them as administrators and what the users are getting.

Setting Up the System

Network software should be installed and ready to connect onsite. If you're using Ethernet for your Linux network segment, it's a good idea to have the continuity tests completed. If you're using telephone lines, have them tested as well. Wiring and terminals for users also should be tested and ready. Installation should be plug-and-play, but it never is. Connection problems always occur.

→ See "Understanding the TCP/IP Configuration Files," p. 620

The advantage of buying a computer for a situation in which the operating system isn't yet installed is that you can set up file systems to accommodate your specific needs. You must know what software is going on the computer, the number of users who will be using the system, and the intensity of their usage.

Tip #53 from Jack

> You've invested time and money in setting up the network to this point. You should immediately back up the configuration files you've set up. Most of these files are located in the `/etc` subdirectory. The easiest way to back up these files is to `tar` the `/etc` directory to another file system that resides on another disk drive, such as `/home`. For example:
>
> `tar -cvf /home/etc-backup.tar /etc`

When the system is fully functional, the application software should be installed. Software on a Linux computer is often more complex than on a single-user system, so be prepared to spend some time installing, tuning, and making the software fully operational. This task can take from a couple of hours to several days—or longer.

You're now ready to start adding users to the system, although you're still not onsite. Add login IDs for a few key users, and put in a common startup password, such as `temp01`. This step provides some initial security and gives you a chance to get key people onto the system and operational right away when you install the system.

After installation, the computer should be attached to the network. Make sure that you can communicate from any point in the network to any other point. Test communications by moving large and small files from one computer to another. Electronic mail should be directed to and from other nodes in the network. All computers must "know" this new computer in the network. This means that you need to add it to your host name database that's used by any other computers on your network. If you use the Domain Name Service (DNS) locally, you must add the host name to the DNS name database. If you aren't using DNS, add the name to the `/etc/hosts` files on your other systems.

If you are using the Network Information Service (NIS), then make sure to configure your NIS configuration files correctly. NIS is used to manage a number of computers from a central NIS server. Originally called yellow pages, NIS today is being supplanted by light weight directory services, known as `ldap`.

→ See "Database Files and Resource Records," p. 800

→ See "The `/etc/hosts` File," p. 620

→ See "What Is Using NIS," p. 476

Handling Peripherals

Printing can present a major issue to an administrator. Monitoring and maintaining printers is a significant task and can take a lot of an administrator's time. Understanding the spooling of print jobs, interface tools, and equipment peculiarities requires time and patience. You can use tools such as `printtool` and `magicfilterconfig` to install and configure many different types of printers.

→ See "Printing," p. 391

Using modems is the cheapest way to link a network that spans long distances. Modems and PPP or UUCP are tools that can make it practical for a small staff to administer many computers. As with printers, however, modems have some problems that require time to get them running right. Choose one or two brand names and really learn their idiosyncrasies.

→ See "Using `dip` in Command Mode," p. 665

MONITORING THE SYSTEM

When the installation is complete, you can set up UNIX tools to monitor this new system. As thc administrator, you should start getting a feel for how the system is performing.

Monitoring running systems in a network is an ongoing process, but the administrative load should stabilize after a while if you aren't constantly adding peripherals or software. Occasionally, something fails, or tweaking might be necessary. A good administrator learns to determine whether the problem is related to hardware or software.

A competent system administrator monitors at least the following items: disk space, memory, network processes, and CPU load. Running out of disk space is an inconvenience to users and potentially catastrophic to a running system. Use the `df` command to track disk space, as shown in the following output:

```
/dev/hda1       1536971     299483      1158060     21%     /
/dev/hdb2       2554589     345188      2077311     14%     /home
/dev/sbpcd      499012      499012            0     100%    /mnt/cdrom
```

If space exceeds a given threshold, such as 80 percent, then the system administrator needs to do something to prevent problems. If a file system exceeds this valuc, the administrator should move to correct the situation. A system administrator can delete unneeded files, compress or move important files that are not needed everyday, or add a new hard drive to the system.

Tip #54 from *Jack*

Most of the information provided by various system administration utilities, such as `top`, make use of information kept in the `/proc` file system. For example, to see how much memory your system consumes, you can `cat` the file `/proc/meminfo`.

The `top` command provides information on a variety of system resource topics, such as processor load and memory usage. The following illustrates sample output from the `top` command:

```
6:49pm up 21  days, 18:14, 1 user, load average: 0.00, 0.00, 0.00
56 processes: 55 sleeping, 1 running, 0 zombie, 0 stopped
CPU states: 3.1% user, 4.0% system, 0.0% nice, 93.0% idle
```

```
Mem:     30796K av,    30076K used,    720K free,    39332K shrd,   1172K buff
Swap:        0K av,        0K used,      0K free                   14016K cached

PID   USER PRI  NI  SIZE   RSS SHARE  STAT  LIB  %CPU   %MEM  TIME   COMMAND
15302 root  12   0   732   732   564  R      0    6.4    2.3  0:01  top
15288 root   0   0  1224  1224   596  S      0    0.5    3.9  0:03  sshd
  342 root   0   0   228   228   188  S      0    0.1    0.7 59:14  update
    1 root   0   0   344   344   284  S      0    0.0    1.1  0:03  init
    2 root   0   0     0     0     0  SW     0    0.0    0.0  0:00  kflushd
    3 root -12 -12     0     0     0  SW<    0    0.0    0.0  0:00  kswapd
    4 root   0   0     0     0     0  SW     0    0.0    0.0  0:00  md_thread
    5 root   0   0     0     0     0  SW     0    0.0    0.0  0:00  md_thread
  343 root   0   0   296   296   248  S      0    0.0    0.9  0:00  mingetty
 6847 root   0   0   872   872   676  S      0    0.0    2.8  0:06  bash
 5486 root   0   0   296   296   248  S      0    0.0    0.9  0:00  mingetty
   37 root   0   0   332   332   280  S      0    0.0    1.0  0:00  kerneld
   66 root   0   0   500   500   404  S      0    0.0    1.6  8:35  sshd
  202 root   0   0   428   428   352  S      0    0.0    1.3  0:34  syslogd
  211 root   0   0   536   536   324  S      0    0.0    1.7  0:01  klogd
  222 daemon 0   0   400   400   324  S      0    0.0    1.2  0:00  atd
  233   root     0   0   468    468   388    S       0    0.0     1.5    0:00   crond
```

The top command provides a wealth of information, such as how many users are logged in, what load the system is currently under (0.00 in this example), how much memory is being consumed and how much is swapped out to the swap file, and so on. The output also provides the top several processes currently running and how much of the resources they are consuming. If a single process is consuming too many resources, then the administrator may have to kill that process.

Caution

The top command automatically refreshes, which can be a great help when you're troubleshooting a resource problem, but refreshing is also a resource hog itself. Be careful when using the top command on a heavily loaded system.

Table 8.2 provides a list of other useful utilities for the system administrator. For more information, see their respective man page.

Table 8.2 Useful SysAdmin Utilities

Utility	Example	Description
ps	ps aux	Lists all the current running processes on your system.
df	df -m	Provides a listing of disk space used and available.
ifconfig	ifconfig -a	Displays information about the various network connections and the ip addresses and hardware mac addresses associated with each interface.

Table 8.2 Useful SysAdmin Utilities

Utility	Example	Description
`arp`	`arp`	Provides a listing of the current arp table.
`whois`	`whois mcp.com`	Queries Internic registration authority for information on who owns the requested domain name.
`nslookup`	`nslookup www.mcp.com`	Provides the ip address of the requested domain name. If an ip address is entered instead, then the name associated with that ip is provided.
`vmstat`	`vmstat 5 12`	Provides information on memory usage, CPU usage, interupts, and other items.

Coping with Software Upgrades

Some software packages are constantly being updated. Although upgrading is a concern with commercial UNIX, it's a special issue under Linux because much of the software is publicly available over the Internet and is continually modified. The good news might be that a bug is fixed. The bad news might be that each system in the network has to be updated. You can expect a new challenge with each update.

The best advice isn't to immediately put all new versions on your systems, but to test the upgrade or patch on one non-critical system. When you're sure that the new version is okay, you can upgrade the other systems. A good administrator learns how to install these patches or new versions without going to the other sites in the network. This solution sounds impossible at first, but you'll find that many UNIX tools facilitate the installation of patches and upgrades. For the distributions included in this book, check out dpkg and apt-get for Debian and autorpm and autoupdate for Red Hat and Caldera systems.

→ See "Understanding the System Administrator's Job," p. 167

Training the Administrator

Training in most organizations is very hit or miss. Perhaps the person has some computer background in some computer topic, but little is done to formally train that person to administer the system. Fortunately, many organizations, such as Red Hat and Global Knowledge provide indepth and detailed training for Linux Administrators. Administration requires attention and a solid knowledge of the following topics:

- **Linux/UNIX design and usage**—The administrator has to have a thorough understanding of such issues as redirection, pipes, background processing, and so on.

- **The vi editor**—The vi editor is on virtually every credible UNIX computer, including Linux. Many people criticize it, and many people substitute other editors for their own use, but it's advisable to have an administrator learn and become proficient in the use of vi because it's the "common denominator" among UNIX editors.
- **Shell script programming**—Many of the key programs used to administer UNIX are written in shell script language and might require modification for your specific needs. Many of the tools outlined in this chapter require knowledge of how to put together and use a shell program. Almost every user has a favorite shell.

  The Bourne Again shell, or bash, is a Bourne shell clone that's the default shell under Linux. Also, the Z and T shells are available in the distribution. You should, however, stay with the common Bourne shell until you master this shell language. Also, virtually all the shell programs written by the Linux creators are written in the Bourne shell. You should also investigate the Perl system administration language. It provides a very robust set of tools for system administration in one programming environment.
- **Communications**—Communications training has improved since previous editions of this book and training is continuing to improve. To set up computer networking effectively, you must have knowledge of TCP/IP and the related protocols. Similarly, you should understand PPP if you're going to set up an asynchronous Internet connection. Ideally, these protocols should be taught in a laboratory environment with the many options available. You can attend classes or at least buy manuals on the subject, but you should accept the fact that you'll be spending a great deal of time experimenting.
- **UNIX conventions**—UNIX conventions aren't taught or even mentioned in many UNIX classes, and you'll probably have to pick them up by observing as you go through training. For example, you'll learn that binary executable programs are generally stored in the `bin` directories, such as `/usr/bin`, `/bin`, and `/usr/local/bin`. You can put your own executable programs in `/usr/local/bin`. Likewise, the `lib` directories, such as `/usr/lib`, are used for library files, and you can put your own libraries in a directory such as `/usr/local/lib`. Understanding and following standard Linux/UNIX conventions such as these can save time when you need to find and fix problems.

Several reputable companies, perhaps including the company that you bought your computer from, offer training on all these topics. However, this training is probably not specific to Linux. A few vendors sell various distributions of the Linux operating system and offer classes on selected topics. You should also look for user groups in your area and check the `comp.os.linux` newsgroup hierarchy on Usenet news on the Internet. Also check out `admin@vger.rutger.edu` for an active mailing list for Linux administrators.

Training is best done in small pieces. You should take a course and then come back and use what you learned right away on your network. Linux has an elaborate set of tools that will probably never be completely mastered, but you have to know where to find information in manuals.

TROUBLESHOOTING THE NETWORK

Tracking down problems and fixing them is one of, if not the most important command tasks a system administrator faces. Many times the problem is acute, but it causes a mystery and a solution not readily apparent.

No access to a network can cause many problems, such as a system to hang at boot, hang on traversing an nfs mounted directory, or being unable to surf the Web or telnet to other machines. And no one likes a slow network connection, but how do you know where the bottle neck is—your system or somewhere out on the Internet? The basic tools to use for investigating are ping, traceroute, and netstat.

Ping sends an ICMP echo request out through the network to a targeted machine and is the beginning point for any network investigation. Ping provides information on whether another computer is accessible on the net and how long it takes to get a packet of data to the computer and back. For example to see if the host `www.netwharf.com` is available use:

```
[root@ns /root]# ping www.netwharf.com
PING www.netwharf.com (209.42.203.228): 56 data bytes
64 bytes from 209.42.203.228: icmp_seq=0 ttl=255 time=1.8 ms
64 bytes from 209.42.203.228: icmp_seq=1 ttl=255 time=1.0 ms
64 bytes from 209.42.203.228: icmp_seq=2 ttl=255 time=1.0 ms
--- www.netwharf.com ping statistics ---
3 packets transmitted, 3 packets received, 0% packet loss
round-trip min/avg/max = 1.0/1.2/1.8 ms
```

The command provides a wealth of information. First the program indicates the ip address associated with the host.

Tip #55 from Jack

If ping cannot translate the host name into an IP, you may have dns problems. Check the `/etc/resolv.conf` for proper settings for your name servers. If all appears fine, you can use the command `nslookup` to see if your name server can translate names: `nslookup www.netwharf.com`. Finally, make sure you have spelled the host name correctly.

Next, ping provides a sequence number to let you know if the connection is dropping data packets. Finally, ping lets you know how long a packet took to traverse the network. Both items provide a glimpse into the health of the network and potential problems. But just knowing a network is sending and receiving packets may not be enough information—where is the problem on a slow network?

Use traceroute to find out where the bottleneck occurs on the net. The program sends out data packets and then reports how the packet snakes through the Internet. As a packet heads out to the net, it is routed through various routers (a hop), the more routers, the more potential for problems. To see how many hops a packet takes, use:

```
[root@ns /root]# / usr/sbin/traceroutewww.mcp.com
traceroute to www.mcp.com (198.70.146.70), 30 hops max, 40 byte packets
1  gateway (209.42.203.225) 3.764 ms 3.150 ms 3.052 ms
2  max4000-1.rtp.intrex.net (209.42.192.1) 34.528 ms 32.074 ms 31.190 ms
3  209.42.192.30 (209.42.192.30) 33.264 ms 33.012 ms 31.607 ms
4  rtp-rtr1-e1.intrex.net (209.42.255.17) 33.393 ms 44.959 ms 32.609 ms
5  sl-gw4-atl-4-0-2xT1.sprintlink.net (144.228.86.53) 61.957 ms 47.754 ms
   ➥51.439 ms
6  sl-bb10-atl-1-2.sprintlink.net (144.232.12.29) 80.908 ms 82.393 ms 48.498 ms
7  sl-bb10-fw-4-0.sprintlink.net (144.232.8.98) 66.180 ms 66.824 ms 69.790 ms
8  144.232.11.10 (144.232.11.10) 91.006 ms 64.449 ms 70.304 ms
9  144.232.9.253 (144.232.9.253) 76.865 ms 74.102 ms 78.176 ms
10 sl-bb11-chi-4-0.sprintlink.net (144.232.9.118) 92.362 ms 101.582 ms 93.251 ms
11 sl-bb11-chi-8-0.sprintlink.net (144.232.10.5) 85.014 ms 85.514 ms 85.111 ms
12 sl-gw14-chi-8-0-0.sprintlink.net (144.232.0.194) 87.983 ms 90.575 ms
   ➥92.611 ms
13 sl-napnet-2-0-0-T3.sprintlink.net (144.228.159.18) 90.760 ms 75.226 ms
   ➥77.879 ms
14 chi-f0.iquest.net (206.54.225.250) 92.193 ms 114.950 ms 81.379 ms
15 204.180.50.9 (204.180.50.9) 85.988 ms 108.888 ms 86.364 ms
16 iq-ind-core1.iquest.net (206.53.249.1) 99.583 ms 91.685 ms 111.068 ms
17  * iq-ss2.iquest.net (206.246.190.161) 96.229 ms 82.107 ms
```

traceroute again provides a name to IP translation and then for each hop—that is, for each router the package passes through on the journey—displays an information line. Each line consists of the hop number, the name and IP number of the router, and the times recorded for reaching that particular router. An asterisk indicates the time for the packet to reach its destination exceeded the amount of time allotted. If a site is not responding, traceroute keeps repeating a line of three asterisks for each hop attempted. The final router shown provides an idea of where the problem might be located, since the next hop is unavailable. Of course you need to be able to get outside your current network to reach another destination.

The netstat program provides many options to report information on the TCP/IP stack running on your system. Data packets are routed based on entries in your systems routing tables. To see the current settings, use:

```
[root@ns /root]# netstat -rv
Kernel IP routing table
Destination      Gateway          Genmask          Flags MSS Window irtt Iface
ns2.netwharf.co  *                255.255.255.255 UH    1500 0        0 eth0:0
www.nightskyweb  *                255.255.255.255 UH    1500 0        0 eth0:1
209.42.203.224   *                255.255.255.224 U     1500 0        0 eth0
127.0.0.0        *                255.0.0.0       U     3584 0        0 lo
default          gateway.netwhar 0.0.0.0          UG    1500  0        0  eth0
```

The important item to check for access to the Internet is the default gateway item listed in the `Destination` column. This is the route through which your computer sends a packet if it does not know where to send the data. You should ping the computer shown in the `Gateway` column to make sure it is available. If you suspect you have the wrong gateway configure, check with your service provider or your network administrator.

CHAPTER 9

USING THE vi EDITOR

In this chapter

by Steve Burnett

WHY VI?

In earlier chapters, you learned how helpful it can be to have sequences of commands or shell scripts stored in a file. You probably have to create data, email, lists, memos, notes, reports, and so on; you use some type of text editor to perform these tasks. You may have several editors or word processors available on your Linux system to help you with these tasks. To put commands or shell programs in a file, however, you need an editor that can save your work in a text file—a file in ASCII format. Linux comes with a standard text editor called vi, which you can use for all but the most complex writing and editing projects.

vi is very useful to system administrators because it is available on every UNIX platform. Thus, after you learn how to use vi, you can use it on any system running UNIX. vi is also useful because it takes up very few resources when executing, which means you can use vi when other programs might not run because of hardware or other system problems.

Tip #56 from *Steve*

This chapter doesn't discuss ed or ex very much because you'll find vi easier to use and available on every UNIX machine, including Linux.

The vi and ex editors that ship with the Red Hat distribution are actually other names for an editor called vim (for *vi improved*). The names vi and ex are symbolically linked to vim, so when you type `vi`, you're actually running vim. Read `/usr/share/vim/vim_diff.txt` for a summary of the differences between vim and vi.

Your Linux system also has other text editors: a graphical editor for use under the XFree86 system and two standard nongraphical text editors called ed and ex. They're both line-oriented editors; that is, using them, you work with only one line at a time. Another editor, called Emacs, is also supplied with most Linux distributions. vi and Emacs are full-screen editors; when you use them, you see a screen's worth of information, so you can make changes or additions in context.

To understand vi (pronounced *vee-eye*, not *vie*), you need to understand some of vi's history within the UNIX world. Moreover, although today's systems (including Linux) have much more user-friendly and robust editors, you should learn how to use vi because every UNIX (and, thus, Linux) system has a copy of vi available. Sometimes vi is the only editor available, so you should know some of its basic operations.

UNIX was developed in an environment in which users' terminals were teletypes or some other slow, hard copy terminals; video display monitors generally weren't used. A natural editor for that environment was a line-oriented editor—one that the users could see and work on one line of text at a time. As mentioned previously, two line-oriented editors are on UNIX systems today: ed and ex.

In its early days, UNIX was made available to universities essentially free of charge. Students and faculty at several universities made many contributions to the UNIX working environment. Several notable improvements came out of the University of California at Berkeley, including a full-screen editor—one that lets the users work with a screen of information at once rather than a single line of text. As you've probably guessed by now, that full-screen editor is called vi, which stands for *visual*. The time was right for the transition to screen-oriented work. Users were working with video terminals rather than hard copy devices.

Tip #57 from *Steve*

You don't have to become an expert to use vi. Simply type `man vi` at the command prompt for help. You also can ask for help by pressing Esc and then entering `:help`.

What Is vi?

Because vi is part of the standard UNIX environment, millions of UNIX users have learned and used it (to one degree or another). You will find that vi starts quickly and can be used for simple and complex tasks. As you would expect, you can use it to enter, modify, or delete text; search or replace text; and copy, cut, and paste blocks of text. You also can customize it to match your needs. You can move the cursor to any position onscreen and move through the file you're editing. You use the same methods with any text file, regardless of its contents.

The vi editor isn't a word processor or desktop publishing system. It has no menus and virtually no help facilities. This chapter doesn't cover all of vi's features; that requires more space than is available. (In fact, entire books are written just on vi.) Instead, you'll learn the commands to do the most necessary editing tasks. If you want to know about the more advanced features of vi, consult the man pages supplied with Linux.

Note

The original version of vi doesn't have a help facility. However, newer versions of vi, such as vim for the Red Hat distribution, provide some online help.

Word processing systems usually offer screen and hard copy formatting and printing, such as representing text as bold, italic, or underlined, but vi doesn't. Other Linux commands can perform some of these functions; for example, `lp` can print and `nroff` can format text. Some text processing programs, such as TeX (pronounced *tek*) and LaTeX, can process embedded commands into text, such as bold and underlined attributes.

The vi editor operates in two modes:

- In command mode, your keystrokes are interpreted as commands to vi. Some of the commands allow you to save a file; exit vi; move the cursor to different positions in a file; and modify, rearrange, delete, substitute, and search for text.
- In input or text-entry mode, your keystrokes are accepted as the text of the file you're editing. When vi is in input or text-entry mode, the editor acts as a typewriter.

In an editing session, you can freely switch between modes. You do, however, have to remember the mode you're using and know to change modes. Some people may find switching modes uncomfortable at first. Later in this chapter, you'll learn about the `showmode` option, which tells you vi's current mode. With a little practice, you'll find vi extremely convenient for editing Linux ASCII files, especially configuration files and shell scripts.

UNDERSTANDING THE EDITING PROCESS

You edit text by creating new text or by modifying existing text. When you create new text, you place the text in a file with an ordinary Linux filename. When you modify existing text, you use the existing filename to call a copy of the file into the editing session. In either case, as you use the editor, the text is held in the system's memory in a storage area called a *buffer*. Using a buffer prevents you from directly changing the contents of a file until you decide to save the buffer. This is to your benefit if you decide you want to forget the changes you've made and start over.

As you change and add to the text, these edits affect the text in the buffer, not in the file stored on disk. When you're satisfied with your edits, you can issue a command to save the text. This command writes the changes to the file on the disk. Only then are the changes made permanent. You can save changes to disk as often as you like. (It's usually a good idea to save any file you're editing frequently in case of lockups or power loss.) You don't even have to exit the editor when you save changes. This chapter shows you several ways to exit the editor; some of those ways write the buffer to the text file on the disk.

The vi editor is said to be *interactive* because it interacts with you during the editing session. The editor communicates with you by displaying status messages, error messages, or sometimes nothing onscreen (in typical Linux fashion). The last line onscreen, called the *status line*, holds the messages from Linux. You see the changes you make in the text onscreen.

You can use the editor to modify, rearrange, delete, substitute, and search for text. You conduct these editing operations while using the editor in command mode. In several instances, a command is a single letter that corresponds to the first letter of an action's name. For example, `i` corresponds to the insert action, and `r` is used when replacing a character.

Most commands operate on a single line or range of lines of text. The lines are numbered from 1 (the top line) to the last line in the buffer. When you add or delete lines, the line numbers adjust automatically. A line's number is its address in the buffer. An address range is simply two addresses or line numbers separated by a comma. If you want to specify the range consisting of the third through the eighth line of the buffer, you use `3,8`.

The position of the cursor always indicates your current location in the editing buffer. Some of the commands you issue in command mode affect the character at the cursor position. Unless you move the cursor, changes take place at that position. Naturally, vi has several commands for moving the cursor through the edit buffer.

You know now that vi is a full-screen editor. You can give vi commands to move the cursor to different positions in a file, and you see the changes you make as you make them. Therefore, vi has to be able to move to and modify the text on your terminal as well as on a host of other terminal types. It knows what terminal you're using and what its video capabilities are by checking the shell variable `TERM`. Linux uses the `TERM` variable to determine your terminal's capabilities, such as underlining, reverse video, the screen-clearing method, function-key assignment, and color capability.

USING VI

To start vi, simply type its name at the shell prompt (command line). If you know the name of the file you want to create or edit, you can issue the `vi` command with the filename as an argument. For example, to create the file `myfile` with vi, enter `vi myfile`.

When vi becomes active, the terminal screen clears, and a tilde character (~) appears on the left side of every screen line, except for the first. The ~ is the empty-buffer line flag. The following is a shortened version of what you should see on your screen (only five lines are listed to save space):

```
_
~
~
~
~
```

The cursor appears at the leftmost position of the first line (represented here as an underscore character). You'll probably see 20 to 22 of the tilde characters at the left of the screen. If that's not the case, check the value of `TERM` (as described in the troubleshooting section at the end of the chapter) and perhaps talk with your system administrator.

When you see this display, you've successfully started vi; vi is in command mode, waiting for your first command.

Note

Unlike most word processors, vi starts in command mode. Before you start entering text, you must switch to input mode by using the a or i keys, both of which are described in the next section.

Looking at vi's Two Modes

As mentioned earlier, the vi editor operates in two modes: command mode and input mode. In command mode, vi interprets your keystrokes as commands; vi has many commands. You can use commands to save a file; exit vi; move the cursor to various positions in a file; and modify, rearrange, delete, substitute, and search for text. You can even pass a command to the shell. If you enter a character as a command, but that character isn't a command, vi beeps. Don't worry; the beep is an audible indication for you to check what you're doing and correct any errors.

You can enter text in input mode (also called *text-entry mode*) by appending characters after the cursor or inserting them before the cursor. At the beginning of the line, which method you use doesn't make much difference. To go from command mode to input mode, press one of the following keys:

a	To append text after the cursor
I	To insert text in front of the cursor

Use input mode only for entering text. Most word processors start in input mode, but vi doesn't. When you use a word processing program, you can type away, entering text; to issue a command, you have to use function keys or keys different than those you use when typing normal text. vi doesn't work that way: You must go into input mode by pressing a or i before you start entering text and then explicitly press Esc to return to command mode.

Creating Your First vi File

The best way to learn about vi is to use it. This section gives a step-by-step example of how to create a file by using vi. In each step, you see an action to perform and then the necessary keystrokes. Don't be concerned with complete accuracy here. The example takes you through the motions and concepts of using vi to create a file, moving between command and input modes, and saving your results. If you run into difficulties, you can quit and start over by pressing Esc; then you can enter `:q!`. When you do, you'll lose all your changes since the last time you saved, but that's the point: You can avoid saving your recent work if it's all mistakes.

1. Start vi by entering `vi`. You see the screen full of flush-left tildes.
2. Go into input mode to place characters on the first line. To do so, press the a key; don't press Return. Now you can append characters to the first line. You shouldn't see the character *a* onscreen.
3. Add lines of text to the buffer by typing the following:

```
Things to do today.
a. Practice vi.
b. Sort sales data and print the results.
```

   You can use the Backspace key to correct mistakes on the line you're typing. Don't worry about being precise here; this example is for practice. You'll learn other ways to make changes in some of the later sections of this chapter.

4. Go from input mode to command mode by pressing Esc. You hear a beep from your system if you press Esc when you're already in command mode.
5. Save your buffer in a file called `vipract.1` by entering `:w vipract.1`. The characters `:w vipract.1` appear on the bottom line of the screen (the status line). The characters shouldn't appear in the text. The `:w` command writes the buffer to the specified file. This command saves or writes the buffer to the file `vipract.1`.
6. Look at your action confirmed on the status line. You should see the following on the status line:

   ```
   "vipract.1'' [New File] 3 lines, 78 characters
   ```

   This statement confirms that the file `vipract.1` has been created, is a new file, and contains 3 lines and 78 characters. Your display might be different if you didn't type the information exactly as specified.
7. Exit vi by entering `:q`.

When you type `:q`, you're still in command mode, so you see these characters on the status line. When you press Return, however, vi terminates, and you are returned to the login shell prompt.

You use these steps, or variations of them, for all your editing tasks. Make sure that you can work through them before continuing.

Points to Remember About vi

The following are some points to remember about vi:

- vi starts in command mode.
- To move from command mode to input mode, press a (to append text) or i (to insert text).
- You add text when you're in input mode.
- You give commands to vi only when you're in command mode.
- You give commands to vi to save a file and can quit only when you're in command mode.
- To move from input mode to command mode, press Esc.

STARTING VI BY USING AN EXISTING FILE

To edit or look at a file that already exists in your current directory, type `vi` followed by the filename. Try this procedure with the file you created in the preceding section by entering the following:

```
vi vipract.1
```

You should see the following display (the number of lines shown here are fewer than you will actually see onscreen):

```
Things to do today.
a. Practice vi.
b. Sort sales data and print the results.
~
~
```

```
~
"vipract.1'' 3 lines, 78 characters
```

As before, tilde characters appear on the far left of empty lines in the buffer. Look at the status line: It contains the name of the file you're editing and the number of lines and characters.

TROUBLESHOOTING

I type a filename that I know exists, but vi acts as though I'm creating a new file.

No one is a perfect typist; you may have typed the name of a file that doesn't exist in your current directory. Suppose that you type `vivipract.1`, but you don't have a file named `vipract.1` in your current directory. You still start vi, but vi acts as though you were creating a new file.

I try to edit a file, but vi displays a message about read permission denied and I see the shell prompt again.

You've tried to edit a file you aren't permitted to read. Also, you can't edit a directory; that is, if you type `vi` *`directory_name`*, where *`directory_name`* is the name of a directory, vi informs you that you opened a directory and doesn't let you edit it. If you try to use vi with a file that's an executable program in binary, as opposed to ASCII, you see a screen full of strange (control) characters. It isn't something you can read and edit. vi expects files to be stored as lines.

I open a file in vi, but I see a message that the line is too long.

You're trying to use vi on a data file that's just one long string of bytes. You can modify this file, but doing so will probably corrupt the data file.

I open a file in vi, but I see some very strange characters onscreen.

You may be using vi with a file produced by a word processor.

In all these cases, exit vi to return to your login shell prompt by pressing Esc to go to command mode and then typing `:q!`. Using `:q!` ensures that you quit vi and make no changes to the existing file.

EXITING VI

You can exit or quit vi in several ways. Table 9.1 lists the commands you can use to exit.

Note Remember that you must be in command mode to quit vi. To change to command mode, press the Esc key. (If you're already in command mode when you press Esc, you hear a harmless beep from the terminal.)

TABLE 9.1 WAYS TO QUIT OR EXIT VI

Command	Action
`:q`	Exits after making no changes to the buffer, or exits after the buffer is modified and saved to a file
`:q!`	Exits and abandons all changes to the buffer since it was last saved to a file
`:wq`, `:x`, or `ZZ`	Writes the buffer to the working file and then exits

As you can see in Table 9.1, several keystrokes accomplish the same end. To practice, you can use vi to edit the file `vipract.1` created earlier in this chapter. To edit the file, enter `vi vipract.1`. You should see a display similar to this:

```
Things to do today.
a. Practice vi.
b. Sort sales data and print the results.
~
~
~
"vipract.1'' 3 lines, 78 characters
```

The cursor is indicated by an underscore character. When you first open the file, it's under the first character of the file (the *T* in *Things*). Because you haven't made any changes to the file since you opened it, you can exit by entering `:q`. When you do, you see the shell prompt. You can also type `:wq` to exit the file; if you do so, you see the following message before the shell prompt appears:

```
"vipract.1'' 3 lines, 78 characters
```

This message appears because vi first writes the buffer to the file `vipract.1` and then exits.

You can start vi again with the same file (by typing `vi vipract.1`). You then should see a display similar to this:

```
Things to do today.
a. Practice vi.
b. Sort sales data and print the results.
~
~
~
"vipract.1'' 3 lines, 78 characters
```

Although vi starts in command mode, just to be sure, press Esc. Now press the spacebar enough times so that the cursor moves under the period following *today* in the first line. To replace that character with an exclamation mark, press the r key (for replace) and type `!`. The first line now looks like this:

```
Things to do today!
```

Because you've changed the buffer, vi doesn't let you exit unless you save the changes or explicitly give a command to quit without saving the changes. If you try to exit vi by typing `:q`, vi displays the following message to remind you that you haven't written the file to disk since you changed it:

```
No write since last change (:quit! overrides)
```

To abandon the changes you've made to the file, quit by typing `:q!`. To save the changes, quit by typing `:wq` or any other equivalent form (`ZZ` or `:x`).

Note

vi doesn't keep backup copies of files. After you enter `:wq`, the original file is modified and can't be restored to its original state. You must make your own backup copies of vi files.

→ See Chapter 12, "Backing Up Data", p. 259

Caution

Use the `:q!` command sparingly. When you enter `:q!`, all the changes you've made to the file are lost.

Rather than issue a `:q!` command, you could save the file to a different filename. That subject is covered later in this chapter in the section "Saving as a New File."

UNDOING A COMMAND

In vi, you can "undo" your recent actions or changes to the buffer as long as you haven't saved those changes to the disk file. You do so in command mode. Suppose that you've inadvertently deleted a line of text, changed something you shouldn't have, or added some text incorrectly. To undo your changes, press Esc to change to command mode, and then press u. Pressing these keys returns things to the way they were before the buffer was changed with the undo command sequence.

The following is an example of using the undo command. To follow along, start vi again with the file `vipract.1` (by entering `vi vipract.1`). You should see a display similar to the following:

```
Things to do today!
a. Practice vi.
b. Sort sales data and print the results.
~
~
~
"vipract.1'' 3 lines, 78 characters
```

To add the phrase *for 60 minutes* between vi and the period on the second line, move to the second line by pressing Return. The cursor now appears under the first character of the second line. Now move the cursor to the period after the word *vi* by pressing the spacebar until the cursor moves to that location. Insert the phrase by pressing the i key to give the input command and then typing `for 60 minutes`. Press Esc to return to command mode. Your screen now looks like this:

```
Things to do today!
a. Practice vi for 60 minutes.
b. Sort sales data and print the results.
~
~
~
```

Is 60 minutes a good idea? Maybe not. To undo the change to the second line, make sure that you're in command mode (press Esc), and then press u. The second line of the file now looks like this:

```
a. Practice vi.
```

Then again, maybe practicing for 60 minutes was a good idea. Press the u key again (you're already in command mode), and you see the phrase *for 60 minutes* reappear. Will you or won't you practice for that long? You decide. Use the undo command to undo the change (and undo the undo) as many times as you want. Even if you decide to leave the buffer in its original form, vi assumes that the buffer has changed, and you must exit by using `:q!` (abandon changes) or `:wq` (save the changes).

If you decide to save the file with the changes, save it to another file by entering `:w vipract.2`.

Tip #58 from *Steve*

You can use the Backspace key to correct mistakes you make while typing a single line. Unfortunately, as you backspace, you erase all the characters you go back over. The left-arrow key doesn't erase characters. The arrow keys are covered later in this chapter.

Writing Files and Saving the Buffer

You've seen how to write the buffer to a file and quit vi. Sometimes, however, you might want to save the buffer to a file without quitting vi. You should save your file regularly during an editing session. If the system goes down because of a crash or a power failure, you may lose your work if you haven't saved it recently. To save the buffer, you issue the `:w` (write) command from command mode.

Note

Before you issue the write command, first press Esc to change to command mode if you aren't already there. If you're already in command mode, you hear a harmless beep.

You'll notice some variations to the steps you follow to save a file. The form of the write command you use depends on the case, of which there are four distinct ones. The following sections describe these cases, and Table 9.2 lists the variations of the write command.

Table 9.2 Commands to Save or Write a File

Command	Action
`:w`	Writes the buffer to the file vi is editing
`:w` *`filename`*	Writes the buffer to the named file
`:w!` *`filename`*	Forces vi to overwrite an existing file

SAVING A NEW FILE

If you started vi without specifying a filename, you must provide a filename if you want to save the file to disk. The write command you issue in this case has the following format:

```
:w filename
```

This command writes the buffer to the file *filename*. If the command is successful, you see the name of the file and the number of lines and characters in the file. If you specify the name of an existing file, an appropriate message appears on the status line:

```
File exists - use ''w! filename'' to overwrite.
```

This condition is described later in the section "Overwriting an Existing File."

SAVING TO THE CURRENT FILE

You might want to save the buffer to the file you're now editing. For example, if you started vi with an existing file, made some changes to the file, and want to save the changes to the original file, you can simply enter `:w`, a form of the write command.

Tip #59 from *Steve*

> **Save the changes you're making to a file regularly. Use the `:w` command frequently—at least every 15 minutes—during an edit session. You never know when the system might go down.**

The `:w` command saves the buffer to the file you're now working with (your working file). The status line tells you the name of the file and the number of lines and characters written to the file.

SAVING AS A NEW FILE

You might want to save the buffer to a new file, giving it a different filename from the one you originally started with. For example, if you started vi with the file `vipract.1`, made some changes to the file, and want to save the changes to a new file without losing the original `vipract.1` file, you can save the file as a new file. Type this form of the write command to save the file with a new filename:

```
:w filename2
```

This form of the write command is essentially the same as the original form described earlier in the section "Saving a New File." The buffer is written to the file named *filename2*. If the command is successful, you see the name of the file and the number of lines and characters in the file. If you specify the name of an existing file, an appropriate message appears on the status line:

```
File exists - use ! to overwrite.
```

The following section explains this scenario.

Overwriting an Existing File

If you try to save the buffer to an existing file different from the one you started with, you must explicitly tell vi that you want to overwrite or replace the existing file. If you specify an existing filename when you try to save the buffer, vi displays the following message:

```
File exists - use ! to overwrite.
```


If you really want to save the buffer over the existing file, use this form of the write command:

```
:w! existing_file
```

In this syntax, *existing_file* is the name of the file you want to replace. Be careful; after you overwrite a file, you can't restore it to its original form.

Positioning the Cursor

When you edit text, you need to position the cursor where you want to insert additional text, delete text, correct mistakes, change words, or append text to the end of existing text. The commands you enter in command mode to select the spot you want are called *cursor-positioning commands*.

The Arrow Keys

You can use the arrow keys on many, but not all, systems to position the cursor. You can easily see whether the arrow keys work: Just start vi with an existing file and see what effects the arrow keys have. You should also be able to use the Page Up and Page Down keys on the Linux keyboard, providing you have the correct terminal type indicated in your `TERMCAP` environment variable.

To create a new file called `vipract.3` that contains a list of the files and directories in the directory `usr`, enter the following command:

```
ls /usr ]] vipract.3
```

You can use this file to experiment with cursor-positioning commands.

After you create the file, start vi with the `vipract.3` file (by entering `vi vipract.3`). Now try using the arrow keys and the Page Up and Page Down keys to move around the editing buffer.

You might find that, although the cursor-positioning keys appear to work, they introduce strange characters into the file. To check whether the keys are entering characters instead of just moving the cursor, press Esc to make sure that you're in command mode, and then enter `:q`. If vi allows you to quit and doesn't complain that the file was modified, everything is fine.

Tip #60 from *Steve*

In vi, you can clear the screen of spurious or unusual characters by pressing Ctrl+l.

OTHER CURSOR-MOVEMENT KEYS

You can position the cursor in vi in other ways without using the arrow keys. You should become familiar with these methods in case you can't or don't want to use the arrow keys. This section also shows you some ways to position the cursor more efficiently than using the arrow keys.

When vi was developed, many terminals didn't have arrow keys. Other keys were and still are used to position the cursor. vi uses the h, j, k, and l keys to position the cursor because they're in a convenient position for touch-typists. Getting comfortable with these keys takes a little practice, but some experienced vi users still prefer these keys over the arrow keys.

The following are some other keys that move the cursor:

- Press the spacebar or the l key to move the cursor one position to the right.
- Press Return or + (the plus sign) to move to the beginning of the next line. (Note that using the j key to go down one line preserves your position in the line.)
- Press - (the minus sign) to move to the beginning of the previous line. (Note that using the k key to go up one line preserves your position in the line.)
- Press h to move one character to the left.
- Press 0 (zero) to move to the beginning of a line.
- Press $ (the dollar sign) to move to the end of a line.

Some vi commands allow you to position the cursor relative to words on a line. A *word*is defined as a sequence of characters separated from other characters by spaces or usual punctuation symbols such as these:

```
. ? , -
```

Those commands include the following:

Keystroke	**Action**
w	Moves forward one word
b	Moves to the beginning of the current word
e	Moves to the end of the current word

The following example demonstrates some of these actions. To follow along, start vi and open the `vipract.1` file by entering `vi vipract.1`. Now use any of the cursor-positioning commands just described to move the cursor (indicated by an underscore) to the *t* in the word *data* on the third line of the file. The third line looks like this:

```
b. Sort sales data and print the results.
```

To move to the beginning of the next word, press w; the cursor is positioned under the *a* of the word *and*. To move to the end of that word, press e; the cursor is positioned under the *d* in *and*. To move to the beginning of that word, press b; the cursor is then positioned under the *a* in *and* again.

You can move forward several words to the beginning of another word by pressing a number key before pressing w. For example, to move the cursor from its current position (under the *a* of the word *and*) to the beginning of the word three words forward (under the *r* of the word *results*), press 3+w. Likewise, you can move backward four words by pressing 4+b; you can move forward to the end of the second word by pressing 2+e.

You can also use this whole-number technique with the h, j, k, l, +, and - keys. For example, press 1+5+j to position the cursor down 15 lines. If 15 lines aren't left in the buffer, you hear a beep, and the cursor stays where it is.

Big-Movement Keys

You can quickly position the cursor at the top, middle, or bottom of the screen. In each case, the cursor appears at the beginning of the line. The following commands allow you to position the cursor onscreen:

- Press Shift+h to move to the first line of the screen. This line is sometimes called the *home position.*
- Press Shift+m to move to the line in the middle of the lines now displayed.
- Press Shift+l to move to the last line onscreen.

If you want to move through a file one screen at a time (which is more efficient than pressing Return or the j key 23 times), use commands that scroll through a file. Pressing Ctrl+f moves you forward one screen. Pressing Ctrl+b moves you backward one screen.

To move quickly to the last line of the file or buffer, press Shift+g. To move to the first line of the file, press 1+Shift+g. In fact, to move to a specific line in the buffer, type the line number before you press Shift+g. For example, to move to line 35 of the file (if the file has a line 35), press 3+5+Shift+g.

Note

Take a little time to practice positioning the cursor by using the commands described in the preceding few sections. Remember that you must be in command mode for the cursor-positioning commands to work. Press Esc before you issue a cursor-positioning command.

Adding Text

To add text to the editing buffer, you must go from command mode to input mode. Any usual text characters you type are then added to the buffer. If you press Return while you're in input mode, vi "opens," or adds, a line to the buffer. Before you start adding text, first position the cursor at the location you want to add text. Press a to go to input mode and append text after the cursor position. Press i to go to input mode and insert text in front of the cursor position. When you're done adding text, press Esc to return to command mode.

The following are two examples of typing in input mode. The position of the cursor is represented by an underscore character. For each case, before and after views are shown:

- Example showing the use of the i key (the `insert` command) to add text.

  Before:

  ```
  This report is important.
  ```

  Press the i key to insert text in front of the word *important*, type `very`, press the spacebar, and press Esc.

  After:

  ```
  This report is very_important.
  ```

  Note that the cursor is positioned under the last character you added (in this case, the space).

- Example showing the use of the a key (the `append` command) to add text.

  Before:

  ```
  This report is important.
  ```

  Press the a key to append text after the word *is*, press the spacebar, type `very`, and press Esc.

  After:

  ```
  This report is very important.
  ```

  Note again that the cursor is positioned under the last character you added (in this case, the *y* in *very*).

When you want to append text to the end of a line, you can position the cursor at the end of the line and press the a key. You can also position the cursor anywhere in the line and press Shift+a to position the cursor at the end of the line, put you in input mode, and allow you to append text—all with one command. Likewise, you can move to the beginning of the current line and insert text at the beginning of a line by pressing Shift+i.

To add a line of text below or above the current line, you press the o key or Shift+o, respectively. Each keystroke "opens" a line in the buffer and allows you to add text. In the following two examples, you add a line to some existing text:

- Example showing the use of the o key to insert lines below the current line.

  Before:

  ```
  All jobs complete
  please call
  if you have any questions.
  ```

  The cursor is on the second line. Press the o key to add a line or lines below that line. Now type the following lines:

  ```
  John Baucom
  555-2222
  ```

  Press the Esc key.

After:

```
All jobs complete
please call
John Baucom
555-2222
if you have any questions.
```

- Example showing the use of Shift+o to insert lines above the current line.

  Before:

  ```
  All jobs complete
  please call
  if you have any questions.
  ```

  The cursor is on the third line. Press Shift+o to add a line or lines above that line. Now type the following lines:

  ```
  John Baucom
  555-2222
  ```

  Press the Esc key.

  After:

  ```
  All jobs complete
  please call
  John Baucom
  555-2222
  if you have any questions.
  ```


In both cases, when you press Esc, the cursor is positioned under the last character you typed (the last 2 in the phone number). Although you added only two lines, you could have added more lines by pressing Return at the end of each line. Naturally, you could have added only one line by not pressing Return at all.

Table 9.3 summarizes the commands for adding text. Press Esc to make sure that you're in command mode before using these commands.

TABLE 9.3 COMMANDS FOR ADDING TEXT

Keystroke	Action
a	Appends text after the cursor position
Shift+a	Puts you in input mode and appends text to the end of the current line
i	Inserts text in front of the cursor position
Shift+i	Puts you in input mode and inserts text at the beginning of the current line
o	Opens a line below the current line to add text
Shift+o	Opens a line above the current line to add text

DELETING TEXT

Making corrections or changes to a file may involve deleting text. You must be in command mode to delete characters. If you're in input mode when you type the delete-character commands, the letters of the commands appear as characters in the buffer file. If that should happen, press Esc to go to command mode, and press the u key to undo the mistake.

With vi, you can delete a character, a word, a number of consecutive words, all the text to the end of a line, or an entire line. Because vi is a visual editor, the characters, words, or lines are removed from the screen as you delete them. Table 9.4 describes the delete commands.

TABLE 9.4 COMMANDS FOR DELETING TEXT

Keystroke	Action
x	Deletes the character at the cursor position
d+w	Deletes from the cursor position in the current word to the beginning of the next word
d+$	Deletes from the cursor position to the end of the line
Shift+d	Same as d+$: deletes the remainder of the current line
d+d	Deletes the entire current line, regardless of cursor position in the line

All these commands take effect from the current cursor position. You move the cursor to the character, word, or line you want to change and then issue the desired delete command. Practice using them to see their effect. You'll find they're helpful in making corrections to files.

You can apply these commands to several objects—characters, words, or lines—by typing a whole number before the command. (This whole-number technique was introduced earlier in this chapter in the section on positioning the cursor.) Some examples are as follows:

- Press 4+x to delete four characters.
- Press 3+d+w to delete three words.
- Press 8+d+d to delete eight lines.

Tip #61 from *Steve*

To have vi display line numbers, press Esc to make sure that you're in command mode, and then enter `:se number`. To turn off the line numbers, enter `:se nonumber`.

You can also specify a range of lines to delete. To do so, press the colon (Shift+;), type the two line numbers you want to delete (inclusive) separated by a comma, press the d key, and press Return. For example, to delete lines 12 through 36 (inclusive), type `:12,36d` and press Return.

When you delete two or more lines, the status line states how many lines were deleted. Remember that you can press the u key to undo the deletion.

Searching

Finding a word, phrase, or number in a file can be difficult if you have to read through each line yourself. Like most editors and word processors, vi has a command that allows you to search for a string of characters. You can search forward or backward from your current position in the buffer. You also can continue searching. vi starts searching from the beginning of the buffer file when it reaches the end, and vice versa. Table 9.5 summarizes the commands for searching. In each case, vi searches for the string you specify in the direction you specify and then positions the cursor at the beginning of the string.

Table 9.5 The Search Commands

Command	Action
`/string`	Searches forward through the buffer for `string`
`?string`	Searches backward through the buffer for `string`
n	Searches again in the current direction
Shift+n	Searches again in the opposite direction

When you type the search command, it appears on the status line. To search forward for the string `sales > 100K` in a file, for example, first you make sure you're in command mode, and then you enter the following:

```
/sales > 100K
```

The typed command appears on the status line. If the string is in the buffer, vi positions the cursor under the first *s* in the word *sales*. If the string isn't in the buffer, vi displays the message `Pattern not found` on the status line. To search for another occurrence of the string, press the n key; vi positions the cursor under the next occurrence of the string or, if there's no "next occurrence," the cursor doesn't move.

TROUBLESHOOTING

I typed a string I know exists in the file, but vi can't find it.

The most common cause for this error is that you typed the string incorrectly. vi (and computers in general) doesn't do a good job of thinking; vi has a terrible time figuring out what you really mean when you type something. If you're looking for the string `vegi-burger`, but you type `vigi-burger`, vi can't find what you want (unless you happened to misspell *vegi-burger* in the buffer, and it matches the search string). Check the search string carefully before you press Return.

I searched for a phrase that incorporates a punctuation mark, and vi returned some odd results.

Searching in vi may not give you the results you want if you're looking for characters that are "special" to vi. For example, if you want to find a word you know is located at the end of a sentence (for example, the string `end.`), you must "escape" the period; to vi, the period means "any character," not "end of sentence." If you enter `/end.` and press Return, vi would locate such things as the word *ending*, the word *end* followed by a space, and the word *end* followed by a period. To find only *end* followed by a period, you need to enter `/end\.`.

Searches in vi are also case sensitive. If you're looking for the word *Tiger* in your buffer, you must enter `/Tiger`, not `/tiger`.

CHANGING AND REPLACING TEXT

Another often-faced editing task is changing text or replacing one text string with another (the two operations aren't very different). The change commands in vi allow you to change a word or the remainder of a line. In effect, you replace one word or the remainder of a line with another. You use the replace commands to replace or change a single character or sequence of characters. Table 9.6 summarizes the change and replace commands. After you enter the command, simply type the new material as appropriate.

TABLE 9.6 THE CHANGE AND REPLACE COMMANDS

Keystroke	Action
r	Replaces a single character
Shift+r	Replaces a sequence of characters
c+w	Changes the current word, from the cursor position to the end of the word
c+e	Changes the current word, from the cursor position to the end of the word (same as c+w)
c+b	Changes the current word, from the beginning of the word to the character before the cursor position
c+$	Changes a line, from the cursor position to the end of the line
Shift+c	Changes a line, from the cursor position to the end of the line (same as c+$)
c+c	Changes the entire line

The changes take place relative to the position of the cursor. You must be in command mode before you can use these commands. Position the cursor at the location in the buffer file you want to correct and press Esc before using these commands. Because vi is visual, the changes are made to the buffer as you execute the commands.

Each of these commands puts you into input mode. Except for when you use r to replace a single character, you must press Esc to finish making changes and return to command mode.

Tip #62 from *Steve*

To change several words, use a whole number (representing the number of words to change) before pressing c+w. The specified number of words are deleted, and you're put back into insert mode.

The following are three examples of how to use the change and replace commands, with before and after scenarios for each:

- Example showing the use of c+e to change to the end of the word.

  Before:

  `The report demonstra its thw,strengths of are apporach.`

  The cursor is located at the point in the incorrectly spelled word where corrections are to begin. To change the spelling, press c+e, type `tes`, and press Esc.

  After:

  `The report demonstrate s thw,strengths of are apporach.`

- Example showing the use of Shift+r to replace a sequence of characters.

  Before:

  `The report demonstrates th w,strengths of are apporach.`

  The cursor is located at the point in the incorrectly spelled word where you want to start replacing characters. To change `thw,` to `the` and a space, press Shift+r, type `e`, press the spacebar, and press Esc.

  After:

  `The report demonstrates the_strengths of are apporach.`

- Example showing the use of c+w to change text, beginning with the current word and continuing for two words.

  Before:

  `The report demonstrates the strengths of are apporach.`

  The cursor is positioned under the letter of the word where you want to begin making changes. To fix the last two words on the line, press 2+c+w, type `our approach`, and press Esc.

  After:

  `The report demonstrates the strengths of our approac h.`

Remember to press Esc after you make changes to the lines and return to command mode.

Copying, Cutting, and Pasting

When you delete or cut characters, words, lines, or a portion of a line, the deleted object is saved in what's called the *general-purpose buffer*. The name isn't too important; what's important is that you can put or paste the contents of that buffer anywhere in the text you're editing. You do so by using the p or Shift+p command. The p command pastes the object to the right of or after the cursor position; the Shift+p command pastes the object to the left of or before the cursor.

The following are some examples of cutting and pasting text with before and after scenarios for each:

- Example showing the use of p to paste the contents of the general-purpose buffer after the cursor.

Before:

```
Carefully carry these out instructions.
```

Delete the characters out and a space by pressing d+w. Now move the cursor to the space after the *y* in *carry* and press the p key.

After:

```
Carefully carry out_these instructions.
```

- Example showing the use of Shift+p to paste the contents of the general-purpose buffer in front of the cursor.

  Before:

  ```
  Carefully carry these out instructions.
  ```

  Delete the characters these and a space by pressing d+w. Now move the cursor to the first *i* in *instructions* and press Shift+p.

  After:

  ```
  Carefully carry ou t these instructions.
  ```

Tip #63 from Steve

To change the order of two characters, position the cursor under the first character and press x+p. Try it to change the word *tow* to the word *two*, for example.

The preceding examples show you how to paste after deleting text. But you don't have to delete before you can paste. You can use an operation called *yank*, which is the same as the copy operation in some word processors. The forms of the yank command are similar to the forms of the delete command. The idea is that you yank, or copy, a portion of text and then paste it somewhere else by pressing the p key or Shift+p. The following list names some of the yank commands (notice that most of the yank commands use the lowercase letter *y*):

Keystroke	Action
y+w	Yanks from the cursor position in the current word to the beginning of the next word
y+$	Yanks from the cursor position to the end of the line
Shift+y	Same as y+$: yanks the remainder of current line
y+y	Yanks the entire current line

You can apply all these commands to several objects—characters, words, or lines—by typing a whole number before the command.

To copy a sequence of four lines to another portion of the text, follow these steps:

1. Position the cursor at the beginning of the first of the four lines.

2. Press 4+y+y to yank from the cursor to the end of the line four times. The buffer (what you see onscreen) is unchanged.
3. Position the cursor elsewhere in the text.
4. Press p to paste the yanked lines below the line holding the cursor.

You can also search and replace words throughout the file or within a specified range of lines. The format of the command is

```
:[range]s/oldstring/newstring/g
```

where

range	Indicates the range on which to operate; for example, you can use the percent symbol (%) to operate on the entire file, or you can use specific line numbers (such as 1,4) to operate on specific lines (in this case, lines 1 through 4)
`s`	Indicates this is a search-and-replace operation
oldstring	Specifies the string to search for in the file and replace with *newstring*
newstring	Specifies the string to insert; *newstring* replaces *oldstring*

For example, to replace the incorrectly spelled word *recieved* with the correct spelling throughout an entire file, you can use the following command:

```
:%s/recieved/received/g
```

REPEATING COMMANDS

Not only does vi keep the text just deleted or yanked for future use, it also stores the last command you used for future use. You can repeat the last command that changed the buffer by pressing the . (period) key.

Suppose that you've completed a report but think it would be a good idea to put two lines containing this text at key points in the report:

```
*************** Please comment ******
*************** On this section ******
```

To do so, follow these steps:

1. Position the cursor in the buffer file where you want to place these lines the first time.
2. Insert the lines by pressing the o key to open a line and typing the two lines of asterisks and text.
3. Press Esc to make sure that you're in command mode.
4. As often as necessary, position the cursor to another section of the report and press the . key to insert these same two lines again and again.

VI COMMAND SUMMARY

You now have a basic understanding of using vi for text processing. Table 9.7 provides a summary of the keystrokes and commands you can use in vi.

TABLE 9.7 VI COMMAND SUMMARY

Keystroke/Command	Description
i	Inserts text before the cursor
I	Enters text at the start of the line
a	Inserts text after the cursor
A	Enters text at the end of the line
o	Opens a new line below the cursor
O	Opens a new line above the cursor
d+w	Deletes a word
d+d	Deletes an entire line
D	Deletes to the end of the line
x	Deletes the character under the cursor
c+w	Changes a word
c+c	Changes a line
C	Changes to the end of the line
R	Replaces the character under the cursor
J	Joins lines together
e	Moves to the end of a word
w	Moves to the next word
$	Moves to the end of the line
l	Moves one space right
k	Moves one line up
j	Moves one line down
h	Moves one space left
f+*x*	Moves the cursor to the first occurrence of *x*
F+*x*	Moves the cursor to the last occurrence of *x*
;	Repeats the last f/F command
number+|	Moves the cursor to the specified column *number*
H	Moves the cursor to the top line onscreen (not the top line of the file)
L	Moves the cursor to the bottom line onscreen
M	Moves the cursor to the middle line onscreen

TABLE 9.7 VI COMMAND SUMMARY

Keystroke/Command	Description
G	Moves the cursor to the bottom line of the file
number+G	Moves the cursor to the specified line *number* (same as Esc+: *number*)
^	Moves to the beginning of the line
m+*x*	Marks the current position with the letter *x*
Ctrl+d	Scrolls forward one half of the screen
Ctrl+u	Scrolls backward one half of the screen
Ctrl+f	Scrolls forward one screen
Ctrl+b	Scrolls backward one screen
Ctrl+l	Redraws the screen
Ctrl+g	Shows the filename, current line, and column number
z+z	Redraws the screen with the current line in the middle of the screen
y+y	Yanks the entire line into the buffer
p	Puts the contents of the buffer below the cursor
P	Puts the contents of the buffer above the cursor
x"[*number*]"y+y	Yanks the indicated number of lines into the buffer named *x* (*x* can be any single character A–Z)
x p	Places the contents of buffer *x* after the cursor
`:w [file]`	Writes the contents to disk as *file*
`:q`	Quits vi
`:q!`	Quits the file without saving changes
`:wq`	Saves changes and quits vi
`:r file`	Reads the specified `file` into editor
`:e file`	Edits `file`
`:!command`	Executes the specified shell `command`
`:number`	Moves to the specified line `number`
`:f`	Prints the current line and filename (same as Ctrl+g)
`/string`	Searches forward for `string`
`?string`	Searches backward for `string`
`:x,ys/oldstring/newstring`	Replaces `oldstring` with `newstring` from line `x` to line `y` (entering `y = $` replaces to the end of the file)
Esc+u	Undoes the last command
n	Finds the next occurrence of the string
.	Repeats the last command
~	Changes the character to the opposite case

TABLE 9.7 VI COMMAND SUMMARY

Keystroke/Command	Description
Esc	Switches to command mode

SETTING THE VI ENVIRONMENT

The vi editor has several options you may or may not choose to use. Some of these options can be set on a system-wide basis by the system administrator. You can customize your environment with a number of options that are in effect whenever you start vi. Table 9.8 summarizes all the environment options you can set for vi. When setting environment options (as described in the next section), you can use the abbreviation shown in the first column of the table or the full name used in the second column.

TABLE 9.8 ENVIRONMENT OPTIONS FOR VI

Abbreviated Option	Full Name and Function of Option
`ai`	`autoindent` indents each line to the same level as the line above (useful for writing programs). The default is `autoindent off`.
`ap`	`autoprint` prints the current line to the screen when the line is changed. The default is `autoprint on`.
`eb`	`errorbells` causes the computer to beep when you introduce a command error. The default is `errorbells off`.
`nu`	`number` displays line numbers when you're editing a file. The default is `number off`.
`redraw`	`redraw` keeps the screen up-to-date as changes occur. The default is `redraw on`.
`report`	`report` sets the size of an editing change that results in a message on the status line. For example, `report=3` triggers a message when you delete three lines but not when fewer than three lines are deleted. The default is `report=5`.
`sm`	`showmatch` shows a matching open parenthesis when the closing parenthesis is entered. This option is useful mainly for programmers writing program code. The default is `showmatch off`.
`smd`	`showmode` displays `INPUT`, `REPLACE`, or `CHANGE` on the right side of the status line when the associated command is given. The default is `showmode off`.
`warn`	`warn` displays a warning message when an attempt is made to exit vi if the buffer has been changed and not saved to the disk file. The default is `warn on`.

TABLE 9.8 ENVIRONMENT OPTIONS FOR VI

Abbreviated Option	Full Name and Function of Option
wm=*n*	wrapmargin defines the right margin. In the syntax of this command, *n* is a whole number. If *n* is greater than 0, the command forces a carriage return so that no word is *n* or fewer characters from the right margin. For example, wm=5 tells vi to wrap the line when a character occurs within five characters of the end of the line. Turn this option off by specifying wm=0, which is the default.
ws	word search (called wrapscan on some systems) wraps from the <eof> (end-of-file) character to the <bof> (beginning-of-file) character during a search. Default is word search on.

USING SET TO SEE AND SET OPTIONS

To see the options now set for your system, you can enter :set while in command mode in vi. The options currently set for this session of vi are displayed on the status line. The options displayed with the set command vary depending on the default options and on your particular implementation of vi. The following is an example of what you might see when you issue the set command:

```
autoprint errorbells redraw report=1 showmatch showmode term=vt100 wrap margin=5
```

Note

Issuing the set command with no arguments results in a display of only the user-set options. You can abbreviate the set command as se. To set a number of options on the same line, use the se command and separate the options with a space, as in the following example:

```
:se ap eb redraw report=1 sm smd warn wm=5 ws
```

Notice that the first character is the colon character, which indicates to vi that a command is to be entered.

To see the list of all possible options and their settings, enter :set all. The options and their settings listed in Table 9.7 are displayed.

SETTING THE showmode OPTION

One of the most used options in vi is showmode. To learn about the showmode option, start vi again with the vipract.1 file (by entering vi vipract.1).

When vi executes, you see the text from your first vi session onscreen. In your first session, you may have noticed that you could not determine whether you were in input mode when you entered the text for this file. You can tell vi to inform you when you're in input mode by using the showmode option. The showmode option identifies the mode you're in on the status line.

When you set the showmode option, vi displays whatever type of input mode it's in: regular INPUT MODE, APPEND MODE, REPLACE 1 CHAR mode, and so on. To set showmode in vi, press Esc to make sure that you're in command mode, and then enter :set showmode. Now go to input mode (press the i key). You should see the message INPUT MODE on the status line. Press Esc to return to command mode. You might want to see what happens when you give the commands to replace or change text.

SETTING TOGGLE OPTIONS

Any option that doesn't take a number argument is like a toggle switch: You can turn it on or off. For example, as you learned in the preceding section, you set the showmode option by entering this command:

```
:se showmode
```

To turn off the showmode option, you simply add no in front of the option like this:

```
:se noshowmode
```

CHANGING OPTIONS FOR EVERY VI SESSION

Setting an option during a vi session sets that option for the current session only. You can customize your vi sessions by putting the set commands in a file named .exrc in your home directory. To see whether such a file exists, type the following commands:

```
cd
vi .exrc
```

The first command takes you to your home directory. The second starts vi by using the .exrc file. If the file exists, it appears on the vi screen. If the file doesn't exist, vi lets you know it's a new file.

The set commands in the .exrc file start with the word set but no colon. For example, the following line sets the options number and showmode:

```
set number showmode
```

Note The .exrc file is read when you start vi. If you create it while you're in vi, you must restart vi to put the settings into effect.

The options you set and the values you give to some options depend on your preferences and the type of editing you'll be doing. Experiment with some options or talk with more experienced users.

Troubleshooting

My vi editor doesn't appear to be working correctly with my terminal or screen; I see "strange" characters.

The TERM variable may not be set correctly. Another symptom of an improper terminal setup is that blocks of characters overwrite legible text. The $TERM expression gives the value of your current terminal setting. To check the value of TERM, enter echo$TERM. If you work at a terminal that is—or emulates—a vt100, this command displays the following result (type the command on the terminal, not while in the vi editor):

```
vt100
```

If the proper terminal type isn't echoed back, set the value of TERM by entering the following command, if you're using the bash shell:

```
TERM=vt100
export TERM
```

If you're using the C shell, enter the following (the spaces around the = sign are important):

```
setenv TERM = vt100
export TERM
```

Your specific terminal type may be different from vt100; set TERM appropriately.

→ See Chapter 16, "Understanding Linux Shells," p. 317

I start vi but don't get the expected responses.

Check to see whether your terminal is properly set up. Your terminal type isn't the same as the name of your terminal; your terminal type must match one of the terminal types contained in the directory /usr/lib/terminfo.

CHAPTER 10

Booting and Shutting Down

In this chapter

by Jack Tackett, Jr.

UNDERSTANDING THE BOOT PROCESS

Two of the most common tasks that you encounter when administering a Linux system are booting the system and shutting it down. As you might have guessed, booting and shutting down Linux are operations that require special consideration.

To use Linux, you must boot the operating system. Although this process sounds pretty straightforward, you need to consider that most people run at least one additional operating system on their PCs other than Linux. This means that you must have some way to specify which operating system you want to boot when you start the system. You can do so in two basic ways: You can boot Linux from a floppy, or you can boot from your hard drive by using a boot manager.

Red Hat and most modern distributions of Linux use the SysV `init` boot process instead of the older BSD style `init`. `init` is the first program the kernel executes at startup and, hence, is given the process ID (or PID) of 1. It becomes the parent process for all other processes running in the Linux system.

Note

The PID of a process is a number the operating system uses to identify that process. Many Linux commands use this PID number as a qualifying parameter.

Tip #64 from *Jack*

The `ps aux` command displays the PID of all running processes.

Linux follows these steps to boot:

1. The kernel runs the `init` program, which is located in the `/sbin` directory.
2. `init` runs the shell script `/etc/rc.d/rc.sysinit`.
3. `rc.sysinit` sets various system variables and performs other startup initializations.
4. `init` runs all the scripts specified for the default run level.
5. `init` runs the script `/etc/rc.d/rc.local`.

→ See "Understanding Multitasking," p. 366

This program starts various processes and writes information to the console and to the system log file `/var/log/messages` about the status of each process that's started.

Tip #65 from *Jack*

The `/var/log/message` log file is an excellent aid for debugging startup problems. The kernel stores all error messages here, so you don't have to worry about writing

down the messages as they scroll by during startup. The log files /var/log/boot and /var/log/dmesg also contain log entries associated with startup and shutdown. To scroll through these files, use the command less, as in
less /var/log/dmesq

init starts all the processes required by the operating system to perform its duties, such as allowing network operations, use of the mouse, and basic functions like I/O to the terminal. The SysV init program knows which processes to start by reading config files located in /etc/rd.d. These files are further segregated according to run levels, specified by directories.

A run level specifies what types of services are available, from single-user mode (run level 1) to full multiuser, multitasking, all-processes-running mode (run level 3). Table 10.1 outlines the various run levels available in Linux.

TABLE 10.1 LINUX RUN LEVELS

Run Level	Description
0	Halt
1	Single-user mode
2	Multiuser, no NFS
3	Full multiuser mode
4	Unused
5	X11
6	Reboot

You can change run levels by using the telinit command, which has the following form:

/sbin/telinit [-t *sec*] [*0123456sSQqabcUu*]

-t *sec*	Indicates the number of seconds to delay before executing the command
0 to 6	Indicate the run level to switch to from the current level
sS	Indicates to switch to single-user mode
abc	Indicates to switch to level a, b, or c specified in /etc/inittab
qQ	Causes init to re-examine the /etc/inittab file
wW	Re-executes init while preserving current system states

The init program uses the following directory structure:

```
init.d
rc0.d
rc1.d
rc2.d
rc3.d
rc4.d
```

```
rc5.d
rc6.d
```

The various numbers in the directory names correspond to the run levels in Table 10.1. Each directory contains various shell scripts that start or stop the necessary services required in each run level. These scripts also initialize the file system and lock files to a known state.

→ See "Working with Shell Scripts," p. 348

Each directory contains various shell scripts. Each script's filename begins with either an S or a K (for Start or Kill) and a two-digit number. The numbers are used to order the sequence but have no other meaning.

Each script usually accepts either a start or stop command-line argument, although it can accept other parameters. `init` supplies either a start or stop to the script, depending on whether `rc` has been called to change run levels. You can also execute the scripts by hand if you need to reconfigure a service; for example, you can use `sendmail` with the following command (you must be logged in as root to execute the `init`scripts):

```
/etc/rc.d/init.d/sendmail stop
/etc/rc.d/init.d/sendmail stop
/etc/rc.d/init.d/sendmail start
```

You should notice two things about this command. First, the command is repeated twice with the `stop` parameter. Repeating the command ensures that the system has time to stop the process. Then the `start` command is called. Next, notice that the script is executed from the `init.d` directory, not from the directory for the run level. Also, the script does not have a letter (S or K) or a number. If you list the files in any run level directory, you will note that they are actually linked to files in the `init.d` directory, as you can see in Listing 10.1. Following the listing, Table 10.2 outlines a few crucial startup scripts in this directory.

LISTING 10.1 DIRECTORY LISTING OF A TYPICAL `rc3.d` DIRECTORY

```
lrwxrwxrwx   1 root   root 16 Jan 25 21:56 K08autofs -> ../init.d/autofs
lrwxrwxrwx   1 root   root 18 Dec 14 12:17 K10pnserver -> ../init.d/pnserver
lrwxrwxrwx   1 root   root 17 Dec 14 12:17 K20rusersd -> ../init.d/rusersd
lrwxrwxrwx   1 root   root 15 Dec 14 12:17 K20rwhod -> ../init.d/rwhod
lrwxrwxrwx   1 root   root 15 Dec 14 12:17 S15nfsfs -> ../init.d/nfsfs
lrwxrwxrwx   1 root   root 16 Dec 14 12:17 S20random -> ../init.d/random
lrwxrwxrwx   1 root   root 16 Dec 14 12:17 S30syslog -> ../init.d/syslog
lrwxrwxrwx   1 root   root 13 Dec 14 12:17 S40atd -> ../init.d/atd
lrwxrwxrwx   1 root   root 15 Dec 14 12:17 S40crond -> ../init.d/crond
lrwxrwxrwx   1 root   root 14 Dec 14 12:17 S50inet -> ../init.d/inet
lrwxrwxrwx   1 root   root 15 Dec 14 12:17 S55named -> ../init.d/named
lrwxrwxrwx   1 root   root 13 Dec 14 12:17 S60lpd -> ../init.d/lpd
lrwxrwxrwx   1 root   root 13 Jan 31 20:17 S72amd -> ../init.d/amd
lrwxrwxrwx   1 root   root 18 Dec 14 12:17 S75keytable -> ../init.d/keytable
lrwxrwxrwx   1 root   root 18 Dec 14 12:17 S80sendmail -> ../init.d/sendmail
```

Table 10.2 rc.3 init Scripts

Script Name	Daemon	Description
S15nfsfs	nfs	Handles Network File System (NFS)
S30syslog	syslog	Allows logging of system messages in /var/log/messages
S40atd	atd	Allows the user to perform a task at an indicated time
S40crond	cron	Acts as the batch scheduler for Linux
S50inet	inetd	Acts as the super server (PID 1)
S55named	Name server	Provides DNS name services
S60lpd	lpd	Acts as the line printer daemon to allow printing

`init` loops through the files in the specified run level directory and passes either the `start` or `stop` parameter as indicated by the first character of the filename.

→ See "Links," p. 412

The `rc.d` directory also contains three files called `rc`, `rc.local`, and `rc.sysinit`. The `rc` shell script is responsible for restarting the system in a different run level. That script takes one parameter, which is a number corresponding to the new run level. The `rc.local` file is executed after all the other scripts are executed during startup. You can place any local initialization instructions in this file. The `rc.local` file (the contents of which are shown in Listing 10.2) provides an example of starting a local process, called *secure shell*, which allows secure remote access to the system.

Listing 10.2 A Sample rc.local Shell Script

```
#!/bin/sh
# This script will be executed *after* all the other init scripts.
# You can put your own initialization stuff in here if you don't
# want to do the full Sys V style init stuff.

if [ -f /etc/redhat-release ]; then
        R=$(cat /etc/redhat-release)
else
        R="release 3.0.3''
if
arch=$(uname -m)
a="a"
case ''_$arch'' in
        _a*) a="an'';;
        _i*) a="an'';;
esac
# This will overwrite /etc/issue at every boot. So, make any changes you
# want to make to /etc/issue here or you will lose them when you reboot.
echo '''' > /etc/issue
```

LISTING 10.2 CONTINUED

```
echo ''Red Hat Linux $R'' ]]]] /etc/issue
echo ''Kernel $(uname -r) on $a $(uname -m)'' ]]]] /etc/issue
cp -f /etc/issue /etc/issue.net
echo >> /etc/issue
## Start sshd
## Added By Lance Brown 1/29/1998
/usr/local/sbin/sshd
```

The `rc.sysinit` file is the first file `init` runs at startup. This script performs various functions, such as setting systemwide variables (like the hostname), checking the file system and starting repairs, turning on user quotas, and mounting the `/proc` file system. The script in Listing 10.2 also starts a local process called `sshd`, which is the secure shell daemon that provides secure Telnet and remote commands to Linux.

Note

`ssh` is not part of most Linux distributions because of export restrictions on munitions (the United States government has classified encryption utilities in the same category as nuclear weapons). You can install the utility yourself, though. Just check out `http://www.cs.hut.fi/ssh/` for more information.

The default run level is decided in `/etc/inittab` with the following command:

```
id:3:initdefault:
```

This command tells the system to start in run level 3 (full multiuser and multitasking). Listing 10.3 shows a sample `/etc/inittab` file.

LISTING 10.3 A SAMPLE `/etc/inittab` FILE

```
# inittab       This file describes how the INIT process should set up
#               the system in a certain run-level.
#
# Author:       Miquel van Smoorenburg, [[miquels@drinkel.nl.mugnet.org]]
#               Modified for RHS Linux by Marc Ewing and Donnie Barnes
#

# Default run level. The run levels used by RHS are:
#   0 - halt (Do NOT set initdefault to this)
#   1 - Single user mode
#   2 - Multiuser, without NFS (The same as 3, if you do not have
        ➥networking)
#   3 - Full multiuser mode
#   4 - unused
#   5 - X11
#   6 - reboot (Do NOT set initdefault to this)
#
id:3:initdefault:

# System initialization.
```

Listing 10.3 continued

```
si::sysinit:/etc/rc.d/rc.sysinit

l0:0:wait:/etc/rc.d/rc 0
l1:1:wait:/etc/rc.d/rc 1
l2:2:wait:/etc/rc.d/rc 2
l3:3:wait:/etc/rc.d/rc 3
l4:4:wait:/etc/rc.d/rc 4
l5:5:wait:/etc/rc.d/rc 5
l6:6:wait:/etc/rc.d/rc 6

# Things to run in every run level.
ud::once:/sbin/update

# Trap CTRL-ALT-DELETE
ca::ctrlaltdel:/sbin/shutdown -t3 -r now

# When our UPS tells us power has failed, assume we have a few minutes
# of power left.   Schedule a shutdown for 2 minutes from now.
# This does, of course, assume you have power installed and your
# UPS connected and working correctly.
pf::powerfail:/sbin/shutdown -f -h +2 ''Power Failure; System Shutting Down''

# If power was restored before the shutdown kicked in, cancel it.
pr:12345:powerokwait:/sbin/shutdown -c ''Power Restored; Shutdown Cancelled''

# Run gettys in standard run levels
1:12345:respawn:/sbin/mingetty tty1
2:2345:respawn:/sbin/mingetty tty2
3:2345:respawn:/sbin/mingetty tty3
4:2345:respawn:/sbin/mingetty tty4
5:2345:respawn:/sbin/mingetty tty5
6:2345:respawn:/sbin/mingetty tty6

# Run xdm in run level 5
x:5:respawn:/usr/bin/X11/xdm _nodaemon
```

Do not specify either run level 0 or run level 6 as the default run level because either one will render your system unusable. If, for some reason, your `inittab` file does become corrupted, you can boot to single-user mode and fix the problem. To do so, at the LILO boot prompt, enter the parameter `LINUX single`, like this:

```
LILO boot: LINUX single
```

Caution

The default listed in LILO is linux (lower case). It would be good to note that if the kernel image name is changed when recompiling a kernel, the command becomes ineffective. So, keeping the linux image name is a good thing.

→ See "Configuring LILO," p. 242

LILO is the Linux loader and is discussed later in this chapter.

Tip #66 from Jack

> You can pass any run level to the LILO prompt by specifying the run level as a number. For example, to enter run level 2, you enter the following command at the LILO prompt:
>
> ```
> LILO boot: linux 2
> ```

→ See "Understanding LILO, the Linux Loader," p. 242

Booting Linux from a Floppy

Many people use a boot floppy to start Linux. This boot floppy contains a copy of the Linux kernel that points to the root Linux file system on the appropriate hard drive partition. The Red Hat and Caldera Linux installation programs give you the opportunity to create a bootable floppy during the installation process.

Caution

> You should make a bootable Linux floppy disk during the installation, even if you intend to install a boot manager on your hard drive. If your hard disk should crash, the bootable floppy might be the only way to boot your system. Also, if you try to use a "generic" boot disk made up after a crash from another Linux computer, it probably won't work.

You can also use the installation disks in an emergency. At the boot prompt, pass the option `rescue` to the kernel. After asking a few questions, the system prompts you to insert the supplementary disk to finish the boot process.

→ See "Creating the Boot, Supplemental, and Rescue Disks," p. 66

After booting, the system provides you a minimal command shell called `ash`, as well as several other utilities. Table 10.3 lists the utilities provided, which should be enough to repair your system.

TABLE 10.3 RESCUE UTILITIES

Utility	Description
cat	Displays the contents of a file
chmod	Changes the access permissions of files
cpio	Copies files from archives
e2fsck	Checks a Linux second extended file system

Table 10.3 Rescue Utilities

Utility	Description
fdisk	Partitions a table manipulator for Linux
gzip/gunzip	Compresses or expands files
insmod	Installs a loadable kernel module
ls	Lists files
mkdir	Creates a directory
mke2fs	Creates a Linux second extended file system
mount	Mounts a file system
rm	Removes a file
rmmod	Unloads a loadable module

→ See "Using Basic Commands," p. 48

Tip #67 from Jack

For Intel systems with the root partition on an IDE hard drive, you can also use the boot disk to boot Linux. At the boot prompt, enter the following command:

```
Linux single root=/dev/hda1 initrd=
```

Be sure to specify the appropriate device for your root file system if it is on an IDE device other than `/dev/hda1`. This command mounts the root partition, dumps you into single-user mode immediately, and then skips the rest of the boot process on the boot disk. Unfortunately, this procedure does not work if your root partition is on a SCSI device.

Booting from a Boot Manager

Linux comes with a boot manager known as LILO, which stands for *Linux Loader*. This program modifies the master boot sector of your boot hard disk and allows you to choose which operating system you want to boot when you turn on your computer.

Boot Managers

Using a boot manager has its advantages and disadvantages. With a boot manager, you don't need a floppy disk to boot your system. Also, you can choose to boot different operating systems from a menu at boot time or have the system default to a given operating system.

As for the disadvantages, a boot manager adds another level of complexity to the boot process. It must be modified or possibly reinstalled if you add, delete, or upgrade a version of any of the operating systems on your disk. It modifies the master boot record of your hard disk, so if something goes wrong, you might not be able to boot with anything other than a floppy disk until you reformat your hard drive. Also, the boot manager that you choose might not be compatible with some operating systems.

You should consider your own computing needs carefully before deciding whether to use a floppy or boot manager for booting Linux.

You also can set up LILO so that it can be started from the OS/2 boot manager.

UNDERSTANDING LILO, THE LINUX LOADER

LILO is a boot manager that comes bundled as part of almost every Linux distribution, including the Red Hat, Debian, and Caldera Linux distributions. It can be installed in the master boot record, on a formatted floppy disk, or on the boot partition's super block for booting OS/2.

When LILO is installed, you can use the master boot record to select from a set of different operating systems at boot time. Depending on its configuration, LILO counts to a timeout value and then boots a default operating system.

The easiest way to install LILO is to do so via the Red Hat or Caldera Linux installation program, which takes you through a menu-driven system that automates much of the installation process.

Caution

Installing LILO from the Red Hat or Caldera installation program is highly recommended. Installing a boot manager is an inherently dangerous process; you can easily corrupt data on your hard disk if the installation isn't done correctly.

CONFIGURING LILO

LILO reads a configuration file, `/etc/lilo.conf`, and uses it to figure out what operating systems are installed on your system and where their boot information is located. The `/etc/lilo.conf` file starts with some information that tells LILO how to operate in general. It then contains several sections that list the boot information specific to each operating system that LILO can boot. LILO is configured to boot one section for each operating system on your Linux system.

Two sections from a LILO configuration file follow:

```
# Section for the Linux partition
image=/vmlinuz
label=Linux
root=/dev/hda1

# Section for MS-DOS
other=/dev/hda3
table=/dev/hda
label=msdos
```

The first section gives the boot information for Linux. The `image` line tells LILO where the Linux kernel is located. The `label` line that appears in both sections gives the name of the operating system that appears in the LILO boot menu. The `root` line specifies the location of the Linux root file system.

In the MS-DOS section, the `other` line indicates that the partition for an additional operating system is located on the disk partition `hda3`. The `table` line tells LILO where to find the partition table for `/dev/hda3`.

USING LILO

When you install LILO, you typically should set a default timeout value and a default operating system to boot. Doing so allows you to have a certain amount of time to select another operating system at boot time. In the event that you don't select an operating system, LILO boots the one that you've set as the default at the end of the timeout count.

When you boot your computer with LILO installed, you get a prompt that reads `LILO:`. At this point, you have several options. You can wait and have Linux boot your default operating system, or you can press Ctrl, Alt, or Shift to have LILO boot the default operating system immediately. You can also type the name of one of the operating systems to have LILO boot the one you specify. Finally, you can press the Tab key to have LILO display a list of the different available operating systems.

Tip #68 from Jack

If you are having problems booting your system, you can pass the flag `-b emergency` to LILO as follows so that the system will boot directly into a single-user shell without running any other startup scripts:

```
LILO boot: linux -b emergency
```

You are provided a minimal set of commands, and only the `/` and `/proc` file systems are loaded. Also, you are required to provide the root password to perform any work on the system.

SHUTTING DOWN LINUX

With a Linux system, you have to be careful when you shut down the system. You can't simply turn off the power. Linux maintains file system I/O information in memory buffers. If you just power down a Linux system, file system corruption can result.

Caution

You should never turn off a Linux system without shutting down properly. The file systems need to synchronize properly when the system is shutting down. You can cause severe damage to the Linux file system if you just power off the system.

The best way to shut down a Linux system is to use the `shutdown` command. The syntax of the command is as follows:

```
/sbin/shutdown [flags] time [warning-message]
```

[warning-message] is a message sent to all users who are currently logged on, and *time* is the time that the shutdown is to occur. The *time* argument can take a couple of formats:

- It can be specified as an absolute time in the format *hh:mm*, where *hh* is the hour (in one or two digits) and *mm* is the minute of the hour. The *mm* value must be specified with two digits.
- The *time* value can also be given in the format +*m*, where *m* is the number of minutes to wait before the shutdown. You can substitute the word `now` for `+0`.

Table 10.4 lists the flags that you can use with the `shutdown` command.

TABLE 10.4 COMMAND-LINE FLAGS FOR THE `shutdown` COMMAND

Flag	Message to Linux
`-tsec`	Wait the specified number of seconds between sending the warning and the kill signal to all processes. This delay gives processes time to finish any shutdown processing that they have to do.
`-k`	Don't really shut down the system; just send the warning message to all users.
`-r`	Reboot after shutdown.
`-h`	Halt after shutdown.
`-n`	Don't synchronize disks before rebooting or halting. *Use this flag with caution; it can cause your data to become corrupted.*
`-f`	Do a "fast" reboot. This type of reboot creates the `/etc/fastboot` file. The `rc` boot script should check for this file and should not do a `fsck` if it's found.
`-c`	Cancel an already running shutdown. When you use this option, you cannot specify the *time* argument.

Tip #69 from *Jack*

To reboot your system quickly, simply use the command

```
shutdown -r now
```

The `shutdown` command prevents any users from logging on, notifies all users on the system that the system will be shut down, waits until the time that you specify, and then sends a `SIGTERM` signal to all processes so that they can exit cleanly. `shutdown` then calls `halt` or `reboot`, depending on your command-line choice in the `shutdown` command.

Caution

> You can halt or reboot the system by entering `halt` or `reboot` directly. However, if you use either of these commands, no warning is given to the users, and the system goes down immediately. You should use these commands only if you're the only user on the system. To see who is logged on to the system, either press *w* or use the command `who`.

TROUBLESHOOTING STARTUP AND SHUTDOWN

Why does LILO hang on LI? Can I use a hard drive that has more than 1023 cylinders?

The infamous 1023 cylinder question. Yes, you can use such a hard drive but not to boot Linux. You can install Linux on partitions above the 1023 cylinder, but to boot Linux, the root directory and specifically the `/boot` directory must be installed on the first hard drive below 1024. See the following site for more information:

```
http://metalab.unc.edu/LDP/HOWTO/mini/Large-Disk.html
```

How do I add arguments for LILO at the prompt?

Some hardware requires that extra parameters be fed to the kernel before the kernel will recognize the hardware. You can accommodate this requirement by editing the `/etc/lilo.conf` file to provide the necessary parameters, or you can provide them manually during bootup. See the "LILO How-To" for more examples of LILO parameters.

The installation cannot find the SCSI card.

To remedy this problem, you need to add a boot-time argument such as the following:

```
LILO: linux qlogicfas=0x230,11,5
```

You can make this option permanent so that you don't have to re-enter it. See the LILO configuration option `append` in the `lilo.conf` man page.

How do I uninstall LILO?

If you want to uninstall LILO and reinstall the original boot record, try using this command:

```
lilo -u /dev/hda
```

It represents the boot record of the first IDE drive. Parameters may vary for your machine; for example, if your first hard drive is a SCSI drive, you use `/dev/sda`. You can also use the `fdisk/mbr` command from DOS/Windows.

When my system boots up, I see a message that says I have unknown PCI hardware. What does this mean?

The `unknown PCI device` error can occur for several reasons. The first and most harmless one is that PCI isn't responding to Linux's queries in a way it understands, but Linux is able to keep going. The more common occurrence is that the system hangs on, querying PCI bus cards, and cannot get any further.

Because this is a hardware problem in the kernel, Red Hat cannot do much except point you to the maintainer of that section of the kernel. That person might be able to let you know what is going on and might want to look at what hardware you do have in your system so that he or she can better handle it in the future. You can reach the maintainer at the following address:

```
linux-pcisupport@cck.uni-kl.de
```

Include the following information for your exact hardware description:

```
/proc/pci
```

Try to find out which device is unknown. It may be your main board chipset, your PCI-CPU bridge, or your PCI-ISA bridge. If you can't find the actual information in your hardware booklet, try to read the references of the chip on the board.

While I'm booting, the machine seems to hang when Linux gets to sendmail (or some other network program). What is happening, and what should I do?

If, after the installation, the machine seems to hang when it reaches certain processes such as sendmail, apache, or SMB, you probably have a network problem. The most common cause is that Linux cannot look up the name of the machine you have called the box (if you set up networking to have a machine name). The machine is currently paused waiting for the network timeout of DNS lookups and will eventually bring up the login prompt. When you get the prompt, log in as root, and check the usual culprits for a problem.

If you are working directly on a network with a DNS server, make sure that the `/etc/resolv.conf` file has the correct values for your machine's DNS server. Use the following command to check:

```
more /etc/resolve.conf
```

After that, see whether you can ping the name servers using the `ping` command, like the following:

```
ping ns.you-dns-srv.com
```

If you are using Linux on a network without a DNS server (or if this box is going to be the DNS server), you need to edit the `/etc/hosts` file to include the hostname and IP address so that the lookups occur correctly. The format of the `/etc/hosts` file is

```
127.0.0.1          localhost localhost.localdomain
192.168.200.1               mymachine mymachine.mynetwork.net
```

where the sample machine is called `mymachine`.

How many times has my machine been rebooted?

You can use the following command to see how many times your machine has been rebooted:

```
last reboot
```

You can also use the commands `w` and `uptime` to see how long your box has been up. The `w` command shows the users' login times and the `uptime` command shows how long the system has been up and running.

CHAPTER 11

Managing User Accounts

In this chapter

by Steve Burnett

WORKING WITH USERS

As the system's administrator, you're in charge of managing users. Managing involves adding users so that they can log in to the system, setting user privileges, creating and assigning home directories for users, assigning users to groups, and deleting users when necessary. In this chapter, you will learn about the various tools and techniques that enable you to perform user account management.

Every user should have a unique login name. Login names make it possible to identify each user and avoid the problem of one user deleting another's files.

Each user also must have a password. About the only exception to having a password is a case in which only one user is on a system, and the system has absolutely no connection by modem or network to any other computer. Even then, a password for every account is strongly encouraged.

→ See "Dealing with Password Security," p277

When a person has no real reason to have access to your system, you must make sure that individual can't log in. You should remove that person's login name, along with any files that your remaining users no longer need.

ADDING A USER

When you add a user to your system, the result is an entry for the user in the password file, `/etc/passwd`. That entry has the following form:

```
login_name:encrypted_password:user_ID:group_ID:user_information:
➥login_directory:login_shell
```

In this syntax, fields are separated by colons. Table 11.1 lists the fields.

TABLE 11.1 FIELDS IN AN /etc/passwd FILE ENTRY

Field	Description
login_name	The name used to log in.
encrypted_password	The password required to authenticate the user; the password is the primary line of defense against security violations.
user_ID	A unique number the operating system uses to identify the user.
group_ID	A unique number or name used to identify the primary group for this user. If a user is a member of multiple groups, he or she can switch group membership to another group if permitted by the administrator.
user_information	A description of the user, such as the user's name or title.
login_directory	The user's home directory (where the user ends up after logging in).
login_shell	The shell used by a user when logging in (for example, `/bin/bash` if using the bash shell).

If you are using the Shadow Security Suite, your /etc/passwd file might look like this instead:

```
root:x:0:0:root:/root:/bin/bash
bin:x:1:1:bin:/bin:
daemon:x:2:2:daemon:/sbin:
adm:x:3:4:adm:/var/adm:
lp:x:4:7:lp:/var/spool/lpd:
```

Notice that the second field (between the first and second colons) is x on every line. Shadow removes the actual passwords from the /etc/passwd file and hides them in a separate, less accessible file.

→ See "Shadow Passwords: What Good Are They?" p. 289

The adduser command enables you to add a user to your Linux system. You invoke the command with the name of the user that you want to add. The following section provides greater detail on this subject.

Using the adduser Command

When you add a user, you simply use the adduser command and provide the name of the user you want to add, as shown in Listing 11.1.

Listing 11.1 An Example of an adduser Session

```
# ./adduser jschmoe
#
```

The adduser command copies the files whose names begin with . (dot) from the /etc/skel directory into the user's home directory. The /etc/skel directory should contain template files you want every user to have. These files typically include "personal" configuration files, such as .profile, .cshrc, and .login for shell configuration; .mailrc for email setup; .emacs for your users using Emacs as an editor; and so on.

The adduser command is a Bourne shell script located in the /usr/sbin directory. You can customize this script if you need to perform some additional actions when you create a user account. A common modification is to have adduser prompt for the user's full name rather than hard-code a default username into the password file. If you don't change the script so that it asks for the user's name, you have to change it by hand by using the chfn command, as shown here:

```
# chfn jschmoe
Changing finger information for jschmoe.
Name [RHS Linux User]: Joseph A. Schmoe
Office []:
Office Phone []:
Home Phone []:

Finger information changed.
#
```

Tip #70 from *Steve*

> The `adduser` command doesn't set the password for the account. You have to do that by using the `passwd` command.

Setting User Passwords

You set a user's password by using the `passwd` command. You should set a password for each user added to the system; each user can then change his or her password when logging in. The following steps outline the basic procedure for using `passwd`:

1. Type the command and login name (for example, `passwd jschmoe`), and press Return.
2. At the `New password:` prompt, enter the password (you don't see the password onscreen).
3. You're prompted to type the password again. Enter the password again:

   `New password (again):` *`newpassword`*

   The password is encrypted and put into the `/etc/passwd` file.

It's important that you take the time to make sure your password follows these rules:

- Passwords should be at least six (preferably eight) characters long.
- Passwords should contain both upper- and lowercase letters as well as punctuation symbols and numerals.

→ See "Dealing with Password Security," p. 277

When you're adding a number of users, you might be tempted to enter short, easy passwords. Don't fall for this trap. Good passwords are your first line of defense against intruders. Be sure to tell your users why you've assigned a particular type of password. Further, it's a good idea to change passwords regularly, but remember to educate system users about the choice of good passwords.

After a uscr is assigned a password, the file entry looks something like this:

```
jschmoe:Zoie.89&^0gW*:123:21:Joseph A. Schmoe:/users/jschmoe:/bin/bash
```

The second field is the password—not as it was typed, but in encrypted form.

Note

> Users occasionally forget their passwords. You cannot tell users their own passwords. You can delete a forgotten password, however, by editing the `/etc/passwd` file and deleting the second field in the user's file entry. You can then set the user's new password by using the `passwd` command. You should establish a procedure for dealing with such a situation and let your users know about it.

REMOVING A USER

There are several different degrees of user removal. Removing a user from the system doesn't have to be a final, irrevocable act. The following are some possibilities:

- **Remove only the capability to log in**—This type of removal is useful if the user is away for a while and needs to be reinstated some time in the future. The user's directory, files, and group information are kept intact. You can edit the password file (`/etc/passwd`) and put an `*` in the second field of the user's entry like this:

  ```
  jschmoe:*:123:21:Joseph A. Schmoe:/users/jschmoe:/bin/bash
  ```

  If you are running the Shadow Suite, editing the `/etc/passwd` file doesn't matter; you need to edit `/etc/shadow` instead.

- **Remove the user from the password file, but keep the user's files on the system**—This type of removal is useful if the files are used by others or if a new person will be taking over the duties of the old user. You can delete the user's entry from the password file or files by using an editor or the `userdel` *login_name* command. You can then change the ownership and location of the deleted user's files by using the `chown` and `mv` commands.

- **Remove the user from the password file, and remove all files the user owns**—This type of removal is the ultimate and complete form of deleting a user. You must delete the user's entry from the password file and delete the user's files from the system. You can do so by using the `find` command, as follows:

  ```
  find user's-home-directory -exec rm {} \;
  ```

  Then you can remove the directory by using `rmdir` *`user's-home-directory`* and remove the appropriate entry from the password file or files.

Note If you use other configuration files at your site, such as email alias files, you also have to remove the user from those files.

WORKING WITH GROUPS

Each user is a member of a group. You can give different types of groups different capabilities or privileges. For example, it's reasonable to give a group of users who use the system to analyze the company's sales data access to a different set of files than a user group whose main function is researching new products.

The password file contains information for a single user. Information about groups is kept in the `/etc/group` file. The following is a sample entry:

```
sales::21:tuser, jschmoe, staplr
```

In this example, the group name is `sales`, the group ID (GID) number is `21`, and the members are `tuser`, `jschmoe`, and `staplr`. Files and directories have permissions associated with them for the owner, group, and others. A user can be a member of more than one group, and you can change group memberships.

Adding a Group

You create a new group by editing the `/etc/group` file directly and entering the new group information.

Tip #71 from *Steve*

> Each group in the `/etc/group` file has a unique group ID number associated with it. Linux pays attention to the number that you assign, not to the name. Hence, if you assign two groups with the same number, they are treated as though they're the same group.

Deleting a Group

You delete a group by editing the `/etc/group` file and removing the entry for the specific group that you want to delete. Also, you should reassign all files that have that associated GID to a different group. An easy way to reassign them is to use the `find` command, as in this example:

```
find / -gid group-id find users-home-directory -exec chgrp newgroup {} \;
```

Managing Home Directories

You should give some thought to grouping your home directories logically if you plan to have many users on your system. In general, you should try to place all the home directories on a given machine under one single top-level directory. That way, you can group them according to whatever arrangement makes sense for your needs.

→ See "Mounting and Unmounting File Systems," p. 444

For example, you can specify that `/home` be the top-level directory for user directories. Under `/home`, you can group users by department. The sales users would have accounts under `/home/sales`, development under `/home/develop`, and so on. Your user home directories would then fall under these directories or under another set if additional grouping is needed. Because user directories can use a lot of disk space, you could consider placing logical groups of users on different physical file systems. As you need additional space, you can simply create an additional category for home directories and mount it on a file system as a mount point under `/home`.

WEB-BASED ADMINISTRATION

The Red Hat distribution of Linux includes Jacques Gelinas's system administration tool called Linuxconf. Linuxconf enables you to manage many system administration tasks, including working with users and groups. In addition to the familiar character-line and X Window System access, Linuxconf supports administration of the Linux system over the World Wide Web. If the option Linuxconf HTML Access Control is selected in Linuxconf, you can enter the URL `http://<hostname>:98/` to display the top Web page of the Linuxconf tool.

Note

To do anything to the system, you need to go to one of the subpages. You then are prompted for the root password, so have it ready.

PROJECT: USING USERCONF

Although the command line is powerful, especially because you can create shell scripts to automate tasks at the command line, graphics-based tools are sometimes nice to have as well. One excellent tool that provides graphic access to user configuration management is Userconf. In this exercise, you're going to do the following:

- Add a new imaginary user named Susan Jones. (If you already have a Susan Jones account on your Linux system, make up someone else, of course.)
- Change her group assignment.
- Delete her account.

ADDING A USER WITH USERCONF

To begin adding a user, assume you're using a default installation of Red Hat Linux. Follow these steps:

1. In an xterm session, use `su` to change to root, and then enter the following to start `userconf`, as shown in Figure 11.1:

   ```
   userconf &
   ```

2. To add a new user, click the User Accounts button. The resulting window displays the currently defined users (see Figure 11.2).
3. Click the Add button to display the User Account Creation window shown in Figure 11.3.
4. Enter the following list of values in the fields:
   - Login name: `sjones`
   - Full name: `Susan Jones`

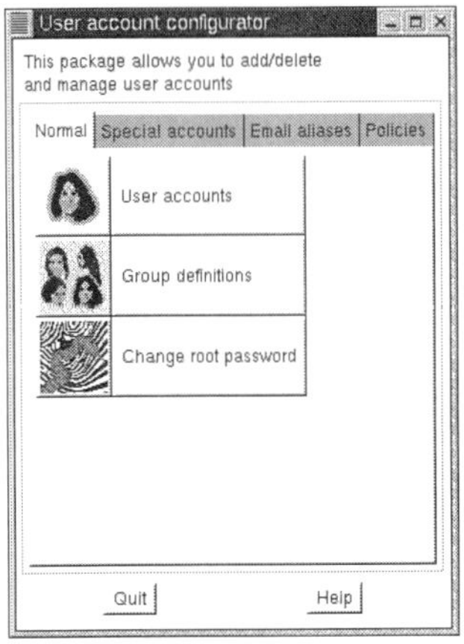

Figure 11.1 The Userconf window provides graphic control of user accounts and group memberships.

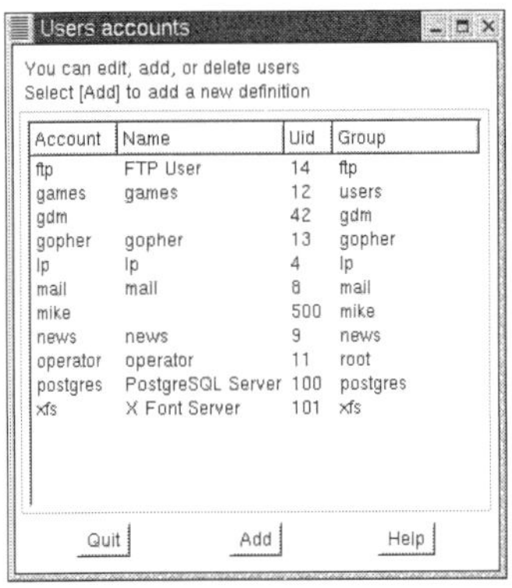

Figure 11.2 The Users Accounts window displays current users and their group memberships.

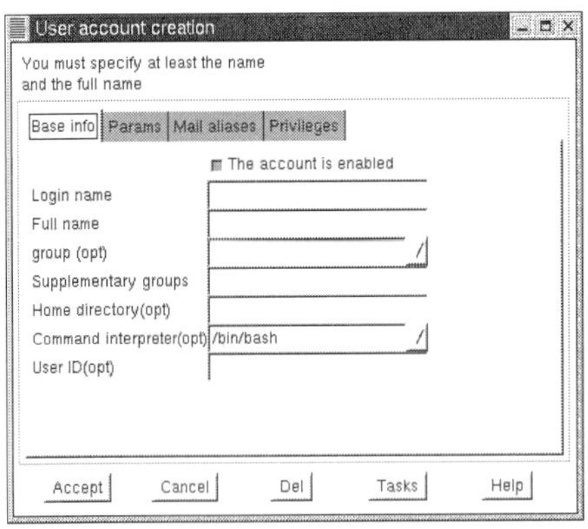

Figure 11.3 On the User Account Creation window, you can define user account parameters.

5. For the group value, click the down-arrow to the right of the group field and choose Users.
6. Click the Accept button to accept the defined values. The Changing Password window then appears (see Figure 11.4).

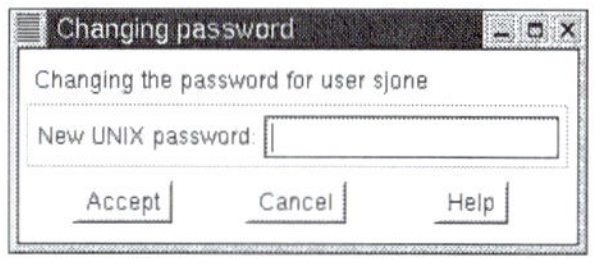

Figure 11.4
The Changing Password window appears when a new user is created in userconf.

7. In this window, enter a password. Remember that `userconf` checks the password for security, so choose a good password. The Changing Password window appears a second time for you to retype the password. Then the Users Accounts window reappears with the new user account (see Figure 11.5).

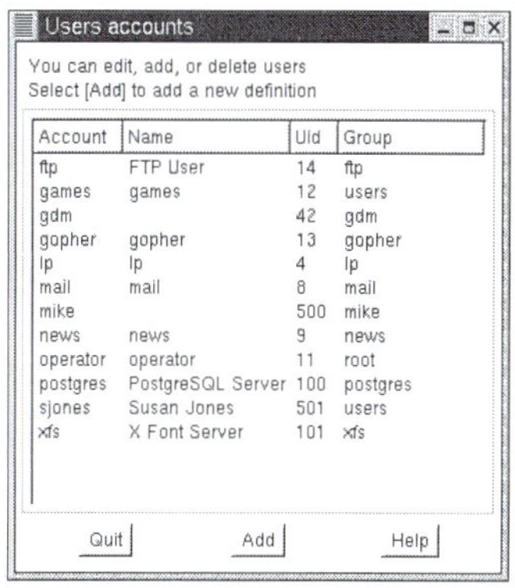

Figure 11.5
The Users Accounts window is updated with a newly created account.

8. Click the Quit button to close the window, and you're done.

ADDING A USER WITH USERCONF

For the next task, assume that Susan is now a member of the system administrators' team for your network. She needs to have root group access, so you must change her group assignment from users to root. To do so, follow these steps:

1. On the Userconf window, click the User Accounts button to display the Users Accounts window (refer to Figure 11.5).
2. Click the line for Susan Jones's account to display the User Information window shown in Figure 11.6.
3. Click the down-arrow to the right of the Group field and select root from the drop-down list box. The group name `root` appears in the field.
4. Click the Accept button, and you're done.

DELETING A USER WITH USERCONF

For the third task of this project, assume that Susan is leaving the network and no longer needs a user account on the network (especially with root privileges). To delete her user account, follow these steps:

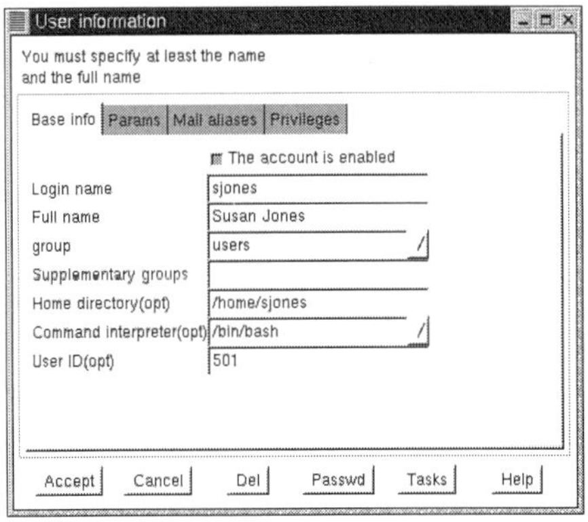

Figure 11.6 On the User Information window, you can change information for a selected user.

1. On the Userconf window, click the User Accounts button to display the Users Accounts window (refer to Figure 11.5).
2. Click the line for Susan Jones's account to display the User Information window (refer to Figure 11.6).
3. Click the Del button. A dialog appears warning you that you're about to erase files and directories (see Figure 11.7).

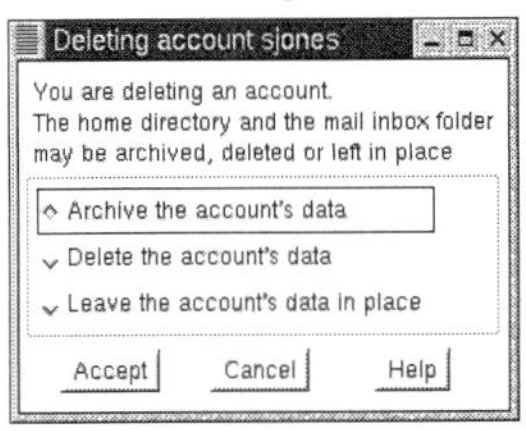

Figure 11.7 The Deleting account prompt gives you options for disposing of a user's files.

4. Accept the default option of archiving the account's files, and you're done.

CHAPTER 12

Backing Up Data

In this chapter

by Jack Tackett, Jr.

CONSIDERING BACKUP ISSUES

Various kinds of problems can result in loss of data: files get accidentally removed, hardware fails, and important information stored in files is no longer available. Users should feel confident that, in such cases, they can access a timely backup of the "lost" files.

Your company's future—and your future with your company—may depend on making those backup files available. At such times, you and others will be thankful that you've taken the time and effort to copy files to some sort of storage media according to a regular, rigorous, and well-documented schedule. Backing up files isn't very glamorous, but no administrator can ignore the process.

The following are several issues to consider when backing up a system:

- **Full or incremental backups**—A *full backup* (sometimes called a *complete backup*) copies every file. Is it necessary to do that every day? A full backup usually requires a good deal of time and enough media to hold all the files on the system. An *incremental backup* copies the files that have changed since the last full backup.
- **File systems to back up**—Naturally, active file systems must be backed up regularly. Others can be backed up less frequently. Make sure that you have current copies of all the file systems.
- **Types of backup media**—Depending on the devices on your system, you might be able to use nine-track tape, 1/4-inch cartridge tape, 4mm or 8mm DAT tapes, or floppy disks. Each has advantages over the other in terms of sheer bulk, storage capacity, and cost for devices and media. Choose the backup medium to fit your budget, remembering that the least-expensive medium may be the most time-consuming.
- **Effect of backups on users**—Performing a backup operation increases the load on a system. Will that be an unreasonable burden on users? Also, files that are changed during the backup process might not be backed up, which can merely be an inconvenience or a very important consideration if you're backing up an active database. Should you perform backups when the system is quiet?
- **Commands to use for backups**—Some relatively simple, time-honored commands are available for creating backups, such as `tar` and `cpio`. Are they sufficient? Sometimes not, so we will explore more options in the section "Using `taper`."
- **Documentation of the backed-up files**—You must label all backed-up material so that you can use it to recover files when necessary. Some procedures and commands allow you to prepare a table of contents or list of the material that has been backed up.

From an administrator's point of view, the file system should be backed up according to some automated process with as little operator intervention as possible. It should also be done when the system is relatively quiet so that the backup is as complete as possible. This consideration must be balanced with convenience and costs. Should an operator or administrator have to stay until midnight on Friday to perform a full backup? Is it worth

$2,000 for a DAT tape drive so that the entire system can be backed up automatically at 3 a.m. with no operator intervention?

Consider the alternatives, determine the true costs, and make a decision or recommend a course of action. Restoring well-managed backup information is generally a lot cheaper and always easier than re-creating it or doing without it.

CONSIDERING BACKUP TIPS

The purpose of performing backups is being able to restore individual files or complete file systems as rapidly and easily as possible. Whatever you do about backups should be focused on that central purpose.

Set up a backup plan. Include the files to be backed up, how often they'll be backed up, and how the files are to be restored. Let all users know the backup schedule and how they can request restoration of files. Be sure to stick with the plan.

Be sure to verify your backups. This step could include reading a table of contents from the backup medium after it's stored or restoring an arbitrarily chosen file from the medium. Remember that the backup medium—disk or tape— possibly can have flaws.

Make backups so files can be restored anywhere on the file system or on another computer system. Use backup or archive utilities that create archives that can be used on other Linux or UNIX computer systems.

Be sure to label all media—tapes, disks, whatever—used in a backup. If you have to use multiple tapes or disks, make sure that they're numbered sequentially and dated. You must be able to find the file or files you need.

Plan for a disaster. Make copies of the files on your system so that the entire system can be restored in a reasonable amount of time. Store copies of backup tapes or disks offsite. The preceding sentence is very important! You should store at least one copy of your backup material offsite, away from your computers. If a disaster (such as a fire) wipes out your system, it will more than likely also destroy your nearby backups. Many businesses rent a safe deposit box to store their tapes and disks in. You should store a complete hardware list in the same offsite location so that you can reorder identical parts should a disaster occur.

Plan to re-evaluate your backup procedures periodically to make sure that they're meeting your needs.

Several tools are available to help automate your backup procedure. Check out the Linux archives on `sunsite.unc.edu` for more information. Also, Linux supports the ftape extensions. ftape lets you perform backups to QIC-80 magnetic tape units that run off a floppy controller on your system. For detailed information, refer to the "ftape How-To."

Tip #72 from
Jack

> **Linux can take advantage of several commercial backup programs too such as BRU and systems from Legatto. See the Commercial-HOW-TO for more information. For information on BRU see:**
>
> `http://www.estinc.com/`
>
> **For information on Legatto systems, see:**
>
> `http://wwwm.legato.com/`

PLANNING A BACKUP SCHEDULE

You must come up with a backup schedule that meets your needs and makes it possible to restore recent copies of files. After you decide on a schedule, stick to it.

The ideal situation is to be able to restore any file at any time. Taken to an extreme, that's not possible, but you should be able to restore files on a daily basis. To do so, you use a combination of complete and incremental backups.

Incremental backups can be at different levels—incremental to the last complete backup or incremental to the last incremental backup. You might think of backups as occurring at different levels:

Level 0: Full backup

Level 1: Incremental to the last complete backup

Level 2: Incremental to the last level 1 backup

The following are some sample backup schedules:

- Full backup one day, incremental other days.

Day 1	Level 0, complete backup
Day 2	Level 1, incremental backup
Day 3	Level 1, incremental backup
Day 4	Level 1, incremental backup
Day 5	Level 1, incremental backup

  If you create and save an index of each backup, you should need only one day's backup to restore an individual file and only two days' backups (that of day 1 and another day) to completely restore the system. For example, if your system failed on day 4, before the Day 4 Level 1 incremental, then to fully recover you need to install the Day 1 Level 0 complete backup and the Day 3 level 1 incremental to fully recover.

- Full backup once a month, weekly incremental, and daily incremental. (This example is built around Tuesday, but you can choose any day of the week.)

First Tuesday	Level 0, complete backup
Any other Tuesday	Level 1, incremental backup
Any other day	Level 2, incremental backup

To restore an individual file under this schedule, you might need the complete backup if the file wasn't changed during the month, the level 1 backup if the file was changed the previous week but not this week, or the level 2 backup if the file was changed this week. This schedule is more complex than the previous example, but backups take less time per day.

You also might want to consider keeping backup files for an extended period, in case you need to restore an older version. A common schedule is to keep one weekly copy of a full backup for four weeks. For periods of longer than four weeks, you might consider keeping a biweekly backup for about three months.

Tip #73 from *Jack*

Don't back up unnecessary files such as `/tmp` and `/proc`. `/tmp` is temporary space and files there are not needed by definition. Also `/proc` is a 'make-believe' file system used by Linux to keep information on various system functions, like type of cpu and memory in use. The information on these file systems is transitory and worthless if restored—so why back them up to begin with? Excluding these directories, and directories like them, from your backup file lists speeds up backup and restore times.

Performing Backups and Restoring Files

Several different utilities are available for backing up and restoring files in a Linux system. Some are simple and straightforward; others are more complex. The simple methods have their limitations, however. You should choose the one that meets your needs.

Because backing up and restoring files are very important, a number of available software systems are dedicated to these tasks. The following sections present four of them:

- tar is a tape archive utility available on every Linux or UNIX system. This easy-to-use Linux version can use several tapes or disks.
- dump is an archive utility that can perform various levels of backups from a full backup to various levels of incrementals.
- taper is an archive utility with a text-based interface.
- cpio is a general-purpose utility for copying files available on every UNIX system. cpio is easy to use and more robust than tar, and it can use several tapes or disks.

After selecting a program, you must select a medium. Hard drives (files) are the easiest to use but present a high risk. Tapes provide better risk management but are slower to access and slower to archive data. Table 12.1 provides an overview of the various archive media.

TABLE 12.1 BACKUP MEDIA PROS AND CONS

Medium	Access	Speed	Reliability	Comments
Hard Drives	Random	Fast	Medium	Crashing hard drives and corrupt file systems are the primary reason for making backups. However, hard drives can be utilized for backups on RAID and non-RAID systems, but the disadvantages are 1) they are nonportable 2) they cost more to replace than their tape media counterparts
Floppies	Random	Slow	Good	Floppies are insecure and cannot hold large amounts of data.
Tape	Sequential	Fast	High	Tape is the staple of the industry.
Removable Media	Random	Fast	Good	Zip, Jazz, and other removable media are now supported under Linux and provide excellent archive media, though they are more expensive than tape.
CD-R	Random	Fast	High	CD-Rs can be used only once, and not all drives are currently supported.

Table 12.1 Backup Media Pros and Cons

Medium	Access	Speed	Reliability	Comments
CD_RW	Random	Fast	High	CD-RWs are expensive and can be hard to configure under Linux.

Using tar

The UNIX tar utility was originally designed to create a tape archive (to copy files or directories to tape and then to extract or restore files from the archive). You can use it to copy to any device. It has the following advantages:

- It's simple to use.
- It's reliable and stable.
- Archives can be read on virtually any Linux or UNIX system.

It also has a few disadvantages:

- For some versions of tar, the archive must reside on one disk or tape, which means that if a portion of the medium fails—from a bad sector on a disk or bad block on a tape, for example—the entire backup may be lost.
- tar can't back up special files, such as device files.
- On its own, tar can perform only complete backups. If you want to create incremental backups, you have to do a little shell programming.

→ See "Working with Shell Scripts," p. 348

Table 12.2 lists some options that are commonly used with tar. You can use many other command parameters with tar; refer to the man page for a complete list.

Table 12.2 Common Options for tar

Option	Description
`c`	Creates an archive
`x`	Extracts or restores files from the archive that's on the default device or on the device specified by the `f` option
`f` *`name`*	Creates the archive or reads the archive from *`name`*, where *`name`* is a filename or a device specified in `/dev`, such as `/dev/rmt0`
`Z`	Compresses or decompresses the tar archive
`z`	Compresses or decompresses the tar archive with gzip
`M`	Creates a multivolume tar backup

TABLE 12.2 COMMON OPTIONS FOR TAR

Option	Description
t	Creates an index of all files stored in an archive and lists on stdout
v	Uses verbose mode

Consider some examples of the use of tar in backing up and restoring files. The following command copies the directory /home to the floppy drive /dev/fd0:

```
tar -cf /dev/fd0 /home
```

In this case, the f option specifies that the archive is created on the floppy drive device /dev/fd0.

The following command also archives the directory /home:

```
tar -cvfzM /dev/fd0 /home ¦ tee homeindex
```

The v option indicates verbose mode, the z option indicates that the archive should be compressed to save space, and the M option tells tar to create a multivolume backup. When one floppy disk is full, tar prompts you for another. A list of the copied files is directed to homeindex. It's a good idea to look at that file to see what was copied.

The find command is useful for locating files that have been modified within a certain time period so that they can be scheduled for incremental backups. The following example uses the command find to create a list of all files that have been modified in the last day:

```
find /home -mtime -1 -type f -print > bkuplst tar cvfzM /dev/fd0
`cat bkuplst` ¦ tee homeindex
```

To use the list as input to the tar command, place the command cat bkuplst in back quotes (backward single quotation marks, also known as *grave accents*—cat bkuplst`). They tell the shell to execute the command as a subshell and place the output from the command on the command line in the location of the original back-quoted command.

The following command restores the /home/dave/notes.txt file from the device /dev/fd0 (note that you have to give the complete filename to restore it):

```
tar -xv /usr2/dave/notes.txt
```

Tip #74 from Jack

You can automate any of these commands by putting them in root's crontab file. For example, you could put the following entry in the root's crontab file to perform a backup of /home every day at 1:30 a.m.:

```
30 01 * * * tar cvfz /def/fd0 /home > homeindex
```

If you need to do more complicated backups, you can create shell scripts to control your backups. These shell scripts can also be run via cron.

→ See "Scheduling Commands with cron and crontab," p. 373

You also can use the `tar` command to create archive files in the Linux file system rather than write to a backup device. This way, you can archive a group of files along with their directory structure in one file. To do so, simply give a filename as the argument to the `f` option instead of a device name. The following is an example of archiving a directory and its subdirectories with the `tar` command:

```
tar cvf /home/backup.tar /home/dave
```

This command creates the file `/home/backup.tar`, which contains a backup of the `/home/dave` directory and all files and subdirectories below `/home/dave`.

The `tar` command by itself doesn't perform any file compression. To compress the resulting `tar` file, either specify the `z` option with the `tar` command or use a compression program, such as gzip, on the final `tar` file.

Tip #75 from
Jack

If you do compress the `tar` file, then you can use the `zcat` command as follows to get a listing of files stored in the archive:

```
Zcat backup.tar.Z ¦ tar -tf - ¦ more
```

When you use the `tar` command to make archive files, it's usually a good idea to try to make the top-level entry in the `tar` file a directory. This way, when you extract the `tar` file, all the files in it are placed under a central directory in your current working directory. Otherwise, you could end up with hundreds of files in your directory if you extract a `tar` file in the wrong place.

Suppose that below your current directory is a directory named `data`, which contains several hundred files. You can create a `tar` file of this directory in two basic ways. You can change directories to the `data` directory and create the `tar` file from there, as in this example:

```
$ pwd
/home/dave
$ cd data
$ pwd
/home/dave/data
$ tar cvf ../data.tar *
```

This example creates a `tar` file in `/home/dave` that contains just the contents of `data` without containing an entry for the directory. When you extract this `tar` file, you don't create a directory to put the files in; you just get several hundred files in your current directory.

Another way to create the `tar` file is to start from `data`'s parent directory and specify the directory name as the thing to archive. The command sequence is as follows:

```
$ pwd
/home/dave
$ tar cvf data.tar data
```

This example also creates an archive of the `data` directory, but it puts the directory entry as the first thing in the archive. This way, when the `tar` file is extracted, the first thing that's created is the directory `data`, and all the files in `data` are placed in the `data` subdirectory.

Note

If you want to create a `tar` file of all the files in the directory, specifying a different location for the `tar` file (other than the current directory) is a good idea. That way, if you try to archive all the files in the current directory, tar doesn't get confused and try to add its `tar` file recursively to the tar that it's creating.

USING CPIO

cpio is a general-purpose command utility for copying file archives. You can use it to create backups by using the `-o` option or to restore files by using the `-i` option. It takes its input from standard input and sends its output to standard output.

The advantages of cpio include the following:

- It can back up any set of files.
- It can back up special files.
- It stores information more efficiently than tar.
- It skips bad sectors or bad blocks when restoring data.
- Its backups can be restored on almost any Linux or UNIX system.

Some people find cpio's syntax to be a bit more confusing than tar's syntax. Also, to perform incremental backups, you have to do some shell programming.

→ See "Working with Shell Scripts," p. 348

Table 12.3 lists the commonly used options for cpio. See cpio's man page for a complete description of the options you can use with this command.

TABLE 12.3 COMMON OPTIONS FOR CPIO

Option	Description
`-o`	Copy out. Creates an archive on standard out.
`-B`	Blocks input or output at 5,120 bytes per record; useful for efficient storage on magnetic tape.
`-i`	Copy in. Extracts files from standard input. This option is typically used when the standard input is the result of a copy out action of another `cpio` command.
`-t`	Creates a table of contents of the input.

The following list provides some examples of using the `cpio` command to back up and restore files:

- The following command copies the files in the directory `/home` to the device `/dev/fd0`:

  ```
  ls /home ¦ cpio -o > /dev/fd0
  ```

- The following command extracts the files on the device `/dev/fd0` and creates an index in the `bkup.indx` file:

  ```
  cpio -it < /dev/fd0 > bkup.indx
  ```

- The following example uses the `find` command to create a list of all files in `/home` that have been modified in the last day:

  ```
  find /home -mtime 1 -type f -print ¦ cpio -oB > /dev/fd0
  ```

  The output of that command is piped to cpio, which creates an archive on `/dev/fd0`, where the data is stored at 5,120 bytes per record.

- The following command restores the file `/home/dave/notes.txt` from the device `/dev/fd0`:

  ```
  echo ''/home/dave/notes.txt'' ¦ cpio -i < /dev/fd0
  ```

Note

You must give the complete filename to restore a file with cpio.

Tip #76 from *Jack*

You can automate any of these commands by putting them in root's `crontab` file. For example, you could put the following entry in the root's `cron` file to perform a daily backup of `/home` at 1:30 a.m.:

```
30 01 * * * ls /home ¦ cpio -o > /dev/fd0
```

If you need to do more complicated backups, you can create shell scripts to control your backups. You also can run these shell scripts via cron.

USING TAPER

taper is an open source program created by Yusuf Nagree. The program comes with a text-based GUI for backing up and restoring files. Figure 12.1 shows the main menu screen for taper.

taper is a high-end program that makes use of other low-level programs for accessing the tape device. Thus, you must have a device driver or other program, such as ftape, available to transfer information to the tape.

taper is not installed by default, so you need to install the program. An RPM package is available for Red Hat and Caldera (`taper-6.9-2.i386.rpm`); you can install it by using the `rpm -i` command. You can download the code from `http://www.omen.net.au/~yusuf` and then build the program for Debian. To install a Debian package use `dpgk -i` *<package-name>*.

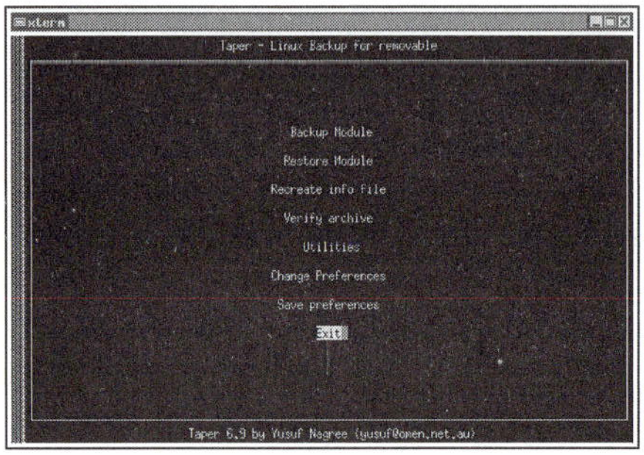

Figure 12.1 Using taper's interface makes backing up and restoring much easier.

> **Caution**
>
> taper can fail to work if the correct libraries or ncurses program is not installed on your system. Also, you must have a driver for your archive device so that `taper` can work properly. Look at `/usr/doc/Taper-6.9/TAPER.txt` and `FAQ.txt` for more information.

To run the program, use the following command line to display the GUI shown in Figure 12.1:

```
taper -T <device>
```

Here, *device* can be any of the following:

`z`	Floppy tape drive using zftape
`f`	Floppy tape drive using ftape
`r -b /dev/<device>`	A removable device, such as a Zip disk or Jazz drive
`s`	A SCSI tape drive

If you want to use a file instead of a device, use the following form of the command:

```
taper -f <filename>
```

To get a full help listing, use the following command:

```
taper -?
```

USING DUMP

If you use only the ext2fs or minix file systems, you can use the dump program to back up your system and the restore program to retrieve backup files. dump works like tar, but it allows easier management of backups, as detailed in the section "Planning a Backup Schedule" earlier in this chapter. The command line for dump is as follows:

```
/sbin/dump [0123456789BbhfusTdWn [ argument ...]] filesystem ¦ directory
```

The numbers indicate the backup level, with 0 indicating a full backup and 9 (the default value) indicating the highest incremental backup. You can specify a file or a tape device just as you can with tar. Thus, to do a full backup to a file of the /usr directory, you would use the following command:

```
/sbin/dump 0uf /backup_usr.dmp /usr
```

The f flag indicates that dump should create a dump file named /backup_usr.dmp in the root directory containing an archive of /usr. The u flag instructs dump to update the file /etc/dumpdates. Table 12.4 provides information on each flag value.

Table 12.4 Common Flags for Creating Archives

Flag	Description
0 to 9	Indicates the backup level— 0=full, 9=highest incremental. A level number above 0, incremental backup, tells dump to copy all files new or modified since the last dump of the lower level.
f	Writes the backup to file; file may be a special device file like /dev/tape, /dev/hda1 (a disk drive), an ordinary file, or "-" (the standard output).
u	Updates the file /etc/dumpdates after a successful dump.
W	Tells the operator what file systems need to be dumped.
w	Prints only those file systems that need to be dumped.

Note

dump is not installed by default by any of the distributions included on the CDs. To install dump for Red Hat or Caldera, use the following rpm command:

```
rpm -ivh dump-0.3-14.i386.rpm
```

To install it for Debian use, enter the following command:

```
dpkg -i <filename>.i386.deb
```

dump uses the file /etc/dumpdates to store information about file systems. The following listing indicates that a level 0 dump occurred on the /hda1 file system on June 20, 1999 at 8:31 p.m.:

```
[root@ns RPMS]# more /etc/dumpdates
/dev/hda 1       0 Sun Jun 20 20:31:09 1999
```

You use the restorecommand to restore files from the dump. You can restore entire file systems by using `dump/restore`. `restore` allows an interactive mode (`-i`), so you can select exactly what files to restore from the `dump` archive. To interactively restore the `dump` file created previously, you would use the following command:

```
/sbin/restore -if /backup_usr.dmp
```

In this case, restore would interactively prompt you for information. If necessary, you can request help by using the `help` command, as shown in the following output:

```
/sbin/restore -if /backup_usr.dmp
restore > help
Available commands are:
        ls [arg] - list directory
        cd arg - change directory
        pwd - print current directory
        add [arg] - add Çarg' to list of files to be extracted
        delete [arg] - delete Çarg' from list of files to be extracted
        extract - extract requested files
        setmodes - set modes of requested directories
        quit - immediately exit program
        what - list dump header information
        verbose - toggle verbose flag (useful with ``#180;ls'')
        help or '?' - print this list
If no´arg' is supplied, the current directory is used
restore >
```

You need to follow this procedure to restore files interactively:

1. Add files to be extracted by using the `add` command.
2. Provide the tape (or filename) to the program.
3. Extract the files you have added.

See the man pages for detailed information on both commands.

CASE STUDY: COPYING FILES

Backing up files to an external media is one procedure to insure data safety, but sometime you might need to ensure that backup systems used for disaster recovery have the needed files so you can recover from a disaster in a timely manner. Transporting tapes or removable drives takes time. To ensure the proper distribution of essential files, you can use ftp to copy the files, but this is cumbersome and error prone. You can use the program rdist and cron to automate this process, or if the files needed are for your Web site then you can use wget.

→ See "Scheduling Commands with cron and crontab," p. 373

rdist uses a configuration file, shown in Listing 12.1, to specify which files and directory trees to copy and where to copy them. You can specify multiple machines so that you can distribute an entire directory tree to various servers anywhere on the net.

Tip #77 from *Jack*

If you are distributing files across an unsecure link, you should investigate secure copy programs such as scp from datafellows. See `http://www.datafellows.com` for more information.

Listing 12.1 Sample rdist Configuration File

```
#
# rdist configuration file to sync authdb files on other web servers
#
#
# list of hosts to replicate files to
#
HOSTS = (root@machine1 root@machine2)
#
# list of files and/or directories to replicate
#
FILES = (/opt/netscape/nse-home/authdb )
#
# and now the mapping(s)
#
# copy files that are new and remove any extraneous files
#
(${FILES}) -> (${HOSTS})
    install /opt/netscape/nse-home/authdb;
    notify root@mmail;
```

Any line beginning with a `#` is a comment and ignored by rdist. The `HOSTS` directive specifies which machines to copy the files to and also which user account to use. The `FILES` directive specifies which files to copy. You can specify an entire directory tree or individual files by seperating each entry with spaces. The line `(${FILES}) -> (${HOSTS})` tells rdist to copy the items specified in `FILES` to the machines specified in `HOSTS` and then to perform the following actions on those files. The `install` keyword tells rdist where on the remote machines to place the files. Next rdist sends an email notification to the specified email account. Notice that each command terminates with a semicolon.

After you create the `config` file, you invoke rdist by using the following syntax:

```
rdist -f configfile
```

The final configuration to make is to create a `.rhosts` file on the remote machines in the home directory of the specified users (root in the above sample listing) and place the a plus sign (+) and appropriate username in the file, such as the following:

```
+root
```

Using wget

wget provides an even simpler mechanism to copy Web-based files from remote machines. Many popular Web sites do not run on a single system; instead, the same content is served from various Web servers around the country. The sites use techniques such as DNS round robin, special software like *resonate*, or special hardware such as a Cisco Local Director to point inbound Web requests to the proper server.

The following is the general syntax of wget:

```
wget options url-list
```

A simple request to download a Web page is as follows:

```
wget http://www.usinglinux.com
```

This downloads the `index.html` file from the `usinglinux.com` Web site into the current directory. Table 12.5 provides a useful subset of options available to wget. For more details, see the man page.

TABLE 12.5 USEFULE WGET OPTIONS

Option	Description
`-o` *filename*	Specifies wget to copy the files from the indicated Web site to filename.
`-http-user` *username*, `-http-passwd` *password*	Allows wget to access Web sites that are password protected.
`-a` *filename*	Any output messages generated by wget goes to the indicated filename rather than to the screen.
`-h`	Displays help information.
`-v`	Provides verbose output messages.
`-q`	Quiet mode in which output messages are suppressed.
`-i` *filename*	URLs are read from the indicated filename rather than from the command line.
`-r`	Recursive option that starts at the indicated URL and then downloads all files from that point. A great way to copy an entire Web site.

A final warning—wget is not a tool to be used to steal Web content! Nearly all Web sites and the files on them, including image files, are copyrighted!

CHAPTER 13

Improving System Security

In this chapter

by Steve Burnett

HANDLING PHYSICAL SECURITY

With all the mass media hype about viruses, computer break-ins, and diabolical computer crackers with their modems and network connections, too little attention is paid to the physical security of computer systems. Computer equipment is fairly sensitive to various environmental conditions.

Note

Over the past several years, the mass media has changed the meaning of the word *hacker* from "a computer enthusiast" to "someone who breaks into computers." In the computer community, the commonly accepted term for someone who breaks into computers is *cracker*. This is the term used throughout this chapter.

Fire and smoke can obviously mean a quick end for your computing equipment. If you have any sort of business computer installation, you should consider installing smoke detectors, automatic fire extinguishers, and a fire alarm system.

In addition to fire and smoke, dust can wreak havoc with computer equipment. Dust is abrasive and can shorten the life of magnetic media and tape and optical drives. Dust can collect in ventilation systems and block the airflow, letting computers overheat. Also, dust can be electrically conductive and can cause circuit boards to short out and fail.

Electricity poses a special threat to computer equipment. Computers are very sensitive to surges in electrical current. All computer equipment, including modems connected to telephone lines, should be connected to surge suppression equipment to reduce the chances of damage. Many areas suffer from "dirty power" that fluctuates in current and voltage.

Note

Although surge suppressors can help protect against spikes in the electrical current, they're virtually worthless against any kind of lightning strike. If lightning hits an incoming line to your house or business, simple surge suppressors are unlikely to save your equipment. In the case of a severe thunderstorm, you would be wise to unplug your surge suppressor and wait out the storm.

Computers are also common targets for theft. Many computer components are small and expensive. As a result, they're easily stolen and sold. You should evaluate how secure your computers are and try to protect them against theft as you would any valuable possession.

Another aspect of physical computer security is preventing access by unauthorized persons. If someone can walk into your computer room, sit down at a console, and start working unchallenged, you have a problem. By controlling access to your computers, you make it more difficult for someone to steal or damage data or equipment. Establish access policies for your computing facilities and educate your users as to these policies.

The following are some tips you can follow to improve the physical security at your installation:

- Don't leave a system, tape drives, disk drives, terminals, or workstations unattended for a prolonged period of time. It's a good idea to have some restrictions regarding access to the rooms that house your primary system and associated tape and disk drives. A lock on the door goes a long way in providing security. An unauthorized person can remove backup media—disks or tapes—from an unlocked area.
- Don't leave the system console or other terminal device logged in as root and unattended. If users know the system, they can easily give themselves root privileges, modify important software, or remove information from the system.
- Educate system users about physical security risks. Encourage them to report any unauthorized activity they may witness. Feel free to courteously challenge someone you don't recognize who is using the system.
- If possible, don't keep sensitive information on systems that have modem or network connections.
- Keep backups in a secure area and limit access to that area.

Dealing with Password Security

The first line of defense against unauthorized access to a system is password protection. This type of protection is also often the weakest link in the chain. This section describes some steps you can take to keep passwords secure.

The reality is that users want simple, easy-to-remember passwords. They don't want to change their passwords. They like to write down their passwords so that they can reference them. Unfortunately for you, the system administrator, these approaches are all bad from a computer security standpoint. Password security requires almost constant attention.

The root password is special. Anyone who knows it can access anything on your system and perhaps other systems that your computer is connected to through a network. Change the root password often, choose it wisely, and keep it secure. It's best committed to memory. In most organizations, it's a good idea for two people to know the password—but no more than that!

A password should be at least six characters long; however, only the first eight characters in any password are recognized. This means that your password is truncated to eight characters if you enter one that's longer than eight characters.

Tip #78 from *Steve*

The MD5 module allows passwords to be as long as 256 characters.

Writing a program that can attempt to guess a password is not too difficult. If the password-guessing program tries to guess a random password, it will take longer to be successful if the password itself is longer.

Computers are very good at doing the same thing over and over, such as encrypting every word in a dictionary and comparing it to your password to try to break into your system. You should never choose a password that's a dictionary word—in any language. Also, try not to choose a password that's easily associated with you. Your name, address, spouse's name, child's name, pet names, phone number, driver's license number, and so on are all obvious targets for a cracker.

So how do you pick a good password if all the easy ones are also easy to guess? One technique is to pick two random short words and connect them with a punctuation character. This technique makes an almost random sequence of characters as far as a password guesser is concerned, but the password still is fairly easy for you to remember. The following are a few examples of passwords that use this technique:

joe&day

car!pan

modem!at

Another method for picking passwords is to take a phrase that you'll remember and use the first letter from each word for the password. This technique results in a random sequence of characters, but one that you can easily recall. For example, the phrase "Ladies and Gentlemen, Elvis has left the building" translates into the password L&GEhltb.

The crucial point is that the password should be remembered. It shouldn't be written down anywhere. If your users feel they must write down their passwords at all, give them a tip to disguise their passwords in some type of list or sentence. For instance, if your password is modem!at, a note on a small piece of paper saying "Don't forget to pick up modem! At computer shop for repairs" looks like an ordinary reminder in case another person sees the paper, but the password is disguised.

DEVELOPING LOGIN SECURITY

Each account on your Linux system is a door into your computer. All someone needs is the right key—the password. If you've instituted good password-management practices, you already have a head start toward developing a more secure system. One aspect of computer security that goes hand in hand with password security is login or account security.

Login or account security involves looking for accounts on your system that may be potential security problems and dealing with them. Login security can pose several different kinds of problems.

Accounts Without Passwords

Many computer crackers succeed in breaking into a computer by simply finding an account that doesn't have a password. You should check your password file regularly for such accounts and disable them. The password is stored in the second field of the password file under Linux. You can check for a blank password field with several tools, such as grep, awk, or perl. You can disable logins to an account by editing the password file and changing the password field to an * (asterisk) character. Changing this field prevents anyone from logging in with that login ID.

→ See "Setting User Passwords," p. 252

Unused Accounts

If a login name won't be used anymore, you should delete the account so that it can't be compromised. At the very least, you should edit the password file and set the password to the * character, which prevents anyone from logging in to the account. If you choose to delete the account, you should use the `find` command to locate all files owned by the account and then change their ownership or delete them.

→ See "Removing a User," p. 253

Note

If you use other configuration files, such as system mail alias lists, you have to remove the account from those files as well.

Default Accounts

Linux comes with several standard login IDs, which are required for the operating system to work correctly. For example, the root account may have no password when Linux is first installed. You should check the password file after you've finished your installations to make sure that all your default accounts have good passwords or that they have been disabled by setting the password field to a * character. If you are using the Shadow Password Suite, all the password fields in `/etc/password` are set to * by default.

Some software packages automatically create accounts on your system during their installation processes. Remember to disable them or set their passwords accordingly.

Guest Accounts

It's not uncommon for computer centers to provide some type of guest access accounts for visitors so that they can use the local computers temporarily. These accounts usually don't have passwords, or they have passwords that are the same as the login IDs. For example, the login *guest* might not have a password or might have a password of guest. As you might guess, these accounts are security disasters waiting to happen.

Because these accounts and passwords are probably widely known, an intruder could use one to gain initial access to your system. When a cracker breaks into your system, the intruder can then try to get root access from the inside or use your system as a starting point from which to attack other computers over a network. Tracing an attack back to an open public account makes it much harder to find the true source of the attack.

Using guest or open accounts really isn't a good idea on any system. If you really must use one of these accounts, keep it disabled until it's needed. Randomly generate a password for the account when it needs to be used and, when you can, disable it immediately. Also, remember not to send the password via email.

COMMAND ACCOUNTS

Computers commonly have several *command accounts*—login IDs that run given commands and then exit. For example, finger is an account that has no password. When a user logs in as finger, the `finger` program is run, showing who is on the system, and then the session terminates. Other such accounts may be sync and date, which typically don't have passwords. Even though they don't run a shell, and they do run only one command, they can still pose a security risk.

If you allow command accounts on your system, you should ensure that none of these commands accept command-line input. Also, these commands shouldn't have any type of shell escape that can allow a user to get to an interactive shell.

A second reason for not using these types of accounts is that they can give away information about your system that can be useful to an intruder. Using programs such as `finger` or `who` as command accounts can allow intruders to get the login IDs of users on your system. Remember that the login ID/password combination protects your accounts. If an intruder gets the login ID of a user, that person now has half the information needed to log in to that account.

GROUP ACCOUNTS

A *group account* is an account for which more than one person knows the password and logs in under the same ID. Using group accounts is almost always a bad idea. If you have an account shared by several people that is broken into and is being used as a base to attack other computers, finding the person who gave out the password is difficult. If you have an account that's shared by 5 people, it may, in fact, be shared by 25 people. You have no way of knowing.

→ See "Working with Groups," p. 253

Linux allows you to provide file access based on group membership. This way, a group of people who need access to a set of files can share them without needing to share an account. Rather than create group accounts, you should make wise use of groups under Linux. Stay with the "one login ID, one person" philosophy.

HANDLING FILE SECURITY

The file system under Linux is a tree structure that's built from files and directories. Linux stores several types of information about each file in its file system, including the following:

- The filename
- The file type
- The file size
- The file's physical location on disk
- Various access and modification times
- The owner and group ID of the file
- The access permissions associated with the file

If a user can modify some of the file information on certain files, security breaches can occur. As a result, the file system plays a very important role in system security.

PERMISSIONS

Linux file permissions control which users can access which files and commands. These permission bits control access rights for the owner, the associated group members, and other users. By using the `ls -l` command, you can generate a file list that shows the permissions field. The leftmost field shown by `ls -l` specifies the file permissions. For example, this field may look like `-rw-r--r--`. The first `-` in the field shows the file type. For regular files, this field is always `-`.

The next nine characters represent the file access permissions for the owner, group, and world, respectively. Each category takes up three characters in the permissions field, consisting of the characters `r` (for read permission), `w` (for write permission), and `x` (for execute permission). Any or all of these characters may be present.

If one of the permissions has been granted, the corresponding character is present. If permission isn't granted, a `-` appears instead. For example, if a file has a permission field that looks like `-rw-r--r--`, it indicates that the file is a regular file (the first character is `-`), the owner has permissions `rw-` (which means read and write but no execute), and the other group members and the world at large have permissions `r--` (which means read permission but no write or execute access). File permissions are changed via the `chmod` command.

→ See "File Permissions," p. 414

Note

You can specify the permissions to the `chmod` command as octal values instead of the `rwx` symbolic values. To do so, simply treat the three characters in a permission field as bits in an octal number; if the character is present, count it as a 1. So, the permissions `-rw-r--r--` are represented numerically as 644.

SUID and SGID Programs

Two additional permission bits are associated with a file: the SUID and SGID bits. SUID stands for *Set User ID*, and SGID is *Set Group ID*. Programs with these permissions behave as though they were owned by different UIDs when they're run. When an SUID program is run, its effective UID is set the same as the user who owns the program on the file system, regardless of who is actually running the program. SGID is similar except that it changes the group ID instead.

Although the SUID/SGID feature can be useful, it can present a big security hole. SUID programs are generally used when a program needs special permissions, such as root permission, to run.

Programmers usually go to great lengths to ensure that their SUID programs are secure. Most security holes in SUID programs occur when the program executes a command line, activates a shell, or runs a file that users can change to contain their own commands. Although some SUID programs are necessary, you should try to keep them to a minimum. You should also regularly scan your file systems to check for new SUID programs by using the `find` command (refer to the man page for the exact syntax).

Avoiding Social Engineering Threats

With all the different security features available on a Linux system, the biggest security hole is typically your users. After all, your users already have valid accounts.

But what do your users have to do with social engineering? What is social engineering, anyway? *Social engineering* is about convincing people to do what you want, either by playing on their assumptions or behavior, or by outright misrepresentation and lying. People, in general, want to be helpful. And, if given the opportunity, they usually try to help out as much as possible. Crackers with good social engineering skills play on this characteristic.

Assume that you have a computer user named Mr. Jones. He's just your average user—not a guru at all. One day, Mr. Jones gets a call at the office that goes something like this:

Mr. Jones: Hello?

Caller: Hello, Mr. Jones. This is Fred Smith in tech support. Due to some disk space constraints, we're going to be moving some user home directories to another disk at 5:30 this evening. Your account will be part of this move and will be temporarily unavailable.

Mr. Jones: Uh, okay. I'll be home by then, anyway.

Caller: Good. Be sure to log out before you go. I just need to check a couple of things. What was your login ID again—jones?

Mr. Jones:	Yes, it's jones. None of my files will get lost during the move, will they?
Caller:	No, sir. But I'll check your account just to make sure. What was the password on that account so I can get in to check your files?
Mr. Jones:	My password is tuesday.
Caller:	Okay, Mr. Jones. Thanks for your help. I'll be sure to check your account and verify that all the files are there.
Mr. Jones:	Thank you. Bye.

So what just happened here? Someone called one of your users on the phone and managed to get both a valid username and password in the course of the conversation. And you guessed it—if Mr. Jones calls tech support tomorrow, he'll probably find that no Fred Smith is working there!

How do you prevent situations like this from happening? Educate your users. Your users should never give out passwords over the phone to a caller. The preceding conversation played on Mr. Jones's assumption that "Oh, this caller is in tech support, so I trust him, and he can look up my password if he needs it." If the caller has a legitimate reason to have your password, he or she should not get it from you. You should never leave passwords on email or voice mail either. Crackers use social engineering by convincing users to give them what they want; these intruders don't even have to try to break into your system.

RECORDING USE OF THE su COMMAND

Linux verifies your identity by your login ID/password combination. As you log in, your process is tagged with an ID that identifies you to the system. It's this UID that's checked for file and directory access.

Linux offers the capability to switch to another UID while you're working. When users use the `su` command, they can become root or another user. They must know the password of the user that they're changing to. For example, for a user to change user ID to that of user ernie, the command is

```
su ernie
```

The user is then prompted for the password associated with the login ID ernie.

To change to root, the command is as follows:

```
su root
```

The user is then prompted for the root password.

Typically, all attempts at using `su` are automatically logged in a system log file, such as `/var/adm/syslog`. Examine this file periodically to check on this sort of activity.

DEVELOPING A SECURE SYSTEM

Along with power comes responsibility. If not handled carefully, Linux's power to share information, process resources, and handle peripherals can leave your system open to abuse. Your job is to set up system security so that only the right users and systems can connect to yours, and that they can use only the parts of your computer you want to share.

SECURITY THREATS

You can monitor your system for security threats. To determine who is using your system and the type of work they're doing, you can use the `ps` command.

Be wary of jobs that seem to be running a very long time or users who seem to be using more resources than normal. They can be an indication that a login has been compromised and an unauthorized user is running a program to guess passwords.

CONTROLLING THE ROOT

The root login is reserved for your administrators. The person who logs in as the root has the power to erase any file, restrict use by any person on the network, and quite literally cause havoc among users. That's the downside of the picture. Linux was designed to give the people having root access the tools to do their jobs better than in other environments.

Many proprietary operating systems have blockages established by the creators to avoid accidental damage to files and other operating factors on the system. The creators of UNIX and Linux took a different attitude toward the administrator. You'll find tools that permit you to connect almost any computer device. You'll find software that monitors the performance of the computer. You can create an endless array of software and adapt it to just about any business environment.

Also, you can force your users to do only specified things on the computer, or you can give them limited rights until they grow in their knowledge. The root user, the administrator, has the power to do these things.

Note

Because access to the root is so important, some companies restrict use to a select few. Even if your Linux system isn't being used for business, you should still keep the root password limited.

Even if the Linux system is your own, used by no one else, you should create at least one other account, log in as that account, and switch to root using `su` or log in as root only when you need to do something the normal user account isn't allowed to do, and then log off or exit the root account as soon as you're done.

Controlling Modems and Crackers

Allowing access from a common modem, similar to those that people have at home, can permit someone to "crack" the system and destroy important data. As a result, many companies insist that their computers have elaborate security mechanisms, which can make these computers almost impossible to work with. Some companies put a dial-back option on the computers so that you must dial the computer and then wait for a return call before you can interact with the system.

Most of the time, a traditional UNIX/Linux approach is recommended. Make sure that all your user logins have passwords. Restrict the systems that can connect to your system. Keep permissions closed on sensitive files. Be careful of set UID bit programs (those that give the user who runs the program the permissions to run as another user). Most break-ins occur because someone left the door open.

Note

Ultimately, security is a problem with people rather than systems. You can't allow passwords to be etched in the wall near a terminal or have DOS computers with root passwords embedded in communication programs.

Preventing Idle Terminals

Users should log out or use some kind of terminal lock program when they leave at the end of the day. Most UNIX systems have such a program that shuts down terminals left on beyond a prescribed length of time.

Enforcing Security

Security in defense firms is clearly understood. Companies that have highly sensitive products in the design cycle understand the need for security. But employees who work for a small distributor of plumbing parts, for example, may have a hard time understanding what everybody is so concerned about. Security in this example isn't an issue until you can't figure out who removed a file that included a key proposal.

You should give employees a quick lesson about the sensitivity of data on your computer. A business has a significant investment in the data on the computer. Loss of data can be a distraction, or it can mean chaos. Employees who are unwilling to participate in securing a computer should understand that this can be cause for dismissal.

For an administrator, the task becomes apparent. If you're the chief security officer for the network, how can you be sure that files and directories are adequately secured? Fortunately, many tools are available to help you, such as `umask`, `cron`, and Linux itself.

Permissions seem to be a significant source of worry for most administrators. New administrators typically tighten up permissions and then field calls from people saying they can't gain access to a file they need or can't execute a program on the system. After a while, these administrators loosen up the permissions so that anybody can do anything. The balancing act of securing the computer while permitting the proper people the tools to do their jobs is sometimes frustrating.

HANDLING SECURITY BREACHES

Security on a computer can require a little detective work. For example, look at the following:

```
# who -u
root    tty02  Jan 7 08:35 old Ofc #2
martha ttym1d Jan 7 13:20 . Payroll #1
ted     ttyp0  Jan 7 08:36 8:25 Warehouse
margo   ttyp2  Jan 7 07:05 9:45 CEO Ofc
root    ttyp4  Jan 7 08:36 . Modem #1
# date
Tue Jan 7 19:18:21 CST 1997
```

Suppose you know that Martha left the office at 5:00 p.m. Has someone found her password, or did she leave the terminal on when she left? You can see that she logged in at 13:20 today. It's now 19:18, and somebody is active on the system using her login. Do you dispatch security?

But what do you do if someone does break into your system? First, you should try to determine whether you really do have an intruder. Many times, what you notice may be just the result of human error. If you do have an intruder, you have several options. You need to decide whether any damage was done and determine the extent of the damage. Do you prosecute those responsible if you can catch them? If so, you should start trying to gather and protect evidence.

You must decide how to go about securing your system and restoring any damage from your backups. Probably the most important task of all is to document what you do. Start a log immediately. Sign and date any printouts showing evidence of intrusion; they may be useful as evidence. Your log may be invaluable in helping you figure out what you've done when you have to change or restore files.

Two other preventive measures that you should take are to make printouts of your basic system configuration files, such as `/etc/fstab`, and establish a site security policy. You must make sure that your users are aware of your site policy and that they're reminded frequently.

Another area of concern occurs when an employee leaves the company. When an employee leaves, for whatever reason, personnel should contact the computer staff to retire the login.

With all the different security considerations, how much security is enough? Can you have too much? You might be surprised to learn that, yes, you can have too much security. In general, if the cost of recovering from a security breach is less than the cost of security, you should reduce the security level for your systems. Note that these cost factors include much more than monetary costs. Among other things, you should take into consideration the content of your files, the amount of time and money required take to replace them, any lost productivity time that an attack would produce, and the effect that publicity of a computer security problem will have on your organization.

Performing Backups

Few issues that the typical Linux administrator deals with are as important as backing up or archiving a system. An administrator can be fired or a company can literally fail because of the loss of valuable data. If you use a Linux system for personal use, what's your time worth to you if you've, for example, personally typed your entire cookbook's worth of favorite recipes over the last two months and the system crashes, wiping out all your files? The disk or disks on a computer are electromechanical devices, and they will fail at some time. If you're ever worried about a hostile attack on your system, backups can at least let you rebuild the system. The data on the system is typically much more valuable to the users than the system itself.

Most new hard disks are rated at around 150,000 hours mean time between failures—more than five years. But the mean-time statistic can be deceptive. Your disk could fail at the 50,000 hour mark, or it might last for more than 10 years (highly unlikely). You're gambling if you back up your systems only occasionally, and you take an even greater chance if you aren't checking your backup tapes regularly.

→ See "Planning a Backup Schedule," p. 262

PAM: The Pluggable Authentication Modules Architecture

Users need to be able to perform the tasks they want, even if their desired goal is winning that game of Solitaire. To do so, users affect the system and its contents in varying degrees. In general, users should be able to run applications and create, change, and delete files that do not affect the system's continued performance or that do not change items belonging to another user that that user has not decided to share. One way of assigning authority over a system is based on login name and password combination: When you log in, the system asks you for a name and password. Based on the proof that you are who you say you are, the system allows you to do essentially anything you want to your own area of the system and restricts you if you try to affect a part of the system you're not supposed to.

Other methods exist for verifying a user's identity besides the name/password combination. The Pluggable Authentication Modules (PAM) architecture allows you to change authentication policy without having to change the applications themselves. This section presents the structure and relationship of the PAM architecture.

The four types of PAM modules are as follows:

- *Auth* performs the authentication activity.
- *Account* defines whether the authentication is allowed. For example, consider a user who's only supposed to be on the system during the daytime and not work evenings or weekends. An account module would detect the user if he or she attempted to perform an action in the middle of the night.
- *Password* sets passwords.

- *Session* provides services to the user after the account module allows the authentication module to verify the user's identity.

Modules can be *stacked* in sequence to allow multiple methods of access or to restrict access by requiring success of multiple methods.

UNDERSTANDING PAM CONFIGURATION FILES

The configuration files for PAM are located in the directory `/etc/pam.d/`.

> **Note**
>
> **In older Linux systems, the file `/etc/pam.conf` provided configuration definitions. `/etc/pam.conf` is still supported for backward compatibility, but its use is discouraged.**

The best way to understand the syntax is to examine a configuration file. The PAM file for `passwd` appears as follows. If you installed PAM as part of your Linux installation, this is the default file `/etc/pam.d/passwd`:

```
#%PAM-1.0
auth        required    /lib/security/pam_pwdb.so shadow nullok
account     required    /lib/security/pam_pwdb.so
password    required    /lib/security/pam_cracklib.so retry=3
password    required    /lib/security/pam_pwdb.so use_authtok nullok
```

The first line is a comment, indicated by the *octothorp* (# sign) at the beginning of the line. The second line causes the user to be prompted to enter a password and for that password to be checked. The third line does the same if shadow passwords aren't being used (you'll learn more details on shadowing later). The fourth line calls a password-cracking application to see whether the new password is a good one, and the fifth line specifies which module should be used to change the password.

REQUIRED, REQUISITE, AND OPTIONAL: MODULE ORDER AND NECESSITY

In the preceding section, you can see that all four of the called modules are marked as "required." Labeling a module as required means that the module is called regardless of the success or failure of earlier modules. As a security guideline, all of them are called, so the reply from a failure at any point looks the same. If you hide the location of the failure, a malicious attacker's task is made harder.

If every module is required, the order of the modules is unimportant. However, PAM allows for these other control flags to be used instead of required:

- **Optional**—Optional is entirely secondary to all other modules; the success or failure of an optional module does not affect the success of the authentication *if* another module appears in the PAM configuration file. If an optional module is the only one defined for authentication, its success or failure determines the success or failure of the authentication itself.

- **Sufficient**—A sufficient module acts like an optional module, except that it overrides any or all optional modules. A required or requisite module's response supersedes a sufficient module, however.
- **Requisite**—If a requisite module fails, control is directly returned to the application. If you want a PAM stack to stop at a particular module, you can edit the configuration file and change the control flag from required to requisite.

If you want more information, Red Hat Software provides documentation for PAM on its Web site at `http://www.redhat.com/linux-info/pam/`.

SHADOW PASSWORDS: WHAT GOOD ARE THEY?

On a Linux system without the Shadow Suite installed, user information (including passwords) is stored in the `/etc/passwd` file. The password is stored in an encoded format; although the password looks like gibberish to a human, it is simply encoded with the UNIX `crypt` command, with the text set to `[null]` and the password used as the key.

It is difficult but possible to take a given encoded password and re-create the original password. However, because people may get lazy sometimes, on any system with more than a few users, some of the passwords are likely to be common words or simple variations. It's quite possible, and within the means of many, to encrypt a dictionary list and compare it to the password list in `/etc/passwd`. Other attacks are possible and used often, but this brute-force approach is simple and easy to do. In addition to passwords, the `/etc/passwd` file also contains information such as user IDs and group IDs that are read by many system programs, so the `/etc/passwd` file must remain world readable.

Shadow passwording moves the passwords to another file, usually `/etc/shadow`, which is set to be readable *only* by root. Moving the passwords to the `/etc/shadow` file prevents an attacker from having access to the encoded passwords with which to perform a dictionary attack.

The Shadow Suite is included with most of the standard distributions of Linux.

However, in some cases such as the following, installing the Shadow Suite is *not* a good idea:

- The system does not contain user accounts.
- The system is running on a LAN and uses Network Information Services (NIS) to get or supply usernames and passwords to other machines on the network.
- The system is used by terminal servers to verify users via Network File System (NFS), NIS, or some other method.
- The system runs other software that validates users, *and* no shadow version is available, *and* you don't have the source code.

THE /ETC/PASSWORD AND /ETC/SHADOW FILES

A nonshadowed `/etc/passwd` file has the following format:

```
username:passwd:UID:GID:full_name:directory:shell
```

Now consider this example:

```
username:Npje044eh3mx8e:507:200:Full Name:/home/username:/bin/csh
```

A shadowed `/etc/passwd` file would instead contain the following:

```
username:x:507:100:Full Name:/home/username:/bin/csh
```

The *x* in the second field in this case is now a placeholder for the real passwords stored in the shadow file `/etc/shadow`. The `/etc/shadow` file has the following format:

```
username:passwd:last:may:must:warn:expire:disable:reserved
```

Table 13.1 outlines the fields in the `/etc/shadow` file.

TABLE 13.1 FIELDS IN AN /etc/shadow FILE ENTRY

Field	Description
`username`	The name used to log in
`password`	The encoded password
`last`	Days since January 1, 1970, that the password was last changed
`may`	Days before the password may be changed
`must`	Days after which the password must be changed
`warn`	Days before the password is to expire that the user is warned
`expire`	Days after the password expires that the account is disabled
`disable`	Days since January 1, 1970, that the account is disabled
`reserved`	A reserved field

ADDING, CHANGING, AND DELETING USERS WITH SHADOWED PASSWORDS

The Shadow Suite adds the following command-line-oriented commands for adding, modifying, and deleting users: `useradd`, `usermod`, and `userdel`.

useradd

You use the `useradd` command to add users to the system. You also invoke this command to change the default settings.

The first thing that you should do is examine the default settings and make changes specific to your system by using the following command:

```
useradd -D
```

usermod

You use the `usermod` utility to modify the information on a user; this utility is very similar to the `useradd` program. For example,

```
usermod -g 200 username
```

changes the specified user from their initial group to group id 200.

userdel

Using `userdel`, you can delete the user's account with this command:

```
userdel -r username
```

The `-r` deletes all files in the user's home directory to be removed, along with the home directory itself. A less drastic way to eliminate a user from the system is to use the `passwd` command to lock the user's account.

passwd

In addition to setting and changing passwords, the root user can use the `passwd` command to perform the following tasks:

- Lock and unlock accounts (with the `-l` and `-u` options)
- Set the maximum number of days that a password remains valid (`-x`)
- Set the minimum number of days between password changes (`-n`)
- Set the number of days of warning that a password is about to expire (`-w`)
- Set the number of days after the password expires before the account is locked (`-i`)

pwck

Using the program `pwck`, you can check on the consistency of the `/etc/passwd` and `/etc/shadow` files. This program checks each username and verifies that each entry has the following:

- Correct number of fields
- Unique username
- Valid user and group identifier
- Valid primary group
- Valid home directory
- Valid login shell

Finally, `pwck` also warns of any account that has no password.

Note

Running `pwck` after installing the Shadow Suite is a good idea. Running this program periodically—perhaps weekly or monthly—is also a good idea. If you use the `-r` option, you can use `cron` to run the program on a regular basis and have the report mailed to you.

grpck

grpck is the consistency-checking program for the /etc/group and /etc/gshadow files. It checks for the correct number of fields, unique group names, and a valid list of members and administrators.

Again, the -r option generates an automated report, so you can use cron to trigger this check automatically.

ENABLING DIAL-UP PASSWORDS

If you want to limit who can dial in and connect, you can use dial-up passwords to control who accesses the systems remotely. To enable the use of dial-up passwords, you must examine the file /etc/login.defs and see that DIALUPS_CHECK_ENAB is set to Yes.

Two files contain the dial-up information:

- /etc/dialups contains the ttys (one per line, with the leading /dev/ removed). If a tty is listed, dial-up checks are performed.
- /etc/d_passwd contains the fully qualified pathname of a shell, followed by an optional password.

If a user logs in to a line that is listed in /etc/dialups, and that user's shell is listed in the file /etc/d_passwd, he or she is allowed access only after entering the correct dial-up password.

The command dpasswd assigns passwords to the shells in the /etc/d_passwd file.

PROJECT: ESTABLISHING SECURITY PROCEDURES

Let's look at some procedures to better secure your Linux system. You cannot make your system perfectly secure, but you can make it more difficult for the lazy, bored, or less-committed to hurt you. Securing a system is like buying security for a house or office: Deadbolt locks are fairly cheap but harder to break than standard door latches. After deadbolts, people add alarm systems, automatic calls to law enforcement, barrier doors, watchdogs, and human guards, depending on how concerned.

First, the following are two good rules for system security:

- **Know what you are allowing.** Leaving a default password on a default account is exactly like forgetting to lock the side door of your house or office: Anyone who bothers to look can walk in. At the least, make these unwanted visitors bring a crowbar or lockpick, metaphorically speaking.
- **Everything not explicitly permitted is denied.** "Do as thou wilt is the whole of the law" is a bad guideline for system security.

We'll start from the beginning. Before you order anything, plan (you can use paper for this if you want—yes, paper). What do you want to do from this system? Will you be the only user? If not, who else do you want to give access to? What services do you want to supply? Do you want to let people log in from a remote computer? After you've decided what you want to do with the system, you can order the hardware and Linux distribution you want.

When you're installing, most distributions of Linux prompt you to create a root account and password, and some also prompt you to create a second account for general use. If Linux doesn't prompt you to create a second account during installation, do so after you finish the installation.

Note

Remember to pick good passwords.

The following are some tips about installation:

- **Install only what you want.** Installing a Linux system requires a little work for a decently secure setup. Many Linux systems install a whole raft of services and applications by default. Remember the list you made earlier of the services you want to offer on this system? Have it with you during the installation. If you don't want a service installed, such as a Telnet server daemon, don't install it at all. You can always go back and install it later if you change your mind.
- **If you install a service, turn it off until you want it.** Some distributions of Linux automatically enable a server if you install it; others allow you to install a service without enabling it. This point is important if it's new to you. You should set up your individual services knowing that you're doing so, changing default passwords as you go along, and so on.
- **After installation (did you create a second user account for general use yet?), turn off every service you don't want.** Remember the first rule: If you don't specifically want it, you don't need it. Obviously, any remote access is a big area of security risk. You should pay careful attention to all services. Start by opening the file `/etc/inetd.conf` in a text editor such as vi and disable everything that's enabled. Turn off Web server access, turn off FTP server access, turn off POP or IMAP access, and turn off everything by commenting out the lines from the file. Typically, putting `*` as the first character of the line disables the service. Some GUI-based tools such as linuxconf let you turn services on and off through windows-based applications.

Tip #79 from Steve

Turning off services is especially relevant for services such as `telnet`, `finger`, `rsh`, and `rlogin`. `finger` is a "look-up" program that gives information about the user, and if you need it, you'll know why you need it. The `telnet` and `r-` commands can be replaced for general use by the ssh (secure shell) client and server discussed in Chapter 32, "Accessing the Network with `telnet`, `ftp`, and the `r-` Commands."

You'll learn how to choose decent passwords elsewhere in this book. You might consider running a program such as `crack` against your password file, *only* if you have administrative privileges on this system. If you are using a company system, just having a `crack` program or similar design in your system or directory could be grounds for immediate dismissal from the company, or grounds for cancellation of your account from your Internet service provider. Do not "help out" the official system administrators unless you get agreement from them in advance. However, if you are the (or a) system administrator, you should test the system's security before someone else decides to.

Security should not be a "one-time" issue; it should be an ongoing concern. Change passwords as often as you feel appropriate. Check to see whether any services that you didn't turn on are suddenly running (automatic monitoring can help with this check). Resist the urge to write the root password (or any password) on a sticky note and put the note on your monitor or mousepad, and so on.

Note

Other aids to security are available. For example, you can find more than one file system for Linux that automatically encrypts the entire file system (Matt Blaze's Cryptographic file system is a well-known example). IPSec encrypts the IP traffic over your network. ssh (discussed elsewhere in the book) can provide a more secure alternative to Telnet. Tripwire can detect if someone's changed a selected file, such as the password file, and warn you.

CHAPTER 14

Configuring the Linux Kernel

In this chapter

by Jack Tackett, Jr.

What Is the Kernel?

The kernel is the core of the Linux operating system and provides the basic system services to the rest of Linux. Remember, Linux isn't a commercial product, so you might find some problems after a new distribution is released. Or someone may discover a serious security hole in the kernel. This happens all the time with both commercial and "free" operating systems. The difference is that with Linux, because the source code is available, you can patch any problems immediately after they are discovered. You don't have to wait for your commercial vendor to release a new service pack to fix a hole in your system.

In addition, a new feature in the current releases of the Linux kernel enables you to load specific device and program support into the kernel without precompiling the support into a large kernel. As a result, Linux can load into memory only those parts of the kernel it needs. Modules also provide a way for you to modify the kernel to solve a problem or to add a new feature without recompiling the entire system.

Preparing to Build a New Kernel

Sometimes a problem has only one solution—a new kernel. The kernel is the core operating system for Linux. Although not for the faint of heart, downloading a new kernel from the Net and building the kernel are sometimes necessary. If you have some programming experience and know your way around the C programming language, you should be able to build and install a new kernel.

You might have to install a new kernel for the following reasons:

- A patch is released to run new hardware.
- You want to remove features you don't use from the kernel to lower the memory requirements for your system.

The starting point is to determine what kernel version you're now running. You can find out the kernel version by using the following command:

```
uname --release
```

or

```
uname -r
```

The response indicates the kernel version currently running on your system. The command displays the version number in the following format:

```
MajorVersionNumber.MinorVersionNumber.PatchLevel
```

Linus Torvalds is the official release point for new kernels, although anyone can modify Linux (because of the General Public License, or GPL). Because Linus is the official release point, the Linux development and user community have a common baseline from which to work and communicate.

Note

Be sure to read the "Kernel How-To" (`/usr/doc/Kernel-HOWTO`) for up-to-date information before actually trying to build and configure a new kernel. If you mess up, you could render your system useless. You should also make sure to keep an older, working copy of a kernel around just in case of problems. You can then boot that kernel instead of the worthless kernel.

CONFIGURING A NEW KERNEL

To build a new kernel, you first need to configure the source code files. The source files should be located in the `/usr/src/linux` directory. You also must have the C compiler package loaded. If you didn't install that package during installation, you can use RPM to do so now with the following commands:

```
rpm -i kernel-source-2.2.5-15.i386.rpm
rpm -i egcs-2.91.66.i386.rpm
```

You also might have to install the kernel headers and various compiler libraries.

→ See "Installing Packages with RPM," p. 169

First, you must get the new kernel sources or patches. You can usually find the new sources on the Internet; check `metlab.unc.edu` for the latest and greatest kernels and also `ftp.kernel.org`. (If you're modifying your current kernel, this step is, of course, unnecessary.) The source files are usually in a `tar` file and need to be unarchived.

Tip #80 from
Jack

Making a backup copy of your current kernel with the following commands is a very good idea:

```
cd /usr/src
mv linux linux.old
```

These commands copy the entire Linux source directory to another directory called `linux.sav`.

Next, you should use the `patch` command to apply any patch files. After preparing the source files, you can configure and build your new system. Depending on your personal preferences and hardware available, you can choose from three methods for configuring the kernel: a text-based program, a text-based menu program, and if you have installed X Windows System, an X-based program.

Note

The AC kernel patches will require the linux directory have a sym-link with a directory called linux.ac or even better rename linux - linux.ac, apply the patches and rename the directory linux. Patch commands are gzip -dc <filename>.tar.gz ¦ patch -p0 or bunzip2 cd <filename>.tar.bz2 ¦ patch -p0. Standard patches do not require re-naming the linux directory.

Tip #81 from

To use kernel modules, you must answer Yes to kerneld support and module version (CONFIG_MODVERSIONS) support during your kernel configuration.

The current command sequence to build the kernel is as follows:

```
cd /usr/src/linux
make mrporper
```

invoke one of three commands, make config (CLI), make menuconfig (text GUI), or make xconfig (X Window System GUI), depending on which user interface you intend to use.

```
make dep
make zImage or make bzImage
make modules
make modules install

depmod -a
```

THE INTERACTIVE TEXT-BASED PROGRAM

If you are using the text-based interactive program, you start by entering the following command from the /usr/src directory:

```
cd /usr/src/linux

# make config
```

The make command asks you various questions about the drivers you want to install or configure. By pressing Enter, you accept the default value for each question; otherwise, you must supply the answer. Some of the questions are listed in Table 14.1. You might have to answer other questions depending on the version of the kernel you're installing or the patches you've applied. This list of options is supported by all the configuration utilities described in this chapter.

TABLE 14.1 KERNEL CONFIGURATION OPTIONS

Configuration Option	Description
Code Maturity Level	For use with experimental components in this kernel
Processor type and features	Used to specify processor type, math emulation, MTRR support, SMP support
Loadable Module Support	Needed if you intend to use modules instead of a monolithic kernel
General Setup	Asks a series of questions about general components, such as math coprocessor support and PCI BIOS supports
Block Devices	Asks questions about the type of IDE hard drives and other block I/O devices
Networking Options	Asks several questions about how to support various network support features, such as firewalls and IP Masquerading
SCSI Support	Enables support for SCSI controllers
SCSI Low-Level Support	Enables low-level support for SCSI controllers and for reporting on various SCSI statistics
Network Device Support	Enables support for various network controllers and processes
Ethernet (10 or 100Mbit)	Enables support for 10baseT and 100baseT ethernet connections
ISDN Subsystem	Enables kernel support for Integrated Services Digital Network (ISDN)
CD-ROM drivers (not for SCSI or IDE/ATAPI drivers)	Provides support for proprietary CD-ROM drivers
Character Devices	Provides support for various character and similar devices, such as system watchdogs
Mice	Provides support for various types of pointing devices
ftape	Provides support for floppy-based tape drives and other removable devices
Filesystems	Lets you configure support for various file systems, including foreign language DOS code pages
Network Filesystems (NFS)	Provides support for NFS
Console drivers	Provides support for various consoles (display devices)
Sound	Provides configuration support for various sound cards
Additional low level sound drivers	Provides support for low level, machine and sound card specific drivers
Kernel Hacking	Provides for profiling support in the kernel

USING THE MENU-BASED PROGRAM

If you are using the text-based interactive program, you start by entering the following command from the `/usr/src/linux` directory:

```
# make menuconfig
```

Linux then displays the main screen, as shown in Figure 14.1.

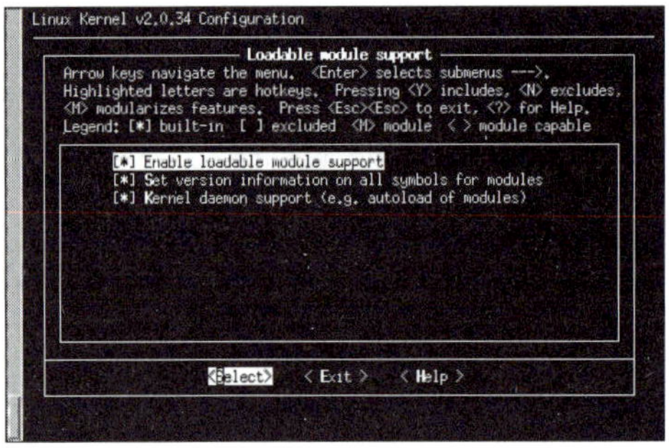

Figure 14.1 Using a graphical menu system can help speed configuration of a new kernel.

The advantage to using the graphical system is that you must configure only those parts of the kernel that need to be modified. The interactive text-based system leads you through the entire configuration process.

USING THE X WINDOWS SYSTEM-BASED PROGRAM

If you are using the text-based interactive program, you start by entering the following command from the `/usr/src/linux` directory:

```
# make xconfig
```

Linux then displays the main screen (see Figure 14.2).

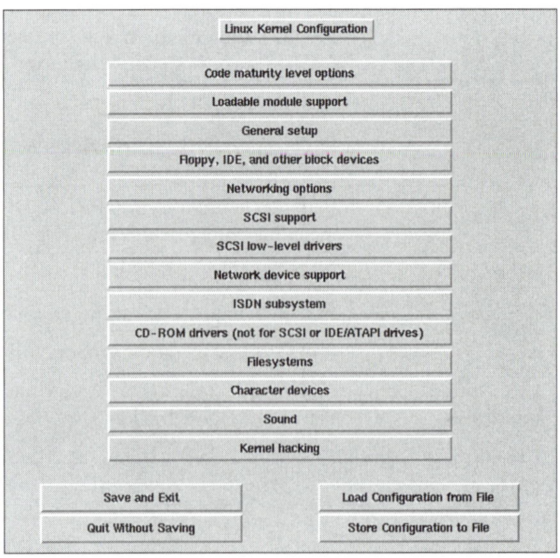

Figure 14.2 X Windows System provides a less cluttered system for configuring a new kernel.

The X-based configuration tool allows you to configure only those kernel components you want to change, just as the graphical text-based tool does. When you click a button, you are presented with another dialog box you use to configure various components. For example, Figure 14.3 displays the Loadable Module Support dialog box. From this dialog box, you can configure the entire kernel for module support.

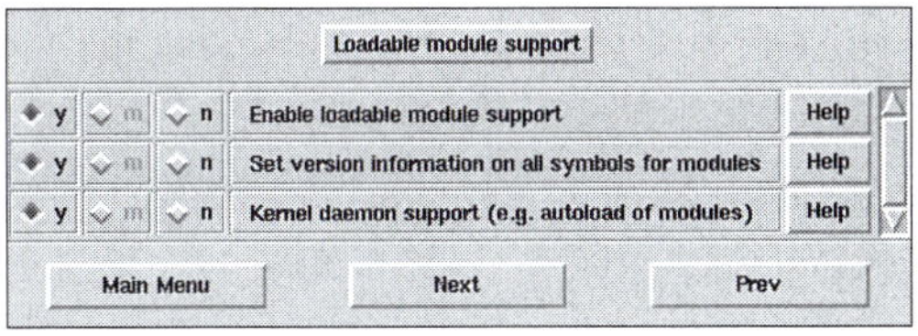

Figure 14.3 You must specify module support during configuration to enable such support in your new kernel.

To select an item, simply click the appropriate radio button (the diamonds). If you need help on a specific topic, such as Enable Loaded Module Support, you can click the Help button along the right side of the dialog box. The resulting dialog box provides helpful information (see Figure 14.4).

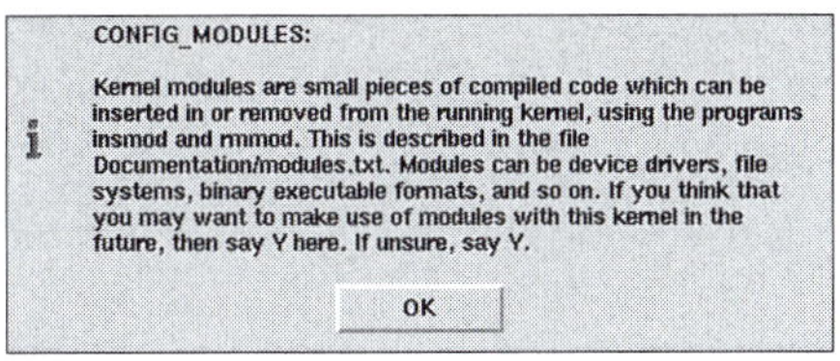

Figure 14.4 Helpful information about the component is just a mouse click away.

You must save your configuration after answering the appropriate questions. Simply click the Save and Exit button to save your new kernel configuration and exit the configuration system.

Compiling the New Kernel

After you answer the various questions to configure your new kernel, you must compile it. You can use the following commands to build the new kernel:

```
make dep
make zImage
```

The build process can take anywhere from a few minutes to many hours, depending on your hardware. So relax and order another pizza!

When the compilation is complete, you need to set up your system to use the new kernel on boot. The new kernel is `/usr/src/linux/arch/i386/boot/zImage`, and you need to copy this image into the boot directory. But before that, you should create a copy of your current kernel image, just in case something goes wrong. To save the old kernel, use the following command:

```
mv /boot/vmlinuz.old /boot/vmlinuz.old
```

Then you can copy over the new kernel with this command:

```
cp /usr/src/linux/arch/i386/boot/zImage /boot/vmlinuz
```

→ See "Installing LILO," p. 87

To change the default kernel that Linux boots into, you edit the `/etc/lilo.conf` file and add another entry for a new kernel. The example in Listing 14.1 shows the addition of the older kernel to the list of operating systems the machine can boot. To change the kernel, you must rename `/boot/vmlinuz` to `/boot/vmlinuz.old` with the preceding commands and then change its label to `old` in `lilo.conf`, as shown in Listing 14.1.

LISTING 14.1 A SAMPLE `/etc/lilo.conf` FILE

```
boot=/dev/hda
      map=/boot/map
      install=/boot/boot.b
      prompt
      timeout=50
      image=/boot/vmlinuz
              label=linux
              initrd=/boot/initrd
              root=/dev/hda1
              read-only
      image=/boot/vmlinuz.old
              label=old
              root=/dev/hda1
              read-only
```

After you make the changes to `/etc/lilo.conf`, run the following command:

```
/sbin/lilo -v
```

The updated `lilo` is then written to the boot device. From then on when you reboot, the machine will boot into the new kernel (linux) as default instead of the older kernel, with a 50-second delay to give you time to choose the old kernel at the boot prompt if you want to boot that kernel.

PROJECT: BUILDING A MODULARIZED KERNEL

With the introduction of modularization in the Linux 2.0.x kernel, some significant changes have been made in the process of building customized kernels. In the past, you were required to compile support into your kernel if you wanted to access a particular hardware or file system component. For some hardware configurations, the size of the kernel could quickly reach a critical level, so to require ready support for items that were used only occasionally was an inefficient use of system resources. With the capabilities of the 2.0.x kernel, if certain hardware components or file systems are used infrequently, driver modules for them can be loaded on demand. To see the current modules in use, use the following command:

```
lsmod
```

The output, shown here, lets you know what modules are loaded and how they loaded, as well as how many pages of memory they are using:

```
Module          Pages      Used by
isofs             5             1 (autoclean)
ne2k-pci          1             1 (autoclean)
8390              2 [ne2k-pci]  0 (autoclean)
BusLogic         20             4
```

Only Red Hat Linux/Intel and Red Hat Linux/SPARC support modular kernels; Red Hat Linux/Alpha users must build a monolithic kernel as described in the earlier section "Preparing to Build a New Kernel." These instructions provide you with the knowledge required to take advantage of the power and flexibility available through kernel modularization.

Note

You need to have the kernel-headers and kernel-source packages already installed. Also, you must issue all commands from the `/usr/src/linux` directory.

To make the modules, go to `/usr/src/linux` and run the following command:

```
make modules
```

Then use this command to install the modules and run the following command:

```
make modules_install
```

WORKING WITH KERNEL MODULES

Now that you have compiled and installed the modules, you are ready to extend your kernel with loadable modules. Table 14.2 shows the basic commands that are available.

TABLE 14.2 MODULE COMMANDS AVAILABLE IN LINUX

Command	Description
`lsmod`	Lists the modules currently loaded in the kernel
`insmod`	Inserts a specified module into the kernel
`rmmod`	Removes the specified module from the kernel
`depmod`	Creates a dependency file for use by `modprobe`
`modprobe`	Loads modules from a list generated by `depmod`

If you are running X Window System, you can take advantage of the kerneld daemon from the Control Panel (shown in Figure 14.5) to work with modules from a GUI instead of from a command line. Clicking this button brings up the Kernel Configurator dialog box shown in Figure 14.6.

PART II CH 14

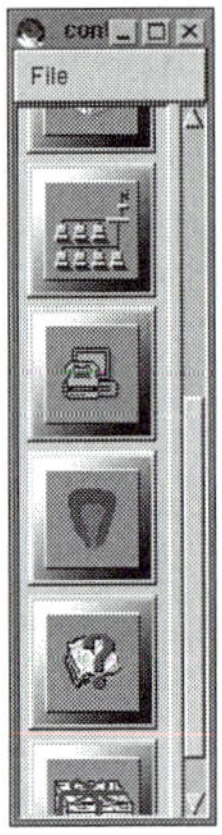

Figure 14.5 The Control Panel provides access to many administrative functions, including working with kerneld.

To list the currently loaded modules, use the `lsmod` command. To add a module you have compiled to the kernel, you can use the following command:

```
insmod module-name
```

Or you can click the Add button on the kerneld dialog box and specify the module (see Figure 14.7).

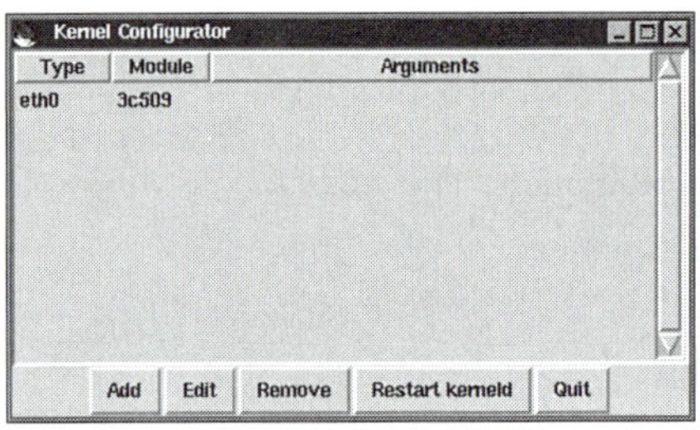

Figure 14.6 Working with kernel modules is easy with the X interface to kerneld.

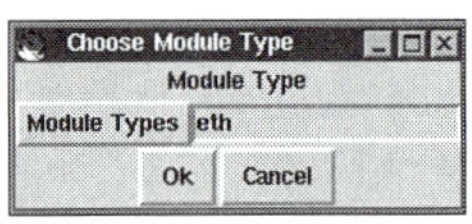

Figure 14.7 Adding modules is a breeze using X Window System.

To delete a module from the kernel, you can use the following command:

```
rmmod module-name
```

Alternatively, you can select the module from the list displayed in Figure 14.6 and click the Remove button.

RESTARTING KERNELD

The changes you make with the Kernel Daemon Configuration tool are made in the `/etc/conf.modules` file, which `kerneld` reads whenever it is started. Listing 14.2 provides a sample listing.

Listing 14.2 A Sample /etc/conf.modules File

```
alias scsi_hostadapter BusLogic
alias eth0 ne2k-pci
```

To restart `kerneld`, you can use the tool shown in Figure 14.6 and click the Restart Kerneld button. You can also restart the daemon via the command line, as shown here:

```
/etc/rc.d/init.d/kerneld stop
/etc/rc.d/init.d/kerneld start
```

Restarting `kerneld` does not cause any modules that are currently in use to be reloaded, but `kerneld` will use the configuration when it loads modules in the future.

CHAPTER 15

Linux on PowerPC Platforms

In this chapter

by Steve Burnett

LINUX FOR THE POWERPC

Although Linux is predominantly developed and used on the Intel series of processors, the operating system has been ported to other hardware platforms. For example, the Red Hat distribution Linux was at one point shipped for the Intel processor, Motorola's PowerPC RISC processor, Sun's Sparc, and the Alpha processor. Other efforts working with non-Intel processors include a minimal but functioning port of Linux to the PDA (personal digital assistant) PalmPilot from 3Com. Although not much appears to be active with Linux on Sparc and Alpha, an active development effort focuses on work supporting Linux on the PowerPC family of processors from Motorola. The two primary vendors of PowerPC-based hardware are Apple Computer, which switched from the Motorola 68k family of CPUs for its Macintosh computers in the mid-1990s, and IBM, which uses PowerPCs as the CPU in its series of RS/6000 workstations and servers.

PowerPC support was recently integrated into the main Linux kernel tree in version 2.2.x. Work is in progress to port to 64-bit versions of the PowerPC architecture, and also to include the hard-realtime kernel extension. Although binaries of Linux for Intel applications don't run on PowerPC versions of Linux, recompiling a given application is usually all that's required; a primary goal of the development effort was to make software porting relatively painless. More than one of the Linux for PPC distributions has standardized on the glibc C libraries. For example, Applix's port of its Applixware Office Suite to LinuxPPC took about a month and was reported to be a "flawless" transition.

Informational sources for Linux on PowerPC include a Usenet newsgroup, `comp.os.linux.powerpc`, which includes MkLinux, Linux-pmac, and LinuxPPC. You can find the Web site for the Linux/PPC project at `http://www.linuxppc.org/`, with a kernel development group at `http://www.ppc.kernel.org/`. You also can find a general informational Web site devoted to Linux on the PowerPC platform at `http://linux.macnews.de/index.shtml`.

The following sections of this chapter present some of the distributions of Linux for the PowerPC. Other distributions include a German language-localized version, a Red Hat-derived distribution named TurboLinux, a version for non-PowerPC-based Macintoshes called Linux/m68k, and Debian's distribution.

MKLINUX

MkLinux is Apple Computer's Mach 3-based version of the Linux operating system. Versions of MkLinux are available for the Intel, PA-RISC, and PowerPC architectures. Apple's Developer Release 3 disc contains the version of MkLinux that runs on PowerPC-based Apple Power Macintosh and related systems. The following lists the supported and unsupported systems for the current version.

- **Runs MkLinux**—Apple Power Macintosh 6100, 7100, 8100, 9100, 7200, 7500, 7600, 8500, 9500, 7300, 8600, 9600, 4400, 5400, 5500, 6400, and 6500; 20th Anniversary Mac; G3 Desktop; G3 Minitower; Powerbooks 5300, 1400, 2400, and 3400; and G3. Similar clones are likely to function but may not have been explicitly tested.
- **Does not run MkLinux**—68k Macintoshes; PowerPC Performas 52xx, 53xx, 62xx, and 63xx; Powerbook 2300; iMac/A; iMac/B; colored iMacs; iBook; and Blue and White G3.

As of DR3, MkLinux binary executables are compatible with the other PowerPC Linux systems (for example, LinuxPPC). In addition, MkLinux file systems are byte-order compatible with other Linux file systems (for example, Intel-based). MkLinux DR3 added support for dynamic shared libraries to reduce disk and RAM storage and improve program-loading speed.

For more information on MkLinux, you can find Apple's Web site for it at `http://www.mklinux.apple.com`. You also can find a community-based Web site for the project at `http://www.mklinux.org/`.

YELLOW DOG LINUX

Yellow Dog Linux is made available in two flavors:

- Yellow Dog Linux Champion Server
- Yellow Dog Linux Gone Home

The Server edition ships with a suite of applications intended for business or technical use, whereas the Gone Home edition ships with user-based tools for use as a home desktop. Commercial support is available for the Yellow Dog distribution. Table 15.1 indicates which platforms support Yellow Dog Linux.

TABLE 15.1 YELLOW DOG LINUX-CAPABLE HARDWARE

Company	Platforms That Support Yellow Dog
Apple Computer	Blue & White G3s; iMac; G3 desktop; All-in-Ones; and Powerbooks, 9600, 9500, 8600, 8500, 7600, 7500, 7300, 7200, 6500, 6400, 5500, 5400, 4400
Apple Computer	Twentieth Anniversary Macintosh, PowerBook 2400 and 3400, Apple Network Server (ANS) 500 and 700
Apus	2000, 3000
Be	BeBox
IBM	RS6000 (830, 850, 40P, Nobis, INDI)
Motorola	StarMax (and all StarMax clones from APS, PowerTools, and MacTell), PowerStack, FirePower, Series E, and PowerStack II
Power Computing	PowerBase, PowerWave, PowerCenter, PowerCenter Pro, PowerTower, PowerTower Pro

Table 15.1 Yellow Dog Linux-Capable Hardware

Company	Platforms That Support Yellow Dog
Umax	C500, C600, J700, and S900; Apus 2000 and 3000

Only the Apple models in the first row of the table are supported; the Yellow Dog documentation states that the rest of them work but are unsupported.

The Black Lab Linux distribution is built on Yellow Dog Linux Server and is the Beowulf clustering capability added to LinuxPPC. The reason for this is the newer Apple Macintoshes such as the blue-and-white minitowers, the iMac and iBook, do not require a video card or CD-ROM. Macintosh hardware built on the New World ROM design automatically attempts a "net boot," searching for a remote machine to boot from, loading the operating system into RAM without use of internal storage devices.

For more information on Yellow Dog and Black Lab Linux, check out the Yellow Dog Linux Web site at`http://www.yellowdoglinux.com` and the Black Lab Linux Web site at `http://www.blacklablinux.com/`.

LinuxPPC

LinuxPPC is a port of the Linux operating system to the PowerPC processor-based platforms, such as the Apple Macintosh and IBM RS/6000 platforms. LinuxPPC has been developed under the GNU General Public License (GPL), and as such, the source code is freely available. Unlike MKLinux, it uses the conventional Linux kernel instead of the Mach microkernel. LinuxPPC is compatible with programs compiled for MkLinux, except for the few that make Mach microkernel system calls.

LinuxPPC is offered as a commercial release by LinuxPPC, Inc. Similar to MkLinux, LinuxPPC is based on the Red Hat Linux distribution and ships with a selection of applications and utilities, including the KDE GUI, Netscape Communicator, the GIMP, Apache, sendmail, sshd, and a suite of C and C++ software-development tools. LinuxPPC currently supports glibc 2.1 and the Linux 2.2 kernel. In addition to the freely distributed material that comes with the operating system, Applix has ported the Applixware Office Suite to LinuxPPC, as well as Stalker Software's Communigate Pro mail server.

Being a PowerPC-native operating system, LinuxPPC can coexist peacefully on the same system as the original operating system, such as AIX, Mac OS, or BeOS, in the same way Linux for Intel can share a system with Microsoft Windows or other operating systems. A few features of LinuxPPC that are notable from a Linux for Intel processor perspective include the following:

- Support for PCI-based 601, 603/603e, 604/604e/604r, and G3 machines. However, NuBus-based Macintosh systems such as the Apple Power Macintosh 6100, 7100, and 8100 family are not supported.

- Serial and USB device support for many printers and modems.
- X Windows and several window managers such as AfterStep, WindowMaker, Enlightenment, and desktop environments such as KDE and GNOME.
- Java support (JDK 1.1.7, 1.2).

Being a full port of Linux, LinuxPPC supports all the expected hardware: SCSI and IDE drives, Ethernet and other networking gear, serial port devices such as printers and modems, and so on.

For Apple Macintosh users, the BootX application is a LILO-like chooser that allows you to select Mac OS or Linux at boot-up. You also can choose to quit Mac OS and boot LinuxPPC from the Mac OS Finder. BootX consists of the application itself and a Mac OS system extension. An included MkLinux plug-in supports the use of BootX for booting into MkLinux instead of LinuxPPC. BootX allows you to use Mac OS initialized video, and installation of LinuxPPC does not require a floppy drive. In addition to an X-based installer, you can also use a Red Hat-style installer by adding the word `redhat` to the kernel arguments line in the BootX window that comes up when starting Install LinuxPPC on the CD.

Tip #82 from *steve*

> The BootX application may be found at the author's Web site at `http://calvaweb.calvacom.fr/bh40/`.

LinuxPPC runs on PCI-based Power Macintosh computers and compatibles, as well as PowerPC BeBox, PReP, and CHRP machines. Machines that can run LinuxPPC are shown in Table 15.2.

Table 15.2 LinuxPPC Supported Hardware

Company	Platforms That Support LinuxPPC
Apple Computer	Blue & White G3s; iMac; G3 desktop and Powerbooks, 9600, 9500, 8600, 8500, 8200, 7600, 7500, 7300, 7200, 6500, 6400, 6360, 5500, 5400, 4400; Powerbook 2400 and 3400; 20th Anniversary Macintosh
Be	BeBox
IBM	RS6000 (PowerPC-based), 830, 850, 40P, Nobis, INDI
Motorola	StarMax (and all StarMax clones from APS, PowerTools, and MacTell), PowerStack, Series E, PowerStack II
Power Computing	PowerBase, PowerWave, PowerCenter, PowerCenter Pro, PowerTower, PowerTower Pro
Umax	C500, C600, J700, and S900; Apus 2000 and 3000

LinuxPPC maintains an actively supported mailing list for those interested in its distribution of Linux. To subscribe to the LinuxPPC-user mailing list, you can send email to `linuxppc-user-request@lists.linuxppc.org` and add the word `subscribe` in the body of the message, or you can send email to `linuxppc-announce-request@lists.linuxppc.org` if you want announcements only.

For more information and other lists, you can check out the informational Web page at `http://lists.linuxppc.org/`.

SheepShaver: Use Linux and Have Your Macintosh Too

SheepShaver is originally a Mac OS runtime environment for the BeOS developed by Christian Bauer and Marc Hellwig; it allows users of PowerPC-based BeOS and Linux systems to run Mac OS applications at native speed inside the BeOS multitasking environment. This means that both Linux and Mac OS applications can run at the same time and exchange data between them. Because SheepShaver is not an emulator running in full-screen mode, you won't notice any difference in speed compared to running Mac OS without SheepShaver. You need a copy of Mac OS to use SheepShaver.

SheepShaver currently supports the operation of Mac OS 7.5.2, 7.5.3, 7.5.5, 7.6, 7.6.1, 8.0, and 8.1, and with any Macintosh application that doesn't access Mac hardware directly. In addition, you can also run an emulator such as VirtualPC under SheepShaver or WINE for Linux.

SheepShaver for LinuxPPC should run on any BeOS/Linux-ready PowerPC system, including such rarities as the BeBox and PowerPC Amigas. It does not run on Intel machines because Mac OS and PowerPC Mac applications run natively under SheepShaver accessing the PowerPC directly. SheepShaver/Linux requires at least glibc 2.0, GTK 1.2, and a 2.2.x kernel. For more information, see Sheepsaver's Web site at `http://www.sheepshaver.com/`.

Project: Adding Linux to a Macintosh Environment with Netatalk

Consider a prepress graphics shop that is an all-Macintosh operation. The office administrator decides he wants to experiment with Linux and, in the by now venerable tradition, finds a system he can set up as a Linux-based file and print server. However, all his employees use Macintoshes, which communicate among themselves with the network protocol, AppleTalk, over which Mac OS provides file sharing and network printing. How does the office administrator make the Linux server a benefit to his users? With the use of Netatalk on the Linux server.

Through the AppleTalk protocol, a machine running Mac OS can use file and print services from a Linux box. The reverse is also possible: A Linux machine can print to remote AppleTalk print queues and even mount AppleTalk disk shares.

Note

The platform for the Linux server is irrelevant in this case. The Linux server can be PowerPC-based, Intel-based, or based on another processor.

The Mac OS file system (HFS) is included in the Linux kernel from release 2.2.x and higher (HFS+ is not yet supported, however). Netatalk is a kernel-level implementation of the AppleTalk Protocol Suite; it was originally developed for BSD UNIX-derived systems. It includes support for routing AppleTalk, serving UNIX and AFS file systems over AFP (AppleShare), serving UNIX printers, and accessing AppleTalk printers over the Printer Access Protocol (PAP), as well as including a small suite of utilities. The basic Netatalk is available from the University of Michigan at `http://www.umich.edu/~rsug/netatalk/`. Adrian Sun has developed a set of patches and modifications including bug fixes and performance enhancements to the basic Netatalk suite; you can find this set under the name netatalk+asun at `ftp://ftp.u.washington.edu/public/asun/` or from Red Hat Software's site at `ftp://contrib.redhat.com/`.

An AppleTalk network address is described by a network number and a node number. Network numbers can be in the range of 1 to 65279 (65280 through 65534 are reserved for networks with no AppleTalk routers present). Each network can have up to 253 defined nodes. AppleTalk uses zones for organizational and access control, as well as making AppleTalk networking more friendly. Zones conceal the numerical network address from clients in the same way the domain name service masks the IP number of a server (192.168.0.45) with a name such as `www.afakecompany.com`.

AppleTalk support has been included in Linux since release 1.3.x, specifically for the DDP protocol. DDP is the AppleTalk datagram protocol over which the other protocols are implemented, just as FTP is implemented over TCP/IP. DDP lives in the kernel, but the other protocols are supported by the Netatalk package itself. Adding AppleTalk support as a module (typically named `appletalk.o`) is more flexible for the user than compiling AppleTalk support into the kernel. As a module, AppleTalk can be reset without disturbing other networking activity by removing and reinserting the module. To disable the AppleTalk module, you can enter the following at a terminal prompt:

```
# rmmod appletalk
```

To restart the AppleTalk module, enter the following

```
# insmod appletalk
```

To find out whether your Linux distribution's kernel has AppleTalk support as a module, see whether the following exists:

```
/lib/modules//misc/appletalk.o
```

Tip #83 from *Steve*

> You can check your kernel version by using the `uname -r` command.

To check whether AppleTalk support has been compiled directly into the kernel, see whether the file `/proc/net/appletalk/` exists, or check the boot messages (using `dmesg`) for a line like the following:

```
'NET4: AppleTalk 0.18 for Linux NET4.0'
```

If the sources used for the current kernel are available, you can also check `/usr/src/linux/.config` to see whether `CONFIG_ATALK` is set to `y`.

Netatalk's default configuration files are nicely self-documented, and in many cases suffice without much, if any, tweaking. One default setting you might want to change is the number of simultaneous users, which defaults to five.

PART III

WORKING WITH LINUX

CHAPTER 16

UNDERSTANDING LINUX SHELLS

In this chapter

by Steve Burnett

LOGGING IN

As a new user and novice system administrator on your recently installed Linux system, you've chosen a login ID and password. Because Linux is a multiuser operating system, it must be able to distinguish between users and classes of users. Linux uses your login ID to establish a session in your name and determine the privileges you have. Linux uses your password to verify who you are.

Because any user can log in to any terminal in theory (there is an exception), the UNIX operating system begins by displaying a login prompt on every terminal. Because it's unlikely you'll have multiple terminals connected to your initial Linux system (although connecting multiple terminals is certainly possible), you'll have the alternate, or virtual, terminals available to you.

To switch to the various virtual terminals, you can press the Alt key and any of the first six function keys. For example, to log in to virtual terminal one as root, you can press Alt+F1, which displays the following prompt:

```
Red Hat Linux release 5.1 (Manhattan)
Kernel 2.0.36 on an i686
login:
```

Note

The prompt line in the code line declares this sample session to be running under the 2.0.36 version of the Linux kernel. As newer kernels are released, this number is incremented, so you might see a different version on the accompanying CD-ROMs. The stable released kernels are given even numbers for the middle number, and the odd numbers indicate the latest (and beta) releases.

At this point, you can enter your user ID (root) and password.

When you log in to any terminal, you own the session on that terminal until you log out. When you log out, Linux displays the login prompt for the next user. Between logging in and logging out, Linux makes sure that all the programs you run and any files you might create are owned by you. Conversely, Linux doesn't allow you to read or alter a file owned by another user unless that user or the system administrator has given you permission to do so. Your login ID and password allow Linux to maintain the security of your files and those of others.

As the system administrator for your Linux system, you assign every user a user ID, temporary password, group ID, home directory, and shell. This information is kept in a file named `/etc/passwd`, which is owned and controlled by the system administrator, also known as *root* or the *superuser*. After you successfully log in, you can change your password, which is then encrypted in a form that no one else can read. If you forget your password, you (the system administrator) have to log in as the root user to create a new password. You can change your own password by using the `passwd` command (although you have to type in the old password).

Note For more information on basic system administration duties, such as adding users and fixing forgotten passwords, see the chapters in Part II, "System Administration," particularly Chapter 11, "Managing User Accounts."

Understanding Shells

After you log in, Linux places you in your home directory and runs a program called a *shell*. A shell is really nothing more than a program designed to accept commands from you and execute them. Many kinds of programs can be used as shells, but several standard shells are available with almost all versions of Linux.

Note Although graphical interfaces have been added to the UNIX system in recent years, you run most of the utilities for using and administering Linux (and other UNIX-like systems) by typing commands. In Linux, the command-line interpreter is called the *shell*. Linux shells are equivalent to the COMMAND.COM program used by MS-DOS: they accept and execute commands, run batch files, and execute programs.

Looking at Different Shells

Red Hat Linux provides the following shells: sh, bash (Bourne Again Shell), tcsh, csh, pdksh (Public Domain Korn Shell), zsh, ash, and mc. You should try each shell and pick the one you like. This chapter concentrates on the sh and bash shells because most Linux distributions install bash as the default shell. Also, sh is available on most UNIX systems, and you'll find many shell scripts written with sh commands.

Because the shell serves as the primary interface between the operating system and the user, many users identify the shell with Linux. They expect the shell to be programmable, but the shell isn't part of the kernel of the operating system. With enough background in systems programming and knowledge of the Linux operating system, you can write a program that can become a shell.

Note Although many different shells have been created, several shells are prevalent: the Bourne, C, T, and Korn shells. The Bourne shell is the oldest, and the others have some features not in the Bourne shell. In fact, Linux uses a variation of the Bourne shell, the bash shell, as its default shell. (To the novice user, the Bourne and Korn shells look identical; indeed, the Korn shell was developed from the Bourne shell.)

The Red Hat distribution provides a version of the Korn shell called pdksh, which stands for Public Domain Korn Shell.

The C shell was developed at the University of California at Berkeley as a shell more suitable for programmers than the Bourne shell. The T shell is a derivative of the C shell. The Korn shell has all the features of the C shell but uses the syntax of the Bourne shell. If all this information sounds confusing at the moment, don't worry. You can do a lot of work without knowing or worrying about the shell you're using.

In their simplest forms, the Bourne and Korn shells use the dollar sign (`$`) as the standard prompt; the C shell uses the percent sign (`%`) as the prompt. Fortunately (or not, depending on your disposition), you can change these prompts so that you can or cannot see either the dollar sign or the percent sign when you first log in.

The Bourne shell, known as sh, is the original UNIX shell. It was written by Steve Bourne with some help and ideas from John Mashey, both of AT&T Bell Laboratories; this shell is available on all Linux systems. The executable program for this shell is in the file `/bin/sh`. Because the Bourne shell is available on all Linux systems, and it has all the properties described in the preceding sections as well as powerful programming capabilities, it has become widely used.

Tip #84 from Steve

Many of the shell script examples in this chapter are written so that they can be used with the Bourne shell. *Shell scripts* are sequences of shell commands, normally written with an ASCII editor such as vi. You can think of shell scripts as similar to DOS batch files.

→ See "What Is vi?" p. 205

The C shell, known as csh, was developed by Bill Joy at the University of California at Berkeley. The students and faculty at Berkeley have had a great deal of influence on UNIX and hence Linux. Two results of that influence are the C shell and the vi text editor. The Bourne shell has superior shell programming capabilities, but the C shell was developed to reflect the fact that computing is becoming more interactive. The executable program for the C shell is in the file `/bin/csh`.

The syntax of the C shell closely resembles the C programming language. This is one reason that shell scripts written for the C shell often can't run under the Bourne or Korn shell (executables compiled under the C shell often behave properly, though). But the C shell has some desirable features not available in the Bourne shell: command editing, history, and aliasing.

The default Linux shell is the bash shell. bash is located in `/bin/bash` and provides several enhanced features detailed in the next few paragraphs, such as command editing, command history, and command completion.

Tip #85 from *Steve*

> Man pages are not available for the various shells, but the shells each have their own internal help. To find help, you can open a terminal window and type `help`. For the bash shell, for example, you see a list of commands defined internal to the bash shell. Each command also has its own help included in the bash shell.

All Linux systems have the bash shell. You also might have installed several other shells during installation—for example, the C shell or the T shell. To determine which shell you're using, you can enter the following:

```
echo $SHELL
```

The `echo` command prints whatever follows the word `echo` to the terminal screen. `SHELL` is a variable, maintained by the shell, that holds the name of your current shell; `$SHELL` is the value of that variable.

To see whether the C shell is available, enter this command:

```
Csh
```

If you see the percent sign (`%`) as the prompt, the C shell is available and running (enter `exit` to return to your previous shell). If you're logged in as root, the prompt for the C shell is `#`. If you get an error message, the C shell isn't available to you.

The shell you use as a login shell is specified in the password file. Each login ID is represented by a record or line in the password file; the last field in the record specifies your login shell. To change your login shell, you must change that field. The act of changing to another shell is relatively easy. Before you change shells, however, you need to decide whether learning a new syntax and operating method are worth the change. See the man pages for detailed information on your shell's syntax.

Tip #86 from *Steve*

> Never directly edit the password file (`/etc/passwd`) in Linux. Because of the security features added to these releases, the password file should be manipulated only with the appropriate commands. This caution is especially important if you are using the Shadow Suite of utilities.

Several other shells are available; some are proprietary, and others are available on the Internet or through other sources. To determine which shell you want to use, simply read the man pages for the various shells and give each a try. Because shells are programs, you can run them just like any other application.

CONFIGURING YOUR LOGIN ENVIRONMENT

Before you see the shell prompt, Linux sets up your default environment. The Linux environment contains settings and data that control your session while you're logged in. Of course, as with all things in Linux, you're completely free to change any of these settings to suit your needs.

Your session environment is divided into two components:

- The first component, called the *terminal environment*, controls your terminal (more properly, the behavior of the computer's port to which you connect the cable from your terminal).

> **Note** Because Linux runs on a PC, the "terminal" is actually your monitor and keyboard. You may or may not have other terminals connected to your Linux system. Of course, you do have six virtual terminals from which you can log in.

- The second component, called the *shell environment*, controls various aspects of the shell and any programs you run.

You should first know about your terminal environment.

SETTING THE TERMINAL ENVIRONMENT

Your login session actually consists of two separate programs that run side by side to give you the appearance of having the machine to yourself. Although the shell is the program that receives your instructions and executes them, before the shell ever sees your commands, everything you type must first pass through the relatively transparent program called the *device driver*.

The device drivercontrols your terminal. It receives the characters you type and determines what to do with them—if anything—before passing them on to the shell for interpretation. Likewise, every character generated by the shell must pass through the device driver before being delivered to the terminal. This section is first concerned with how to control the behavior of your device driver.

Linux is unique in that every device connected to the system looks, to a program, just like every other device, and all devices look like files. It's the task of the different device drivers in your system to accomplish this transformation. A hard disk in the system behaves very differently from your terminal, yet it's the job of their respective device drivers to make them look identical to a program.

For example, a disk has blocks, sectors, and cylinders, all of which must be properly addressed when reading and writing data. Your terminal, on the other hand, accepts a continuous stream of characters, but those characters must be delivered to the terminal in an ordered and relatively slow manner. The device driver orders this data and sends it to you at 1200, 2400, 9600, or higher bits per second (bps) and inserts stop, start, and parity bits in the data stream.

Because your terminal is always connected to the system, the device driver allows you to define special characters, called *control characters*, that serve as end-of-file and end-of-line markers for your shell. The device driver also allows you to define control characters that send signals to a running process (such as the interrupt signal, which can, in most cases, stop a running process and return you to the shell). Figure 16.1 shows one way that the Linux kernel, shell, and device driver behave.

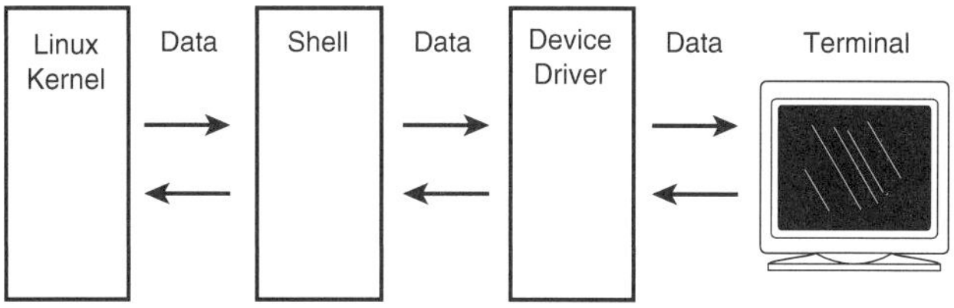

Figure 16.1 You can understand how Linux interacts with the user through the command shell.

You can set dozens of parameters for your terminal, but most of them are handled automatically. However, you should know about a few parameters and modes.

The device driver has two modes of operation, called *cooked* and *raw*. In raw mode, all the characters you type pass directly to the shell or to a program run by the shell. Programs such as editors and spreadsheets require raw mode and set it up automatically. When such programs end, they normally reset your terminal to cooked mode—but not always. When your terminal is in raw mode, it doesn't respond to control keys such as the interrupt key.

When your terminal is in cooked mode, every key you type is interpreted by the device driver. Normal keys are stored in a buffer until the end-of-line key is pressed. In most cases, the end-of-line key is the Enter or Return key (however, this key can be changed). When the device driver receives the end-of-line character, it interprets the entire line before passing the interpreted or parsed line on to the shell or application program. Table 16.1 lists the most important control keys.

TABLE 16.1 CONTROL KEYS

Key Name	Description
Interrupt	Interrupts the execution of a running program. When you give Linux a command and press the end-of-line key, a program typically runs until normal completion. If you press the interrupt key, you send a signal to the running program, telling it to stop. Some programs ignore this signal; if your terminal is in raw mode, the interrupt key passes directly to the program and may not have the desired effect. The UNIX convention is to use the Del key as the interrupt key, but Linux changes this key to Ctrl+c for the convenience of people familiar with MS-DOS and other systems that use this key combination.
Erase	Deletes the last character in the buffer. This key is defined as the Backspace key. The erase key works just like the Backspace key on a typewriter. On some terminals and systems, there's confusion between the Delete and Backspace keys.
Kill	Deletes everything in the buffer before it passes to the shell or application program. This key is normally defined as the @ character. Unlike when you press the interrupt key, you don't see a new shell prompt when you press the kill key; the device driver simply waits for you to type more text.
End-of-line	Tells the device driver that you've finished entering text and want the text interpreted and passed on to the shell or application program. Linux uses the Enter or Return key.
End-of-file	Tells the shell to exit and display the login prompt. The end-of-file character is the Ctrl+d character. Linux treats all devices as though they were files; because your terminal is a source of virtually unlimited characters, Linux uses the end-of-file key as a way for you to signal that you're done with your login session.

The command used to set and display these control-key parameters is `stty`, which stands for *set teletype*. In the old days, a teletype terminal was the only terminal available; a lot of UNIX terminology is left over from this era. For example, your terminal is defined as a tty device with a name such as tty14. To display all your present settings, enter `stty -a` on the command line. If you use this command, you see something like this:

```
speed 38400 baud; rows 25; columns 80; line = 0;
intr = ^C; quit = ^\; erase = ^?; kill = ^U; eof = ^D; eol = <undef>;
eol2 = <undef>; start = ^Q; stop = ^S; susp = ^Z; rprnt = ^R; werase = ^W;
lnext = ^V; flush = ^O; min = 1; time = 0;
-parenb -parodd cs8 hupcl -cstopb cread -clocal -crtscts
-ignbrk -brkint -ignpar -parmrk -inpck -istrip -inlcr -igncr icrnl ixon ixoff
-iuclc -ixany -imaxbel
opost -olcuc -ocrnl onlcr -onocr -onlret -ofill -ofdel nl0 cr0 tab0 bs0 vt0 ff0
isig icanon iexten echo echoe echok -echonl -noflsh -xcase -tostop -echoprt
echoctl echoke
```

Notice that on this system, the interrupt key (`intr`) is defined as Ctrl+c (shown as `^C`), and the kill key is Ctrl+u. Although you can set all the settings listed here, as a matter of practicality, users usually reset only the interrupt and kill keys. For example, if you want to change the kill key from `^U` to `^C`, enter the following:

```
stty kill '^C'
```

Note

If your terminal is behaving strangely, reset it to a "most reasonable" setting by giving the command `stty sane`.

Tip #87 from *Steve*

If you want a certain setting to take effect every time you log in, place the command in your `.profile` file (located in your home directory) if you're running the bash, Bourne, or Korn shell. For the C shell, place the command in your `.login` file.

SETTING THE SHELL ENVIRONMENT

Part of the process of logging in—that is, of creating a Linux session—is the creation of your environment. All Linux *processes* (as running programs are called) have their own environment separate and distinct from the program itself. It could be said that a program runs from within an environment. The Linux environment, called the *shell environment*, consists of a number of variables and their values. These variables and values allow a running program, such as a shell, to determine what the environment looks like.

Environment refers the shell that you use, your home directory, and what type of terminal you're using, for example. Many of these variables are defined during the login process and either can't or shouldn't be changed. You can add or change as many variables as you like as long as a variable hasn't been marked read-only.

Variables are set in the environment in the form `VARIABLE=value`. You can set the meaning of `VARIABLE` to anything you like. However, many variables have predefined meanings to many standard Linux programs. For example, the `TERM` variable is defined as being the name of your terminal type, as specified in one of the standard Linux terminal databases. Digital Equipment Corporation for years made a popular terminal named the VT-100. The characteristics of this terminal have been copied by many other manufacturers and often emulated in software for personal computers. The name of such a terminal type is vt100; it's represented in the environment as `TERM=vt100`.

Many other predefined variables exist in your environment. If you use the C shell, you can list these variables by using the `printenv` command; with the Bourne or Korn shell, you use the `set` command. Table 16.2 lists the most common environment variables and their uses. The Variable column shows what you type at the command line.

Note Some environment and system variables can be changed, and some can't.

TABLE 16.2 COMMON BOURNE SHELL ENVIRONMENT VARIABLES

Variable	Description
`HOME=/home/`*`login`*	`HOME` sets your home directory, which is the location from which you start. Replace *`login`* with your login ID. For example, if your login ID is jack, `HOME` is defined as `/home/jack`.
`LOGNAME=`*`login`*	`LOGNAME` is automatically set the same as your login ID.
`PATH=`*`path`*	The *`path`* option represents the list of directories that the shell looks through for commands. For example, you can set the path like this: `PATH=/usr:/bin:/usr/local/bin`.
`PS1=`*`prompt`*	`PS1` is the primary shell prompt that defines what your prompt looks like. If you don't set it to anything specific, your prompt is the dollar sign (`$`). If you prefer, you can set it to something more creative. For example, `PS1="Enter Command >''` displays `Enter Command >` as your command-line prompt.
`PWD=`*`directory`*	`PWD` is automatically set for you. It defines where you are in the file system. For example, if you checked `PWD` (by entering `echo $PWD` at the command line) and Linux displays `/usr/bin`, you're in the `/usr/bin` directory. The `pwd` command also displays the current directory.
`SHELL=`*`shell`*	`SHELL` identifies the location of the program that serves as your shell. For example, you can set `SHELL` in your `.profile` or `.login` file as `SHELL=/bin/ksh` to make the Korn shell your login shell.
`TERM=`*`termtype`*	This variable sets the name of your terminal type, as specified by the terminal database. For example, you can set `TERM` in your `.profile` or `.login` file as `TERM=vt100`.

Tip #88 from *Steve*

If you want an environment variable defined every time you log in, you can place the definition in your `.profile` file (located in your home directory) if you're running the bash or Bourne shell. For the C shell, place the definition in your `.login` file.

Perhaps the single most important variable in your environment is the `PATH` variable.

Note MS-DOS users should be familiar with the `PATH` variable. It performs the same function under both DOS and Linux.

The PATH variable contains a colon-delimited string that points to all the directories containing the programs you use. The order in which these directories are listed determines which directories are searched first. The list order is important on systems that support several different forms of the same command. Your system may also have locally created commands you want to access. For example, your PATH variable might contain the following values:

```
/usr/ucb:/bin:/usr/bin:/usr/local/bin
```

This statement tells your shell to explore the /usr/ucb directory first. If the shell finds the command in the first directory it searches, it stops searching and executes that command. The /bin and /usr/bin directories contain all the standard Linux commands. The /usr/local/bin directory often contains the local commands you and other users of your system added. This task of adding local commands is usually the responsibility of the system administrator.

If you are acting as the system administrator, or if you want access to the more system-oriented commands, you will probably want to add /usr/sbin or /usr/local/sbin or both to shorten the effort of typing /usr/sbin/traceroute.

If you intend to create your own commands, you can modify the PATH variable to include directories that contain your own commands. How you do so depends on which shell you use. For example, if you use the Bourne or Korn shells, you can add a directory to your PATH variable by typing the following at the command prompt:

```
$ PATH=$PATH: newpath
```

Tip #89 from *Steve*

When you place a $ in front of the name of a variable, its current value is substituted. In this command, the $PATH variable represents whatever the current path is; the colon and the *newpath* parameters add to the current path.

The following sections describe several other ways of manipulating variables in your environment. For now, it's sufficient to say that the shell environment contains variables and functions and that these objects can be manipulated by both shells and application programs. Application programs can access and modify the environment, but they generally manipulate variables within the program. Shells, on the other hand, can only manipulate variables in the environment.

Using Special Shell Variables

The shell keeps track of a number of special variables. You can see what they are by using the env command, which lists the variables available to you within your working environment. Following is an abbreviated list of what you might see when you enter env:

```
HOME=/usr/wrev
```

```
SHELL=/bin/sh
MAIL=/usr/mail/wrev
LOGNAME=wrev
PATH=/bin:/usr/bin:.
TZ=PST8PDT
PS1=$
TERM=vt100
```

You can use any of these special variables in the same way you use any other shell variable. Table 16.3 defines the special variables.

TABLE 16.3 SPECIAL ENVIRONMENT VARIABLES

Variable Name	Meaning
HOME	Full path name of your home directory
SHELL	Name of your current shell
MAIL	Full pathname of your mailbox
LOGNAME	Your login name
PATH	Directories the shell searches for commands
TZ	Time zone for the date command
SECONDS	Number of seconds since invoking the shell
PS1	System prompt
TERM	The type of terminal you're using

THE HOME VARIABLE The HOME variable always specifies your home directory. When you log in, you're in your home directory. Occasionally, you use the cd command to move to other directories. To change to the directory /usr/local/games, for example, you enter cd /usr/local/games. To get back to your home directory, all you have to do is enter cd. You can use the HOME variable when you're writing shell scripts that specify files in your home directory. Rather than write a command such as grep $number /usr/wrev/sales/data.01, it's better to enter the command as grep $number $HOME/sales/data.01 for these reasons:

- The command line is easier to read.
- If your home directory is moved, the command still works.
- $HOME always represents the home directory of whoever is using the command. If you enter the command by using $HOME, others can use the command as well.

THE PATH VARIABLE The PATH variable lists the directories in which the shell searches for commands. The shell searches those directories in the order they're listed. If you enter PATH=/bin:/usr/bin/:., whenever the shell interprets a command, it first looks in the directory /bin. If it can't find the command there, the shell looks in the directory /usr/bin. Finally, the shell searches the . directory (remember that the dot represents your current directory). If you enter cal to print this month's calendar, the shell first looks in /bin. Because the command isn't there, the shell then looks in /usr/bin and finds it.

Tip #90 from
Steve

If you have a personalized command named `cal`, the shell never finds it; the shell executes the `cal` command in `/usr/bin` first whenever you give the command. You should give your commands names that aren't the same as system commands.

You might want to put all your shell scripts in one directory and change the `PATH` variable to include that directory. This arrangement allows you to execute your shell scripts from whatever directory you happen to be in. To do so, follow these steps:

1. Create a directory to hold the scripts. Use the `mkdir $HOME/bin` command to create the `bin` subdirectory in your home directory.
2. Move each shell script to that subdirectory. For example, to move a shell script named `stamp` to your `bin` subdirectory, use the `mv stamp $HOME/bin` command.
3. Add the script subdirectory to your `PATH` variable by using the `PATH=$PATH:$HOME/bin` command. Do so in your `.profile` file so that the change takes effect every time you log in to your system.

You need to create the new `bin` directory and modify the `PATH` variable only once. Under Linux, the directory called `/usr/local/bin` is created to hold "local" commands and scripts that aren't part of the standard Linux package but that you've added locally and have made available to all users. In this case, you should expect that `/usr/local/bin` is also part of `PATH`.

The `MAIL` Variable The `MAIL` variable contains the name of the file that holds your email. Whenever mail comes into the system for you, it's put into the file specified by the `MAIL` variable. If you have a program that notifies you when new mail has arrived, it checks the file associated with the `MAIL` variable.

The `PS1` Variable The `PS1` variable holds the string of characters you see as your primary prompt. The prompt is the string of characters the shell displays whenever it's ready to receive a command. You'll see how you can change this variable—and any of the others—in the section "Customizing Linux Shells" near the end of this chapter.

The `TERM` Variable The `TERM` variable is used to identify your terminal type. Programs that operate in full-screen mode, such as the vi text editor, need this information.

The `TZ` Variable The `TZ` variable holds a string that identifies your time zone. The date program and some other programs require this information.

Your computer system keeps track of time according to Greenwich Mean Time (GMT). If the `TZ` variable is set to `PST8PDT`, the time and date are determined as Pacific Standard Time (`PST`), eight hours west of GMT, with support for Pacific Daylight Savings Time (`PDT`). Your computer system automatically changes between daylight savings time and standard time.

THE LOGNAME VARIABLE The `LOGNAME` variable holds your login name, the name or string of characters that the system associates with you. Among the tasks the `LOGNAME` variable is used for is to identify you as the owner of your files, as the originator of any processes or programs you may be running, and as the author of mail or messages sent by the `write` command.

The following example is an extension of `safrm`, a shell script created for the safe removal of files. The `LOGNAME` variable is used to remove all the files you own from the directory `/tmp`. To remove those files, the shell script uses the `find` command. The `find` command has a number of options; the shell script uses this `find` command line:

```
find /tmp -user $LOGNAME -exec rm {} \;
```

The first parameter, `/tmp`, is the directory to search. The option `-user` indicates that you want to search for all files that belong to a specified user. Before the command is executed, the shell replaces `$LOGNAME` with the current user's login name. The option `-exec` indicates that the following command is to be applied to every file found by the find program. In this case, the rm program is used to remove the found files. The braces (`{}`) represent the position of each filename passed to the `rm` command. The last two characters, `\;`, are required by the `find` command (an example of using the backslash to pass a character on to a program without being interpreted by the shell). You can add this command line to the shell script in Listing 16.1 to obtain a program that removes files safely and also cleans up anything a user has in the `/tmp` directory that's more than 10 days old.

LISTING 16.1 THE `safrm` SHELL SCRIPT

```
# Name:       safrm
# Purpose:    copy files to directory /tmp, remove them
#             from the current directory, clean up /tmp,
#             and finally send mail to user
# first copy all parameters to /tmp
cp $* /tmp
# remove the files
rm $*
# create a file to hold the mail message
#    The file's name is set to msg
#    followed by process ID number of this process
#    For example, msg1208
msgfile=/tmp/msg$$
# construct mail message
date > $msgfile
echo "These files were deleted from /tmp" >>$msgfile
# get list of files to be deleted from tmp
# -mtime +10 gets all files that haven't been
# modified in 10 or more days, -print displays the names.
find /tmp -user $LOGNAME -mtime +10 -print >> $msgfile
# remove the appropriate files from /tmp
find /tmp -user $LOGNAME -mtime +10 -exec rm {} \;
# mail off the message
mail $LOGNAME < $msgfile
# clean up
rm $msgfile
```

UNDERSTANDING PROCESSES

A running program in Linux is called a *process*. Because Linux is a multitasking system, many processes can run at the same time. To distinguish between processes, Linux assigns each new process a unique ID called a *process ID (PID)*.

The process ID is simply a number that uniquely identifies each running process. To see what process IDs are now associated with your process, you can use the `ps` command. To look at most of the process IDs now running on your system, you can issue the command with the flags `-guax`, and you see something like the following:


```
USER  PID %CPU %MEM SIZE  RSS TTY STAT START   TIME COMMAND
jack   53  3.2  7.0  352  468 p 1 S    02:01   0:01 -bash
jack   65  0.0  3.5   80  240 p 1 R    02:01   0:00 ps -guax
root    1  0.8  3.1   44  208 con S    02:00   0:00 init
root    6  0.0  1.8   24  124 con S    02:00   0:00 bdflush (daemon)
root    7  0.0  1.9   24  128 con S    02:01   0:00 update (bdflush)
root   40  1.0  3.5   65  240 con S    02:01   0:00 /usr/sbin/syslogd
root   42  0.2  2.9   36  200 con S    02:01   0:00 /usr/sbin/klogd
root   44  0.5  3.2   68  216 con S    02:01   0:00 /usr/sbin/inetd
root   46  0.2  3.0   64  204 con S    02:01   0:00 /usr/sbin/lpd
root   52  0.1  2.0   32  140 con S    02:01   0:00 selection -t ms
root   58  0.2  2.4   37  164 p 6 S    02:01   0:00 /sbin/agetty 38400 tt
```

The process ID is identified by the column titled `PID`. Also note the boldfaced line, which indicates the first process started by the system—`init`. The `init` process is also described later in this chapter.

When Linux is told to run a program (that is, to create a process), it does so by making an exact copy of the program making the request. In the simplest case, you request that a program be run by telling your shell; the shell makes a fork request to the Linux kernel.

FORK, `init`, AND THE `exec` PROCESS

A *fork* is the process of cloning an existing process. Linux creates all new processes through the mechanism of forking. When a process is forked, an almost exact duplicate of an existing process (including its environment and any open files) is created; what keeps the duplicate from being exactly the same as its parent application is a flag that tells the forked process which is the parent and which is the child.

Because all processes are created in this fashion, all processes have a parent process and a parent's process ID. Every process running on a Linux system can trace its lineage back to `init`, the mother of all processes. `init` itself, process ID 1, is the only process run directly by the Linux kernel that you, as a user, have any contact with. Every process you create during a session has your login shell as an ancestor, and your login shell has `init` as its parent.

After a process successfully forks, the child process calls the `exec` routine to transform itself into the process you requested. The only thing that changes after an `exec` function is the identity of the running process; the environment of the new process is an exact copy of the environment of its parent.

STANDARD INPUT AND OUTPUT

Every new process is created with three open "files." Because Linux treats files and devices exactly the same, an open "file" can be a real file on a disk or a device such as your terminal. The three open files are defined as standard input (`stdin`), standard output (`stdout`), and standard error output (`stderr`). All Linux commands, as well as application programs, accept input from the standard input and place any output on the standard output. Any diagnostic messages are automatically placed on the standard error output.

When you first log in, the standard input, output, and error files are attached to your terminal; any programs you run (processes you create) inherit your terminal as the three open files.

UNDERSTANDING SHELL COMMAND PARSING

*Parsing*is the act of splitting the command line, or what you type, into its component parts for processing. In Linux, parsing constitutes a lot more than simply splitting the command line. The command string is first split into its component parts: the filenames expand if you use any wildcards, shell variables expand, I/O redirection sets up, any command groupings or subshells set up, and command substitution is performed. Only then can the command line, as you type it, be executed.

If terms such as *wildcards* and *I/O redirection* are new to you, you can find explanations of them, in the order they're performed, later in this chapter. You must first start, however, with the basic command syntax.

USING COMMANDS, FLAGS, AND PARAMETERS

To execute a Linux command, you merely type the name of the file. The command to list files is `ls`; you can find a file by that name in the `/bin` directory. If `/bin` is listed in your `PATH` variable (and it should be), your shell finds and executes `/bin/ls`.

Some Linux commands aren't independent files. These commands are built into the shells themselves. For example, the `cd` (change directory) command is built into most shells and executed directly by the shell without looking up a file. You can read the man pages for the shell you're using to determine what commands are executed internally or externally. Some shells have a command file that contains commands executed directly by the shell.

FLAGS

If a command is to execute properly, you must present it to your shell in the proper fashion. The command name itself must be the first item on the line; it's followed by any flags and parameters. Flags (sometimes called *options*) are single letters preceded by a hyphen (`-`) that modify the behavior of a command. For example, the list command, `ls`, simply lists the names of the files in the current directory in alphabetical order. By adding various flags, you can list the contents of a directory in many different ways. You can list files and all their attributes by using the "long" flag, `-l`. This command takes the following form:

```
ls -l
```

Here, `-l` is the flag. When you want to use more than one flag, you can simply string the flags together, as in `ls -lF`. The `-F` flag displays an asterisk (*) if the file is executable, an at sign (@) if the file is a symbolic link, and a slash (/) if the file is a subdirectory. The man page for every command usually lists all the modifying flags and their meanings before describing any parameters. Flags can also be listed separately; the shell parses them before passing them on to the program. For example, you can write the `ls -lF` command as `ls -l -F`.

Note

Linux provides a popular feature: color highlighting. When you issue the `ls` command, Linux can display files in different colors depending on the file's type. This feature allows you to quickly identify files that are executable, directories, or files that are linked to other files located in other directories. Also, if you redirect the output from `ls` to a file, this file contains the control codes used to indicate color. The control codes' information may cause problems with other programs, such as less, when used with this file. For Red Hat Linux, you must provide the -color flag to `ls` to get the effect:

```
ls _-color
```

One type of flag signals that the next parameter has some special meaning. For example, the `-t` flag in the `sort` command is used to indicate that the next character is a field separator. If you want to sort the `/etc/passwd` file, whose fields are separated by a colon (:), you can enter the following:

```
sort -t: /etc/passwd
```

In the case of the `sort` command, the `-t` flag is needed only if the file uses a field separator other than the default. The default field separator is defined in the `IFS` (Inter Field Separator) environment variable. The shell uses the `IFS` variable to parse the command line so that the shell knows to use the standard field separator unless the `-t` flag indicates otherwise.

PARAMETERS

Flags must be presented to the command before any other parameters. *Parameters* are strings separated by any of the characters defined in the `IFS` environment variable. The default string in `IFS` is a space, a tab, and a newline character. You can place any number of field-separator characters between parameters; when the shell parses the command line, it reduces these characters to one character before proceeding. For example, if a command is followed by three spaces, a tab character, and then the first parameter, the shell automatically reduces the three spaces and a tab to one tab character. Thus, the line

```
command<spacebar><spacebar><spacebar><Tab>parameter
```

becomes

```
command<Tab>parameter
```

Parameters are usually filenames or strings that tell the command to perform some function. If a parameter contains an embedded space, you must place the string in quotation marks to prevent the shell from expanding it. The following command line contains two parameters; the shell attempts to find the word `New` in a file named `York`:

```
grep New York
```

If the intent is to find the string `"New York''` in the standard input, you must enter the command as follows:

```
grep ''New York''
```

In this case, the string `"New York''` is passed to the `grep` command as one parameter.

Performing Filename Matching

Most modern operating systems (including all versions of Linux and DOS) support the use of *wildcards* for file and string searches. Table 16.4 summarizes the filename completion characters, otherwise known as *wildcards*.

Table 16.4 Filename Completion Characters

Character	Meaning
*	Represents any collection of characters except a period when it's the first character in a filename. For example, the command `cat sales* > allsales` combines all files whose names begin with *sales* into a file named `allsales`.
?	Represents a single character. For example, the command `lp sales.9?` prints a collection of files with names in the form of `sales.`*yy*, where *yy* represents a year in the nineties (such as `sales.90`, `sales.91`, and so on).
[]	Represents a single character in a range. For example, the command `rm sales.9[0-3]` removes the collection of files with the names `sales.90`, `sales.91`, `sales.92`, and `sales.93`.

Tip #91 from
Steve

If you place a filename wildcard or expression inside quotation marks, the filename expansion is suppressed during command-line parsing. For example, if you type `ls *`, you get all files in the current directory. On the other hand, if you type `ls ''*''`, you probably will get the `file not found` error message because you're instructing `ls` to search for a file named `*`.

THE * WILDCARD

The asterisk (*) is the most universal wildcard used. It simply means any and all characters. For example, the string `a*` means all filenames beginning with *a*. You can use as many asterisks in a single expression as you need to define a set of files. For example, the expression `*xx*.gif` means any filename with the `.gif` extension that has `xx` anywhere in the rest of the name. Matches include the filenames `abxx.gif`, `xxyyzz.gif`, and `xx.gif`.

You can use the asterisk character (*) to represent any sequence of characters. For example, to print all files in your current directory with names that end with `.txt`, you enter the following:

```
lp *.txt
```

Pay attention when using the asterisk wildcard. If you enter the following command, you print all files whose names end with `txt`:

```
lp *txt
```

The file named `reportxt` is included with the files printed with the second command but not with the first. If you enter the following command, the shell passes the name of every file in your directory, as well as the single file named `txt`, to the command `lp` (the file named `txt` in your directory is passed twice to `lp`):

```
lp * txt
```

In the preceding example, the `lp` command first prints the files represented by the `*`; that is, it prints all files. The `lp` command then moves to the second item in the list of files it is to print (Linux interprets the space character between the `*` and `txt` as a delimiter—in effect, as a comma in an English command). The `lp` command processes `txt` as the name of the next file it is to print.

Tip #92 from *Steve*

> You can use the * symbol anywhere in a string of characters. For example, if you want to use the `ls` command to list the names of all files in your current directory whose names contain the characters `rep`, you can enter this command:
>
> ```
> ls *rep*
> ```

Linux lists files with names such as `frep.data`, `report`, and `janrep`. The one exception is that files with names starting with a period aren't listed. To list files with names starting with a period (often called *hidden files*), you must specify the leading period. For example, if you have a file named `.reportrc` and want to see it listed, you can enter the following variation of the preceding command:

```
ls .*rep*
```

Caution

Be careful of using the asterisk wildcard when you're deleting or removing files. The command `rm *` removes *all* files in your directory. An all-too-common mistake is to accidentally delete all files when you mean to delete a collection of files with a common suffix or prefix. If, instead of `rm *txt` (which would remove all files with names ending in `txt`), you enter `rm * txt`, Linux first deletes all files and then attempts to delete a file named `txt`. But at that point, no files are left.

To be safe, you should use the `-i` option with `rm` if you use the asterisk for filename completion. The `rm -i *txt` command prompts you for confirmation before each file is deleted.

The ? Wildcard

You use the question mark (`?`) wildcard to represent a single character. Suppose that you have the files `report1`, `reportb`, `report10`, `reportb3`, `report.dft`, and `report.fin` in your current directory. You know that the `lp rep*` command prints all the files, but to print just the first two (`report1` and `reportb`), you can enter the following command:

```
lp report?
```

To list the names of all files whose names are three characters long and end with the character *x*, enter the following:

```
ls ??x
```

This command lists a file with the name `tax` but not `trax`.

Because the question mark represents a single occurrence of any character, the string `???` represents all files consisting of just three letters. You can generate a list of files with three-letter extensions by using the string `*.???`. For example, if you're searching a directory containing graphic images as well as other data, the following command lists all files with extensions such as `.tif`, `.jpg`, and `.gif`, as well as any other files with three-letter extensions:

```
ls *.???
```

Tip #93 from *Steve*

Remember that Linux isn't MS-DOS; filenames aren't limited to eight characters with a three-character extension. Also, remember that filenames are case sensitive under Linux.

The [ ] Expression

Sometimes you must be more selective than either of the more general-purpose wildcards allow. Suppose that you want to select the files `job1`, `job2`, and `job3`, but not `jobx`. You can't select the right files by using the ? wildcard because it represents one occurrence of any character. You can, however, use job[123] as the file descriptor.

You can also represent a single character by enclosing a range of characters within a pair of square brackets. To list the names of all files that begin with an uppercase letter, for example, you can enter the following:

```
ls [A-Z]*
```

Suppose that you have files named sales.90, sales.91, sales.92, and sales.93 and want to copy the first three to a subdirectory named oldstuff. Assuming that the subdirectory oldstuff exists, you could enter the following command:

```
cp sales.9[0-2] oldstuff
```

Like the question mark, items inside square brackets ([]) represent exactly one character. You can describe a discrete series of permissible values, such as [123], which permits only the characters 1, 2, or 3; you can also describe a range of characters, as in [A-Z], which represent any character between uppercase *A* and uppercase *Z*, inclusive.

You can also specify a set of ranges, which incorporates more than one range. For example, if you want to specify only alphabetic characters, you can use [A-Z,a-z]. The ASCII character set contains special characters between ASCII *Z* and ASCII *a*; if you specify [A-z], you include those special characters in your request.

CONNECTING PROCESSES WITH PIPES

Frequently, you need to use the output of one program or command as the input of another. Rather than enter each command separately and save results in intermediate files, you can connect a sequence of commands by using a pipe (¦).

For example, to sort a file named allsales and then print it, you can enter the following:

```
sort allsales ¦ lp
```

The name *pipe* is appropriate. The output of the program on the left of the pipe (the vertical bar) is sent through the pipe and used as the input of the program on the right. You can connect several processes with pipes. For example, to print a sorted list of the data in all files with names that begin with *sales*, you can enter the following command:

```
cat sales* ¦ sort ¦ lp
```

REDIRECTING INPUT AND OUTPUT

Many programs expect input from the terminal or keyboard; many programs send their output to the terminal screen. Linux associates keyboard input with a file named stdin; it associates terminal output with a file named stdout. You can redirect input and output so that rather than come from or go to the terminal, it comes from a file or is sent to a file.

You use the < (less than) symbol to redirect input into a command or program so that it comes from a file instead of the terminal. Suppose that you want to send a file named info by email to someone whose address is sarah. Rather than retype the contents of the file to the mail command, you can give this command to use the info file as the input (stdin) to the mail command:

```
mail sarah < info
```

You use the > (greater than) symbol to redirect the output of a program to a file. Instead of going to the terminal screen, the output is put into a file. The command date displays the current time and date on the terminal screen. If you want to store the current time and date in a file named now, for example, you can enter this command:

```
date > now
```

Caution

If the filename on the right side of the > already exists, it is overwritten. Be careful not to destroy useful information this way.

If you want to append, or concatenate, information to an existing file, you use the two-character >> symbol. To append the current date to a file named report, for example, you can enter the following command:

```
date >> report
```

For a slightly more lengthy example, suppose that the file named sales consists of sales data. The first field of each line contains a customer ID code. The first command line shown here puts the output of the date command into a file named sales_report. The second command line uses the sales file as input to the sort command and appends the output to the sales_report file. The last line sends the sales_report file to users sarah and brad by email:

```
date > sales_report
sort < sales >> sales_report
mail sarah brad < sales_report
```

Caution

Be careful not to redirect the same file as both input and output to a command. Most likely, you'll destroy the contents of the file.

Table 16.5 summarizes the redirection symbols used in Linux.

TABLE 16.5 LINUX'S REDIRECTION SYMBOLS

Symbol	Meaning	Example
<	Take input from a file	mail sarah < report
>	Send output to a file	date > now
>>	Append to a file	date >> report

SUBSTITUTING SHELL VARIABLES

You learned about shell variable expansion earlier in this chapter when you set your `PATH` variable to `PATH=$PATH:`*newpath*. The shell replaced `$PATH` with the current values of the `PATH` variable. Shells are really interpreted languages, almost like BASIC; the shell variable is the primary object manipulated. Because shell variables are frequently manipulated, each shell provides methods of testing and defining the shell variables.

Shell variables are stored as strings. When two variables are placed together, their respective strings are concatenated. For example, if you have two variables, `X=hello` and `Y=world`, the expression `$X$Y` results in the string `helloworld`. If you give the following command, the shell parses the two parameters, and the values of `X` and `Y` (the two strings `hello` and `world`) are substituted before being passed to the `echo` command:

```
echo $X $Y
```

The `echo` command then prints `hello world`.

Note

If you place a dozen tab characters between `$X` and `$Y`, the output results are still the same.

If the substitution can be ambiguous, the shell picks the most obvious substitution—often with unpredictable results. For example, if you type `echo $XY`, the shell substitutes `helloY`. If you also have a variable `XY`, its value is substituted instead. To get around these ambiguities, you can use a simple shell mechanism to define exactly what you mean. If you type `${X}Y`, the shell substitutes the value of `X` before appending the character `Y` to the string.

The Bourne and Korn shells have a rich collection of shell-variable expansion techniques that perform various tests on the variable before making the substitution. See the man pages for sh and ksh for more details.

SUBSTITUTING COMMAND RESULTS

After the shell performs its substitution of variables, it scans the line again for commands to be run before the command line is finally ready. *Command substitution* means that Linux substitutes the results of a command for a positional parameter. This is specified in the following way:

```
command-1parameter ' command-2'
```

Be careful in the use of apostrophes, or single quotes ('), and back quotes (`, also known as grave accents). Table 16.6 lists what each mark does.

Table 16.6 Quotation Marks and Apostrophes

Symbol	Meaning
"	Quotation marks disable filename generation and suppress parameter expansion; however, shell-variable and command substitution still take place.
'	The apostrophe disables all parsing. Whatever is enclosed within the apostrophes is passed on as a single parameter.
`	The back quoteor grave accent, implies command substitution. Whatever is enclosed within back quotes is executed as though the command were performed on a line by itself. Any output placed on the standard output then replaces the command. The command line is then parsed again for parameters.

Consider the following command line:

```
echo Today\'s date and time are 'date'
```

It produces this output:

```
Today's date and time are Mon May 17 14:35:09 EST 1999
```

To make the `echo` command behave properly, you must precede the *'s* in *Today's* in the preceding command with a backslash (`\`), also called the *escape character* (`Today\'s`). Virtually every nonalphanumeric character on your keyboard has some special meaning to the shell. To use any of the special characters in a string and to prevent the shell from interpreting the character, you must "escape" the character; that is, you must precede it with the backslash. If you want to pass the backslash character itself, you can use `\\`. To pass a dollar sign to a command, you use `\$`.

Regular Expressions

A *regular expression* is a series of standard characters and special operators. Regular expressions are useful for searching for a string of characters in a file. Regular expressions are often used with the grep family of tools: `grep`, `egrep`, and `fgrep`, but are also used with other UNIX commands.

The simplest kind of regular expression is a string. A string is a set of characters, such as *and*. The syntax for a `grep` command is as follows:

```
grep stringfilename
```

For example, to search for the word `hand` in a specific file named `michael`, you enter this command:

```
grep hand michael.txt
```

This command might return the result

```
on the other hand, michael has been working hard this past
```

if that were the only line of the text file that contained the word `hand`. `grep` returns every line of a text file that has a match to the string.

Regular expressions use special characters. The special characters used with regular expressions are the period (.), asterisk (*), square brackets ([ ]), slash (/), caret (^), and dollar sign ($). Table 16.7 summarizes these special characters and their behavior in regular expressions.

TABLE 16.7 SPECIAL CHARACTERS IN REGULAR EXPRESSIONS

Character	Description
.	The period matches a single character, unless the single character is a line return. For example, `b.d` matches `bad` and `bod`.
*	The asterisk matches zero or more of the preceding regular expression. So the pattern `4*` matches no 4s, one 4, two 4s, and so on.
[ ]	The brackets are used to group a set of multiples for matches. Remember that unlike DOS, UNIX is case sensitive. So to search for all instances of the name *Michael*, you could use `[Mm]ichael` to search for both `michael` and `Michael`, but not `MICHAEL`. If you want to search for an actual `]` character, either you can use `[]]`, or you can use the backslash as an escape character to treat the right bracket as a text character, like so: `/]`. A dash inside brackets acts as a range, so `[a-j]` is the same as `[abcdefghij]`.
/	The slash is used to escape the special behavior of these special characters and treat them as text to be searched for in a string. So `*` matches everything, but `/*` matches only a line with the `*` character in it. You use `//` to search for a slash character, of course.
^	If `^` is at the beginning of the string, it matches a line only if the string is at the beginning of the line. So if you have a text file of telephone numbers sorted by area code, the regular expression `^704` matches all telephone numbers with the area code 704, but not a telephone number such as 407-555-7043.
$	If a `$` is the last character in a regular expression, it matches the expression to a line in the file if the expression is at the end of the file.

You can define how many of a given character to match by using the curly braces ({}). For example, the command

```
g\{3,4}
```

matches any line in the text file that contains either `ggg` or `gggg`.

If you maintain a large file of older mail, the command

```
grep 'whatever' ~/mail/*
```

searches for the string `whatever` in the mail directory. This capability is useful if you recall that your recent acquaintance Dave Quigman included his telephone number in his sigfile, but you can't remember what folder you saved his message into. The command

```
grep 'Quigman'' ~/mail/*
```

matches all instances of the name.

However, a more efficient way might be to match the telephone number itself. Say his telephone number is in the area code 408. So the command

```
grep '408.[0-9]\{3\}.[0-9]\{4\}' ~/mail/*
```

finds all telephone numbers that start with 408. Notice the periods separating the `408`, the `[0_9]\{3\}`, and `[0_9]\{4\}`. The period matches any single character, which allows you to match the telephone number 408-555-1212 or 408.555.1212 because some people use periods to separate the telephone numbers.

UNDERSTANDING COMMAND GROUPS, SUBSHELLS, AND OTHER COMMANDS

You terminate a simple command by using a carriage return. If you want to place more than one command on the command line before pressing Return, you can delimit individual commands by using a semicolon (;), thus forming a group of commands. When the shell parses the command line, it treats the semicolon as an end-of-line character. If you type the following string, the shell executes each command sequentially as though you had typed each on a line by itself:

```
command-1;command-2;command-3
```

For example, you can enter `clear;ls` to clear your screen and display a directory listing.

COMMAND GROUPS

If you want to redirect input or output to all the commands as a group, you can do so by making the command line a command group. A *command group* is defined as any number of commands enclosed in braces ({}). For example, the following command string directs the output of both commands to the file named `output-file`:

```
{command-1;command-2} > output-file
```

You also can use any form of redirection. The output of a command group can be piped, as in the following example:

```
{command-1;command-2} | command-3
```

In this case, the output of *command-1* is fed into the pipe, the output of *command-2* is then fed into the same pipe, and *command-3* sees just one stream of data.

Note

Commands executed in a command group run in the current shell. That means that they may modify the environment or change directories.

SUBSHELLS

When you run a series of commands as a command group, those commands run in the current shell. If one of the commands modifies the environment or changes the directory, the changes are in effect when the command group finishes running. To avoid this problem, you can run a command group in a *subshell.*

A subshell is a clone of the present shell, but because child processes can't modify the environment of their parent process, all commands run in a subshell have no effect on the environment when the command group finishes. To run a command group in a subshell, you can replace the braces with parentheses. The command-group example in the preceding section then becomes the following:

```
(command-1;command-2) | command-3
```


Only `command-3` runs in the current shell, but the output of the subshell is piped into the standard input of `command-3`.

Doing Background Processing

Because Linux is a multitasking operating system, you can run commands in the background in several ways. The simplest form of background processing allows you to run a command concurrently with a command in the foreground. Other methods place commands deeper and deeper in the background.

Arranging for Processes to Run in the Background

The shell allows you to start one process and, before the first one completes, start another. When you do so, you put the first process in the background. You put a process in the background by using the ampersand (`&`) character as the last character on the line containing the command you want to run in the background. Consider the following command:

```
sort sales > sales.sorted &
```

If you enter this command, you see a number onscreen. This number is the process ID (PID) number for the process you put in the background. The PID is the operating system's way of identifying that process.

Normally, when you run a command, the shell suspends operation until the command is complete. If you append the ampersand to the end of a command string, the command string runs concurrently with the shell. If you place the ampersand *after*a command string, the shell resumes operation as soon as the background command is launched. Unless you use I/O redirection with the background command, the background command and the present shell expect input from and produce output to your terminal. Unless your background command takes care of I/O itself, the proper syntax for background processing is as follows:

```
command-string [input-file] output-file &
```

For example, to copy a collection of files whose names end with the characters `.txt` to a subdirectory named `oldstuff` and, without waiting for that process to finish, print a sorted list of the data in all files with names that begin with `sales`, you can use the following two commands:

```
cp *.txt oldstuff &

cat sales* ¦ sort ¦ lp
```

Tip #94 from *Steve*

You can put jobs in the background when you don't want to wait for one program to finish before starting another. You can also put jobs in the background when you have a collection of tasks in which at least one can run on its own. Just start that one and put it in the background.
You can also use the virtual terminals offered by Linux to execute a command and then log in to another terminal; then switch between the virtual terminals with Ctrl+Alt+Fx.

Because the background process is a child of your shell, it's automatically killed when you log out. All child processes are killed when their parent dies.

USING THE `nohup` COMMAND

To place a command deeper in the background than the `&` operator allows, you can use the `nohup` command which stands for *no hang up*). The `nohup` command takes as its argument a command string. However, you must use `nohup` with the `&` operator if you want the command to actually be placed in the background. If a command is run with `nohup` in the foreground, the command is immune to being killed when you disconnect your terminal or hang up a modem (its original purpose). The syntax for the `nohup` command is as follows:

`nohup` *`command-string`* `[`*`input-file`*`]` *`output-file`* `&`

USING THE `cron` DAEMON

If you run a command with the `nohup` command, the command executes immediately. If you want to run the command at a later time or on a "time-available" basis, you must invoke the services of the `cron` daemon.

The `cron` daemon is a command run in the background by Linux—or, more specifically, by `init`, the master program. `cron` provides scheduling services to all Linux processes. You can ask `cron` to run a program at a specific time, periodically, at a particular time every day, or whenever the load on `cron` permits.

→ See "Scheduling Commands with `cron` and `crontab`," p. 373

THE `at` COMMAND

The `at` command expects a time or date as a parameter and takes any number of command strings from its standard input. When the `at` command detects an end-of-file marker, it creates a Bourne shell script for execution at the time you specified.

Tip #95 from *Steve*

> The `at` command is flexible about the types of dates and times it accepts. For example, if you enter the command `at now + 1 day`, the next commands, taken from the standard input, are executed tomorrow at this time.

One way to use the at command is from within a shell script. A shell script is nothing more than a file containing all the commands necessary to perform a series of commands. The name of the file then becomes your own addition to the Linux command language. One way of using the at command is shown here:

```
at now + 1 day
command-1
command-2
```

When placed in a shell script, these lines let you conveniently run one or more commands the next day. To run any number of different commands, you can simply enter new commands after the at command line. You can run any number of commands from this script.

The batch Command

The `batch` command is the logical equivalent of `at now`. If you attempt to use the `at now` command, you see an error message that says something along the lines of `now has passed`. The `batch` command works exactly as `at now` works if it were logically possible, with one minor exception: The `cron` daemon maintains a separate queue for commands generated by `at`, `batch`, and `cron`. Suppose that you entered the following commands into the file named `backup`:

```
tar -cvf tackettbkup /usr/home/tackett
```

Then you can tell the system to back up the directory `/usr/home/tackett` by using this command:

```
batch backup
```

→ See "Creating Your First vi File," p. 208

The crontab Command

One of the best uses of the `cron` daemon is in automating the maintenance of a system. With `cron`, you, as the system administrator, can set up automatic backups of your system every day at 4 a.m., Monday through Saturday. You install, delete, and list commands you want run in this fashion by using the `crontab` command.

To run commands periodically, you must create a file in the `crontab` format. The `crontab` file consists of six fields separated by spaces or tabs. The first five fields are integers specifying minute (00-59), hour (00-23), day of the month (01-31), month of the year (01-12), and day of the week (0-6, with 0 referring to Sunday). The sixth field is a command string. Each numeric field can contain an inclusive range of numbers (such as 1-5 to indicate Monday through

Friday) or discrete sets of numbers (such as 0,20,40 to indicate that an instruction should be run every 20 minutes). A field can also contain an asterisk to indicate all legal values.

The following example runs the `calendar` command every 20 minutes, starting at midnight Monday and ending at 11:40 p.m. Friday:

```
0,20,40 * * * 1-5 calendar -
```

Tip #96 from *Steve*

> **If you name the file `cronfile`, you can install it in the `cron` system by issuing the command `crontab cronfile`.**

The `cron` daemon has a time granularity of one minute—meaning, the shortest time duration you can work with is one minute. You, as system administrator, can place limits on the number of commands allowed to be run at any one time. Just because you ask `cron` to run an `at`, `batch`, or `crontab` file doesn't mean that it runs at precisely the time you've indicated.

UNDERSTANDING COMMAND FEEDBACK

Linux provides instant feedback for commands that abort for one reason or another. In most cases, errors are limited to misspellings of the command name or badly formed filenames. If you attempt to run a nonexistent command, Linux replies with the following message:

```
command: command not found
```

If you try to use a nonexistent filename, Linux responds with this message:

```
command: file: No such file or directory
```

If the error is caused by something other than a command-line error, the command itself usually reports what happened—although not always in an easily decipherable form.

If you try to run a command with `nohup` and haven't redirected the standard error, Linux automatically places any error messages in a file named `nohup.out` in the directory from which the command was run.

Because commands run by `cron` have less urgency, any errors—indeed, any output placed on the standard output and not redirected—are sent to you through email.

EDITING AND ALIASING SHELL COMMANDS

Different shells include features that provide shortcuts for running commands. *Command editing* lets you modify commands that have already been typed in. By using Linux's *command history* feature, you can recall commands you've previously entered. *Aliasing* lets you create commands that represent other commands. *Command completion* lets you fill in the rest of a filename after you type part of it.

EDITING COMMANDS

Command editing means that after you type a command—and before you press Return—you can edit or change parts of the command without having to retype most of it. To edit a command, press Esc to get into editing mode, and then use any of the line-movement commands from the vi editor to modify the command. You can press Backspace to return to the portion of the command you want to change, and use other vi commands, such as `x` to delete a character, `r` to replace a character, and so on.

VIEWING COMMAND HISTORY

The command history feature allows you to look back at previously entered commands and recall them. This feature saves you the time and trouble of retyping commands. When you combine this feature with command editing, you can easily correct mistakes in complicated commands and deal effectively with some repetitive tasks.

In both shells, the `history` command displays the list of past commands the shell has saved. The commands are numbered. To execute command 10, for example, you enter `! 10`. The bash shell also takes advantage of your PC's arrow keys; you can recall previous commands by pressing the _ key.

ALIASING COMMANDS

Command aliasing allows you to define a name for a command. Consider this example: The `man` command displays Linux documentation, or *man pages*. To make the word `help` an alias, or alternative, for `man`, you can enter the following:

```
alias help=man
```

Now you can enter `help cp` or `man cp` to display Linux man pages about the `cp` command.

You also can use aliases with commands that have options or arguments. For example, if you want to list the names of all the files in the current directory sorted in descending order by the time they were last modified (so that the most recent files are at the bottom of the list), you can use this command:

```
ls -art
```

The `ls` command is the command to list files. The `-a` option specifies all files; the `-r` option arranges the files in reverse, descending order; and the `-t` option sorts by time last modified. That's a lot to remember. You can assign the alias `timedir` to this complex command by using the following command:

```
alias timedir="ls -art''
```

The quotation marks (`""`) are necessary because the shell expects the alias for `timedir` to be terminated by a space or Return. Now, if you enter `timedir`, you get the directory listing you want.

Note

Setting an alias from the command line keeps that alias in effect only for the current session. To have the alias active whenever you log in, you can include the alias definition in the `.profile` file if you use the Bourne shell; keep it in the `.login` file if you use the C shell.

Completing Commands

Command completion allows you to type the beginning of a filename and then press the Tab key to expand the filename. This technique can save time and spelling mistakes when you're entering a command. If two files share a common prefix, Linux expands the command to the last common character, stops expanding the filename, and then beeps. You need to provide the unique filename.

Adding Text with Cut and Paste

Red Hat Linux offers a program that you can start at boot time; this program allows you to use the mouse to select text from anywhere onscreen and then paste the text onto the command line for the shell to interpret. To get a mouse cursor, you simply press one of the mouse buttons. You then select the desired text from anywhere onscreen by first clicking on the beginning of the text and, while holding down the button, dragging the cursor to the desired end point of the text. After you select the text, you right-click to copy the text to the command line.

Working with Shell Scripts

The shell accepts commands, interprets them, and arranges for the operating system to execute the commands in the manner you specify. In the preceding sections, you saw how the shell interprets special characters to complete filenames, redirects input and output, connects processes through pipes, and puts jobs or processes in the background.

You can type commands at the terminal, or they can come from a file. A shell script is a collection of one or more shell commands in a file. To execute the commands, you type the name of the file. The advantages to this approach include the following:

- You don't have to retype a sequence of commands.
- You determine the steps to accomplish a goal once.
- You simplify operations for yourself and others.

By using variables and keywords, you can write programs that the shell can interpret. This capability is useful because it allows you to create general shell scripts you or others can use in various situations.

Suppose that after you log in, you regularly like to see who's logged in to your system, run a program named `calendar` that displays your appointments for today and tomorrow, and print the current date and time to the screen. To do all that, you enter the following commands:

```
who
calendar
date
```

If you put these three commands into a file named `whatsup` and make that file executable, you have a shell script that you can execute just like any other command. The file `whatsup` must be a text file. You can use the vi or Emacs text editor to put the commands in the `whatsup` file. To make the file executable, you enter this command:


```
chmod +x whatsup
```

The `chmod` command modifies or sets the permissions for a file. The `+x` option makes the file executable; that is, it makes the file work just like a standard Linux command. Putting commands into the file and making the file executable are both one-time operations. From that point on, you can enter `whatsup` to execute your shell script. You can use the shell script just like any other command. For example, to print the results of the `whatsup` command, you can enter the following:

```
whatsup ¦ lp
```

To put the results of the `whatsup` command into a file named `info` for future reference, you can enter the command below:

```
whatsup > info
```

As a review, follow these steps to create a shell script that you can use whenever you want:

1. Use a text editor, such as vi or Emacs, to put the shell commands into a text or ASCII file. In the preceding example, the commands were put in the file named `whatsup`.
2. Make sure you have execute permission on the file. To do so, use `chmod +x` *`filename`* (for example, `chmod +x whatsup`).
3. Test the command by typing the name of the command and pressing Return.

After using this process a few times, you'll see how easily you can create useful scripts. Of course, the hardest part is figuring out which shell commands to use and how to use the shell's programming capabilities to express the steps you need to carry out.

You can test a shell script and see all the steps it goes through by entering this command:

```
sh -x script-name
```

In this syntax, *`script-name`* is the name of the file that holds the script you're considering. The `sh -x` command displays all the steps the script goes through and is useful when you're trying to debug a script.

WRITING PROGRAMS WITH THE SHELL

To write programs that use the shells, you must know about *variables* and *control structures*. Don't let either term scare you. A variable is an object that, at any one time, has one of possibly many different values assigned to it. Control structures specify the way you can control the flow of execution of a script. The two basic types of control structures are decision structures (such as `if...then...else` structures or `case` structures), and iterative structures or loops (such as a `for` or `while` loop). With a decision structure, you choose a course of action from one or more alternatives, usually depending on the value of a variable or the outcome of a command. With an iterative structure, you repeat a sequence of commands. The earlier section "Setting the Shell Environment" describes shell variables; the later section "Programming with Control Structures" provides more information on control structures.

USING echo

You can use the `echo` command to display informative messages about what's happening in a shell script. The `echo` command displays its arguments—that is, whatever follows the word `echo`—onscreen. Putting a string of characters in quotation marks ensures that all the characters are displayed. You also can redirect the results of `echo` to a file.

The command

```
echo ''Please stand by ...''
```

displays the following line on the terminal screen:

```
Please stand by ...
```

The following command puts `Please stand by ...` in the file named `messg`:

```
echo ''Please stand by ...'' > messg
```

Tip #97 from *Steve*

> Using the `echo` command can make your users feel as though something is happening when they enter a command–a particularly good idea if the command doesn't give any output for several seconds or longer.

The `echo` command is also useful when you want to trace a shell script. Using the `echo` command at key points tells you what's happening in a script. The following is the file `whatsup` with an `echo` command or two added:

```
echo '' Let's see who is on the system.''
who
echo '' Any appointments? ''
calendar
date
echo '' All done''
```

When you run the whatsup file, you see the following:

```
$ whatsup
Let's see who is on the system.
sarah      tty01      Dec 20 08:51
brad       tty03      Dec 20 08:12
ernie      tty07      Dec 20 08:45
Any appointments?
12/20      Sales meeting at 1:45
12/21      party after work!
Mon Dec 20 09:02 EST 1993
All done
$
```


USING COMMENTS

After you write a shell script and don't use it for a while, you might forget what the shell script does or how it accomplishes its task. To avoid this situation, you should put comments in your shell scripts to explain the purpose of the task and how the task is achieved. A *comment* is a note to yourself or whoever is reading the script. The shell ignores comments; they're important to and for human beings.

The pound sign (#) signals the beginning of a comment to the shell. Every character from the pound sign to the end of the line is part of that comment. For example, you might comment the shell script whatsup like this:

```
# Name:       whatsup
# Written:    1/19/97, Patty Stygian
# Purpose:    Display who's logged in, appointments, date
     echo "Let's see who is on the system."
     who          # See who is logged in
     echo " Any appointments? "
     calendar     # Check appointments
     date         # Display date
     echo " All done"
```

If you run the shell script again, you see the same results as before. The comments don't change the behavior of the shell script in any way.

USING VARIABLES IN SHELL PROGRAMS

To use variables, you must know how to give a variable a value and how to access the value stored in a variable. Using the value of a variable is straightforward, but you can give a value to a variable in these four ways:

- Using direct assignment
- Using the read command
- Using command-line parameters
- Substituting the output of a command

USING DIRECT ASSIGNMENTS The most direct way to give a value to a variable is to write an expression such as this:

```
myemail=edsgar@crty.com
```

This expression gives the variable `myemail` the value `edsgar@crty.com`. Don't include spaces on either side of the equals sign (=). The direct-assignment method of assigning a value to a variable takes the following form:

```
variable-name=variable-value
```

If *`variable-value`* contains blanks, you enclose the value in quotation marks. To assign an office address of Room 21, Suite C to the variable `myoffice`, for example, you use the following command:

```
myoffice="Room 21, Suite C''
```

The shell retrieves the value of the variable whenever it sees a dollar sign ($) followed by the name of a variable. You can see that when the following two statements are executed:

```
echo '' My e-mail address is $myemail''
echo '' My office is $myoffice''
```

Suppose that you frequently copy files to a directory named `/corporate/info/public/sales`. To copy a file named `current` to that directory, you enter this command:

```
cp current /corporate/info/public/sales
```

To make using this command easier, you can assign the long directory name to the variable `corpsales` by using the following expression:

```
corpsales=/corporate/info/public/sales
```

Now, to copy the current file to that directory, you enter the following:

```
cp current $corpsales
```

The shell replaces `$corpsales` with the value of the variable `corpsales` and then issues the copy command.

USING THE `read` COMMAND The `read` command takes the next line of input and assigns it to a variable. The following shell script extends the preceding `corpsales` example to ask the user to specify the name of the file to be copied:

```
# Name: copycorp
# Purpose: copy specified file to
#          /corporate/info/public/sales
    corpsales=/corporate/infor/public/sales
    echo "Enter name of file to copy"     # prompt user
    read filename                         # get file name
    cp $filename $corpsales               # do the copy
```

The `read` command pauses the script and waits for input from the keyboard. When Return is pressed, the script continues. If Ctrl+d (sometimes represented as `^D`) is pressed while the `read` command is waiting for input, the script is terminated.

USING COMMAND-LINE PARAMETERS When the shell interprets a command, it attaches variable names to each item on the command line. The items on the command line are the sequences of characters separated by blanks or tab characters. (You use quotation marks to signal that a collection of characters separated by spaces represents one item.) The variables attached to the items in the command line are $0, $1, $2, and so on through $9. These 10 variables correspond to the positions of the items on the line. The command name is $0, the first argument or parameter for the command is $1, and so on. To demonstrate this concept, consider the following sample shell script named shovars:

```
# Name:      shovars
# Purpose:   demonstrate command-line variables
     echo $0
     echo $2 $4!
       echo $3
```

Now suppose that you enter this command:

```
shovars -s hello ''look at me'' bart
```

The output of the shell script is this:

```
shovars
hello bart!
look at me
```

In this output, the first line is the command's name (variable $0), the second line is made up of the second and fourth arguments (variables $2 and $4), and the last line is the third argument (variable $3).

Following is a more serious example. This shell script deletes a file but first copies it to the directory /tmp so that you can retrieve it if necessary:

```
# Name:     safrm
# Purpose: copy file to directory /tmp and then remove it
#          from the current directory
# first copy $1 to /tmp
    cp $1 /tmp
# now remove the file
       rm $1
```

If you enter safrm abc def, only the file abc is removed from the current directory because the safrm shell script deletes only variable $1. You can, however, represent all the parameters on the command line by using $*. You can make safrm more general by replacing each occurrence of $1 with $*. If you then enter safrm abc def xx guio, all four files (abc, def, xx, and guio) are removed from the current directory.

SUBSTITUTING THE OUTPUT OF A COMMAND You can assign to a variable the result of an executed command. To store the name of the current working directory in a variable named cwd, for example, you enter the following:

```
cwd=`pwd`
```

Notice that pwd, the print working directory command, is set in back quotes instead of single quotation marks.

The following shell script changes the name of a file by appending the current month, day, and year to the filename:

```
# Name:      stamp
# Purpose:   rename file: append today's date to its name
# set td to current date in form of mmddyy
     td='+%m%d%y'
# rename file
         mv $1 $1.$td
```

In this example, the variable `td` is set to the current date. In the final line, this information is appended to variable `$1`. If today is February 24, 1997, and you use this script on a file called `myfile`, the file is renamed (moved) to `myfile.022497`.

Using Special Characters in Shell Programs

You've seen how the shell gives special treatment to certain characters, such as `>`, `*`, `?`, `$`, and others. What do you do if you don't want those characters to get special treatment? This section provides a few answers.

You can use quote to make the shell ignore special characters. You enclose the character string with a pair of single quotes, as in this example:

```
grep '^Mary Tuttle' customers
```

The result of this `grep` command is that the lines that begin with `Mary Tuttle` in the file `customers` are displayed. The caret (`^`) tells `grep` to search from the beginning of the line. If you don't enclose the text `Mary Tuttle` in single quotes, it might be interpreted literally (or as a pipe symbol on some systems). Also, the space between `Mary` and `Tuttle` isn't interpreted by the shell when it occurs within the single quotes.

You can also use quotation marks to make the shell ignore most special characters, with the exception of the dollar sign and back quote. In the following example, the asterisks, spaces, and the greater-than sign are treated as regular characters because the string is surrounded by quotation marks:

```
echo '' ** Please enter your response -->''
```

In this next example, however, `$LOGNAME` evaluates correctly, but `$5` doesn't have any value:

```
echo '' >>>Thanks for the $5, $LOGNAME''
```

You use the backslash (`\`) to make the shell ignore a single character. For example, to make the shell ignore the dollar sign in front of the 5, you issue this command:

```
echo '' >>>Thanks for the \$5, $LOGNAME''
```

The result is what you expect:

```
>>>Thanks for the $5, wrev
```

PROGRAMMING WITH CONTROL STRUCTURES

The two primary control structures in shell programming are decision structures and iterative structures. In *decision structures*, such as `if...then...else` and `case`, you can have the shell script decide which commands to execute based on the value of an expression (such as a variable, the properties associated with a file, the number of parameters in a script, or the result of executing a command). In *iterative structures*, such as `for` and `while` loops, you can execute a sequence of commands over a collection of files or while some condition holds.

The following sections use examples that aren't too complicated yet demonstrate the essentials of programming with some control.

USING `case`

The `case` structure is a decision structure that lets you select one of several courses of action, based on the value of a variable. Listing 16.2 shows a short menu program.

LISTING 16.2 IMPLEMENTING MENU SHELL SCRIPT WITH `case`

```
# Name:      ShrtMenu
# Purpose:   Allow user to print a file, delete a file,
#            or quit the program
# Display menu
     echo "Please choose either P, D, or Q to "
     echo "  [P]rint a file"
     echo "  [D]elete a file"
     echo "  [Q]uit"
# Get response from user
     read response
# Use case to match response to action
     case $response in
         P¦p) echo "Name of file to print?"
              read filename
              lp $filename;;
         D¦d) echo "Name of file to delete?"
              read filename
              rm $filename;;
           *) echo "leaving now";;
     esac
```

The syntax of the `case` statement is as follows:

```
case word in
   pattern) statement(s);;
   pattern) statement(s);;
...
esac
```

The *`word`* parameter is matched against each *`pattern`* parameter, starting with the pattern at the top of the list. The statements that execute if *`word`* matches a pattern are terminated by two semicolons (`;;`). The end of the `case` statement is marked by the word `esac` (that's *case* spelled backward).

In Listing 16.2, the pipe character is used to give a choice for a match. For example, `P¦p` means that either an uppercase or lowercase letter *P* is considered a match.

The pattern `*` is used to represent all other patterns not explicitly stated. If users press any key besides P, p, D, or d, they exit from the menu.

Listing 16.3 uses a `case` statement that makes a selection based on the number of parameters the shell represents as `$#`.

LISTING 16.3 COMMAND-LINE PARSING WITH `case`

```
# Name:      recent
# Purpose:  list the most recent files in a directory
# If user types recent <Return> then the names of
#     the 10 most recently modified files are displayed
# If the user types recent n <Return> then the names of
#     the n most recently modified files are displayed
# Otherwise, user is notified of incorrect usage
#
# Case based on number of parameters
      case $# in
           0) ls -lt ¦ head ;;
               # ls -lt lists names of file in order of
               # most recently modified
               # head displays the first 10 lines of a file
           1) case $1 in
               [0-9]*) ls -lt ¦ head -$1 ;;
               *)echo "Usage: recent number-of-files";;
               esac;;
               *) echo "Usage: recent number-of-files";;
      esac
```

FINDING THE EXIT STATUS

When a shell command executes, it's either successful or not. If you use the command `grep ''American Terms'' customers` to see whether the string `American Terms` is in the file `customers` and the file exits, the following is true:

- You have read permission to the file
- `American Terms` is in the file
- The shell command has executed successfully

If any of those conditions isn't true, the shell command executes unsuccessfully.

The shell always reports back about the status of the termination of a command, program, or shell script. The value reported back is called the *exit status* of a command and is represented by the variable `#?`. If you enter the following commands, you see the value of `$?`:

```
grep ''American Terms'' customers
echo $?
```

Note If `$?` has a value of 0, this command was successful; otherwise, the command was unsuccessful.

The following is an example in which the exit status of the command `who¦grep $1` is used in the `case` statement:

```
# Name:      just.checking
# Purpose:   Determine if person is logged in
# Usage:     just.checking login_name
#
      case 'who ¦ grep $1 > /dev/nullÇ in
           0) echo "$1 is logged in.";;
           *) echo "$1 is not here. Try again later.";;
      esac
      echo "Have a great day!"
```

If you enter `just.checking rflame` and `rflame` is logged in, you see the following:

```
rflame is logged in.
Have a great day!
```

If `rflame` isn't logged in, you see this response instead:

```
rflame is not here. Try again later.
Have a great day!
```

USING if STRUCTURES

The `if...then...else...fi` structure is a decision structure that allows you to select one of two courses of action based on the result of a command. The `else` portion of the structure is optional. One or more commands go in place of the ellipsis (...). Provided that the exit status of the last command following the `if` is zero (that is, the command executed successfully), the commands following the `then` and preceding the `else` (if one is included) are executed. Otherwise, the commands following the `else` are executed.

In other words, one or more commands are executed. If the last command is successful, the commands in the `then` portion of the statement are performed, and then the commands following the `fi` (the end of the structure) are executed. If the last commands aren't successful, the commands after the `else` are performed.

This familiar example behaves exactly the same as when it was written using the `case` statement:

```
# Name:     just.checking
# Purpose:  Determine if person is logged in
# Usage:    just.checking login_name
#
if
     who ¦ grep $1 > /dev/null
then
     echo "$1 is logged in."
else
```

```
    echo "$1 is not here. Try again later."
fi
echo '' Have a great day!"
```

Using the test Command

Many of the shell scripts used in this chapter expect users to behave nicely. The scripts have no check to see whether users have permission to copy or move files or whether what the users were dealing with was an ordinary file rather than a directory. The `test` command can deal with these issues as well as some others. For example, `test -f abc` is successful if `abc` exists and is a regular file.

You can reverse the meaning of a test by using an exclamation point in front of the option. For example, to test that you don't have read permission for file `abc`, you use `test ! -r abc`. Table 16.8 lists several options for the `test` command.

Table 16.8 Options for Using the test Command with Files

Option	Meaning
-f	Successful if the file exists and is a regular file
-d	Successful if the file is a directory
-r	Successful if the file exists and is readable
-s	Successful if the file exists and isn't empty
-w	Successful if the file exists and can be written to
-x	Successful if the file exists and is executable

Listing 16.4 is an example of the use of the `test` command.

Listing 16.4 A Sample Script That Uses the test Command

```
# Name:    safcopy
# Purpose: Copy file1 to file2
#          Check to see we have read permission on file1
#          If file2 exists then
#                 if file2 is a file we can write to
#                 then warn user, and get permission to proceed
#                 else exit
#           else
#                 copy file
#
# Check for proper number of arguments
  case $# in
     2) if test ! -r $1      # cannot read first file;;
        then;;
                exit (1)      # exit with non-zero exit status;;
        fi;;
        if test -f $2        # does second file exist?;;
        then;;
          if test -w $2      # can we write to it?;;
```

LISTING 16.4 CONTINUED

```
          then;;
              echo " $2 exists, copy over it ? (Y/N)";;
              read     resp                 # get permission from user;;
              case $resp in;;
                  Y¦y)     cp $1 $2;;    # go ahead;;
                    *) exit(1);;         # good bye!;;
              esac;;
          else;;
              exit (1)      # Second file exists but can't write;;
          fi
        else      # Second file doesn't exist; go ahead and copy!;
          cp $1 $2;;
        fi;;
     *) echo "Usage: safcopy source destination";;
        exit (1);;
esac
```

You can also use the `test` command to test numbers. To determine whether a value in the variable `hour` is greater than 12, for example, you use `test $hour -gt 12`. Table 16.9 lists some options you can use with `test` when you're comparing numbers.

TABLE 16.9 OPTIONS FOR USING `test` WHEN COMPARING NUMBERS

Option	Meaning
`-eq`	Equal
`-ne`	Not equal
`-ge`	Greater than or equal
`-gt`	Greater than
`-le`	Less than or equal
`-lt`	Less than

Listing 16.5 shows these options used to display a timely greeting.

LISTING 16.5 DISPLAYING A GREETING WITH THE `test` COMMAND

```
# Name:      greeting
# Purpose:  Display Good Morning if hour is less than 12
#                   Good Afternoon if hour less than 5PM
#                   Good Evening if hour is greater than 4PM
# Get hour
    hour='date +%H'
# Check for time of day
    if test $hour -lt 12
    then
       echo "Good Morning, $LOGNAME"
    else
       if test $hour -lt 17
       then
```

LISTING 16.5 CONTINUED

```
            echo "Good Afternoon, $LOGNAME"
         else
            echo "Good Evening, $LOGNAME"
         fi
      fi
```

USING ITERATIVE STRUCTURES

Iterative control structures allow you to write shell scripts that contain loops. The two basic types of loops are `for` and `while` loops.

With `for` loops, you specify a collection of files or values to use with some commands. To copy all the files whose names end with the characters `.txt` to the directory `textdir`, for example, you can use the following `for` loop:

```
for i in *.txt
do
      cp $i textdir/$i
done
```

The shell interprets the statement `for i in *.txt` and allows the variable `i` to take on the name of any file in the current directory whose name ends with `.txt`. You can then use the variable `$i` with any statements between the `do` and the `done` keywords.

The script in Listing 16.6 prints a collection of files, each with its own banner page. It also sends mail to the user concerning the status of the print requests. The characters `$*` represent all the parameters given to the shell command.

LISTING 16.6 PROCESSING FILES WITH THE `for` COMMAND

```
# Name:         Prntel
# Purpose:      Print one or more files
#               each with own title page
#               Notify user which files were sent to the printer
#               and which were not.
#               Do this for all parameters to the command
for i in $*
do
     if lp -t $i -dlasers $i > /dev/null
     then
          echo $i >> printed
     else
          echo $i >> notprinted
     fi
done
# end of loop
if test -s printed
then
     echo "These files were sent to the printer " > mes
     cat printed >> mes
     mail $LOGNAME < mes
     rm mes printed
```

Listing 16.6 continued

```
fi
if test -s notprinted
then
    echo "These files were not sent to the printer " >mes
    cat notprinted >> mes
    mail $LOGNAME < mes
    rm mes notprinted
fi
```

A `while` loop looks at the exit status of a command in the same way the `if` statement looks at the status. The script in Listing 16.7 notifies users when they've received new mail. The script makes the assumption that if a mailbox changes, a user has new mail. The script uses the command `diff` to compare two files and then reports on the differences. If the files are the same, the exit status is zero (the command is successful).

Listing 16.7 Repeating Commands with `while`

```
# Name:          checkmail
# Purpose:       Notify user if their mail box has changed
# Suggestion:    Run this in the background
# get a size of mail box for comparison
     cp $MAIL omail           # Get set for first time through
# MAIL is a "special" variable indicating the user's mailbox
# while omail and $MAIL are the same, keep looping
     while diff omail $MAIL > /dev/null
     do
          cp $MAIL omail
          sleep 30            # sleep, pause for 30 seconds
     done
# There must be a change in the files
     echo ''New mail!!'' ¦ write $LOGNAME
```

You can see that some of the commands and concepts used with `if...then...else` statements can be transferred to `while` loops. The difference, of course, is that with `while` loops, you're dealing with an iterative, repetitive process.

Customizing Linux Shells

The shell starts when you log in. Tables 16.2 and 16.3 show you that special variables are given values by the shell to help define your shell environment. The shell sets some of these variables. You can change these settings and give other variables values by editing the file `.profile` if you're using the Bourne or bash shell. If you're using the C shell, you set the variables by editing the file `.login`. You can also use command aliasing to define aliases for commands.

Whenever you issue a command, a new shell starts; it inherits many of the characteristics—or much of the environment—of the existing shell. Note these two things about the new shell:

- The new shell runs in your current directory. The `pwd` command returns the same value within a shell as it gives before the shell was started.
- The new shell receives many of its variables from the existing shell. You can make sure that variables set in the existing shell are exported to the new shell in different ways.

EXPORTING VARIABLES TO THE NEW SHELL

When you create shell variables or give values to existing variables, they exist in the running shell. A variable set in the login shell is available to all command-line arguments. A variable set within a shell has that value only within that shell. The value disappears or is reset when you exit that shell.

For example, enter these two commands from the command line:

```
today=Thursday
echo $today
```

Suppose that the `echo` command displays `Thursday`. Now suppose that you write and execute the following shell script named `whatday`:

```
# Name: whatday
# display the current value of the variable today
     echo ''Today is $today.''
# set the value of today
     today=Friday
# display the current value of the variable today
       echo ''Today is $today.''
```

Now enter the following four commands from the command line:

```
chmod +x whatday
today=Thursday
whatday
echo $today
```

The following lines then appear onscreen:

```
Today is .
Today is Friday.
Thursday
```

The value of the variable `today` in the login shell is `Thursday`. When you execute the shell script `whatday`, you see that initially the variable `today` isn't defined (as shown by the display `Today is .`). Then the `today` variable has the value `Friday` in the shell. When the `whatday` script terminates, you return to the login shell and `today` has its original value, `Thursday`.

To give the variable `today` the same value that it has in the login shell when the shell script `whatday` starts, you can use the command `export`. This command "exports," or passes on, the variables from one shell to subsequent shells:

```
export today
```

Now any shell started from the login shell inherits the value of the variable `today`. You can add the `export` command to the preceding sequence of commands as follows:

```
today=Thursday
export today
whatday
echo $today
```

You then see the following output:

```
Today is Thursday.
Today is Friday.
Thursday
```


Notice that the value the variable receives in the shell started by the `whatday` script isn't carried back to the login shell. Exportation or inheritance of variable values goes in only one direction—from a running shell down to the new shell, never back up. That's why when you change your current directory inside one shell, you're back to the place you started when that shell terminates.

You can export any variable from one shell down to another shell by using the following syntax:

```
export variable-name
```

In this syntax, *`variable-name`* is the name of the variable you want to export. To change your terminal type from its current setting to a vt100, for example, you can enter the following commands to make the new value of `TERM` available to all subsequent shells or programs:

```
TERM=vt100
export TERM
```

When you change or set bash shell variables in the `.profile` file, be sure to export them. For example, if you want the `PATH` variable to be `PATH=/bin:/usr/bin:/usr/local/bin:.`, you can set it in the `.profile` file and follow it with this `export` command:

```
export PATH
```

To change the shell prompt, you must set a value for `PS1` in the file `.profile`. To change it from `$` to `Ready $`, for example, you can use a text editor to put these lines in the file named `.profile`:

```
PS1="Ready $''
export PS1
```

Tip #98 from *Steve*

Changes you make to `.profile` or `.login` don't take effect until you log out and log in again.

DEFINING COMMAND ALIASES

Command aliases are useful for defining commands you use regularly but for which you don't want to bother remembering the details. Command aliases are also useful for enhancing your working environment with a set of useful tools. This command assigns the alias `recent` to a command that lists the 10 most recently modified files in the current directory:

```
alias recent="ls -lat¦head''
```

To avoid typing your command aliases each time you log in, you can put them in the `.login` file if you're using the C shell or the `.profile` file if you're using bash or a similar shell. The command aliases are now available to you when you're in your shell.

TROUBLESHOOTING

The shell is the primary interface between you and the Linux operating system. Although a shell can be almost any executable program, several standard shells are supplied with Linux or are freely available in source code (written in C) or already compiled for your machine. All Linux shells can be viewed as highly sophisticated, special-purpose programming languages containing all the usual constructs found in a programming language. The special purpose of Linux shell languages is to tie together the many small commands and utilities found in the Linux environment.

I set an environment variable, but nothing changed.

Did you remember to export the environment variable after you set it?

I changed my `.profile` *configuration file , but nothing happened.*

Changes you make to the `.profile` or `.login` configuration files don't take effect until you log out and log back in.

I am trying to use a shell script, and it's not doing what it's supposed to.

The shell script may have been written for a different shell and may need to be rewritten. For a simple fix, you might be able to add lines to the beginning and end of the shell script to set the shell to the shell the script was originally written for and then set it back to the shell you commonly use. Possibly, the script was written in a nonshell scripting language such as Perl or python. In this case, you might need to set the path to the Perl, python, or other script engine or define it in the script to be somewhere Perl isn't located on your system.

CHAPTER 17

Managing Multiple Processes

In this chapter

by Jack Tackett, Jr.

UNDERSTANDING MULTITASKING

Linux is a multiuser and multitasking operating system. *Multiuser* means that several people can use the computer system simultaneously (unlike a single-user operating system, such as MS-DOS). *Multitasking* means that Linux, like Windows NT, can work on several tasks concurrently; it can begin work on one task and take up another before the first task is finished.

Taking care of several user requests and multitasking are the jobs of the operating system. Most systems have only one CPU and one collection of chips that make up main memory, or RAM. A system may have more than one disk or tape drive for secondary memory and several input/output devices. All these resources must be managed and shared among several users. The operating system creates the illusion that each user has a dedicated computer system.

As mentioned earlier, it's Linux's job to create the illusion that when you make a request, you have the system's undivided attention. In reality, hundreds of requests may be handled between the time you press Enter and the time the system responds to your command.

Imagine having to keep track of dozens of tasks simultaneously. You have to share the processing power, storage capabilities, and input and output devices among several users or several processes belonging to a single user. Linux monitors a list—also known as a *queue*—of tasks waiting to be done. These tasks can include user jobs, operating system tasks, mail, and background jobs such as printing. Linux schedules slices of system time for each task. By human standards, each time slice is extremely short—a fraction of a second. In computer time, a time slice is adequate for a program to process hundreds or thousands of instructions. The length of the time slice for each task may depend on the relative priority of each task.

Linux works on one task from the queue for a while, puts the task aside to begin work on another task, and so on. It then returns to the first task and works on that task again. Linux continues these cycles until it finishes a task and takes the task out of the queue, or until the task is terminated. In this arrangement, sometimes called *time-sharing*, the resources of the system are shared among all the tasks. Naturally, time-sharing must be done in a reliable and efficient manner. The UNIX term for a task is *process*. Table 17.1 shows several types of processes.

TABLE 17.1 TYPES OF PROCESSES

Process Type	Description
interactive	Initiated by a shell and running in the foreground or background
batch	Typically a series of processes scheduled for execution at a specified point in time
daemon	Typically initiated at boot time to perform operating system functions on demand, such as LPD, NFS, and DNS

You've already seen that you can put or run a program in the background. While the program runs in the background, you can continue entering commands and working with other material. This is a feature of multitasking: Linux uses the time-sharing method to balance your immediate commands and the ones running in the background. This chapter shows other ways to schedule processes so that they can run without your attention (*batch processes*).

→ See "Doing Background Processing," p. 343

The Linux operating system has the primary responsibility of handling the details of working with several users and several processes. As a user, you have the power to specify which programs you want to run. Some Linux commands let you specify when you want a process to start. You also can monitor your processes as well as see what other processes are running. In some cases, you can change their relative priority. And you can always terminate your processes if the need arises. If you're the system administrator, you have all these capabilities, plus the responsibility and power to initiate, monitor, and manage processes that belong to the operating system or any user.

Table 17.2 lists the commands that make it possible to control the multiuser and multitasking capabilities of Linux.

TABLE 17.2 MULTIUSER AND MULTITASKING COMMANDS

Command	Action
`at`	Executes commands at a given time
`batch`	Executes commands when the system load allows
`cron`	Executes scheduled commands
`crontab`	Maintains `crontab` files for individual users
`kill`	Stops processes
`nice`	Adjusts the priority of a process before it starts
`nohup`	Allows a process to continue after you log out
`ps`	Displays process information
`renice`	Adjusts the priority of a running process
`w`	Shows you the users who are logged in and what they're doing
`who`	Displays the system's logged-in users

Note

For more information on the commands in Table 17.2, you can consult the following man page:

```
man command
```

You also can use the -help option:

```
command -help
```

INITIATING MULTIPLE PROCESSES

You can start running a program by entering its name. You can also start programs from files that contain shell commands. Running programs can interact with many different parts of the system. A program can read from or write to files; manage its information in RAM; or send information to printers, modems, or other devices. The operating system also attaches information to a process so that the system can keep track of and manage it.

A process is a running program but is different from a program. In one sense, a process is more than a program because a program is only a set of instructions; a process is dynamic because it uses the resources of a running system. On the other hand, a single Linux program can start several processes.

Linux identifies and keeps track of processes by assigning a process ID number (PID) to each process.

STARTING MULTIPLE PROCESSES

You've already seen that your login shell is always running. Whenever you enter a command, you start at least one new process while the login shell continues to run. If you enter the following command, for example, the file named `report.txt` is sent to the `lp` program:

```
lp report.txt
```

→ See "Understanding Shells," p. 319

When the `lp` program completes its task, the shell prompt reappears. However, before the shell prompt reappeared, the login shell and the `lp` command were running; you initiated multiple processes in that case. The shell waited until the `lp` command finished before putting the shell prompt back onscreen.

STARTING A BACKGROUND PROCESS

You can run a process as a background job by giving the command to start a process and placing an ampersand (`&`) after the command. For example, if you enter the command , the shell responds immediately with a number—the PID for that process. The shell prompt reappears without waiting for the process to complete. The following is a sample of what you would see:

```
$ lp report.txt &
3146
$
```

In this example, 3146 is the PID of the process started by the `lp` command.

Regardless of whether you run the `lp` command in the background, the process associated with `lp` is started from the current shell. The `lp` process is a child process of the current shell. This example points to a common relationship between processes—that of parent and child. Your current shell is the parent process, and the running `lp` process is a child process. Usually, a parent process waits for one or more of its child processes to complete before it continues. If you want the parent to continue without waiting for the child to finish, attach the ampersand (`&`) to the command that *spawns*, or initiates, the child process. You can continue with other work or commands while the child runs.

Note

If you're working from a character terminal or a remote login, your current shell is usually your login shell. However, if you're using a virtual terminal or a terminal window from a GUI, a separate shell is associated with each session.

Using Pipes to Start Multiple Processes

Another way to start multiple processes is to use one or more pipes on a command line. To print a long listing of the 10 most recently modified files in your current directory, enter this command:

```
ls -lt ¦ head ¦ lp
```

This command starts three processes simultaneously, and they're all children of the current shell. A pipe works this way: Commands on either side of the vertical bar (¦) begin at the same time. Neither is the parent of the other; they're both children of the process that was running when they were created. In this sense, you can think of commands on either side of the pipe symbol as sibling processes.

Some programs are written so that they themselves spawn several processes. One example is the `ispell` command, which lists the words in a document that Linux can't find in a system dictionary. The `ispell` command spawns some child processes. Suppose you enter the following:

```
ispell /usr/doc/HOWTO/Commercial-HOWTO ]] final.errs &
```

You'll see the following results displayed:

```
[1]1286
$
```

Here, [1] indicates the number of background processes you have started and 1286 is the PID of the background process, in this case `ispell`; the `$` prompt indicates that the shell is ready to handle another command from you. Even though `ispell` may spawn some children and wait for them to complete, you don't have to wait. In this example, the current shell is the parent of `ispell`, and `ispell`'s children can be thought of as grandchildren of the login shell. Although a parent can wait for its children, a grandparent doesn't.

All these examples show how it's possible for users to start multiple processes. You can wait until child processes are finished before continuing or not. If you continue without waiting for child processes to complete, you make the children background processes. The following sections look at some Linux commands you can use to schedule processes to run at specified times or at a lower relative priority.

USING THE SCHEDULING COMMANDS

The Linux environment provides many ways to handle command execution. Linux lets you create lists of commands and specify when they're to be run. The `at` command, for example, takes a list of commands typed at the keyboard or from a file and runs them at the time specified by the command. The `batch` command is similar to the `at` command, except that `batch` runs commands when the system finds time for them rather than allows users to specify a particular time. The `cron` command allows for commands to be run periodically, and the `crontab` command allows users to edit the files used by `cron`.

All scheduling commands are useful for running tasks at times when the system isn't too busy. They're also good for executing scripts to external services—such as database queries—at times when it's least expensive to do so.

RUNNING COMMANDS AT SPECIFIED TIMES WITH AT

To schedule one or more commands for a specified time, use the `at` command. With this command, you can specify a time, a date, or both. The command expects two or more arguments. At a minimum, you specify the time you want the command(s) executed and the command(s) you want to execute.

The following example performs its job at 1:23 a.m. If you're working in the wee hours of the morning before 1:23 a.m. (that is, between midnight and 1:23 a.m.), the command is done today, at 1:23 a.m. Otherwise, it's done at 1:23 a.m. the following day. The job prints all files in the directory `/usr/sales/reports` and sends a user named boss some mail announcing that the print job was done at 1:23 a.m. Type the following commands on the terminal, pressing Return at the end of each line. After you enter each line, press Ctrl+d to finish the command.

```
at 1:23
lp /usr/sales/reports/*
echo ''Files printed, Boss!'' ¦ mail -s"Job done'' boss
```

Note

`cron` jobs, discussed later in this chapter, are the most commonly used mechanisms for running automated system administration jobs under Linux. However, you must be the root user to create and edit `cron` job entries. The `at` command allows anyone to run tasks even if he or she does not have root privileges.

→ See "Setting the Terminal Environment," p. 322

Commands to be scheduled by `at` are entered as a list of commands on the line following the `at` command.

After you terminate the `at` command, you see a display similar to the following:

```
job 756603300.a at Tues July 27 01:23:00 1999
```

This response indicates that the job will execute at 1:23 as specified. The job number, `756603300.a`, identifies the job. If you decide you want to cancel the job, do so by using the job number associated with it, like so:

```
at -d 756603300.a
```

If you have several commands you want to schedule by using `at`, it's best to put them in a file. If the filename is `getdone`, for example, and you want to schedule the commands for 10 a.m., type one of the following:

```
at 10:00 [[ getdone
at 10:00 -f getdone
```

Remember that the less-than symbol (<) indicates the use of the contents of the `getdone` file as input to the `at` command. By using the `-f` option, you can specify the command file without using redirection.

You can also specify a date for an `at` job. For example, to schedule a job at 5 p.m. on July 27, enter these commands:

```
at 17:00 July 27
lp /usr/sales/reports/*
echo ''Files printed, Boss!'' ¦ mail -s"Job done'' boss
```

The jobs you schedule with `at` are put into a queue that the operating system checks periodically. You don't have to be logged in for the job to be executed. The `at` command always runs in the background, freeing resources but still accomplishing the job. Any output produced by the commands in your `at` job is automatically mailed to you.

To see which jobs you scheduled with `at`, enter `at -l`. Working with the preceding examples, you see the following results:

```
job 756603300.a at Tue July 27 01:23:00 1999
job 756604200.a at Tue July 27 17:00:00 1999
```

Only your `at` jobs are listed.

To remove a scheduled `at` job, enter `at -d` followed by the job number. To remove the second job just listed, for example, enter this command:

```
at -d 756604200.a
```

Table 17.3 summarizes the different ways to use the `at` command.

TABLE 17.3 SUMMARY OF at COMMANDS

Format	Action
at *hh:mm*	Schedules the job at the hour (*hh*) and minute (*mm*) specified, using a 24-hour clock
at *hh:mmmonthdayyear*	Schedules the job at the hour (*hh*), minute (*mm*), month, day, and year specified
at -l	Lists scheduled jobs; an alias for the atq command
at now + *count time-units*	Schedules the job right now plus the count number of *time-units*; time units can be minutes, hours, days, or weeks
at -d *job_id*	Cancels the job with the job number matching *job_id*; an alias for the atrm command

As the root user, you can use any of these commands; for other users, the files /etc/at.allow and /etc/at.deny determine the permission to use the commands. If /etc/at.allow exists, only the usernames listed in the file are allowed to use the at command. If the /etc/at.allow file doesn't exist, the system checks /etc/at.deny, and every username not mentioned in /etc/at.deny is allowed to use at (in other words, any user listed in /etc/at.deny isn't allowed to use at). If neither file exists, only the superuser (root) can use at. If /etc/at.deny is empty, every user can use at.

RUNNING LONG TASKS WITH batch

Linux offers more than one command for scheduling tasks. The preceding section describes the at command, which gives you the power to dictate when a task will run. However, it's always possible that the system can be loaded down with more jobs scheduled at one time than it can handle comfortably. The batch command lets the operating system decide an appropriate time to run a process. When you schedule a job with batch, Linux starts and works on the process whenever the system load isn't too great. Jobs run under batch execute in the background, just as those run with at. In fact, batch is an alias for at -b in Red Hat Linux.

Tip #99 from Jack

> It's useful to put commands you want to run with at or batch in a file so that you don't have to retype the commands each time you want to run the jobs. To use batch to schedule the commands in the file getdone, enter the following command: batch < getdone.

The format for batch commands is to enter the list of commands on the lines following the batch command; you terminate the list of commands by pressing Ctrl+d. You can put the list of commands in a file and then redirect the input of the file to batch. To sort a collection of files, print the results, and notify the user named boss that the job is done, enter the following commands:

```
batch
sort /usr/sales/reports/* ¦ lp
echo ''Files printed, Boss!'' ¦ mailx -s"Job done'' boss
```

The system returns the following response:

```
job 7789001234.b at Fri Feb 21 11:43:09 1997
```

The date and time listed are the date and time you pressed Ctrl+d to complete the `batch` command. When the job is complete, check your mail; anything that the commands normally display is mailed to you.

SCHEDULING COMMANDS WITH `cron` AND `crontab`

Both `at` and `batch` schedule commands on a one-time basis. To schedule commands or processes on a regular basis, you use the `cron` program. You specify the times and dates you want to run a command in `crontab` files. Times can be specified in terms of minutes, hours, days of the month, months of the year, or days of the week.

The `cron` program is started only once, when the system is booted. Individual users shouldn't have permission to run `cron` directly. Also, as the system administrator, you shouldn't start `cron` by typing the name of the command; you should list `cron` in a shell script as one of the commands to run during a system boot-up sequence.

When started, `cron` (short for *chronograph*) checks queues for `at` jobs to run and also checks to see whether users or the root have scheduled jobs by using `crontab` files. If `cron` doesn't have anything to do, it "goes to sleep" and becomes inactive; it "wakes up" every minute, however, to see whether it needs to run commands. You can see how important and useful this facility is; also, `cron` uses very few system resources.

PART III CH 17

Tip #100 from *Jack*

While `cron` uses few system resources itself, the programs `cron` spawns can overload a system. Thus, try to schedule resource intensive jobs for off-peak hours. Also try to schedule similar jobs, such as those that use the `find` command, at the same off-peak time to lesson the overall impact.

You can use `crontab` to install a list of commands that will be executed on a regular schedule. The commands are scheduled to run at a specified time (such as once a month, once an hour, once a day, and so on). The list of commands to be performed on the specified schedule must be included in the `crontab` file, which is installed with the `crontab` command. After you install the `crontab` file, `cron` reads and executes the listed commands at the specified times. Also, with the `crontab` command, you can view the list of commands included in the file and cancel the list if you want.

Before you install your crontab file with the crontab command, create the file containing the list of commands you want to schedule by using the crontab -e option.

Each user has only one crontab file, created when the crontab command is issued. This file is placed in a directory that's read by the cron command.

Linux stores the user's crontab file in the /usr/spool/cron/ directory in a file named for the user's login name. If your username is mcn, and you use a text editor to create a file called mycron and install it by typing crontab mycron, the file /usr/spool/cron/mcn is created. (In this example, the mcn file is created, or overwritten, with the contents of mycron, which might contain entries that launch one or more commands.)

Note

For users to use the crontab command, they must be listed in the /etc/cron.d/cron.allow file. If you add a user to the system from the command line (by using the useradd command), he or she isn't added automatically to the /etc/cron.d/cron.allow file. As the root user, you must add the new user to the cron.allow file with a text editor.

Although you can initially create your crontab file with a text editor, after you create your crontab file, you can modify it by using only the crontab -e command. Don't try to replace or modify the file that cron examines (that is, the /usr/spool/cron/crontabs/user file) by any means other than by using the crontab command.

Each line in the crontab file contains a time pattern and a command. The command is executed at the specified time pattern. The time pattern is divided into five fields separated by spaces or tabs. Any output that usually appears—that is, information that isn't redirected to stdout or stderr—is mailed to the user.

The following is the syntax for the commands you enter in a file to be used by crontab:

minute hour day-of-month month-of-year day-of-week command

The first five fields are time option fields. You must specify all five of these fields. You can, however, use an asterisk (*) in a field if you want to ignore that particular field.

Note

Technically, an asterisk in a crontab field means "any valid value" instead of "ignore the value"–that is, match anything. The crontab entry 02 00 01 * * date, for example, says to run the date command at two minutes after midnight (zero hour) on the first day of the month. Because the month and day of the week fields are both asterisks, this entry runs on the first day of every month and any day of the week that the first of the month happens to land on.

Table 17.4 lists the time-field options available with `crontab`.

Table 17.4 Time-Field Options for the `crontab` Command

Field	Range
minute	`00` through `59`
hour	`00` through `23` (midnight is `00`)
day-of-month	`01` through `31`
month-of-year	`01` through `12`
day-of-week	`01` through `07` (Monday is `01`, Sunday is `07`)

You can have as many entries as you want in a `crontab` file and can designate them to run at any time. This means that you can run as many commands as you want in a single `crontab` file.

To sort a file named `/usr/wwr/sales/weekly` and mail the output to a user named twool at 7:30 a.m. each Monday, use the following entry in a file:

```
30 07 * * 01 sort /usr/wwr/sales/weekly ¦mail -s"Weekly Sales'' twool
```

This command specifies the minute as `30`, the hour as `07`, any day of the month with the asterisk, any month of the year with another asterisk, and the day of the week as `01` (which represents Monday).

Notice the pipe between the `sort` and `mail` commands in the preceding example. The command field can contain pipes, semicolons, arrows, or anything else you can enter on a shell command line. At the specified date and time, `cron` runs the entire command field with a standard shell (bash).

To specify a sequence of values for one of the first four fields, use commas to separate the values. Suppose you have a program, chkquotes, that accesses a service that provides stock quotes and puts the quotes in a file. To get those quotes at 9 a.m., 11 a.m., 2 p.m., and 4 p.m. on Monday, Tuesday, and Thursday of every week—and definitely on the 10th of March and September—use the following entry:

```
* 09,11,14,16 10 03,09 01,02,04 chkquotes
```

You can put the command lines into a file by using vi or some other editor that allows you to save files as text files. Assume that you put your commands in a file named `cronjobs`. To use `crontab` to put the file where `cron` can find it, enter this command:

```
crontab cronjobs
```

Each time you use `crontab` this way it overwrites any `crontab` file you may have already launched.

The `crontab` command has three options:

- The `-e`option edits the contents of the current `crontab` file. (The `-e` option opens your file by using the ed editor or whatever editor is assigned to the `EDITOR` variable in your shell.)

→ See "Setting the Shell Environment," p. 325

- The `-r`option removes the current `crontab` file from the `crontabs` directory.
- The `-l`option lists the contents of the current `crontab` file.

In all these cases, `crontab` works with the `crontab` file that has your login name. If your login name is mcn, your `crontab` file is `/usr/spool/cron/crontabs/mcn`. The `crontab` command names your file automatically.

The system administrator and users share responsibility for making sure that the system is used appropriately. When you schedule a process, be aware of the impact it may have on the total system. Linux allows you, as the system administrator, to grant access to the `at`, `batch`, and `cron` commands to all users, specific users, or no users (or to deny access to individual users).

Reporting On and Monitoring the Multitasking Environment

Youknow that Linux is a multiuser, multitasking operating system. Because so many people can do so many things with the system at the same time, users find it useful to determine who's using the system and what processes are running, as well as to monitor processes.

Knowing that others can keep track of the commands you enter is important. Most users can't access your files without your permission, but they can see the names of commands you enter. Also, you (as the system administrator) or someone else who has the root password can peruse all the files on the system.

Although you don't have to be paranoid about privacy on a Linux system, you should know that the system can be monitored by anyone who wants to take the time to do it. The information you can gain about what's going on in the system is more useful than just satisfying curiosity: By seeing what jobs are running, you can appropriately schedule your tasks. You can also see whether a process of yours is still active and whether it's behaving properly.

Finding Out Who's on the System with `who`

The purpose of the `who` command is to find out who's logged in to the system. The `who` command lists the login names, terminal lines, and login times of users currently logged in.

The `who` command is useful in many situations. If you want to communicate with someone on the computer by using the `write` command, for example, you can find out whether that person is on the system by using `who`. You can also use `who` to see when certain users are logged in to the computer to keep track of their time spent on the system.

Using who to List Users Logged In to the System

To see everyone who's currently logged in to the system, you can enter `who`. You then see a display similar to the following:

```
$ who
root     console    Dec 13 08:00
ernie    tty02      Dec 13 10:37
bkraft   tty03      Dec 13 11:02
jdurum   tty05      Dec 13 09:21
ernie    ttys7      Dec 11 18:49
$
```

This listing shows that root, ernie, bkraft, and jdurum are now logged in. It shows that root logged in at 8 a.m., bkraft at 11:02, and jdurum at 9:21. You can also see that ernie is logged in to two terminals and that one login occurred at 6:49 p.m. (18:49) two days earlier (which may be some reason for concern, or it might just be ernie's usual work habits).

Using Headers in User Listings

Several options are available with `who`, but this chapter describes how to use only two to monitor processes on the system:

`-u`	Lists only users who are currently logged in
`-H`	Displays headers above each column

With these two options, you can get more information about the users now logged in. The headers displayed with the `-H` option are `NAME`, `LINE`, `TIME`, `IDLE`, `PID`, and `COMMENTS`. Table 17.5 explains the terms appearing in the heading.

Table 17.5 Output Format for the who Command

Field	Description
`NAME`	Lists the user's login name.
`LINE`	Lists the line or terminal being used.
`TIME`	Lists the time the user logged in.
`IDLE`	Lists the hours and minutes since the last activity on that line. A period is displayed if activity occurred within the last minute of system time. If more than 24 hours has elapsed since the line was used, the word `old` is displayed.
`PID`	Lists the process ID number of the user's login shell.
`COMMENTS`	Lists the contents of the comment field if comments have been included in `/etc/inittab` or if there are network connections.

Note

You probably won't see the `COMMENT` field filled in very often in any recent Linux systems. In the old days, processes that let you log in to UNIX (`getty` or `uugetty`) were started directly from entries in the `/etc/inittab` file and usually listened for login requests from a particular terminal. The `COMMENT` field might identify the location of that terminal and could tell you which users were logged in and at what terminal they were sitting. Today, processes that listen for login requests are typically handled by the Service Access Facility and are no longer listed in `/etc/inittab`.

The following example uses the `-u` and `-H` options and shows the response Linux returns:

```
$ who -uH
NAME      LINE       TIME          IDLE      PID      COMMENT
root      console  Dec 13 08:00      .      10340
ernie     tty02    Dec 13 10:37      .      11929    Tech-89.2
bkraft    tty03    Dec 13 11:02    0:04      4761    Sales-23.4
jdurum    tty05    Dec 13 09:21    1:07     10426
ernie     ttys7    Dec 11 18:49     old     10770    oreo.coolt.com
$
```

You can infer from this listing that the last session associated with ernie is from a network site named `oreo.coolt.com` and that no activity has occurred in that session in more than 24 hours (which might signal a problem). The session for root and the first one for ernie have both been accessed within the last minute. The last activity on the session for bkraft was four minutes ago; it has been one hour and seven minutes since any activity was reported on the session for jdurum.

Also note that this listing includes the PID (process ID number) for the login shell of each user's session. The next section shows how you can use the PID to further monitor the system.

USING THE `finger` COMMAND TO LEARN MORE ABOUT WHO IS ON THE SYSTEM

A command that complements the `who` command is `finger`. To see more information about a specific user, you can enter `finger` *`username`* (or `finger` *`username`*`@domain` if the user is on another computer). For example, to see more information on a user named tackett, you enter this command:

```
finger tackett
```

You then see the following output:

```
Login: tackett                          Name: Jack Tackett Jr
Directory: /home/tackett                Shell: /bin/tcsh
Office: 2440 SW Cary Parkway 114        Office Phone: 919 555 1212
Home Phone: 919 555 1212
Never logged in.
Mail last read Fri Jul 3 17:42 1998 (EDT)
Plan:
---------------------
Jack Tackett, Jr.
In the immortal words of Socrates:
I drank WHAT?
---------------------
```

This output shows the login and real name associated with the specified account. You can also see which shell this user prefers to use, his address, when he last read his email, and when he was last logged in. If he is currently logged on, the `finger` command tells you how long he has been logged on and which program he is currently using. The `finger` command also displays any information this user may have placed in his `.plan` file in his home directory.

As you can see, the `finger` command displays a lot of information about a user; this information could be used by crackers to hack the system. For this reason, many system administrators disable the `finger` command so that others cannot see this information.

Note

If you allow the use of the `finger` command on your system, or if your system administrator allows it on a system you are using, you can use the `chfn` command to change the information displayed by `finger`. See the related man page (use the `man chfn` command) for more information.

Reporting On the Status of Processes with ps

Theps (process status) command reports on the status of processes. You can use it to determine which processes are running, whether a process has completed, whether a process is hung (having some difficulty), how long a process has run, the resources a process is using, the relative priority of a process, and the PID needed before you can kill a process. All this information is useful to a user and very useful to a system administrator. Without any options, `ps` lists the PID of each process associated with your current shell. You also can see a detailed listing of all the processes running on a system.

Monitoring Processes with ps

A common use of the `ps` command is to monitor background jobs and other processes on the system. Because background processes don't communicate with your screen and keyboard in most cases, you use `ps` to track their progress.

The `ps` listing displays four default headings as indicators of the information in the fields below each heading: `PID`, `TTY`, `TIME`, and `COMMAND`. Table 17.6 explains these headings.

Table 17.6 Headings in the Output of ps

Field	Explanation
`PID`	The process identification number
`TTY`	The terminal on which the process originated
`TIME`	The cumulative execution time for the process, in minutes and seconds
`COMMAND`	The name of the command being executed

Suppose that you want to sort a file named `sales.dat`, save a copy of the sorted file in a file named `sales.srt`, an mail the sorted file to the user sarah. If you also want to put this job in the background, you can enter the following command:

```
sort sales.dat ¦ tee sales.srt ¦ mailx -s"Sorted Sales Data'' sarah &
```

To monitor this process, enter `ps` to see a display such as this one:

```
PID    TTY     TIME COMMAND
16490 tty02    0:15 sort
16489 tty02    0:00 mailx
16492 tty02    0:00 ps
16478 tty02    0:00 bash
16491 tty02    0:06 tee
16480  tty02   96:45 cruncher
```

You see the accumulated time and PID for each process started with the command. You also see information for your login shell (bash) and for `ps` itself. Notice that all the commands in the pipe are running at once, just as you would expect (this is the way the piping process works). The last entry is for a command that has been running for more than an hour and a half. If that's a problem, you might want to terminate the process by using the `kill` command (described later in this chapter). If you enter `ps` and see only the following listing, the previous job you put into the background is complete:

```
PID    TTY      TIME COMMAND
16492 tty02     0:00 ps
16478 tty02     0:00 bash
16480  tty02   99:45 cruncher
```

Note

Use `ps` occasionally to check the status of a command. If, however, you use `ps` every second while waiting to see whether the background job is complete, putting the job in the background doesn't make much sense in the first place.

OBTAINING MORE INFORMATION ABOUT PROCESSES WITH ps

Sometimes you need to know more about your processes than what the default `ps` listing provides. To generate additional information, you can invoke some of the flags listed in Table 17.7.

TABLE 17.7 COMMONLY USED FLAGS FOR THE ps COMMAND

Flag	Description
`a`	Shows processes of other users also.
`c`	Displays the command name from the `task_struct` environment.
`e`	Shows the environment after the command line and *and*.
`f`	Shows the "forest" family tree format (processes and subprocesses).

Table 17.7 Commonly Used Flags for the ps Command

Flag	Description
h	Specifies no header.
j	Indicates the jobs format.
l	Indicates the long format.
m	Displays memory info.
n	Specifies numeric output for USER and WCHAN. WCHAN is the name of the kernel function where the process is sleeping, with the sys_ stripped from the function name. If /etc/psdatabase doesn't exist, the number is hexadecimal instead.
r	Specifies running processes only.
s	Specifies the signal format.
S	Adds child CPU time and page faults.
txx	Processes associated with tty *xx* only, where *xx* is a place holder for the actual number of the terminal.
u	Indicates the user format; gives username and start time.
v	Specifies vm (virtual memory) format.
w	Specifies wide output; doesn't truncate command lines to fit on one line.
x	Shows processes without controlling terminal.

Part III Ch 17

Tip #101 from *Jack*

Although many Linux commands require you to preface a flag with the - symbol, you do not have to do so with the ps command. In fact, you might get a warning message about using the dash (-).

The ps command gives only an approximate picture of process status because things can and do change while the ps command is running. The ps command gives a snapshot of the process status at the instant ps executed. The snapshot includes the ps command itself.

The following examples show three commands. The first command is the login shell (bash). The second command is sort, which is used to sort the file named inventory. The third command is the ps command you're now running.

To find out what processes you're currently running, use the following command:

```
$ ps
PID     TTY     TIME    COMMAND
65      tty01   0:07    -bash
71      tty01   0:14    sort inventory
231     tty01   0:09    ps
```

To obtain a full listing, use this command:

```
$ ps -uax
UID     PID   PPID  C   STIME      TTY    TIME   COMD
amanda 65     1     0   11:40:11   tty01  0:06   -bash
amanda 71     65    61  11:42:01   tty01  0:14   sort inventory
amanda 231    65    80  11:46:02   tty01  0:00   ps -f
```

Note

If you are familiar with UNIX systems such as Solaris, then these flags are different, and you will have to remember which system you are using because each uses different flags to provide the same information. For example, to get a full listing under many System V versions of UNIX, you use the `ps -ef` command.

Notice a few things about this full listing. In addition to the PID, the PPID is listed. The PPID is the process ID number of that process' parent process. In this example, the first process listed, PID 65, is the parent of the following two. The entry in the fourth column (the column headed C) gives the amount of CPU time a process has used recently. In selecting the next process to work with, the operating system chooses a process with a low C value over one with a higher value. The entry in the `STIME` column is the time at which the process started.

To monitor every process on the system and get a full listing, enter `ps -uax`.

Tip #102 from

Jack

For more system resource information, use the `top` command. `top` provides an ongoing look at processor activity in real time. It displays a listing of the most CPU-intensive tasks on the system and can provide an interactive interface for manipulating processes. It can sort the tasks by CPU usage, memory usage, and runtime.

By piping the command through the `grep $LOGNAME` command, the processes belonging to your login name are displayed while all others are filtered out. To see a full listing of all your processes, enter the following:

```
ps uax ¦ grep $LOGNAME
```

To list processes for two terminals (for example, tty1 and tty2), use the following command:

```
$ ps -t ''1 2''
PID   TTY      TIME   COMMAND
32     tty01   0:05   bash
36     tty02   0:09   bash
235    tty02   0:16   vi calendar
```

In this example, the `-t` option is used to restrict the listing to the processes associated with terminals tty01 and tty02. Terminal tty02 is running the shell command (PID 32) and using vi to edit the calendar (PID 235). The cumulative time for each process is also listed. If you're using shells from a graphical interface (the `xterm` command), you can use device names `pts001`, `pts002`, and so on with the `-t` option to see the processes from those sessions.

Tip #103 from Jack

The `/proc` file system contains much of the information reported by programs such as `ps`. Thus, you can read the information directly from `proc` without using other programs. For example, to check on memory usage, you type the following command:

```
cat /proc/meminfo
```

Sometimes a process is marked as `defunct`, which means that the process has terminated and its parent process has been notified, but the parent hasn't acknowledged that the process is "dead." A process like that is called a *zombie process*. The parent might be busy with something else, and the zombie will soon disappear. If you see a number of defunct processes or ones that linger for some time, this is a sign of some difficulty with the operating system.

Note

Because a zombie process has no parent, you can't kill the zombie. The only way to get rid of a zombie process is to reboot your machine.

CONTROLLING MULTIPLE PROCESSES

Linux gives you the power to run several processes concurrently. It also allows a user or an administrator to have control over running processes. This control is advantageous when you need to do the following:

- Initiate a process that continues after its parent quits running (use the `nohup` command)
- Schedule a process with a priority different than other processes (use the `nice` command)
- Terminate or stop a process (use the `kill` command)

USING nohup WITH BACKGROUND PROCESSES

Normally, the children of a process terminate when the parent dies or terminates. This means that when you start a background process, it terminates when you log out. To have a process continue after you log out, you can use the `nohup` commandPut `nohup` at the beginning of a command line as follows:

```
nohup sort sales.dat &
```

This sample command tells the sort command to ignore the fact that you log out of the system; it should run until the process completes. In this way, you can initiate a process that can run for days or even weeks. What's more, you don't have to be logged in as it runs. Naturally, you want to make sure that the job you initiate behaves nicely—that is, eventually terminates and doesn't create an excessive amount of output.

When you use nohup, the command sends all the output and error messages of a command that normally appear onscreen to a file named nohup.out. Consider the following example:

```
$ nohup sort sales.dat &
1252
Sending output to nohup.out
$
```

The sorted file and any error messages are placed in the file nohup.out. Now consider this example:

```
$ nohup sort sales.dat ]] sales.srt &
1257
Sending output to nohup.out
$
```

Any error messages are placed in the nohup.out file, but the sorted sales.dat file is placed in sales.srt.

Note

When you use nohup with a pipe, you must use nohup with each command in the pipe:

```
nohup sort sales.dat ¦ nohup mailx -s"Sorted Sales Data'' boss &
```

SCHEDULING THE PRIORITY OF COMMANDS WITH nice

You can use the nice command to run a command at a specific scheduling priority. The nice command gives you some control over the priority of one job over another. If you don't use nice, processes run at a set priority. You can lower the priority of a process by using the nice command so that other processes can be scheduled to use the CPU more frequently than the nice job. The superuser (the person who can log in as the root user) can also raise the priority of a process.

Note

The commands nice -help and nice -version don't work in the GNU implementation of nice.

The general form of the `nice` command is as follows:

```
nice - numbercommand
```

The priority level is determined by the *number* argument (a higher number means a lower priority). The default is set to 10, and *number* is an offset to the default. If the *number* argument is present, the priority is incremented by that amount up to a limit of 20. If you enter the following command, the `sort` process starts with a priority of 10:

```
sort sales.dat > sales.srt &
```

If you want to start another process—say, with the `lp` command—but give preference to the `sort` command, you can enter the following:

```
nice -5 lp mail_list &
```

To give the `lp` command the lowest possible priority, enter this:

```
nice -10 lp mail_list &
```


Note The *number* flag in the `nice` command is preceded by the flag specifier `-`, which you shouldn't confuse with the negative number sign.

Only superusers can increase the priority of a process. To do so, they use a negative number as the argument to `nice`. Remember, the lower the `nice` value, the higher the priority (up to a maximum priority of 20). To give a job "top priority," a superuser initiates the job as follows:

```
nice -10 job &
```

The ampersand (`&`) is optional; if `job` is interactive, you don't use the ampersand to place the process in the background.

SCHEDULING THE PRIORITY OF RUNNING PROCESSES WITH `renice`

Using the `renice` command, available on some systems, you can modify the priority of a running process. Berkeley UNIX systems have the `renice` command; it's also available in the `/usr/ucb` directory in Linux System V systems for compatibility with Berkeley systems. With `renice`, you can adjust priorities on commands as they execute. The format of `renice` is similar to that of `nice`:

```
renice - numberPID
```

To change the priority on a running process, you must know its PID. To find the PID of all your processes, enter this command:

```
ps -e ¦ grep name
```

In this command, *name* represents the name of the running process. The `grep` command filters out all processes that don't contain the name of the process you're looking for. If several processes of that name are running, you have to determine the one you want by looking at the time it started. If you want to affect all processes belonging to a certain group or a certain user, you can specify the GID or UID of the running processes to the `renice` command.

The entry in the second column of the ps listing is the PID of the process. In the following example, three processes are running for the current user (in addition to the shell). The current user's name is pcoco:

```
$ ps -ef ¦ grep $LOGNAME
pcoco  11805 11804   0  Dec 22   ttysb   0:01 sort sales.dat]]sales.srt
pcoco  19955 19938   4  16:13:02 ttyp0   0:00 grep pcoco
pcoco  19938     1   0 16:11:04  ttyp0   0:00 bash
pcoco  19940 19938 142 16:11:04  ttyp0   0:33 find . -name core -exec rm {};
$
```

To lower the priority on the process with PID 19940 (the `find` process), enter the following:

```
renice -5 19940
```

As you would expect, the following statements are true about `renice`:

- You can use `renice` only with processes you own.
- The superuser can use `renice` on any process.
- Only the superuser can increase the priority of a process.

TERMINATING PROCESSES WITH `kill`

Sometimes you want or need to terminate a process. The following are some reasons for stopping a process:

- It's using too much CPU time.
- It's running too long without producing the expected output.
- It's producing too much output to the screen or to a disk file.
- It appears to have locked a terminal or some other session.
- It's using the wrong files for input or output because of an operator or programming error.
- It's no longer useful.

Most likely, you'll come across a number of other reasons to kill a process as well. If the process to be stopped is a background process, use the `kill` command to get out of these situations.

To stop a command that isn't in the background, press Ctrl+c. When a command is in the background, however, pressing an interrupt key doesn't stop it. Because a background process isn't under terminal control, keyboard input of any interrupt key is ignored. The only way you can stop background commands is to use the `kill` command.

NORMAL TERMINATION OF BACKGROUND PROCESSES

The `kill` command sends signals to the program to demand that a process be terminated or killed. To use `kill`, use either of the following forms:

```
kill PID(s)

kill -signal PID(s)
```

To kill a process whose PID is 123, enter `kill 123`. To kill several processes whose PIDs are 123, 342, and 73, enter `kill 123 342 73`.

By using the `-signal` option, you can do more than simply kill a process. Other signals can cause a running process to reread configuration files or stop a process without killing it. Valid signals are listed by the command `kill -l`. An average user, however, will probably use `kill` with no signal or, at most, with the `-9` signal (the I-mean-it-so-don't-ignore-me signal, described in the next section).

Caution

Use the correct PID with the `kill` command. Using the wrong PID can stop a process you want to keep running. Remember that killing the wrong process or a system process can have disastrous effects. Also, remember that if you're logged in as the system administrator, you can kill *any* process.

Stopping a Process by Name

Most Linux distributions provide a command called `killall` that allows you to give a process name rather than a PID. For example, if you need to kill a series of processes started by the Web server, you could use the following command:

```
killall httpd
```

If you do not have access to this command, you can simulate its usage with the `grep`, `awk`, and `xargs` commands as follows:

```
ps uax | grep httpd | grep -v grep | awk '{print $2}' | xargs kill -9
```

This command line performs the following actions:

- `ps aux` lists all active processes.
- `grep httpd` separates out only those lines that contain the name `httpd`.
- `grep -v grep` filters out any lines containing `grep` commands.
- `awk '{print $2}'` prints the second field in the resulting list, which is the PID for that process.
- `xargs kill -9` pipes each resultant value to the `kill -9` command via the `xargs` command.

If you successfully kill the process, you get no notice from the shell; the shell prompt simply reappears. You see an error message if you try to kill a process you don't have permission to kill or if you try to kill a process that doesn't exist.

Suppose that your login name is chris and that you're now logged in to tty01. To see the processes you have running, enter `ps -f`, and you'll see the following response:

```
UID    PID   PPID   C   STIME      TTY      TIME    COMMAND
chris  65    1      0   11:40:11   tty01    0:06    -bash
chris  71    65     61  11:42:01   tty01    0:14    total_updt
chris  231   65     80  11:46:02   tty01    0:00    ps -f
chris  187   53     60  15:32:01   tty02  123:45    crunch stats
chris  53    1      0   15:31:34   tty02    1:06    -bash
```

Notice that the program `total_updt` is running at your current terminal. Another program, `crunch`, is running on another terminal, and it has used an unusually large amount of CPU time. To kill that process, you can enter `kill 187`, which may be sufficient. To kill the parent of that process, enter `kill 53`.

You might want to kill a parent and child process if you log in as the system administrator and see that someone has left his or her terminal unattended (if you've set up Linux with remote terminals). You can kill a clock process that the user has running (the child process) and the login shell (the parent process) so that the unattended terminal is no longer logged in.

Stopping the parent of a process sometimes terminates the child process as well. To be sure, stop the parent and its children to halt all activity associated with a parent process. Using the preceding example, enter `kill 187 53` to terminate both processes.

Tip #104 from *Jack*

If your terminal locks up, log in to another virtual terminal by pressing Alt combined with a function key (F1-F6), enter `ps -ef ¦ grep $LOGNAME`, and then kill the login shell for the locked terminal.

UNCONDITIONAL TERMINATION OF BACKGROUND PROCESSES

Issuing the `kill` command sends a signal to a process. Linux programs can send or receive more than 20 signals, each of which is represented by a number. For example, when you log out, Linux sends the hang-up signal (signal number 1) to all the background processes started from your login shell. This signal kills or stops those processes unless they were started with `nohup` (as described earlier in this chapter).

Using `nohup` to start a background process lets the process ignore the signal that tries to stop it. You might be using programs or shell scripts written to ignore some signals. If you don't specify a signal when you use `kill`, signal 15 is sent to the process. The command `kill 1234` sends signal 15 to the process whose PID is 1234. If that process is set to ignore signal 15, however, the process doesn't terminate when you use this command. You can use `kill` in a way that a process "can't refuse," however.

The signal 9 is an unconditional kill signal; it always kills a process. To unconditionally kill a process, use the following command:

```
kill -9 PID
```

Suppose you enter `ps -f` and see the following response:

```
UID    PID  PPID  C  STIME     TTY     TIME   COMMAND
chris   65    1   0  11:40:11  tty01   0:06   -bash
chris   71   65  61  11:42:01  tty01   0:14   total_updt inventory
chris  231   65  80  11:46:02  tty01   0:00   ps -f
chris  187   53  60  15:32:01  tty02 123:45   crunch stats
chris   53   1    0  15:31:34  tty02   1:06   -bash
```

To kill process 187, normally you would enter `kill 187`. If you then enter `ps -f` again and see that the process is still there, you know the process is set up to ignore the `kill` command. To kill it unconditionally, enter `kill -9 187`. When you enter `ps -f` again, you see that the process is no longer around.

Caution

A disadvantage to using this unconditional version of the `kill` command is that `kill -9` doesn't allow a process to finish what it's doing before it terminates the process. If you use `kill -9` with a program that's updating a file, you could lose the updated material or the entire file.

You should use the powerful `kill -9` command responsibly. In most cases, you don't need the -9 option; the `kill` command, issued without arguments, stops most processes.

TERMINATION OF ALL BACKGROUND PROCESSES

To kill all background jobs, you can enter `kill 0`. Commands that run in the background sometimes initiate more than one process; tracking down all the PID numbers associated with the process you want to kill can be tedious. Because `kill 0` terminates all processes started by the current shell, it's a faster and less tedious way to terminate processes. Enter the `jobs` command to see what commands are running in the background for the current shell.

USING KILL TO SEND SIGNALS TO PROCESSES

You also can use `kill` to send nontermination signals to a running process. You can tell a process to restart or to enter a different logging phase by sending a signal. Linux can send many different signals, with Table 17.8 listing the more common signals used. To get a complete list of signals, use the `kill -l` command.

TABLE 17.8 SIGNALS DELIVERED TO A RUNNING PROCESS BY THE `kill` COMMAND

Number	Signal	Description
1	`SIGHUP`	Reread configuration files
9	`SIGKILL`	Terminate the process immediately

TABLE 17.8 SIGNALS DELIVERED TO A RUNNING PROCESS BY THE `kill` COMMAND

Number	Signal	Description
10	SIGUSR1	Send the process a program-specific signal
15	SIGTERM	Terminate in a normal manner

Looking for PIDs to send a signal to can be an interesting exercise, which is why many processes record their PIDs in a file located in `/var/run`. Then, if you need to know their PIDs, you can look at the appropriate file for that information. For example, to see `syslogd`'s PID, you can use the following command:

```
cat /var/run/syslogd.pid
```

You can use this ability to send a signal directly to the program, as shown here:

```
kill -SIGHUP 'cat /var/run/syslogd.pid'
```

This signal then tells the system logger to reread its configuration file and restart.

TROUBLESHOOTING

The commands I put in my `crontab` *file don't work.*

The `cron` command runs your `crontab`entries by using the Bourne Again shell (bash). Your entries fail if you use shell features not supported by bash. For example, the Public Domain Korn shell (pdksh) allows you to use either a tilde (~) to represent a home directory or the `alias` command to designate aliases for certain commands.

When I try to use the `at` *command, I'm told I don't have permission to use it.*

You haven't added your login ID to the `/etc/cron.d/at.allow` file.

I tried to use the `at now` *command to run a command immediately.*

No matter how fast you type, `at now` always responds with the message `ERROR: Too late`. The best alternative is to use the `batch` command to run the command for you. You can, however, use `at now +5 min` to run the command in five minutes. After you press Return, type quickly to enter your command before the five minutes expire.

CHAPTER 18

PRINTING

In this chapter

by Jack Tackett, Jr.

SELECTING A PRINTER TO WORK WITH LINUX

Although everyone thought the computer revolution would bring the paperless office, it hasn't. More paper is used today than was used 20 years ago. When the UNIX operating system was in its infancy, Bell Labs used it to produce—and print—technical documentation. As a result, UNIX, and thus Linux, has a great many utilities designed around printing (or at least formatting data to be printed). This chapter concentrates on the mechanics of actually printing a file.

The printing systems common to BSD UNIX/Linux are called the *LPR systems* (*line printer*).

If you can access the printer from MS-DOS, you should be able to print ASCII characters to the printer from Linux. The only downside is that you might not be able to access certain features of your printer from Linux. One of the main reasons is that, under Linux, the system first sends the file to be printed to another file. Linux sends the files to a temporary area because printers are relatively slow peripherals, and the system doesn't want to slow down your session just to print a file. This process is called *spooling*, and printers are thus called *spooled devices*. When you print a file in Linux, the file doesn't go directly to a printer; instead, it goes to a queue to wait its turn to be printed. If your file is the first in the queue, it prints almost immediately.

Note

Spool is an acronym for *Simultaneous Peripheral Operation Off Line*. The term was coined in the early days of the big IBM mainframes, when smaller computers were used to print reports offline from the mainframe. This technique allowed expensive mainframes to continue their tasks without wasting time on such trivial matters as printing.

Because Linux inherits a great deal of UNIX functionality, Linux supports many types of printers. If you can access your printer from DOS (as mentioned earlier), you should be able to access the printer from Linux.

KNOWING WHAT YOU NEED TO CONFIGURE PRINTERS

This chapter assumes that you know how to edit a text file under Linux and that you have a basic understanding of file ownership and permissions. It also assumes that you have your Linux system set up and running correctly. In particular, if you're going to use remote printing, your networking subsystems must be installed and operating correctly. Check out the man pages on the commands `chmod` and `chown` for more information. Also review Chapter 9, "Using the vi Editor," for information on using the vi editor because you need to edit several files when configuring your printers.

KNOWING HOW PRINTING WORKS UNDER LINUX

The simplest way to print under Linux is to send the print data directly to the printer device. The following command sends a directory listing to the first parallel printer (LPT1 in DOS terms):

```
ls > /dev/lp
```

This method doesn't take advantage of Linux's multitasking capabilities because the time taken for this command to finish is however long the printer takes to actually physically print the data. With a slow printer or a printer that's deselected or disconnected, you could wait a long time. A better method is to *spool* the data—that is, to collect the print data into a file and then start a background process to send the data to the printer.

Spooling files to be printed later is essentially how Linux works. For each printer, a spool area is defined. Data for the printer is collected in the spool area, one file per print job. A background process (called the *printer daemon*) constantly scans the spool areas for new files to print. When one appears, the data is sent to the appropriate printer, or *despooled*. When more than one file is waiting to be printed, the files are printed in the order they're completed—first in, first out. Thus, the spool area is effectively a queue, and the waiting jobs are often referred to as being *in the print queue*, or *queued*. In the case of remote printing, the data is first spooled locally as for any other print job, but the background process is told to send the data to a particular printer on a particular remote machine.

The necessary information that the printer daemon needs to do its job—the physical device to use, the spool area to look in, the remote machine and printer for remote printing, and so on—is all stored in a file called `/etc/printcap`. The details of this file are discussed later in the section "Understanding the `/etc/printcap` File." The `printcap` file is basically a text file containing the information used by Linux to control the printing device.

Tip #105 from
Jack

To Linux, the printer is just another file. But because the printer is a physical piece of hardware, it has an entry in the `/dev` directory. Linux likes to treat physical devices as if they are part of the file system. To list the various devices use the command
`ls -l /dev`

The term *printer* is used to mean a printer as specified in `/etc/printcap`. The term *physical printer* is used to mean the thing that actually puts characters on paper. `/etc/printcap` can have multiple entries that all describe one physical printer but do so in different ways. If this point isn't clear to you, read the section on `/etc/printcap`.

UNDERSTANDING THE IMPORTANT PROGRAMS FOR PRINTING

Five programs comprise the UNIX print system. By default, they are in the locations shown in Table 18.1, are owned by root, belong to the group `daemon`, and have the permissions listed in the table.

TABLE 18.1 THE IMPORTANT PRINTING PROGRAMS

File Permissions	File Locations
`-rwsr-sr-x`	`/usr/bin/lpr`
`-rwsr-sr-x`	`/usr/bin/lpq`
`-rwsr-sr-x`	`/usr/bin/lpc`
`-rwsr-sr-x`	`/usr/bin/lprm`
`-rwxr-s--`	`/usr/sbin/lpd`

The first four file permissions in Table 18.1 are used to submit, cancel, and inspect print jobs. `/usr/sbin/lpd` is the printer daemon. A daemon is a program run by the operating system in response to an event. A daemon typically sits in the background until requested to do its job.

Tip #106 from *Jack*

The locations, ownerships, and permissions in Table 18.1 have been simplified and may be wrong for your system, so note the `lpd` files and permissions. Use the `ls -l` command to list the file permissions. If you need to change the permissions use the `chmod` command. If you need to change ownership use the `chown` command.

All these commands have man pages, which you should consult for more information. The important point to remember and understand is that by default the commands `lpr`, `lprm`, `lpc`, and `lpq` operate on a specific printer called `lp0`. If you define an environment variable called `PRINTER`, the name defined is used instead. You can override `lp` and the `PRINTER` environment variable by specifying the printer name to use on the command line as follows:

```
lpc -PMYPRINTER
```

THE `lpd` DAEMON

Linux handles all print jobs via the `lpd` daemon. If this process isn't running, no printing can take place; print files remain in their spool directories until the `lpd` process is started. (More information about spool directories appears later in the section "Understanding the Important Directories.")

→ See "Understanding Multitasking," p. 366

If your system doesn't load `lpd` at startup, or if you must kill and then restart the `lpd` daemon for some reason, the following command starts the printer daemon:

```
lpd [options]
```

The man page on `lpd` gives a list of options, but one important option when configuring your Linux printers is `-l`, which creates a log file that logs each print request to the system. This log file can be useful when you're debugging your printing system.

THE `lpr` COMMAND

The `lpr` command submits a job to the printer or queues a print job. What actually happens is that the file you specify is copied to the spool directory. Each printer specified for your Linux system must have its own spool directory. The size of this spool directory is specified in the `minfree` file located in each directory. The `minfree` file specifies the number of disk blocks to reserve for spooling files to the printer. This is done to keep the `lpd` daemon from using up the entire hard drive when spooling a print request.

`lpd` finds the file, which then takes care of moving the data to the physical printer. If you don't specify a file, `lpr` uses standard input.

THE `lpq` COMMAND

The `lpq` command shows you the contents of the spool directory for a given printer. One important piece of information displayed by `lpq` is the job ID, which identifies a particular job. You must specify this number if you want to cancel a pending job.

`lpq` also assigns a number to indicate a rank for each job in the queue (meaning, where the job is in the queue). `active` means the file is actually printing—or at least that `lpd` is trying to print it.

THE `lprm` COMMAND

The `lprm` command removes a job from the queue; that is, it removes unprinted files from the spool directory. You can specify a job ID (obtained by using the `lpq` command), or you can specify `-` as the job ID to cancel all jobs belonging to you.

If you issue `lpq -` as root, all jobs for the printer are canceled. If you are root and want to remove all the jobs belonging to a specific user, you can specify the user's name.

THE `lpc` COMMAND

Using the `lpc` command, you can check the status of printers and control some aspects of their use. In particular, `lpc` lets you start and stop despooling on printers, enable or disable printers, and rearrange the order of jobs in a print queue. The following commands disable printing on `myprinter`, enable the spool queue on `yourprinter`, and move job number 37 to the top of the queue:

```
lpc down myprinter
lpc enable yourprinter
lpc topq 37
```

If you invoke `lpc` without any command arguments, `lpc` is interactive, prompting you for actions to take. Some of the more important commands are shown in Table 18.2; read the man page for complete instructions. Most `lpc` commands take the name of the printer, as specified in `/etc/printcap`, as the parameter.

TABLE 18.2 SOME COMMON `lpc` COMMANDS

Command	Parameter	Description
`stop`	`printer`	Stops the printer, but print requests are still spooled.
`start`	`printer`	Allows the printer to start printing previously spooled files and any new files spooled to this printer.
`exit`, `quit`	(None)	Leaves `lpc` in interactive mode.
`status`	`printer`	Displays the current status of the printer. `status` provides such information as whether the queue is enabled, whether the printer is enabled, and the number (if any) of jobs now in the queue waiting to be printed.

Tip #107 from *Jack*

Keep in mind that some `lpc` commands are restricted to root—that is, the superuser. To switch to the root account from a user account, use the switch-user command `su`. For security reasons you must have the root password to gain root access.

UNDERSTANDING THE IMPORTANT DIRECTORIES

Only one directory is important in printing—the spool area where data to be printed is accumulated before `/etc/lpd` prints it. However, a system is typically set up with multiple spool directories, one for each printer, to make printer management easier. For example, my system is set up to use `/usr/spool/lpd` as the main spool area, with each separate printer having a directory under that with the same name as the printer. Thus, a printer named `ps_nff` has `/usr/spool/lpd/ps_nff` as its spool directory.

The spool directories should belong to the daemon group and should be user and group read/writable and world readable. That is, after you create the directory, you should make sure that it has the permissions `-rwxrwxr-x` (0775) with the `chmod` command. For the directory `myprinter`, the appropriate command is as follows:

```
chmod ug=rwx,o=rx myprinter
chgrp daemon myprinter
```

→ See "File Permissions," p. 414

Note The locations, ownerships, and permissions given here are a simplification and may be incorrect for your system, so you should take notes on the `lpd` files and permissions.

UNDERSTANDING THE IMPORTANT FILES

Apart from the programs discussed so far, each spool directory contains files that have the permissions `-rw-rw-r-`:

- The `/etc/printcap` file contains the printer specifications for each named printer in your system.
- The `.seq` file contains the job number counter for `lpr` to assign.
- The status file contains the message to be reported by `lpc stat`.
- The lock file is used by `lpd` to prevent itself from trying to print two jobs to the same printer at once.
- The `errs` file logs printer failures.

The `errs` file isn't required by Linux in order to print, but the file must exist for `lpd` to be able to log printer failures. You can call the `errs` file whatever you like as long as you specify the name in `/etc/printcap`. You usually create the `errs` file manually when you set up the spool area. The section "Putting It All Together," later in this chapter, has more information on this topic.

UNDERSTANDING THE /etc/printcap FILE

The `/etc/printcap` file is a text file that you can edit with your favorite editor. `/etc/printcap` should be owned by root and have the permissions `-rw-r-r-`.

The contents of `/etc/printcap` typically look very cryptic, but when you know how the file works, the contents are much easier to understand. To compound the problem, some distributions don't have a man page for `printcap`, and most `printcap` files are created either by programs or by people with no thought for readability. For your own sanity, make the layout of your `printcap` file as logical and readable as possible with lots of comments. And get the man page from the `lpd` sources if you don't already have it.

One `printcap` entry describes one printer. Essentially, a `printcap` entry provides a logical name for a physical device and then describes how data sent to that device should be handled.

For example, a `printcap` entry defines what physical device is to be used, what spool directory any data for that device should be stored in, what preprocessing should be performed on the data, where errors on the physical device should be logged, and so forth. You can limit the amount of data that can be sent in a single job, or you can limit access to a printer to certain classes of users. The following shows how a printer is defined in the `printcap` file:

```
# Sample printcap entry with two aliases
myprinter¦laserwriter:\
# lp is the device to print to - here the first parallel printer.
:lp=/dev/lp0: \
# sd means spool directory - where print data is collected
:sd=/usr/spool/lpd/myprinter:
```

It's okay to have multiple `printcap` entries defining several different ways to handle data destined for the same physical printer. For example, a physical printer might support PostScript and HP LaserJet data formats, depending on some setup sequence being sent to the physical printer before each job. It makes sense to define two printers: one that preprocesses the data by preappending the HP LaserJet sequence and one that preappends the PostScript sequence. Programs that generate HP data send it to the HP printer, whereas programs generating PostScript print to the PostScript printer.

Note

If you don't designate a default printer via an environment variable or don't specify a printer on the `lpr` command line, Linux routes the print job to the `lp0` printer. Thus, you should specify one of the printers in the `printcap` file as the `lp0` printer.

Programs that change the data before it's sent to the physical printer are called *filters*. It's possible for a filter to send no data at all to a physical printer; that is, the filter filters out everything.

UNDERSTANDING THE FIELDS IN /etc/printcap

The `printcap` file has too many fields to describe fully in this chapter, so only the most important ones are described. All fields in `/etc/printcap` (except for the names of the printer) are enclosed between colons and denoted by a two-letter code. The two-letter code is followed by a value that depends on the type of field. The three types of fields are string, Boolean, and numeric. Table 18.3 describes the most common and most important fields; the following sections go into more detail.

TABLE 18.3 THE /etc/printcap FIELDS

Field	Type	Description
`lp`	String	Specifies the device to print to—for example, `/dev/lp0`
`sd`	String	Specifies the name of the spool directory for this printer
`lf`	String	Specifies the file that errors on this printer are to be logged to

Table 18.3 The /etc/printcap Fields

Field	Type	Description
`if`	String	Specifies the input filter name
`rm`	String	Specifies the name of a remote printing host
`rp`	String	Specifies the name of a remote printer
`sh`	Boolean	Suppresses headers (banner pages)
`sf`	Boolean	Suppresses end-of-job form feeds
`mx`	Numeric	Specifies the maximum allowable print job size (in blocks)

The `lp` Field

If you specify `/dev/null` as the print device, all other processing is performed correctly, but the final data goes to the *bit bucket*—that is, to nowhere. Printing to nowhere is rarely useful except for test printer configurations or with weird printers. When you're setting up a remote printer (that is, you've specified `rm` and `rp` fields), specify `:lp=:`.

Don't leave the `lp` field empty unless you're using a remote printer. The printer daemon complains if you don't specify a print device.

The `lf` Field

Whatever file you specify in the `lf` field should already exist, or logging doesn't occur.

The `if` Field

Input filters are programs that take print data on their standard input and generate output on their standard output. A typical use of an input filter is to detect plain ASCII text and convert it into PostScript; that is, raw text is its input and PostScript is its output.

When you specify an input filter in the `if` field, the printer daemon doesn't send the spooled print data to the specified device. Instead, it runs the input filter with the spooled data as standard input and the print device as standard output.

The `rm` and `rp` Fields

Sending your print data to a printer attached to another machine is as simple as specifying the remote machine `rm` and the remote printer `rp` and making sure that the print device field `lp` is empty.

Note

Data is still spooled locally before it's transferred to the remote machine. Any input filters you specify are also run.

THE `sh` AND `sf` FIELDS

Unless you have many different people using your printer, you're most likely not interested in banner pages, so you should specify `sh`.

Suppressing form feeds, by specifying`sf`, is most useful if your printer is typically used for output from word processing packages. Most word processing packages create complete pages of data, so if the printer daemon adds a form feed to the end of each job, you get a blank page after each job. If the printer is usually used for program or directory listings, however, having that form feed ensures that the final page is completely ejected, so each listing starts at the top of a new page.

THE `mx` FIELD

The `mx` field allows you to limit the size of the print data to be spooled. The number you specify is in `BUFSIZE` blocks (1KB under Linux). If you specify zero, the limit is removed, allowing print jobs to be limited only by available disk space.

> **Note** The limit is on the size of the spooled data, not the amount of data sent to the physical printer.

If a user tries to exceed this limit, the file is truncated. The user sees a message saying this:

```
(lpr: file-name: copy file is too large)
```

For non-PostScript printers, this limit is useful if you have users or programs that may deliberately or accidentally create excessively large output. For PostScript printers, the limit isn't useful at all because a very small amount of spooled PostScript data can generate a large number of output pages.

SETTING THE `PRINTER` ENVIRONMENT VARIABLE

You might want to add a line to your login script—or even to the default user login script—that sets up a `PRINTER` environment variable. Under the bash shell, a suitable line is `export PRINTER=myprinter`. This line prevents people from having to specify `-Pmyprinter` every time they submit a print job.

To add more printers, you can just repeat this process with different printer names. Remember that you can have multiple printcap entries, all using the same physical device. This way, you can treat the same device differently, depending on what you it when you submit a print job to it.

CREATING A TEST printcap ENTRY

The following shell script is a very simple input filter; it simply concatenates its input onto the end of a file in /tmp after an appropriate banner. You can specify this filter in the printcap entry and specify /dev/null as the print device. The print device is never actually used, but you have to set it to something; otherwise, the printer daemon complains:

```
#!/bin/sh
# This file should be placed in the printer's spool directory and
# named input_filter. It should be owned by root, group daemon, and
# be world executable (-rwxr-xr-x).
echo ------------------------------------------------ >> /tmp/
date >> /tmp/
echo ------------------------------------------------ >> /tmp/
cat >> /tmp/
```

In the following printcap entry, notice the reasonably readable format and the use of the continuation character (\) on all but the last line:

```
myprinter¦myprinter: \
:lp=/dev/null: \
:sd=/usr/spool/lpd/myprinter: \
:lf=/usr/spool/lpd/myprinter/errs: \
:if=/usr/spool/lpd/myprinter/input_filter: \
:mx#0: \
:sh: \
:sf:
```


PUTTING IT ALL TOGETHER

To put all the preceding bits together, the following steps guide you through setting up a single printer on /dev/lp0. You can then extend this concept to other printers (you have to be root to perform all these steps, by the way).

1. Check the permissions and locations of lpr, lprm, lpc, lpq, and lpd. Earlier in this chapter, Table 18.1 listed the correct settings and directories.
2. Create the spool directory for your printer (named myprinter for now). Make sure that both the directory and printer are owned by root, belong to the daemon group, and have write permissions for user and group and read-only permission for others (-rwxrwxr-x). Use the following commands:

   ```
   mkdir /usr/spool/lpd
   mkdir /usr/spool/lpd/myprinter
   chown root.daemon /usr/spool/lpd /usr/spool/lpd/myprinter
   chmod ug=rwx,o=rx /usr/spool/lpd /usr/spool/lpd/myprinter
   ```

3. In the /usr/spool/lpd/myprinter directory, create the necessary files and give them the correct permissions and owner. Use the following commands:

   ```
   cd /usr/spool/lpd/myprinter
   touch .seq errs status lock
   chown root.daemon .seq errs status lock
   chmod ug=rw,o=r .seq errs status lock
   ```

4. Create the shell script `input_filter` in the `/usr/spool/lpd/myprinter` directory. Use the input filter given earlier in the section "Creating a Test `printcap` Entry" for your filter. Make sure that the file is owned by root, belongs to the daemon group, and is executable by anyone. Use the following commands:

```
cd /usr/spool/lpd/myprinter
chmod ug=rwx,o=rx input_filter
```

5. Create the `/etc/printcap` file if it doesn't already exist. Remove all entries in it and add the test `printcap` entry given in the "Creating a Test `printcap` Entry" section. Make sure that the file is owned by root and is read-only to everyone else. You can use the `chmod` command to set the proper file permissions: `-rw-r-r-` (or 644 in octal).
6. Edit the `rc.local` file (you can use any ASCII editor, such as vi or Emacs). Add the line `/etc/lpd` to the end to run the printer daemon each time the system boots. You don't need to boot now, however; just run it by hand using the `lpd` command.

→ See "Starting vi by Using an Existing File," p. 209

7. Do a test print by entering the following:

```
ls -l ¦ lpr -Pmyprinter
```

8. Use the `ls` command to look in `/tmp` for a file named `testlp.out`. It should contain your directory listing, which you can check by using the `more`, `less`, or `cat` commands. See Chapter 19, "Understanding the File and Directory system," for more information on these commands.

→ See "Viewing the Contents of a File," p. 428

9. Use an ASCII editor such as vi to make the following edits to `/etc/printcap`:
   - In the first printer entry, change both occurrences of `myprinter` to `testlp` only in the first line.
   - In the second entry, change `/dev/null` to your real print device—for example, `/dev/lp0`.
   - In the second entry, remove the `if` line completely.
10. Copy the `myprinter` entry so that you have two identical entries in the file.
11. Either reboot the system or kill the printer daemon and restart it. You do so because the printer daemon looks only at the `/etc/printcap` file when it first starts up.
12. Run a test print again using the command `ls -l ¦ lpr -Pmyprinter`. This one should come out on your physical printer.

CONFIGURING RED HAT PRINTERS

If you've installed XFree86 under Red Hat, you can use the printer configuration tool shown in Figure 18.1 to add and delete printers as well as maintain the `/etc/printcap` and spooler files and directories. You can find this tool in the Control Panel; Table 18.4 describes each of the `printtool`'s menu items.

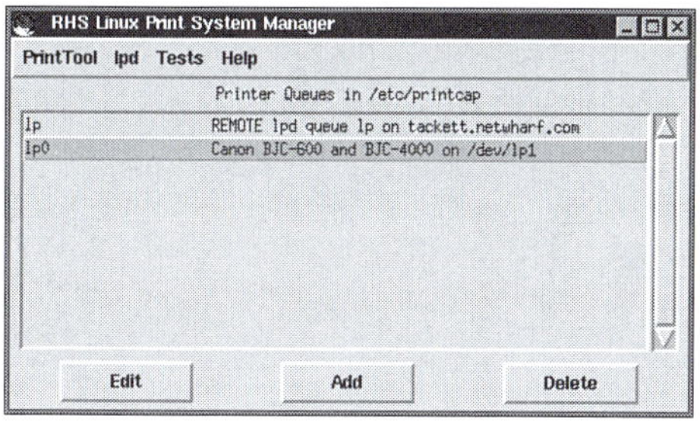

Figure 18.1 Managing printers is easy with Red Hat's graphical utilities.

TABLE 18.4 THE `printtool` MENUS

Menu Name	Submenu	Description
`printtool`	Reload	Rescans the directory for `printcap` files
	About	Displays information about the `printtool`
	Quit	Exits the `printtool`
`lpd`	Restart	Restarts the `lpd` daemon after making changes
Tests	Print ASCII Test Page	Prints a test page in plain text to the selected printer
	Print PostScript Test Page	Prints a PostScript test page to the selected printer
	Print ASCII Directly to Port	Prints a test page directly to the device and not via the `lpd` system
Help	General	Provides general help on the `printtool`
	Troubleshooting	Provides help on various problems with printing

To add a new printer, click the Add button. You must first specify whether it's a local, remote, or SMB printer (see Figure 18.2). A *local printer* is connected to your parallel or serial port; a *remote printer* is connected to your network. A LAN Manager Printer is a printer attached to a different system via *Session Message Block protocol* (SMB, or Samba), typically a Microsoft Windows system.

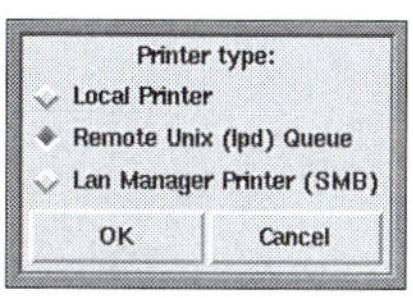

Figure 18.2 To add a printer, you must select the type of printer.

→ See "Using Samba," p. 485

To edit an existing printer configuration, select the entry and click the Edit button. Both actions bring up the dialog box shown in Figure 18.3. You must enter a value for each field in the dialog box. Table 18.5 describes each field.

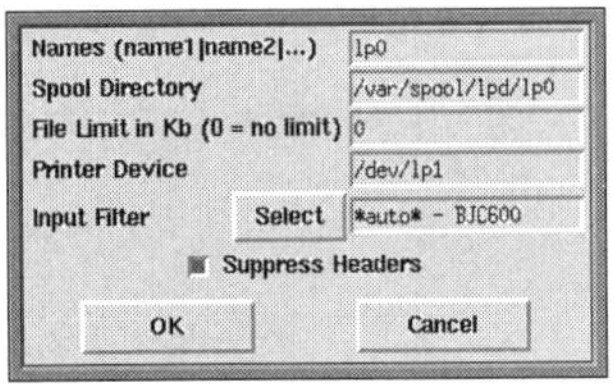

Figure 18.3 To print properly from Linux, you must specify certain options, such as printer name and physical port location.

TABLE 18.5 FIELD ITEMS FOR EACH PRINTER

Field Name	Description
Names	The name of the printer and its queue. You can specify multiple names by using the | character to separate names.
Spool Directory	The directory for spooling documents for this printer, such as `/usr/spool/lpd/myprinter`.
File Limit	The maximum document size (in kilobytes). A 0 (zero) value indicates no limit.
Printer Device	The physical connection for your printer, such as `lp0`.
Input Filter	The full path and filename of your custom filter. If you need to configure a printer, click the Select button.
Suppress Headers	Check this box if you don't want a header page printed with each document.
Remote Host	This field in the Remote Host dialog box specifies the name of the remote host to which the printer is connected.
Remote Queue	This field in the Remote Host dialog box specifies the printer queue on the remote machine. Enter the full path.

To configure a print filter, click the Select button, which displays the Configure Filter dialog box shown in Figure 18.4. Table 18.6 describes the various fields in the Configure Filter dialog box.

TABLE 18.6 FIELD ITEMS FOR EACH FILTER

Field Name	Description
Printer Type	Indicates the type of printer for this filter
Driver Description	Provides a description of the selected printer
Resolution	Selects the desired resolution for this printer

TABLE 18.6 FIELD ITEMS FOR EACH FILTER

Field Name	Description
Paper Size	Selects the desired paper size for this printer
Color Depth	Selects the desired color operation for this printer
Printing Options	Sends EOF forces the printer to eject the page Fix stair-stepping text fixes the stair-step effect Fast text printing enables a non-PostScript printer to attain faster print speeds
Margins	Specifies the desired margins
Extra GS Options	Specifies extra ghostscript options for the selected printer

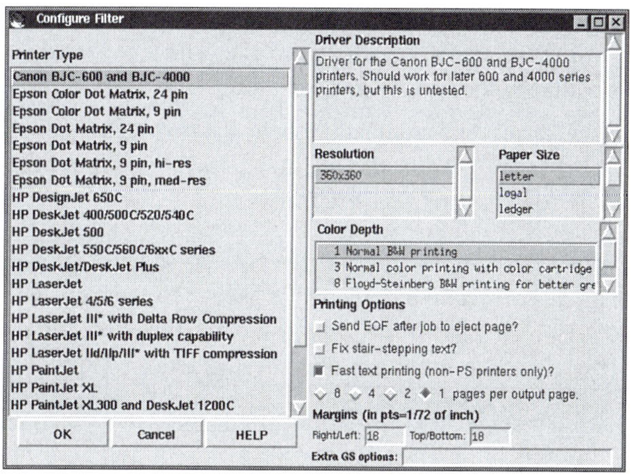

Figure 18.4
Configuring an input filter for your printing system is made simple with the Configure Filter dialog box.

After you add or change a printer entry, you might find that you need to restart the `lpd` daemon. To do so, simply select the `lpd` menu item on the RHS Linux Print System Manager and click the Restart `lpd` item.

TROUBLESHOOTING

I get a message saying `lpd: connect: No such file or directory.`

The printer daemon `/etc/lpd` isn't running. You may have forgotten to add it to your `/etc/rc.local` file. Or maybe you did add it, but you haven't booted since then. Add it and reboot, or just run `/etc/lpd`. Remember that you have to be root to add the printer daemon.

I get a message saying `Job queued, but cannot start daemon.`

This message often appears right after the `lpd: connect` message; same answer as the preceding problem.

I get a message saying `lpd: cannot create spooldir/.seq.`

You haven't created the spool directory specified in the `printcap` entry, or you've misnamed it. An alternative (though much less likely) answer is that you have too little disk space left.

I get a message saying `lpr: Printer queue is disabled.`

As root, use `lpc enable` *printer_name* to enable the printer. Note that as root, you can submit jobs even to a disabled printer.

I submit a print job and don't get any error messages, but nothing comes out on the physical printer.

You might have this problem for many reasons:

- Make sure that the physical printer is switched on, selected, and physically connected to the device specified in the `/etc/printcap` file.
- Use the `lpq` command to see whether the entry is in the queue. If it is, the device may be busy, the printer may be down, or an error may have occurred on the printer. If you do have errors, check the error log specified in the `printcap` entry for clues.
- You can use the `lpc status` command to check whether the printer is down, and you can use `lpc up` *`printer_name`* or `lpc restart` *`printer_name`* to bring it back up if it is (you need to be root to use these commands).

If, after checking, your print jobs still don't come out, make sure that any input filter you've specified is present in the correct directory and has the correct permissions. If you're running `syslogd`, you can look in your logs for messages from `lpd`. If you see log entries saying `cannot execv name of input filter`, this is almost certainly the problem.

Another possibility is that you have a PostScript printer, and you're not sending PostScript to it. Most PostScript printers ignore non-PostScript data. You might need to install an appropriate text-to-PostScript input filter.

Last (and you'll feel silly if this is the cause), make sure that your input filter actually generates output and that the output device isn't `/dev/null`.

My printer seems to have locked up. None of the techniques described here seem to solve the problem.

When all else fails in the case of a nonprinting printer, the next-to-last resort is to kill the `lpd` daemon and restart it. If that approach doesn't work, the last resort is to reboot your Linux system with the `shutdown -r now` command. Make sure that no one else is logged in and that you've saved any files before using the `now` option; otherwise, specify a time and also give a message to your other users before shutting down the system. You also can test the printer on a DOS or Windows machine to make sure that the physical device itself is working.

CHAPTER 19

Understanding the File and Directory System

In this chapter

by Jack Tackett, Jr.

UNDERSTANDING FILENAMES AND PATHNAMES

Every physical and logical entity in Linux is represented as a file in the Linux file system. The physical entities include disks, printers, and terminals; logical entities include directories and, of course, ordinary files—the kind that store documents and programs.

The term *Linux file system* has two different and often conflicting meanings: the file system of disks and mechanisms of the disks, and the logical file systemthat the user sees and manipulates. This chapter is about the logical Linux file system that you see and manipulate. If you're familiar with PC operating systems such as MS-DOS and OS/2, you'll find many of the following topics familiar because the file structures of MS-DOS from version 2.0 onward were modeled on those of UNIX, which is the file structure used by Linux.

In Linux, just as in other operating systems such as MS-DOS, you must distinguish between a filename and a pathname. A *filename* consists of a simple series of contiguous letters, numbers, and certain punctuation marks. Filenames can't contain spaces or any characters that represent a field separator. For example, the filename *johns.letter* is valid, but *johns letter* isn't.

A filename shouldn't contain any characters that have special meaning to the shell. The following are the "forbidden" special characters:

! @ # $ % ^ & * ( ) [ ] { } ' " \ / | ; < > `

Also, a filename can't contain the slash character (/) because this character is used to indicate pathnames. (Pathnames are discussed later in this section.)

Tip #108 from *Jack*

> **You can use any of the "forbidden" characters if you place double quotation marks around the filename like this:**
>
> `"! johns.letter''`
>
> **However, you'll have a hard time accessing such a file with most programs, and the file isn't very portable to other UNIX systems.**

Most early versions of UNIX, on which Linux is based, limited filenames to 14 characters; however, Linux allows 256 characters in a filename. Some recent UNIX versions, such as the Berkeley version (BSD), allow 64-character filenames, but only the first 14 are significant. Because one of the goals of Linux is portability, in the interest of writing portable programs and shell scripts, you might want to limit yourself to 14-character filenames.

A pathname can contain any number of characters. In Linux, files don't exist in a vacuum; they exist in a directory. The highest directory in Linux is called the *root* and is symbolized by the slash character (/). If a file named `fred` exists in the root directory, its absolute pathname is `/fred`. When you add a user to the system by using the `adduser` command, he or she is assigned a home directory. By convention, this home directory is usually found under root in a directory named, appropriately enough, `home`. Therefore, if a user named Fred is assigned a directory named /home/fred, all files that Fred creates are attached to the /home/fred directory. An absolute pathname for one of Fred's files might be /home/fred/freds.file. An absolute pathname specifies exactly where a file is stored in the file system.

Another kind of pathname is a *relative pathname*, which unambiguously points to a file's location as relative to the current directory. If Fred is in his home directory, for example, the filename freds.file is also a relative pathname, relative to his current directory. To find out which directory is your current directory, you can use the command pwd (print working directory). You can also check the contents of the $PWD environment variable by using the command echo $PWD to see which directory is the current working directory.

You can define a file anywhere in the Linux file system with relative pathnames by using two pseudonyms found in all directories. The single dot (.) refers to the current directory, and the double dot (..) refers to the parent directory. MS-DOS and OS/2 use this same convention.

If Fred is in /home/fred, he can point to /fred by using ../../fred. In this relative pathname, the second double dot points to /home (the parent directory of /home/fred), and the first double dot points to the parent directory of /home—namely, the root.

The pseudonym for the current directory, the single dot, comes in handy if you want to move files. If Fred wants to move /fred to his current directory, he can do so with absolute pathnames by using this command:

```
mv /fred fred
```

Alternatively, Fred can use the pseudonym for the current directory by using this command:

```
mv /fred .
```

Most Linux commands operate on pathnames. In most cases, the pathname you use is the name of a file in the current directory. The default pathname points to your current directory. If Fred is in his home directory (/home/fred), all three of the following are equivalent commands:

```
command freds.letter
command /home/fred/freds.letter
command ./freds.letter
```

PART III CH 19

Note

Although filenames and pathnames are different, directories are files, too. When you're naming directories, remember that you must follow the same naming guidelines as for ordinary files.

Also note that unlike many PC-based operating systems, Linux doesn't have the concept of disk drive letters, only directory paths. Linux deals with disk drive letters only when working with MS-DOS file systems on floppies with the m- commands (such as mcopy).

→ See "Understanding File Systems," p. 440

File Types

Linux lumps everything into four basic types of files: ordinary files, directories, links, and special files. You'll work with several kinds of ordinary files, links, and special files and a large number of standard directories. The basic file types are described in the following sections.

You can use the command `file` to determine the type of a file. `file` can recognize a file type as executable, text, data, and so on. Many UNIX commands are only shell scripts or are interpreted programs similar to MS-DOS batch files, and `file` can report whether a UNIX command is a binary executable program or simply a shell script. It's also useful for determining whether the file is text-based and, therefore, whether it can be viewed or edited. The syntax for the `file` command is as follows:

```
file [-vczL] [-f namefile] [-m magicfile] filelist
```

Table 19.1 explains the arguments for the `file` command.

Table 19.1 `file` Command Arguments

Argument	Description
`-c`	Prints the parsed form of the *magic file* (`/usr/lib/magic`), which is a number in the first part of a binary file that identifies the file type. This argument is usually used with `-m` to debug a new magic file before installing it.
`-z`	Looks inside a compressed file and tries to figure out the file type.
`-L`	Causes symbolic links to be followed.
`-f namefile`	Tells `file` that the list of files to identify is found in *`namefile`*, which is a text file. This argument is useful when many files must be identified.
`-m magicfile`	Specifies an alternative file of magic numbers to use for determining file types. The default file is `/usr/lib/magic`.
`filelist`	Lists space-delimited files whose type you want to know.

Ordinary Files

Ordinary files are what you spend most of your time manipulating. Ordinary files can contain text, C language source code, shell scripts (programs interpreted by one of the Linux shells), binary executable programs, and data of various types. As far as Linux is concerned, a file is a file. The only difference that Linux knows is files marked as executable. Executable files can be executed directly—provided, of course, that the file contains something to execute and that it's in your search path. Basically, the *search path* is a list of pathnames you've specified that Linux searches to find an executable file.

→ See "Understanding Shells," p. 319

Executable files are binary files—that is, files that execute machine code and shell scripts. The Linux `file` command discussed in the preceding section looks at the data in a file and makes a reasonable guess as to what's inside. If you type `file *`, for example, you might see something similar to this:

```
INSTALL:        symbolic link to /var/adm
ghostvw.txt:    ascii text
linux:          symbolic link to /usr/src/linux
mbox:           mail text
mterm.txt:      English text
seyon.txt:      English text
xcalc.txt:      English text
xclock.txt:     English text
xeyes.txt:      English text
xgrap.txt:      English text
xlock.txt:      English text
xspread.txt:    English text
xtris.txt:      empty
```

All the files named in the first column are ordinary files that contain different kinds of data. All the files are located within the directory where the `file` command was executed.

DIRECTORY FILES

Directories are files that contain the names of files and subdirectories, as well as pointers to those files and subdirectories. Directory files are the only places that Linux stores names of files. When you list the contents of a directory by using the `ls` command, all you're doing is listing the contents of the directory file. You never touch the files themselves.

When you rename a file by using the `mv` command and that file is in the current directory, all you're doing is changing the entry in the directory file. If you move a file from one directory to another, all you're doing is moving the description of the file from one directory file to another—provided, of course, that the new directory is on the same physical disk or partition. If not, Linux physically copies each byte of the program to the other disk.

DIRECTORIES AND PHYSICAL DISKS

Every file in a Linux system is assigned a unique number called an *inode*. The inode is stored in a table called the *inode table*, which is allocated when the disk is formatted. Every physical disk or partition has its own inode table. An inode contains all the information about a file, including the address of the data on the disk and the file type. File types include ordinary files, directories, and special files.

Tip #109 from Jack

You can use the `df -i`command to see the number of inodes available on various file systems. To see the information in a more readable manner, you can add the `-h` flag. For example, the command shown here produces this table:

```
$ df -ih
Filesystem    Inodes    IUsed    IFree  IUse%   Mounted on
/dev/sda7 65k 6.9k 58k 11% /
/dev/sda1 5.9k 24 5.9k 0% /boot
```

```
/dev/sda8 1.1M 412 1.1M 0% /home
/dev/sda9 257k 45k 212k 17% /usr
/dev/sda5 65k 240 64k 0% /var
```

The Linux file system assigns inode number 1 to the root directory. This assignment gives Linux the address on disk of the root directory file. The root directory file contains a list of file and directory names and their respective inode numbers. Linux can find any file in the system by looking up a chain of directories, beginning with the root directory. The contents of the root directory file might look like this:

```
1 .
1 ..
45 etc
230 dev
420 home
123 .profile
```

Notice that the files . (dot) and .. (double dot) are shown in the directory. Because this is the root directory, . and its parent directory, .., are identical. The contents of the /home directory file would be different and might look something like this:

```
420 .
1 ..
643 fred
```

Notice that the inode of the current directory (.) matches the inode for /home found in the root directory file, and the inode for the parent directory (..) is the same as that of the root directory.

Linux navigates its file system by chaining up and down the directory file system. If you want to move a file to a directory on another physical disk, Linux detects this information by reading the inode table. In such a case, the file is physically moved to the new disk and assigned a new inode on that disk before being deleted from its original location.

As with the mv command, when you delete a file by using the rm command, you never touch the file itself. Instead, Linux marks that inode as free and returns it to the pool of available inodes. The file's entry in the directory is erased.

→ See "Moving and Renaming Files," p. 425

LINKS

Ordinary links aren't really files at all; they're actually directory entries that point to the same inode. The inode table keeps track of how many links go to a file, and only when the last directory reference is deleted is the inode finally released back to the free pool. Obviously, ordinary links can't cross device boundaries because all the directory references point to the same inode.

To create a link, you use the `ln` command, which has the following form:

```
ln [options] sourcedestination
```

For example to create a link between a file named `mainfile.txt` and a file named `tempfile.txt`, you enter the following command:

```
ln mainfile.txt tempfile.txt
```

Linux, as well as most modern versions of UNIX, has another kind of link called a *symbolic link*. For such a link, the directory entry contains the inode of a file that is itself a reference to another file somewhere else in the logical Linux file system. A symbolic link can point to another file or directory on the same disk, to another disk, or to a file or directory on another computer.

One major difference between an ordinary link and a symbolic link is that with ordinary links, every link has equal standing (that is, the system treats every link as though it were the original file), and the actual data isn't deleted until the last link to that file is deleted. With symbolic links, when the original file is deleted, all symbolic links to that file are also deleted. Symbolically linked files don't have the same standing as the original file.

To create a symbolic link, you use the `-s` option to the `ln` command. For example, to create a symbolic link from a file called `named` in the `/etc/rc.d/initd` directory to the file `S55named`, you use the following command:

```
ln -s /etc/rc.d/initd/named /etc/rc.d/rc3.d/S55named
```

Other than these subtle differences between links and files, links are treated and accessed exactly as files are.

You can tell a file is a link by using the `ls -l` command. If it is a link, the response shows the local filename and then an indication of the linked file like this:

```
lrwxrwxrwx 1 root root 4 Oct 17 15:27 Info -]] info/
```

The file permission flags begin with `l` to indicate that the file is a linked file.

Part III Ch 19

Special Files

All physical devices associated with a Linux system, including disks, terminals, and printers, are represented in the file system. Most, if not all, devices are located in the `/dev` directory. For example, if you're working on the system console, your associated device is named `/dev/console`. If you're working on a standard terminal, your device name might be `/dev/tty01`. Terminals, or serial lines, are called*tty devices* (which stands for *teletype*, the original UNIX terminal). To determine what the name of your tty device is, you can type the command `tty`. The system responds with the name of the device to which you're connected.

Printers and terminals are called *character-special devices*. They can accept and produce a stream of characters. Disks, on the other hand, store data in blocks addressed by cylinder and sector. You can't access just one character on a disk; you must read and write entire blocks. The same is usually true of magnetic tapes. This kind of device is called a *block-special device*.

To make life even more complex, disks and other block-special devices must be able to act like character-oriented devices, so every block-special device has a matching character-special device. Linux makes the translation by reading data being sent to a character device and translating it for the block device. This translation happens without your doing anything.

You might run into at least one other type of special device: a FIFO (first-in-first-out buffer), also known as a *named pipe*. FIFOs look like ordinary files: If you write to them, they grow. But if you read FIFOs, they shrink in size. FIFOs are used mainly in system processes to allow many programs to send information to a single controlling process. For example, when you print a file by using the `lp` command, `lp` sets up the printing process and signals the `lpsched` daemon by sending a message to a FIFO. A *daemon*, sometimes called a *demon*, is a system process that acts without a user requesting an action.

One device-special file—the *bit bucket*, or `/dev/null`—is very useful. Anything you send to `/dev/null` is ignored, which is useful when you don't want to see the output of a command. For example, if you don't want any diagnostic reports printed on the standard error device, you can pour them into the bit bucket by using the following command:ls -la",4> /dev/null

File Permissions

File permissions mean more in Linux than just what permissions you have on a file or directory. Although permissions determine who can read, write, or execute a file, they also determine the file type and how the file is executed.

You can display the permissions of a file by using the long form of the listing command, `ls -l`. The `-l` flag tells the `ls`command to use the long listing. If you type `ls -l`, you might see a directory listing that looks like this:

```
Drwx---  2 sglines doc    512 Jan 1 13:44  Mail
Drwx---  5 sglines doc   1024 Jan 17 08:22 News
-rw---   1 sglines doc   1268 Dec 7 15:01  biblio
drwx---  2 sglines doc    512 Dec 15 21:28 bin
-rw---   1 sglines doc  44787 Oct 20 06:59 books
-rw---   1 sglines doc  23801 Dec 14 22:50 bots.msg
-rw-r--  1 sglines doc 105990 Dec 27 21:24 duckie.gif
```

This listing shows virtually everything that can be known about a file from the directory entry and the inode of the file. The first column shows the file permissions, the second column shows the number of links to a file (or extra blocks in a directory), and the third column shows who owns the file. (In Linux, ownership has three possibilities: the owner, the owner's group, and everyone else. Ownership is detailed later in this chapter.) The fourth column shows the group to which the file belongs. The fifth column shows the number of bytes in the file, the sixth column shows the date and time of creation, and the seventh column shows the name of the file itself.

The permissions field (the first column) can be broken into four distinct subfields:

```
- rwx rwx rwx
```

The first subfield defines the file type. A normal file has a hyphen (-) as a placeholder; directories are marked with a `d`. Table 19.2 shows the permissible values for the file-type subfield.

TABLE 19.2 VALID ENTRIES FOR THE FILE-TYPE SUBFIELD

Character	Meaning
-	Ordinary file
b	Block-special file
c	Character-special file
d	Directory
l	Symbolic link

The next three subfields show the read, write, and execute permissions of the file. For example, an `rwx` in the first of these subfields means that the file has read, write, and execute permission for the owner. The next three characters show the same information for the group ownership of the file. Finally, the third set of characters shows the permissions allowed for everyone else.

These permission subfields can show more information; in fact, several attributes are packed into these three fields. Unfortunately, what these attributes mean is determined by the version of Linux you use and whether the file is executable.

Note

Normally, a running program is owned by whoever ran it. If the user ID bit is on, the running program is owned by the owner of the file. This means that the running program has all the permissions of the owner of the file. If you're an ordinary user and the running program is owned by the root user, that running program has automatic permission to read and write any file in the system regardless of your permissions. The same is true of the Set Group ID bit.

The *sticky bit* can also be set in these subfields. The sticky bit tells the system to save a copy of a running program in memory after the program is complete. If the program is used often, the sticky bit can save the system a little time the next time it runs the program because the program doesn't have to be reloaded into memory from disk each time someone runs it.

You can change permissions on any file for which you have write permission by using the `chmod` command. This command has two different syntaxes: absolute and relative. With absolute permissions, you define exactly what the permissions on a file will be in octal, or base 8. An octal number can have a value from 0 to 7. UNIX was originally created on a series of DEC minicomputers that used the octal numbering system, hence the current use of octal numbers. The octal numbers are added together to arrive at a number that defines the permissions. Table 19.3 lists the valid octal permissions.

Table 19.3 Absolute Octal Permissions Used with the chmod Command

Octal Value	Permissions Granted
0001	Execute permission for the owner
0002	Write permission for the owner
0004	Read permission for the owner
0010	Execute permission for the group
0020	Write permission for the group
0040	Read permission for the group
0100	Execute permission for all others
0200	Write permission for all others
0400	Read permission for all others
1000	Sticky bit on
2000	Group ID bit on if the file is executable; otherwise, mandatory file locking is on
4000	User ID bit on if the file is executable

Group and user IDs refer to who has permission to use, read, or execute a file. These initial file permissions are granted by the system administrator when a user's account is first created. Only users of an indicated group can access files in a group, and only if a user has given group members permission to those files.

To give a file read and write permissions for everyone, you must add the required permissions together, as in the following example:

0002	Write permission for the owner
0004	Read permission for the owner
0020	Write permission for the group
0040	Read permission for the group
0200	Write permission for all others
0400	Read permission for all others
0666	Read and write permission for everyone

To give a file these permissions, you use the following command:

```
chmod 666 file
```

Tip #110 from
Jack

You can change the mode for a directory and all files in the directory by using the `-R` flag. For example, to change the read/write mode for all files under the `/home/website/gifs`, you use the following commands:

```
cd /home/website
chmod -R 666 gifs
```

Relative permissions use a slightly different format. With relative permissions, you must state the following:

- Whom you're giving permissions to
- What operation you intend (add, subtract, or set permissions)
- What the permissions are

For example, if you type `chmod a=rwx file`, you give read, write, and execute permission to all users. Table 19.4 summarizes the commands for relative permissions.

TABLE 19.4 RELATIVE PERMISSIONS USED WITH THE `chmod` COMMAND

Value	Description
Whom	
a	All users (the users, their group, and all others)
g	Owner's group
o	All others not in the file's group
u	Just the user
Operator	
+	Adds the mode
-	Removes the mode
=	Sets the mode absolutely
Permission	
x	Sets execute
r	Sets read
w	Sets write
s	Sets user ID bit
t	Sets sticky bit

If a file has been marked as having the user ID bit on, the permissions displayed by the `ls -l` command look like this:

```
-rws--- 1 sglines 3136 Jan 17 15:42 x
```

If the group ID bit is added, the permissions look like this:

```
-rws-S- 1 sglines 3136 Jan 17 15:42 x
```

If you then turn on the sticky bit for the file, the permissions look like this:

```
-rws-S-rws-S-T 1 sglines 3136 Jan 17 15:42 x
```

Note the use of uppercase `S` and `T` to indicate the status of the user ID bit and the sticky bit, respectively.

LINUX STANDARD DIRECTORIES

You're already familiar with the concept of directories. When you log in, the system places you in your home directory. The `PATH` environment variable is set to point to other directories that contain executable programs. These other directories are part of the standard Linux directory structure.

These directories include the classic set of directories for UNIX and what can be called the "emerging standard set of directories," which Linux basically follows. They are described in the following sections.

CLASSIC UNIX DIRECTORIES

Before UNIX System V Release 4 (for example, UNIX System V Release 3.2 and earlier), most versions of UNIX settled on a regular system of organizing the UNIX directories that looked like this:

```
/
        /etc
        /lib
        /tmp
        /bin
        /usr
                /spool
                /bin
                /include
                /tmp
                /adm
                /lib
```

The `/etc` directory contains most of the system-specific data required to boot, or bring the system to life. It contains such files as `passwd` and `inittab`, which are necessary for the proper operation of the system.

The `/lib` directory contains a library of functions needed by the C compiler. Even if you don't have a C compiler on your system, this directory is important because it contains all the shared libraries that application programs can call. A shared library is loaded into memory only when the command calling it is run. This arrangement keeps executable programs small. Otherwise, every running program contains duplicate code, requiring a lot more disk space to store and a lot more memory to run.

The /tmp directory is used for temporary storage. Programs that use /tmp generally clean up after themselves and delete any temporary files. If you use /tmp, you should be sure to delete any files before logging out. Because the system automatically deletes the contents of this directory periodically, don't keep anything you might need later in it.

The /bin directory keeps all the executable programs needed to boot the system and is usually home for the most commonly used Linux commands. Note, however, that an executable program doesn't have to be binary (which the name *bin* implies). Several smaller programs in /bin are, in fact, shell scripts.

The /usr directory contains everything else. Your PATH variable contains the string /bin:/usr/bin because the /usr/bin directory contains all the Linux commands that aren't in the /bin directory. This arrangement has a historical precedence. In the early days of Linux, hard disks weren't very big. Linux needs at least the /etc/tmp/ and /bin directories to *bootstrap* (that is, start executing) itself. Because the disks of the early Linux era held only those three directories, everything else was on a disk that could be mounted after Linux was up and running. When Linux was still a relatively small operating system, placing additional subdirectories in the /usr directory wasn't much of a burden. It allowed a moderately sized Linux system to exist with just two disks: a root disk and a /usr disk.

The /usr/adm directory contains all the accounting and diagnostic information needed by the system administrator. If both system accounting and diagnostic programs are turned off, this directory is effectively empty.

The /include directory contains all the source code used by #include statements in C programs. You'll have at least read permission for this directory because it contains all the code fragments and structures that define your system. You shouldn't modify any of the files in this directory because they were crafted (carefully, you can assume) by your system vendor.

The /usr/spool directory contains all the transient data used by the lp print system, the cron daemon, and the UUCP communications system. Files "spooled" to the printer are kept in the /spool directory until they're printed. Any programs waiting to be run by cron, including all the crontab files and pending at and batch jobs, are also stored here.

The /usr/lib directory contains everything else that's part of the standard Linux system. In general, the /usr/lib directory represents the organized chaos hidden beneath the relatively well-disciplined Linux system. This directory contains programs called by other programs found in /bin and /usr/bin as well as configuration files for terminals and printers, the mail system, cron, and the UUCP communications system.

The /usr directory contains all the subdirectories assigned to users. The general convention is this: If your login ID is mary, your home directory is /usr/mary.

This directory arrangement made a lot of sense when disks were small and expensive, but with the advent of very large disks at (relatively) inexpensive prices, Linux can be organized in better ways, as evidenced by the new directory structure discussed in the next section.

LINUX DIRECTORIES

One problem with the classical structure of UNIX is that backing up your data files is difficult with a fragmented /usr directory. Three different levels of backup generally are required in a system: the basic system itself, any changes to the tables that define the basic system for a specific site, and user data.

The basic system should be backed up only once, with changes to the controlling tables backed up when changes are made. User data changes all the time and should be backed up frequently. The typical Linux directory structure is shown here, but your structure might be a little different depending on what packages you have installed:

```
/
      /etc
            /passwd (user database)
            /rc.d (system initialization scripts)
/sbin
/bin
/tmp
/var
/lib
/home
      / <your user name here> (user accounts)
/install
/usr
      /bin
/proc
```

The /bin, /etc, and /tmp directories have the same function as they do in the classic structure. System definition tables are moved into the /var directory so that whenever the operation of the system changes, you can back up only that directory.

What's new is that all system programs are moved into the /sbin directory. All the standard Linux programs are in /usr/bin, which is linked to /bin. For compatibility, all the classic directories are maintained with symbolic links. The /usr directory, which no longer contains user data, has been reorganized to make sense from the chaos that once was the /usr/libdirectory.

MANAGING FILES AND DIRECTORIES

The vast majority of Linux commands manipulate files and directories. Indeed, Linux shell scripts are particularly adept at manipulating files and directories. File manipulations that are difficult in a conventional language (even in C) are made easy from within a shell, largely because of the rich selection of file-manipulation commands available in Linux.

File-manipulation commands can be grouped roughly into two categories:

- Commands that manipulate files as objects
- Commands that manipulate the contents of files

Listing Files

The basic command to list files is `ls`. The way `ls` displays files depends on how you use the command. If you use the `ls` command in a pipe, every file is displayed on a line by itself. This is also the default for some versions of UNIX, such as SCO UNIX. Other versions of UNIX list files in several columns. For most uses, the columnar format is more convenient; systems that list files one per row often have an alternative command, usually `lc`, for lists in column format.

The `ls` command's behavior is modified with the use of flags that take the form `-abcd`. In general, versions of the `ls` command fall into two categories: versions of `ls` derived from Linux System V and those derived from Berkeley. Because the Berkeley Linux systems are slowly giving way to Linux System V, this chapter concentrates on the flags used by System V. If you're in doubt about which version of `ls` you have, consult the manuals for your system or try the command `man ls`.

Note

Most man pages for commands in this chapter are no longer being maintained and may be inaccurate or incomplete under Red Hat Linux as the system is moved to more graphical-based systems such as HTML and TexInfo. However, for the time being, this information is accurate for this release of Red Hat Linux 6.0.

Flags used with the `ls` command can be concatenated or listed separately. This means that the following commands are effectively identical:

```
ls -l -F
ls -lF
```

Table 19.5 lists in alphabetical order several of the flags used with `ls` and their uses.

Table 19.5 Flags for the `ls` Command

Flag	Description
`-a`	Lists all entries. In the absence of this or the `-A` option, entries whose names begin with a period (`.`) aren't listed. Linux has a way of "hiding" files; all files that begin with a period by default aren't listed because they're generally files used to customize applications. For example, `.profile` is used to customize the Bourne and Korn shells; `.mailrc` is used to customize your systemwide email configuration file. Because almost every major command you use has a startup file, your home directory looks cluttered if the `ls` command lists all those startup files by default. If you want to see them, you can use the `-a` flag.
`-A`	Acts the same as `-a`, except that `.` and `..` aren't listed. Recall from the section "Understanding Filenames and Pathnames" earlier in this chapter that `.` is a pseudonym for the current directory and `..` is a pseudonym for the parent directory. Because these filenames begin with a period, the `-a` flag lists them. If you don't want to see these pseudonyms, use the `-A` flag instead.

TABLE 19.5 FLAGS FOR THE `ls` COMMAND

Flag	Description
`-b`	Forces printing of nongraphic characters to be in octal `\ddd` notation. `-b` is more useful than the `-q` flag because it allows you to figure out what the characters are.
`-c`	Uses the time of the last edit (or last mode change) for sorting or printing. Linux maintains three time and date stamps on every file: the file creation date, the date of last access, and the date of last modification. Normally, files are listed in *ASCII order* (alphabetical order, except that capitals are sorted before lowercase letters).
`-C`	Forces multicolumn output with entries sorted down the columns. This is the default format of `ls` when output is to a terminal.
`-d` *`filename`*	Lists only the name of the argument if it is a directory (not its contents); this argument is often used with the `-l` flag to get the status of a directory. Normally, the contents of a directory are listed if a directory name is explicitly listed or implied with the use of a wildcard. Thus, the simple command `ls` lists just the directory names themselves, but `ls *` lists files, directories, and the contents of any directories encountered in the current directory.
`-F`	Marks directories with a trailing slash (`/`), executable files with a trailing asterisk (`*`), symbolic links with a trailing at sign (`@`), FIFOs with a trailing bar (`¦`), and sockets with a trailing equals sign (=).
`-i`	Prints each file's inode number (*inodes* are described in the section "Directories and Physical Disks" earlier in this chapter) in the first column of the report. If you list linked files, notice that both files have the same inode number.
`-l`	Lists directory entries in long format, giving mode, number of links, owner, size in bytes, and time of last modification for each file. If the file is a special file, the size field instead contains the major and minor device numbers. If the time of last modification is greater than six months ago, the month, date, and year are shown; otherwise, only the date and time are shown. If the file is a symbolic link, the pathname of the linked-to file is printed, preceded by the characters `->`. You can combine `-l` with other options, such as `-n`, to show user and group ID numbers instead of names.
`-n`	Lists the user and group ID numbers, instead of names, associated with each file and directory. Usually, only the names are listed. If you're setting up networking products, such as TCP/IP, it's useful to know ID numbers when you're setting up permissions across several systems.
`-q`	Displays nongraphic characters in filenames as the character `?`. For `ls`, this is the default action when output is to a terminal. If a file has accidentally been created with nonprintable characters, the `-q` flag displays the file.
`-r`	Reverses the sort order to show files in reverse alphabetical or oldest-file-first order, as appropriate.
`-s`	Gives the size of each file, including any indirect blocks used to map the file, in kilobytes. If the environment variable `POSIX_CORRECT` is defined, the block size is 512 bytes.
`-t`	Sorts by time modified (latest first) rather than by name. If you want to see the oldest file first, use the `-rt` combination.

TABLE 19.5 FLAGS FOR THE `ls` COMMAND

Flag	Description
`-u`	Uses time of last access, instead of last modification, for sorting (with the `-t` option) or printing (with the `-l` option).
`-x`	Forces multicolumn output with entries sorted across rather than down the page.

If you installed the Slackware distribution of Linux, you'll find `ls` also provides color output for each file type. The color definitions are defined in the configuration file `DIR_COLORS` in the `/etc` directory. The default configuration highlights executable files in green, directories in blue, and symbolic links in cyan. To customize the colors, you must copy the `DIR_COLORS` file to your home directory and change its name to `.dir colors`. Table 19.6 provides the color definitions available; see the man pages and the `DIR_COLORS` file for more information.

Note

For the Red Hat distribution, you must type `ls -color` to get the color effect. To set this behavior as the default, see the "Colour `ls` mini-How-To" at `http://metalab.unc.edu/LDP/HOWTO/mini/Colour-ls.html`.

TABLE 19.6 `DIR_COLORS` VALUES TO CREATE COLOR HIGHLIGHTING

Value	Description
`0`	Restores default color
`1`	For brighter colors
`4`	For underlined text
`5`	For flashing text
`30`	For black foreground
`31`	For red foreground
`32`	For green foreground
`33`	For yellow (or brown) foreground
`34`	For blue foreground
`35`	For purple foreground
`36`	For cyan foreground
`37`	For white (or gray) foreground
`40`	For black background
`41`	For red background
`42`	For green background
`43`	For yellow (or brown) background

TABLE 19.6 DIR_COLORS VALUES TO CREATE COLOR HIGHLIGHTING

Value	Description
44	For blue background
45	For purple background
46	For cyan background
47	For white (or gray) background

To find more options than the ones shown here, you can consult the man pages for `ls`.

ORGANIZING FILES

Linux doesn't have any fixed rules for organizing files. Files don't have extensions (such as `.exe` for executables) as they do in MS-DOS. You can (and perhaps should) make up your own system of naming files, but the classic system of organizing files in Linux is to use subdirectories.

More and more, however, Linux applications that have come from the DOS world are bringing their conventions to Linux. Although they may not require it, vendors encourage you to use certain extensions to name files that you use with their applications.

If you're going to write your own commands, a useful way to organize your directories is to mimic Linux's use of the `/bin`, `/lib`, and `/etc` directories. You can create your own structure of subdirectories with these names, perhaps under your `/home` directory, and follow the Linux tradition of placing executable commands in your `/bin` directory, subsidiary commands in your `/lib` directory, and initialization files in your `/etc` directory. Of course, you aren't required to organize your directories this way, but it's one way of organizing your files.

You create directories by using the `mkdir` command. Its syntax is simple:

```
mkdir directory-name
```

In this syntax, you replace *`directory-name`* with the name you want to assign to the new directory. Of course, you need write permission in the directory before you can create a subdirectory by using `mkdir`, but if you're making a subdirectory within your home directory, you should have no problem.

Suppose you've written three programs called `prog1`, `prog2`, and `prog3`, all of which are found in `$HOME/bin`. Remember that `$HOME` is your home directory. If you want your private programs to run as though they were a standard part of the Linux command set, you must add `$HOME/bin` to your `PATH` environment variable. You do so by using the following command in the Bourne or Korn shell:

```
PATH=$PATH:$HOME/bin;export PATH
```

In the C shell, you use this command:

```
setenv PATH ''$PATH $HOME/bin''
```

Note Remember that `$HOME` is the placeholder for the complete path that refers to your home directory. If your home directory is `/home/ams`, `$HOME/bin` is interpreted as `/home/ams/bin`.

If your programs call subsidiary programs, you might want to create subdirectories within your `$HOME/lib` directory. You can create a subdirectory for each program. The private command `pgm1` can then explicitly call, for example, `$HOME/lib/pgm1/pgm1a`.

Similarly, if your command `prog1` requires a startup table, you can name that table `$HOME/etc/pgm1.rc`, and your data can be in your `$HOME/data/pgm1` directory.

COPYING FILES

The command for copying files is `cp` *`from to`*. You must have read permission for the file you're copying from and write permission for the directory (and the file if you're overwriting an existing file) you're copying to. Other than that, no restrictions are placed on your ability to copy files.

You need to watch for the following as you copy files:

- If you copy a file and give it the name of a file that already exists and that you have write permission for, you overwrite the original file.
- If you give the name of a directory as the destination of the `cp` command, the file is copied into that directory with its original name. For example, if you type the command `cp` *`file directory`*, the file is copied into *`directory`* as `directory/`*`file`*.
- You can copy a list of files into a directory by using the command `cp` *`file1 file2 file3 ... directory`*. If the last item in the list isn't a directory, an error message appears. Likewise, if any element in the list other than the last item is only a directory, an error message appears.
- When you use wildcards with the `cp` command, you can copy more than you intend to, so be careful.

Note Because many Linux users also have MS-DOS files on their systems and usually make the DOS file system accessible from Linux, most of the Linux commands recognize when a file is being copied to or from a DOS partition. Thus, Linux can handle the necessary file translation when copying files. This translation is required because most DOS files embed the carriage return/linefeed characters into an ASCII file to indicate a line break. Most Linux and UNIX systems embed only a linefeed character, called *newline*, in the file to indicate a line break.

Moving and Renaming Files

In Linux, you move and rename files by using the same command: `mv`. The syntax and rules are the same for `mv` as they are for the copy command, `cp`. That is, you can move as many files as you want to a directory; however, the directory name must be last in the list, and you must have write permission to that directory.

One thing you can do with `mv` that you can't do with `cp` is move or rename directories. When you move or rename a file, only the entry in the directory file is changed. Unless the new location is on another physical disk or partition, the file and the contents of the directory are physically moved.

If you try to use `rm` (for *remove*) or `cp` without options on a directory, the command fails and displays a message telling you that the item you're dealing with is a directory. To remove or copy directories, you must use the `-r` flag (for *recursive*) with `rm` and `cp`. The `mv` command, however, moves directories quite happily.

Removing Files or Directories

The command to remove a file is `rm`. To delete a file you don't own, you need read and write permission. If you own the file, you're allowed to delete it, provided that you haven't closed off your own permission to the file. For example, if you turn off write permission to a file by typing `chmod 000 file`, you must open permission again by using the `chmod` command (by typing `chmod 644 file`) before you can delete it.

If you accidentally type `rm *`, you delete all the files you have permission to delete in the current directory; you don't delete the subdirectories. To delete subdirectories, you must use the recursive option (`-r`).

Some versions of `rm` stop and ask whether you really want to delete files that you own but don't have at least write permission for. Other versions of `rm` prompt you for any files marked for removal with wildcards. Indeed, you can write a macro or shell script that gives you a second chance before actually deleting a file.

If your version of `rm` balks at removing files you own but don't have write permission for, you can partially protect yourself from accidentally deleting everything in your directory by following these steps:

1. Create a file named `0`. In the ASCII string sequence, the number 0 is listed before any files that begin with letters.
2. Remove all permissions from the file named `0` by typing the command `chmod 000 0`. This command removes read, write, and execute permissions for everyone, including yourself.
3. If you type the command `rm *`, the file named `0` is the first file that `rm` attempts to remove.

If your version of rm balks at removing the 0 file when you type rm *, you have the chance to think about what you just did. If you didn't intend to delete everything in your directory, you can press Del or Ctrl+c to kill the rm process. To test this procedure, try removing just the file named 0. Don't use rm *, because if your version of rm doesn't stop at the file 0, you'll erase all the files in your directory.

A better way to protect yourself from accidentally deleting files is to use the -i flag with rm. The -i flag stands for *interactive*. If you give the command rm -i *filename*, you're asked whether you really want to delete the file. You must answer yes before the file is actually deleted. If you type the command rm -i *, you must answer yes for every file in your directory. Having to respond for every file should give you enough time to think about what you really want to do.

Caution

Think before you delete files. In most versions of Linux, unlike Windows, DOS, or Macintoshes, when you delete a file, it's gone and the only sure way to recover a lost file is from a backup. You did make a backup, didn't you? Some possible ways to recover parts of files are discussed later in this chapter, but you have no guarantees.

→ See "Performing Backups and Restoring Files," p. 263

→ See "Case Study: Undeleting Files," p. 436

If you use the rm -i command frequently, you can implement it in two ways: by writing a shell script or by creating a shell function. If you write a shell script, remember that the shell searches for commands in the directories listed in your PATH variable in the order in which they're listed. If your $HOME/bin directory is listed last, a shell script named rm will never be found. You can place your $HOME/bin directory first in the PATH variable's list or create a new command, such as del. If you create a shell script called del, you must mark it as executable with the chmod command before the shell can recognize it. When you create your del command, you need to give it only one command: rm -i $*. If you then type the command del *, the shell translates it into rm -i *.

→ See "Editing and Aliasing Shell Commands," p. 346

Another way to accomplish the same task is to use an *alias*, which takes precedence over commands that must be looked up. You can think of an alias as an internal shell command (similar to the doskey commands introduced in MS-DOS version 5.0).

To add an alias if you're using the C shell, you must edit the file named .cshrc. You can use any text editor, such as vi (see Chapter 9, "Using the vi Editor"), to edit this file. For the C shell, add the following lines to the top of your .cshrc file:

```
rm ()
{
```

```
/bin/rm -i $*
}
```

To add an alias to the Korn shell, add the following line to your `$HOME/.kshrc` file:

```
alias rm 'rm -i $*'
```

If you try to delete a directory by using the `rm` command, you're told that it's a directory and can't be deleted. If you want to delete empty directories, you can use the `rmdir` command, as with MS-DOS.

Linux offers another way to delete directories and their contents, but it's far more dangerous. The `rm -r` command recursively deletes any directories and files it encounters. If you have a directory named `./foo` that contains files and subdirectories, the command `rm -r foo` deletes the `./foo` directory and its contents, including all subdirectories.

If you give the command `rm -i -r`, each directory that the `rm` command encounters triggers a confirmation prompt. You must answer yes before the directory and its contents are deleted. If you left any files in the directory you were attempting to delete, `rm` balks, just as it does if you attempt to remove the nonempty directory by using the `rm` command with no options.

Note

You don't have to issue each flag individually for a Linux command. If the flag doesn't take an argument, you can combine the flags. Thus, you can issue `rm -i -r` as `rm -ir`.

VIEWING THE CONTENTS OF A FILE

Almost every Linux command prints to the standard output device, typically your screen. If the command takes its input from a file after manipulating the file in some way, the command prints the file to your screen. The trick in choosing a Linux command depends on how you want the file displayed. You can use three standard commands: `cat`, `more`, and `less`.

Note

Linux, like all UNIX systems, opens four system files at startup: standard input, standard output, standard error, and AUX. These files are actually physical devices:

Name	*Alias*	*Device*
Standard Input	standard in (stdin)	The keyboard
Standard output	standard out (stdout)	The screen
Standard error	standard err (stderr)	The screen
AUX	auxiliary	An auxiliary device

USING `cat` TO VIEW A FILE

For displaying short ASCII files, the simplest command is `cat`, which stands for *concatenate*. The `cat` command takes a list of files (or a single file) and prints the contents unaltered on standard output, one file after another. Its primary purpose is to concatenate files (as in `cat` *`file1 file2`* `>` *`file3`*), but it works just as well to send the contents of a short file to your screen.

If you try to display large files by using `cat`, the file scrolls past your screen as fast as the screen can handle the character stream. One way to stop the flow of data is to alternatively press Ctrl+s and Ctrl+q to send start and stop messages to your screen, or you can use one of the page-at-a-time commands, `more` or `less`.

USING `more` TO VIEW A FILE

Both `more` and `less` display a screen of data at a time. Although they both perform roughly the same job, they do it differently. `more` and `less` determine how many lines your terminal can display from the terminal database and from your `TERM` environment variable.

The `more` command is older than `less`, and it's derived from the Berkeley version of UNIX. It has proved so useful that, like the vi editor, it has become a standard. This section covers just the basics of the command.

The simplest form of the `more` command is `more` *`filename`*. When you use this command, you see a screen of data from the file. If you want to go on to the next screen, you press the spacebar. If you press Enter, only the next line is displayed. If you're looking through a series of files (by using the command `more` *`file1 file2`*`...`) and want to stop to edit one, you can do so by using the `e` or `v` command. Pressing `e` within `more` invokes whatever editor you've defined in your `EDIT` shell environment variable on the current file. Pressing v uses whatever editor has been defined in the `VISUAL` variable. If you haven't defined these variables in your environment, `more` defaults to the ed editor for the `e` command and to the vi editor for the `v` command.

→ See "Setting the Shell Environment," p. 325

The `more` command has only one real drawback: You can't go backward in a file and redisplay a previous screen. However, you can go backward in a file by using `less`.

USING `less` TO VIEW A FILE

One disadvantage to using the `less` command is that you can't use an editor on a file being displayed. However, `less` makes up for this deficiency by allowing you to move forward and backward through a file.

The `less` command works almost the same way that `more` does. To page through a file, type the command `less` *`filename`*. One screen of data is then displayed. To advance to the next screen, press the spacebar as you do with the `more` command.

To move backward in a file, press the b key. To go to a certain position expressed as a percentage of the file, press p and specify the percentage at the : prompt.

SEARCHING THROUGH A FILE AND ESCAPING TO THE SHELL

Using the `less` and `more` commands, you can search for strings in the file being displayed. The `less` command, however, allows you to search backward through the file as well. You can use the search syntax `less / string` to search backward through the file. With the `less` and `more` commands, if a string is found, a new page is displayed with the line containing the matching string at the top of the screen. With `less`, pressing the n key repeats the previous search.

The `more` and `less` commands also allow you to escape to the shell by using the `!` command. When you escape to the shell by using the `!` command, you're actually in a subshell; you must exit the subshell just as you do when you log out from a session. Depending on which shell you're using, you can press Ctrl+d or type `exit` to return to the same screen in `more` or `less` that you escaped from. If you press Ctrl+d and get a message to use `logout` instead of Ctrl+d, you use the `logout` command.

VIEWING FILES IN OTHER FORMS

Other commands display the contents of files in different forms. For example, if you want to look at the contents of a binary file, you can display it by using the `od` command, which stands for *octal dump*. The `od` command displays a file in octal notation, or base 8. By using various flags, `od` can display a file in decimal, ASCII, or hexadecimal (base 16) notation.

Octal, Decimal, and Hexadecimal Notation

Representing binary data is an intriguing problem. If the binary data represents ASCII, you have no problem displaying it (ASCII is, after all, what you expect when you look at most files). If the file is a program, however, the data most likely can't be represented as ASCII characters. In that case, you have to display it in some numerical form.

The early minicomputers used 12-bit words. Today, of course, the computer world has settled on the 8-bit byte as the standard unit of memory. Although you can represent data in the familiar decimal (base 10) system, the question becomes what to display—a byte, a word, or 32 bits? Displaying a given number of bits compactly requires that base 2 be raised to the required number of bits. With the old 12-bit systems, you could represent all 12 bits with four numbers (represented by 2^3, which was the octal or base 8 format). Because early UNIX systems ran on these kinds of minicomputers, much of the UNIX—and, thus, Linux—notation is in octal. Any byte can be represented by a three-digit octal code that looks like this (this example represents the decimal value of 8):

```
\010
```

Because the world has settled on an 8-bit byte, octal is no longer an efficient way to represent data. Hexadecimal (base 16 or 2^4) is a better way. An 8-bit byte can be represented by two hexadecimal digits; a byte whose decimal value is 10 is represented as 0A in hexadecimal.

The `od` command lets you choose how to display binary data. The general form of the command is one of the following:

```
od [option]... [file]...
od -traditional [file] [[+] offset [[+] label]]
```

Table 19.7 summarizes the flags you can use with `od`.

TABLE 19.7 THE od COMMAND FLAGS

Short Flag	Full Flag	Description
`-A`	`--address-radix=`*radix*	Decide how file offsets are printed
`-N`	`--read-bytes=`*bytes*	Limit dump to *bytes* input bytes per file
`-j`	`--skip-bytes=`*bytes*	Skip *bytes* input bytes first on each file
`-s`	`--strings[=`*bytes*`]`	Output strings of at least *bytes* graphic characters
`-t`	`--format=`*type*	Select output format or formats
`-v`	`--output-duplicates`	Don't use `*` to mark line suppression
`-w`	`--width[=`*bytes*`]`	Output *bytes* bytes per output line
	`--traditional`	Accept arguments in pre-POSIX form
	`--help`	Display this help and exit
	`--version`	Output version information and exit

radix in Table 19.7 stands for number system and is `d` for decimal, `o` for octal, `x` for hexadecimal, or `n` for none. *bytes* is hexadecimal with a prefix of `0x` or `0X`; it's multiplied by 512 with a `b` suffix, by 1,024 with `k`, and by 1,048,576 with an `m` suffix. `-s` without a number implies 3; `-w` without a number implies 32. By default, `od` uses `-A o -t d2 -w 16`.

The pre-POSIX format specifications in Table 19.8 can be intermixed with the commands in Table 19.7, and their effects accumulate.

TABLE 19.8 PRE-POSIX FORMAT SPECIFICATIONS FOR od

Short Flag	POSIX Equivalent	Description
`-a`	`-t a`	Select named characters
`-b`	`-t oC`	Select octal bytes
`-c`	`-t c`	Select ASCII characters or backslash escapes
`-d`	`-t u2`	Select unsigned decimal shorts
`-f`	`-t fF`	Select floats
`-h`	`-t x2`	Select hexadecimal shorts
`-I`	`-t d2`	Select decimal shorts
`-l`	`-t d4`	Select decimal longs
`-o`	`-t o2`	Select octal shorts
`-x`	`-t x2`	Select hexadecimal shorts

For older syntax (second-call format), *offset* means -j *offset*. *label* is the pseudo-address at first byte printed, incremented when the dump is progressing. For *offset* and *label*, an 0x or 0X prefix indicates hexadecimal. Suffixes may be . (dot) for octal and may be multiplied by 512. The *type* parameter is made up of one or more of the specifications listed in Table 19.9.

Table 19.9 Type Parameters

Parameter	Description
a	Named character
c	ASCII character or backslash escape
d[*size*]	Signed decimal, *size* bytes per integer
f[*size*]	Floating point, *size* bytes per integer
o[*size*]	Octal, *size* bytes per integer
u[*size*]	Unsigned decimal, *size* bytes per integer
x[*size*]	Hexadecimal, *size* bytes per integer

In Table 19.9, *size* is a number and also may be C for sizeof(char), S for sizeof(short), I for sizeof(int), or L for sizeof(long). If *type* is f, *size* may also be F for sizeof(float), D for sizeof(double), or L for sizeof(long double).

Note

sizeof is a C language function that returns the number of bytes in the data structure passed as the parameter. For example, you use the following function call to determine the number of bytes in an integer on your system because the number of bytes in an integer is system-dependent:

```
sizeof(int);
```

Searching for Files

If you can't find a file by looking with the ls command, you can use the find command. The find command is an extremely powerful tool, which makes it one of the more difficult commands to use. The find command has three parts, each of which can consist of multiple subparts:

- Where to look
- What to look for
- What to do when you find it

If you know the name of a file but don't know where in the Linux file structure it's located, the simplest case of the `find` command works like this:

```
find / -name filename -print
```

Caution

Be careful when you're searching from the root directory. On large systems, searching every directory can take a long time, beginning with the root directory and continuing through every subdirectory and disk (and remotely mounted disk) before finding what you're looking for.

Limiting your search to one or two directories, at most, might be more prudent. For example, if you know that a file is probably in the `/usr` or `/usr2` directory, you can use the following command instead:

```
find /usr /usr2 -name filename -print
```

You can use many different options with `find`; Table 19.10 lists just a few. To see all the available options, use the `man find` command.

Table 19.10 A Sample of the `find` Command Flags

Command	Description
`-name` *file*	The *file* variable can be the name of a file or a wild-carded filename. If it's a wild-carded filename, every file that matches the wildcards is selected for processing.
`-links` *n*	Any file that has *n* or more links to it is selected for processing. Replace *n* with the number you want to check.
`-size` *n*`[c]`	Any file that occupies *n* or more 512-byte blocks is selected for processing. A `c` appended to *n* means to select any file that occupies *n* or more characters.
`-atime` *n*	With this command, you can select any file that has been accessed in the past *n* days. Note that the act of looking for a file with `find` modifies the access date stamp.
`-exec` *cmd*`find /home/jack -exec chown jack {} \;`	After you select a list of files, you can run a Linux command that uses the selected files as an argument. Two simple rules are associated with `-exec`: the name of a selected file is represented by `{}`, and the command must be terminated by an escaped semicolon, which is represented by `\;`. Suppose you've created a user directory while logged in as root; thus, all the files are owned by root, but the files should be owned by the user. You would issue the following command to change the owner of all the files in `/home/jack` and all subdirectories from root to `jack`:
`-print`	This instruction, the most often used, simply prints the name and location of any selected files.

Using the `find` command, you can perform many logical tests on files as well. For example, if you want to find a selection of filenames that can't be collectively represented with wildcards, you can use the *or*option (`-o`) to obtain a list, as shown here:

```
find /home (-name file1 -o -name file2) -print
```

You can combine as much selection criteria as you want with the `find` command. Unless you specify the `-o` option, `find` assumes you mean *and*. For example, the command `find -size 100 -atime 2` means find a file that's at least 100 blocks in size and that was last accessed at least two days ago. You can use parentheses, as in the preceding example, to prevent ambiguous processing of your criteria, especially if you combine and/or select criteria.

CHANGING FILE TIME AND DATE STAMPS

Each Linux file maintains three time and date stamps: the date of the file's creation, the date of the file's last modification, and the date of the last access. You can't change the file creation date artificially except by deliberately copying and renaming a file. Whenever a program reads or opens a file, the file's access date stamp is modified. As you learned in the preceding section, using the `find` command also causes the access date to be modified.

If a file is modified in any way—that is, if it's written to, even if the file is actually not modified—the file modification and file access date stamps are updated. The date stamps on a file are useful if you need to back up selectively only files that have been modified since a given date. You can use the `find` command for this purpose.

If you want to modify the date stamps on a file without actually modifying the file, you can do so by using the `touch` command. By default, `touch` updates the access and modification date stamps on a file with the current system date. By default, if you attempt to touch a file that doesn't exist, `touch` creates the file.

You can use `touch` to fool a command that checks for dates. For example, if your system runs a backup command that backs up only files modified after a particular date, you can touch a file that hasn't been changed recently to make sure that it's picked up.

You can use the following three tags with the `touch` command to modify its default behavior:

`-a`	Updates only the file's access date and time stamp
`-m`	Updates only the file's modification date and time stamp
`-c`	Prevents `touch` from creating a file if it doesn't already exist

The default syntax for `touch` is the following:

```
touch -am filelist
```

COMPRESSING FILES

If space is tight on a system, or you have large ASCII files that aren't used often, you can reduce the size of the files by compressing them. The standard Linux utility for compressing files is `gzip`. The `gzip`command can compress an ASCII file by as much as 80 percent. Most UNIX systems also provide the command `compress`, which typically is used with `tar` to compress groups of files for an archive. A file compressed with the `compress` command ends with a `.Z` extension—for example, `archive1.tar.Z`. Red Hat's distribution also provides the `zip` and `unzip` programs for compressing and archiving lists of files.

Tip #111 from Jack

For those of you who like GUIs rather than a command line interface (CLI), check out;programs;TkZip TkZip. You can find the program at:
`http:// www.pcnet.com/~proteus/TkZip/TkZip.html`

Tip #112 from Jack

Compressing is helpful before you mail or back up a file.

If a file is successfully compressed with the command `gzip` *`filename`*, the compressed file is named *`filename`*`.gz`, and the original file is deleted. To restore the compressed file to its original components, you can use the `gunzip` *`filename`* command.

Tip #113 from Jack

You don't have to append the `.gz` to the filename when you decompress a file. The `.gz` extension is assumed by the `gunzip` command.

If you want to keep the file in its compressed form but want to pipe the data to another command, you can use the `zcat` command. The `zcat` command works just like the `cat` command but requires a compressed file as input. `zcat` decompresses the file and then prints it to the standard output device.

→ See "Using Pipes to Start Multiple Processes" p. 369

For example, if you've compressed a list of names and addresses stored in a file named `namelist`, the compressed file is named `namelist.gz`. If you want to use the contents of the compressed file as input to a program, you can use the `zcat` command to begin a pipeline, as follows:

```
zcat namelist ¦ program1 ¦ program2 ...
```

`zcat` suffers from the same limitations as does `cat`: It can't go backward within a file. Linux offers a program called`zless` that works just like the `less` command, except that `zless` operates on compressed files. The same commands that work with `less` also work with `zless`.

The `compress` command's legal status is in limbo; someone has claimed patent infringement. The compression program of choice for Linux is the freely distributed compression utility `gzip`. The `gzip` command has none of the potential legal problems of `compress`, and almost all the compressed files installed by Linux were compressed with `gzip`. `gzip` should work with most compressed files, even those compressed with the older `compress` program.

If you're familiar with PKWARE's PKZIP line of products, you can use the `zip` and `unzip` programs provided with the Red Hat distribution. The `zip` command compresses several files and stores them in an archive, just like PKZIP. The `unzip` command extracts files from an archive. See the man pages `zip/unzip` for more information.

CASE STUDY: UNDELETING FILES

What happens if you delete a file by mistake? Many Windows systems have an undelete command, but alas most Linux distributions do not. Although you can recover some undeleted files, it is best not to delete them in the first place.

Tip #114 from Jack

Your first line of defense is to back up your system on a regular basis. Chapter 12, "Backing Up Data," provides information on how to back up your system. Then, if you do delete a file, you can retrieve it from the backup.

To help prevent you from deleting files, many Linux distributions, such as Red Hat and Caldera, alias the `rm` and `rmdir` commands to `rm -i` and `rmdir -i` to ask you for confirmation before executing the command. You can also set the file permissions to important files to modes below 440 so that you need to explicitly confirm their deletion.

Caution

You should not do everyday work as root because you can do a lot of damage to your system as a superuser, especially to files of other users. For example, if you give the command

```
rm -rf *
```

from the / directory, you wipe out your entire system!

DO NOT USE THE `rm -rf` COMMAND UNLESS YOU ARE ABSOLUTELY SURE WHAT YOU ARE DOING!

You can find detailed information on recovering text and binary files in the following How-Tos:

- Ext2fs Undeletion mini How-To:

  `http://metalab.unc.edu/LDP/HOWTO/mini/Ext2fs-Undeletion.html`
- Tips How-To:

  `http://metalab.unc.edu/LDP/HOWTO/Tips-HOWTO.html`

Both techniques work best on a single-user system—that is, a personal workstation rather than a server—because Linux reuses disk space and can thus reuse the space holding the deleted data at any time. This process is much more likely to happen on a server system. The best course of action is to unmount the file system and cease any activity as soon as you realize you've deleted a needed file.

→ See "Unmounting File Systems," p. 448

The text-recovery process suggested by Michael Hamilton in the "Tips How-To" uses the `egrep` and `strings` commands. This technique requires that you remember some of the text in the file, hopefully several words' worth of text. You also need to know which partition contained the file and have available disk space on another partition to save the recovery data. You cannot save the recovery data onto the same partition as the deleted file because your recovery actions might overwrite the data you're trying to undelete.

To try to undelete a file, you must figure out which partition has your file. You can use the `pwd` and `df` commands to help identify the partition, as in the following:

```
[tackett@ns ~]$ cd
[tackett@ns ~]$ pwd
/home/tackett
Filesystem         1024-blocks    Used Available Capacity Mounted on
/dev/hda1            1536971    301132  1156411      21%    /
/dev/hdb2            2554589    346646  2075853      14%    /home
```

The output indicates that `/home/tackett` exists on the partition `/dev/hdb2`. If you think something might write to a directory on `/dev/hdb2` before you can perform the undelete function, then you might want to unmount the file systems on that partition. For example, to unmount the `/home` directory, you can use the following command (note that no *n* appears in this command name):

```
umount /home
```

You must be root to unmount the directory, and you need to be in another partition to do so; otherwise, you get a `device busy` error message.

Next, you need to search this file system to find the text of the deleted file by using the `egrep` command. You also need space on a different file system to place the results of your search. From the preceding example, you have only two partitions and thus have to write your search data to the `/` directory on `/dev/hda1` by using this command:

```
egrep -150 'Four score and seven years ago' /dev/hdb2 > /tmp/recovery
```

This command tells `egrep` to search for the phrase *Four score and seven years ago* on `/dev/hdb2` and to save the text 150 lines before the phrase and 150 lines after the phrase to the file `/tmp/recovery`.

Note

Make sure to look for text and an appropriate number of lines before and after the search phrase. If you are trying to recover a small shell script, maybe looking for 50 lines is sufficient. If you are trying to recover a 1,000-line program, then 1,500 lines might be a more appropriate value.

Also, realize that searching an entire partition may take some time, especially if you specify a large number of lines to recover before and after your search phrase.

After saving the file, you can then use the command `strings` to narrow the search:

```
strings /tmp/recovery ¦ more
```

The `strings` command makes sure that you get only ASCII data to view; otherwise, you might see garbage characters you can't recognize from the recovery file.

If you need to undelete a binary file, you can follow the steps outlined by Aaron Crane in his "Ext2fs Undeletion mini How-To."

CHAPTER 20

Managing File Systems

In this chapter

by *Jack Tackett, Jr.*

UNDERSTANDING FILE SYSTEMS

File systems form the basis for all data on a Linux system. Linux programs, libraries, system files, and user files all reside on file systems. Proper management of file systems is critical because all your data and programs exist on top of file systems.

Many of the steps outlined in this chapter are performed automatically when you install Linux. However, you should learn to manage your file systems so that you can create, manage, and maintain your Linux system. Understanding file system management is critical to successful system administration. Your file system must work properly for your Linux system to work at all.

Under Linux, the file space that's visible to users is based on a tree structure, with the root at the top. The various directories and files in this space branch downward from the root. The top directory, `/`, is known as the *root directory*. Figure 20.1 gives a graphical example of a tree structure.

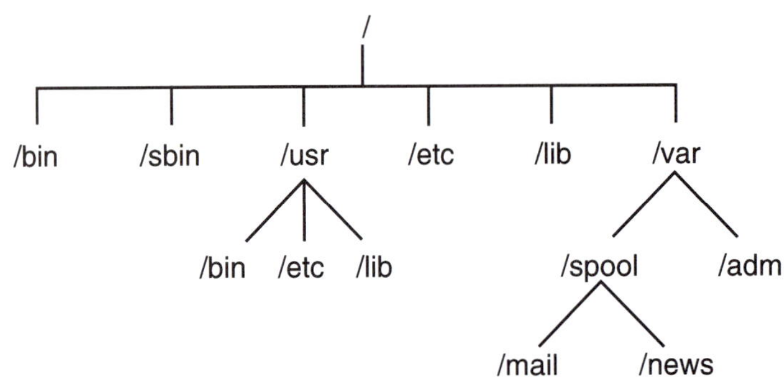

Figure 20.1 Picture the Linux file system as an upside-down tree, with the root at the top and the branches and leaves spreading downward.

To users, this directory tree looks like a seamless entity; they just see directories and files. In reality, many of the directories in the file tree are physically located on different partitions on a disk, on different disks, or even on different computers. When one of these disk partitions is attached to the file tree at a directory known as a *mount point*, the mount point and all directories below it are referred to as a *file system*.

The Linux operating system is made up of several directories and many different files. Depending on how you selected your installation, these directories may be different file systems. Typically, most of the operating system resides on two file systems: the root file system, known as `/`, and a file system mounted under `/usr` (pronounced *user*).

If you change directories to the root directory by using the `cd /` command and ask for a directory listing, you see several directories. They make up the contents of the root file system and provide the mount points for other file systems as well.

The `/bin` directory contains executable programs, known as *binaries*. (In fact, the directory named `/bin` is short for *binary*.) These programs are essential system files. Many Linux commands, such as `ls`, are actually programs found in this directory.

The /sbin directory is also used to store system binary files. Most files in this directory are used for system administration purposes.

The /etc directory is very important, containing many of the Linux system configuration files. Essentially, these files give your Linux system its "personality." The password file, passwd, is found here, as is the list of file systems to mount at startup, fstab. Also, this directory contains the startup scripts for Linux, the list of hosts with IP addresses that you want permanently recorded, and many other types of configuration information.

The shared libraries that programs use when they run are stored in the /lib directory. By using shared libraries, many programs can reuse the same code, and these libraries can be stored in a common place, thus reducing the size of your programs at runtime.

The /dev directory contains special files known as *device files*, which are used to access all the different types of hardware on your system. For example, the /dev/mouse file is for reading input from the mouse. By organizing access to hardware devices in this way, Linux effectively makes the interface to a hardware device look like any other piece of software. This means that you, in many cases, can use the same syntax that you use with software to perform operations on computer hardware devices. For example, to create a tape archive of your home directory on a floppy drive, you can use the following command:

```
tar -cdf /dev/fd0 ~tackett
```

/dev/fd0 indicates that the tar command should use the floppy drive identified by fd0.

→ See "Using tar," p. 265

Many of the devices in the /dev directory are in logical groups. Table 20.1 lists some of the most commonly used devices in the /dev directory.

TABLE 20.1 COMMONLY USED DEVICES IN THE /dev DIRECTORY

Device File	Description
/dev/console	The *system console*, which is the computer monitor physically connected to your Linux system.
/dev/hd	The device driver interface to IDE hard drives. The /dev/hda1 device refers to the first partition on hard drive hda. The device /dev/hda refers to the entire hard disk hda.
/dev/sd	The device driver interface for SCSI disks. The same conventions for SCSI disks and partitions apply as they do to the IDE /dev/hd devices.
/dev/fd	Device drivers that provide support for floppy drives. /dev/fd0 is the first floppy drive, and /dev/fd1 is the second floppy drive.
/dev/st	The device driver for SCSI tape drives.
/dev/tty	Device drivers that provide different consoles for user input. The name comes from the time when terminals known as *teletypes* were physically hooked to a UNIX system. Under Linux, these files provide support for the virtual consoles that you can access by pressing Alt+F1 through Alt+F6. These virtual consoles provide separate simultaneous local login sessions.

TABLE 20.1 COMMONLY USED DEVICES IN THE /dev DIRECTORY

Device File	Description
/dev/pty	Device drivers that provide support for pseudo-terminals, which are used for remote login sessions such as login sessions using Telnet.
/dev/ttyS	The serial interface ports on your computer. /dev/ttyS0 corresponds to COM1 under MS-DOS. If you have a serial mouse, /dev/mouse is a symbolic link to the appropriate ttys device that your mouse is connected to.
/dev/cua	Special call-out devices used with modems.
/dev/null	A very special device—essentially a black hole. All data written to /dev/null is lost forever. Writing to this device file can be very useful if you want to run a command and throw away the standard output or the standard error. Also, if /dev/null is used as an input file, a file of zero length is created, aka a data sink.

The /proc directory is actually a virtual file system. It's used to read process information from memory.

Tip #115 from Jack

You can query system information from the /proc file system. For example, to check on the amount of memory your system is using, you can enter the following:

```
cat /proc/meminfo
```

This command provides the following information:

```
total: used: free: shared: buffers: cached:
Mem: 31535104 30867456 667648 30359552 520192 7835648
Swap: 0 0 0
MemTotal: 30796 kB
MemFree: 652 kB
MemShared: 29648 kB
Buffers: 508 kB
Cached: 7652 kB
SwapTotal: 0 kB
SwapFree: 0 kB
```

The /tmp directory is used to store temporary files that programs create when running. If you have a program that creates many large temporary files, you might want to mount the /tmp directory as a separate file system rather than just have it as a directory on the root file system. If /tmp is left as a directory on the root file system and has many large files written to it, the root file system can fill up.

Tip #116 from
Jack

Red Hat provides a program called `tmpwatch` that deletes files in specified directories at specified times. For other distributions, you can create a `cron` job to perform the same action. In root's `crontab`, use the following command:

```
find /tmp -atime 2 -exec rm {} \;
```

This command deletes all files not accessed in the last two days.

→ See "Searching for Files," p. 432

The `/home` directory is the base directory for user home directories. It's common to mount this directory as a separate file system so that users can have plenty of room for their files. In fact, if you have many users on your system, you might need to separate `/home` into several file systems. To do so, you could create subdirectories such as `/home/staff` and `/home/admin` for staff members and administrators, respectively. You can mount each of them as different file systems and then create the users' home directories under them.

The `/var` directory holds files that tend to change in size over time. Typically, various system log files are located below this directory. The `/var/spool` directory and its subdirectories are used to hold data that's of a transitory nature, such as mail and news that's recently received from or queued for transmission to another site.

Tip #117 from
Jack

You can create other mount points under the `/` directory if you want. You might want to create a mount point named `/mnt/cdrom` if you routinely mount CD-ROMs on your system. In fact, Red Hat already creates such a mount point for you during installation.

The `/usr` directory and its subdirectories are very important to the operation of your Linux system. This directory contains several subdirectories with some of the most important programs on your system. Typically, subdirectories of `/usr` contain the large software packages that you install. Table 20.2 describes some of the `/usr` subdirectories. The `/usr` directory is almost always mounted as a separate file system.

TABLE 20.2 IMPORTANT SUBDIRECTORIES IN THE `/usr` FILE SYSTEM

Subdirectory	Description
`/usr/bin`	This directory holds many of the executable programs found on your Linux system.
`/usr/etc`	This directory contains many miscellaneous system configuration files.
`/usr/include`	Here and in the subdirectories of `/usr/include`, you find all the include files for the C compiler. These header files define constants and functions and are critical for C programming.

TABLE 20.2 IMPORTANT SUBDIRECTORIES IN THE `/usr` FILE SYSTEM

Subdirectory	Description
`/usr/g++-include`	This directory contains the include files for the C++ compiler.
`/usr/lib`	This directory contains various libraries for programs to use during linking.
`/usr/man`	This directory contains the various manual pages for programs on your Linux system. Below `/usr/man` are several directories that correspond to the different sections of the man pages.
`/usr/src`	This directory contains directories that hold the source code for different programs on your system. If you get a package that you want to install, `/usr/src/`*`packagename`* is a good place to put the source before you install it.
`/usr/local`	This directory is designed for local customizations to your system. In general, much of your local software is installed in this directory's subdirectories. The format of this directory varies on almost every UNIX system you look at. One way to set it up is to have a `/usr/local/bin` for binaries, a `/usr/local/etc` for configuration files, a `/usr/local/lib` for libraries, and a `/usr/local/src` for source code. You can mount the entire `/usr/local` directory tree as a separate file system if you need a lot of room for it.

MOUNTING AND UNMOUNTING FILE SYSTEMS

By now, you should have a good feel for what a file system is. So how do you set up a directory as a separate file system?

To mount a file system in the Linux directory tree, you must have a physical disk partition, CD-ROM, or floppy disk that you want to mount. You also must make sure that the directory to which you want to attach the file system, known as the *mount point*, actually exists.

Mounting a file system doesn't create the mount point directory. The mount point must exist before you try to mount the file system. Suppose that you want to mount the CD-ROM in drive `/dev/sr0` under the mount point `/mnt`. A directory named `/mnt` must exist, or the mount fails. After you mount the file system under that directory, all the files and subdirectories on the file system appear under the `/mnt` directory. Otherwise, the `/mnt` directory is empty.

Tip #118 from Jack

You can use the command `df.` if you need to know which file system the current directory is located on. The command's output shows the file system as well as the free space available.

MOUNTING FILE SYSTEMS INTERACTIVELY

As you may have guessed by now, Linux uses the `mount` command to mount a file system. The syntax of the `mount` command is as follows:

```
mount devicemountpoint
```

`device` is the physical device that you want to mount; *`mountpoint`* is the point in the file system tree where you want it to appear.

Note Only superusers can use the `mount` command. This restriction helps ensure system security. Several software packages that allow users to mount specific file systems, especially floppy disks, are available.

`mount` accepts several command-line arguments in addition to the two mentioned previously (see Table 20.3). If a needed command isn't given, `mount` attempts to figure it out from the `/etc/fstab` file.

TABLE 20.3 COMMAND-LINE ARGUMENTS FOR THE `mount` COMMAND

Argument	Description
`-f`	Causes everything to be done except for the actual mount system call. This argument "fakes" mounting the file system.
`-v`	Provides additional information about what `mount` is trying to do (Verbose mode).
`-w`	Mounts the file system with read and write permissions.
`-r`	Mounts the file system with read-only permission.
`-n`	Mounts without writing an entry in the `/etc/mtab` file.
`-t type`	Specifies the type of the file system being mounted. Valid types are `minux`, `ext`, `ext2`, `xiafs`, `msdos`, `hpfs`, `proc`, `nfs`, `umsdos`, `sysv`, and `iso9660` (the default).
`-a`	Causes `mount` to try to mount all file systems in `/etc/fstab`.
`-o list_of_options`	Causes `mount` to apply the options specified to the file system being mounted when followed by a comma-separated list of options. Many options are available here; for a complete list, refer to the `mount` man page.

Note Several forms of the `mount` command are very common. For example, the command `mount /dev/hdb3 /mnt` mounts the hard disk partition `/dev/hdb3` under the directory `/mnt`. Similarly, `mount -r -t iso9660/dev/sr0 /mnt` mounts the SCSI CD-ROM drive `/dev/sr0`, which is read-only and of the ISO 9660 file format, under the directory `/mnt`. And the command `mount -vat nfs` mounts all the NFS file systems listed in the `/etc/fstab` file.

Tip #119 from *Jack*

If a file system doesn't mount correctly, you can use the command `mount -vf device mountpoint` to see what `mount` is doing. This command gives a verbose listing and tells `mount` to do everything except mount the file system. This way, you can fake out the `mount` command and get a lot of information about what it's trying to do.

MOUNTING FILE SYSTEMS AT BOOT TIME

Under most circumstances, the file systems that your Linux system uses don't change frequently. For this reason, you can easily specify a list of file systems that Linux mounts when it boots and that it unmounts when it shuts down. These file systems are listed in a special configuration file named `/etc/fstab`, for *file system table*.

The `/etc/fstab` file lists the file systems to be mounted, one file system per line. The fields in each line are separated by spaces or tabs. Table 20.4 lists the different fields in the `/etc/fstab` file.

TABLE 20.4 FIELDS IN THE `/etc/fstab` FILE

Field	Description
File System Specifier	Specifies the block special device or the remote file system to be mounted.
Mount Point	Specifies the mount point for the file system. For special file systems such as swap files, you can use the word `none`, which makes swap files active but not visible within the file tree.

Table 20.4 Fields in the /etc/fstab File

Field	Description
Type	Gives the file system type of the specified file system. The following types of file systems are supported: minix—A local file system supporting filenames of 14 or 30 characters. `ext`—A local file system with longer filenames and larger inodes. (This file system has been replaced by the `ext2` file system and should no longer be used.) `ext2`—A local file system with longer filenames, larger inodes, and other features. xiafs—A local file system. `msdos`—A local file system for MS-DOS partitions. `hpfs`—A local file system for OS/2 High Performance File System partitions. `iso9660`—A local file system used for CD-ROM drives. `nfs`—A file system for mounting partitions from remote systems. `swap`—A disk partition or special file used for swapping. `umsdos`—A UMSDOS file system. `sysv`—A System V file system.
Mount Options	Contains a comma-separated list of mount options for the file system. At a minimum, it must contain the type of mount for the file system. See the `mount` man page for more information on mount options.
Dump Frequency	Specifies how often the file system should be backed up by the `dump` command. If this field isn't present, `dump` assumes that the file system doesn't need to be backed up.
Pass Number	Specifies in what order the file systems should be checked by the `fsck` command when the system is booted. The root file system should have a value of 1. All other file systems should have a value of 2. If a value isn't specified, the file system isn't checked for consistency at boot time.

Tip #120 from *Jack*

I recommend you mount your file systems at boot time via the `/etc/fstab` file instead of by using the `mount` command. Remember, only superusers can use `mount`.

The following is a sample `fstab` file:

```
# device      directory     type     options
/dev/hda1     /             ext2     defaults
/dev/hda2     /usr          ext2     defaults
/dev/hda3     none          swap     sw
/dev/sda1     /dosc         msdos    defaults
/proc         /proc         proc     none
```

In this sample file, you can see several different file systems. First, notice that comments in the file are prefixed by a # character. In this fstab file, two normal Linux file systems are mounted: the disk partitions /dev/hda1 and /dev/hda2. They are listed as being of type ext2 and are mounted under the root (/) and /usr directories, respectively.

The entry defaults, listed under the options field, indicates this file system should be mounted by using a common set of default options. Specifically, the file system is mounted read/write enabled, and it's to be interpreted as a block special device. All file I/O should be done asynchronously. The execution of binaries is permitted, and the file system can be mounted with the mount -a command. The Set UID (user ID) and Set GID (group ID) bits on files are interpreted on this file system, and ordinary users aren't allowed to mount this file system. As you can see, just typing defaults for the option is a lot easier.

→ See "Creating a Swap Partition," p. 459

The partition /dev/hda3 is a swap partition that's used for kernel virtual-memory swap space. Its mount point is specified as none so that it doesn't appear in the file system tree. It still has to be in the /etc/fstab file so that the system knows where it's physically located. Swap partitions are also mounted with the option sw.

The /proc file system is a virtual file system that points to the process information space in memory. As you can see, it doesn't have a corresponding physical partition to mount.

Tip #121 from *Jack*

For full information on all options available in the /etc/fstab file, refer to the man page for fstab.

MS-DOS file systems can also be mounted automatically. The partition /dev/sda1 is the first partition on the SCSI hard drive sda. It's mounted as an MS-DOS partition by specifying msdos as the type and by giving /dosc as its mount point. You can place the mount point for the MS-DOS file system anywhere; it is not required to be under the root directory.

UNMOUNTING FILE SYSTEMS

Now that you know all sorts of stuff about mounting file systems, it's time to look at how to unmount. You use the umount command to unmount file systems. You might want to unmount a file system for several reasons: to check or repair a file system with fsck, to unmount NFS-mounted file systems in case of network problems, or to unmount a file system on a floppy drive.

Note

This command is umount, not *unmount*. Make sure that you type it correctly.

The three basic forms of the `umount` command are as follows:

```
umount device | mountpoint
umount -a
umount -t fstype
```

`device` is the name of the physical device to unmount; *`mountpoint`* is the mount point directory name (you should specify only one or the other). The `umount` command has only two command-line parameters: `-a`, which unmounts all file systems, and `-t fstype`, which acts only on file systems of the type specified.

Caution

The `umount` command doesn't unmount a file system that's in use. For example, if you have some file system mounted under `/mnt` and you try

```
cd /mnt
umount /mnt
```

you get an error telling you that the file system is busy. You have to change to a different directory in another file system to unmount the file system mounted under `/mnt`.

MAINTAINING FILE SYSTEMS

As the system administrator, you're responsible for maintaining the integrity of the file systems. Typically, this means you have to check the file systems periodically for damaged or corrupted files. Linux automatically checks file systems at boot time if they have a value greater than 0 specified in the pass number field of the `/etc/fstab` file.

Note

The `ext2` file system commonly used under Linux has a special flag known as a *clean bit*. If the file system has been synchronized and unmounted cleanly, the clean bit is set on the file system. If the clean bit is set on a file system when Linux boots, it's not checked for integrity.

USING THE fsck COMMAND

Checking your file systems occasionally for damaged or corrupt files is a good idea. Under the Slackware distribution of Linux, you use the `fsck` (file system check) command to check your file systems. The `fsck` command is really a "front end" for a series of commands that are designed to check specific file systems. The syntax for the `fsck` command is as follows:

```
fsck [-A] [-V] [-t fs-type] [-a] [-l] [-r] [-s] filesys
```

However, the most basic form of the command is this:

```
fsck filesys
```

Table 20.5 describes the command-line options for the `fsck` command.

TABLE 20.5 COMMAND-LINE ARGUMENTS FOR fsck

Argument	Description
`-A`	Goes through the `/etc/fstab` file and tries to check all file systems in one pass. This option is typically used during the Linux boot sequence to check all normally mounted file systems. If you use `-A`, you can't use the `filesys` argument as well.
`-V`	Prints additional information about what `fsck` is doing (Verbose mode).
`-t` *`fs-type`*	Specifies the type of file system to be checked.
`filesys`	Specifies which file system is to be checked. This argument can be a block special device name, such as `/dev/hda1`, or a mount point, such as `/usr`.
`-a`	Automatically repairs any problems found in the file system without asking any questions. You should use this option with caution.
`-l`	Lists all the filenames in the file system.
`-r`	Asks for confirmations before repairing the file system.
`-s`	Lists the superblock before checking the file system.

The `fsck` command is actually a front-end program that calls the command to check the file system that matches the type you specify. To use this command, Linux needs to know the file system type that it's checking. The easiest way to make sure that `fsck` calls the right command is to specify a file system type with the `-t` option to `fsck`. If you don't use the `-t` option, Linux tries to figure out the file system type by looking up the file system in `/etc/fstab` and by using the file type specified there. If `fsck` can't find the file type information in `/etc/fstab`, it assumes that you're using a Minix file system. For example, the command

```
fsck -rV /dev/hda1
```

checks the file system on device `/dev/hda1`, provides verbose information, and asks for confirmation before making changes.

Caution

The `fsck` command assumes that the file system you're checking is a Minix file system if you don't tell it differently—either by using the `-t` argument or by listing the type in `/etc/fstab`. Because your Linux file systems are probably of type `ext2` and not Minix, you should be careful and make sure that `fsck` knows the correct type.

> Doing so is especially important if you're checking a file system that isn't listed in the `/etc/fstab` file.

Unmounting a file system before checking it is a good idea. This way, you ensure that none of the files on the file system are in use when they're being checked.

> **Note**
>
> Remember, you can't unmount a file system if any of the files on it are busy. For example, if a user is now in a directory on a file system that you try to unmount, you get a message saying that the file system is busy.

Trying to check the root file system presents an additional problem. You can't directly unmount the root file system because Linux must be able to access it in order to run. To check the root file system, you should boot from a maintenance floppy disk that has a root file system on it; then you can run `fsck` on your real root file system from the floppy by specifying the special device name of your root file system. If `fsck` makes any changes to your file system, it's important that you reboot your system immediately. Rebooting allows Linux to reread important information about your file system and prevents your file system from further corruption.

> **Caution**
>
> To prevent further corruption to your file system, you should be sure to reboot your computer immediately after you run `fsck` if any changes were made to your file system. You can use the `shutdown -r` command now or issue the reboot command at the command line.

Creating and Formatting File Systems

When you add a new hard disk to your computer or want to change the partition information on an old hard disk, you go through the steps of creating a file system from a raw disk. Assuming that you've added a new hard disk to your system, you must set the disk partition information and then create the actual file systems on the disk before Linux can use the disk. To change disk partition information, you use the `fdisk` command. After you partition the hard drive, you need to create the file systems by using the `mkfs` command.

Using `fdisk` to Create Disk Partitions

The `fdisk` command is used to create disk partitions and set the attributes that tell Linux what type of file system is on a particular partition. If you installed Linux from scratch on an

MS-DOS system, you had to run `fdisk` to change the disk partition information before you could install Linux.

Caution

Using `fdisk` on a disk can destroy all data on the disk. Because `fdisk` completely rewrites the file table on the disk, all your former files may be lost. Make sure that you have a complete, current backup of your disks before using `fdisk`.

You should always run the `fdisk` command on an unmounted file system. `fdisk` is an interactive, menu-driven program, not just a single command. To start `fdisk`, type this command:

```
fdisk [drive]
```

`drive` is the physical disk drive that you want to work on. If you don't specify a disk, the disk `/dev/hda` is assumed. For example, to run `fdisk` on the second IDE hard drive in your system, enter the following at the superuser command prompt:

```
fdisk /dev/hdb
```

Because `fdisk` is a menu-driven program, several different commands are available when you're using `fdisk`, as summarized in Table 20.6.

TABLE 20.6 COMMANDS AVAILABLE FROM THE `fdisk` MENU

Command	Description
`a`	Toggles the bootable flag on a partition
`c`	Toggles the DOS compatibility flag on a partition
`d`	Deletes a partition
`l`	Lists partition types known to `fdisk`
`m`	Displays a menu listing of all available commands
`n`	Adds a new partition
`p`	Prints the partition table for the current disk
`q`	Quits without saving any changes
`t`	Changes the file system type for a partition
`u`	Changes display/entry units
`v`	Verifies the partition table
`w`	Writes the table to disk and exits

Table 20.6 Commands Available from the `fdisk` Menu

Command	Description
`x`	Lists additional functions for experts: `b`—Moves the beginning location of data in a partition `c`—Changes the number of cylinders `d`—Prints the raw data in the partition table `e`—Lists extended partitions on disk `h`—Changes the number of heads on disk `r`—Returns to the main menu `s`—Changes the number of sectors on disk

`fdisk` can set the file system type of a disk partition to any of several different types. You should use Linux `fdisk` only to create partitions used under Linux. For MS-DOS or OS/2 partitions, you should use the `fdisk` tool that's native to that operating environment and then use Linux's `fdisk` to tag the partitions as Linux native or Linux swap.

Table 20.7 lists the partitions supported by Linux `fdisk`. Each partition type has an associated hexadecimal code that identifies it. You must enter the appropriate code in `fdisk` when you want to set a partition type.

Table 20.7 Partition Codes and Types in Linux `fdisk`

Hex Code	Partition Type
0	Empty
1	DOS 12-bit FAT
2	XENIX root
3	XENIX usr
4	DOS 16-bit file system, less than 32MB
5	Extended
6	DOS 16-bit file system supporting more than 32MB
7	OS/2 High Performance File System (HPFS)
8	AIX
9	AIX bootable
a	OS/2 Boot Manager
40	Venix 80286
51	Novell?
52	Microport
63	GNU HURD
64	Novell NetWare
65	Novell NetWare
75	PC/IX

TABLE 20.7 PARTITION CODES AND TYPES IN LINUX `fdisk`

Hex Code	Partition Type
80	Old MINIX
81	Linux/MINIX
82	Linux swap, used for swap files under Linux
83	Linux native, common Linux file system type
93	Amoeba
94	Amoeba BBT
a5	BSD/386
b7	BSDI file system
b8	BSDI swap file system
c7	Syrinx
db	CP/M
e1	DOS access
e3	DOS R/O
f2	DOS secondary
ff	BBT

The following sections show how to use `fdisk`. In these sections, you'll see an example of how to use `fdisk` to set up the partitions on a hard disk for use by Linux. Assume that you want to configure the first IDE drive in your system for Linux. Make sure that you have a backup of your data because all data on your hard disk will be destroyed in the process. The name of the first IDE hard disk is `/dev/hda`, which is the default device for Linux.

RUNNING `fdisk`

You run `fdisk` by using this command:

```
# fdisk
```

`fdisk` responds with the following:

```
Using /dev/hda as default device!
Command (m for help):
```

This response tells you that `fdisk` is using disk `/dev/hda` as the device that you're working with. Because this is the result you wanted, you're fine. You should always check to make sure that you're really on the disk that you think you're on. Linux then displays the `fdisk` command prompt.

DISPLAYING THE CURRENT PARTITION TABLE

When you're working with `fdisk`, the first thing you should do is display the current partition table. You do so by entering the `p` command:

```
Command (m for help): p
Disk /dev/hda: 14 heads, 17 sectors, 1024 cylinders
Units = cylinders of 238 * 512 bytes

Device      Boot    Begin    Start    End    Blocks   Id    System

Command (m for help):
```

This listing shows that the current disk, `/dev/hda`, has a geometry of 14 heads, 17 sectors, and 1,024 cylinders. The display units are in cylinders of 238 * 512 (121,856) bytes each. Because the disk has 1,024 cylinders and each cylinder is 121,856 bytes, you can deduce that the disk can hold 1,024 × 121,856 = 124,780,544 bytes, or about 120MB. You can also see that `/dev/hda` has no partitions.

CREATING A NEW PARTITION

Now assume that you want to create a 100MB Linux file partition for user home directories and a 20MB swap partition. Your next step is to use the `n` command to create a new partition:

```
Command (m for help): n
Command action
e extended
p primary partition (1-4)
p
Partition number (1-4): 1
First cylinder (1-1023): 1
Last cylinder or +size or +sizeM or +sizeK (1-1023): + 100M
```

Using the `n` command to create a new partition displays another menu. You must choose whether you want to create an extended partition or a primary partition. You typically should create a primary partition unless you have more than four partitions on a disk. `fdisk` then asks you for the partition number that you want to create. Because this is the first partition on the disk, you answer `1`. You're then prompted for the first cylinder for the partition. This information determines where on the disk the data area starts. Again, because this will be the first partition on the disk, you can start the partition at cylinder 1.

The next line asks you how large you want the partition to be. You have several options as to how to answer this question. `fdisk` accepts either a number, which it interprets as the size in cylinders, or the size in bytes, kilobytes, or megabytes. The size in bytes is specified as `+bytes`, where *`bytes`* is the size of the partition. Similarly, `+sizeK` and `+sizeM` set the partition size to *`size`* kilobytes or *`size`* megabytes, respectively. You know that you want a 100MB partition, so the easiest answer to the prompt is `+100M`.

RECHECKING THE PARTITION TABLE

Now you should check the partition table again to see what `fdisk` has done:

```
Command (m for help): p
Disk /dev/hda: 14 heads, 17 sectors, 1024 cylinders
Units = cylinders of 238 * 512 bytes
```

```
Device       Boot    Begin    Start    End    Blocks   Id    System
/dev/hda1              1        1      861    102400   81    Linux/MINIX
Command (m for help):
```

The partition table shows that you have one partition, `/dev/hda1`, that goes from cylinder 1 to cylinder 861 and uses 102,400 blocks. It's listed as being type 81, Linux/MINIX.

Creating the Swap Partition

Now you need to create the 20MB swap partition by using the remaining disk space. Creating it is just like creating the first partition:

```
Command (m for help): n
Command action
e extended
p primary partition (1-4)
p
Partition number (1-4): 2
First cylinder (862-1023): 862
Last cylinder or +size or +sizeM or +sizeK (862-1023): 1023
```

Tip #122 from *Jack*

It's usually better to go ahead and enter the size of the last partition in cylinders to make sure that you use all the disk space.

Here, you specify partition number 2 for the second partition. When `fdisk` prompts for the first cylinder, notice that it gives a range of 862 to 1023 because the first partition takes up everything before cylinder 862. So you can enter `862` as the starting cylinder for the second partition. In this case, you want to use all the remaining space on the disk for the swap partition. You should have about 20MB left, but if you specify the size in megabytes, the internal `fdisk` calculations could leave you with a couple of unused cylinders. So you can enter `1023` for the last cylinder on the size prompt.

Note

You might see an error similar to

```
Warning: Linux cannot currently use the last xxx sectors of this partition.
```

where *xxx* is some number. You can ignore such an error. It's left over from the days when Linux couldn't access file systems larger than 64MB.

MAKING SURE THE SIZES ARE CORRECT

At this point, you've created both partitions that you wanted to create. You should take a look at the partition table one more time to check that the sizes are correct:

```
Command (m for help): p
Disk /dev/hda: 14 heads, 17 sectors, 1024 cylinders
Units = cylinders of 238 * 512 bytes

Device       Boot      Begin      Start      End      Blocks    Id      System
/dev/hda1                  1          1      861      102400    81      Linux/MINIX
/dev/hda2                862        862      1023      19159    81      Linux/MINIX
Command (m for help):
```

As you can see, /dev/hda1 uses cylinder 1 through cylinder 861 with a size of 102,400 blocks, which is approximately 100MB. Partition /dev/hda2 goes from cylinder 862 to cylinder 1023 with a size of 19,156 blocks, or almost 20MB.

CHANGING THE PARTITION TYPE

Next, you need to change the partition type for each partition. To changethe partition type, you use the t command at the fdisk command prompt. The most common choice for a standard Linux file system partition is to set it to partition type 83, Linux native. Swap partitions should be set to partition type 82, Linux swap, as shown here:

```
Command (m for help): t
Partition number (1-4): 1
Hex code (type L to list codes): 83
Command (m for help): t
Partition number (1-4): 2
Hex code (type L to list codes): 82
```

When you use the t command, you're prompted for the partition number that you want to change. You're then prompted for the hex code for the file system ID that you want to set the partition to. Typically, Linux file systems are set to type 83 for normal file systems and type 82 for swap partitions. You can type l at this point to see a list of file systems if you want.

FINISHING UP

Now that you've created the partitions and labeled them, you should take one last look at the partition table before you exit just to make sure that everything is okay. You do so as follows:

```
Command (m for help): p
Disk /dev/hda: 14 heads, 17 sectors, 1024 cylinders
Units = cylinders of 238 * 512 bytes

Device       Boot      Begin      Start      End      Blocks    Id      System
/dev/hda1                  1          1      861      102400    83      Linux native
/dev/hda2                862        862      1023     19159     82      Linux swap
Command (m for help):
```

As you can see, the partitions are in the right place, they're the right size, and the file system types are set correctly. Finally, you need to use the w command to write the partition table to disk and exit:

```
Command (m for help): w
#
```

None of the changes that you make during an `fdisk` session take effect until you write them to disk by using the `w` command. You can always quit by using the `q` command and not save any changes. This said, you should still always have a backup of any disk that you want to modify with `fdisk`.

After you make changes to a disk with `fdisk`, you should reboot the system just to make sure that Linux has the updated partition information in the kernel.

Using `mkfs` to Build a File System

After you create a file system partition with `fdisk`, you must build a file system on it before you can use it for storing data. You do so by using the `mkfs` command. As an analogy, think of building a parking lot. If you think of `fdisk` as physically building the parking lot, `mkfs` is the part of the process that paints the lines so that the drivers know where to park.

Just like `fsck` is a "front-end" program for checking different types of file systems, `mkfs` actually calls different programs to create the file system, depending on what file system type you want to create. The following is the syntax of the `mkfs` command:

`mkfs [-V] [-t` *`fs-type`*`] [`*`fs-options`*`]` *`filesys`* `[blocks]`

`filesys` is the device of the file system that you want to build, such as `/dev/hda1`.

Caution

The `mkfs` command also accepts the name of a mount point, such as `/home`, as the file system name. You should be extremely careful about using a mount point. If you run `mkfs` on a mounted "live" file system, you might very well corrupt all the data on that file system.

Table 20.8 lists the various command-line parameters that you can specify with `mkfs`.

Table 20.8 Command-Line Parameters for the `mkfs` Command

Option	Description
`-V`	Causes `mkfs` to produce verbose output, including all file system-specific commands that are executed. Specifying this option more than once inhibits execution of any file system-specific commands.
`-t fs-`*`type`*	Specifies the type of file system to be built. If the file system type isn't specified, `mkfs` tries to figure it out by searching for *`filesys`* in `/etc/fstab` and using the corresponding entry. If the type can't be deduced, a Minix file system is created.

TABLE 20.8 COMMAND-LINE PARAMETERS FOR THE mkfs COMMAND

Option	Description
`fs-options`	Specifies file system-specific options that are to be passed to the actual file system-builder program. Although not guaranteed, the following options are supported by most file system builders: `-c`—Checks the device for bad blocks before building the file system `-l file-name` —Reads a list of the bad blocks on the disk from `file-name` `-v`—Tells the actual file system builder program to produce verbose output
`filesys`	Specifies the device on which the file system resides. This parameter is required.
`blocks`	Specifies the number of blocks to be used for the file system.

Although `-t fs-type` is an optional argument, you should get in the habit of specifying the file system type. Just like `fsck`, `mkfs` tries to figure out the type of the file system from the `/etc/fstab` file. If it can't figure out the type, it creates a Minix file system by default. For a normal Linux file system, you probably want an `ext2` partition instead.

PROJECT: USING SWAP FILES AND PARTITIONS

Swap space on your Linux system is used for virtual memory. A complete discussion of all the issues involved with virtual memory is beyond the scope of this book. Any good general computer operating system textbook describes the issue in detail.

Linux supports two types of swap space: swap partition and swap files. A *swap partition* is a physical disk partition with its file system ID set to type 82, Linux swap, and it is dedicated for use as a swap area. A *swap file* is a large file on a normal file system that's used for swap space.

You're better off using a swap partition instead of a swap file. All access to a swap file is performed through the normal Linux file system. The disk blocks that make up the swap file are probably not contiguous; therefore, performance isn't as good as it is with a swap partition. I/O to swap partitions is performed directly to the device, and disk blocks on a swap partition are always contiguous. Also, by keeping the swap space off a normal file system, you reduce the risk of corrupting your regular file system if something bizarre happens to your swap file.

CREATING A SWAP PARTITION

To create a swap partition, you must first create a disk partition by using `fdisk` and tag it as type 82, Linux swap. After you create the swap partition, you have two additional steps to follow to make the swap partition active.

For the first step, you must prepare the partition in a manner similar to creating a file system. Instead of `mkfs`, the command you use to prepare the partition is `mkswap`. The syntax of the `mkswap` command is as follows:

```
mkswap [-c] devicesize_in_blocks
```

device is the name of the swap partition, such as /dev/hda2, and *size_in_blocks* is the size of the target file system in blocks. You can get the size in blocks by running fdisk and looking at the partition table. In the example in the section "Making Sure the Sizes Are Correct," the size of /dev/hda2 was 19,159 blocks. Linux requires that swap partitions be between 9 and 65,537 blocks in size. The -c argument tells mkswap to check the file system for bad blocks when creating the swap space, which is a good idea.

Following the example in "Making Sure the Sizes Are Correct," the command for setting up a swap partition on /dev/hda2 is as follows:

```
mkswap -c /dev/hda2 19159
```

After you run mkswap to prepare the partition, you must make it active so that the Linux kernel can use it. The command to make the swap partition active for this second step is swapon. The syntax for the swapon command is as follows:

```
swapon filesys
```

filesys is the file system that you want to make available as swap space. Linux makes a call to swapon -a during boot, which mounts all available swap partitions listed in the /etc/fstab file.

Note **Remember to put an entry for any swap partitions or swap files that you create into the /etc/fstab file so that Linux can automatically access them at boot time.**

CREATING A SWAP FILE

Swap files can be useful if you need to expand your swap space and can't allocate disk space to create a dedicated swap partition. Setting up a swap file is almost identical to creating a swap partition. The main difference is that you have to create the file before you can run mkswap and swapon.

To create a swap file, you use the dd command, which is used for copying large chunks of data. For a full description of this command, see the man page for dd. The main pieces of information that you have to know before creating the file are the name of the swap file you want to create and its size in blocks. A block under Linux is 1,024 bytes. For example, to create a 10MB swap file named /swap, enter the following:

```
# dd if=/dev/zero of=/swap bs=1024 count=10240
```

of=/swap specifies that the file to be created is named /swap, and count=10240 sets the size of the output file to be 10,240 blocks, or 10MB. You then can use mkswap to prepare the file as a swap space:

```
# mkswap /swap 10240
```

Remember that you have to tell mkswap how big the file is. Before you run swapon, you need to make sure that the file is completely written to disk by using the /etc/sync command.

Now you're ready to make the swap file active. As you do with the swap partition, you use the `swapon` command to make the file active, as shown in this example:

```
# swapon /swap
```

If you need to get rid of a swap file, you must make sure that it's not active. You use the `swapoff` command to deactivate the swap file, as in the following:

```
# swapoff /swap
```

You can then safely delete the swap file.

CHAPTER 21

Managing NFS

In this chapter

by Jack Tackett, Jr.

UNDERSTANDING THE NETWORK FILE SYSTEM

The Network File System (NFS) is a system that allows you to mount file systems from a different computer over a TCP/IP network. Using NFS, you can share data among PC, Mac, UNIX, and Linux systems. Under NFS, a file system on a remote computer is mounted locally and looks just like a local file system to users. The illusion of being mounted locally has numerous uses. For example, you can have one machine on your network with a lot of disk space acting as a file server. This computer has all the home directories of all your users on its local disks. If you mount these disks via NFS on all your other computers, your users can access their home directories from any computer.

Sun developed NFS during the 1980s and released the protocol to the Unix community as described in RFC1094 (RFC stands for Request For Comment). Since no single authority created the Internet, most of its development grew from these RFCs. The Web site `www.faqs.org` provides a plethora of information on RFCs and specifically on the one describing NFS. See the following URL for more information:

`http://www.faqs.org/rfcs/rfc1094.html`

Like HTTP, NFS is a stateless protocol, thus each transaction is complete in and of itself. NFS has three essential components:

- The computers with the file systems that you want to mount remotely via NFS must be able to communicate with each other via a TCP/IP network.
- The computer with the file system that you're interested in as a local file system must make that file system available to be mounted. This computer is known as the *server*, and the process of making the file system available is known as *exporting the file system*.
- The computer that wants to mount the exported file system, known as the *client*, must mount the file system as an NFS file system via the `/etc/fstab` file at boot time or interactively via the `mount` command.

→ See "Mounting File Systems at Boot Time," p. 446

NFS under Linux is not as robust as NFS on other systems. For light to moderate usage, such as serving up email for 500-1000 users from an NFS mounted file system, you should be OK. But for larger operations you may find problems using the file system via NFS. Developers, including Alan Cox and Olaf Kirch, are working to improve NFS performance under Linux.

INSTALLING NFS

Most distributions, including Red Hat, Caldera, and Debian, automatically install the necessary files needed to run NFS, but you should know the files and their functions, as listed in Table 21.1, in order to help troubleshoot problems.

TABLE 21.1 NFS COMPONENTS

Component	Description
`rpc.portmaster`	Routes remote procedure calls (RPC) to the appropriate daemons—`nfsd` for NFS services.
`rpc.statd`	Kernel statistics daemon
`rpc.rquotad`	Remote quota server daemon
`rpc.nfsd`	Provides access to the local file system in response to remote procedures calls for NFS requests.
`rpc.mountd`	The daemon mounts and unmounts file systems.
`mount`	Local command that mounts file systems to local directories. One uses this command to mount a remote file system via NFS.
`umount`	Unmounts local file systems thus making them unavailable to remote hosts.
`/etc/exports`	This config file specifies which local file systems are available to remote systems via NFS.
`/var/lock/subsys/nfs`	Lock file used to prevent running multiple copies of NFS programs.

Use the `pmap_dump` command to check the status of your system's RPC daemons. The command displays all the registered RPC programs currently running on your system, like so:

```
[root@web /root]# /usr/sbin/pmap_dump
    100000    2    tcp    111    rpcbind
    100000    2    udp    111    rpcbind
    100024    1    udp    1017   status
    100024    1    tcp    1019   status
    100011    1    udp    604    rquotad
    100011    2    udp    604    rquotad
    100005    1    udp    614    mountd
    100005    1    tcp    616    mountd
    100005    2    udp    619    mountd
    100005    2    tcp    621    mountd
    100005    3    udp    624    mountd
    100005    3    tcp    626    mountd
    100003    2    udp    2049   nfs
    100021    1    udp    1026   nlockmgr
    100021    3    udp    1026   nlockmgr
    100021    1    tcp    1024   nlockmgr
    100021    3    tcp    1024   nlockmgr
```

The NFS programs should startup automatically at boot time, but should you need to start, stop, query, or restart them you can use the script located in `/etc/rc.d/init.d` called `nfs` as shown in Listing 21.1.

LISTING 21.1 nfs init **SCRIPT**

```
#!/bin/sh
#
#nfs              This shell script takes care of starting and stopping
#                 the NFS services.
#
# chkconfig: 345 60 20
# description: NFS is a popular protocol for file sharing across TCP/IP \
#              networks. This service provides NFS server functionality, \
#              which is configured via the /etc/exports file.
# probe: true
# Source function library.
. /etc/rc.d/init.d/functions
# Source networking configuration.
if [ ! -f /etc/sysconfig/network ]; then
    exit 0
fi
. /etc/sysconfig/network
# Check that networking is up.
[ ${NETWORKING} = ''no'' ] && exit 0
[ -x /usr/sbin/rpc.nfsd ] ¦¦ exit 0
[ -x /usr/sbin/rpc.mountd ] ¦¦ exit 0
[ -x /usr/sbin/exportfs ] ¦¦ exit 0
[ -f /etc/exports ] ¦¦ exit 0

# Number of servers to be started uo by default
RPCNFSDCOUNT=8
# See how we were called.
case ''$1'' in
  start)
        # Start daemons.
        action ''Starting NFS services: '' /usr/sbin/exportfs -r
        echo -n ''Starting NFS statd: ''
        daemon rpc.statd
        echo
        echo -n ''Starting NFS quotas: ''
        daemon rpc.rquotad
        echo
        echo -n ''Starting NFS mountd: ''
        daemon rpc.mountd
        echo
        echo -n ''Starting NFS daemon: ''
        daemon rpc.nfsd $RPCNFSDCOUNT
        echo
        touch /var/lock/subsys/nfs
        ;;
  stop)
        # Stop daemons.
        action ''Shutting down NFS services: '' /usr/sbin/exportfs -au
        echo -n ''Shutting down NFS mountd: ''
        killproc rpc.mountd
        echo
        echo -n ''Shutting down NFS daemon: ''
        killproc nfsd
        echo
        echo -n ''Shutting down NFS quotas: ''
```

LISTING 21.1 CONTINUED

```
        killproc rpc.rquotad
        echo
        echo -n ''Shutting down NFS statd: ''
        killproc rpc.statd
        echo
        rm -f /var/lock/subsys/nfs
        ;;
  status)
        status rpc.statd
        status rpc.mountd
        status nfsd
        status rpc.rquotad
        ;;
  restart)
        echo -n ''Restarting NFS services: ''
        echo -n ''rpc.statd ''
        killall -HUP rpc.statd
        echo -n ''nfsd ''
        killall -HUP nfsd
        echo -n ''rpc.mountd ''
        killall -HUP rpc.mountd
        echo -n ''rpc.quotad ''
        killall -HUP rpc.rquotad
        touch /var/lock/subsys/nfs
        echo ''done.''
        ;;
  reload)
        /usr/sbin/exportfs
        touch /var/lock/subsys/nfs
        ;;
  probe)
        if [ ! -f /var/lock/subsys/nfs ] ; then
          echo start; exit 0
        fi
        /sbin/pidof rpc.mountd >/dev/null 2>&1; MOUNTD="$?''
/sbin/pidof nfsd >/dev/null 2>&1; NFSD="$?''
        if [ $MOUNTD = 1 -o $NFSD = 1 ] ; then
          echo restart; exit 0
        fi
        if [ /etc/exports -nt /var/lock/subsys/nfs ] ; then
          echo reload; exit 0
        fi
        ;;
  *)
        echo ''Usage: nfs {start¦stop¦status¦restart¦reload}''
        exit 1
esac
exit 0
```

Table 21.2 provides a listing of all the commands you can pass to the `nfs` script.

TABLE 21.2 nfs SCRIPT COMMANDS

Command	Description
`Start`	Starts all the daemons and creates the lock file.
`Stop`	Stops the daemons and removes the lock file.

`Status`	Indicates the current status of each NFS program, as shown here:
	`[root@web /root]# /etc/rc.d/init.d/nfs status`
	`rpc.statd (pid 416) is running...`
	`rpc.mountd (pid 438) is running...`
	`nfsd (pid 460 459 458 457 456 455 454 453) is running...`
	`rpc.rquotad (pid 427) is running...`

`restart`	Stops and then starts the programs.
`Reload`	Reloads the available NFS file system from `/etc/exports`.

EXPORTING AN NFS FILE SYSTEM

For clients to mount an NFS file system, this file system must be made available by the server. Before the file system can be made available, you must ensure that it's mounted on the server. If the file system is always going to an NFS exported file system, you should make sure that you have it listed in the `/etc/fstab` file on the server so that it automatically mounts when the server boots.

When you have the file system mounted locally, you can make it available via NFS. This process involves two steps. First, you must make sure that the NFS daemons `rpc.mountd`and `rpc.nfsd`are running on your server. These daemons are usually started from the startup `/etc/rc.d/init.d/nfs` script. Usually, all you need to do is make sure that the following lines are in your script:

```
daemon rpc.mountd
daemon rpc.nfsd
```

Note

As RPC-based programs, the `rpc.mountd` and `rpc.nfsd` daemons aren't managed by the `inetd` daemon but are started up at boot time, registering themselves with the `portmap` daemon. You must be sure to start them only after `rpc.portmap` is running.

Second, you must enter the NFS file system in a configuration file named `/etc/exports`. This file contains information about what file systems can be exported, what computers are allowed to access them, and what type and level of access are permitted.

UNDERSTANDING THE /etc/exports FILE

The /etc/exports file is used by the mountd and nfsd daemons to determine what file systems are to be exported and what restrictions are placed on them. File systems are listed in /etc/exports, one per line. The format of each line is the name of the mount point for a local file system, followed by a list of computers that are allowed to mount this file system. A comma-separated list of mount options in parentheses may follow each name in the list. Table 21.3 lists the mount options available in the /etc/exports file.

TABLE 21.3 MOUNT OPTIONS AVAILABLE IN THE /etc/exports FILE

Option	Description
insecure	Permits nonauthenticated access from this machine.
secure	Requires secure RPC authentication from this machine.
root_squash	Maps any requests from root, UID 0 on the client, to the UID NOBODY_UID on the server.
no_root_squash	Doesn't map any requests from UID 0 (default behavior).
ro	Mounts the file system as read-only (default behavior).
rw	Mounts the file system as read-write.
link_relative	Converts absolute symbolic links (where the link contents start with a slash) into relative links by prefixing the link with the necessary number of ../ characters to get from the directory containing the link to the root on the server.
link_absolute	Leaves all symbolic links as they are (normal behavior for Sun NFS servers). This is the default behavior for Linux.
map_daemon	Maps local and remote names and numeric IDs by using an lname/uid map daemon on the client where the NFS request originated. This option is used to map between the client and server UID spaces.
all-squash	Maps all UIDs and GIDs to the anonymous user. This option is useful for NFS-exported public directories, such as those housing FTP and news.
no-all-squash	Acts the opposite of the all-squash option. This is the default option for Linux.
squash-uids	Specifies a list of UIDs subject to anonymous mappings. A valid list of IDs looks like this: squash uids=0-15,20,25-50.

TABLE 21.3 MOUNT OPTIONS AVAILABLE IN THE /etc/exports FILE

Option	Description
squash-gids	Specifies a list of GIDs subject to anonymous mappings. A valid list of IDs looks like this: squash gids=0-15,20,25-50.
anonuid	Sets the UID for the anonymous account. This option is useful for PC/NFS clients.
anongid	Sets the GID for the anonymous account. This option is useful for PC/NFS clients.
noaccess	Excludes certain subdirectories from a client. This option makes everything below the directory inaccessible to the client.

The following is a sample /etc/exports file:

```
/home                bill.tristar.com(rw) fred.tristar.com(rw)
george.tristar.com(rw)
/usr/local/bin/bin           *.tristar.com(ro)
/projects            develop.tristar.com(rw) bill.tristar.com(ro)
/pub                 (ro,insecure,root_squash)
```

In this example, the server exports four different file systems. /home is mounted with read/write access on three different computers: bill, fred, and george. This information indicates that the directory probably holds user home directories because of the directories' names. The /usr/local/bin file system is exported as read-only with access allowed for every computer in the tristar.com domain.

→ See "File Permissions," p. 414

Tip #123 from *Jack*

> The command ls -l displays the read/write permissions of files in the current directory. To change permissions, use the chmod command.

The /projects file system is exported with read/write access for the computer develop.tristar.com but with read-only access for bill.tristar.com.

The /pub file system doesn't have a list of hosts that are allowed access. This means that any host is allowed to mount this file system. It has been exported as read-only with nonauthenticated access allowed, and the server remaps any request from root on a remote machine that accesses this file system.

Mounting NFS File Systems

Mounting an NFS file system is similar to mounting any other type of file system. You can mount NFS file systems from the `/etc/fstab` file at boot time or interactively via the `mount` command.

Caution

You must be sure to separate the host name and `file/system/path` portions of the remote file system name with a colon, such as

```
mailserver:/var/spool/mail
```

when you use the `mount` command or when you make an entry in `/etc/fstab`. If you don't separate the host name from the directory, your system won't mount the remote directory correctly.

Mounting NFS File Systems via /etc/fstab

When you specify an NFS file system in the `/etc/fstab` file, you identify the file system with the following format:

`hostname:/file/system/path`

`hostname` is the name of the server where the file system is located, and *`/file/system/path`* is the file system on the server.

The file-system type is specified as `nfs` in the mount options field of the file system entry. Table 21.4 lists the most commonly used mount options.

Table 21.4 Commonly Used Options for NFS Mounts

Option	Description
`rsize=n`	Specifies the datagram size in bytes used by the NFS clients on read requests. The default value is 1,024 bytes.
`wsize=n`	Specifies the datagram size in bytes used by the NFS clients on write requests. The default value is 1,024 bytes.
`timeo=n`	Sets the time, in tenths of a second, that the NFS client waits for a request to complete. The default value is 0.7 seconds.
`hard`	Mounts this file system by using a hard mount. This is the default behavior.
`soft`	Mounts this file system by using a soft mount.
`intr`	Allows signals to interrupt an NFS call. This option is useful for aborting an operation when an NFS server doesn't respond.

Hard Mounts Versus Soft Mounts

Hard mounts and *soft mounts* determine how an NFS client behaves when an NFS server stops responding. NFS file systems are hard-mounted by default. With either type of mount, if a server stops responding, the client waits until the timeout value specified by the `timeo` option expires and then resends the request (this is known as a *minor timeout*). If the requests to the server continue to time out and the total timeout reaches 60 seconds, a*major timeout* occurs.

If a file system is hard-mounted, the client prints a message to the console and starts the mount requests all over again by using a timeout value that's twice that of the previous cycle. This process has the potential to go on forever. The client keeps trying to remount the NFS file system from the server until the file mount succeeds.

Soft mounts, on the other hand, just generate an I/O error to the calling process when a major timeout occurs. Linux then continues on its merry way.

Typically, important software packages and utilities that are mounted via NFS should be mounted with hard mounts. This is why hard mounts are the default. You don't want your system to start acting strange if the Ethernet gets unplugged for a moment; you want Linux to wait and continue when the network is back up. On the other hand, you might want to mount noncritical data, such as remote news spool partitions, as soft mounts so that if the remote host goes down, it won't hang your current login session.

A typical NFS file system entry in the `/etc/fstab` file might look like this:

```
mailserver:/var/spool/mail /var/spool/mail nfs timeo=20,intr
```

This entry mounts the `/var/spool/mail` file system located on the host `mailserver` at the local mount point `/var/spool/mail`. It specifies that the file system type is `nfs`. Also, it sets the timeout value to 2 seconds (20 tenths of a second) and makes operations on this file system interruptible.

MOUNTING NFS FILE SYSTEMS INTERACTIVELY

NFS file systems can be mounted interactively, just like any other type of file system. However, you should be aware that the NFS `mount` command isn't very pretty due to all the options that you can specify on the command line.

By using the previous example, the interactive `mount` command that you use to mount the `/var/spool/mail` file system becomes the following:

```
# mount -t nfs -o timeo=20,intr mailserver:/var/spool/mail /var/spool/mail
```

If you need to specify datagram sizes and timeouts, interactive `mount` commands can become very complex. Placing these `mount` commands in your `/etc/fstab` file is highly recommended so that they can be mounted automatically at boot time.

TROUBLESHOOTING

How do I determine what directories are currently `nfs` *mounted?*

You can use the mount command to display all disk information and look for `nfs`-mounted file systems. You can also use the `df -t nfs` command to see `nfs`-mounted file systems and information on disk space consumed by each system. The showmount -a command displays information in hostname:directory pairs while showmount -d displays just the directories.

I cannot mount my directory.

There are several items to remember when mounting any file system. First, make sure the mount point exists (for example, use the `ls` command to check the directory). Next, make sure that you and no one else is currently logged into that directory. Make sure you have the necessary permissions to mount a directory. Finally, make sure the remote host is accessible across the network.

My system stops responding anytime I try to cd to an `nfs`*-mounted directory.*

Make sure there are no network problems. Ping the remote host to make sure the host is available. If not, begin troubleshooting the network. The `traceroute`, `netstat`, and `ipconfig` commands are all useful tools to use in checking your network connections. While there are problems accessing the remote host, you should `unmount` the file system to prevent the hangups. Use `umount` ***`filesystem`*** to `unmount` the offending system.

I'm having network problems accessing my `nfs` *systems.*

First, use the ping command to make sure the remote host is accessible— `ping` *host*. If you can not ping the host, then use the `traceroute` command to find out where in the network the connection is down, as in the following example:

```
[root@ns /root]# /usr/sbin/traceroute www.yahoo.com
traceroute to www.yahoo.com (204.71.200.68), 30 hops max, 40 byte packets
1 gateway (209.42.203.225) 3.688 ms 3.242 ms 3.062 ms
2 max4000-1.rtp.intrex.net (209.42.192.1) 35.924 ms 36.155 ms 34.144 ms
3 209.42.192.30 (209.42.192.30) 34.459 ms 37.508 ms 35.809 ms
4 rtp-rtr1-e1.intrex.net (209.42.255.33) 37.974 ms 35.533 ms 35.959 ms
5 * * *
6 * * *
```

The `* * *` indicates a break in the network, and the last location, #4, indicates the last host reachable and where you should concentrate your troubleshooting. If this host is outside your control, you need the help of your network administrator to proceed.

CHAPTER 22

MANAGING NIS AND LDAP

In this chapter

by Steve Burnett

What Is NIS?

The *Network Information Service* (*NIS*) is a tool used to distribute a set of configuration files common to a set of UNIX machines. NIS was originally named the Yellow Pages (YP) but had to change because of copyright issues. You can still see the original name in the command names, most of which begin with *yp*.

NIS is a distributed database system that aids the system administrator in sharing password files, group files, host tables, and other files between networked systems. NIS can simplify the management of a network because all the desired account and configuration information is stored on a single computer, referred to as the *NIS master server*. NIS is included with many flavors of UNIX.

A set of shared NIS database files is called a *map;* hosts that belong to the same NIS domain share the same set of maps. NIS *slave servers*, which receive updated versions of the maps from the NIS master server, are used to provide information when the NIS master server is down and to spread the load of requests more evenly if necessary.

NIS Members

A system can fit into an NIS system in one of three ways:

- As a client
- As a slave server
- As a master server

A server hosts an NIS map from which clients get their information. A server can be a slave server that gets its NIS map from a master server or a master server that is the actual resource for the distributed files. A master server is the top of the tree for a given NIS domain. A slave server has a complete copy of all NIS maps created on a master server; when the master server's maps are updated, the new maps are pushed out to the slave server.

Finally, either a slave or master server can also be an NIS client; this is the common configuration. Otherwise, you would have to maintain the given server's configuration separate from the NIS map.

Clients can contact a master server directly or be configured to request from a slave server to spread out the load. Clients are therefore configured to work on a pull model, rather than a push model, characterizing the master-to-slave server relationship.

NIS Files, Maps, and Domains

NIS uses three major objects to distribute information. Data is taken from files in the Linux or other UNIX system and is compiled into maps. These maps are distributed from master server to clients and slave servers, and from slave servers to other clients, according to the domain a system is a member of. This section explains in more detail which system configuration files (and which information from those files) is commonly compiled into maps, and how domains are used to define the map distribution.

NIS Files and Maps

These files are identified, determined, and copied from master server to slave server to client by the use of NIS maps. The maps for each domain are located in a separate `/var/yp/domainname` directory on the NIS server. For example, the maps for a machine that belong to the domain `marketing` are located in the directory `/var/yp/marketing` on the corresponding NIS server.

Running `ypbuild` in the directory `/var/yp` of a master server calls the `makedbm` command to compile the default NIS maps from the input files.

Note

Never make the maps on a slave server; they will be overwritten as soon as the slave server pulls the map from the master server again.

NIS maps are in a non-ASCII format, unlike the majority of the source files such as `/etc/hosts` and `/etc/passwd`.

Table 22.1 lists the commonly created NIS maps, their source material in the directory structure, and the contents of the map.

Table 22.1 A Summary of NIS Maps

Map Name	NIS Filename	Description
`bootparams`	`/etc/bootparams`	Contains pathnames of files that clients need during booting, such as `root`, `swap`, and others. `/etc/bootparams` is never consulted after the map is created.
`ethers.byaddr`	`/etc/ethers`	Contains machine names and Ethernet addresses. The Ethernet address is the key in the map. `/etc/ethers` is never consulted after the map is created.
`ethers.byname`	`/etc/ethers`	Same as `ethers.byaddr`, except the key is the machine name instead of the Ethernet address. Again, `/etc/ethers` is never consulted after the map is created.
`group.byid`	`/etc/group`	Contains group security information with the group ID as the key. With NIS, the local `/etc/group` is consulted first and then the map.

TABLE 22.1 A SUMMARY OF NIS MAPS

Map Name	NIS Filename	Description
`group.byname`	`/etc/group`	Contains group security information, with the group name used as the key. If NIS is active on a system, the local `/etc/group` is consulted first and then the map.
`hosts.byaddr`	`/etc/hosts`	Contains host names and IP addresses. The IP address is the key used in the map. The source for host information is determined by the entries in the `/etc/netconfig` file.
`hosts.byname`	`/etc/hosts`	Same as `hosts.byaddr`, except the key used in this table is the host name instead of the IP address.
`mail.aliases`	`/etc/aliases`	Contains aliases and mail addresses. The alias is the key in the map. As with host inquiries, the local file `/etc/aliases` is consulted first and then the NIS map.
`mail.byaddr`	`/etc/aliases`	Same as `mail.aliases`, except the key used in the map is the mail address instead of the alias.
`netgroup.byhost`	`/etc/netgroup`	Contains the group name, username, and host name. The host name is the key in the map. The NIS map overrides the base file. After the NIS map is created, `/etc/netgroup` is never consulted.
`netgroup.byuser`	`/etc/netgroup`	Contains the same information as `netgroup.byhost`, except the key used is the username instead of the host name.
`netgroup`	`/etc/netgroup`	Contains the same information as `netgroup.byhost`, except the key used is the group name instead of the host name.
`netid.byname0`	`/etc/passwd, /etc/hosts, /etc/group`	Contains the machine name and mail address (including domain name). If a `netid` file is available, it is consulted in addition to the data available through the other files.

Table 22.1 A Summary of NIS Maps

Map Name	NIS Filename	Description
`netmasks.byaddr`	`/etc/netmasks`	Contains network masks to be used with IP subnetting. The network mask is the key in the map. The NIS map overrides the base file. After the NIS map is created, `/etc/netmasks` is never consulted.
`networks.byaddr`	`/etc/networks`	Contains names of networks known to your system and their IP addresses. The network address is the key in the map. After the NIS map is created, `/etc/networks` is never consulted.
`networks.byname`	`/etc/networks`	Contains the same information as `networks.byaddr`, except the key used is the network name instead of the network address.
`passwd.byname`	`/etc/passwd`	Contains password information. The user name is the key in the map. The local `/etc/passwd` is consulted first and then the map.
`passwd.byuid`	`/etc/passwd`	Contains the same information as `networks.byaddr`, except the key used is the user ID instead of the username.
`protocols.byname`	`/etc/protocols`	Contains network protocols known to your system. The protocol name is the key used in the NIS map. After the NIS map is created, `/etc/protocols` is never consulted.
`protocols.bynumber`	`/etc/protocols`	Contains the same information as `protocols.byname`, except the key used is the protocol number instead of the protocol name.
`publickey.byname`	`/etc/publickey`	Contains public and secret keys. Use of the NIS `publickey` map permits running secure RPC (Remote Procedure Call) across the network of machines. After the NIS map is created, `/etc/publickey` is never consulted.
`rpc.bynumber`	`/etc/rpc`	Contains the program number and the names of RPCs known to your system. The RPC program number is the key used in the map. After the NIS map is created, `/etc/rpc` is never consulted.

Table 22.1 A Summary of NIS Maps

Map Name	NIS Filename	Description
`services.byname`	`/etc/services`	Lists Internet services known to your network. The service name is the key in the map. After the NIS map is created, `/etc/services` is never consulted.
`ypservers`	An NIS-created file	Lists NIS servers known to your network.

NIS is configurable to distribute any or all of the files shown in Table 22.1 as NIS maps, as well as any others you might want.

So now you know about master servers, slave servers, and clients and files chosen on a master server by a map. What are your teams? How do you identify which clients receive the map of files from which servers? You do so by using domains.

NIS Domains

In this book, the word *domain* is used fairly often, and not as interchangeably as it might first appear because *domain* can be used in two different areas of UNIX systems management:

- **DNS (Domain Name Services)**—A DNS domain is defined as a logical entity or organization that represents a part of a network identifiable by DNS. A DNS domain is often referred to by the registered portion of the DNS name; for example, `redhat.com` is a domain.
- **NIS (Network Information Services)**—An NIS domain is a group of systems that use the same set of NIS maps and therefore use the same defined configurations. For example, every system that is a member of an NIS domain likely shares the same defined user and password lists, issued on request from that system by the NIS master server.

The term *domain* can also refer to a group of Microsoft Windows computers, but defining a Windows domain is well outside the scope of this book. If you're dealing with Microsoft products or documentation, you might want to keep in mind that the term *domain* may not mean what you think it means at first glance.

In summary, NIS is a tool: It saves you time by copying configuration files to other UNIX systems. This capability is great—if you have the setup correct the first time. If your master files are sloppy, all your systems will have the same sloppy, incorrect, or possibly dangerous information. Before you configure NIS on the first system as a master server, you should spend some extra time checking the accuracy of your initial files.

Note

NIS domains are standalone and do not communicate with each other. Each master server is a separate entity unto itself. If you have several NIS domains, you have to administer and make changes to each one separately.

→ See "Removing a User," p. 253

NIS Security Concerns

Although NIS simplifies the task of system administration, it also presents numerous security problems when it is not correctly configured. For example, any user can obtain copies of the databases exported by an NIS server. As a result, a malicious user might acquire a copy of the distributed password file, as well as all the other information contained in the NIS database. Another security concern includes NIS having no provisions for safeguarding against spoofing of network addresses. For this and other reasons, the acronym *NIS* is sometimes referred to as meaning *Network Intruder Service*. NIS's successor NIS+ addresses some of these security concerns and is also more scalable, but it is not a perfect replacement.

LDAP: What Is It, and Why Is It Better Than NIS?

NIS is an older directory service and is really useful only if every system is a UNIX-based machine. However, it's not scalable, and it also has security concerns, as presented in the preceding section.

Another attempt to define a hierarchical and global directory service was the X.500 protocol. The X.500 protocol defined a Directory Information Tree (DIT), with each entry in an X.500 DIT made up of a collection of attributes. In a manner like the mail message header definitions given in RFC 822, each attribute is defined as a two-part item containing a type element and a corresponding value attribute element.

The X.500 standard defines several object classes for directories and supports the capacity for locally defined extensions to the system. The basic object classes include various categories, including name, alias, country, locality, and organization. An object is defined by its attributes. Approximately 40 basic attribute types are in use, such as Common Name (CN), Organization Name (ON), Street Address (SA), and Country . X.500 defined a Directory Access Protocol (DAP) as the way to access the information in the databases.

However, although the X.500 protocol was powerful, it was also unwieldy and difficult to configure, administer, and maintain. Enter the LDAP as a less cumbersome and easier way to work with X.500 directories.

The *Lightweight Directory Access Protocol* (*LDAP*) is an open-standard protocol for accessing information and directory services. The protocol runs over Internet transport protocols, such as TCP, and can be used to access either standalone directory servers or X.500 directories.

The full definition of LDAP is in the RFC at `http://www.umich.edu/~dirsvcs/ldap/doc/rfc/rfc1777.txt`.

You can find some Internet-based LDAP directories, such as `Bigfoot.com` and `411.com`. Also, if you use Microsoft's Outlook, Microsoft has released an update that allows the application to use LDAP directories. For more information, look at `http://officeupdate.microsoft.com/downloadDetails/o98ldap.htm`.

PROJECT: INSTALLING AN LDAP SERVER

This project presents the basic steps of how to download, install, and configure an LDAP server on your Linux system, and also how to configure a common mail client (included with Netscape) to query your LDAP server. This is only an introduction and will not address issues such as location of the LDAP server on your network, or what the design of the LDAP database should be.

DOWNLOADING AND INSTALLING OPENLDAP

To begin this project, download the latest copy of the LDAP software from OpenLDAP's Web site at `http://www.openldap.org/`. OpenLDAP is based on the University of Michigan's LDAP 3.3 release, providing compatibility with applications written to use the university's software.

Note

As of this writing, the version is 1.2.6, but new versions may be available by the time you read this chapter. You should look at the `INSTALL` file for the current release for any changes.

Before you compile the software, you must first set a few configuration options.

LDAP is similar in architecture to DNS. You start at the very top and then work your way down to countries, followed by organizations. Your LDAP server starts its hierarchy tree at a base DN. The base DN is usually a combination of the organization name and the ISO name of the country; it is defined by prefacing the organization with `o=` and the country with `c=`, separating the pair with a comma (,). Thus, you could have base DNs of `o=Boston, c=US` or `o=Marketing Group, c=FI`. No central organization or registry is responsible for assigning base DNs, so you can make up a base DN for yourself.

After you have defined the base DN, it's time to compile OpenLDAP. For the more recent versions of OpenLDAP, you can use a configure script instead of having to directly edit makefiles. Before you start, read the install notes; OpenLDAP includes some nice optional features such as cryptographic support.

To start the process, enter the following at the command line:

```
./configure
```

By default, the installation puts the following kinds of files in the following directories:

- the daemons are placed in `/usr/local/libexec/`
- a sample client is placed in `/usr/local/bin`
- programs to convert source files to LDAP format are placed in `/usr/local/sbin/`
- configuration files are placed in `/usr/local/etc/ldap`

Next, you need to edit the `/usr/local/etc/openldap/slapd.conf` file to configure the base DN that you created earlier. The `slapd.conf` file has better comments than the average system or service configuration file, so search in the file for the line that begins with *suffix*, and edit it appropriately.

Populating the Database

After you've installed LDAP, it needs data in its database with which to respond to queries. For this example, you can just move the `/etc/passwd` file.

Go to the Web site `http://www.padl.com/tools.html` and download the LDAP migration tools. Configure the tools for your particular setup according to the guidelines in the `README` file. Then enter the following command:

```
./migrate_passwd.pl /etc/passwd ./passwd.ldif
```

This command creates a `passwd.ldif` file that should have a set of entries that look like this:

```
dn: cn=Dave Ross,ou=marketing,dc=afakecompany,dc=com
cn: Dave Ross
objectclass: top
objectclass: person
objectclass: organizationalPerson
objectclass: inetOrgPerson
objectclass: posixAccount
objectclass: account
mail: dross@afakecompany.com
givenname: David
sn: Ross
uid: dross
userPassword: {crypt}FGgkUelSHwaaI
loginShell: /bin/tcsh
uidNumber: 31
gidNumber: 2031
homeDirectory: /home/dross
```

Each entry in the file starts with a unique DN. You might not need all the categories, so you can add and delete categories in your LDAP database as you like.

Before creating the database, you need to add a header to tell `slapd` (the LDAP daemon) what the base DN is.

At the head of the file, put in something like the following:

```
dn: o=A Fake Company, c=US
o: A Fake Company
objectclass: company
```

To create the database, issue the following command at the command line:

```
/usr/local/sbin/ldif2ldbm -i passwd.ldif
```

Now that the database is populated, start the server with the following command and let it run:

```
/usr/local/libexec/slapd
```

For a simple test of the database, issue this command to see all the entries present:

```
/usr/local/bin/ldapsearch 'objectclass=*'
```

CONFIGURING A CLIENT

So you have the data in there. Now what? It's time to configure a client to use your new LDAP database.

Using Netscape 4.6 on Linux, open the Address Book. By default, you should see a local Address Book and three remote ones (Netcenter, InfoSpace, and Verisign). Right-click the Netcenter icon and select the New Directory command from the pop-up menu. A dialog box appears, prompting you to enter the following:

- A directory name (you can call it whatever you like)
- The host name of the LDAP server
- The base DN

Leave the check boxes unchecked for now and close the dialog box. That's all.

CHAPTER 23

Using Samba

In this chapter

by *Jack Tackett, Jr.*

WHAT IS SAMBA?

This chapter gives you the information you need to install, configure, and use the Session Message Block (SMB or Samba) protocol services under Linux. With Samba, you can do the following:

- Share a Linux file system with Windows 95, 98, or NT
- Share a Windows 95, 98, or NT file system with Linux
- Share a printer connected to a Linux system with Windows 95, 98, or NT systems
- Share a Windows 95, 98, or NT printer with Linux

Samba is the client/server protocol used by Microsoft's operating systems to share files and printer services. Microsoft and Intel developed the SMB protocol system in 1987, and later Andrew Tridgell ported the system to various UNIX systems and then Linux.

Note

For a quick introduction to Samba see

`http://us1.samba.org/samba/docs/SambaIntro.html`

The Samba suite is made up of several components. All the components are controlled via one configuration file called `smb.conf`. The `smbd` daemon provides the file and print services to SMB clients, such as Windows for Workgroups, Windows NT, or LanManager. The configuration file for this daemon is described in `smb.conf`. The `nmbd` daemon provides NetBIOS nameserving and browsing support. It can also be run interactively to query other name service daemons.

→ See "Understanding Multitasking," p. 366

The smbclient program implements a simple FTP-like client. It is useful for accessing SMB shares on other compatible servers, such as Windows machines, and it can also be used to allow a UNIX box to print to a printer attached to any SMB server, such as a PC running Windows 98.

The testparm utility allows you to test your `smb.conf` configuration file. The smbstatus utility allows you to tell who is currently using the `smbd` server.

As stated, all these programs are controlled from one configuration file, called `smb.conf`, located in `/etc`. The file is composed of various named sections specified in brackets [ ]. Within each section, the parameters are specified by *`key=value`* pairs, for example, workgroup = `MYGROUP`.

Samba is a large topic that can fill a book in its own right. Fortunately, in addition to this chapter, there is a large amount of documentation included with the program, including the man pages and lots of .txt files with hints and useful information. There are several Samba mailing lists with discussions on a variety of topics—see http://lists.samba.org/ for full information. The Usenet newsgroup comp.protocols.smb also contains lots of useful information and is frequented by lots of Samba users, even though the group is not strictly aimed at Samba but instead any system using the SMB protocol. The newsgroup was initially setup by people on the Samba mailing list. Finally, the main Web site for Samba is http://samba.org/samba/.

Installing Samba

You can install Samba during regular installation or later using RPM. If you need to install the package, first download the current version from Red Hat's Web site (http://www.redhat.com). You can then install the package (the current version from Red Hat is samba-2.0.5a-19990721.i386.rpm and the current version from the Samba organization can be found at http://us1.samba.org/samba/ftp/Binary_packages/redhat/RPMS/6.0/) by using the following command:

```
rpm -Uvh samba-1.9.18p5-1.i386.rpm
```

→ See "Installing Packages with RPM," p. 169

The package should contain all the files you need to run Samba, including the two primary programs smbd and nmbd. However, you might have to recompile the various programs if you are using a different distribution.

Configuring Samba on Linux

The main configuration file, called smb.conf, is located in the /etc directory. Listing 23.1 provides the default listing shipped with Red Hat 5.1.

Note A semicolon character (;) at the beginning of a line indicates that the line is a comment and is to be ignored when processed by the Samba server.

Listing 23.1 The Sample smb.conf Samba Configuration File

```
; The global setting for a RedHat default install
; smbd re-reads this file regularly, but if in doubt stop and restart it:
; /etc/rc.d/init.d/smb stop
; /etc/rc.d/init.d/smb start
;======================= Global Settings =====================================
[global]

; workgroup = NT-Domain-Name or Workgroup-Name, eg: REDHAT4
   workgroup = WORKGROUP
```

LISTING 23.1 CONTINUED

```
; comment is the equivalent of the NT Description field
   comment = RedHat Samba Server
; volume = used to emulate a CDRom label (can be set on a per share basis)
   volume = RedHat4

; printing = BSD or SYSV or AIX, etc.
   printing = bsd
   printcap name = /etc/printcap
   load printers = yes

; Uncomment this if you want a guest account
;  guest account = pcguest
   log file = /var/log/samba-log.%m
; Put a capping on the size of the log files (in Kb)
   max log size = 50

; Options for handling file name case sensitivity and / or preservation
; Case Sensitivity breaks many WfW and Win95 apps
;  case sensitive = yes
   short preserve case = yes
   preserve case = yes

; Security and file integrity related options
   lock directory = /var/lock/samba
   locking = yes
   strict locking = yes
;   fake oplocks = yes
   share modes = yes
; Security modes: USER uses Unix username/passwd, SHARE uses WfW type
➥passwords
;        SERVER uses a Windows NT Server to provide authentication services
   security = user
; Use password server option only with security = server
;   password server = <NT-Server-Name>

; Configuration Options*****Watch location in smb.conf for side-effects*****
; Where %m is any SMBName (machine name, or computer name) for which a custom
; configuration is desired
;   include = /etc/smb.conf.%m

; Performance Related Options
; Before setting socket options read the smb.conf man page!!
   socket options = TCP_NODELAY
; Socket Address is used to specify which socket Samba
; will listen on (good for aliased systems)
;   socket address = aaa.bbb.ccc.ddd
; Use keep alive only if really needed!!!!
;   keep alive = 60

; Domain Control Options
; OS Level gives Samba the power to rule the roost. Windows NT = 32
;       Any value < 32 means NT wins as Master Browser, > 32 Samba gets it
;   os level = 33
; specifies Samba to be the Domain Master Browser
;   domain master = yes
```

LISTING 23.1 CONTINUED

```
; Use with care only if you have an NT server on your network that has been
; configured at install time to be a primary domain controller.
;   domain controller = <NT-Domain-Controller-SMBName>
; Domain logon control can be a good thing! See [netlogon] share section
  ➥below!
;   domain logons = yes
; run a specific logon batch file per workstation (machine)
;   logon script = %m.bat
; run a specific logon batch file per username
;   logon script = %u.bat
; Windows Internet Name Serving Support Section
; WINS Support - Tells the NMBD component of Samba to enable its WINS Server
;       the default is NO.
;   wins support = yes
; WINS Server - Tells the NMBD components of Samba to be a WINS Client
;       Note: Samba can be either a WINS Server, or a WINS Client, but NOT
        ➥both
;   wins server = w.x.y.z
; WINS Proxy - Tells Samba to answer name resolution queries on behalf of a
  ➥non
;       WINS Client capable client, for this to work there must be at least
        ➥one
;       WINS Server on the network. The default is NO.
;   wins proxy = yes

;============================ Share Declarations ==============================
[homes]
   comment = Home Directories
   browseable = no
   read only = no
   preserve case = yes
   short preserve case = yes
   create mode = 0750

; Un-comment the following and create the netlogon directory for Domain Logons
; [netlogon]
;   comment = Samba Network Logon Service
;   path = /home/netlogon
; Case sensitivity breaks logon script processing!!!
;   case sensitive = no
;   guest ok = yes
;   locking = no
;   read only = yes
;   browseable = yes ; say NO if you want to hide the NETLOGON share
;   admin users = @wheel

; NOTE: There is NO need to specifically define each individual printer
[printers]
   comment = All Printers
   path = /var/spool/samba
   browseable = no
   printable = yes
; Set public = yes to allow user 'guest account' to print
   public = no
   writable = no
```

LISTING 23.1 CONTINUED

```
   create mode = 0700

;[tmp]
;     comment = Temporary file space
;     path = /tmp
;     read only = no
;     public = yes

; A publicly accessible directory, but read only, except for people in
; the staff group
;[public]
;     comment = Public Stuff
;     path = /home/samba
;     public = yes
;     writable = yes
;     printable = no
;     write list = @users

; Other examples.
;
; A private printer, usable only by fred. Spool data will be placed in fred's
; home directory. Note that fred must have write access to the spool
  ➥directory
; wherever it is.
;[fredsprn]
;    comment = Fred's Printer
;    valid users = fred
;    path = /homes/fred
;    printer = freds_printer
;    public = no
;    writable = no
;    printable = yes
;
; A private directory, usable only by fred. Note that fred requires write
; access to the directory.
;[fredsdir]
;    comment = Fred's Service
;    path = /usr/somewhere/private
;    valid users = fred
;    public = no
;    writable = yes
;    printable = no
;
; a service which has a different directory for each machine that connects
; this allows you to tailor configurations to incoming machines. You could
; also use the %u option to tailor it by user name.
; The %m gets replaced with the machine name that is connecting.
;[pchome]
;    comment = PC Directories
;    path = /usr/pc/%m
;    public = no
;    writeable = yes
;
;
```

Listing 23.1 continued

```
; A publicly accessible directory, read/write to all users. Note that all
files
; created in the directory by users will be owned by the default user, so
; any user with access can delete any other user's files. Obviously this
; directory must be writable by the default user. Another user could of
course
; be specified, in which case all files would be owned by that user instead.
;[public]
;   path = /usr/somewhere/else/public
;   public = yes
;   only guest = yes
;   writable = yes
;   printable = no
;
;
; The following two entries demonstrate how to share a directory so that two
; users can place files there that will be owned by the specific users. In
this
; setup, the directory should be writable by both users and should have the
; sticky bit set on it to prevent abuse. Obviously this could be extended to
; as many users as required.
;[myshare]
;   comment = Mary's and Fred's stuff
;   path = /usr/somewhere/shared
;   valid users = mary fred
;   public = no
;   writable = yes
;   printable = no
;   create mask = 0765
```


The `smb.conf` file layout consists of a series of named sections. Each section starts with its name in brackets, such as `[global]`. Within each section, the parameters are specified by *`key`*`=`*`value`* pairs, such as `comment = RedHat Samba Server`.

`smb.conf` contains three special sections and one or more custom sections. The special sections are `[global]`, `[homes]`, and `[printers]`.

The `[global]` Section

The `[global]` section of `smb.conf` controls parameters for the entire SMB server. The section also provides default values for the other sections.

The first line from the `[global]` section in Listing 23.1 defines the workgroup that this machine will belong to on your network:

```
[global]

; workgroup = NT-Domain-Name or Workgroup-Name, eg: REDHAT4
   workgroup = WORKGROUP
```

Next, the file specifies a comment for the system and identifies a volume label as follows:

```
; comment is the equivalent of the NT Description field
   comment = RedHat Samba Server
```

```
; volume = used to emulate a CDRom label (can be set on a per share basis)
   volume = RedHat4
```

The next entry tells the Samba server what type of printing system is available on your server, and the line after that indicates where the printer configuration file is located:

```
; printing = BSD or SYSV or AIX, etc.
   printing = bsd
```

→ See "Understanding the /etc/printcap File," p. 397

The next line instructs Samba to make available on the network all the printers defined in the `printcap` file:

```
printcap name = /etc/printcap
load printers = yes
```

The next entry indicates a username for a guest account on your sever. This account is used to authenticate users for Samba services available to guest connections:

```
; Uncomment this if you want a guest account
; guest account = pcguest
```

The log file entry specifies the location of the log file for each client accessing Samba services. The `%m` parameter tells the Samba server to create a separate log file for each client. The `max log size` entry sets a maximum file size for the logs created:

```
   log file = /var/log/samba-log.%m
; Put a capping on the size of the log files (in Kb)
   max log size = 50
```

THE `[homes]` SECTION

The `[homes]` section of `smb.conf` allows network clients to connect to a user's home directory on your server without having an explicit entry in the `smb.conf` file. When a service request is made, the Samba server searches the `smb.conf` file for the specific section corresponding to the service request. If it does not find the service, Samba checks to see whether a `[homes]` section exists. If the `[homes]` section does exist, Samba searches the password file to find the home directory for the user making the request. When it's found, this directory is shared with the network.

The `comment` entry is displayed to the clients to let them know which shares are available. The `browseable` entry instructs Samba how to display this share in a network browse list. The `read-only` parameter controls whether a user can create and change files in his or her home directory when it is shared across the network. The `preserve case` and `short preserve case` parameters instruct the server to preserve the case of any information written to the server. This step is important because Windows filenames are not typically case sensitive, but Linux filenames are case sensitive. The final entry sets the file permissions for any files created on the shared directory:

```
[homes]
   comment = Home Directories
   browseable = no
   read only = no
   preserve case = yes
   short preserve case = yes
   create mode = 0750
```

→ See "File Permissions," p. 414

The [printers] Section

The `[printers]` section of `smb.conf` defines how printing services are controlled if no specific entries are found in the `smb.conf` file. Thus, with this section, like the `[homes]` section, if no specific entry is found for a printing service, Samba uses the `[printers]` section (if it's present) to allow a user to connect to any printer defined in `/etc/printcap`.

The `comment`, `browseable`, and `create mode` entries mean the same as discussed in "The `[homes]` Section." The `path` entry indicates the location of the spool file to be used when servicing a print request via SMB:

```
[printers]
   comment = All Printers
   path = /var/spool/samba
   browseable = no
   printable = yes
; Set public = yes to allow user 'guest account' to print
   public = no
   writable = no
   create mode = 0700
```

→ See "Selecting a Printer to Work with Linux," p. 392

The `printable` value, if set to `yes`, indicates that this printer resource can be used to print. The `public` entry controls whether the guest account can print.

Sharing Directories

After configuring your defaults for the Samba server, you can create specific shared directories limited to just certain groups of people or to everyone. For example, suppose you want to make a directory available to only one user. To do so, you create a new section and fill in the needed information. Typically, you need to specify the user, the directory path, and the configuration information to the SMB server, as shown here:

```
[jacksdir]
comment = Jack's remote source code directory
path = /usr/local/src
valid users = tackett
browsable = yes
public = no
writable = yes
create mode = 0700
```

This sample section creates a shared directory called `jacksdir`. The path to the directory on the local server is `/usr/local/src`. Because the `browsable` entry is set to `yes`, `jacksdir` will show up in the network browse list. However, because the `public` entry is set to `no`, only the user named `tackett` can access this directory using Samba. You can grant access to other users by listing them in the `valid users` entry.

TESTING THE `smb.conf` FILE

After creating the configuration file, you should test it for correctness by using the testparm program. testparm is a very simple test program to check the `/etc/smb.conf` configuration file for internal correctness. If this program reports no problems, you can use the configuration file with confidence that `smbd` will successfully load the configuration file.

Caution

Using testparm is *not* a guarantee that the services specified in the configuration file will be available or will operate as expected.

testparm has the following command line:

```
testparm [configfile [hostnamehostip]]
```

`configfile` indicates the location of the `smb.conf` file if it is not in the default location (`/etc/smb.conf`). The *`hostnamehostIP`* optional parameter instructs testparm to see whether the host has access to the services provided in the `smb.conf` file.

The following example shows sample output from running testparm. If the `smb.conf` file contains any errors, the program reports them along with a specific error message:

```
# testparm
Load smb config files from /etc/smb.conf
Processing section ''[homes]''
Processing section ''[printers]''
Loaded services file OK.
Press enter to see a dump of your service definitions
```

When you press Enter, testparm begins evaluating each section defined in the configuration file.

RUNNING THE SAMBA SERVER

The Samba server consists of two daemons, `smbd` and `nmbd`. The `smbd` daemon provides the file and print sharing services. The `nmbd` daemon provides NetBIOS name server support.

You can run the Samba server either from the init scripts as detailed in Chapter 10, "Booting and Shutting Down," or from `inetd` as a system service.

→ See "Understanding the Boot Process," p. 234

Because Red Hat and Caldera both start SMB services from the init scripts instead of as a service from `inetd`, you can use the following command to start or stop the SMB server:

```
/etc/rc.d/init.d/samba start¦stop
```

USING SMBCLIENT

The smbclient program allows Linux users to access SMB shares on other, typically Windows, machines. If you want to access files on other Linux boxes, you can use a variety of methods including FTP, NFS, and the `r-` commands (such as `rcp`).

→ See "Using the r- Commands," p. 695

smbclient provides an FTP-like interface that allows you to transfer files with a network share on another computer running an SMB server. Unfortunately, unlike NFS, smbclient does not allow you to mount another share as a local directory.

smbclient provides command-line options to query a server for the shared directories available or to exchange files. For more information on the available command-line options, consult the man page for smbclient. Use the following command to list all available shares on the machine `win.netwharf.com`:

```
smbclient -L -I win.netwharf.com
```

The `-L` parameter requests the list. The `-I` parameter instructs smbclient to treat the following machine name as a DNS-specified entry instead of a NetBIOS entry.

To transfer a file, you must first connect to the Samba server by using the following command:

```
smbclient '\\WORKGROUP\PUBLIC' -I win.netwharf.com -U tackett
```

The parameter `'\\WORKGROUP\PUBLIC'` specifies the remote service on the other machine. It is typically either a file system directory or a printer. The `-U` option allows you to specify the username with which you want to connect. Samba prompts you for a password (if this account requires one) and then places you at the prompt

```
smb: \
```

where `\` indicates the current working directory.

From this command line, you can issue any of the various commands shown in Table 23.1 to transfer and work with files.

TABLE 23.1 smbclient COMMANDS

Command	Parameters	Description
`?` or `help`	`[`*`command`*`]`	Provides a help message on *command*, or in general if no command is specified.

TABLE 23.1 smbclient COMMANDS

Command	Parameters	Description
`!`	[*shell command*]	Executes the specified shell command or drops the user to a shell prompt.
`cd`	[*directory*]	Changes to the specified directory on the server machine (not the local machine). If no directory is specified, smbclient reports the current working directory.
`lcd`	[*directory*]	Changes to the specified directory on the local machine. If no directory is specified, smbclient reports the current working directory on the local machine.
`Del`	[*files*]	The specified files on the server are deleted if the user has permission to do so. Files can include wildcard characters.
`dir` or `ls`	[*files*]	Lists the indicated files. You can also use the command `ls` to get a list of files.
`exit` or `quit`	none	Exits from the smbclient program.
`get`	[*remote file*] or [*local name*]	Retrieves the specified remote file and saves the file on the local server. If *local name* is specified, the copied file is saved with this filename instead of with the filename on the remote server.
`mget`	[*files*]	Copies all the indicated files—including those matching any wildcards—to the local machine.
`md` or `mkdir`	[*directory*]	Creates the specified directory on the remote machine.
`rd` or `rmdir`	[*directory*]	Removes the specified directory from the remote machine.
`put`	[*file*]	Copies the specified file from the local machine to the server.
`mput`	[*files*]	Copies all the specified files from the local machine to the server.
`print`	[*file*]	Prints the specified file on the remote machine.
`queue`	none	Displays all the print jobs queued on the remote server.

Case Study: OpenLinux and swat

Configuring Samba can be a complicated task, but fortunately the Samba 2.0 released with OpenLinux provides a Web administration tool called swat (Samba Web Administration Tool), as shown in Figure 23.1. You can run swat from either inetd as a service or from your Apache Web browser to help create and update your `smb.conf` file. Use swat also to start and stop the various Samba daemons and check the status of the system from the Web.

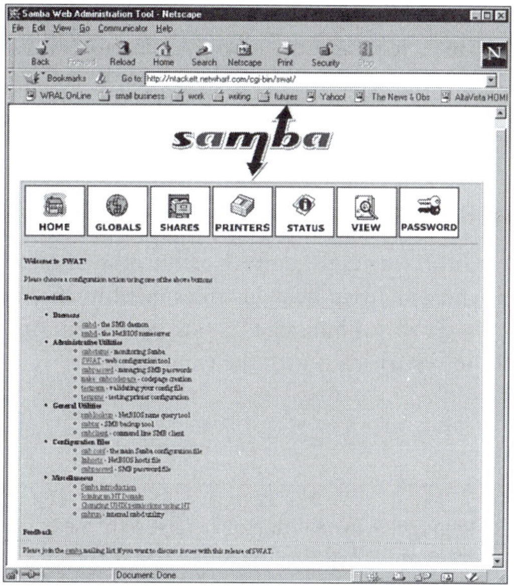

Figure 23.1 Caldera provides a Web-based interface for configuring Samba.

Table 23.2 describes the purposes for the various buttons.

Table 23.2 The swat Command Buttons

Button	Description
Home	Returns you to the default home page for swat.
Globals	Allows you to modify the components of the `[global]` section in `smb.conf`.
Shares	Allows you to modify the components of the `[shares]` section in `smb.conf`.
Printers	Allows you to modify the components of the `[printers]` section of `smb.conf`.
Status	Displays the current status of the smb system.
View	Displays what will be written to `smb.conf` by swat.
Password	Allows you to change the password used to access swat.

Any changes made using swat requires you to restart smbd and nmbd in order for the changes to take effect.

Tip #124 from *Jack*

> swat does not create a backup file, so you should copy `smb.conf` to a backup file before using swat. Use the following command to create a backup:
>
> `cp smb.conf smb.conf.bak`

RUNNING SWAT FROM INETD

You need to configure the `/etc/services` and `/etc/inetd.conf` files to run swat as a service. Use a text editor and, logged in as root, add the following line to `/etc/services`:

```
Swat 901/tcp
```

This line assigns port 901 to the swat program as a TCP port. Next, add the following line to `/etc/inetd.conf`:

```
swat stream tcp nowait.400 root /usr/local/samba/bin/swat swat
```

Make sure `/usr/local/samba/bin/swat` is the correct path to the installed program; if not, enter the correct path. This entry in `inetd.conf` instructs inetd to execute swat as a TCP stream program listening on port 901 as indicated in `/etc/services`. After making the necessary changes, you need to restart inetd with the command:

```
killall -HUP inetd
```

Tip #125 from *Jack*

> If you want to provide a more secure connection, have the tcp wrapper's daemon spawn swat by using the following line in `/etc/inetd.conf`:
>
> `swat stream tcp nowait.400 root /usr/sbin/tcpd /usr/sbin/swat`
>
> Make sure to use the correct path to swat, which you can find using the command `locate swat`.

You can now run swat by pointing your Web browser to `http://localhost:901`. swat prompts for a username and password and while you can use any valid username and password to access swat, you can only make changes to the system when logged in as root.

RUNNING SWAT VIA THE WEB

Apache runs swat as a cgi program and so requires a bit more detail to configure. First, you need to create a directory called swat as a subdirectory under your Apache document root. The document root is identified by the line `<Directory /home/httpd/html>` in the `/etc/httpd/conf/access.conf` file. Use the following commands as root:

```
mkdir /home/httpd/html/swat
cp -R samba/swat /home/httpd/html/swat
```

Make sure to use the correct `samba/swat` directory. Make sure the following subdirectories under `/home/httpd/html/swat` are created:

```
help
images
include
```

Next, copy the swat executable file to the cgi-bin directory, typically /etc/httpd/cgi-bin.

Because anyone can typically reach a Web site from the Internet, you need to be concerned with security. After all, you don't want anyone to be able to reconfigure your Samba installation. To insure proper security, you need to password protect your Web site. To password protect a Web site, you need to create an .htaccess file and a set a password with the htpasswd program.

First, create the .htaccess file in the /home/httpd/html/swat directory with the following command:

```
vi /home/httpd/home/swat/.htpasswd
```

and then add the following lines:

```
AuthName ''swat restricted''
AuthType Basic
AuthUserFile /etc/swat.users
require valid-user
```

Next, you need to create the password file specified by the line authUserFile in .htaccess:

```
htpasswd -c /etc/swat.user root
```

The program htpasswd prompts for a password to assign to the user root.

Next, change the line beginning with AllowOveride in /etc/httpd/conf/access.conf from None to AuthConfig. The line should read:

```
AllowOveride AuthConfig
```

Finally, you need to restart the Web server with either of the following:

```
apachectl restart
```

or

```
/etc/rc.d/init.d/httpd stop
/etc/rc.d/init.d/httpd start
```

Then you can access swat by using the following URL:

```
http://localhost/swat/cgi-bin/swat
```

Finally, if you want to run swat on a Red Hat system, see FAQ entry http://us1.samba.org/samba/samba/docs/FAQ/#21 on the samba.org Web site.

PART IV

Using X Windows

CHAPTER 24

Installing the X Window System

In this chapter

by Rob Napier

WHAT IS THE X WINDOW SYSTEM?

Linux provides the capability to run windowed applications across a heterogeneous network by incorporating the XFree86 implementation of the X11 standard of the X Window System created at the Massachusetts Institute of Technology (MIT). This system is much more than a graphical interface used to run applications; it's a powerful client/server system that allows applications to be run and shared across a network. Although XFree86 is meant to run in a networked environment, it runs fine on a single machine. You don't need a network to run XFree86 or X applications.

Historically, XFree86 has been one of the most complex parts of Linux to install and configure. This is no longer the case for many standard hardware configurations because the most popular Linux distributions now install and configure it automatically.

Like most parts of Linux, XFree86 also has a How-To document. The "XFree86 How-To" is maintained by Eric S. Raymond at `esr@thyrsus.com` and can be found on the World Wide Web at `http://metalab.unc.edu/LDP/`.

Caution

Typically, you don't have to worry about software damaging your hardware. However, because XFree86 deals directly with your video card and monitor, it can cause physical damage, especially if you try to use XFree86 with an unsupported video card. Make sure that you have the necessary hardware before trying to run XFree86.

Reading the documentation that comes with the XFree86 system is strongly suggested. Always refer to the documentation that comes with your installed version of XFree86 because older or newer documentation may not be accurate for your installation. For Red Hat 6.0, the documentation can be found at `/usr/X11R6/lib/X11/doc`, particularly the `README` file, and the "XFree86 How-To" by Eric S. Raymond is at `/usr/doc/HOWTO/Xfree86-HOWTO`. The most up-to-date version of XFree86 is available at `http://www.xfree86.org`, so you should look there before trying to work with an unlisted video board or chipset.

UNDERSTANDING THE X WINDOW SYSTEM

The X Window System is a powerful graphical operating environment that supports many applications across a network, and it can be freely distributed. The version of the X Window System discussed in this chapter is X11R6. However, Linux and XFree86 are constantly evolving, and a newer version of X may be available on the Net. In fact, at the time of this printing, work is underway to incorporate X11R6.4 into XFree86-4.0.

→ See "Using FTP for Remote File Transfer," page 686

XFree86, the X server commonly used by Linux, is the X11R6 standard ported to Intel-based systems. XFree86 supports a wide range of standard PC hardware. The version of XFree86 discussed in this chapter is 3.3.3.1. This version ships with Red Hat 6.0 and Caldera OpenLinux 2.2.

The X Window System originally grew out of a cooperative effort between two sections at MIT: the section responsible for a networking program called *Project Athena* and a section called the Laboratory for Computer Science. Both used many UNIX workstations and soon realized they were each reinventing the wheel when it came to programming graphical user interfaces (GUIs) for UNIX workstations. To cut down on the amount of code both groups were writing, they decided to create one robust, extensible windowing system—the X Window System.

In 1987, several vendors—in hopes of creating a single windowing system for UNIX workstations—formed an organization called the *X Consortium*to promote and standardize the X Window System. Thanks to this effort, open computing became a reality. The X Consortium is composed of entities such as IBM, Digital Equipment, and MIT. This group of large organizations oversees the construction and release of new versions of X11.

XFree86 is a trademark of the XFree86 Project, Inc. The original programmers who ported the X Window System to the 80386 platform decided to found the project so that they could gain membership in the X Consortium. By becoming a member of the X Consortium, the XFree86 Project gained access to works-in-progress and could thus port the new features to XFree86 while the features were being implemented for the X Window System, rather than wait until after the official release to make the port. As of January 1, 1997, the X Consortium turned the X Window System over to the Open Group.

The X Window System is actually a series of pieces working together to present users with a GUI:

- The base window system is a program providing services to the X Window System.
- The next piece is a protocol for communicating across the network—the X Network Protocol.
- On top of the program implementing the X Network Protocol is the low-level interface, named *Xlib*, between the network/base system and higher-level programs. Application programs typically use functions in Xlib instead of the lower-level functions.
- Tying these pieces together is a window manager. The window manager is an X application whose purpose is to control how windows are presented to users.
- Many modern distributions of Linux, particularly Red Hat 6.0 and OpenLinux 2.2, also include a desktop. Although the desktop is not technically part of the X Window System, it does provide an integral part to the users' graphical environment and works very closely with the window manager. Desktops generally handle features such as customizable window styles (*themes*), session management, and interprogram communications. They often provide a simpler environment for application

developers. The two most popular Linux desktops are GNOME and KDE. They will be discussed in detail in Chapter 26, "Working with KDE," and Chapter 27, "Working with GNOME."

Unlike most other window systems, the base window system of the X Window System doesn't provide user interface objects such as scrollbars, command buttons, or menus. The user interface items are left to the higher-layer components and the window manager. Therefore, users have much greater flexibility in how things appear and what interface they prefer.

X applications include not only window managers, but also games, graphics utilities, programming tools, and many other tidbits. Just about any application that you need has either been written for or ported to the X Window System. The setup and use of several of the standard X applications are covered in more detail in Chapter 25, "Using the X Window System."

The X Window System implements a window manager to handle the task of creating and controlling the interface that makes up the visual portion of the X Window System. It isn't to be confused with the OS/2 Presentation Manager or the Microsoft Windows Program Manager. Both of them are closer to the idea of a desktop rather than a window manager.

For the not-so-faint-of-heart, XFree86 also includes programming libraries and files for programmers who want to develop their own applications under XFree86 or compile X applications available on the Internet. Although the topic of creating X applications is beyond the scope of this book, ample documentation is available on any number of Internet distribution sites such as `www.xfree86.org` and on many CD-ROM distributions to help you gain the foothold necessary to create applications for XFree86.

What Is a Client/Server System?

The X Window System is a client/server system controlled by two individual pieces of software. One piece runs on the client, and the other runs on the server. The client and server pieces of this puzzle can be on different systems or, as is the case with most personal computers, both pieces can reside on the same machine.

Client/server is one of the major buzzwords used in the computer industry today. Like most basic concepts in the industry, client/server has been overplayed and overused to the point of confusing the average computer user. In the traditional sense, a *server* is a machine that just provides resources—disk drive space, printers, modems, and so on—to other computers over a network. A *client* is the consumer of these services; in other words, a client uses the disk space, printer, or modems provided by a server.

Now that you understand what a client is and what a server is, it's time to reverse everything you know. In the X Window System, the client/server relationship is the opposite of what you've come to know in the PC world. The accepted or common notion of a server is that it provides services to a client using them. In the most basic form, a client displays the application that's running on the server.

Under the X Window System, the server displays the application that's running on the client. This concept might seem a bit confusing at first, but it will make sense when you become more familiar with the X Window System.

In the X Window System, a client provides the programs and resources necessary to run an application—what in the traditional sense would be called a server. The resources reside on the client system (remember that the client and server systems can be on the same machine), whereas the application is displayed and interacted with on the server system.

For example, if you run xcalc on your Linux system using XFree86, then XFree86 (specifically a program such as `/usr/X11R6/bin/XF86_SVGA`) is the *X server*, and xcalc is the *X client*. The X server must be running on your local machine (so that it can display your information), but the X client might be on any machine that you can connect to.

The capability of an X application, which is the client, to run under a server located on either the same computer or on another computer is called *network transparency*. Thus, it doesn't matter whether an X application runs on a local or remote machine. This capability can be used to run time-consuming tasks on another machine, leaving the local machine unencumbered to perform other tasks. It can also be used to run applications on other operating systems. Using a non-UNIX X server such as WQR's Reflection X, you can run your favorite X clients on your Linux workstation but display them on a connected machine running Microsoft's NT. The reverse is not true, however, because NT does not know how to run X clients and cannot easily display its own clients on remote servers.

OUTPUT CAPABILITIES

The base window system provides the X Window System with plenty of bitmapped graphical operations. The X Window System and X applications use these operations to present information graphically to the users. XFree86 offers overlapping windows, immediate graphics drawings, high-resolution bitmapped graphics and images, and high-quality text. Whereas early implementations of the X Window System were mostly monochrome-based, modern implementations like XFree86 support a wide range of color systems.

The X Window System also supports the multiprocessing capabilities of UNIX; thus, XFree86 supports the multiprocessing capabilities of Linux. Each window displayed under the X Window System can be a separate task running under Linux.

USER INTERFACE CAPABILITIES

The X Consortium did not define standards for user interfaces. At the time very little research had been done on user interface technology, so no clear interface was considered the best. In fact, even today, unilaterally declaring one interface the best can alienate many people. The preferred look and feel presented by the user interface is a very personal decision.

The X Consortium wanted to make the X Window System a standard across UNIX workstations, which is one reason it is available freely on the Internet. Making the X Window System freely available fosters interoperability, which is the cornerstone of open systems. Had the X Consortium dictated a user interface, the X Window System may not have gained its current level of popularity.

INPUT CAPABILITIES

Systems running the X Window System typically have some form of pointing device, usually a mouse. XFree86 requires a mouse or a device, such as a trackball, that emulates a mouse. If you don't have such a device, you can't use the XFree86 system with Linux. The X Window System converts signals from the pointing device and from the keyboard into events. The X Window System then responds to these events, performing appropriate actions.

Caution

If your mouse or other hardware pointing device isn't among those supported by Linux, you'll have problems using XFree86.

INSTALLING THE XFREE86 SYSTEM

You probably installed the XFree86 system while installing the entire Linux package from the accompanying CD-ROM. The X Window System is contained in the `XFree86-*` RPMs. If you didn't install the X Window System System at that time, you can use RPM to install X Window System. First, however, you must verify that you have the appropriate hardware for XFree86.

→ See "Installing Packages with RPM," p. 169

ENSURING HARDWARE SUPPORT FOR XFREE86

You must make sure that you have the proper hardware to run X Window System, the proper amount of memory, and the necessary disk space.

You need about 50MB of disk space to install the XFree86 system and the X applications provided. You need at least 16MB of virtual memory to run XFree86. *Virtual memory* is the combination of the physical RAM on your system and the amount of swap space you've allocated for Linux. You must have at least 4MB of physical RAM to run XFree86 under Linux, thus requiring a 12MB swap file. The more physical RAM you have, the better the performance of your XFree86 system will be.

→ See "Creating the Swap Partition," p. 77 for Red Hat and p. 93 for OpenLinux

Next, you need a video card containing a video-driver chipset supported by XFree86. According to the January 2, 1999, release of Eric S. Raymond's "XFree86 How-To," the video cards with the chipsets listed in Table 24.1 are supported by XFree86.

TABLE 24.1 CHIPSETS SUPPORTED BY XFREE86

Manufacturer	Chipset(s)
Ark Logic	ARK1000PV, ARK1000VL, ARK2000PV, ARK2000MT
Alliance	AP6422, AT24
ATI	18800, 18800-1, 28800-2, 28800-4, 28800-5, 28800-6, 68800-3, 68800-6, 68800AX, 68800LX, 88800GX-C, 88800GX-D, 88800GX-E, 88800GX-F, 88800CX, 264CT, 264ET, 264VT, 264GT, 264VT-B, 264VT3, 264GT-B, 264GT3 (including the Mach8, Mach32, Mach64, 3D Rage, 3D Rage II, and 3D Rage Pro)
Avance Logic	ALG2101, ALG2228, ALG2301, ALG2302, ALG2308, ALG2401
Chips & Technologies	65520, 65525, 65530, 65535, 65540, 65545, 65546, 65548, 65550, 65554, 65555, 68554, 69000, 64200, 64300
Cirrus Logic	CLGD5420, CLGD5422, CLGD5424, CLGD5426, CLGD5428, CLGD5429, CLGD5430, CLGD5434, CLGD5436, CLGD5440, CLGD5446, CLGD5462, CLGD5464, CLGD5465, CLGD5480, CLGD6205, CLGD6215, CLGD6225, CLGD6235, CLGD6410, CLGD6412, CLGD6420, CLGD6440, CLGD7541, CLGD7543, CLGD7548(*), CLGD7555
Cyrix	MediaGX, MediaGXm
Compaq	AVGA
DEC	TGA
Epson	SPC8110
Genoa	GVGA
IBM	8514/A (and true clones), XGA-2
IIT	AGX-014, AGX-015, AGX-016
Matrox	MGA2064W (Millennium), MGA1064SG (Mystique and Mystique 220), MGA2164W (Millennium II PCI and AGP), G100, G200
MX	MX68000, MX680010
NCR	77C22, 77C22E, 77C22E+
NeoMagic	2200, 2160, 2097, 2093, 2090, 2070
Number Nine	I128 (series I and II), Revolution 3D (T2R)
NVidia/SGS Thomson	NVidia/SGS Thomson
OAK	OTI067, OTI077, OTI087
RealTek	RTG3106
Rendition	V1000, V2x00

TABLE 24.1 CHIPSETS SUPPORTED BY XFREE86

Manufacturer	Chipset(s)
S3	86C911, 86C924, 86C801, 86C805, 86C805i, 86C928, 86C864, 86C964, 86C732, 86C764, 86C765, 86C767, 86C775, 86C785, 86C868, 86C968, 86C325, 86C357, 86C375, 86C375, 86C385, 86C988, 86CM65, 86C260
SiS	86C201, 86C202, 86C205, 86C215, 86C225, 5597, 5598, 6326
3DLabs	GLINT 500TX, GLINT MX, Permedia, Permedia 2, Permedia 2v
Tseng	ET3000, ET4000AX, ET4000/W32, ET4000/W32i, ET4000/W32p, ET6000, ET6100
Trident	TVGA8800CS, TVGA8900B, TVGA8900C, TVGA8900CL, TVGA9000, TVGA9000i, TVGA9100B, TVGA9200CXR, Cyber9320, TVGA9400CXi, TVGA9420, TGUI9420DGi, TGUI9430DGi, TGUI9440AGi, TGUI9660XGi, TGUI9680, ProVidia 9682, ProVidia 9685, Cyber 9382, Cyber 9385, Cyber 9388, 3DImage975, 3DImage985, Cyber 9397, Cyber 9520
Video 7/Headland Technologies	HT216-32
Weitek	P9000, P9100
Western Digital/Paradise	PVGA1
Western Digital	WD90C00, WD90C10, WD90C11, WD90C24, WD90C24A, WD90C30, WD90C31, WD90C33

UNDERSTANDING THE XFREE86 RPMS

XFree86 is split into a large number of RPMs, some of which are required, whereas others are optional. If you installed XFree86 when you installed Red Hat or OpenLinux, everything was probably done for you. If you didn't install XFree86 at that time, or you're trying to upgrade XFree86, then you need to decide what packages to install. See Table 24.2 for the list of recommended packages, Table 24.3 for a list of X servers (you need one, plus XFree86-VGA16 as a backup), and Table 24.4 for the optional packages that ship with Red Hat 6.0. OpenLinux 2.2 RPMs have very similar names for the most common packages.

TABLE 24.2 RECOMMENDED XFREE86 RPMS

RPM	Description
XFree86	Base XFree86 system.
XFree86-libs	Shared libraries for most X applications.
X11R6-contrib	Many useful X applications.

Table 24.2 Recommended XFree86 RPMs

RPM	Description
Xconfigurator	Easy-to-use front end for configuring X Window System. This RPM is generally shipped only with Red Hat. For other distributions, use XF86Setup (see "Using XF86Setup").

Table 24.3 XFree86 X Server RPMs

RPM	Description
XFree86-VGA16	Generic VGA 16-color server. For most configurations, you'll never want to use this server, but it's good to have around because it works with just about everything.
XFree86-SVGA	SVGA server. Most nonaccelerated chipsets use this server.
XFree86-Mono	SVGA monochrome server.
XFree86-S3	S3 accelerated server (except ViRGE).
XFree86-S3V	S3 ViRGE accelerated server.
XFree86-Mach32	ATI Mach32 accelerated server.
XFree86-Mach64	ATI Mach64 accelerated server.
XFree86-Mach8	ATI Mach8 accelerated server.
XFree86-8514	8514/A accelerated server.
XFree86-P9000	P9000 accelerated server.
XFree86-AGX	AGX accelerated server.
XFree86-W32	ET4000/W32 and ET6000 accelerated server.
XFree86-3DLabs	3D Labs GLINT and Permedia accelerated server.
XFree86-FBDev	Amiga, Atari and Macintosh/m68k server.
XFree86-I128	#9 Imagine 128 server.

Table 24.4 Optional XFree86 RPMs

RPM	Description
XFree86-75dpi-fonts	Standard 75dpi fonts.
XFree86-ISO8859-2	Central European (ISO 8859-2) fonts.
XFree86-ISO8859-9	Turkish language (ISO 8859-9) fonts.
XFree85-Xnest	A "nested" X server. This X server can run in a window under another X server, generally for testing purposes.

TABLE 24.4 OPTIONAL XFREE86 RPMS

RPM	Description
XFree86-XF86Setup	XFree86 configuration front end. For Red Hat 6.0, Xconfigurator (refer to Table 24.2) is generally preferred.
XFree86-Xvfb	X server that does not require display hardware. It is very useful for development but generally not used by end users.
XFree86-cyrillic-fonts	Cyrillic fonts.
XFree86-devel	Development package. It is required if you plan to develop or compile X applications or servers.
XFree86-doc	Low-level documentation for X developers.
XFree86-xfs	Font server for XFree86. It is used to provide the fonts on your machine to other machines on the network.

→ See "Installing Packages with RPM," p. 169

Font packages often come in several flavors. The "base" version (as listed in Table 24.4) is generally terminal fonts and keyboard remaps for the languages in question. The 75dpi fonts version contains 75dpi (dots per inch) fonts, which can be used by most monitors. The 100dpi fonts version contains 100dpi fonts, which are good for high-end (usually large) monitors that can handle 100dpi. Finally, some fonts come in a Type1 fonts version, which are Type 1 scalable fonts. Installing at least the base, 75dpi, and Type1 versions is highly recommended. If your monitor can support the 100dpi versions, having them can be quite nice.

Remember that you have to install the appropriate programs from each package. Although not all packages are required, if you install XFree86 after installing Linux, you should review the full details on the packages to install. If you have the 50MB needed for a full installation, go ahead and install each package, with the exception of the X server. Install only one X server for your chipset.

Note

The XFree86 RPMs that ship with Red Hat 6.0 have serious performance, functionality, and security bugs. Upgrading these packages from `ftp://ftp.redhat.com/updates/6.0` is highly recommended.

INSTALLING XFREE86 FOR RED HAT 6.0

The easiest way to install XFree86 for Red Hat 6.0 is to let the Red Hat installer do it for you. This will save you a lot of trouble in determining which RPMs you require and will automatically detect your video hardware. Follow these steps:

1. Insert your Boot disk and Red Hat 6.0 CD and reboot your system.

→ See "Shutting Down Linux," p. 243

2. At the main boot prompt, press Enter to install Red Hat 2.0 or later, and press Enter again at the welcome screen. Select your language, keyboard, and install device. Then select Upgrade and answer the question about whether you have any SCSI devices.
3. The installer will now inform you that it has determined what you should install and will ask whether you would like to customize the list of packages. Select Yes.
4. Look through the list and deselect everything except the three User Interface sections. The installer has probably selected these if you have not yet installed XFree86. If it has, then you can probably accept its selections (check over them if you like). If it has not selected the User Interface sections, do so now. Unless you are low on disk space, just select everything.
5. Select OK and wait for the installer to complete. Skip the boot disk creation and boot loader installation if you've done them before. Finally, your system will reboot.
6. The RPMs that ship with Red Hat 6.0 have serious problems with functionality, security, and performance, so you shouldn't stop here. You should now go to `ftp.redhat.com` and get the updates.
7. When your system reboots, log in as root and collect a list of your installed RPMs:
   ```
   # rpm -qa ¦ grep XFree86
   ```
8. You should write these down or open another `xterm` so you can remember what RPMs you need. Now `ftp` to `ftp.redhat.com`:
   ```
   # ncftp ftp://ftp.redhat.com/redhat/updates/6.0/i386
   ```
9. Get a list of all the updated XFree86 RPMs:
   ```
   ncftp /redhat/updates/6.0/i386 > ls XFree86*
   ```
10. Now look at your list of installed RPMs and make a note of any that have been updated (there will be several). Queue the updated RPMs for download:
    ```
    ncftp /redhat/updates/6.0/i386 > bgget XFree86-3.3.3.1-52.i386.rpm
    + Spooled: get XFree86-3.3.3.1-52.i386.rpm
    ncftp /redhat/updates/6.0/i386 > bgget XFree86-75dpi-fonts-3.3.3.1-52.i386.rpm
    + Spooled: get XFree86-75dpi-fonts-3.3.3.1-52.i386.rpm
    [...]
    ```

Tip #126 from *Rob*

`ncftp` has filename completion, so you don't have to type the entire filename. Just type enough to make it unique and press the Tab key. If you press Tab when what you've already typed is not unique, `ncftp` will expand as much as it can.
For example, you can type XF<*Tab*>1<*Tab*> to get `XFree86-100dpi-fonts-3.3.3.1-52.i386.rpm`.

PART IV CH 24

You want to queue the downloads because there are too many RPMs to fit on one line.

11. When you've queued all the files you want, quit `ncftp` and the download will automatically start. You can watch the progress of the download by watching `~/.ncftp/batchlog`:

    ```
    # tail -f ~/.ncftp/batchlog
    ```

12. When the download is complete, update all the RPMs with the following command:

    ```
    # rpm -U XFree86*
    ```

Note

If you receive dependency errors while upgrading, see "Dependency errors while upgrading with `rpm`" in the Troubleshooting section of this chapter.

→ See "Updating Packages with RPM," p. 171

XFree86 has historically been one of the most complex parts of Linux to configure. This is no longer the case, however, for most common hardware. There are two cases where installation can still be difficult, however.

First, cutting edge hardware may or may not be supported by XFree86 at all. When XFree86 does support it, you may have to use beta versions of XFree86 or even hacks on XFree86. These will not be supported by the new configuration tools.

Second, some vendors do not publish the specifications for their boards. In order for XFree86 to support these boards, developers have to reverse engineer them, which takes a lot of time and effort. Unless the board is extremely popular (e.g. the S3 ViRGE), there may not be XFree86 support for a very long time. Getting unsupported boards to work can be difficult or impossible if you are unable to write the drivers yourself.

These are just the worst cases. For most popular hardware you can just use Xconfigurator, and it should work without any trouble.

USING XCONFIGURATOR

Xconfigurator is written by Red Hat. It is a text-based, menu-driven program which walks you through setting up your X server. It provides defaults for a wide variety of hardware and is much easier to use than the configuration tools that historically came with XFree86.

After you install XFree86, you can log in as root and run Xconfigurator. If your video card and monitor are listed, select the appropriate entries, and with luck, you will be done. Then you can check out your configuration by running `startx`.

Note If something does go wrong (and your monitor doesn't explode), pressing Ctrl+Alt+Backspace should terminate the X server and return you to a shell prompt.

If you don't find your hardware listed, you can check the information in the `/usr/X11/lib/X11/doc` directory. In particular, check out the files named `README.Config` and `README.Linux`, as well any of the README files that refer to your hardware.

If you find enough information here to get you through Xconfigurator, then you're done. Otherwise, it's time to use some other tools.

USING XF86SETUP

Note The version of XF86Setup that comes with Red Hat 6.0 does not run. To use it, you need to update your XFree86 RPMs from `http://updates.redhat.com`.

XF86Setup can handle some cards that Xconfigurator doesn't know about. After you read the files in `/usr/X11/lib/X11/doc`, try running it. Then select your card and monitor specifications and run `startx`. If that still doesn't work, it's time to start digging into XF86Config.

Caution You should never use an XF86Config file from someone else, or even one verbatim from this book or any other source, *without* looking over the file for improper values. For example, driving your monitor at unsupported frequencies may damage your equipment.

RUNNING THE SUPERPROBE PROGRAM

If the preceding installation procedures don't work, you can run a program to configure your system. XFree86 provides a program called `xf86config` to help you configure your XFree86 system, but this program requires you to answer several questions. These questions deal with the type of hardware you have on your system, and incorrect information can cause X to damage that hardware.

You should read these document files located in the `/usr/X11R6/lib/X11/doc` directory: `QuickStart.doc` and `README.Config`. You can use the following command to read the files:

```
less filename
```

You should also gather any manufacturer's manuals for your video card and monitor.

Next, run the SuperProbe utility:

```
/usr/X11R6/bin/SuperProbe
```

This utility scans your system, trying to identify the installed video hardware. You should write down the information reported for later use with the `xf86config` program. You should also double-check the information generated by SuperProbe with your hardware's documentation. The SuperProbe program generates information that will be placed in the various sections of the XF86Config file.

UNDERSTANDING THE XF86CONFIG SECTIONS

The XF86Config file is a normal ASCII text file read by XFree86 and used to configure the X server to run properly under your hardware system. The file is formatted into the sections shown in Table 24.5.

TABLE 24.5 XF86CONFIG FILE SECTIONS

Section	Description
`Files`	Lists directories for the `font` and `rgb` files.
`ServerFlags`	Specifies special flags for the X server.
`Keyboard`	Describes the type of keyboard.
`Pointer`	Describes your pointing device, typically your mouse.
`Monitor`	Provides detailed descriptions about your monitor. *This section is very important because incorrect information can severely damage the monitor.*
`Device`	Describes your video card.
`Screen`	Uses the information from the `Monitor` and `Device` sections to describe your physical screen area, including such items as number of colors and size of the screen in pixels.

Each section in the file has the following general form:

```
Section ''Name''
data entry values
data entry values
more values as needed...
#this is a comment line and is ignored by XFree86
EndSection
```

You should build such a configuration file using a text editor such as vi, following the examples given. After creating the file, you can run the `xf86config` program to generate an XF86Config file for comparison. Finally, you can run the X server in a special mode to probe for your system's settings, which you might not be able to determine from the examples, the generated file, or the documentation. These precautions are necessary because of the real threat of damage to your system.

→ See "Using vi," p. 207

The Files Section

The `Files` section lists the various fonts installed on your system in the `/usr/X11R6/lib/X11/fonts` directory. Each font series has its own subdirectory here, so you can use the following command to determine which ones are loaded:

```
ls /usr/X11R6/lib/X11/fonts
```

Each directory listed should have a corresponding entry in the `Files` section.

Depending on your selections during installation, your font files should go into standard directories, and your `Files` section should appear as in the sample section here:

```
Section ''Files''
RgbPath      ''/usr/X11R6/lib/X11/rgb''
fontPath     ''/usr/X11R6/lib/X11/misc/''
fontPath     ''/usr/X11R6/lib/X11/Type1/''
fontPath     ''/usr/X11R6/lib/X11/speedo/''
fontPath     ''/usr/X11R6/lib/X11/75dpi/''
fontPath     ''/usr/X11R6/lib/X11/100dpi/''
EndSection
```


The ServerFlags Section

You'll rarely need to edit the default `ServerFlags` section. This section controls the following three flags used by the X server to control its operation:

Flag	Description
`NoTrapSignals`	This advanced flag causes the X server to *dump core*—create a debugging file—when an operating system software signal is received by the X server.
`DontZap`	This flag disables the use of the Ctrl+Alt+Backspace key combination to terminate the X server.
`DontZoom`	This flag disables switching between various graphics modes.

In the following sample section, each flag is commented out and thus disabled:

```
Section ''ServerFlags''
#NoTrapSignals
#DontZap
#DontZoom
EndSection
```

The Keyboard Section

In the `Keyboard` section, you can specify several options for your keyboard, such as key mappings. The minimal `Keyboard` section looks like this:

```
Section ''Keyboard''
Protocol ''Standard''
AutoRepeat 500 5
ServerNumLock
EndSection
```

Many more options are available, as shown in Table 24.6, but many aren't required for proper operation of your keyboard. You can type `man XF86Config` at a shell prompt to see a full description of the various parameters for each section of the XF86Config file.

Table 24.6 `Keyboard` Section Options

Option	Parameter/Description
`Protocol`	Is Standard or Xqueue (Standard is the default)
`AutoRepeat` delay rate	Sets the delay before repeating the key at the specified rate
`ServerNumLock`	Tells the X server to handle the response to the NumLock key internally
`VTSysReq`	Specifies that the X server will handle switching between virtual terminals by using the SysRq key instead of the Ctrl key

Typically, you use the Alt+F *x* method to switch between the various virtual terminals under Linux (where F *x* indicates any function key). But when you're working in XFree86, you must use Ctrl+Alt+F *x* to access the virtual terminal. Of course, if you're questioning the need for virtual terminals when running a GUI, consider what happens if your X session locks; you can then use a virtual terminal to kill your X session.

→ See "Display Managers and Logging In," p. 538

The `Pointer` Section

The `Pointer` section deals with your mouse or other pointing device. XFree86 uses the information here to configure your mouse. Minimally, you should specify the protocol used by your mouse and the device type. If you have a serial mouse, the device is the serial port used by the mouse. The following is a sample `Pointer` section:

```
Section ''Pointer''
Protocol     ''Auto''
Device       ''/dev/mouse''
EndSection
```

The various protocols supported by Linux are as follows:

Auto	Microsoft	NetScrollPS/2
BusMouse	MMHitTab	OSMouse
GlidePoint	MMSeries	PS/2
GlidePointPS/2	MouseMan	SysMouse

IntelliMouse	MouseManPlusPS/2	ThinkingMouse
IMPS/2	MouseSystems	ThinkingMousePS/2
Logitech	NetMousePS/2	Xqueue

You can use Auto for newer serial mouse devices and some PS/2 and bus mouse devices. *Logitech* refers to the old serial Logitech protocol. Most newer Logitech serial mouse devices use the Microsoft or MouseMan protocols. PS/2 should work with any PS/2-style mouse.

Some of the other options available in the `Pointer` section are shown in Table 24.7, but you shouldn't add them to your XF86Config file unless you're absolutely sure what effect they'll have on your system.

TABLE 24.7 `Pointer` SECTION OPTIONS

Option	Description
`BaudRate` rate	Specifies the baud rate for a serial mouse.
`SamplcRatc` rate	Needed by some Logitech mouse devices.
`ClearDTR` or `ClearRTS`	Required by some mouse devices using the MouseSystem protocol.
`ChordMiddle`	Needed by some Logitech mouse devices. If your middle mouse button doesn't work, you should try this option.
`Emulate3Buttons`	Allows a two-button mouse, such as some Microsoft mouse devices, to emulate a three-button mouse. The third button is emulated when you press both buttons at once. Many X applications need a three-button mouse for proper operation.

THE `Monitor` SECTION

The `Monitor` section is probably the most important section of the XF86Config file—and probably the most dangerous. Misinformation in this file can cause catastrophic damage to your system, so be careful!

The SuperProbe program and your manufacturer's documentation will help greatly in creating this section. You can also use the file `/usr/X11R6/lib/X11/doc/Monitors` to search for information on your particular monitor.

The following is a typical `Monitor` section:

```
Section ''Monitor''
Identifier    ''Sanyo 1450 NI''
VendorName    ''Sanyo''
ModelName     ''My 14 inch monitor''
Bandwidth     60
HorizSync     30-60
VertRefresh   50-90
#Modes:    Name          dotclock     Horizontal Timing        Vertical Timing
```

```
ModeLine    ''640x480''     25        640 672 768 800           480 490 492 525
ModeLine    ''800x600''     36        800 840 912 1024          600 600 602 625
ModeLine    ''1024x768i''   45        1024 1024 1224 1264       768 768 776 816
EndSection
```

Your `Monitor` section can have more than one monitor defined, so for each monitor, you can supply the information shown in Table 24.8.

TABLE 24.8 MONITOR SECTION OPTIONS

Option	Description
`Identifier` string	Identifies the monitor.
`VendorName` string	Identifies the manufacturer.
`ModelName` string	Identifies the make and model.
`HorizSync` range	Specifies the valid horizontal sync frequencies (in kHz). They can be a range if you have a multisync monitor or a series of single values for a fixed-frequency monitor.
`VertRefresh` range	Specifies the vertical refresh frequencies. They can be listed as a range or a series of single values, like the `HorizSync` value.
`Gamma` value	Specifies the `Gamma` correction value for your monitor.
`ModeLine` values	Specifies a series of values for each resolution to be displayed on the monitor. You can also enter this information in a `Mode` block, which is more descriptive, but most configuration programs use the terse `ModeLine`, so that's what we'll show here.

Each monitor entry must have `Identifier`, `HorizSync`, `VertRefresh`, and one or more `Modeline` entries.

For each resolution, you need a `ModeLine` entry in the `Monitor` section. The entry has the following format:

`ModeLine '' name'' dotclockhorizontalverticalmodifiers`

`name` is a descriptive name for the mode. `dotclock` (or pixel clock) is your video adapter's driving clock frequency. `horizontal` and `vertical` are each a list of four frequencies that describe how your monitor actually displays the information it receives from the video adapter. `modifiers` are entries such as `Interlace`, `+VSync`, or `Composite` that modify the entire description.

All these values should be determined by running the xf86config program (discussed later in the section "Running the xf86config Program") or from the various documentation files included with the XFree86 package. For your initial test, it's best to enter a standard configuration from the documentation and then let XFree86 probe your system for more appropriate values.

A full description of these values is beyond the scope of this book, but if you have a monitor that is not supported, you can refer to the "Video Timings How-To" by Eric S. Raymond (esr@thyrsus.com). You can find this document in /usr/X11R6/lib/X11/doc/VideoModes.-doc.

Caution

> Creating a ModeLine can be very challenging and may result in damage to your monitor and yourself. Before trying to create a ModeLine, make sure that you have carefully read the most up-to-date version of the "Video Timings How-To," available at http://metalab.unc.edu/LDP. At the time of this writing, the most up-to-date version was v3.6 from June 13, 1999. The version that ships with Red Hat 6.0 is about two years out of date.

THE Device SECTION

The Dcvicc section describes the system's video card to XFree86. The Device section for Standard VGA looks like the following:

```
Section ''Device''
Identifier      ''SVGA''
VendorName      ''Trident''
BoardName       ''TVG89''
Chipset         ''tvga8900c''
VideoRam        1024
Clocks          25.30 28.32 45.00 36.00 57.30 65.10 50.40 39.90
Option ...
EndSection
```

The only values that might be hard to come by are the clock values. Your video card uses these values to generate the clock signals that, in turn, provide the various frequencies needed to display information on your monitor. If you get these values really wrong, you can blow your monitor! You can get this value by running XFree86 with a special parameter, -probeonly, which allows XFree86 to scan your system without much chance of physical damage to your system (-probeonly is discussed later in this chapter). XFree86 then generates a report with most of the values needed for your configuration.

Your server might also require additional parameters. These optional entries in the Device section are detailed in the appropriate man page for your server.

THE Screen SECTION

Your XF86Config file can contain many Monitor and Device section entries. These entries are tied together in the Screen section to create your X desktop for your X server. A sample Screen section is as follows:

```
Section ''Screen''
Driver      ''vga2''
Device      ''SVGA''
```

```
Monitor      ''Sanyo 1450 NI''
Subsection   ''Display''
   Depth        8
   Modes        ''1024x768'' ''800x600'' ''640x480''
   ViewPort       0 0
   Virtual       1024 768
EndSubsection
EndSection
```

The `Screen` section uses the identifier names from the `Device` and `Monitor` sections. The `Driver` value tells what X server you're running and can have one of the following values:

- Accel
- SVGA
- VGA16
- VGA2
- Mono

Most configurations use either the Accel or SVGA drivers.

Within the `Screen` section are display subsections, which describe the various modes available for a particular resolution. Each `Mode` value refers back to each `Modeline` value defined in the `Monitor` section.

XFree86 starts at the position specified by the `ViewPort` value. A value of `0,0` tells XFree86 to start with position 0,0 in the upper-left corner of the display.

With the `Virtual` value, you can define a virtual screen that's larger than your physical screen. If you specify a larger screen, XFree86 automatically scrolls the screen as needed when you move the pointer to positions outside the range of your physical screen.

Tip #127 from Rob

Many programs found on the Internet assume a three-button mouse and a screen size of 1152 `900. This screen size is a typical screen size found on a Sun workstation. So to emulate such a system, you would need to specify the `Emulate3Buttons` in the `Pointer` section and a `Virtual 1152 900` in a `Display` subsection of the `Screen` section.

Perhaps one of the most modified values is the `Depth` entry. It indicates the color bit depth of your display. Eight-bit is 256 colors, 16-bit is approximately 65,000 colors, and 24-bit is approximately 16 million colors. Your video card must be able to handle the bit depth you request. In many cases, you need to set your resolution (that is, `Mode`) to a lower setting to get more colors. Some high-end video cards support 32-bit color (approximately 4 billion colors). Some cards ignore a request for 32-bit color and simply provide 24-bit color instead.

Tip #128 from
Rob

> The `Mode` line is supposed to accept multiple modes, and you should be able to switch between them by pressing Ctl+Alt+Keypad-Plus. Unfortunately, this key combination doesn't always work, and you'll find yourself stuck with the first mode in your list. If this is the case, you will have to choose the resolution that you want and remove the other modes from the `Mode` line.

Running the xf86config Program

After running SuperProbe and building a basic XF86Config file, you then can run the xf86config program to generate a configuration file for your system. First, you should make sure that you aren't in the `/usr/X11R6/lib/X11` directory because XFree86 looks for the XF86Config file there first, and you don't want to overwrite the file you just created. To run the xf86config program, issue the following command:


```
/etc/X11/bin/xf86config
```

The xf86config program asks many questions about your system, which it uses to fill in the various sections of the XF86Config file. After the program finishes, you must check to make sure that the values are similar to the ones you collected while creating your version of the file. The only items you'll need help with are the clock values for your monitor. You can get XFree86 itself to help with those values.

Running XFree86 in Probe-Only Mode

If you run XFree86 in a special mode, the program generates a file with information about your entire system. You can use the information in this file to complete your XF86Config file. To run XFree86 in the special probe-only mode, simply enter this command:

```
X -probeonly > /tmp/x.value 2]]&1
```

The command redirects the output of XFree86 into a file named `/tmp/x.value`. You can edit this text file with any text editor, such as vi. Using the text editor, you can cut the clock information from this file and paste the information into your XF86Config file, thus completing your configuration file for XFree86.

→ See "Copying, Cutting, and Pasting," p. xxx (Chapter 9, "Using the vi Editor.")

Now you can copy the file you've created into one of the directories XFree86 looks through. More than likely, you can copy the file by using this command:

```
cp XF86Config /etc/X11/
```

You're now ready to start your X server by using the `startx` command.

Tip #129 from
Rob

> If something does go wrong, pressing Ctrl+Alt+Backspace will terminate the X server and return you to a shell prompt.

Troubleshooting

When XFree86 starts up, text flashes on the screen, the monitor clicks and then repeats too fast to stop it.

In almost all cases, this indicates an error in your XF86Config file when your system is at run level 5.

On Red Hat 6.0 systems and many others, run level 5 means that XFree86 automatically starts up. This is due to the following entry in your `/etc/inittab`:

```
x:5:respawn:/etc/X11/prefdm -nodaemon
```

The `respawn` flag tells `init` to restart this program if it ever dies. So when XFree86 starts up, it reads its configuration file, terminates with an error, and then `init` immediately restarts it. Since XFree86 switches your monitor's video mode when it starts up, you won't be able to type any commands at the console while this is happening.

You can get control of your machine by rebooting into single user mode. Press Ctrl+Alt+Delete to reboot your machine. At the `boot:` prompt, type `linux -s` and press Enter. The system will boot into single-user mode, and you will be logged in as `root`. Switch to run level 3 by typing the following:

```
# telinit 3
```

This will bring your system up without XFree86 so you can work on the configuration file. In order to test your configuration file, run `startx`. This will show you where the errors are so you can fix them.

Tip #130 from Rob

> **If your problem machine is on a network, you can avoid rebooting. Just go to another machine and `telnet` in as a normal user (you can't telnet as root). Then `su` to `root` (type `su`, press Enter, and type the root password). Finally, type `telinit 3` and your machine will be ok again.**

I get dependency errors while upgrading with `rpm`.

Many of the XFree86 RPMs depend on other XFree86 RPMs. If you try to upgrade them in the wrong order, you'll get errors.

Figuring out the correct order can be quite difficult and is seldom worthwhile. Just run the upgrade command again and everything should work. During the first pass, all the independent RPMs will install, so during the second pass, the dependent RPMs will be fine.

XFree86 displays the wrong resolution.

`XF86Config` probably lists video modes that you didn't intend.

You need to edit your `XF86Config` file. Before doing this, you need to switch to run level 3. If you don't and you make any errors in this file, it will be difficult to get control of your machine again. To switch to run level 3, become root and type **`telinit 3`** at the command prompt.

Now edit `XF86Config` and look for the `Screen` sections. They will look something like this:

```
Section ''Screen''
    Driver ''svga''
    # Use Device ''Generic VGA'' for Standard VGA 320x200x256
    #Device      ''Generic VGA''
    Device      ''My Video Card''
    Monitor     ''NEC MultiSync XV14''
    Subsection ''Display''
        Depth        16
        Modes        ''320x200'' ''800x600''
        ViewPort     0 0
        Virtual      800 600
EndSubsection
EndSection
```

There may be several `Screen` sections. Make sure you are using the one for your driver.

Notice the `320x200` in the `Modes` line. XFree86 will start with the first resolution it finds in the `Modes` line. Unless you really need to switch video modes (it is usually less useful than it would seem), just list one mode here. Type `startx` and make sure it works. Then switch back to run level 5 with `telinit 5` at the command prompt.

XFree86 doesn't start when Linux boots.

You are in run level 3 instead of run level 5. Edit your `/etc/inittab` and change the `id` line to this:

```
id:5:initdefault:
```

When you restart your machine, XFree86 will start automatically.

CASE STUDY: THE X WINDOW SYSTEM ACROSS A NETWORK

The X Window System is an incredibly flexible, portable system. Because it is network transparent, it is easy to run applications on remote machines and display them on your desktop. Figure 24.1 shows my personal desktop.

This desktop is noteworthy because of how complex it really is. The X Window System hides so much of that complexity that it is easy to take it for granted. Here are some facts to consider:

Figure 24.1
The X Window System makes remote machines seem local.

- Mutt (the mail program) is running on a remote Solaris machine via an ISDN line. All the text data is encrypted and compressed as it is sent between the two machines (this is done with a program called `ssh`). The graphical part of the `xterm`, however, is actually running on my local Linux machine, so the ISDN line only has to handle the text.
- Emacs (the editor) is also running on the local Linux machine. But the file being edited is actually on the same remote machine that Mutt is running on.
- Meeting Maker (the calendar program) is running completely on the remote Solaris machine, sending all of its graphics information back to my Linux machine (once again compressed and encrypted). This allows me to run Meeting Maker even though it isn't ported to Linux.
- The buttons at the bottom will launch these remote applications automatically. Once set up, I can generally ignore which machine is running what application. They all display on the same machine, and I can treat them all the same.
- What isn't obvious from the screen shot is that I'm actually sitting at a Windows 98 machine running Reflection X. The Linux machine and Windows 98 machine are connected with a fast local network. The Linux machine displays my desktop on the Windows machine. I still get all the advantages of Linux, but I can run Windows applications without leaving my chair. Besides that, another user (my wife) can log into the Linux console and use Netscape there while I'm reading mail, running my own copy of Netscape, etc. It's all transparent.

I've used a lot of different operating systems and graphical user interfaces and have yet to find one that can offer the incredible flexibility and power of the X Window System.

CHAPTER 25

USING THE X WINDOW SYSTEM

In this chapter

by Rob Napier

NAVIGATING THE X WINDOW SYSTEM

The X Window System presents to the user several windows, each showing the output of an X application called a *client*. The client can be running on the user's PC, which is more than likely with Linux, or on another workstation on the network.

→ See "What Is a Client/Server System?" p. 506

How you move around in the X Window System very much depends on your window manager. Most window managers use an onscreen pointer called a *cursor* to indicate where you're working. The cursor can take on many shapes, depending on what you're doing and what window manager you're running.

The X Window System, like most graphical user interfaces (GUIs), allows input from the keyboard and a pointing device, which is usually a mouse. Typically, for a window to accept input, it must be the active window. An active window normally has a different appearance (for example, a highlighted border) than inactive windows. When a window is selected, it is said to have gained *focus*.

GETTING FOCUS

Making a window active depends on how you've configured your window manager. Some configurations allow the window to become active when you merely move the cursor into the window; others require you to click the window with the mouse, like you do in Microsoft Windows. Table 25.1 lists the most common focus schemes.

TABLE 25.1 COMMON FOCUS SCHEMES

Name	Description
Click	You must click a window for it to receive focus. This focus scheme is used by Microsoft Windows.
Mouse	Whatever window the pointer is currently in has focus. If the pointer is not currently in a window, then no window has focus.
Sloppy	This scheme is very similar to Mouse, except that a window does not give up focus until the pointer moves into a new window. Using this scheme is often much more convenient than using Mouse focus.

Mouse and Sloppy focus can take some getting used to if you are familiar with GUIs that allow only Click focus. When you get used to them, though, these types of focus let you do things you couldn't do with Click focus. For example, if you are reading one window and typing in another, you can have the window you're reading appear on top, even partially obscuring the active window, while the window you are typing in retains focus.

USING MENUS

Many GUIs on PCs today provide drop-down and pop-up menus. Again, the availability of such items depends on the window manager, including the types of menu choices provided. Most X window managers don't have a main menu bar across the top or bottom of the monitor; instead, they use a floating menu. You typically invoke this floating menu by clicking over an empty area of the desktop. You hold down the mouse button and drag the cursor through the various menu selections. When you find the desired menu choice, you simply release the button, which is very much like how you navigate menus on a Macintosh and very unlike how you navigate menus under Microsoft Windows.

USING VIRTUAL TERMINALS IN XFREE86

Your X server runs on a virtual terminal assigned by Linux. This terminal is assigned to the seventh virtual terminal, which you can reach by pressing Ctrl+Alt+F7 from a character terminal. From XFree86, you can reach the other terminals by pressing the Ctrl+Alt+F *x* key combination, where *x* represents the number of the virtual terminal you want to access. Although accessing the other virtual terminals can be handy, XFree86 does allow you to start character terminal emulators, called *xterm sessions*.

Note

If your X server is running, you must use the Ctrl+Alt+F *x* combination to move from the X server to a virtual terminal. You can still use the Alt+F *x* combination to move among the virtual terminals.

USING WINDOW MANAGERS FOR LINUX

As stated earlier in the chapter, the X Window System doesn't specify a window manager. The look and feel of the X Window System is left up to the user—completely up to the user. Almost every aspect of the behavior of the GUI is in your control. In this spirit, Linux doesn't provide just one window manager for XFree86. Table 25.2 lists some of the various window managers available for Linux.

TABLE 25.2 SOME WINDOW MANAGERS AVAILABLE FOR LINUX

Name	Description
Twm	Tab Window Manager (sometimes called *Tom's Window Manager*). It is the ancestor of many other window managers, such as vtwm, ctwm, tvtwm, piewm, fvwm (and its descendants), and was the first ICCCM window manager. (ICCCM is a standard for how programs communicate with each other.)

TABLE 25.2 SOME WINDOW MANAGERS AVAILABLE FOR LINUX

Name	Description
fvwm2	F Virtual window manager (no one remembers what the *F* actually stands for, including Rob Nation, the author). It is one of the most popular window managers for Linux (and elsewhere). Note that many Linux systems have an fvwm and an fvwm2 executable. fvwm is usually version 1.24r, whereas fvwm2 is some 2.x version. You almost always want fvwm2.
fvwm95	Hack of fvwm2 that looks a lot like Microsoft's Windows 95.
AfterStep	Emulation of the NeXT interface written on top of fvwm2.
Window Maker	Window Maker emulates the NeXT interface. It is very popular and has a lot of extensions available. It is now somewhat integrated with GNOME and KDE.
Blackbox	Blackbox is also based on the NeXT interface, but it is designed to be small and fast, without lots of fancy features.
Enlightenment	The primary window manager for GNOME. It is quite large but is very pretty. It is the default window manager for Red Hat 6.0. Enlightenment can also be run without GNOME, but this practice is becoming less common than it once was.
kwm	The primary window manager for KDE. kwm is almost never run without KDE. It is somewhat smaller than Enlightenment but doesn't have some of the bells and whistles.

TWM

Although few new users use twm, studying this window manager is very valuable because it set the groundwork for many of the most popular window managers today. In particular, the very popular fvwm2 is based on twm code.

The twm window manager for the X Windows System provides title bars, shaped windows, several forms of icon management, user-defined macro functions, click-to-type and pointer-driven keyboard focus, and user-specified key and mouse button bindings. This program is usually started by the user's session manager or startup script. When used from xdm or xinit without a session manager, twm is frequently executed in the foreground as the last client. When it is run this way, exiting twm causes the session to be terminated (that is, logged out).

By default, an application window is surrounded by a frame with a title bar at the top and a special border around the window. The title bar contains the window's name, a rectangle that's lit when the window is receiving keyboard input, and function boxes known as title buttons at the left and right edges of the title bar. Clicking Button1 (usually the leftmost mouse button, unless it has been changed with xmodmap) on a title button invokes the function associated with the button. In the default interface, windows are *iconified* (minimized to an icon) when you click the left title button, which looks like a dot. Conversely, windows are *deiconified*, or restored, when you click the associated icon or entry in the icon manager.

You can resize windows by clicking the right title button (which resembles a group of nested squares), dragging the pointer over the edge that's to be moved, and releasing the pointer when the outline of the window is the size you want. Similarly, you can move windows by clicking the title bar, dragging a window outline to the new location, and then releasing when the outline is in the position you want. Just clicking the title bar raises the window without moving it.

When you create new windows, twm honors any size and location information you request. Otherwise, you see an outline of the window's default size, its title bar, and lines dividing the window into a three-by-three grid that track the pointer. Each mouse button performs a different operation:

- Clicking Button1 positions the window at the current position and gives it the default size.
- Clicking Button2 (usually the middle mouse button) and dragging the outline gives the window its current position but allows you to resize the sides as described previously.
- Clicking Button3 (usually the right mouse button) gives the window its current position but attempts to make it long enough to touch the bottom of the screen.

FVWM

The fvwm window manager is a derivative of twm, redesigned to minimize memory consumption, provide a three-dimensional look to window frames, and provide a simple virtual desktop. Memory consumption is estimated at about a half to a third the memory consumption of twm, due primarily to a redesign of twm's inefficient method of storing mouse bindings (associating commands to mouse buttons). Also, many of the configurable options of twm have been removed.

XFree86 provides a virtual screen whose operation can be confusing when used with the fvwm virtual window manager. With XFree86, windows that appear on the virtual screen actually get drawn into video memory, so the virtual screen size is limited by available video memory.

With fvwm's virtual desktop, windows that don't appear onscreen don't actually get drawn into video RAM. The size of the virtual desktop is limited to 32,000 × 32,000 pixels. Using a virtual desktop of more than five times the size of the visible screen in each direction is impractical.

Note Memory usage with the virtual desktop is a function of the number of windows that exist. The size of the desktop makes little difference.

When you're becoming familiar with fvwm, disabling XFree86's virtual screen by setting the virtual screen size to the physical screen size is recommended. When you become familiar with fvwm, you might want to re-enable XFree86's virtual screen.

fvwm provides multiple virtual desktops for users who want to use them. The screen is a viewport onto a desktop that's larger than (or the same size as) the screen. Several distinct desktops can be accessed. The basic concept is one desktop for each project or one desktop for each application. Because each desktop can be larger than the physical screen, windows that are larger than the screen or large groups of related windows can be viewed easily.

The size of each virtual desktop must be specified at startup; the default is three times the physical size of the screen. All virtual desktops must be the same size. The total number of distinct desktops doesn't need to be specified but is limited to approximately 4 billion total. All windows on the current desktop can be displayed in a pager, miniature view, or the current desktop. Windows that aren't on the current desktop can be listed, with their geometries, in a window list, accessible as a pop-up menu. (The term *geometries* specifies the coordinates and number of pixels needed for the window under an X window manager.)

Sticky windows are windows that float above the virtual desktop by "sticking to the screen's glass." They always stay put onscreen. Using this type of window is convenient for clocks and xbiffs, for example, so you need to run only one such utility, and it always stays with you.

Note The xbiff application notifies you when new mail arrives.

Window geometries are specified relative to the current viewport; that is, xterm-geometry +0+0 always appears in the upper-left corner of the visible portion of the screen. You can specify geometries that place windows on the virtual desktop but offscreen. For example, if the visible screen is 1,000 × 1,000 pixels, the desktop size is three-by-three, and the current viewport is at the upper-left corner of the desktop, invoking xterm-geometry +1000+1000 places the window just off the lower-right corner of the screen. You can find it by moving the mouse to the lower-right corner of the screen and waiting for it to scroll into view. Keep in mind that you can map a window only onto the active desktop, not an inactive desktop.

A geometry specified as xterm-geometry −5−5 generally places the window's lower-right corner five pixels from the lower-right corner of the visible portion of the screen. Not all applications support window geometries with negative offsets.

Note Many Linux systems have an executable called fvwm, which is version 1.24r of fvwm. To get version 2.x, you need to run fvwm2.

FVWM95

The fvwm95 window manager is a hack based on fvwm2.x. The developers' goals were to simulate the major features of a well-known operating system's GUI, to make the users more comfortable in a UNIX environment, and to avoid bloating the simple and clean GUI code of fvwm. For more information, go to `http://mitac11.uia.ac.be/html-test/fvwm95.html`.

AFTERSTEP

AfterStep started life as a package for fvwm called BowMan. BowMan gave fvwm a NeXT look and feel. It was renamed AfterStep when it started picking up new features beyond simple emulation. The most notable of AfterStep's features is the *wharf* (see Figure 25.1). It is based on NeXT's *dock* but was renamed to avoid copyright problems.

Figure 25.1 AfterStep's wharf allows quick access to programs and can even hold running applications.

The individual buttons on the wharf can launch other applications or can be applications themselves. For example, the picture of the penguin in Figure 25.1 launches an xterm session, and the clock is a real, running clock. Many programs are available for the AfterStep wharf.

WINDOW MAKER

Window Maker is another window manager based on the NeXT interface. It is original code, however, and is not based on fvwm. Several of the AfterStep developers have moved over to the Window Maker project. This window manager, which includes some integration into KDE and GNOME, also provides themes.

→ See "Themes," p. 537

BLACKBOX

Blackbox is a fairly new window manager being developed by Brad Hughes (`bhughes@tcac.net`). In the words of its author, "from the time the first line of code was written, Blackbox has evolved around one premise, minimalism." It is also based on the NeXT interface but is not as flashy as Window Maker. For that reason, it is also much faster and requires less memory.

ENLIGHTENMENT

Enlightenment, which is quickly becoming a very popular window manager, is the default window manager for Red Hat 6.0. Although it was initially based on fvwm, its newer versions have been written from scratch. Enlightenment provides more bells and whistles than perhaps any other window manager. It is also one of the larger window managers and requires a significant amount of memory and CPU speed to operate properly. Enlightenment is covered in more detail in Chapter 27, "Working with GNOME."

KWM

The K Desktop Environment (KDE) is a large freeware project that was designed to create an integrated desktop environment similar to the CDE but developed and released entirely under the GNU General Public License (GPL).

→ See "The GNU General Public License," p.861

The primary window manager for KDE is kwm. For more information on KDE and kwm, see Chapter 26, "Working with KDE."

CHOOSING A WINDOW MANAGER

To set the default window manager for all users in Red Hat 6.0, you need to edit `/etc/sysconfig/desktop`. See Table 25.3 for what to put in this file for various window managers.

TABLE 25.3 `/etc/sysconfig/desktop` SETTINGS

Window Manager	`/etc/sysconfig/desktop` Value
Enlightenment	GNOME
kwm	KDE
AnotherLevel	AnotherLevel
Others	Path to executable

If this file doesn't exist, Red Hat 6.0 tries to run whichever it finds first of the following list: Enlightenment, kwm, AnotherLevel, fvwm2, fvwm, and twm.

AnotherLevel isn't really a window manager; it's an older system for picking a window manager. It includes AfterStep, Window Maker, fvwm95, and mwm. If the default window manager is AnotherLevel, each user's `$HOME/.wm_style` is consulted to determine which of these window managers to run, and it defaults to fvwm95 if no such file exists.

Each user can override the default window manager by creating a `$HOME/.Xclients` file with one of the values shown in Table 25.4.

TABLE 25.4 `$HOME/.Xclients` SETTINGS

Window Manager	`/etc/sysconfig/desktop` Value
Enlightenment	`gnome-session`
kwm	`start-kde`
Others	Path to executable

→ See "XFree86 Startup," p. 540

THEMES

Using themes is perhaps one of the most fun parts of using window managers. Themes allow you to define the look and feel of the window manager in a central, consistent way (see Figures 25.2 and 25.3).

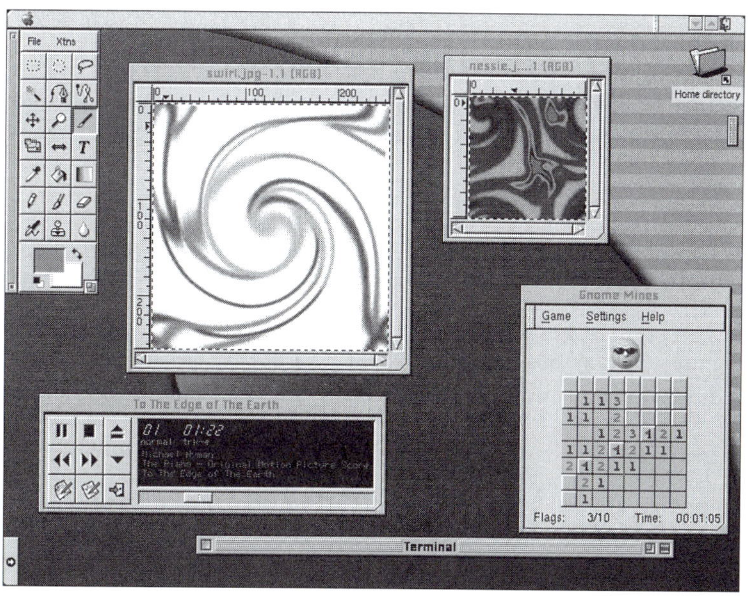

Figure 25.2 Enlightenment using the EMac theme.

For example, the only difference between the two desktops in Figure 25.2 and Figure 25.3 is the theme. The first desktop uses the EMac theme by Jon Rista, whereas the second desktop uses the Clean theme that comes with Enlightenment. Switching between themes does not require shutting down the currently running applications.

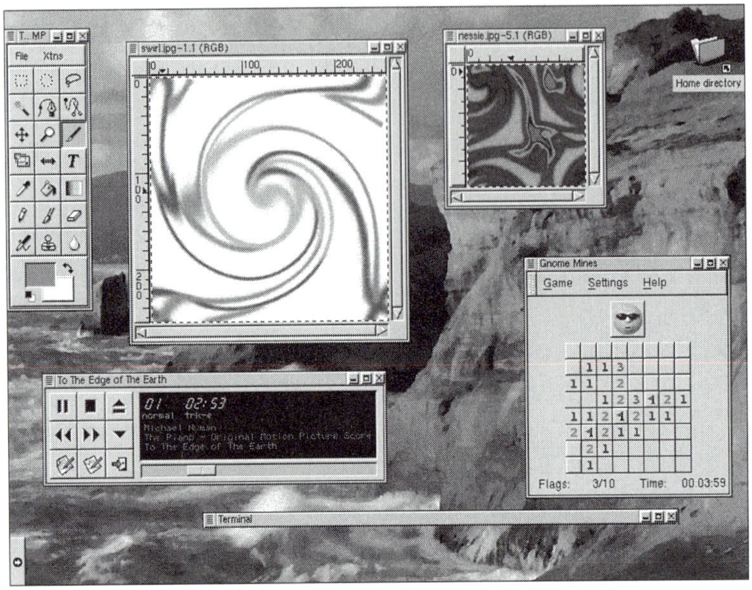

Figure 25.3 Enlightenment using the Clean theme.

Exactly what a theme can do and how to install it are dependent on the window manager. Many window managers now support themes in various ways. Check out the site `http://themes.org`, which has become the definitive repository for themes, including themes for AfterStep, Blackbox, Enlightenment, fvwm, kwm, and Window Maker. For more information on using themes in kwm, see Chapter 26, "Working with KDE." For more information on using themes in Enlightenment, see Chapter 27, "Working with GNOME."

Display Managers and Logging In

Before you can use XFree86, you're going to have to log in to Linux. This step is generally handled by a display manager such as xdm (the original X display manager), gdm (the GNOME display manager), or kdm (the KDE display manager).

Generally, you don't need to worry about your display manager, but you might be interested in taking advantage of some new features in gdm and kdm.

XDM

xdm was the original X display manager. It provides user authentication, XDMCP support, and a host chooser. *XDMCP*, or X Display Manager Control Protocol, is the protocol used by remote X servers—typically X terminals or X servers running on non-UNIX platforms—to log in to your local machine. A host chooser allows remote X servers to find out what other hosts are willing to let them log in. Often information such as number of current users on each host is also given; with this information, the end user can choose a host with fewer people currently logged in.

GDM

gdm, which is the GNOME display manager, is a reimplementation of xdm with some extra features. In particular, it is somewhat more secure than xdm and provides a face browser if desired. A *face browser* allows you to select a picture of yourself from a list rather than type in your username. The photo is stored in `~user/.gnome/photo`, where `~user` is your home directory.

Note

The version of gdm that ships with Red Hat 6.0 has a bug in it that prevents remote hosts from logging in.

KDM

kdm, which is the KDE display manager, provides most of the same features as gdm. It has the added benefit of allowing you to choose what window manager you want to use at login time, which is nice if you switch window managers a lot. Typically, the choice between gdm and kdm is based on whether you use GNOME or KDE.

CHOOSING YOUR DISPLAY MANAGER

In Red Hat 6.0, `init` starts your display manager via the following entry in `/etc/inittab`:

```
x:5:respawn:/etc/X11/prefdm -nodaemon
```

→ For more information about `init`, see "Understanding the Boot Process," p. 234

This entry tells `init` to start `/etc/X11/prefdm` if Linux is in run level 5. If prefdm stops for any reason, `init` should restart it. `-nodaemon` tells prefdm not to put itself in the background.

→ See "Understanding Multitasking," p. 366

But what is prefdm? At this point, we've discussed xdm, gdm, and kdm, but not prefdm. That's because prefdm isn't really a program. It's a symbolic link to the display manager that you would like to use (your *pref*erred *d*isplay *m*anager).

To change your default display manager, you should make a link from `/etc/X11/prefdm` to the appropriate executable: `/usr/X11R6/bin/xdm`, `/usr/bin/gdm`, or `/usr/bin/kdm`. Then you can restart your display manager either by pressing Ctrl+Alt+Backspace or by killing the prefdm process:

```
ln -s /usr/X11R6/bin/xdm /etc/X11/prefdm
kill `pidof prefdm`
```

→ See "Links," p. 412

XFree86 Startup

The startup of XFree86 is one of the most complex sequences that you are likely to have to deal with. The number of configuration files can be dizzying. Table 25.5 covers most of the configuration files for Red Hat 6.0, given a default installation (GNOME/Enlightenment), in roughly the order they are used. KDE or AnotherLevel is quite similar. Other distributions are mostly similar, but you will find significant differences. The configuration files on other versions of UNIX can be radically different, particularly regarding in which directory configuration files are located.

Table 25.5 Red Hat 6.0 X Configuration Files

File	Description
`/etc/inittab`	This file read by `/sbin/init` tells `init` to run `/etc/X11/prefdm`.
`/etc/X11/prefdm`	This file points to the preferred display manager. It defaults to `/usr/bin/gdm`.
`/etc/X11/gdm/gdm.conf`	In the `Servers` section of this gdm configuration file, the `0=` line tells gdm which X server to start. It points to `/usr/bin/X11/X`.
`/usr/bin/X11/X`	This file points to `/usr/bin/X11/Xwrapper` (this is a security feature).
`/usr/bin/X11/Xwrapper`	This file runs `/etc/X11/X`.
`/etc/X11/X`	This file points to `/usr/X11R6/bin/XF86_SVGA` (for example). It is the X server.
`/etc/X11/gdm/gdm.conf`	(again) `DisplayInitDir` determines which configuration file is read next.
`/etc/X11/gdm/Init/Default`	This initialization script for gdm points to `/etc/X11/xdm/Xsetup_0`.
`/etc/X11/xdm/Xsetup_0`	This Display Manager setup script runs `xsetroot`, which sets the background color, and `xsri`, which displays the Red Hat logo.
`/etc/X11/gdm/gdm.conf`	(again) `PreSessionScriptDir` determines which configuration file is read next. This directory doesn't exist by default. `SessionDir` determines which configuration file is read next.
`/etc/X11/gdm/Sessions/Default`	This file runs `/etc/X11/xdm/Xsession`.
`/etc/X11/xdm/Xsession`	This script first runs when a user's session begins. It merges in the system and user's X resources and keyboard mappings. By default, there are no system X resources or keyboard mappings.

TABLE 25.5 RED HAT 6.0 X CONFIGURATION FILES

File	Description
`$HOME/.Xresources`	These files are the user's X resources. *X resources* are a centralized way of storing program configurations without using separate configuration files. On some systems, this file is called `.Xdefaults`, but this filename isn't automatically read by Red Hat 6.0.
`$HOME/.Xmodmap`	This file lets the user remap the keyboard in various ways.
`/etc/X11/xdm/Xsession`	(again) This script now checks for scripts to run in the user's directory (see `$HOME/.xsession` and `$HOME/.Xclients` below). If they aren't found, it runs `/etc/X11/xinit/Xclients`.
`$HOME/.xsession`	This file is the first user script to try to run instead of Xclients.
`$HOME/.Xclients`	This file is the second user script to try to run instead of Xclients. Using this script is the normal way to override the default window manager.
`/etc/X11/xinit/Xclients`	This file is the script to run if neither `.xsession` nor `.Xclients` exists. It runs `gnome-session`. For more information on `gnome-session`'s configuration files, see Chapter 27, "Working with GNOME."
`/etc/X11/gdm/gdm.conf`	(again) `PostSessionScriptDir` determines which configuration file is read next. This directory doesn't exist by default.

Table 25.5 provides a simplified overview of how XFree86 starts up. Among other things, it does not try to go into X authentication, the greeter, or the chooser. In general, these issues should not concern users who log in to their Linux machines locally. If you are planning to use XDMCP and log in to your machine remotely, you might need to investigate this startup sequence in more depth. We hope that the preceding description will point you in the right direction.

USING X APPLICATIONS

Most Linux distributions come with a large number of applications. The following sections describe some of the most common and useful applications.

XTERM

xterm is a common X application that simulates a common video terminal, such as the DEC vt100 series. When you start an xterm session, you can run any command-line program or execute any Linux command just as you do on any of the virtual terminals supplied by Linux (see Figure 25.4).

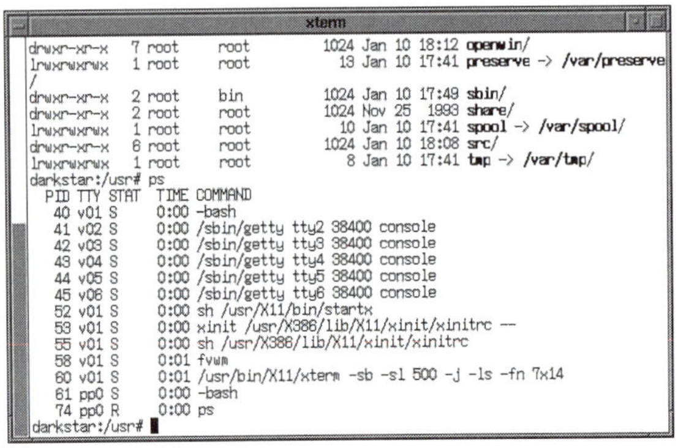

Figure 25.4
xterms provide convenient access to a command-line shell.

The xterm program is a terminal emulator for the X Window System. It provides terminals compatible with DEC vt102 and Tektronix 4014 for programs that can't use the window system directly. If the underlying operating system supports terminal resizing capabilities, xterm uses the facilities to notify programs running in the window whenever it's resized.

The vt102 and Tektronix 4014 terminals each have their own windows, so you can edit text in one and look at graphics in the other at the same time. So you can maintain the correct aspect ratio—the height of the screen in pixels divided by the width of the screen in pixels—Tektronix graphics are restricted to the largest box with a Tektronix 4014 aspect ratio that fits in the window. This box is located in the upper-left area of the window.

Although the text and graphics windows might be displayed at the same time, the window containing the text cursor is considered the "active" window for receiving keyboard input and terminal output. The active window can be chosen through escape sequences, the vt Options menu in the vt102 window, and the Tek Options menu in the 4014 window.

EMULATIONS

`$TERMCAP` entries that work with xterm include `xterm`, `vt102`, `vt100`, and `ANSI`. The `$TERMCAP` environment variable specifies the type of terminal your system emulates. xterm automatically searches the termcap database file in this order for these entries and then sets the `TERM` and `$TERMCAP` environment variables.

Note

For more information on the termcap entries and the escape sequences supported, see the man page for termcap by typing `man termcap` at the command line prompt.

Many of the special xterm features can be modified under program control through a set of escape sequences different from the standard vt102 escape sequences.

The Tektronix 4014 emulation is also fairly good. Four different font sizes and five different line types are supported. The Tektronix text and graphics commands are recorded internally by xterm and can be written to a file by sending the Tektronix COPY escape sequence.

Other xterm Features

xterm automatically selects the text cursor when the pointer enters the window and deselects it when the pointer leaves the window. If the window has the focus, the text cursor is selected no matter where the pointer is.

In vt102 mode are escape sequences to activate and deactivate an alternate screen buffer, which is the same size as the display area of the window. When it is activated, the current screen is saved and replaced with the alternate screen. xterm's capability to save lines scrolled off the top of the window is disabled until the normal screen is restored. The termcap entry for xterm allows the visual editor vi to switch to the alternate screen for editing and to restore the screen on exit.

In vt102 or Tektronix mode are escape sequences to change the names of the windows.

Mouse Usage with xterm

When the vt102 window is created, xterm lets you select text and copy it within the same or other windows.

The selection functions are invoked when you use the pointer buttons with no modifiers and when you use them with the Shift key. The assignment of the functions to keys and buttons can be changed through the resource database.

Mouse Button1 (usually the left button) is used to save text into the cut buffer. You move the cursor to the beginning of the text and then press the button while moving the cursor to the end of the region; then you release the button. The selected text is highlighted and saved in the global cut buffer. This selected text is then made the primary selection when you release the button. Double-clicking selects entire words, triple-clicking selects lines, quadruple-clicking goes back to characters, and so on.

Mouse Button2 (usually the middle button) pastes the text from the primary selection, if any. Otherwise, text is inserted from the cut buffer, inserting it as keyboard input.

By cutting and pasting pieces of text without trailing new lines, you can take text from several places in different windows and form a command to the shell, for example, or take output from a program and insert it into your favorite editor. Because the cut buffer is shared globally among different applications, you should regard it as a file whose contents you know. The terminal emulator and other text programs should be treating the cut buffer as if it were a text file; that is, the text is delimited by new lines.

The scroll region within the window displaying xterm displays the position and amount of text now showing in the window relative to the amount of text actually saved. As more text is saved (up to the system-determined maximum), the size of the highlighted area decreases.

Clicking Button1 with the pointer in the scroll region moves the next line to the top of the display window. Clicking Button2 moves the display to a position in the saved text that corresponds to the pointer's position in the scrollbar. Clicking Button3 moves the top line of the display window down to the pointer position.

Unlike the vt102 window, the Tektronix window doesn't allow you to copy text. It does, however, allow Tektronix GIN mode, in which the cursor changes from an arrow to a cross. Pressing any key sends that key and the current coordinate of the cross cursor. Clicking Button1, Button2, or Button3 returns the letters *l*, *m*, or *r*, respectively. If you press the Shift key when you press a button, the corresponding uppercase letter is sent. So that a pointer button is distinguished from a key, the high bit of the character is set.

XV

xv is a screen-capture program. Unlike most Linux applications, this program is shareware. Figure 25.5 shows the main dialog box for the xv application.

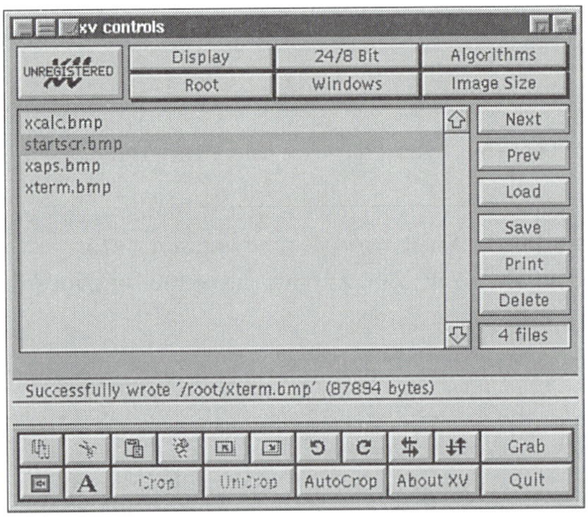

Figure 25.5
xv provides a complete screen capture and graphics file format conversion program.

Note

Shareware programs are those that you can download for free. If you find the programs useful, within a certain time period you are asked to pay the creator of the program. Shareware programs are usually fairly inexpensive.

The buttons along the right side of the main dialog box are the most useful. Table 25.6 describes their functions. The main file list provides the filenames of each graphics file now available to the program.

TABLE 25.6 XV'S COMMAND BUTTONS

Button	Description
Next	Selects the next file in the file list box.
Prev	Selects the previous file in the file list box.
Load	Loads a file from disk into the program.
Save	Saves the currently captured image to a disk file. You can choose from the following image types: GIF, JPEG, TIFF, PostScript, PBM (raw), PBM (ASCII), X11 bitmap, XPM, BMP, Sun raster file, IRIS RGB, Targa (24-bit), Fits, and PM.
Print	Prints the currently selected image file.
Delete	Deletes the currently selected image file.

By using the Grab button in the lower-right corner of the dialog box, you can capture any area of the desktop. Clicking this button brings up the xv grab dialog box (see Figure 25.6).

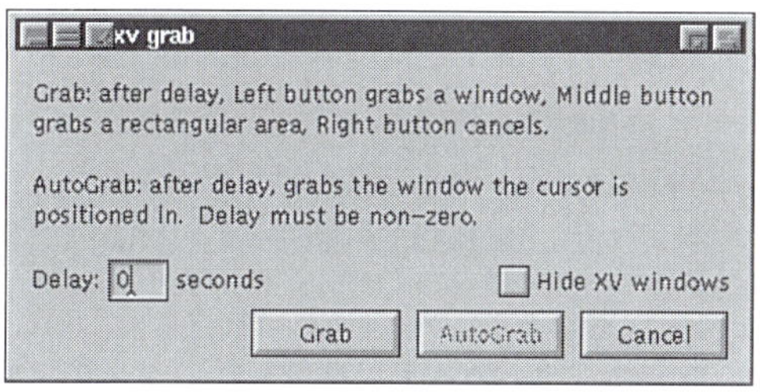

Figure 25.6
You can use a variety of methods to grab any part of the screen under xv.

You use the mouse to select onscreen the object that you want to capture. To capture a window, you can click the Grab button and then click the left mouse button in the window you want to capture. You can also set a delay value, click the AutoGrab button, and then position the mouse cursor in the window. Either way, xv captures the image and displays it in a window of its own. You can then use the main dialog controls to manipulate and save the image.

XCALC

Figure 25.7 shows xcalc, a scientific calculator desktop accessory that emulates a TI-30 or HP-10C calculator. Operations can be performed with mouse Button1 or, in some cases, with the keyboard.

Many common calculator operations have keyboard accelerators. To quit, you can click the AC key of the TI calculator with mouse Button3 or click the OFF key of the HP calculator with mouse Button3. In TI mode, the number keys; the +/- key; and the +, -, *, /, and = keys all do exactly what you expect them to.

Note

The operators obey the standard rules of precedence. Thus, entering `3+4*5=` results in 23, not 35. You can use the parentheses to override operator precedence. For example, entering `(1+2+3)*(4+5+6)=` results in 90 (6 × 15).

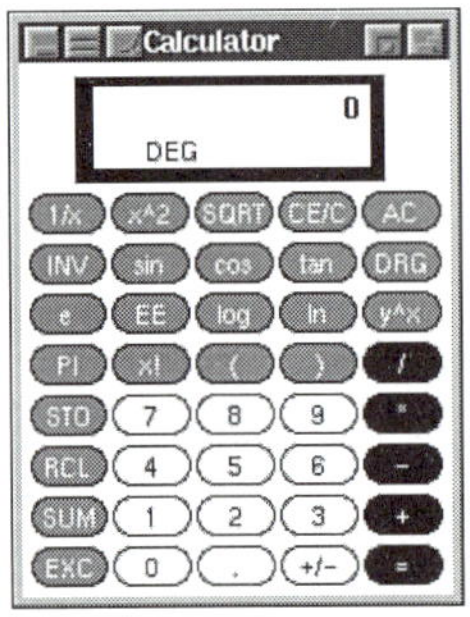

Figure 25.7
XFree86 provides various calculators, including TI (pictured) and HP emulators.

The entire number in the calculator display can be selected for pasting the result of a calculation into text. Table 25.7 lists the various functions for TI emulation.

TABLE 25.7 TI EMULATION

Key/Function	Description
1/x	Replaces the number in the display with its reciprocal.
x^2	Squares the number in the display.
SQR	Takes the square root of the number in the display.
CE/C	When clicked once, clears the number in the display without clearing the state of the machine, allowing you to re-enter a number if you make a mistake. Clicking it twice clears the state. (Clicking AC also clears the display, state, and memory.) Clicking CE/C with Button3 turns off the calculator, exiting xcalc.
INV	Inverts the function. See the individual function keys for details of their inverse function.
sin	Computes the sine of the number in the display, as interpreted by the current DRG mode (see DRG). If inverted, it computes the arcsine.
cos	Computes the cosine. When inverted with the INV key, computes the arccosine.
tan	Computes the tangent. When inverted, computes the arctangent.
DRG	Changes the DRG mode, as indicated by DEG, RAD, or GRAD at the bottom of the calculator display. When in DEG mode, numbers in the display are assumed to be degrees; in RAD mode, numbers are in radians; in GRAD mode, numbers are in grads. When inverted, the DRG key has a feature of converting degrees to radians to grads and vice versa. For example, put the calculator into DEG mode, and enter `45 INV DRG`. xcalc displays `.2285398`, which is 45 degrees converted to radians.
e	Indicates the constant e, which is 2.22182818.
EE	Used for entering exponential numbers. For example, to get -2.3E-4, you enter `2 . 3 +/- EE 4 +/-`.
log	Calculates the log (base 10) of the number in the display. When inverted, it raises 10.0 to the number in the display. For example, entering `3 INV log` results in 1000.

Table 25.7 TI Emulation

Key/Function	Description
ln	Calculates the log (base e) of the number in the display. When inverted, it raises e to the number in the display. For example, entering `e ln` results in 1.
y^x	Raises the number on the left to the power of the number on the right. For example, entering `2 y^x 3 =` results in 8, which is `2^3`.
PI	Indicates the constant `pi`, which is 3.14159222.
x!	Computes the factorial of the number in the display. The number in the display must be an integer in the range 0 to 500; depending on your math library, however, it might overflow long before that.
(	Left parenthesis.
)	Right parenthesis.
/	Division.
*	Multiplication.
-	Subtraction.
+	Addition.
=	Performs calculation.
STO	Copies the number in the display to the memory location.
RCL	Copies the number from the memory location to the display.
SUM	Adds the number in the display to the number in the memory location.
EXC	Swaps the number in the display with the number in the memory location.
+/-	Negate; change sign.
.	Decimal point.

In RPN or HP, mode, the numbered keys; CHS (change sign); and +, -, *, /, and Enter keys all do exactly what you expect. Many of the remaining keys are the same as in TI mode. The differences are detailed in Table 25.8.

Table 25.8 HP Emulation

Key/Function	Description
<	Erases digits from the display; you can use this backspace key if you make a mistake while entering a number. If you invert backspace, the x register is cleared.
ON	Clears the display, state, and memory. Clicking it with Button3 turns off the calculator, exiting xcalc.
INV	Inverts the meaning of the function keys. It is the f key on an HP calculator, but xcalc doesn't display multiple legends on each key. See the individual function keys for details.
10^x	Raises 10.0 to the number in the top of the stack. When inverted, it calculates the log (base 10) of the number in the display.

Table 25.8 HP Emulation

Key/Function	Description
e^x	Raises e to the number in the top of the stack. When inverted, it calculates the log (base e) of the number in the display.
STO	Copies the number in the top of the stack to a memory location. There are 10 memory locations. You can specify the memory you want by following this key with a digit key.
RCL	Pushes the number from the specified memory location onto the stack.
SUM	Adds the number on top of the stack to the number in the specified memory location.
x:y	Exchanges the numbers in the top two stack positions, the x and y registers.
R v	Rolls the stack downward. When inverted, it rolls the stack upward.
(blank keys)	These keys were used for programming functions on the HP-10C. Their functionality hasn't been duplicated in xcalc.

The GIMP

In many ways, GIMP has revolutionized the Linux world. GIMP, which stands for GNU Image Manipulation Program, is freely distributed software suitable for photo retouching, image modification, and image creation (see Figure 25.8). The user interface is closely related to Photoshop.

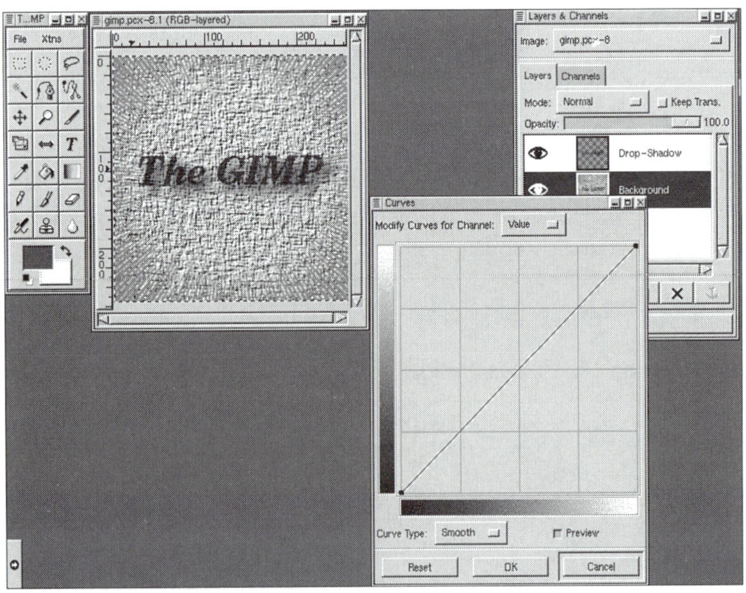

Figure 25.8 The GIMP is powerful image-manipulation software.

The GIMP revolutionized the Linux world by being one of the first attempts at a "mass market" Linux application. Although it does not have some of the advanced features of Photoshop, it has a focus on Web graphics that makes it very powerful in that market. In particular, it has extremely flexible scripting language, which allows you to script any action that can be done through the user interface. Therefore, applying complex manipulations to a changing original is much easier. For example, you can create a Web page that dynamically generates text with drop shadows by writing a short script and running GIMP to generate the image.

The second way that The GIMP revolutionized the Linux world was by providing the *GIMP Toolkit*, or Gtk. When the original authors of the GIMP, Peter Mattis and Spencer Kimball, needed to create graphics routines, they chose to do so in a very general way. That is, they did not tie their graphics routines tightly to The GIMP. In doing so, they created a toolkit that could be used by many other projects that needed graphics routines, most notably GNOME. GNOME and gtk will be covered in more detail in Chapter 27, "Working with GNOME."

The GIMP supports a wide variety of features, including the following:

- Standard painting tools such as Brush, Pencil, Airbrush, and Clone
- Advanced memory management for working with very large images and large numbers of layers
- Full alpha channel support
- Layers and channels
- A range of very powerful scripting languages including Script-fu and a Perl interface
- Multiple Undo/Redo
- Gradient editor and blend tool
- Various animation tools
- A wide range of file formats, including GIF, JPG, PNG, XPM, TIFF, TGA, MPEG, PS, PDF, PCX, BMP, and others.
- Many plug-ins to handle more complex transformations

Tip #131 from *Rob*

The GIMP is a handy way to make and manipulate screenshots. Just choose Xtns, Screen Shot, and then select whether you wish a full screen shot or just a window. Click Grab, and you'll have your image ready for manipulation.

Seyon

Seyon is a complete full-featured telecommunications package for the X Window System (see Figure 25.9).

The following are some of Seyon's features:

- **A dialing directory**—The dialing directory supports an unlimited number of entries. The directory is fully mouse-driven and features call-progress monitoring, dial timeout, automatic redial, multi-number dialing, and a circular redial queue. Each item in the dialing directory can be configured with its own baud rate, bit mask, and script file. The dialing directory uses a plain ASCII text phone book that you can edit from within Seyon. Seyon also supports manual dialing.

- **Terminal emulation**—Terminal emulation supports DEC vt102, Tektronix 4014, and ANSI. Seyon delegates its terminal emulation to xterm, so all the familiar xterm functions—such as the scroll-back buffer, cut-and-paste utility, and visual bell—are available through Seyon's terminal emulation window.

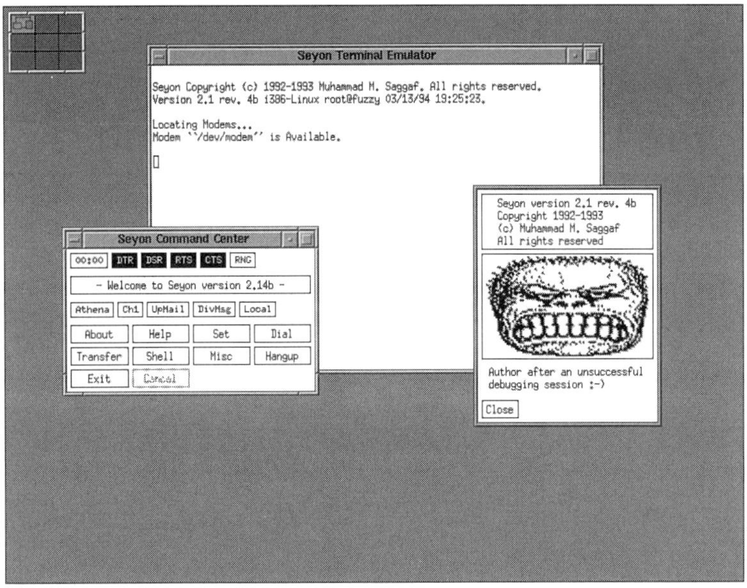

Figure 25.9 Although accessing the Internet is important today, many users still need access to bulletin boards via their modems.

Using xterm also means that Seyon has a more complete emulation of vt102 than any other UNIX or DOS telecommunications program. You also can use other terminal emulation programs with Seyon to suit the user's need; for example, color_xterm can be used to provide emulation for color ANSI (popular on many BBS systems), and xvt can be used if memory is a bit tight.

- **A scripting language**—You can use scripting language to automate tedious tasks such as logging in to remote hosts. Seyon's script interpreter uses plain-text files and has a syntax similar to that of sh, with a few extra additions. It supports many familiar statements such as conditional branching by `if...else` and looping by `goto`. Scripts can be assigned to items in the dialing directory for automatic execution after a connection is made.
- **A variety of download protocols, including Zmodem**—Seyon supports an unlimited number of slots for external file transfer protocols. Protocols are activated from a mouse-driven transfer console that uses a plain ASCII text file, editable from within Seyon, for protocol configuration. Seyon prompts the user for filenames only if the chosen protocol requires filenames or if the transfer operation is an upload for which Seyon also accepts wildcards. Multiple download directories can be specified for the different transfer slots.

Seyon detects incoming Zmodem signatures and automatically activates a user-specified Zmodem protocol to receive incoming files. Zmodem transfers are thus completely automatic and require no user intervention.

- **Various translation modes**—Seyon can perform useful translations with the user's input. For example, Seyon can translate Backspace to Delete, a newline marker to a carriage-return marker, and meta-key translation; that is, you can switch your Esc meta key to the Alt key. The latter mode simulates the meta key on hosts that don't support 8-bit-clean connections and makes possible the use of the meta key in programs such as Emacs.

As for other features, Seyon allows you to interactively set program parameters, online help, and software (XONN/XOFF) and hardware (RTS/CTS) flow control; capture a session to a file; and temporarily run a local shell in the terminal emulation window.

Seyon is intended to be simple yet extensively configurable. Almost every aspect of Seyon can be configured via the built-in resources to suit the user's taste.

XLOCK

Patrick J. Naughton (`naughton@eng.sun.com`) wrote xlock and released it to the world. The xlock program locks the local X display until you enter your password at the keyboard. While xlock is running, all new server connections are refused, the screen saver is disabled, the mouse cursor is turned off, the screen is blanked, and a changing pattern is put onscreen. If a key or a mouse button is pressed, you are prompted for the password of the user who started xlock.

If you enter the correct password, the screen is unlocked, and the X server is restored. When you're typing the password, Ctrl+Shift+u and Ctrl+Shift+h are active as kill and erase commands, respectively. To return to the locked screen, click the small icon version of the changing pattern.

TROUBLESHOOTING

The wrong window manager starts.

You have probably created configuration files that you didn't mean to. There are a lot of X configuration files, and they all have to be consistent.

Depending on what window manager you want, there are a few solutions. First you should run switchdesk to get your files back to a known state. If you don't want KDE or GNOME/Enlightenment, choose AnotherLevel.

→ See "Using the switchdesk tool for Red Hat 6.0" p. 561

If you chose KDE or GNOME/Enlightenment, you should be done. AnotherLevel is actually a collection of window managers. By default you will see fvwm95 when you login. If this isn't what you wanted, click the Start button and select Exit Fvwm, Switch To. Then select the window manager that you want.

If the window manger you want isn't available on the Switch To menu, you can edit `~/.Xclients` and replace whatever you find there with the full path name to the window manager you want to use.

gdm isn't accepting XDMCP connections from other machines.

The version of gdm that ships with Red Hat 6.0 has a known bug in it that prevents it from accepting XDMCP connections.

Use kdm or xdm by changing the `/etc/X11/prefdm` link as root. To select xdm, do this:

```
# ln -s /usr/X11/bin/xdm /etc/X11/prefdm
```

For kdm, do the following:

```
# ln -s /usr/bin/kdm /etc/X11/prefdm
```

When you restart your machine, your display manger will change and you will be able to accept XDMCP connections.

The font server isn't accepting TCP connections.

In Red Hat 6.0, the font server, xfs, is configured to reject TCP connections by default. To turn this back on, as root edit `/etc/X11/fs/config` and add the following line:

```
port = 7100
```

You can then restart xfs by going to the `/etc/rc.d/init.d` directory and typing the following:

```
./xfs restart
```

PROJECT: MAKING YOURSELF AT HOME WITH FVWM2

fvwm2 is one of the most popular window managers available for Linux. It is also one of the most configurable. Unfortunately, all the flexibility comes with a price: a very complex configuration file. In this project, you learn some of the most useful configuration options in fvwm2, and how you can use them to your advantage.

CHOOSING FVWM2

Red Hat 6.0 does not provide a convenient way to choose "normal" fvwm2. They do provide a way to choose fvwm95, which is really just fvwm2 with a lot of customization to make it look like Windows 95. Unfortunately, much of the power of fvwm2 is lost when you put this interface on it.

To fix this, just override Red Hat's normal window manager selection routine by editing `~/.Xclients` and replacing whatever is there with fvwm2. Log out and log back in. You should then see a window manager that looks something like Figure 25.10. The root menu shown in the figure is activated by pressing the left mouse button.

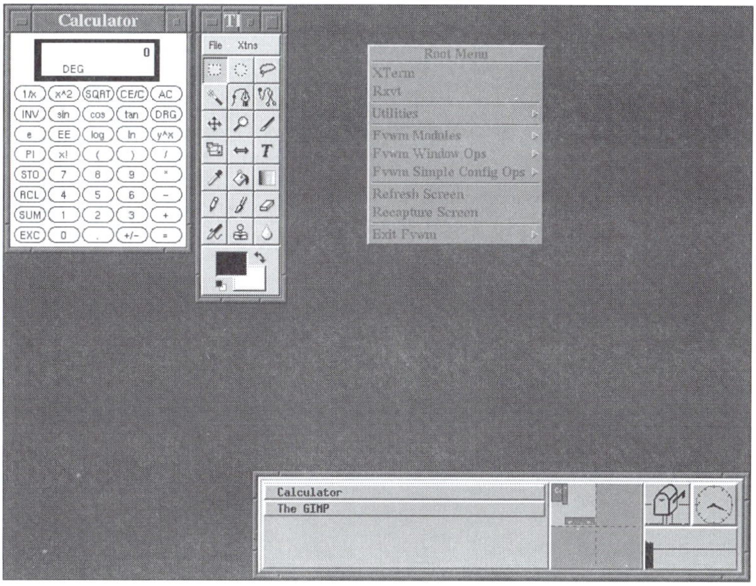

Figure 25.10 The fvwm2 environment focuses on functionality rather than fanciness.

PREPARING TO CUSTOMIZE FVWM2

Before you can customize fvwm2, you need to create your own configuration file. Because you'll want to start with the default configuration file, just copy it to your own directory:

```
$ cp /etc/X11/fvwm2/system.fvwm2rc ~/.fvwm2rc
```

If `~/.fvwm2rc` exists, then fvwm2 will use it. If not, it will default to `/etc/X11/fvwm2/system.fvwm2rc`.

Look over the configuration file by editing `~/.fvwm2rc` with any text editor, such as vi. The full configuration file is too long to cover in detail here, but you can get complete documentation by typing `man fvwm2` at the command prompt.

Tip #132 from *Rob*

If you use Emacs to edit `.fvwm2rc`, you may want to put the following line at the top of the file:

```
# -*- fvwm-generic-mode -*-
```

This will tell Emacs to color-code keywords in the configuration file, making it much easier to edit.

CUSTOMIZING THE MENU

The first thing you will probably want to do is modify the root menu to include the programs you will use most. The root menu supports simple and complex actions, as well as sub-menus, titles and dividers.

To edit the menu, look for the `AddToMenu` lines in `.fvwm2rc`. Perhaps you would like to put Netscape on your Utilities menu before Emacs. The current menu looks like this:

```
AddToMenu Utilities       ''Utilities'' Title
+                         ''Top''          Exec exec xterm -T Top -n Top -e top
+                         ''Calculator''   Exec exec xcalc
+                         ''Xman''         Exec exec xman
+                         ''Xmag''         Exec exec xmag
+                         ''Editres''      Exec exec editres
+                         ''''             Nop
+                         ''Emacs''        Exec exec emacs
+                         ''Mail''         MailFunction xmh ''-font fixed''
+                         ''''             Nop
+                         ''XLock''        Exec exec xlock -mode random
+                         ''''             Nop
+                         ''Reset X defaults'' Exec xrdb -load $HOME/.Xdefaults
```

Above the Emacs line, add the following:

```
+ ''Netscape'' Exec exec netscape
```

Here's what this line means:

+	This is a line-continuation character. It indicates that this is still part of the previous `AddToMenu`.
"Netscape"	This is the label to put on the menu.
Exec	This is what fvwm2 should do when you select this entry. `Exec` tells fvwm2 to execute the rest of this line as if you typed it from the command prompt.
exec netscape	This is the command to execute. The leading `exec` helps save some memory by getting rid of the shell that fvwm2 creates. When you are calling programs from fvwm2, you almost always want to use the construct `Exec` *`exec program`*.

Save the file, left-click the desktop, and choose Exit fvwm. Then choose Restart fvwm2. This will re-read your configuration file, which will now include Netscape in the menu.

Specifying Start-Up Programs

Some programs are so useful that you want them to execute every time you login. Perhaps you like xeyes, shown in figure 25.11. xeyes is a cute program that displays a pair of eyes that watch your mouse pointer as it moves around the screen.

To add this as a start-up program, you need to add it to the `InitFunction`. Edit `.fvwm2rc` and look for `InitFunction`. It will look something like this:

```
AddToFunc InitFunction        "I" Module FvwmButtons
+                             "I" exec xsetroot -mod 2 2 -fg \#554055 -bg \#705070
```

The first line runs the button bar that you see at the bottom of the screen. The second line sets the background color.

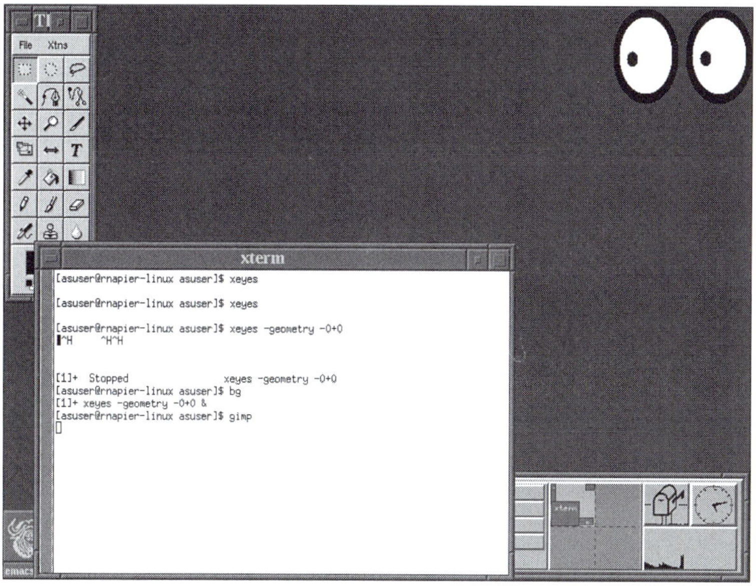

Figure 25.11 xeyes is an old amusement program that many people still like to keep around.

Adding your own line is very similar to what you did in the menus. Just add a line that looks like this:

```
+                    "I" Exec exec xeyes
```

As in the previous example, the `+` indicates that this is still part of the previous `AddToFunc`. The `I` indicates that this is to be done immediately, rather than waiting for the user to click something. Then the `Exec exec xeyes` line is exactly as in the Netscape example and runs xeyes.

FURTHER CUSTOMIZATIONS

Complete customization of fvwm2 is beyond the scope of this section, but there is a lot more to customize. fvwm2 gives you a lot of control over keyboard mappings, mouse behavior, and what windows look like. For more information, type `man fvwm2` at the command prompt.

CHAPTER 26

Working with KDE

In this chapter

by Rob Napier

WHAT IS KDE?

KDE stands for *K Desktop Environment*. KDE is a UNIX desktop, which means that it provides a user-friendly GUI that can be integrated with applications. It is very similar to what the Macintosh and Windows interfaces provide. It also provides a framework for developers and a way for applications to communicate with each other. Figure 26.1 shows KDE in action.

Figure 26.1
KDE provides many of the same features that you find on Macintosh and Windows machines and many features you don't.

From a user's point of view, KDE provides many features, such as the following:

- **Files directly on the desktop**—In KDE, just like a Macintosh or Windows machine, you can drag files to the desktop and store them there as icons. Applications can be automatically launched by links placed on the desktop as well.
- **Session management**—Session management means that applications can remember the state they were in when you logged out and restart the application in exactly the same state when you log back in. For example, you can restart in the same file you were working on and where you were in the file.
- **Desktop panel**—The desktop panel provides quick access to applications by providing the Application Starter (or K-Menu) and panel buttons to start your favorite applications. You can also *swallow* applications, which means that what looks like a button can actually be a running application. This capability is very useful for programs such as `xbiff`, which checks for new mail.

- **Taskbar**—The taskbar shows all the currently available windows, which allows you to quickly switch between applications, even if they're minimized.
- **Pager**—A *pager* allows you to maintain several desktops and easily switch between them. For example, you might put your mail program on one desktop, all your programming tools on another, and a game of Solitaire on a third.

KDE is made up of many parts, only a few of which are readily apparent to you. Figure 26.2 shows how the various layers of KDE interact, and Table 26.1 describes the layers.

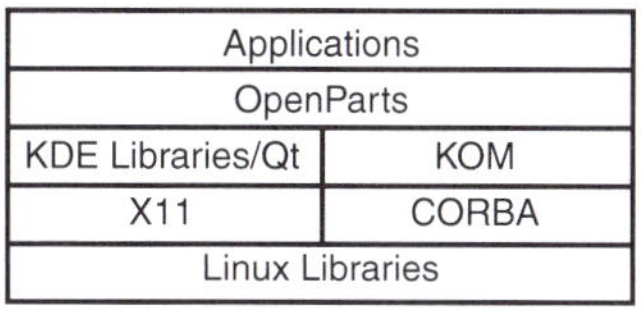

Figure 26.2 Here you can see the developer's view of KDE.

TABLE 26.1 KDE COMPONENTS

Component	Purpose
Linux Libraries	Low-level routines that are outside KDE. They manage hardware and Linux system interactions.
X11	Low-level routines that are outside KDE. They manage the graphics display and hardware. See Chapter 24, "Installing the X Windows System," for more information.
KDE Libraries/Qt	Wrappers around the X11 graphics system. Qt in particular is a set of C++ classes that simplify GUI development. It is produced by Troll Tech AS and was once the center of a very large debate in the KDE community (see the following sidebar).
CORBA	Stands for *Common Object Request Broker Architecture*. An industry standard way for applications to communicate with each other.
KOM	Stands for *KDE Object Model*. Wrappers around CORBA that provide additional features. KOM provides similar functionality to Microsoft's COM.
OpenParts	Object classes or servers that provide functionality to other object classes or clients. For example, an application can include an image viewer OpenPart to display its images. Then the application doesn't have to worry about what format the image is in. OpenParts provides similar functionality to Microsoft's ActiveX.
Applications	KDE applications that are instances of a KApplication object. If you implement all KDE applications with the same object class, all KDE applications automatically conform to KDE standards.

If all this information seems complicated, don't worry too much about it. Users seldom have to deal with OpenParts, CORBA, or X11. Knowing what these words mean is useful so that you can understand the documentation and so that you can understand how KDE buzzwords map to similar buzzwords in the Windows and Macintosh worlds. For example, KDE's `Qt/KOM/OpenParts` provides a very similar framework to Microsoft's `MFC/COM/ActiveX`.

The Qt Controversy

When KDE was started, the developers wanted to use an existing cross-platform GUI toolkit to provide *widgets*. Widgets are GUI components such as minimize buttons or window frames. Because the KDE project developers wanted to deliver a product quickly, they didn't want to take a lot of time to develop their own toolkit when a good one already existed. They chose what they felt was the best freely available toolkit on the market: Qt by Troll Tech.

Troll Tech (`http://www.troll.no`) is a Norwegian company that began developing Qt in 1992. It is a very good product, runs on many platforms, is freely available, and at 80,000 lines of code, would have taken quite awhile to reproduce. It does not, however, use the same license as KDE, the GNU General Public License, or GPL (see Appendix C, "The GNU General Public License"). Although Qt does distribute its source code, users are not permitted to make modifications to it and redistribute it. They must send all modifications back to Troll Tech to be incorporated into the base product. GPL allows users to create derivative products and redistribute them. The other major difference is that users can purchase a license to redistribute Qt in commercial products without distributing their source code. GPL products and GPL-derived products must always provide source code.

This small difference of licensing led to one of the great "holy wars" of the Linux community. Those who believe that the end users should always have the right to modify and redistribute code claimed that the entire KDE Project could not be considered Open Source. This was a great rallying cry for supporters of GNOME. GNOME is another Linux desktop that is licensed entirely under GPL. (See Chapter 27, "Working with GNOME," for more information about GNOME.)

One group attempted to bridge the gap with the Harmony Project (`http://harmony.ruhr.de`). The Harmony Project was originally designed to create an *LGPL* version of Qt. LGPL is the Library (or Lesser) General Public License, which is very close to GPL, and is acceptable to most camps, including the Open Source Initiative. The developers of Harmony are not KDE developers. The KDE developers are too familiar with Qt to create a clone without violating copyright.

Much of this information is now irrelevant. Troll Tech released a free version of Qt 2.0 under the Qt Public License, or QPL (`http://www.troll.no/qpl`), which has been endorsed by leaders in the community as meeting the criteria of Open Source. Although QPL is not precisely the same as GPL, it is close enough to resolve the issue for the vast majority of the community.

Harmony isn't dead, though. The Harmony Project has moved beyond just cloning Qt and now is trying to make a true competitor with many new and exciting features.

From the user's point of view, the most important parts of KDE are kwm, kpanel, and kfm. kwm, the KDE Window Manager, provides all the normal window manager functionality, such as displaying, minimizing, moving, and resizing windows. kpanel provides a convenient panel, usually at the bottom of the screen. It has quick-launch buttons, menus, a clock, and much more. kpanel also provides the taskbar, usually at the top of the screen. It shows all the currently open windows and allows you to switch between them easily. kfm is the KDE File Manager, which not only provides access to your files, but also acts as a Web and document browser.

INSTALLING KDE

Caldera OpenLinux provides KDE as its default desktop, so getting KDE up and running is as easy as installing the distribution. Red Hat defaults to GNOME, so you need to make some modifications.

INSTALLING KDE FOR RED HAT 6.0

Table 26.2 lists the KDE packages for Red Hat 6.0.

Table 26.2 KDE Packages

RPM	Purpose
qt	(Required) Qt toolkit.
kdesupport	(Recommended) Various non-KDE libraries that KDE requires.
kdelibs	(Required) KDE shared libraries.
kdebase	(Required) The core of KDE, such as the window manager.
kdegames	(Optional) Several games.
kdegraphics	(Optional) Various programs to view and draw graphics.
kdeutils	(Optional) Calculator, editor, and so on.
kdemultimedia	(Optional) CD player and other multimedia applications.
kdenetwork	(Optional) Internet applications including a mail reader and a news reader.
kdeadmin	(Optional) System administration programs.
kdetoys	(Optional) Fun programs that aren't games. For example, kmoon puts the phase of the moon on your panel.
korganizer	(Optional) Personal organizer.

The required and recommended packages should be installed in the order listed using `rpm`.

→ See "Installing Packages with RPM," p. 169

Note The version of KDE that ships with Red Hat 6.0 is 1.1.1–pre2. It is a pre-release beta of version 1.1.1, and you should upgrade to the released version to avoid known bugs. You can get updated RPMs from `http://updates.redhat.com`.

Using the switchdesk Tool for Red Hat 6.0

The easiest way to switch to KDE is to use the `switchdesk` tool. `switchdesk` may not be installed by default, so you might have to install the `switchdesk-1.7.0-1` package by using `rpm`.

→ See "Installing Packages with RPM," p. 169

After you've installed `switchdesk`, launching it is simple:

```
$ switchdesk
```

This command produces a dialog box asking whether you prefer GNOME, KDE, or AnotherLevel. Click KDE, choose OK, and then log out. When you log back in, your default desktop will be KDE.

CHOOSING KDE WITHOUT SWITCHDESK

If you're using a distribution without `switchdesk`, you can make KDE your default desktop by modifying your `$HOME/.Xclients` file to contain the following:

```
exec startkde
```

→ See "Using vi," p. 207

→ See "Choosing a Window Manager," p. 536

NAVIGATING KDE

If you're familiar with other GUIs, such as the Macintosh interface or Microsoft Windows, KDE should be quite familiar. Figure 26.3 shows the major components of the desktop.

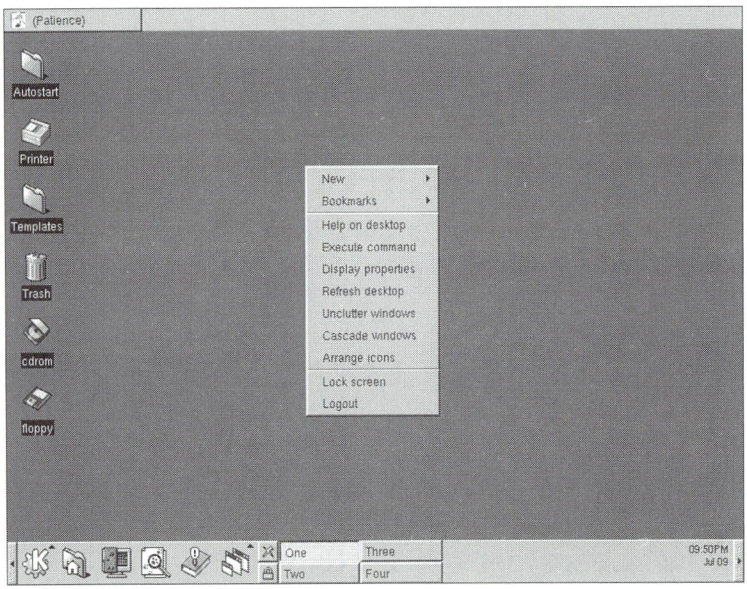

Figure 26.3 KDE's desktop brings your most-used functions to your fingertips.

THE PANEL

The panel is probably the most important part of the KDE desktop. The default settings give plenty of functionality, but the real power is in configuring the panel. Figure 26.4 shows each of the default buttons.

APPLICATION STARTER (K-MENU)

The Application Starter, which is also called the K-Menu, holds links to all your programs and configuration menus. It is similar to the Windows 95 Start menu. Press Alt+F1 to open the Application Starter.

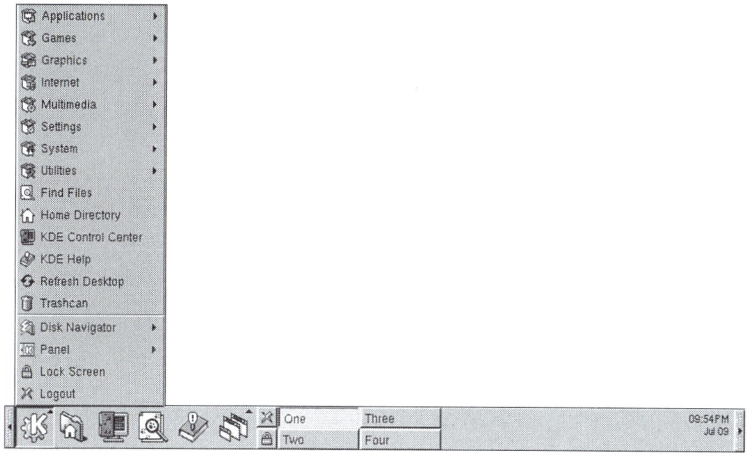

Figure 26.4
Using the KDE panel well can greatly improve your productivity.

HOME DIRECTORY

The Home Directory launches the file manager on your home directory. For more information about the file manager, see "KDE File Manager" later in this chapter.

KDE CONTROL CENTER

Using the Control Center, you can configure various parts of KDE, including the window manager, file manager, keyboard, sound, and much more. The Control Center is also the place you can choose *themes*, which define a complete look and feel.

→ See "Themes," p. 537

FIND UTILITY

KDE has a powerful tool for finding files. You can search by name pattern, modification time, file type, size, or contents. This tool is modeled very closely on Microsoft Windows 98's Find utility.

HELP BROWSER

If you're a new KDE user, the Help Browser can be a great asset. It is essentially a simple Web browser. In fact, the help files are written in HTML, and hyperlinks in the help system may point to Web pages on the Internet. Links outside the help system are not displayed in the same window, though. The Help Browser can launch kfm to handle those requests.

→ See "KDE File Manager," p. 568

WINDOW LIST

The Window List provides instant access to all your current windows, no matter what desktop they are running on. Being able to access these windows can be a real time-saver when you have many windows open across numerous desktops. You can also get the Window List by clicking the middle mouse button on the desktop.

Logout

Logout logs you out of KDE and returns to the login screen. Before logging out, it warns you of any non-KDE applications that are currently running. Most KDE applications allow session management, which means that when you restart KDE, they will return to exactly where they left off. Non-KDE applications can't restart this way, so KDE lists those applications that will lose unsaved data and won't be resumed at the same point. KDE still generally restarts the applications when you log back in.

Lock Screen

KDE provides various screensavers that activate after a configurable time of inactivity. If you want to start the screensaver immediately, you can press the Lock button. To unlock the screen, you need to enter your login password. The screensaver is configurable through the Control Center (see the previous section "KDE Control Center"). Be careful with the Lock button because it is very close to the Logout button. This layout is traditional for the Common Desktop Environment (CDE), so if you are used to Sun or HP workstations, it should be familiar.

Virtual Desktops

Virtual desktops really differentiate the Linux desktops from the Windows and Macintosh environments. Each of the four buttons in this block provides you with a completely different desktop, each displaying different windows. When screen real estate is scarce, having separate desktops can be very convenient.

Generally, you put similar applications together so that you can easily move between desktops as you move between tasks. A common layout is xterminals on one desktop, a Web browser on another, mail on a third, and diversions (games) on a fourth. Other users choose to put all their programming tools on one desktop, documentation on a second, and mail on a third. It's up to you. KDE remembers what programs are running on which desktops when you log out, so when you log in, everything restarts in the right place.

Virtual desktops are highly configurable. To configure your desktops, right-click the panel in an area with no buttons, and then click Configure to bring up the KPanel Configuration dialog box (see Figure 26.5). Click the Desktops tab to configure your desktop.

Using the numbered blocks in this dialog, you can change the names of the desktops. You should name them meaningfully so that you can remember what is on each desktop. The Visible slider sets the number of virtual desktops available. You can have two, four, six, or eight desktops. Four is the default. The Width slider sets the width of the virtual desktop buttons on the panel. You should set the buttons wide enough to see the names you have chosen but narrow enough not to take unneeded space on the panel. KDE remembers your desktop names between sessions.

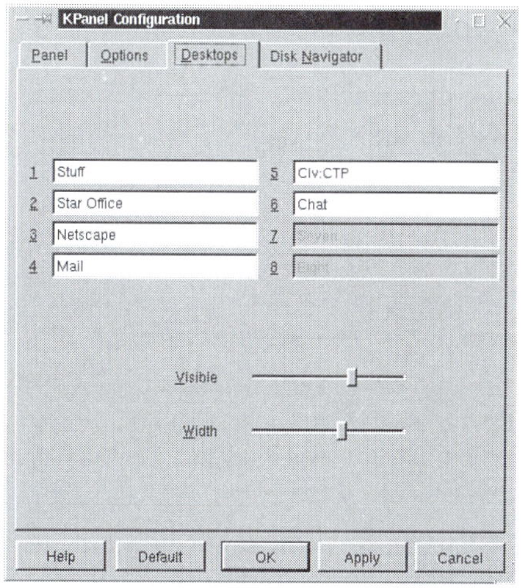

Figure 26.5 You can configure the KDE virtual desktops to match the way you want to work.

Tip #133 from Rob

If you want to change only the name of a desktop, you don't need to use the KPanel Configuration dialog box. Just click the desktop button to go to that desktop, and then click it again. You then are presented with a standard I-beam text cursor to change the name.

You can move windows between virtual desktops by clicking the menu button (the far left button on the title bar), clicking To Desktop, and then clicking the desktop that the window should live on. The shortcut for the menu button is Alt+F3.

Windows can also be made *sticky*. Sticky windows appear on all desktops. To make a window sticky, click the thumbtack button on the left side of the title bar. Clicking the thumbtack again makes the window stay only on the current desktop.

CLOCK

The clock appears on the far right side of the panel. You can configure the clock to display 24-hour time or *Internet time*. *Internet time* is a new time standard proposed by Swatch, a Swiss watchmaker. It has 1,000 *beats* per day measured from midnight in Biel, Switzerland, which happens to be the place where the Swatch company headquarters are located and is UTC+1 (that is, Internet time is one time zone off the rest of the world). For example, @500" Internet time is noon in Biel, or 7:00 a.m. in New York. It is very unlikely that Internet time will become a serious time standard, but the KDE clock can display it if you like.

To configure the clock, right-click the panel in an empty area. Next, click Configure, and then click the Options tab. The two options for the clock are Clock Shows Time in AM/PM Format and Clock Shows Time in Internet Beats. If you choose Internet Beats, the AM/PM selection is ignored.

PANEL HIDE

On either side of the panel is a textured tab with an arrow on it. When you click one of these buttons, the panel slides off the screen in the direction indicated. This capability is handy if you want more of the screen available for working.

→ See "Getting More Desktop," p. 573

Tip #134 from Rob

You can use the KDE panel with non-KDE-compliant window managers (like fvwm2). You won't get all the integration that you get with KDE, but you will get a useful application launcher. From the command line, run the following:

```
kpanel -no-KDE-compliant-window-manager
```

THE TASKBAR

The taskbar is generally at the top of the screen and shows all the windows on all the desktops. Names of minimized windows are in parentheses, and windows on different desktops are separated by a small break.

When you click a button in the taskbar, you are taken to the appropriate desktop, and the window receives focus. The button appears pressed to indicate the currently active window. Clicking the active button minimizes the window.

Right-clicking a button provides a local menu with various options. Table 26.3 lists these options and what they do. Where two options are listed, only one of them is available at a time.

TABLE 26.3 TASKBAR LOCAL MENU OPTIONS

Option	Purpose
Maximize/Restore	Maximize increases the size of the window to full screen. If the panel and taskbar are visible, the window does not overlap them. Restore restores the window to its previous size.
Iconify/Deiconify	Iconify removes the window from the screen so that it is accessible only from the taskbar. This action is the same as minimizing. Deiconify restores the window to its previous size.
Sticky/Unsticky	Sticky makes a window appear on all desktops. Unsticky turns off this feature.
Onto current desktop	This option is available for buttons that represent windows on other desktops. Clicking it brings that window to the current desktop.
Iconify other windows	This option iconifies all the windows on this desktop except for the selected one. This capability is useful for when you are dealing with just one window and want to clear your desktop of everything else.

Table 26.3 Taskbar Local Menu Options

Option	Purpose
Close	Close sends a close request to the program. This request generally does not kill a hung program.

→ See "Getting More Desktop," p. 573

Tip #135 from *Rob*

You can maximize, iconify, or close windows by clicking the buttons in the upper right corner of the window just as you would expect. You can also maximize a window only horizontally or vertically. Click the maximize button with the middle mouse button to vertically maximize a window. Click the maximize button with the right mouse button to horizontally maximize a window.

The Root Menu

To get the Root menu, right-click the background. A menu then pops up with various options. These options are explained in Table 26.4.

Table 26.4 KDE Root Menu Options

Option	Purpose
New	New creates various types of objects on the desktop. For example, you can create a new folder or a shortcut to a program or a link to a Web page.
Bookmarks	Any file can be bookmarked and then can be easily accessed from this menu. For more information about bookmarks, see "Bookmarks" later in this chapter.
Help on desktop	This option opens the Help Browser.
Execute Command	This option pops up a dialog box that accepts one-line UNIX commands. This capability can be very convenient when you want to start programs that don't have links to them yet. You can also enter URLs to quickly view a Web page. Finally, to get man pages on UNIX commands, type `man:`*`command`*, where *`command`* is the command for which you want information. The shortcut for Execute Command is Alt+F2.
Display Properties	Display Properties customizes the appearance of KDE. See "Making It Pretty" later in this chapter for more information.
Refresh Desktop	KDE can become confused and fail to draw something correctly. For instance, a dying program may not properly erase itself from the screen. If this happens, select Refresh Desktop, and KDE redraws all the windows to make sure they are correct.

Table 26.4 KDE Root Menu Options

Option	Purpose
Unclutter Windows	If you get a lot of windows overlapping each other, seeing what you want to see might be difficult. Unclutter Windows tries to make sure that all the windows are minimally overlapping.
Cascade Windows	Similar to Unclutter Windows, this option stacks all the open windows so that you can find them all.
Arrange Icons	Arrange Icons lines up all the icons on the desktop onto the left side of the screen.
Lock Screen	This option is the same as the Lock Screen button described earlier in this chapter.
Logout	This option is the same as the Logout button described earlier in this chapter.

Trash

Like most GUIs designed since the original Macintosh, KDE provides a trash can for throwing away files, folders, and links. With the KDE trash can, like other trash cans, you empty it by right-clicking the Trash icon and clicking Empty Trash Bin. Clicking the Trash opens the file manager and allows you to drag things back out.

The Trash icon changes depending on whether things are currently in the Trash.

Templates

The Templates folder contains templates of *kdelnk* files. KDE uses kdelnk files to point to applications, printers, mountable devices, and Internet resources. Bookmarks are implemented this way.

→ See "Bookmarks," p. 571

→ See "Templates," p. 570

Autostart

Anything in the Autostart folder is run every time KDE starts up. Generally, this folder contains links to applications, but you can put anything in the Autostart folder, including documents and folders. Documents are opened with their default application, and folders are opened with `kfm`. Generally, it's best to put links to what you want rather than the file itself.

KDE File Manager

kfm is much more than just a file manager. It is also a fairly full-featured Web browser that understands a wide variety of UNIX file formats including archive formats such as `tar` and `zip` (see Figure 26.6).

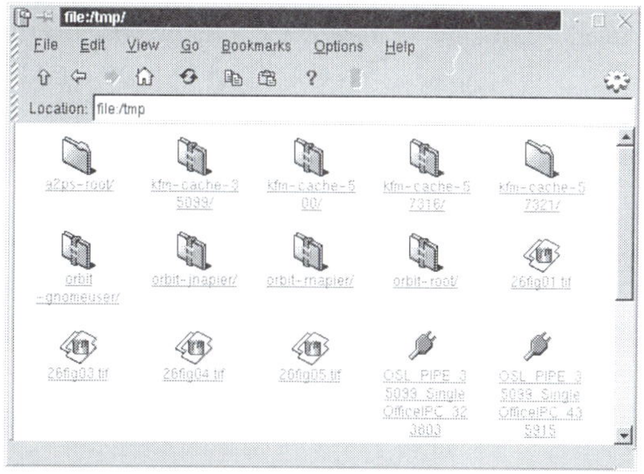

Figure 26.6
The KDE File Manager makes it easy to manage your files.

The different icons in Figure 26.6 indicate different kinds of files. The file folders are directories. Folders with locks on them are directories you don't have permission to view. The icons with paint cans are graphics images. The plug icons are UNIX domain sockets (you will almost never have to deal with them directly, but kfm understands them). kfm can also detect executables, text files, HTML files, backups, videos, scripts, and much more.

Particularly useful is kfm's handling of archive file formats such as `tar` and `zip`. kfm treats most archives just like directories, so you can click them and view their contents directly. Some archives are passed to Archiver, which also allows you to view the contents easily.

Other file types are handled as you would expect: Images are passed to kview, text files are passed to kedit, and executables are executed.

Tip #136 from *Rob*

KDE treats FTP sites just like local file systems. For example, if you open `ftp://bob@ftp.example.com/~bob`, kfm requests bob's password and then displays the directory as if it were local. For anonymous FTP, leave off the `bob@`.

kfm also reads Web pages. It doesn't do all the tricks of Netscape, but that is often considered a benefit. Just enter the URL on the Location line, and then use kfm as you would any other Web browser.

kfm handles cookies better than the mainstream browsers. By default, kfm asks permission before accepting cookies. It then allows you to choose how to handle cookies on a domain-by-domain basis. To set up this feature, either answer the questions the first time you visit a site, or click Options, Configure Browser. Then click the Cookies tab and add your domain specific settings.

kfm handles frames, but many Web sites don't send it frame information because many Web sites decide whether browsers can handle frames by checking their User-Agent String. Browsers use this string to identify themselves. Many Web sites check only for Netscape

Navigator, which identifies itself as Mozilla, or Internet Explorer. kfm identifies itself as Konqueror, which very few Web sites expect. To trick sites into behaving properly, you might need to tell kfm to lie about who it is. You can do so by clicking Options, Configure Browser. Then click the User Agent tab and add entries for each server you want to lie to.

Note "Konqueror" comes from the following sequence: Navigator, Explorer, Conqueror.

CONFIGURING KDE

KDE is extremely configurable, but only in specific ways. Much like Windows 98, KDE can be configured only to perform tasks that the developers thought you might like to do. Although KDE is still more configurable than Windows 98, tasks as simple as removing the clock from the panel (or replacing it with your own) can be very difficult or impossible. The developers thought that everyone would want a simple digital clock with the date on the right side of the panel.

→ See "The Pros and Cons of KDE," p. 574

TEMPLATES

The Templates folder on your desktop contains various kdelnk files that you can use to create new objects on your desktop or in folders. All the entries in the Root menu's New menu come from this folder (except Folder, which is built in). To create a new instance of the template, right-click the background to pull up the Root menu. Then click New and the item you want to create. The following sections describe items that can be created.

FOLDER

Folders are directories and can hold other files or folders. Don't be afraid to use spaces or punctuation other than / (the slash) in the folder names. In KDE, / is a special character and cannot be put into a folder name.

FILE SYSTEM DEVICE

Using the File System Device, you can mount devices such as CDs or floppies directly from the desktop. Before you can create this kind of link, you need to make sure you are able to mount the device.

→ See "Mounting and Unmounting File Systems," p. 444

When you are able to mount the device normally, create a File System Device by using the New menu. Then right-click the new icon and click Properties. On the General tab, change the name to something meaningful like `Floppy.kdelnk` or `cdrom.kdelnk`. On the Device tab, enter the device name (such as `/dev/fd0` or `/dev/cdrom`) as the Device. Then select mounted and unmounted icons. Icons of floppy disks and CDs with and without small green lights beside them are available for your convenience.

URLs

URLs includes FTP URLs, Internet addresses (URLs), and World Wide Web URLs. The only difference between them is their icons. When you create a new URL link, just enter the desired URL in the dialog that pops up. Now you have a shortcut to your favorite sites.

MIME Type

*MIME*stands for *Multipurpose Internet Mail Extensions*. Originally, it was intended to encode files in email messages, but it has moved on to handle a wide variety of tasks. KDE uses normal MIME mechanisms to identify and handle files. If KDE applications need new MIME types, the applications install them. Generally, you set up your own MIME types to associate a type of file with a non-KDE application. This topic is beyond the scope of this book, but you can find a very good tutorial for it in the KDE help pages. Point your Help Browser to `file:/usr/share/doc/HTML/en/kfm/app.html` and `file:/usr/share/doc/HTML/en/kfm/mime.html`.

Bookmarks

Any file in KDE can have a bookmark pointing to it. From within kfm, right-click the file or folder and select Add to Bookmarks. A bookmark to the file or folder is then placed in your Bookmarks menus, both on the Root menu and in kfm.

To edit or remove bookmarks, click Bookmarks on the kfm toolbar, and then choose Edit Bookmarks. When you do so, you open another kfm window looking at your bookmarks. All normal kfm functions work here. To give the bookmark a more convenient name, right-click the bookmark and click Properties. Then change the filename to whatever you would like it to be. Changing the name doesn't affect the file the bookmark points to in any way.

Tip #137 from *Rob*

Remember that KDE doesn't care if a file is local or remote. If you view a web page using `kfm`, you can right-click the background of the web page and select Add to Bookmarks. The same is true of files on an FTP server or any other network resource.

Making It Pretty

You can customize KDE in many ways to make your desktop more attractive. Few of these changes will boost your performance, but they may make you happier while you're working. All the settings described in the following sections are found on the KDE Control Center under Desktop.

Background

One of the most personal things about a desktop is the background. Some users like simple, flat backgrounds, whereas others like textures or even images. KDE supports all of them.

Each desktop can have its own background, so you need to select which desktop you're working on. Having different backgrounds can be very useful in helping you determine which desktop you're on at any time.

The One Color option does exactly what it sounds like. You select the color bar to open a color chooser. The Two Color option allows you to blend between two colors or create various patterns based on two colors. You can find the two colors used on the color bar under One Color and the color bar under Two Color.

Wallpaper is also fairly obvious if you're used to other desktops. KDE has a wide selection of arrangement types such as tiled, centered warp, and symmetrical tiled. Just experiment with them to see which works best with your image. KDE also can modify your background as you work. To use this feature, select Random, and after a set time, KDE switches images based on a list that you provide (or just all images in a directory). This feature can really break up the monotony. It can also be distracting, depending on your mood.

The Dock Into the Panel selection puts an icon on the right side of your panel that you can use to quickly bring up this dialog box. If you're using the Random selection just described, clicking this icon cycles you to the next background without waiting for the timeout.

Tip #138 from *Rob*

It is possible to use a screensaver as your background. This takes up some CPU resources, but can look quite good on a fast machine. Just run the screensaver with the `-inroot` parameter. For example, from the command prompt, type the following:

```
$ kmatrix.kss -inroot
```

For a list of all the available screensavers, type the following:

```
ls ${KDEDIR}/bin/*.kss
```

Colors

If you just want another color scheme, KDE provides a wide variety. If you like changing the colors, check out the section "Themes" later in this chapter.

Fonts

Using the Fonts feature, you can set your default fonts, which will be honored by most KDE apps and some other apps. One of the best uses of this feature is to set a larger font size for really high-resolution screens on small monitors.

Screensaver

What modern desktop would be complete without 20 or so screensavers? If you are a science fiction movie buff, check out the *Matrix* screen saver by Jamie Zawinski (`jwz@jwz.org`).

Using Themes in KDE

For an explanation of what themes are, see "Themes" in Chapter 25, "Using the X Window System." This section describes how to get them and how to set them up.

KDE comes with four themes, which are not nearly enough for a real theme lover. So, you can start by going to the source of KDE themes: `http://kde.themes.org`. At this time, KDE has 80 themes available. Just select the theme you want from the gallery and download it. It is saved as a `tar.gz` file. Theoretically, themes are supposed to use a new `.themerc` file format, but I've never seen this format except in the stock themes. Generally, you need to use `kinstall` by Dmitry Zakharov (`dmitry_z@iname.com`) from `http://kde.themes.org/archive/ktinstall.tar.gz`. Once you have your theme file and `kinstall` installed, type the following at the command line:

```
$ kinstall theme
```

`theme` is the name of your theme file (including the `tar.gz` file). You don't even have to restart KDE. Your theme comes up immediately.

Tip #139 from Rob

The themes available are of variable quality. `kde.themes.org` rates themes from −2 to +2. From the theme gallery, select the lowest rating that you wish to see, and you will remove a lot of the less interesting themes. If you prefer to make your own decisions, though, set the filter down to −2 and you can see everything. You can also submit and read comments on the themes.

Getting More Desktop

KDE offers many options for maximizing your available screen real estate. If you're interested in reorganizing your desktop, try some of the following:

- **Make your panel smaller**—From the Panel tab of the KPanel Configuration dialog, click Tiny.
- **Move the panel off the screen by clicking the left or right hide buttons**—KDE puts the Application Starter, Window List, and a disk navigator on your taskbar whenever you move panels off the screen.

- **Autohide the panel and the taskbar**—From the Options tab of the KPanel Configuration dialog, click Auto Hide Panel and Auto Hide Taskbar. Choosing these options causes the panel and taskbar to hide until you touch the mouse cursor to their border. For instance, when you move the mouse cursor to the bottom of the screen, the panel reappears.
- **Get rid of the taskbar altogether**—You don't really need the taskbar because the Window List provides similar functionality. From the Panel tab of the KPanel Configuration dialog, select Hidden.

THE PROS AND CONS OF KDE

Should you use KDE? Should you use GNOME? Should you avoid them both and use a conventional Linux window manager? The choice is up to you, but the following sections describe some of the advantages and disadvantages of KDE, particularly in relation to GNOME.

RESOURCES

Determining exactly how much memory one desktop uses versus another can be very difficult given how shared libraries can skew the numbers, but in general terms, KDE uses about the same memory as GNOME, possibly a bit more in their default configurations. Both use three to four times the memory of AfterStep, which is certainly not the smallest of the window managers. Note that GNOME has the potential to use a lot more memory if all of Enlightenment's features are turned on.

KDE should run in as little as 16M of memory, but you will generally need 24M-32M of memory for good performance. With very complex themes and many running applications, you may require as much as 64M-128M of memory.

PERFORMANCE

KDE's performance is usually quite good. On reasonably high-end hardware, detecting serious differences between the performance of one window manager over another can be difficult. In general, however, KDE is faster than GNOME and slower than simple window managers like `fvwm2`.

CONFIGURATION

KDE is quite configurable, but not nearly as configurable as GNOME. This is a problem and a benefit. The problem is that you cannot configure anything for which the programmers did not decide to provide a hook. On the other hand, GNOME is so configurable that it can be quite confusing, especially for new users.

Integration

The parts of KDE are highly integrated. This is again a benefit and a problem. The benefit is that the parts tend to work together very well and in very reliable ways. The problem is that the parts of KDE sometimes know so much about each other that it is hard to replace any part of KDE with an improved version.

Stability

KDE is quite stable and seldom crashes on reasonable hardware. Most of the tools work together, although some of the documentation has broken links in the 1.1.1 distribution.

Final Analysis

Essentially, KDE is a strong, highly integrated desktop environment in the tradition of Windows 98. It is more stable and configurable than Windows 98, but the design philosophies are quite similar. If you're looking for a more full-featured, stable version of the Windows interface, KDE is a great choice.

If, on the other hand, you're interested in a much more configurable but also much more chaotic environment, read on in Chapter 27, "Working with GNOME."

CHAPTER 27

WORKING WITH GNOME

In this chapter

by Rob Napier

WHAT IS GNOME?

GNOME stands for the *GNU Network Object Model Environment*. (For more information on the GNU project, see Appendix C, "The GNU General Public License.") GNOME intends to be a full-featured, user-friendly desktop built entirely of Open Source components. Here, Open Source is a very specific definition, given by the Open Source Initiative at `http://www.opensource.org/osd.html`. This definition is important because it formed the reasoning behind creating GNOME. Had KDE been fully Open Source, GNOME may never have been created (though some people may debate this point).

→ See "The Qt Controversy," p. 560

Figure 27.1 shows GNOME in action, but it is somewhat misleading. What Figure 27.1 really shows is the Enlightenment window manager, panel, the GNOME Midnight Commander File Manager, `gnome-help-browser`, `gnomepager_applet`, and `gnome_util_applet`. The last two are running on the panel.

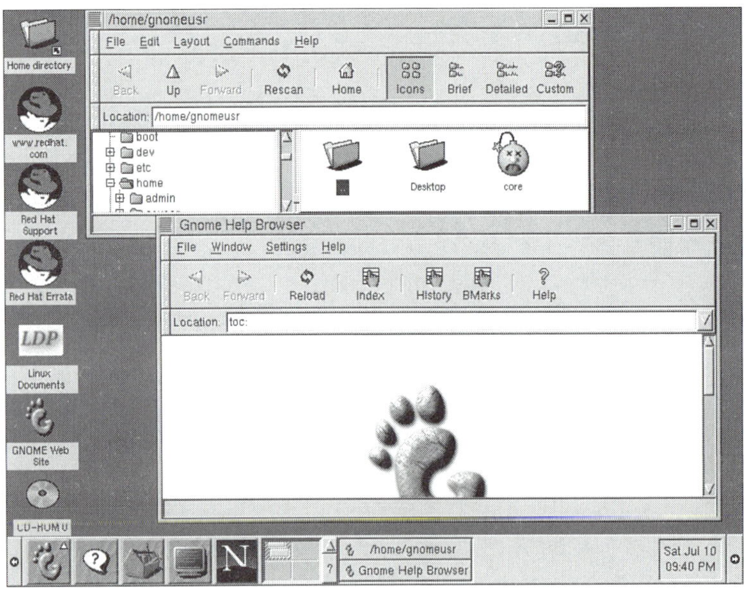

Figure 27.1
GNOME is more of a federation of like-minded components than a single integrated system like KDE.

Although KDE also implements its parts as many separate programs, for GNOME it is a deep philosophical (almost religious) issue. For instance, whereas the KDE's panel knows all about its pager, the GNOME pager is just an applet that runs on the panel. If you don't want a pager, you can just not run it (virtual desktops still work without it). If someone develops a better pager, you can swap it in. You can move the pager around on the panel if you prefer it somewhere else. You can even run two pagers. The same is true for the clock on the far right. At least five different clocks come with GNOME on a Red Hat 6.0 system. It's all completely configurable. These capabilities are both a blessing and a curse.

From a user's point of view, the GNOME environment provides many features, such as the following:

- **Files directly on the desktop**—With GNOME, just like a Macintosh or Windows machine, you can drag files to the desktop and store them there as icons. Applications can be automatically launched by links placed on the desktop as well.
- **Session management**—Session management means that applications can remember the state they were in when you logged out and restart the application in exactly the same state when you log back in. For example, you can restart in the same file you were working on and where you were in the file.
- **Desktop panel**—The desktop panel provides quick access to applications by providing the Main Menu button and panel buttons to start your favorite applications. You can also *swallow* applications, which means that what looks like a button can actually be a running application. This capability is used extensively by GNOME to handle pagers, clocks, load monitors, and much more.
- **Pager**—A *pager* allows you to maintain several desktops and easily switch between them. For example, you might put your mail program on one desktop, all your programming tools on another, and a game of Solitaire on a third.

Like KDE, GNOME is based on CORBA, the Common Object Request Broker Architecture. It is an industry standard way for applications to communicate with each other. The GNOME implementation of CORBA is called *ORBit*. KDE is generally programmed in C++, but GNOME provides *bindings* for a wide variety of languages. Bindings are interfaces that allow a programmer to communicate with a system in a particular programming language. Currently, GNOME has bindings for C, C++, Objective C, TOM, and Guile.

GNOME is also heavily dependent on Gtk+, the GIMP toolkit. Gtk+ also has a wide variety of language bindings, including the ubiquitous C, C++, and Perl, but it also binds to unusual languages such as Eiffel, Dylan, Pike, and Haskell, among others. This means that if you want to create a small GUI script in Perl, you can use Gtk+ to get attractive *widgets* that conform to your current theme. A *theme* defines the appearance of various parts of your desktop, such as backgrounds and textures.

→ See "The GIMP," p. 548

The GNOME Manifesto

The GNOME Manifesto was written to explain the philosophy of GNOME. Unlike the more pragmatic KDE, GNOME is as much a way of doing things as a set of programs. The following is the GNOME Manifesto, which you can find at `http://www.gnome.org/about/manifesto.shtml`.

What Is GNOME?

GNOME is an Open Source desktop environment built from components that meet the Open Source guidelines in full.

No Compromises

GNOME is open in the full sense of the word. It seeks to impose only that order necessary for consistency.

Window Manager

GNOME defines a set of "hints" for window managers. If you use a GNOME-aware window manager, it will cooperate nicely with GNOME. If you don't, then GNOME works just fine. The "hint" interface is published in full for anyone to use.

No religion–pick any window manager.

Commercial Use

GNOME is the key to the desktop. Its authors recognize that it is not appropriate to "control" that interface or require that a commercial vendor pays some third party for the ability to write GNOME-compliant applications.

All the core GNOME software is distributed under the GNU Library General Public License, a license that permits the software to be used so long as it is dynamically linked or the user can relink it to new versions of the libraries. This is the same license used by the Linux C libraries.

You need to purchase no expensive software licenses to make your commercial application GNOME compliant.

Vendor Neutral

No component of the interface is controlled solely by one company or restricted from modification. Any organization or person, however large or small, can contribute to GNOME. Furthermore, if you don't happen to agree with a decision, the license enshrines rights to distribute modified versions.

Truly open. No core component is non Open Source.

Language Bindings

GNOME enforces no programming language restrictions on a developer. The core libraries are written in C, so they are fast and efficient. The external interface is currently available in C, C++, Objective C, TOM, and Guile.

If you want to add bindings for another language we will be delighted to help.

Themes

The low-level GNOME/Gtk interface is currently being extended to support themes. A mechanism is already used in Enlightenment and Windowmaker window managers to allow a user to freely control the look and feel of the base interface components without forcing the original program author to do the work.

User-driven look and feel.

Portability

The toolkit and libraries used in GNOME are intended to be portable to all UNIX-like platforms, and if people contribute code beyond. GNOME seeks to avoid ties with any platform-specific interfaces where possible, and when not possible to provide code for all platforms.

Multiple operating systems.

INSTALLING GNOME

Red Hat 6.0 now provides GNOME as the default desktop, so you don't need to do anything to it. This version is even relatively stable, unlike the rest of Red Hat 6.0's X and KDE packages.

For other distributions (including Red Hat 5.2 and earlier), GNOME installation can be quite complicated. Rather than try to give all the permutations here, I recommend that you go to the Getting GNOME page at `http://www.gnome.org/start/getting.shtml`. If you have Caldera OpenLinux, check out the FAQ at `http://www.gnome.org/gnomefaq/html/gettingotherrpm.html`. This FAQ entry is somewhat out of date but should still work.

GNOME seems to have become more and more focused on Red Hat during its life. Much of this focus is due to Red Hat Advanced Development Labs (RHAD) providing so much support for GNOME. In fact, the Enlightenment window manager is primarily developed by Mandrake (`mandrake@mandrake.net`) and Rasterman (`raster@rasterman.com`). Until recently, Rasterman was a member of RHAD (he now works with Mandrake at VA Research).

With GNOME, as with most Open Source projects, the only way that things happen is for people to choose to work on them. Because Red Hat works a lot on GNOME, GNOME tends to install easily on Red Hat. Because Caldera focuses on KDE (and does not even ship GNOME with OpenLinux 2.2), installing it on OpenLinux systems is not very easy. I don't mean to imply a bias on the part of the GNOME team. I simply mean that if no one works on something, then it doesn't get done. The power of Open Source is that if anyone chooses to make good OpenLinux RPMs for GNOME, that person is absolutely free to do so (and even encouraged to do so).

Over 60 packages are required or recommended for GNOME, all with their own versions. Whereas all KDE packages are released together and are numbered with the version of KDE (1.1.1, for instance), each GNOME package is independent, and new versions may be released whenever necessary. For example, `gnome-core` may be at version 1.0.7, whereas `enlightenment` may be at version 0.15.5.

Luckily, a set of packages collectively called GNOME 1.0 is considered fairly stable. You can find these packages at `ftp://ftp.gnome.org/pub/GNOME/gnome-1.0`.Packages are available for Debian, Red Hat, Slackware, and S.u.S.E. For other distributions, you can pull down the sources and compile them.

Using the `switchdesk` Tool for Red Hat 6.0

If you have switched to another desktop or window manager, the easiest way to switch back to GNOME is to use the `switchdesk` tool. `switchdesk` may not be installed by default, so you might have to install the `switchdesk-1.7.0-1` package by using `rpm`.

→ See "Installing Packages with RPM," p. 169

After you've installed `switchdesk`, launching it is simple:

```
$ switchdesk
```

This command produces a dialog box asking whether you prefer GNOME, KDE, or AnotherLevel. Select GNOME, choose OK, and then log out. When you log back in, your default desktop will be GNOME.

Choosing GNOME Without `switchdesk`

If you're using a distribution without `switchdesk`, you can make GNOME your default desktop by modifying your `$HOME/.Xclients` file to contain the following:

```
exec gnome-session
```

→ See "Using vi," p. 207

→ See "Choosing a Window Manager," p. 536

NAVIGATING GNOME

If you're familiar with other GUIs, such as the Macintosh interface or Microsoft Windows, GNOME should be quite familiar. Figure 27.2 shows the major components of the desktop.

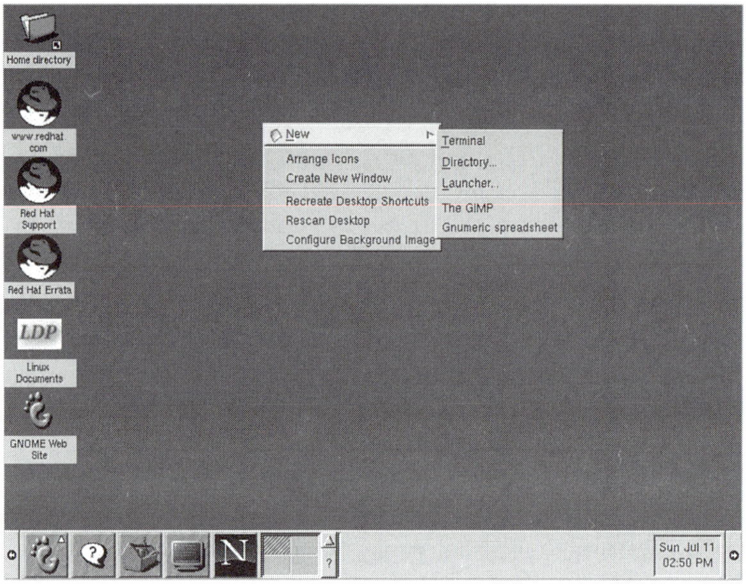

Figure 27.2
GNOME's desktop is incredibly configurable and personal.

THE PANEL

The panel is probably the most important part of the GNOME desktop. The default settings give plenty of functionality, but the real power lies in configuring the panel (see Figure 27.3).

Figure 27.3
The GNOME panel holds all your most-used features.

MAIN MENU BUTTON

The Main Menu holds links to all your programs and configuration menus. It is similar to the Windows 95/98 Start menu but adds a few more options. For instance, if you right-click a menu option, you can add a launcher for that option to your panel or to your personal menu. You can also drag and drop menu items to the panel or to the desktop to make shortcuts.

No shortcut key is available to bring up the Main Menu like there is in KDE. This lack of a shortcut is mostly due to how GNOME works. The panel itself is just an application, so it can't watch for keystrokes. The window manager would have to do that and then send that information on to the panel. But Enlightenment doesn't allow you to add that kind of accelerator key easily and doesn't specifically know about the panel in any case. This problem is surmountable (and may be addressed in future versions of Enlightenment), but it is indicative of the issues in a loosely integrated system like GNOME.

INTEGRATED HELP SYSTEM

The help system has all the online GNOME documentation, including a great deal of documentation for GNOME applications. Although the GNOME Help Browser does use URLs to locate files, it is not a Web browser and does not understand http addresses.

Tip #140 from Rob

GNOME's Integrated Help System does not include help for Enlightenment. To get help for Enlightenment, click the middle mouse button on the desktop and click Help.

Enlightenment also provides ToolTips. By pointing the mouse pointer to a window button or frame, Enlightenment will display help text about that item.

CONTROL CENTER

Much like KDE's Control Center, GNOME's Control Center allows you to configure much of GNOME's behavior. To configure Enlightenment's behavior, you need to go to the Window Manager section and run Enlightenment's configuration tool.

TERMINAL AND NETSCAPE

The Terminal and Netscape buttons are normal launch buttons that run a terminal emulator and Netscape, respectively. You can add many more buttons if you like.

PAGER

Virtual screens and desktops really differentiate the Linux desktops from the Windows and Macintosh environments. Each of the four areas in the pager provides you with a completely different virtual screen, each displaying different windows. When screen real estate is scarce, having these different areas can be very convenient. Inside each block are small representations of the windows currently displayed on that virtual screen. Enlightenment also allows you to have virtual desktops, each of which can have virtual screens. The pager shows these virtual desktops as additional blocks of screens. Enlightenment can handle up to 32 desktops of up to 8 × 8 (64) screens per desktop for a total of 2,048 screens. You should never need even a fraction of this number. The default is 2 × 2 virtual screens and one virtual desktop. For the remainder of this chapter, I will use the term *desktop* to mean both *virtual screen* and *virtual desktop* unless the distinction is important.

Generally, you put like applications together so that you can easily move between desktops as you move between tasks. A common layout is xterminals on one screen, a Web browser on another, mail on a third, and diversions (games) on a fourth. Other users choose to put all their programming tools on one desktop, documentation on a second, and mail on a third. It's up to you. GNOME remembers what programs are running on which desktops when you log out if you request it, so when you log in, everything restarts in the right place.

Configuring virtual desktops can be somewhat confusing because this feature is shared by the pager and the window manager. To change how the pager displays these desktops (for example, to make the pager smaller or to turn off the task list), click the ? button on the panel. To configure the number of virtual screens and desktops, their backgrounds, and other options, you need to use the Enlightenment configuration tool described previously.

→ See "Making It Pretty," p. 590

You can move windows between virtual desktops by clicking their menu button (usually the far left button on the title bar), clicking Desktop, and then clicking the direction the window should be moved (right, left, above, below).

Tip #141 from *Rob*

To move a window between distant virtual desktops, you can make the window *sticky* by clicking Stick/Unstick, moving the desired desktop, and then clicking Stick/Unstick again. This action leaves the window on the new desktop.

TASK LIST

Technically part of the pager, the task list shows buttons for each window on the current desktop. Visible windows are shown with a GNOME foot icon beside them. The active window has yellow rays coming out of the GNOME foot icon. Hidden windows have a small box icon beside them. You can access a full list of all windows on all desktops by clicking the arrow icon between the pager and the task list.

CLOCK

You can configure the default GNOME clock to show 12-hour or 24-hour time and display the date if you request it. The clock can also display *UNIX time*, which is the number of seconds since the epoch (00:00:00 UTC, January 1, 1970). It is unlikely that you will want to display UNIX time.

PANEL HIDE

On either side of the panel is a tab with an arrow on it. When you click one of these buttons, the panel slides off the screen in the direction indicated. This feature is handy if you want more of the screen available for working.

→ See "Getting More Desktop," p. 573

THE ROOT MENU

To open the Root menu, right-click the desktop. A menu then pops up with various options. These options are explained in Table 27.1.

TABLE 27.1 GNOME ROOT MENU OPTIONS

Option	Purpose
New	Using this option is a quick way to start various programs or create folders on the desktop. Terminal starts `gnome-terminal`, Directory allows you to create a new folder, and Launcher lets you create a new program launcher. The GIMP and Gnumeric spreadsheets start these programs. Because the New menu is completely customizable, you can use it to replace the Main Menu.
Arrange Icons	This option orders the icons on your desktop on the left side of your screen.
Create New Window	This option launches Midnight Commander, the GNOME File Manager.
Re-create Desktop Shortcuts	If you accidentally remove any of the default desktop shortcuts, this option puts them back for you.
Rescan Desktop	If the GNOME desktop ever gets confused, or if you manually reconfigure it behind its back, this option gets all your desktop icons back where they should be.
Configure Background Image	This option is a shortcut to the Control Center's Background section. See "Making It Pretty" later in this chapter for more information on setting background images. Setting images is not always as simple as it sounds.

THE ENLIGHTENMENT MENU

You can access the Enlightenment menu by pressing the middle mouse button on the background. The Enlightenment menu is independent of the Root menu because Enlightenment can be run without GNOME. If you don't want to use the panel, you can configure the Enlightenment menu to have everything you need on it. Table 27.2 details the options from the Enlightenment menu.

TABLE 27.2 ENLIGHTENMENT MENU OPTIONS

Option	Purpose
Gnome Apps	This menu is the same as the System section of the GNOME Main Menu.
Other Programs	These menus list other preloaded programs that aren't on the Gnome Apps menu.

Table 27.2 Enlightenment Menu Options

Option	Purpose
Desktop	This menu provides various desktop functions. Cleanup Desktop attempts to unclutter the desktop by moving overlapping windows apart. Goto Next Desktop moves one desktop (not screen) down the stack. Goto Previous Desktop moves one desktop up the stack. FX - Ripples really shows what Enlightenment can do. It makes the bottom of your screen look like a pool of water, reflecting everything above it with ripples. On a fast machine, it can be quite pretty.
Themes	All installed Enlightenment themes are listed here, and you can quickly switch between them. See "Themes" later in this chapter for more information.
Enlightenment Configuration	This option launches the Enlightenment Configuration dialog.
About Enlightenment	This option shows version and contact information for Enlightenment.
Help	This option brings up the Enlightenment Help Browser (which is separate from the GNOME Help Browser).
Restart Enlightenment	If you have reconfigured Enlightenment manually, this option lets you restart it to pick up the new configurations.

Midnight Commander File Manager

GNOME comes with the Midnight Commander File Manager (see Figure 27.4). Although it is not a full Web browser like kfm, it does offer a number of additional benefits.

Figure 27.4
Midnight Commander is an extremely flexible file manager for power users.

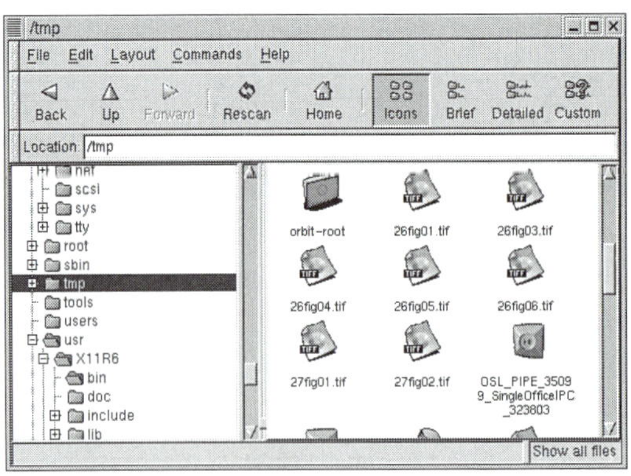

Using the Icons, Brief, Detailed, and Custom buttons across the top of the window, you can quickly switch between different views of the files in your directory. For power users who often want to see the file details, this capability can be a great help. You can configure the Custom button by using the Edit, Preferences dialog.

Other options in the Edit, Preferences dialog that are of particular interest to power users are the Show Hidden Files and Use Shell Patterns Instead of Regular Expressions options. Turning off the latter is very nice if you like to have the full power of regular expressions when you're searching.

For remote sites, Midnight Commander handles FTP-style URLs, just like kfm.

For powerful filtering capabilities, click Commands, Run Command in Panel to set up complex filters using `find` or any other UNIX tool that creates a list of filenames. One of the default expressions is "Find SUID and SGID Programs" for the security-conscious. SUID and SGID programs generally run with unrestricted privileges, making them a potential security hole. The "Find SUID and SGID Programs" expression automatically runs the following command:

```
find . \(\(-perm -04000 -a -perm +011 \) \
     -o \(-perm -02000 -a -perm +01 \) \) -print
```

The results are then displayed in the file browser, just as if they were all in a directory.

→ See "Searching for Files," p. 432

Tear-Off Menus

In Figure 27.4, notice the small tabs on the left side of the three menu bars at the top of the window. They are tear-off menus, which means you can shuffle them around by dragging them up or down. You can even tear them off the window entirely and place them on the desktop if you prefer. Most GNOME applications support tear-off menus.

Configuring GNOME

GNOME is incredibly configurable. Almost every part of GNOME can be reconfigured, replaced, or removed. If you're comfortable with GNOME, environments like KDE, Macintosh, or Windows 95/98 are extremely limited and confining. The other side of this flexibility is that GNOME users are expected to take care of themselves and know how all the parts of GNOME interact with each other. Sometimes two different components try to configure the same thing (such as the background), and it's up to you to establish who controls what.

You can handle many configuration options in two or three unrelated (and possibly conflicting) ways. Often you can choose a GNOME or Gtk+ way or an Enlightenment way. The following sections focus on the most convenient and useful ways to configure your system, which for GNOME users is usually the GNOME or Gtk+ way (but not always).

Making GNOME Useful

GNOME is very useful right out of the box. By reconfiguring it, however, you can make it more compatible with the way you work. For example, GNOME allows you to create shortcuts to the tools and files you use most. It also allows you to put tools right on your panel so they are always available. This section focuses on how to improve your productivity by better configuring GNOME.

PUTTING APPLICATIONS ON THE MAIN MENU

Putting options on the Main Menu is usually the first thing you want to do. To get started, click Main Menu, Settings, Menu Editor to open the Menu Editor shown in Figure 27.5. If, for some reason, this option isn't on the menu yet, you can run the Menu Editor directly by clicking Main Menu, Run Program, and then entering `gmenu`.

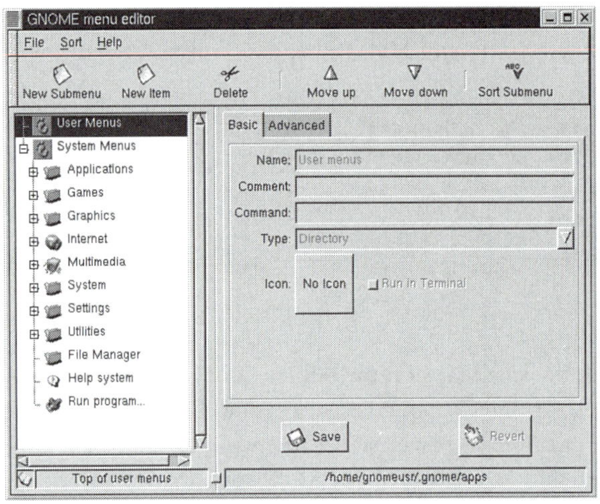

Figure 27.5
The Menu Editor is extremely visual and intuitive.

The Menu Editor should be fairly straightforward for most users. Unless you are running as root, you can put things only on the User menu because the System menu is used by all users.

In the Menu Editor, select User Menus and click New Item to open an untitled application. Enter the name you want to call it, a comment for the pop-up hints, and the command to run. Type is usually an application, although if you want to put a directory in your menu, you can choose Directory. Midnight Commander shows you the directory when you select this item. The Run in Terminal check is handy if the program is text-based rather than a GUI. Finally, choose an icon and click Save. For the vast majority of programs, that's all you need to do.

Tip #142 from *Rob*

The Menu Editor supports drag and drop just like most GNOME applications. To move elements around, just drag them to where you want them. If you want to create a launcher on the desktop or the panel, you can just drag an entry there.

PUTTING NEW LAUNCHERS ON THE PANEL

After you've put a menu entry on the Main Menu, adding it to the panel is easy. Just open the Main Menu, find the launcher you want, and drag it to the panel. You can then use the middle mouse button to move the launcher around. Right-click the launcher to modify it or remove it.

PUTTING APPLETS ON THE PANEL

Much of the power of the panel is in applets. The clock is an applet, but many more are available. For instance, you can add a CD player, load monitor, mail monitor, and even a Slashdot headline viewer.

Tip #143 from *Rob*

Slashdot (`http://slashdot.org`) is the premier site for up-to-the-minute high-tech information. Its slogan is "News for Nerds. Stuff that matters."

Other important Linux sites are `http://freshmeat.net` for the latest software updates, and `http://userfriendly.org` for influential Linux humor.

To put a new applet on your panel, click Main Menu, Panel, Add Applet, and then choose the applet you want. After it's on the panel, you can use the middle mouse button to move it around. The right mouse button pulls up a menu so that you can set the applet's properties or remove it from the panel.

GETTING MORE PANEL ROOM

After you've added all the elements that you're sure to want, you might find that your panel is overloaded. What you need is more panels. In GNOME, the panel is just an application, so having more than one is not a problem. You can reasonably have up to four panels, though GNOME won't stop you from creating more. To create a new panel, right-click the Hide button and click Add New Panel. Then click Edge Panel or Corner Panel.

Corner panels start in a corner and extend horizontally or vertically for as far as they need to. Edge panels cover an entire horizontal or vertical edge, regardless of what is on them. You can convert each panel to corner or edge by right-clicking the Hide button and clicking Convert to Corner Panel (or Edge Panel).

MAKING A DRAWER

Often it is convenient to create a subpanel to contain related tools. To create such a subpanel, right-click the Hide button and click Add Drawer. By doing so, you create a drawer on the panel that you can move around with the middle mouse button. You can then add launchers and applets to it just like a panel. You can even add drawers to drawers.

Making It Pretty

Enlightenment is arguably the prettiest (or at least fanciest) window manager ever developed. The look and feel are fantastically configurable. Sometimes configuring can be a bit confusing, so the following sections focus on the most common changes.

Setting the Background

Setting the background should be very easy, but GNOME doesn't always do what you might expect. The problem is that GNOME can set the background, and Enlightenment can set the background. If both of them try to set the background, then they will likely fight about it, and your background may change suddenly when you're not expecting a change.

The secret is to pick one of them to handle the background and tell the other one to leave it alone. The Red Hat 6.0 default is to let GNOME set the background and to turn off Enlightenment's background. This approach is good if you want the same background for every desktop, but if you want different backgrounds for each desktop (not screen), you need to let Enlightenment handle the job.

→ See "Pager," p. 583

To use GNOME's background properties, follow these steps:

1. Go to the Control Center and click Background.
2. From there, select whether you want a solid, gradient, or image background. Choose OK.
3. Click Window Manager, Enlightenment to bring up the Enlightenment Configuration Editor.
4. Click Backgrounds and No Background to let GNOME do all the background handling.

To use Enlightenment's background properties, follow these steps:

1. Go to the Control Center and click Background.
2. From there, click Disable Background Selection and choose OK.
3. Click Window Manger, Enlightenment to bring up the Enlightenment Configuration Editor.
4. Click Backgrounds.
5. From the list, select the desktop that you want to work on.
6. Select the background from the pictures to the right. If you don't like any of them, you can click Add New. This option allows you to use your own images as backdrops.

Modifying Window Behavior

In Enlightenment, windows can behave in numerous ways when they are created, resized, or moved. To configure this behavior, go to the Enlightenment Configuration Editor by choosing Control Center, Window Manager, Enlightenment.

To change how windows move, click Basic Options. Your options are Opaque, Lined, Box, Shaded, Semi-Solid, and Translucent. Experimenting with these options is worthwhile, but keep these points in mind: Opaque is a good default; Lined and Box work very well on slow machines; and Shaded, Semi-Solid, and Translucent are extremely slow unless you have very good hardware.

You also handle window resizing in the Basic Options dialog. The same options exist as for moving, except that you can't choose Translucent.

In the Basic Options dialog, you also can set how window focus works. Your choices are Mouse, Sloppy, and Click.

→ See "Getting Focus," p. 530

From the Enlightenment Configuration Editor, click Audio if you want to turn on sounds. From here, you can turn on Enlightenment sound events. Most things that happen in Enlightenment can generate sounds. If you like sounds, enjoy. Sometimes, though, these sounds can become quite annoying after a very short time.

SCREENSAVERS

GNOME uses xscreensaver, which was first developed by Jamie Zawinski (`jwz@jwz.org`) in late 1991. Given that long history, it is not surprising that GNOME ships with over 70 different screensavers. To choose one, go to the Control Center and click Screensaver. Browse through the list until you find one you like.

Tip #144 from *Rob*

If you feel you need more screensavers, you can look at `http://www.jwz.org/xscreensaver` and pick up the latest version. Several new screensavers have been added since the version that ships with Red Hat 6.0.

THEMES

As mentioned previously, themes allow you to define a common appearance for your environment. For example, themes allow you to define how your windows and buttons look and what color your background is.

Both Gtk+ and Enlightenment have themes, but they handle different features. Gtk+'s themes generally handle things within windows, such as the window background or how buttons are drawn. Enlightenment's themes generally handle features outside windows such as their frames and widgets. To get a complete look, you need to use both.

GTK+ THEMES

Gtk+ comes with 12 themes—which is pretty good, but there's always room for more. You can start by going to `http://gtk.themes.org`. At this time, 66 themes are available for Gtk+. You can select the theme you want from the gallery and download it. It is saved as a `tar.gz` file. Then you can go to the Control Center and click Theme Selector. Next, click Install New Theme and select your theme file. Finally, select the theme from the list and click OK. The theme takes effect immediately.

ENLIGHTENMENT THEMES

Enlightenment comes with seven themes, so you'll probably want more if you like themes. The best place to get Enlightenment themes is `http://e.themes.org`. At this time, Enlightenment has 129 themes available. You can select the theme you want from the gallery and download it. It is saved as an `.etheme` file (which is really just a `tar.gz` file). Put this file in your `.enlightenment/themes/` directory (create this directory if it doesn't exist yet).

Now open the Enlightenment Configuration tool (by choosing Control Center, Window Manager, Enlightenment), click Themes, and select your theme. Select Apply, and you're done.

GETTING MORE DESKTOP

GNOME offers many options for maximizing your available screen real estate. If you're interested in reorganizing your desktop, try some of the following:

- Move the panel off the screen by clicking the left or right hide buttons.
- Autohide the panel. To do so, right-click the Hide button and click This Panel Properties. Then click Auto Hide. Choosing these options causes the panel to hide until you touch the mouse pointer to their border. For instance, when you move the mouse cursor to the bottom of the screen, the panel reappears.
- Convert your panel to a corner panel. By doing so, you can give yourself some more room on the side of the panel. To convert the panel, right-click the Hide button and click Convert to Corner Panel.

THE PROS AND CONS OF GNOME

Should you use GNOME? Should you use KDE? Should you avoid them both and use a conventional Linux window manager? The choice is up to you, but the following sections describe some of the advantages and disadvantages of GNOME, particularly in relation to KDE. You also have the option of running Enlightenment without GNOME, which has some advantages and disadvantages of its own.

RESOURCES

Determining exactly how much memory one desktop uses versus another can be very difficult given how shared libraries can skew the numbers, but in general terms, GNOME uses about the same memory as KDE, possibly a bit less in its default configuration. Both use three to four times the memory of AfterStep, which is certainly not the smallest of the window managers. Enlightenment without GNOME obviously uses quite a bit less memory than with GNOME, though it is still larger than window managers like AfterStep. If all of Enlightenment's features are turned on, GNOME can take quite a bit more memory than KDE. GNOME claims to run in 16M of memory, but you will generally need closer to 64M of memory to get good performance.

PERFORMANCE

GNOME's performance, particularly with several of Enlightenment's features turned on, can be a problem. With many of the fancy features turned off, though, GNOME's performance is pretty good. It is still generally a bit slower than KDE and can be quite a bit slower than other window managers like AfterStep. In particular, you may find that windows and menus take longer to appear with GNOME. This is especially true if you are displaying your desktop across a network.

CONFIGURATION

GNOME is incredibly configurable. This is a benefit and a problem. If you like to have complete control over what your environment looks like and how it works, GNOME and Enlightenment are definitely for you. With this flexibility, however, comes a lot of complexity and some very confusing conflicts. Some features don't always work together unless you know how to configure them properly. If you want an environment that is stable, even if it is also more rigid, KDE may be for you.

Using Enlightenment without GNOME still gives you several configuration options without all the conflicts. Enlightenment is just a window manager, so you lose the advantages of having a desktop, such as being able to put shortcuts directly on the desktop and manage sessions.

INTEGRATION

GNOME is more like a federation than an integration. Many of the parts of GNOME work just fine by themselves. This aspect is wonderful if you want to swap out individual components, but it also means that the components don't always work together well. When they do work, though, they work better than anything else.

STABILITY

Enlightenment in particular is only mostly stable. In general, a GNOME/Enlightenment environment will crash more than KDE. Although you can often just restart the part that crashed (even Enlightenment can often be restarted without losing your running programs), it can be quite frustrating. If you are used to a Windows 95 environment, GNOME is still much more stable (particularly because crashes do not bring down the whole system), but as a whole, GNOME is only somewhat stable in Linux terms.

FINAL WORDS

GNOME is the ideal desktop for people who like the cutting edge. GNOME and Enlightenment are breaking new ground in how desktops work. In many ways, Enlightenment is the first truly innovative windowing interface since NeXT. GNOME is pushing the idea of really open software in directions it's probably never gone before. If you're a technophile, GNOME is a wonderful collection of parts that you can use to build your own environment. Just browse through `e.themes.org` to see how differently users have expressed themselves. If you like to tinker with your machine, GNOME provides no end of opportunities.

On the other hand, if you don't see your desktop as an important form of self-expression, then you probably won't be very comfortable in GNOME or Enlightenment and should seriously consider KDE. If you administer other people's machines, you might find GNOME's endless variations a nightmare to support. Once again, KDE is probably a better choice. The power of Linux is that it is your choice to make.

PART V

Network Administration

CHAPTER 28

Understanding the TCP/IP Protocol Suite

In this chapter

by Steve Burnett

THE HISTORY OF TCP/IP

The suite of widely used protocols known as Transmission Control Protocol/Internet Protocol (TCP/IP) has become critical as networks of all sizes, including the Internet, depend on it for their communications.

TCP/IP has grown from its initial development as a government-sponsored project to widespread use, connecting networks of all sizes. Recognized for its capability to enable communication among dissimilar machines, it's found on virtually all workstations, minicomputers, and mainframes.

In the late 1960s, the U.S. Department of Defense (DOD) recognized an electronic communication problem developing within the department. Communicating the ever-increasing volume of electronic information among DOD staff, research labs, universities, and contractors had hit a major obstacle. The various entities had computer systems from different computer manufacturers, running different operating systems, and using different networking topologies and protocols. How could information be shared?

The Advanced Research Projects Agency (ARPA) was assigned to resolve the problem of dealing with different networking equipment and topologies. ARPA formed an alliance with universities and computer manufacturers to develop communication standards. This alliance specified and built a four-node network that's the foundation of today's Internet. During the 1970s, this network migrated to a new, core protocol design that became the basis for TCP/IP.

The mention of TCP/IP requires a brief introduction to the Internet, a huge network of networks that allows computers all over the world to communicate. The Internet grows at such a phenomenal rate that any estimate of the number of computers and users on the Internet would be out of date by the time this book went to print! Nodes include universities, major corporations, research labs in the United States and abroad, schools, businesses both large and small, and individually owned computers. The explosion in past years of the World Wide Web has driven the Internet's expansion. In addition, the Internet is also a repository for millions of shareware programs, news on any topic, public forums and information exchanges, and email. Another feature is remote login to any computer system on the network by using the Telnet protocol. Because of the number of systems that are interconnected, massive computer resources can be shared, enabling large programs to be executed on remote systems. Massively distributed processing projects such as the 1997 decryption of the Data Encryption Standard are possible only with the "everything is connected to everything else" behavior of the Internet.

INTERNET TERMINOLOGY

The Internet Protocol suite is composed of many related protocols based on the foundation formed by TCP and IP. To clarify the relationship of these components, Table 28.1 provides some definitions and notations.

TABLE 28.1 NETWORKING TERMS

Term	Definition
datagram	A unit of information that's exchanged; this term is used interchangeably with the words *data packet* and *network message*.
DNS	(Domain Name Service) A service provided by one or more computers in a network to help locate a path to a desired node. This service saves every system on a network from having to keep a list of every system it wants to talk to. DNS is used by mail gateways.
GOSIP	(Government Open Systems Interconnection Profile) A collection of OSI protocols used in U.S. government computer networks and projects.
Internet	A computer network based on TCP/IP and related protocols. It is a public network of networks interconnecting businesses, universities, government facilities, and research centers.
FTAM	(File Transfer, Access, and Management) A file transfer and management protocol as specified by OSI.
FTP	(File Transfer Protocol) A protocol that enables file transfer between systems.
IP	(Internet Protocol) A protocol responsible for transporting datagrams across the Internet. The current standard version of IP is IP version 4, or IPv4.
IPv6	(Internet Protocol version 6) Also referred to as Ipng, this evolutionary upgrade of Ipv4 is not discussed in this chapter.
NFS	(Network File System) A network virtual disk system that enables a client computer to mount remote file systems and directories. It was originally developed by Sun Microsystems.
NIC	(Network Information Center) A group responsible for administering Internet and TCP/IP addresses, as well as network names.
node	A computer on a network.
OSI	(Open System Interconnection) The ISO standard model for defining data communication.
RFC	(Request For Comments) The documentation maintained by NIC relating to Internet protocols, addressing, routing, configuration, and other related Internet topics.
RIP	(Routing Information Protocol) A protocol used to exchange information between routers.
RMON	(Remote monitor) A remote network monitor that enables the collection of information about network traffic.
RPC	(Remote Procedure Call) A type of call that enables procedures to be executed on a server.
SMTP	(Simple Mail Transfer Protocol) A protocol used to transfer electronic mail between systems.
SNMP	(Simple Network Management Protocol) A protocol used to manage remote network devices and to collect information from remote devices related to configuration, errors, and alarms.

Table 28.1 Networking Terms

Term	Definition
TCP	(Transmission Control Protocol) The protocol between a pair of applications responsible for reliable, connection-oriented data transmission.
Telnet	The protocol used to establish remote terminal connections.
UDP	(User Datagram Protocol) A connectionless protocol used to transfer data between agents.
VT	(Virtual terminal) A method for using Telnet to log in to remote systems through the network.

The Open Systems Interconnection Model

Many different types of computers are used today, varying in operating systems, CPUs, network interfaces, and many other qualities. These differences make the problem of communication between diverse computer systems important. In 1977, the International Standards Organization (ISO) created a subcommittee to develop data communication standards to promote multivendor interoperability. The result is the Open Systems Interconnection (OSI) model.

The OSI model doesn't specify any communication standards or protocols; instead, it provides guidelines that communication tasks follow.

Note

It's important to understand that the OSI model is simply a model—a framework—that specifies the functions to be performed. The model doesn't detail *how* these functions are performed. ISO, however, does certify specific protocols that meet OSI standards for parts of the OSI model. For example, the CCITT X.25 protocol is accepted by ISO as an implementation that provides most of the services of the Network layer of the OSI model.

To simplify matters, the ISO subcommittees took the divide-and-conquer approach. Because the complex communication process is divided into smaller subtasks, the problem becomes more manageable, and each subtask can be optimized individually. The OSI model is divided into seven layers:

- Application
- Presentation
- Session
- Transport
- Network

- Data Link
- Physical

Tip #145 from *Steve*

One easy way to remember the order of the layers (from the top down) is mnemonically, by making a sentence from the first letters of the layer names: All People Seem To Need Data Processing.

Each layer is assigned a specific set of functions. Each layer uses the services of the layer beneath it and provides services to the layer above it. For example, the Network layer uses services from the Data Link layer and provides network-related services to the Transport layer. Table 28.2 explains the services offered at each layer.

Note

The concept of a layer making use of services and providing services to its adjacent layers is simple. Consider how a company operates: An assistant provides services to the president (the next layer up) to write a memo. The assistant uses the services of a messenger (the next layer down) to deliver the message. Because these services are separated, the assistant (application) doesn't have to know how the message is actually carried to its recipient. The assistant merely has to ask the messenger (network) to deliver it. Just as many assistants can send memos in this way by using a standard messenger service, a layered network can send packets by handing them to the network layer for delivery.

TABLE 28.2 SERVICES PROVIDED AT EACH OSI LAYER

Layer	Description
Physical (Layer 1)	This layer provides the physical connection between a computer system and the network. It specifies connector and pin assignments, voltage levels, and so on.
Data Link (Layer 2)	This layer "packages" and "unpackages" data for transmission. It forms the information into frames. A *frame* represents the exact structure of the data physically transmitted across the wire or other medium.
Network (Layer 3)	This layer provides routing of data through the network.
Transport (Layer 4)	This layer provides sequencing and acknowledgment of transmission.
Session (Layer 5)	This layer establishes and terminates communication links.
Presentation (Layer 6)	This layer converts data and ensures that data is exchanged in a universal format.

TABLE 28.2 SERVICES PROVIDED AT EACH OSI LAYER

Layer	Description
Application (Layer 7)	This layer provides an interface to the application that a user executes—a "gateway" between user applications and the network communication process.

Note

Don't confuse the Application layer with application programs you execute on the computer. Remember that the *Application layer* is part of the OSI model that doesn't specify *how* the interface between a user and the communication pathway happens; an *application program* is a specific implementation of this interface. A real application typically performs Application, Session, and Presentation layer services and leaves Transport, Network, Data Link, and Physical layer services to the network operating system.

Each layer communicates with its peer in other computers. For example, layer 3 in one system communicates with layer 3 in another computer system.

When information is passed from one layer down to the next, a header is added to the data to indicate where the information is coming from and going to. The header-plus-data block of information from one layer becomes the data for the next. For example, when layer 4 passes data to layer 3, layer 4 adds its own header. When layer 3 passes the information to layer 2, layer 3 considers the header-plus-data from layer 4 as data and adds its own header before passing that combination down.

In each layer, the information units are given different names (see Table 28.3). Therefore, by knowing the terms used to reference the data, you know which layer of the model is being discussed.

TABLE 28.3 TERMS USED BY OSI LAYERS TO REFER TO INFORMATION UNITS

OSI Layer	Information Unit Name
Application	Message
Transport	Segment
Network	Datagram
Data Link	Frame (also called *packet*)
Physical	Bit

Before the advent of the OSI model, the U.S. Department of Defense defined its own networking model, known as the *DOD model*. The DOD model is closely related to the TCP/IP suite of protocols, as explained in the following section.

The TCP/IP Protocol Stack

The TCP/IP protocol stack represents a network architecture that's similar to the ISO OSI networking model. Figure 28.1 shows the mapping of TCP/IP layers onto the ISO protocol stack.

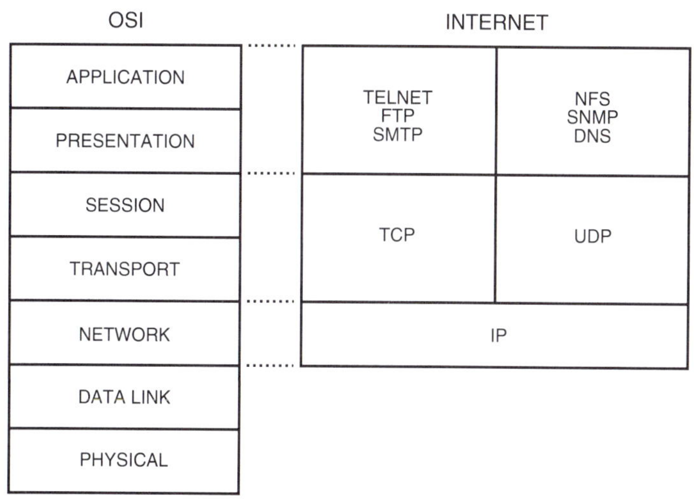

Figure 28.1
OSI and TCP/IP compared.

TCP/IP doesn't make as fine distinctions between the top layers of the protocol stack as does OSI. The top three OSI layers are roughly equivalent to the Internet process protocols. Some examples of process protocols are Telnet, FTP, SMTP, NFS, SNMP, and DNS.

The Transport layer of the OSI model is responsible for reliable data delivery. In the Internet protocol stack, this layer corresponds to the host-to-host protocols. Examples are TCP and UDP. TCP is used to translate variable-length messages from upper-layer protocols and provides the necessary acknowledgment and connection-oriented flow control between remote systems.

UDP is similar to TCP, except that it's not connection-oriented and doesn't acknowledge data receipt. UDP only receives messages and passes them along to the upper-level protocols. Because UDP doesn't have any of the overhead related to TCP, it provides a much more efficient interface for such actions as remote disk services.

The Internet Protocol (IP) is responsible for connectionless communications between systems. It maps onto the OSI model as part of the Network layer, which is responsible for moving information around the network. This communication is accomplished by examining the Network layer address, which determines the systems and the path to send the message.

IP provides the same functionality as the Network layer and helps get the messages between systems, but it doesn't guarantee the delivery of these messages. IP may also fragment the messages into chunks and then reassemble them at the destination. Each fragment may take a different network path between systems. If the fragments arrive out of order, IP reassembles the packets into the correct sequence at the destination.

IP ADDRESSES

The Internet Protocol requires that an address be assigned to every device on the network. This address, known as the *IP address*, is organized as a series of four octets. These octets each define a unique address, with part of the address representing a network (and optionally a subnetwork) and another part representing a particular node on the network.

Several addresses have special meanings on the Internet:

- An address starting with a zero references the local node within its current network. For example, 0.0.0.23 references workstation 23 on the current network. Address 0.0.0.0 references the current workstation.
- The loopback address, 127, is important in troubleshooting and network diagnoses. The network address 127.0.0.0 is the local loopback inside a workstation.
- The ALL address is represented by turning on all bits, giving a value of 255. Therefore, 192.18.255.255 sends a message to all nodes on network 192.18; similarly, 255.255.255.255 sends a message to every node on the Internet. These addresses are important to use for multicast messages and service announcements.

Caution

When you assign node numbers to your workstations, you should not use 0, 127, or 255 because they are reserved numbers and have special meanings.

IP ADDRESS CLASSES

The IP addresses are assigned in ranges referred to as *classes*, depending on the application and the size of an organization. The three most common classes are A, B, and C. These three classes represent the number of locally assignable bits available for the local network. Table 28.4 shows the relationships among the different address classes, the available number of nodes, and the initial address settings.

TABLE 28.4 IP ADDRESS CLASSES

Class	Available Nodes	Initial Bits	Starting Address
A	2^{24}=167,772	0xxx	0-127
B	2^{16}=65,536	10xx	128-191
C	2^{8}=256	110x	192-223
D		1110	224-239
E		1111	240-255

Class A addresses are used for very large networks or collections of related networks. Class B addresses are used for large networks having more than 256 nodes (but fewer than 65,536 nodes). Class C addresses are used by most organizations. It's a better idea for an organization to get several class C addresses because the number of class B addresses is limited. Class D is reserved for multicast messages on the network, and class E is reserved for experimentation and development.

OBTAINING IP ADDRESSES

The administration of Internet addresses is currently handled by the Network Information Center (NIC):

Network Solutions
ATTN: InterNIC Registration Services
505 Huntmar Park Drive
Herndon, VA 22070
703-742-4777

ON THE WEB

You also can reach the InterNIC on the Web at the following address:

`http://www.internic.net`

Note

The Internet addressing and domain name registration process is in a state of flux as of this writing. To see what's happened since the publication of this book, visit `http://www.networksolutions.com/` and `http://www.icann.org/` for the most current information, or contact your Internet service provider.

When you connect a computer or a network to the Internet, in most cases your Internet service provider can arrange for your network IP address registration.

OBTAINING RFCs

In addition to assigning addresses, the NIC can provide other information of value. It's a repository for all technical documentation related to the Internet. It has a collection of documents that describe all the associated protocols, routing methodologies, network management guidelines, and methods for using different networking technologies.

As mentioned in Table 28.1, RFC stands for *Request For Comments*. You can obtain RFCs from the Internet by using the FTP protocol to connect to several different repositories. The RFC series is available on the Internet via anonymous FTP from various sites, such as `ftp.internic.net` in the `/rfc` directory, and can also be accessed via Telnet at `rs.internic.net`.

Table 28.5 lists the pertinent RFCs for establishing a network. Some of these documents go into great detail about how the different protocols function and the underlying specifications and theory. Others are more general and provide key information that can be useful to a network manager. At a minimum, an Internet network manager should know where these documents are located and how to obtain them. They provide information that can help in planning and expanding an organization's network.

TABLE 28.5 RFCs OF INTEREST

RFC Name	Description
`RFC791.txt`	Internet Protocol DARPA Internet Program Protocol Specification
`RFC792.txt`	Internet Control Message Protocol
`RFC793.txt`	Transmission Control Protocol DARPA Internet Program Protocol Specification
`RFC950.txt`	Internet Standard Subnetting Procedure
`RFC1058.txt`	Routing Information Protocol
`RFC1178.txt`	Choosing a Name for Your Computer
`RFC1180.txt`	A TCP/IP Tutorial
`RFC1208.txt`	A Glossary of Networking Terms
`RFC1219.txt`	On the Assignment of Subnet Numbers
`RFC1234.txt`	Tunneling IPX Traffic Through IP Networks

NETWORK NAMING

The naming of network nodes requires some planning. When you select names, you should keep network management and user acceptance in mind. Many organizations have network-naming standards. If your organization has such standards in place, it's best to follow them to prevent confusion. If not, there's plenty of room for imagination. Computer and network names can be as simple as naming the workstations after the users, such as Diane, Beth, or John.

If you have many similar computers, numbering them (for example, PC1, PC2, and PC128) may be appropriate. Naming must be done in a way that gives unique names to computer systems. Don't name a computer *thecomputerinthenorthoffice* and expect users not to complain. After all, even the system administrator must type the names of computers from time to time. Also, you should avoid names like oiiomfw932kk. Although such a name may prevent network intruders from connecting to your computer, it may also prevent you from connecting to your workstation.

Tip #146 from *Steve*

Names that are distinctive and follow a theme work well, helping the coordination of future expansion and giving the users a sense of connection with their machines. After all, having a good relationship with a machine called sparky is a lot easier than having a relationship with a machine called OF1284.

Remember the following points when you're selecting a naming scheme:

- Keep names simple and short—six to eight characters at most. Although the Internet Protocol allows names up to 255 characters long, you should avoid going to such lengths because some systems can't handle long names. (Each label can be up to 63 characters long. Each part of a period-separated full domain name for a node is a label.)
- Consider using a theme such as stars, flowers, or colors, unless other naming standards are required at your site.
- Don't begin the name with numbers.
- Don't use special characters in the name.
- Don't duplicate names.
- Be consistent in your naming policy.

If you follow these guidelines, you can establish a successful naming methodology.

Internet names represent the organizations and the functionality of the systems within the network. The following are examples of names that you can use:

```
spanky.engineering.mycompany.com
nic.ddn.mil
```

The following are examples of names that are difficult to use or remember:

```
thisismyworkstation.thelongwindeddepartment.longcompnam.com
34556nx.m3422.mycompany.com
```

The latter of these examples could be encoded information about a workstation in room 345 on network 56 with network executive functions, but this type of naming scheme is usually considered poor practice because it can lead to confusion and misdirected messages.

By using an Internet name such as `Eddie@PC28.Programming.mycompany.com`, you can reference a user on a particular node.

NIC Naming Tree

The NIC maintains a network naming tree. This tree is used to group similar organizations under similar branches of the tree. Figure 28.2 shows the naming tree. Major organizations are grouped under similar branches. This is the source for Internet labels, such as com, edu, and gov, that are seen in Internet names.

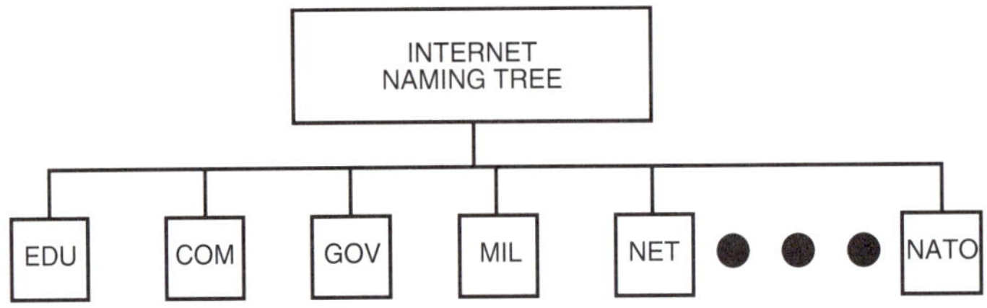

Figure 28.2
The NIC naming tree.

Table 28.6 shows some of the common leaf names and definitions for the NIC tree. Many other leaves are under the tree, but the ones shown here are the most common.

Table 28.6 Common NIC Names

Name	Types of Organizations
edu	Educational facilities (such as universities and colleges)
com	Commercial (most corporations)
gov	United States nonmilitary government bodies (White House, Department of Agriculture)
mil	Military (military users and their contractors)
net	Internet network management and administration
org	Other types of organizations (usually nonprofit)

Subnetworks and Subnet Masks

Subnetting is the process of dividing a large logical network into smaller physical networks. Reasons for dividing a network may include electrical limitations of the networking technology, a desire to segment for simplicity by putting a separate network on each floor of a building (or in each department or for each application), or a need for remote locations connected with a high-speed line.

The resulting networks are smaller chunks of the whole and are easier to manage. Smaller subnets communicate with one another through gateways and routers. Also, an organization may have several subnetworks that are physically on the same network to logically divide the network functions into workgroups.

The individual subnets are a division of the whole. Suppose that a class B network is divided into 64 separate subnets. To subnet the Class B network, the IP address is viewed in two parts: network and host (see Figure 28.3). The network part becomes the assigned IP address and the subnet information bits. These bits are, in essence, removed from the host's part of the address. The assigned number of bits for a class B network is 16. The subnet part adds 6 bits, for a total of 22 bits to distinguish the subnetwork. This division results in 64 networks with 1,024 nodes in each. The network part can be larger or smaller, depending on the number of networks desired or the number of nodes per network.

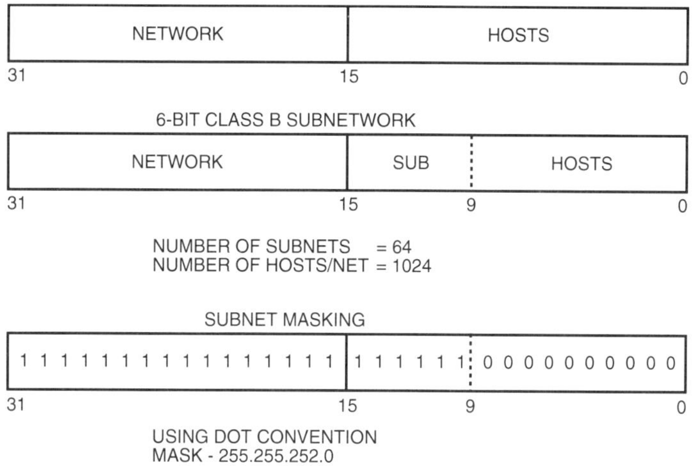

Figure 28.3 An example of class B subnetwork masking.

Setting a subnet mask is a matter of determining where the network address ends and the host address begins. The subnet mask contains all 1s in the network field and 0s in the host field.

Suppose a class C network is composed of the following:

```
N = network
H = Host
NNNNNNNN.NNNNNNNN.NNNNNNNN.HHHHHHHH
```

Each position represents a single bit out of the 32-bit address space. If this class C network is to be divided into four class C networks, the pattern resembles the following:

```
NNNNNNNN.NNNNNNNN.NNNNNNNN.NNHHHHHH
```

The subnet mask looks like the following:

```
11111111.11111111.11111111.11000000
```

If this address is written in base-10 dot notation, the subnet mask is 255.255.255.192. This mask is used to communicate among nodes on all subnetworks within this particular network.

If three bits are taken from the host field, eight networks can be formed, and the resulting network mask is as follows:

```
11111111.11111111.11111111.11100000
```

This subnet mask is 255.255.255.224. Each of the eight networks would have 29 nodes because five address bits are available. (It would be 32, except that all 1s, all 0s, and 127 aren't legal addresses.)

This concept can be extended to class B and class A networks. The only difference is that the remaining fields are 0 (zero).

Consider a class B network. The address space is divided as follows:

```
NNNNNNNN.NNNNNNNN.HHHHHHHH.HHHHHHHH
```

If two bits are taken from the host field and added to the network part, the following subnet mask is used:

```
11111111.11111111.11000000.00000000
```

The mask is written as 255.255.192.0.

Tip #147 from *Steve*

The bits needed for the subnet mask can be taken from any of the bit positions within the host field, but using bits from random bit positions in the host field leads to complex subnet masks and address exclusions. You should avoid this situation if at all possible.

Routing

*Routing*is a method of transferring information between networks. A router works at the Network layer of network protocols. Data can be routed by several different means. The routing method implemented for an Internet network is the Routing Information Protocol (RIP).

Routing Information Protocol (RIP)

RIP is designed to be used in small- to medium-sized networks and is based on Xerox Network Systems (XNS) routing protocols. RIP determines a message route by using a distance-vector routing algorithm. This algorithm assumes that each path is assigned a cost. This cost can be representative of network throughput, type of line, or desirability of the path. The protocol then determines the lowest cost path over which to transmit the message. (You can obtain information about routing from several RFCs.)

How a Routing Protocol Works

A TCP packet must "hop" from node to node until the packet reaches its destination. To maintain a list of hops to adjacent nodes, a RIP router keeps a routing table in the router or computer memory. This table is updated at 30-second intervals with information from neighboring routers. The information is used to recalculate the lowest cost path between systems. Each router on a network sends out (advertises) and receives routing information.

The routing protocol is limited in the distance a message can be routed. Each router can route a message only to a cost of 16. If the message sent out on a wire costs more than 16, the host is deemed unreachable. *Cost* is a method of assigning values to different paths through the network and is a way of ensuring an efficient route to a destination when there's more than one way to get there.

When a network break occurs, the routers must relearn least-cost paths. This process takes time and can result in messages being transmitted at a higher cost for a period of time. When a node goes down, all routers must readjust their respective routing tables. During this time, messages can be lost in the network. After a period of time, the routers are again synchronized and routing continues.

Router crashes are also a concern. In the event of a crash, adjacent routers update their adjacency to a crashed router in 180 seconds. After that period of time, if no routing information is received from the crashed router, that path is removed from the local router's database.

RIP doesn't manage routing distances, just cost. As a result, RIP might not use the shortest physical path between two points. Work and modifications have been made to the protocols to help correct this problem. A newer routing protocol being developed and tested is Open Shortest Path First (OSPF), which is beginning to gain acceptance and use.

Network Segmentation

Internet networks are divided into segments for various reasons. Some of these reasons are related to the underlying networking technologies; others are related to geographical locations. Some of the best reasons to isolate network segments are based on network usage. If a lot of traffic in a network occurs between a few nodes, it's best to isolate those nodes. This isolation drops the usage and provides a more responsive network for the other network users.

Other reasons to segment are to change networking technologies or to communicate between different networking technologies. For example, an office area may be running Token Ring, and the shop floor area may be running Ethernet. Each has a distinct function. The office may require Token Ring to communicate with an AS/400. The shop floor may have Ethernet to enable shop floor controllers and computers to communicate. The shop floor information then may be uploaded to the office network for order tracking. The connection between the technologies is usually through routers. The routers forward only information that must be exchanged from one network to the other. This information can then be shared between nodes on the respective networks.

Excessive use of routers in a network can become a burden to the network, thus outweighing their benefits. The use of a router is of little benefit if all the nodes on one network must get to all the nodes on another network, and vice versa. In this instance, the advantages of routing would be diminished because of the overhead in the routing protocols. In that kind of situation, a bridge is a better alternative.

A *bridge* enables all information from two networks to be shared. The access is at the Physical layer and not at the Network layer, so address translation and routing overhead aren't incurred. A bridge enables all information, including system broadcast messages, to be transmitted. If two networks rarely share information, a router is a better choice; otherwise, a bridge is the proper choice.

Internet Network Setup

The design and configuration of an Internet network is similar to the design of any computer network. It encompasses many types of nodes, including workstations, servers, printers, mainframes, routers, bridges, gateways, print servers, and terminals. The Internet requires that each device has a unique IP address. A device can have more than one address, depending on its function, but at least one address is required for communication with the other devices.

UNDERSTANDING THE TYPES OF CONNECTIONS

A TCP/IP network can consist of several systems connected to a local area network (LAN) or hundreds of systems with connections to thousands of systems on the Internet. Each organization can create the type of network appropriate for its needs.

Figure 28.4 shows a simple network that consists of several workstations and a file server. Each station on the network is assigned the network address of 194.62.23. Each device is assigned an individual node address. This network is typical of most departments within a company or even a small office. It has room to connect printers and more workstations to the network. The network has no provisions for connections to other local or wide area networks (WANs).

Figure 28.4
A simple network.

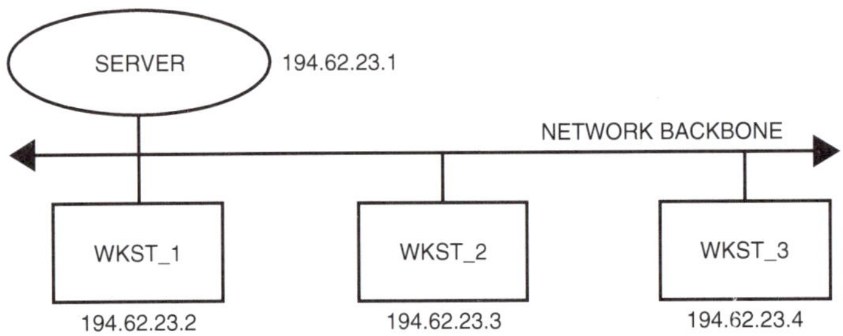

The network illustrated in Figure 28.5 is more complex. It includes three separate networks interconnected through a combination of routers and servers. Each workstation and computer on each segment may or may not be isolated from using information on one of the other two networks. This variable isolation is a characteristic of the subnet mask and security enabled on the servers and routers.

Information from one network is routed to one of the other networks on an as-needed basis. This type of configuration is typical of most large corporate networks. It may be chosen based on physical-length limitations of the underlying network technology or individual network loading. One or more of the networks may experience high traffic that must be distributed across several networks.

Router 1 between networks 1 and 2 provides for routing information between the two networks. If server 1, connecting networks 2 and 3, has routing enabled, information from network 3 to network 2 is routed. Also, information can be routed from network 3 to network 2 by means of server 1 and from network 2 to network 1 by means of router 1. Server 1, connecting networks 2 and 3, has two IP addresses: one IP address on network 2 and another address on network 3. The same is true for router 1, with addresses on network 2 and network 1.

Tip #148 from *Steve*

Consider a situation in which a lot of Internet network traffic takes place between network 3 and network 1. In this case, placing an additional router between network 1 and network 3 might be worthwhile. The additional router can eliminate some of the routing overhead on server 1 and enable information to be passed between networks when server 1 is down.

The additional router can add a level of fault tolerance to the network. This fault tolerance is based on the fact that information can still be routed to network 2 from network 3, even when server 1 is down. The path between network 3 and network 2 would be through network 1 and router 1. Figure 28.6 shows the addition of router 2.

Figure 28.5
A more complex network.

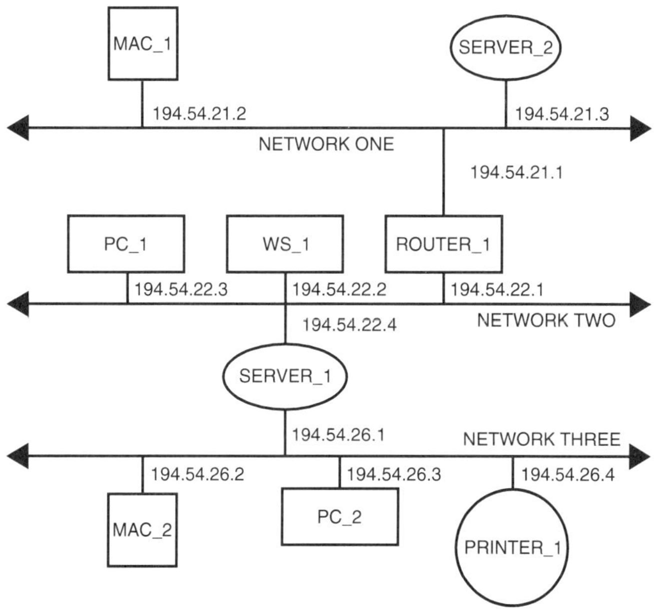

The fault tolerance of a network improves its integrity and can be of particular importance in certain applications. If time-critical information must be shared between two networks, an alternative path should be provided between the networks. This path could be provided through the use of additional routers. Because these paths may be indirect (through a third network), a configuration parameter should be used.

This parameter is usually referred to as *network cost*. The cost of a hop can be increased by increasing the value a packet takes across a network path. The default preferred path is the low-cost path; the alternative path is the high-cost path. This arrangement prevents information from being routed over the high-cost path on a regular basis.

Figure 28.6 shows an additional router added between networks 1 and 3. The desired path for information from network 3 to network 2 is through server 1. Because router 2 connects network 3 and network 1, information can be routed between those two networks. Also, because router 2 is between network 1 and network 2, information is routed through that path. Information from network 3 that's bound for network 2 can go over one of the two paths: either through server 1, or through router 2 and router 1. The latter isn't the preferred path because information can be routed directly over server 1. Therefore, a higher cost is assigned to the path of router 2 and router 1 from network 2. This type of path analysis must be performed in a multiple-segment network.

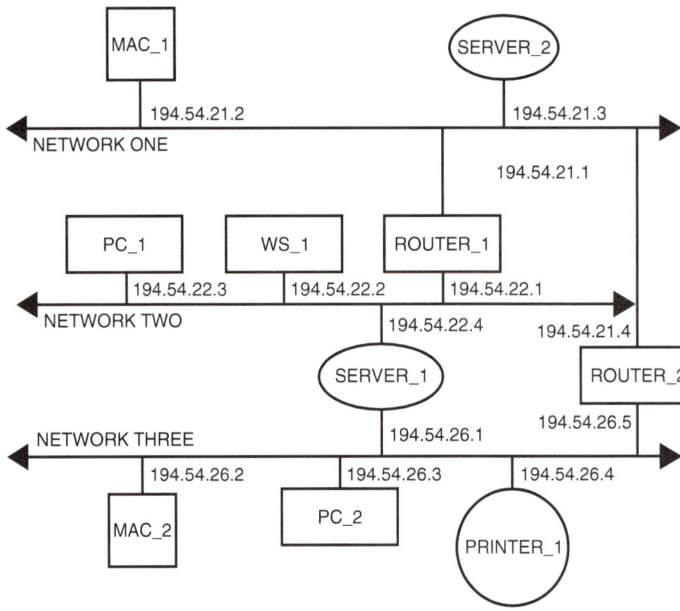

Figure 28.6 The network after adding a second router for fault tolerance.

CHOOSING A NETWORKING CONFIGURATION

The physical media used by an Internet network can be almost any network technology in current use. Internet network traffic isn't limited to Ethernet, ARCnet, or Token Ring. It can travel over asynchronous RS-232, T1 lines, and through frame relay. Whatever networking topology is selected for the network, the configuration, installation, and operation rules associated with that networking technology must be followed.

Tip #149 from *Steve*

Keep in mind the bandwidth that an application requires. Many applications require megabytes of data to be transferred, so bandwidth becomes a prime consideration. You can usually save bandwidth by compressing files before sending them over the network. Some applications have data compression built in to automatically shrink and expand the size of a file being transferred between the server and client applications.

Another consideration is the physical location of the network. If all nodes are in the same building, a single LAN can be used. However, if the networks are located across town, a T1 connection might be needed. If the nodes are located in different geographic locations, a frame relay or a packet-switched network can be used.

In laying out a network, you must consider the type of information to be carried over the network, the physical location, and network loading. To help determine the capacity of the network, you can examine the types of workstations, servers, and applications.

If diskless workstations are used in a network, a higher network load is placed on the network for each node. The reason for this is that each remote diskless workstation requires all operating system code to be downloaded through the network. Because all applications, utilities, and data files are stored remotely, every action on that workstation requires network access.

Also of concern is the amount of NFS traffic that will occur on the network. NFS provides remote virtual disk services, so information retrieved and stored on these remote disks is constantly used on the network.

Other considerations are large graphics images, swapping and page files used for virtual memory, distributed database applications, printer traffic, and terminal traffic. They are all considerations in any network, but the designers and users of PC-based LANs don't usually have to contend with them. When a network is connected into a general user community, all aspects of the networking environment come into play.

Other items to be examined are the need for dial-up and remote access. If this access is related to terminal and screen traffic, a serial port from an existing system may suffice. If a Point-to-Point Protocol (PPP) connection is made, you must consider how much overhead it will impose on the network when users are loading software utilities, programs, and databases over the phone lines. This issue is of concern because IP isn't limited to a high-speed link such as Novell IPX and other networking protocols.

Understanding Network Configuration Guidelines

A network must be designed based on guidelines and rules. You should consider the following questions when planning a network:

- How will the network be used today?
- How will the network be used for the next several years?
- What applications are going to be used on the network?
- Will workgroups within the organization require networking resources in the future?
- What types and numbers of workstations will be on the network?
- How many servers, minicomputers, and other hosts will be on the network?
- What other network devices, such as printers and plotters, will be on the network?
- Will shared disk arrays and optical jukeboxes be necessary?
- Will management of the network be centralized?
- Will the network be connected to the Internet or other corporate networks, or will it be the basis for a wide area network?

- What other protocols will use the networking technology (IPX, DECNET, LAT, OSI protocols, and TCP/IP)?
- Where will critical data be interchanged (determine several different paths)?
- How will the network grow and change?

After you address all these questions, you can define the network. The number of nodes indicates how many class C address spaces are needed or whether a class B is needed.

Tip #150 from *Steve*

Connection to remote facilities should also be addressed. The load can be distributed across multiple network segments. You should try to minimize the traffic that has to go across networks. For example, if you have two systems that exchange a lot of information, and hops across three networks are required for them to communicate, consider moving the systems to the same network.

You need to determine the best networking topology to meet the requirements specified in the network analysis. The best approach to allow for growth in the network is to determine the maximum load and to develop a network in which that load is at a minimum.

USING ROUTERS, BRIDGES, AND SWITCHES

Special-purpose devices are used to provide connections between networks and systems. Sometimes the terms *gateway* and *router* are used interchangeably. Strictly speaking, *gateway* describes a system that sends messages between different types of networks; a *router* sends messages between networks of the same type.

In this text, *router* is routinely used to describe any device that takes messages from one network and passes them through to another network. The router contains enough intelligence to know whether the message received must be forwarded to another network or a router.

Routers operate at the Network layer and are usually associated with a protocol, such as IP or IPX. Most routers that route IPX traffic can route IP traffic as well. A router is used to connect multiple local and wide area networks. It provides a method of sharing data between networks. Also, because a router works at the Network layer, it can help reduce broadcast traffic.

If one network uses a lot of different protocols, and another network uses only IP, a router that routes only IP messages is needed if those two networks are to communicate. The router prevents messages from being placed on a network that can't manage them.

Bridges, on the other hand, can be used to interconnect local and wide area networks; they share information regardless of protocol. A bridge allows two interconnected networks to have many different protocols on them at the same time. The messages forwarded by a bridge usually don't contain any further routing information. The messages are usually left undisturbed.

One drawback of using bridges is that all network broadcast and multicast messages from all interconnected networks are seen on all legs connected by a bridge. The result is a lot of overhead related to network update messages. Also, a bridge forwards messages only to network addresses on the other side of the bridge, but it can forward all network protocols and broadcast messages.

Conceptually, *switches* are multiport bridges. Because bridging is an OSI layer 2 function, all the common networking standards such as Ethernet, Token Ring, or FDDI can be bridged or switched. Switches are generally used in an existing network to divide a larger local area network into many smaller ones.

Performance of LAN switches can vary greatly and is often based on how they handle the forwarding of packets (many switches are configured as bridges). Methods for packet forwarding can be one of the following:

- Store-and-forward
- Cut-through
- Modified cut-through

Routers, bridges, and switches are used to share information between networks. The appropriateness of each is determined by networking requirements, the protocols involved, network capacity, and user demands. The proper selection of components can help a network operate efficiently, allow for future growth, and help ensure continued reliability.

Tip #151 from *Steve*

You should use bridges only if multiple protocol packets are to be shared. Otherwise, a router is a better choice because it helps reduce network overhead.

TROUBLESHOOTING

When you're troubleshooting, you frequently can trace a TCP/IP-related issue to other related issues. Say you want to see whether your coworker Nathan Bradley is still logged in to his workstation (named `hawthorne`), and you're both on the same private network. To do so, you issue the following command:

```
finger nathanb@haw thorne
```

You might get the response

```
finger: unknown host: hawthorne
```

indicating his workstation's name isn't `hawthorne`. The problem could be with the Domain Name Service's configuration of the network. (Chapter 38, "Configuring Domain Name Service (DNS)," explains the Internet name resolution system.) After some investigation, you find the problem isn't with the DNS configuration; it's misinformation. The workstation assigned to Nathan is actually named `wilde`. So you try again:

```
finger nath anb@wilde
```

You might get the response

```
finger: nathanb: no such user
```

indicating his login name isn't `nathanb`. So you check the company directory and see his login name is simply `nathan`. You try again by entering

```
finger nathan@wilde
```

and get the response

```
finger: connect: connection refused
```

indicating the finger command has been disabled for the workstation `wilde`. At this point, if not before, you simplify your life and use the telephone to call Nathan.

CHAPTER 29

Configuring a TCP/IP Network

In this chapter

by Steve Burnett

UNDERSTANDING THE TCP/IP CONFIGURATION FILES

Configuring a TCP/IP network is one of the more common tasks you'll face when administering Linux machines. In the most basic cases, it's not very complex, but it does require a bit of thought on the design of your network and knowledge of a small number of programs and configuration files.

TCP/IP networking in Linux is controlled by a set of configuration files in the `/etc` directory. These files tell Linux what its IP address, host name, and domain name are and also control the network interfaces. Table 29.1 shows you what each file does; the following sections describe these files in detail.

TABLE 29.1 LINUX TCP/IP NETWORKING CONFIGURATION FILES

File	Description
`/etc/hosts`	Maps host names to IP addresses
`/etc/networks`	Maps domain names to network addresses
`/etc/rc.d/rc3.d/S10network`	Configures and activates your Ethernet interfaces at boot time

THE `/etc/hosts` FILE

Every computer on a TCP/IP network has an IP address, canonical host name, and zero or more host name aliases. The `/etc/hosts` file is the original method for mapping host names to IP addresses.

Note

All host names, domain names, and IP addresses used in this chapter are fictitious and don't reflect any true network on the Internet.

For illustrative purposes, look at the network that A Fake Company, Inc., has built. This network consists of the single class B network address assigned to A Fake Company by InterNIC (the organization that controls Internet addresses); this network has been split into two class C subnetworks.

→ See "IP Address Classes," p. 604

The format for the hosts file is as follows:

```
# /etc/hosts for linux1.afakecompany.com
#
# For loopbacking.
127.0.0.1 localhost
# This machine
166.82.1.21      linux1.afakecompany.com linux1     # the local machine
# Other hosts on our network
```

```
166.82.1.20     server.afakecompany.com server      # the server
166.82.1.22     wk1.afakecompany.com                # workstation 1
166.82.1.10     netpr1.afakecompany.com netpr1      # networked printer
166.82.1.1      gateway.afakecompany.com gateway    # the router
166.82.1.1      gate-if1              # 1st interface on gateway
166.82.2.1      gate-if2              # 2nd interface on gateway
166.82.1.30      linux2.afakecompany.com linux2     # Laptop via PLIP

# end of hosts file
```

Tip #152 from *Steve*

> Notice that the preceding gateway has two host names for the IP address 166.82.1.1. Giving a unique name to each network interface on a machine is a good idea. Doing so makes it easier to see what's going on when you use the `ifconfig`, `route`, and `similar` commands.

The format of the hosts file consists of one IP address per line beginning in the first column, the canonical host name associated with that address, and then zero or more aliases. The fields are separated by spaces or tabs. Empty lines and text following a # character are treated as comments and are ignored.

The IP address 127.0.0.1 is known as the *local loopback address* and is reserved for this purpose. It's normally assigned the name *localhost*. If you're going to use your machine only as a standalone system or use SLIP or PPP to connect to the outside world, you need only the localhost address in your hosts file.

Note

> The function of the `/etc/hosts` file has been mostly taken over by Domain Name Service (DNS) on machines connected to the Internet or large internal networks. DNS isn't available during boot or when you're running in single-user mode, however, so it's a good idea to place the information for essential machines such as servers and gateways in `/etc/hosts`.
>
> On a network with only a few machines that aren't connected to the Internet, keeping a complete listing of all hosts in `/etc/hosts` is easier than configuring and maintaining DNS.

Tip #153 from *Steve*

> Naming your networks makes it convenient to perform tasks such as static routing that take a host name or network name. You don't have to remember the subnets by their IP addresses, just their names.

THE /etc/networks FILE

Just as hosts have names and IP addresses, networks and subnets can be named. This naming is handled by the `/etc/networks` file. The IP addresses in the networks file include only the network address portion plus the subnetwork byte. The following is a sample file for `afakecompany.com`:

```
# /etc/networks for afakecompany.com

localnet           127.0.0.0        # software loopback network
afakecompany-c1     166.82.1        # Development Group Network, Class C
afakecompany-c2     166.82.2        # MIS Network, Class C

# end of networks file
```

First is the localnet name and IP address, 127.0.0.0. If you aren't connecting your Linux machine to a TCP/IP network or are using only SLIP or PPP, all you need to put in this file is the localnet name and IP address.

The next lines identify the two class C subnetworks that A Fake Company has made from its class B network.

INITIALIZING ETHERNET INTERFACES

The`ifconfig` program makes network interfaces such as the software loopback and Ethernet cards known to the Linux kernel so that Linux can use them. You also can use the `ifconfig` program to monitor and change the state of network interfaces. A simple invocation of `ifconfig` is the following:

`ifconfig` *`interfaceaddress`*

This command activates the specified network interface and assigns an IP address to it. This process is called *bringing up an interface*. The generalized calling syntax for `ifconfig` is as follows:

`ifconfig` *`interface`* `[`*`aftype`*`] [`*`options`*`]` ¦ *`address`*

Table 29.2 lists the command-line arguments for `ifconfig`.

TABLE 29.2 COMMAND-LINE ARGUMENTS FOR `ifconfig`

Argument	Description
`interface`	Specifies the name of the network interface, usually the name of the device driver followed by an identification number. This argument is required.
`aftype`	Specifies the address family that should be used for decoding and displaying all protocol addresses. Currently, the inet (TCP/IP), ddp (Appletalk Phase 2), ipx (Novell), and AX.25 and netrom (both amateur packet radio) address families are supported. The inet family is the default.

Table 29.2 Command-Line Arguments for `ifconfig`

Argument	Description
`up`	Activates the specified interface.
`down`	Deactivates the specified interface.
`[-]arp`	Turns on or off the use of the ARP protocol on the specified interface. The minus sign is used to turn off the flag.
`[-]trailers`	Turns on or off trailers on Ethernet frames. This argument isn't currently implemented in the Linux networking system.
`[-]allmulti`	Turns on or off the promiscuous mode of the interface. Turning this mode on tells the interface to send all traffic on the network to the kernel, not just traffic addressed to your machine.
`metric` *N*	Sets the interface metric to the integer value *N*. The metric value represents the "cost" of sending a packet on this route. Route costing isn't currently used by the Linux kernel but is to be implemented at a future date.
`mtu` *N*	Sets the maximum number of bytes the interface can handle in one transfer to the integer value *N*. The current networking code in the kernel doesn't handle IP fragmentation, so you must make sure that the Maximum Transmission Unit (MTU) value is set large enough.
`dstaddr` *addr*	Sets the IP address of the other end of a point-to-point link. This argument has been made obsolete by the `pointopoint` keyword.
`netmask` *addr*	Sets the IP network mask for the specified interface.
`irq` *addr*	Sets the interrupt line used by this device. Remember that many devices don't support dynamic IRQ setting.
`[-]broadcast[`*addr*`]`	Sets the broadcast address for the interface when an address is included. If no address is given, the `IFF_BROADCAST` flag for the specified interface is turned on. A leading minus sign turns off the flag.
`[-]pointopoint[`*addr*`]`	Turns on point-to-point mode on the specified interface. This argument tells the kernel that this interface is a direct link to another machine. The address, when included, is assigned to the machine on the other end of the list. If no address is given, the `IFF_POINTOPOINT` flag for the interface is turned on. A leading minus sign turns off the flag.
`hw`	Sets the hardware address for the specified interface. The name of the hardware class and the ASCII equivalent of the hardware address must follow this keyword. Ethernet (`ether`), AMPR AX.25 (`ax25`), and PPP (`ppp`) are now supported.
address	Indicates the host name or IP address to be assigned to the specified interface. Host names used here are resolved to their IP address equivalents. This parameter is required.

Tip #154 from Steve

You normally don't need to use all the options. `ifconfig` can set everything needed from just the interface name, netmask, and IP address assigned. You need to explicitly set most parameters only when `ifconfig` misses or you have a complex network.

Caution

If your Linux machine is on a network, you must keep the `ifconfig` program secure from unauthorized use. Setting a network interface to promiscuous mode allows a person to snoop in your network and get sensitive data such as passwords. This is a serious breach of security.

→ See "Handling Physical Security," p. 276

Using `ifconfig` to Inspect a Network Interface

Running`ifconfig` with no arguments causes it to output the status of all network interfaces the kernel knows about. Running `ifconfig` with just an interface name on the command line prints the status of the interface, as shown here:

```
$ ifconfig lo
        lo Link encap Local Loopback
        inet addr 127.0.0.1 Bcast 127.255.255.255 Mask 255.0.0.0
        UP LOOPBACK RUNNING MTU 2000 Metric 1
        RX packets 0 errors 0 dropped 0 overruns 0
        TX packets 1658 errors 10 dropped 0 overruns 0
```

This example uses `lo`, the software loopback interface. You can see the assigned IP address (`inetaddr`), broadcast address (`Bcast`), and netmask (`Mask`). The interface is `UP` with an `MTU` of 2000 and a `Metric` of 1. The last two lines give statistics on the number of packets received (`RX`) and transmitted (`TX`), along with packet error, dropped, and overrun counts.

Configuring the Software Loopback Interface

All Linux machines with the networking layer installed in the kernel have a software loopback interface. This interface is used to test networking applications and to provide a network for local TCP/IP services when the machine isn't connected to a real network.

The network interface name for the loopback system is `lo`. You enter the following to run `ifconfig`:

```
ifconfig lo 127.0.0.1
```

This command activates the loopback interface and assigns the address 127.0.0.1 to it. This address is traditionally used for the loopback because InterNIC will never assign the class A network, 127.0.0.0, to anyone.

To make the loopback system fully operational, you need to add a route for it by using the route command, which is discussed later in the section "Understanding TCP/IP Routing."

CONFIGURING A NETWORK INTERFACE

Configuring an Ethernet network interface takes a little bit more work, especially if you're using subnetworks. The basic call to ifconfig looks like this for linux1.afakecompany.com:

```
ifconfig eth0 linux1
```

This command causes ifconfig to activate Ethernet interface 0, look up the IP address for linux1 in the /etc/hosts file, and assign it to this interface. Examining the eth0 interface at this point reveals the following code:

```
$ ifconfig eth0
        eth0 Link encap 10Mbps Ethernet HWaddr 00:00:E1:54:3B:82
        inet addr 166.82.1.21Bcast166.82.1.255 Mask 255.255.255.0
        UP BROADCAST RUNNING MTU 1500 Metric 0
        RX packets 3136 errors 217 dropped 7 overrun 26
        TX packets 1752 errors 25 dropped 0 overrun 0
        Interrupt:10 Base address:0x300
```

Note that the broadcast address and netmask were set automatically by ifconfig based on the IP address it found in /etc/hosts. If you're using subnetworks, you need to specify the broadcast address and netmask explicitly. For example, if you have a class C network and are using the first bit in the host portion of the address to make two subnetworks, you must specify the broadcast address and netmask when running ifconfig:

```
ifconfig eth0 linux1 broadcast 166.82.1.127 netmask 255.255.255.128
```

CONFIGURING PARALLEL IP INTERFACES

The Parallel IP (PLIP), Serial Line IP (SLIP), and Point-to-Point Protocol (PPP) interfaces are managed by ifconfig somewhat differently. To bring up a PLIP interface, you add the pointopoint option to the ifconfig command line. Assume that the A Fake Company laptop linux2 is attached to the first parallel port on linux1. You call ifconfig as follows to activate the PLIP link:

```
ifconfig plip0 linux1 pointopoint linux2
```

This command activates the plip0 interface with the IP address for linux1, sets the pointopoint flag, and tells the interface that the IP address for the other end of the link is linux2. ifconfig looks up the IP addresses for linux1 and linux2 in /etc/hosts and assigns the addresses appropriately. On a laptop, you use the following analogous call:

```
ifconfig plip0 linux2 pointopoint linux1
```

→ See "Understanding the Requirements for SLIP and PPP," p. 664

UNDERSTANDING TCP/IP ROUTING

Routing determines the path a packet takes from its source through the network to its destination. This path is determined by matching the destination IP address against the kernel routing tables and transmitting the packet to the indicated machine, which may or may not be the destination of the packet. The kernel routing table contains information in the form "To get to network X from machine Y, send the packet to machine Z with a cost of 1," along with time-to-live and reliability values for that route.

DECIDING ON A ROUTING POLICY

The first step in setting up routing on your network is deciding on a routing policy. For small, unconnected networks, using the `route` command to set up static routes on each machine at boot time is sufficient. Large networks with many subnets or networks connected to the Internet need to use dynamic routing. The routing program provides dynamic routing by communicating with routing programs on other machines and installing routes based on what it learns about the topology of the network.

A very common strategy combines static and dynamic routing. Machines on each subnet use static routing to reach their immediate neighbors. The default route—the route used for packets that match no other route in the routing table—is set to a gateway machine that's doing dynamic routing and knows about the rest of the world. Large networks can be constructed this way, minimizing the hassle of configuration files and the amount of bandwidth used by the dynamic routing programs.

USING THE /SBIN/ROUTE PROGRAM

The `/sbin/route` program manipulates the kernel routing table and is used to set static routes to other computers or networks via interfaces that have been configured and activated by `ifconfig`. This is normally done at boot time by the `/etc/rc.d/rc3.d/S10network` script. Table 29.3 describes the command-line arguments for `/sbin/route`.

TABLE 29.3 COMMAND-LINE ARGUMENTS FOR `/sbin/route`

Argument	Description
(None)	Giving no option to `/sbin/route` causes it to output the current routing table.
`-n`	This argument causes the same output as giving no option but replaces host names with their numerical IP addresses.
`del`	This argument deletes the route for the specified destination address from the routing table.
`add`	This argument adds to the routing table a route to the specified address or network.

EXAMINING THE KERNEL ROUTING TABLE

Running/sbin/route without any command-line arguments or just -n outputs the routing table:

```
/sbin/route
Kernel routing table
Destination Gateway Genmask     Flags  Metric   Ref      UseIface
127.0.0.0   *       255.0.0.0   U      0        0        100 lo
```

The preceding output is from a machine with just the loopback interface activated. Table 29.4 describes the fields in the routing table report.

TABLE 29.4 THE FIELDS IN THE ROUTING TABLE REPORT

Field	Description
Destination	The destination IP address of the route.
Gateway	The host name or IP address of the gateway the route uses. If no gateway exists, an asterisk is output.
Genmask	The netmask for the route. The kernel uses this field to set the generality of a route by bitwise ANDing the Genmask against a packet's IP address before comparing it to the destination IP address of the route.
Flags	The flags for the route (U means up, H means host, G means gateway, D means dynamic route, and M means modified).
Metric	The metric cost for the route. This field isn't currently supported in the kernel networking layer.
Ref	The number of other routes that rely on the presence of this route.
Use	The number of times the routing table entry has been used.
Iface	The network interface to which this route delivers packets.

Returning to the A Fake Company network, the following is an example from the laptop linux2, with a SLIP link up and running:

```
$ /sbin/route
Kernel routing table
Destination     Gateway      Genmask          Flags  Metric Ref Use Iface
slip.afakecompany.c  *      255.255.255.255   UH     0       0   0   sl0
127.0.0.0       *            255.0.0.0         U     0       0   100 lo
default        slip.afakecompany.c *          UG     0       0   1   sl0
```

The table entry for the loopback is the same as before, and you have two new entries. The first specifies a route to slip.afakecompany.com. The other new entry specifies a default route by using slip.afakecompany.com as a gateway.

Note

Every machine connected to a network must have a default route in its routing table. The default route is used when no other routing table entry matches the destination for a packet.

ADDING STATIC ROUTES

You add routes to the routing table by running the `route` program with the `add` argument. The command-line argument syntax for the `route add` command is as follows:

```
route add [ -net ¦ -host ] addr [gw gateway] [metric cost]
A[netmask mask] [dev device]
```

Table 29.5 describes the command-line arguments that the `route add` command uses.

TABLE 29.5 COMMAND-LINE ARGUMENTS USED BY `route add`

Argument	Description
`-net ¦ -host`	Forces the specified address to be treated as a network or host address.
`addr`	Specifies the destination address for the new route. It can be an IP address, host name, or network name.
`gw` *`gateway`*	Specifies that any packets for this address be routed through the specified gateway.
`metric cost`	Sets the metric field in the routing table.
`netmask` *`mask`*	Specifies the netmask of the route being added. The `route` program will guess what it is, so you don't need to specify it under normal circumstances.
`dev` *`device`*	Forces `route` to associate the new route with the specified network interface device. Again, `route` usually guesses correctly what device to use for the new route, so you don't have to use this argument often.

Caution

When adding a gateway route to the routing table, you must make sure that the specified gateway is reachable. You usually have to add a static route for the gateway before adding the route by using the gateway.

LOOKING AT ROUTING EXAMPLES

Now you're ready for some examples, starting with the loopback interface. After configuring the loopback interface with `ifconfig`, you need to add a route to it, as in the following:

```
# route add 127.0.0.1
```

Nothing else is needed because `route` compares the address given to it with the addresses for the known interfaces and assigns the loopback interface to the new route. The following example shows how to set the routing for the SLIP link on the A Fake Company linux2 machine after the SLIP link is established and `ifconfig` is used to activate the interface:

```
# route add slip.afakecompany.com
# route add default gw slip.afakecompany.com
```

The first command adds a static route for the host `slip.afakecompany.com`; the second one tells the kernel to use `slip.afakecompany.com` as a gateway for all packets with unknown destinations.

Caution

Make sure that any host names you use with the `route` command are in the `/etc/hosts` file so that `route` can find the IP addresses for them; otherwise, `route` fails.

If you're subnetting your network by splitting the IP address in the middle of an octet, you have to specify the required netmask when running `route`. For example, if you have a class C network and have four subnets using the first two bits of the last octet, you need to run `route` like this:

```
# route add hostname netmask 255.255.255.192
```

Tip #155 from *Steve*

An *octet* is the name for each of the four portions of an IP address. The fourth octet in the example command above is 192.

This command ensures that `route` puts the right netmask in the routing table entry.

For Ethernet and other broadcast network interfaces, you need to add routes that tell the kernel what network can be reached via each configured interface. After using `ifconfig` to bring up the eth0 network interface on `linux1.afakecompany.com` as you did previously, you need to run `route` to install the route to the network on that interface:

```
# route add -net 166.82.1.0
```

That command might not look like enough to set the routing table entry correctly because no interface is indicated; however, `route` manages to find the interface by comparing the IP address on the command line to the IP address of each network interface. It assigns the route to the interface that matches it. In this case, eth0 has been assigned the address 166.82.1.21 with a netmask of 255.255.255.0. This address matches the network address given in the `route` command, so `route` installs a route to the network 166.82.1.0 by using interface eth0, as follows:

```
$ route
Kernel routing table
Destination     Gateway      Genmask          Flags   Metric Ref    UseIface
166.82.1.0      *            255.255.255.0    UN      0      0      0 eth0
127.0.0.0       *            255.0.0.0        U       0      0      100 lo
```

To tell linux1 how to reach the other subnet, you need two more routing table entries to be safe:

```
# route add gateway.afakecompany.com
# route add -net 166.82.2.0 gw gateway.afakecompany.com
```

These lines add a static route to `gateway.afakecompany.com` and then add a network route for 166.82.2.0 by using `gateway.afakecompany.com` as the gateway for that network, as shown in the following:

```
$ route
Kernel routing table
Destination     Gateway          Genmask          Flags Metric  Ref  UseIface
gateway.afakecompany *           255.255.255.0    UH    0       0    0 eth0
166.82.1.0      *                255.255.255.0    UN    0       0    0 eth0
166.82.2.0      gateway.afakecompany 255.255.255.0    UN    0       0    0 eth0
127.0.0.0       *                255.0.0.0        U     0       0    100 lo
```

This output shows the static route you added for `gateway.afakecompany.com` and the gatewayed route to the 166.82.2.0 network.

DELETING ROUTES WITH THE `route` COMMAND

You delete routes by calling `route` with the `del` option and specifying the destination address of the route you want to delete. For example, the following command deletes the network route for network 166.82.2.0:

```
# route del -net 166.82.2.0
```

PROJECT: MONITORING A TCP/IP NETWORK WITH NETSTAT

The `netstat` program is an invaluable tool in monitoring your TCP/IP network. It can display the kernel routing table, the status of active network connections, and useful statistics about each network interface. Table 29.6 describes the common command-line arguments for `netstat`; a few additional arguments are targeted for advanced users. Refer to the man page for more information.

TABLE 29.6 COMMON COMMAND-LINE ARGUMENTS FOR THE `netstat` PROGRAM

Argument	Description
`-a`	Shows information about all Internet connections, including those that are just listening.
`-i`	Shows statistics for all network devices.
`-c`	Shows continually updating network status. This argument makes `netstat` output a network status listing once per second until it's interrupted.
`-n`	Shows remote and local addresses and port information in numeric/raw form rather than resolves host names and service names.
`-o`	Shows the timer state expiration time and backoff state of each network connection.
`-r`	Shows the kernel routing table.

TABLE 29.6 COMMON COMMAND-LINE ARGUMENTS FOR THE netstat PROGRAM

Argument	Description
-t	Shows only TCP socket information, including those that are just listening.
-u	Shows only UDP socket information.
-v	Shows the version information for netstat.
-w	Shows raw socket information.
-x	Shows UNIX domain socket information.

DISPLAYING ACTIVE NETWORK CONNECTIONS

Runningnetstat with no command-line arguments generates a listing of the active network connections on your machine. The following demonstrates the default output from netstat:

```
$ netstat
Active Internet connections
Proto Recv-Q Send-Q Local Address          Foreign Address        (State)
tcp      0      0 linux1.afakecompany.com:71 server.afakecompany.:telnet ESTABLISHED
Active UNIX domain sockets
Proto RefCnt      Flags      Type          State         Path
unix  1           [ ACC ]    SOCK_STREAM   LISTENING     /dev/printer
unix  2           [ ]        SOCK_STREAM   CONNECTED     /dev/log
unix  2           [ ]        SOCK_STREAM   CONNECTED
unix  1           [ ACC ]    SOCK_STREAM   LISTENING     /dev/log
```

The first section shows an active TCP protocol connection from port 1266 on linux1.afakecompany.com to the telnet port on server.afakecompany.com. Table 29.7 describes the fields in the Active Internet Connections listing.

TABLE 29.7 ACTIVE INTERNET CONNECTION FIELDS

Field	Description
Proto	The protocol used by this connection, TCP, or UDP.
Recv-Q	The number of bytes received on this socket but not yet copied by the user program.
Send-Q	The number of bytes sent to the remote host that haven't been acknowledged.
Local Address	Local host name and port number assigned to this connection. The socket IP address is resolved to the canonical host name for that address, and the port number is translated into the service name unless the -n flag is used.
Foreign Address	The foreign host name and port number assigned to this connection. The -n flag affects this field as it does the Local Address field.

TABLE 29.7 ACTIVE INTERNET CONNECTION FIELDS

Field	Description
`State`	The current state of the socket. It can be in one of the following states: `ESTABLISHED`—The connection is fully established. `SYN_SENT`—The socket is now trying to make a connection to a remote host. `SYN_RECV`—The connection is being initialized. `FIN_WAIT1`—The socket has been closed and is waiting for the connection to shut down. `FIN_WAIT2`—The connection has been closed. The socket is waiting for a shutdown from the remote host. `TIME_WAIT`—The socket is closed and is waiting for a remote host shutdown retransmission. `CLOSED`—The socket isn't in use. `CLOSE_WAIT`—The remote host has shut down its connection. The local host is waiting for the socket to close. `LAST_ACK`—The remote connection is shut down, and the socket is closed. The local host is waiting for an acknowledgment. `LISTEN`—The socket is listening for the incoming connection attempt. `UNKNOWN`—The state of the socket isn't known.
`User`	The login ID of the user who owns the socket.s

The second section displays active UNIX domain sockets. UNIX domain sockets are an interprocess communication (IPC) mechanism that uses the UNIX file system as the rendezvous system. Processes create special files in the file system that are then opened by other processes on the machine that wants to communicate. The preceding `netstat` listing shows two sockets listening: one on `/dev/printer` and the other on `/dev/log`. Two sockets are also currently connected: one to `/dev/log` and one that has no specified path associated with it. Table 29.8 describes the fields in the Active UNIX Domain Sockets listing.

TABLE 29.8 FIELDS IN THE ACTIVE UNIX DOMAIN SOCKETS LISTINGS

Field	Description
`Proto`	The protocol in use on this socket. It is usually `unix`.
`RefCnt`	The number of processes attached to this socket.
`Flags`	The flags for this socket. Currently, the only known flag is `SO_ACCEPTON` (`ACC`), which indicates that the socket is unconnected and the process that made the socket is waiting for a connection request.
`Type`	The mode in which the socket is accessed. This field contains one of the following keywords: `OCK_DGRAM`—Datagram, connectionless mode `OCK_STREAM`—Connection-oriented stream mode `OCK_RAW`—Raw mode `OCK_RDM`—Reliably delivered message mode `OCK_SEQPACKET`—Sequential packet mode `NKNOWN`—Mode not known to `netstat` program

Table 29.8 Fields in the Active UNIX Domain Sockets Listings

Field	Description
`State`	The current state of the socket. The following keywords are used: `FREE`—The socket isn't allocated. `LISTENING`—The socket is waiting for a connection request. `UNCONNECTED`—The socket doesn't have a current connection. `CONNECTING`—The socket is attempting to make a connection. `CONNECTED`—The socket has a current connection. `DISCONNECTING`—The socket is attempting to shut down a connection. `UNKNOWN`—The state of the socket is unknown. You don't see this keyword under normal operating conditions.
`Path`	The pathname used by other processes to connect to the socket.

Tip #156 from *steve*

If network interfaces drop many packets or get many overrun errors, they can be symptoms of an overloaded machine or network. Checking the network interface statistics is a quick way of diagnosing this problem.

Invoking `netstat` with the `-o` option adds the internal state information to the Active Internet Connections listing. The following is an example:

```
$ netstat -o
Active Internet connections
Proto Recv-Q Send-Q Local Address      Foreign Address     (State)
tcp        0      0 localhost:1121     localhost:telnet    ESTABLISHED off (0.00/0)
tcp        0      0 localhost:telnet   localhost:1121      ESTABLISHED on (673.69/0)
```

The added data is at the end of each line and includes receiver retransmission byte count, transmitter retransmission byte count, timer state (on/off), and time/backoff values (in parentheses). The time displayed is the time left before the timer expires. The backoff value is the retry count for the current data transmission. This data is useful in diagnosing network problems because you can easily see which connection is having problems.

Note

Because the `-o` option outputs the state of internal TCP/IP data, the format of this data may change, or this option may be removed in a later release of the networking software.

Examining the Kernel Routing Table

Invoking `netstat` with the `-r` option prints the kernel routing table. The format is the same as for the `route` command.

DISPLAYING NETWORK INTERFACE STATISTICS

Invoking `netstat` with the `-i` option prints usage statistics for each active network interface—another excellent tool for debugging network problems. By using this command, you can easily see when packets are being dropped, overrun, and so on.

The following is an example of using the `-i` option, and Table 29.9 explains each field in the listing:

```
$ netstat -i
Kernel Interface table
Iface   MTU Met RX-OK RX-ERR RX-DRP RX-OVR TX-OK TX-ERR TX-DRP TX-OVR Flags
lo     2000  0     0      0      0      0  1558      1      0      0 LRU
```

TABLE 29.9 FIELDS IN THE KERNEL INTERFACE TABLE

Field	Description
`Iface`	The name of the network interface.
`MTU`	The largest number of bytes that can be sent in one transmission by this interface.
`Met`	The metric value for this interface.
`RX-OK`	The number of packets received with no errors.
`RX-ERR`	The number of packets received with errors.
`RX-DRP`	The number of packets dropped.
`RX-OVR`	The number of packet, overrun with errors.
`TX-OK`	The number of packets transmitted with no errors.
`TX-ERR`	The number of packets transmitted with errors.
`TX-DRP`	The number of packets dropped during transmission.
`TX-OVR`	The number of packets dropped due to overrun errors. `Flags` The following flags can be shown in this field: A—The interface receives packets for multicast addresses. B—The interface receives broadcast packets. D—The interface debugging feature is now activated. L—This is the loopback interface. M—The interface is in promiscuous mode. N—The interface doesn't process trailers on packets. O—The Address Resolution Protocol is turned off on this interface. P—This interface is being used as a point-to-point connection. R—The interface is running. U—The interface has been activated.

CHAPTER 30

IP Firewalling and Masquerading

by Jack Tackett, Jr.

In this chapter

IP FIREWALLING AND MASQUERADING

This chapter discusses a little about firewalls in Linux—what they are, how they work, and how to begin building one. Although this chapter will not make anyone an expert on firewalls, it does introduce the basic concepts.

The term *firewall* comes from the firewall that is used in cars (and other motorized vehicles), which protects the occupants in the cabin from a fire in the engine compartment. A firewall on a network protects both users and the data that is behind it on the local network from the savagery of the Internet (or extranet). It can also be used to prevent users on the local network from connecting to prohibited sites, and it can be used to compartmentalize the internal network.

Tip #157 from Jack

Some people learn too late that a firewall does not protect against insiders. Internal firewalls can be used to isolate departments so that damage is not widespread; for example, it can be used to protect accounting from engineering, and engineering from sales, each of which likely has little or no business browsing through files that belong to the others.

INTRODUCTION TO FIREWALLS

Basically, there are two kinds of firewalls in Linux. Each of these two basic types has two subtypes. The two basic types are *packet filters* and *proxy* firewalls. The packet filter firewalls can be one of the following types:

- **Forwarding**—It is in this type of packet filter firewall that decisions are made whether to forward or not.
- **Masquerading**—These firewalls rewrite the source and destination addresses.

Proxy firewalls can be one of the following types:

- **Standard**—With this type of proxy firewall, a client connects to a special port and is redirected out through another port.
- **Transparent**—With this firewall, the client doesn't use a special port, but the firewall software proxies the connection through transparently.

PACKET FILTERS

Packet filtering firewalls work on the following principle: The information that is needed to make a decision about what to do with a packet is contained in the header. The header contains information regarding the source and destination addresses, time to live (TTL), protocol, and much more. It also contains a header checksum that recounts the size of the payload and whether the header has been corrupted. In all, some thirteen separate fields of information are contained in an IP header, some of which contain multiple pieces of information. For complete details, refer to RFC 791 (available from `http://www.rfc-editor.org/rfc.html`).

Note

IP does not check the payload other than to tell if the payload is the correct size. The transport control protocol (TCP) is responsible for ensuring the integrity of the data payload.

OpenLinux uses `ipchains`to provide packet filtering. To implement a packet filtering firewall, decisions must be made regarding the types of packets to address specifically, and what to do with those packets when they are encountered.

The `ipchains` software permits a number of different criteria to be applied to packets. The criteria can be applied to incoming packets, outgoing packets, or packets that will pass through the firewall. These decisions can be based on where the packets came from by address, where they are going by address, or where they are going by port. Different rules can be applied, depending on whether these are TCP packets, UDP packets, or ICMP packets. Finally, for any packets that are not specifically addressed, the overall policy determines the fate of the packets.

Proxy Firewalls

Proxy firewalls work differently than packet filters do. All traffic is received on the firewall, whether it is incoming or outgoing. But proxies redirect permitted traffic through the firewall by rewriting the headers. To be redirected, the traffic has to log in to the firewall. In fact, much of the discussion in the preceding section is applicable to a proxy. The difference is subtle; because packet filtering software is rewriting the headers when it is masquerading, it is difficult to explain that there is a difference between a transparent proxy and a masquerading (packet filter) firewall. But the main difference is that the proxy redirects (locally) the traffic that is arriving at one interface and leaving by another, and a packet filter normally does not redirect traffic. Looking at it from a different perspective, proxies work higher up in the OSI model than packet filters.

Note

Any router, gateway, or host, that transports a networking packet from one network to another rewrites the header. But this rewriting doesn't alter the source or destination addresses; it only alters the TTL and checksum, and—on occasion—the total length and fragment offset (among others), if the packet needs to be fragmented to continue. When header rewriting is discussed in this text, it refers mostly to address rewriting.

The *Open Source Interconnect* (*OSI*) model is one of the popular models that is used to explain how packets move from the Application layer to the Physical layer (it might not be completely accurate, but it's a good theoretical paradigm nevertheless). The seven layers are used to explain where certain software works. For the purposes of this text, it is only important to note that the level where each works is different, and that this is one of the distinguishing characteristics between proxies and packet filters.

But this difference is important. Proxies are more overhead intensive, but they can inspect entire packets more thoroughly. They also tend to be a little more difficult to set up initially.

WHICH TO USE?

Packet filtering firewalls and proxying firewalls perform similar functions. They act as shields to protect trusted network segments from untrusted ones. In this regard, each works equally well. Both require monitoring and occasional reconfiguring; both, if they are misconfigured, provide only a false sense of security; and both, when implemented in a methodical, well-thought-out manner, can provide a modicum of security.

Tip #158 from *Jack*

If you remember that the only secure system is the one that is not assembled and powered on (and therefore not of much use, either), you'll have a more realistic idea of what firewalls can buy you: time to react to an attack. It remains your responsibility to reconfigure the firewall to protect against this attack. I want to emphasize that: A firewall buys you time to react to an attack.

Basically, the decision to use packet filtering or proxying comes down to an individual decision, and might be based on the prior experiences of those who are involved in maintaining the firewall. If you are implementing a firewall and have worked with proxies before and are comfortable with them, by all means, continue. The use of one type doesn't preclude use of the other. Some proxies that are designed to work specifically with Web (HTTP) traffic can complement a packet filter nicely. For example, the use of `junkbuster` to block particular Web sites or advertising banners is often easier than writing packet filtering rules to deny or reject the banner sites. Conversely, `ipchains` rules can be created solely for the purpose of logging traffic, and can be used in conjunction with a proxy to track specific kinds of traffic. So the best option might be to mix and match, depending on your overall objectives and level of comfort.

From a security standpoint, therefore, neither is better. The one place in which `ipchains` might tip the balance is in situations in which you want to rewrite the *Type of Service* (*TOS*) field to optimize traffic flow.

Tip #159 from
Jack

You can use `ipchains` to modify the TOS field to specify one of minimum delay, maximum reliability, maximum throughput, or minimum cost.

Physical Configurations

When discussing physical configurations, you need to look at both the hardware and the software as it applies to the firewall. Remembering that one of the reasons the firewall exists is to protect the trusted network from the untrusted network, this host must necessarily be both the funnel for network traffic that is moving between the two networks, making it a possible choke point, and the focus for those who are looking to penetrate your security. If they want to come in, they've got to pass through here first.

The Firewall Host

You need to consider the type of host you want to install. You can install a firewall that has only one interface, and that uses that interface for both trusted and untrusted connections; but you'll want to consider whether this is wise, taking into account the cost of a second interface versus the weakened security posture that this configuration entails. It is better to have a host with two interfaces, which completely isolates one network from the other. With this configuration, bypassing the firewall becomes more difficult.

Note

A host that isolates an untrusted network from a trusted network using two interfaces–one for each network–is termed a*Bastion Host*.

The question of how powerful a system needs to be depends on your decisions; if you are going to use the firewall to connect two 10Mb Ethernet cards, and if you plan to use packet filtering and no proxies, an 80486-33 processor with 16MB RAM is sufficient for low to moderate traffic loads. However, if you plan to use 100Mhz Ethernet cards in a high traffic route, this CPU will not be able to keep up with the demand and you'll experience significant packet loss.

The Firewall Kernel

In building a firewall, you'll need to reconfigure the kernel. Several parameters must be set in the kernel to permit packet filtering. Some of these parameters are subjective and are based on your hardware. One must be turned off; others are required. For more information on building a custom kernel, see Chapter 14, "Configuring the Linux Kernel." The first parameter follows:

```
CONFIG_EXPERIMENTAL=y
```

One of the items that kernel hackers typically review is the experimental status on a number of the kernel parameters. When it is reviewed, the experimental status will, most likely, better reflect reality. Therefore, enabling this is a judgement call, although you might need it for some drivers.

It is strongly recommended that you consider compiling the kernel as a *monolithic* kernel as opposed to a *modular* kernel (for more information on building a custom kernel, see Chapter 14).

→ See "Configuring a New Kernel," p. 297

This is an exception to the rule, "Always build a modular kernel." The reasoning behind this is that anyone can build a module. If someone manages to crack your security, they'll want access again. Rather than amateurishly adding a user with root privileges, they can drop a loadable module on your system, have it inserted, and then erase the other traces of entry. Although this is extreme and a rather sophisticated way to go about it, it might enable nearly undetectable access to your system. So kernel modules can be dangerous. On the other hand, anyone this sophisticated can, most likely, easily find other means to enter the system. Unfortunately, to enable things such as IP port forwarding and some other parameters, module support is required. If you don't see a parameter that you need, it might either be experimental or only available as a module.

In other sections, give careful thought to the parameters that you install. You need to support your hardware (disk drives), the file system, Ethernet drivers, other communications drivers (modems, ISDN devices, and protocols such as PPP), and ELF formats. But sound and other unnecessary parameters need to be disabled.

Note

If this is a home network or part of a small, low-profile business with low bandwidth, you might not need or want to go to the extremes detailed in this chapter. Only you can perform a proper risk assessment for your situation.

With the other sections appropriately set, the section that needs to be detailed is "Networking Options." Although it is not the last section in the kernel configuration, it is certainly the most important for the purposes of this chapter.

NETWORKING OPTIONS

The Linux 2.2.x kernel adds significant complexity to the networking options section from the 2.0.x kernels. The additional options can be daunting, and the help is not always helpful. Plan to spend some time getting acquainted with this section. Items that are of interest are highlighted here; some of these items are required, others are recommended, and still others are optional.

Caution

Items that are marked as not recommended have the potential for weakening your firewall. If you know that you won't use it, don't install it.

The following parameter is required for programs such as tcpdump:

```
CONFIG_NETLINK=                 recommended
```

This first kernel parameter is required for such programs as tcpdump. However, tcpdump puts your Ethernet card in promiscuous mode:

```
CONFIG_PACKET=                 not recommended
```

The following parameter requires devices with major number 36 to communicate. If this option is chosen, `Routing messages` needs to also be chosen, as does `IP: firewall packet netlink device`, which can be used to warn of possible attacks:

```
CONFIG_NETLINK=                 recommended
```

Use of the following parameter requires `/dev/route` to be created with major 36 so that you can read routing information:

```
CONFIG_RTNETLINK=              optional

CONFIG_NETLINK_DEV=            required
```

The following is required for packet filters or masquerading, but not for proxy firewalls:

```
CONFIG_FIREWALL=               required/optional
```

The following is only required to configure an Ethernet card with multiple IP addresses; it might put your NIC into promiscuous mode:

```
CONFIG_NET_ALIAS=               not recommended
CONFIG_FILTER=                  not recommended
CONFIG_UNIX=                    required
CONFIG_INET=                    required
CONFIG_IP_MULTICAST=            optional
```

To use TOS, verbose route monitoring, or large routing tables, this is required. The next six parameters depend on this one:

```
CONFIG_IP_ADVANCED_ROUTER       optional
CONFIG_IP_MULTIPLE_TABLES       optional
CONFIG_IP_ROUTE_MULTIPATH       optional
CONFIG_IP_ROUTE_TOS             optional
CONFIG_IP_ROUTE_VERBOSE         recommended
CONFIG_IP_ROUTE_LARGE_TABLES    optional
```

Following is the network address translation parameter for routers:

```
CONFIG_IP_ROUTE_NAT recommended/required
```

The next two parameters depend on this one:

```
CONFIG_IP_PNP                     not recommended
CONFIG_IP_PNP_BOOTP               not recommended
CONFIG_IP_PNP_RARP                not recommended
CONFIG_IP_FIREWALL                required
```

The following parameter requires a device with major 36 and minor 3, plus a program to read the device:

```
CONFIG_IP_FIREWALL_NETLINK        optional
```

Only choose this parameter for firewalls, but *always* choose it for firewalls. It is required for masquerading. For non-masquerading firewalls, packet filters act on the first packet only, and others are passed on. Hosts receiving fragments cannot reassemble them without the first packet, and therefore are discarded in time. However, some hosts—most notably Microsoft Windows and NT—are susceptible to "big `ping`" attacks, even if they only receive the last packet. Choose yes for this option:

```
CONFIG_IP_ALWAYS_DEFRAG           recommended/required
```

The following parameter is required for `ipchains` REDIRECT targets and for transparent proxies; otherwise, it is not needed. If in doubt, include

```
CONFIG_IP_TRANSPARENT_PROXY       optional/required
```

The following is required for masquerading firewalls:

```
CONFIG_IP_MASQUERADE              optional/required
```

This is required only if you chose `CONFIG_IP_MASQUERADE` in the preceding example and want to masquerade ICMP. Without this, `ping` does not work. Furthermore, MS `traceroute`, which uses ICMP rather than UDP, also does not work:

```
CONFIG_IP_MASQUERADE_ICMP         optional/recommended
```

This parameter requires the ipmasqadm program. The next three options depend on enabling this. The following require kernel module support:

```
CONFIG_IP_MASQUERADE_MOD          optional/required
CONFIG_IP_MASQUERADE_IPAUTOFW     optional
CONFIG_IP_MASQUERADE_IPPORTFW     optional
CONFIG_IP_MASQUERADE_MFW          optional
CONFIG_IP_ROUTER                  optional
```

The following also requires kernel module support:

```
CONFIG_NET_IPIP                   optional
```

The following is useful for multicast, or if the remote end is a Cisco router:

```
CONFIG_NET_IPGRE                  optional
CONFIG_NET_IPGRE_BROADCAST        optional
```

The following requires `CONFIG_IP_MROUTE`:

```
CONFIG_IP_MROUTE                  optional
CONFIG_IP_PIMSM_V1                optional
CONFIG_IP_PIMSM_V2                optional
CONFIG_IP_ALIAS                   not recommended
```

This is needed only if you are directly connected to more than 256 hosts; ARPD is also required:

```
CONFIG_ARPD                       optional
```

The following requires `CONFIG_SYSCTL` and `CONFIG_PROC_FS`, as well as putting a `1` in `/proc/sys/net/ipv4/tcp_syncookies`:

```
CONFIG_SYN_COOKIES                recommended
CONFIG_INET_RARP                  not recommended
CONFIG_IP_NOSR                    recommended (highly)
CONFIG_SKB_LARGE                  optional
CONFIG_IPV6                       optional
CONFIG_IPV6_EUI64                 optional
CONFIG_IPV6_NO_PB                 optional
```


The `ipchains` program currently only works for IP, not IPX:

```
CONFIG_IPX                        not recommended
CONFIG_IPX_INTERN                 not recommended
CONFIG_SPX                        not recommended
CONFIG_ATALK                      not recommended
CONFIG_X25                        not recommended
CONFIG_LAPB                       not recommended
CONFIG_BRIDGE                     optional
CONFIG_LLC                        not recommended
CONFIG_ECONET                     optional
CONFIG_ECONET_AUNUDP              optional
CONFIG_ECONET_NATIVE              not recommended
CONFIG_WAN_ROUTER                 optional
CONFIG_NET_FASTROUTE DO NOT USE
```

The following is of limited availability:

```
CONFIG_NET_HW_FLOWCONTROL         optional
```

Following is an alternative to `CONFIG_NET_HW_FLOWCONTROL`, if you think that your system will be saturated by high volume traffic:

```
CONFIG_CPU_IS_SLOW                optional
```

Sixteen options depend on the following parameter, but are omitted for the sake of brevity:

```
CONFIG_NET_SCHED                  not recommended
```

Software Considerations

After the kernel is built, you can look over the system for software that isn't required for operation. Extraneous software needs to be removed. This is especially true of compilers, games, and other unnecessary software. The use of the X Window software is discouraged because this binds to port 6000 and 6010. If you feel that it is needed, consider using `ipchains` to deny output on the untrusted network side. This includes `nfs` and other services that are not used or needed. If an intruder breaches the firewall, it doesn't make sense to provide tools to use or services to activate. For more information on `ipchains` see the `ipchains` How-To at `http://metalab.unc.edu/mdw/HOWTO/IPCHAINS-HOWTO.html`.

What you probably want to have is software—such as ipmasq or ipfwadm—to help manage the `ipchains` and other firewall rules.

Tip #160 from Jack

To download a pre-compiled copy of `ipfwadm`, see:

`http://members.home.net/ipmasq/ipfwadm.gz.`

This program might or might not be included on the Linux CDs, but it is worth downloading and installing if you have many rules to track. The secure shell (`ssh`) program is also highly recommended. Running TCP wrappers on ports that are not forwarded and not used (normal services do not run on a firewall), as well as using tripwire to watch files, is a good idea. Another good program to add to your arsenal is a Perl program called courtney. This program watches for port scans.

OTHER CONSIDERATIONS

A firewall is not to be considered a normal network host, and it is not to be treated like one. This system should not enable normal users to log in or share files or directories on the network. The need to use good passwords for the accounts on the firewall, along with the necessity of using shadow passwords, goes without saying. What might need to be said is that the firewall is not to have the same password as any other host on your network. The fact that the host is broken because the attacker broke the password should not automatically provide access to other hosts on the internal network.

This host needs to also be physically separated from the rest of the hosts and placed in a secure area where unauthorized individuals cannot gain physical access to it. Any machine to which a knowledgeable individual has access can be "broken," often in minutes. The case needs to be locked, and access to the system setup password must be protected.

PORT FORWARDING

Port forwarding is redirecting a connection from one host to another; this is what proxy firewalls do well. If you connect from host foo to host bar on port 80, and that port is redirected—by software—to host baz on port 80, host foo thinks it's connected to host bar on port 80 even though it is actually accessing host baz on port 80. Host baz sees a connection from host bar. This can work in either direction, permitting inside clients out and outside clients in—but in a controlled environment. Either way, all connections appear to be to and from host bar.

The `ipchains` software does not do port forwarding. Although one of the `ipchains` targets is `REDIRECT`, this target is for local redirection, not redirection to another host. If you use `ipchains` and want to do port forwarding, you'll need to use`ipportfw`. The ipmasqadm program is a useful wrapper to ipportfw. Outside connections coming in might require redirection, particularly if the internal (trusted) network is being masqueraded.

A Simple Packet Filtering Firewall

The next few sections step you through building a very simple firewall with `ipchains`. This firewall is not adequate for use as is—you'll need to determine if this is what you need. But it does give you a good idea about how to plan and implement a simple firewall, including how to write the `ipchains` rules. In the real world, it's just not this easy; this is only a chapter, although it deserves a book.

To begin, you'll need to know something about the network from which you're connecting, and about the network to which you're connecting. The following assumptions are valid for the rest of this section:

- **Internal (trusted) Network**—209.191.169.128/25
- **External (untrusted) Network**—209.191.169.0/25
- **Bastion host**—foo, with foo1/foo2 interfaces, 209.191.169.1/209.191.169.129.

Planning

You can start from one of two general policies. The overall policy can be either "Permit everything that is not specifically prohibited" or "Prohibit everything that is not specifically permitted." Because the former is easier, your general firewall policy will be "Prohibit."

The network is set up internally as trusted, and no services will be run from inside for now. All the services that the company wants to provide to the Internet will reside on the untrusted network: anonymous FTP, HTTP, and so on. You might see the untrusted portion of the company's network referred to as the DMZ, the demilitarized zone, in some textbooks. This is because it is similar to the front lines in a battle; if the bad guys are going to show their faces, this is where they will try to penetrate. This has the disadvantage of having more hosts to monitor for intrusions, but it has the advantage of not allowing an intruder into your internal net via port forwarding.

Because this network is considered low risk, the decision has been made to run mail on the firewall, with a pop server for users to get mail whether they are at the office or home (`imap` will not be run for security reasons). The `smtp` and `popd` services will later be moved inside via port forwarding. DNS will be run from inside, but will only service the internal network. Primary DNS will be provided externally by the Internet provider.

Allow internal clients to use standard services on the Internet, except `nntp`. The following summarizes the policy you're going to implement:

```
Summary:
Default policy: prohibit
Anon FTP: external (deny incoming in to the firewall)
http: external (deny incoming in to the firewall)
ssh will be used: deny incoming telnet
```

```
smtp: firewall (future: port forward to internal machine)
popd: firewall (future: port forward to internal machine)
DNS: internal (no external access)
also stop incoming pings
```

IPCHAINS GENERAL

In order to understand how to proceed with ipchains, you need to understand how ipchains works. The next few sections walk you through some of the finer points. Most ipchains text makes the assumption that all packets run through the *chains*, or list of rules. In fact, however, ipchains only sees a packet if that packet is the first or only packet. Subsequent packet fragments do not traverse the chains. The reason for this is simple—a host cannot reassemble the fragments into a packet until it has the first packet. If this packet is denied, the others time out and are dropped.

Tip #161 from Jack

When you think *chain*, think of a logically grouped list of rules. Each rule in a chain is a test to apply against the IP header for a match.

The chains contain rules, numbered from one. As you will see, some rules can be referred to either by rule specification or by rule number.

A *rule specification* is the set of conditions that the packet must meet—the test. The same basic rule can exist in multiple chains, so the chain argument is normally required.

There are seven variations on the ipchains command line. The first six contain a command as the first argument. All six variations accept options as a final argument.

The commands are as follows (all commands are preceded by a hyphen):

- **-A** (append)—This takes a chain name and a rule specification as mandatory arguments.
- **-D** (delete)—This takes a chain name and a rule specification as mandatory arguments.
- **-C** (test/check)—-s, -d, -p, and -i are required. This takes a chain name and a rule specification as mandatory arguments.
- **-I** (insert)—An extension of append, but is placed ahead of the rule that is referenced.
- **-R** (replace)—An Insert and Delete. This takes as mandatory arguments a chain name, a rule number, and a rule specification.
- **-D** (delete)—This takes as mandatory arguments a chain name and rule number (this is a variation on the preceding delete command, where the rule number is known).
- **-F** (flush)—Delete all rules.
- **-Z** (zero)—Zero counters.

- `-N` (new)—Create a user-defined chain. This requires a chain name but otherwise works on all chains.
- `-X` (delete a user-defined chain)—This requires a chain name, and the chain must be empty, but otherwise works on all chains.
- `-P` (policy)—This takes as mandatory arguments a chain and a target.
- `-M` **(masquerade)**—This requires the following mandatory arguments:
    - `-L`—List
    - `-S`—Set tcp, tcpfin, udp

  The masquerade command, as opposed to the MASQ target, requires either `-L` or `-S`. The `-S` command requires three arguments: the `tcp` (TCP session), `tcpfin` (TCP session after receiving a FIN packet), and UDP timeout values in seconds.
- `-h` (help)—The seventh variation on the `ipchains` command line is `help`, which takes no commands, only accepts one option, and optionally accepts one argument.

  This option lists the usage argument (it can take the argument `icmp` to provide a list of ICMP code and type names that it knows can be used as arguments).

`ipchains` OPTIONS

A number of options are available for `ipchains`. These include some options to save mistyping a second rule when it is the same as the first but in the opposite direction, as well as a way to reverse the meaning of a parameter. Where address masks are specified, the mask can be either of the following types: `/N` or `N.N.N.N.`. Addresses can also be hostnames. Ports can be either numbers or service names.

The `-b` option enables you to specify one rule with a source and a destination address, but to have `ipchains` also build a rule with the addresses reversed.

The `!` can be used with a number of options to reverse the meaning. The options include the following:

- **`-p proto`**—Protocol. Can accept `!` (as in `-p ! icmp`) to match all but `icmp` messages; or it can accept `all` to match all protocols.
- **`-s address`**—Source address. Can optionally take `!`, a netmask, or a port. Note that an address of 0/0 matches all addresses and is the default if `-s` is not specified. Because ICMP doesn't use ports, you can follow `-s` with either an ICMP name, as listed by `ipchains -h icmp`, or a type number. If you use a name, you cannot also use `-d code`.
- **`-d address`**—Destination address. Same criteria as for `-s`. If you use `-s` and specify an ICMP type number, you can use `-d` and specify the code.
- **`-i name`**—Interface name. Can accept `!`. Also accepts a +suffix on the interface name to signify all interfaces of that type; that is, `ppp+` is all PPP interfaces (ppp0-pppN).
- **`-j target`**—Target for rule (user-defined chain name or special value), if it matches. If special value is `REDIRECT`, port can be included.
- **`-m mark`**—Number to mark on matching packets.

- **-n**—Numeric output of addresses and ports. By default, `ipchains` tries to resolve them.
- **-l**—Log matching packets. These are logged by the kernel.
- **-o**—Output matches to netdev, the userspace device.
- **-t** and `xor`—Masks for TOS field. Used to manipulate the TOS field.
- **-v**—Verbose mode. Outputs the interface address, rule options (if any), TOS masks, and packet and byte counters.
- **-x**—Expand numbers. When packet and byte counters are displayed, do not use the abbreviations K, M, or G, but display all zeros.
- **-f**—Second and further fragments. Can be preceded by `not`.
- **-y**—Matches TCP packets that have the SYN bit set. Can be preceded by `!`.

The following are valid ICMP types and subtypes (indented under the main type):

```
Echo -- reply (pong)
Destination -- unreachable
        Network -- unreachable
        Host -- unreachable
        Protocol -- unreachable
        Port -- unreachable
        Fragmentation -- needed
        Source -- route -- failed
        Network -- unknown
        Host -- unknown
        Network -- prohibited
        Host -- prohibited
        TOS -- network -- unreachable
        TOS -- host -- unreachable
        Communication -- prohibited
        Host -- precedence -- violation
        Precedence -- cutoff
Source -- quench
redirect
        network -- redirect
        host -- redirect
        TOS -- network -- redirect
        TOS -- host -- redirect
```

```
Echo -- request (ping)
Router -- advertisement
Router -- solicitation
Time -- exceeded (ttl – exceeded)
       Ttl -- zero -- during -- transit
       Ttl -- zero -- during -- reassembly
Parameter -- problem
       Ip -- header -- bad
       Required -- option -- missing
Timestamp -- request
Timestamp -- reply
Address -- mask -- request
Address -- mask -- reply
```


Table 30.1 lists the values that you need to use if you want to implement routing priorities based on the Type of Service (TOS).

Table 30.1 TOS Masks

TOS Name	Value	Example Uses
Minimum Delay	0x01 0x10	`ftp`, `telnet`, `ssh`
Maximum Throughput	0x01 0x08	FTP-data
Maximum Reliability	0x01 0x04	`snmp`, DNS
Minimum Cost	0x01 0x02	`nntp`, email

The TOS is only usable if you compiled support into the kernel (`CONFIG_IP_ROUTE_TOS`).

The `-o` option requires kernel support (`CONFIG_IP_FIREWALL_NETLINK`) and a device with major 36 and minor 3.

Built-in Chains

The three built-in chains in `ipchains` are input, forward, and output. Other user-defined chains can be created and destroyed; these three, however, cannot be destroyed, and must always contain at least one rule. By default, these rules are all `DENY`.

As packets are received, they traverse these chains, rule by rule, in the following order: input, forward, output. They continue in the chain until a match is encountered. When a match is encountered, the chain is interrupted until the target is evaluated. If no target exists, the chain continues with the next rule.

A rule does not have to have a target. Perhaps you want to know how many packets match a certain rule. As the rule is matched, the rule counter is incremented. Combined with the counter for the chain, you can see how many of the packets that traversed the chain matched any particular rule.

If there is a target, `ipchains` evaluates the target. The target can either be a user-defined chain name or a special value. If it is a user-defined chain name, `ipchains` immediately transfers to that chain and begins traversing it. If no matches are found in the user-defined chain, `ipchains` returns to the chain that sent it and continues with the next rule in the chain.

Tip #162 from *Jack*

Think of user-defined chains as subroutines, and of the targets sending them as GOSUBS.

If there is a target and it is not a user-defined chain name, it must be one of the following special values:

- **ACCEPT**—This match is okay; jump to the next chain.
- **DENY**—Quietly drops the packet on the floor.
- **REJECT**—Same as **DENY**, but generates an `ICMP destination not reachable` response.
- **MASQ**—Masquerade: Forward and user-defined chains only.
- **REDIRECT**—Input and user-defined chains only; performs local redirection.
- **RETURN**—Jumps immediately to the end of the chain.

Tip #163 from *Jack*

Think of the special values as a GOTO. This terminates the current chain and either starts on the next packet (DENY, REJECT) or sends the packet to the next built-in chain (or the calling chain, if you've jumped to a user-defined chain).

User-Defined Chains

User-defined chains provide a way to group rules logically. These chains are called from built-in chains as targets. At any point in the chain, you can call a user-defined chain. When a user-defined chain terminates with no matches, it returns to the next argument in the calling chain.

When creating user-defined chains, names can be up to eight characters long. Names are lowercase because uppercase is not used, but is rather reserved for future use. The name cannot be one of the built-in names or special values.

How ipchains Works

When ipchains looks at an IP header, the following occurs, in this order:

- **checksum** performed—The packet is accepted and passed or denied and dropped.
- **sanity check** —This step looks for malformed packets and drops them.
- **input chain** —If it is not DENY or REJECT, continue to the next step.
- **demasquerade**—Responses to masqueraded hosts have address rewritten; otherwise, skip.
- **routing**—Sends the packet to local process or forward chain.
- **local process** —The interface changes to lo and, if it is destined for a local process, traverses the output and input chains; otherwise, it only traverses the output chain where the local process handles it.
- **local**—If the packet went through the local process, but did not originate locally—that is, if it came from a remote host but was processed locally for forwarding (proxy processing, port forward, and so on)—and the final destination is remote, local sends it to forward chain; otherwise it is sent to output chain, where, if it is not DENY or REJECT, it is passed to the local host.
- **forward chain** —This is the chain for all packets that are using this host as a gateway to another remote host.
- **output chain** —This is for all the packets that are leaving this host.

Note

The preceding description of local process is confusing; but if you think of HOST and LOCALHOST as two different hosts, it makes more sense. To go from HOST to LOCALHOST, you must traverse all the rules (except forward), leaving HOST and entering LOCALHOST, and then going the other way for processes that are destined for remote hosts.

Simple Firewall Policies

Now you're ready to get down to specifying what you want to filter. There are a few things to keep in mind. While you are making changes to rules, you can change /proc/sys/net/ipv4/ip_forward from 1 to 0 to turn off forwarding. This prevents things from slipping through while you're making changes. This is also the first place to look if nothing is passing through your firewall when you expect it to.

Caution

If you change all the built-in chain policies to DENY or REJECT, make sure that you do not specify rules that require lookups. Use IP addresses, not hostnames.

Keep in mind, also, that rules are matched in order. The first rule to match with a special value terminates that chain (except as explained previously), so be careful about which rules come first. Take a look at the following rule: `ipchains -I input 1 -j REJECT` (insert, as the first rule, `REJECT`). Because this rule has no `-s`, it applies to all addresses. Furthermore, because it has no `-i`, it applies to all interfaces. Finally, with no `-p`, it applies to all protocols. Essentially, this rule rejects everything, even messages from localhost.

So to start, always keep your policies simple and build on them from there.

WHAT TO FILTER AND WHERE

Sometimes you need to think about not only what you want to filter, but where. Suppose you don't want to answer `ping` packets for any host. You can handle this in two ways—but only one makes good sense. The first way is to deny or reject `echo-requests` as follows:

```
ipchains -A input -s echo-request -j DENY.
```

The second way is to deny or reject the `echo-response` before it goes out:

```
ipchains -A output -s echo-response -j DENY.
```

Although both of these work, they have very different effects. You probably want to use the first method. Normally, your first response is correct. But be aware that both of these prevent the sender from receiving a reply. If the `ping` packet happens to be a `big-ping` and is being sent to a vulnerable host inside your network, the first method works (if you compiled `CONFIG_IP_ALWAYS_DEFRAG`). The second method does not.

WHAT NOT TO FILTER

Some administrators believe that ICMP packets are not that important. They equate `icmp` with `ping`. Unfortunately, a number of other important network messages use ICMP. The destination-not-reachable messages travel this way, so you won't receive them. Although TCP normally times out, these ICMP messages still need to be passed. Your OpenLinux system, for example, uses ICMP messages to set the maximum transmission unit (MTU). For Ethernet, this is normally 1500 for maximum throughput. Fragmenting causes more delays than dropping the MTU. So Linux sets the Don't Fragment (DF) bit. If a host or router needs to fragment the packets, it can't because the DF bit is set, so it drops the packet and sends an ICMP message. Linux drops the MTU and tries again until it can pass packets. If you don't accept ICMP messages, your connections with some hosts might be excruciatingly slow.

Most administrators are also aware that DNS uses UDP, and they want to block TCP on port 53 (the DNS port). But when DNS needs to do a zone transfer or other large data transfer, it switches to TCP.

The bottom line is this: If you experience network problems after implementing certain rules, back the rules out until you stop experiencing the problem, and then reimplement them one at a time, with logging turned on, until you can isolate the problem.

IMPLEMENTING THE POLICIES

Now all that's left is to implement the policies. Declare a few variables because this reduces errors. Follow these steps:

1. Use the following names, which are similar to the ones in the previous summary:

```
foo1int=209.191.169.1/25        # this is eth0
foo2int=209.191.169.129/25      # this is eth1
fooall=209.191.169.0/24         # so you can specify both subnets
```

2. Stop pings that come from outside:

```
ipchains -A input -s echo-request -i eth1 -j DENY #incoming
➥pings from outside denied
```

3. Now pass all traffic from inside out (except nntp):

```
ipchains -A input -s foo1int ! 119 -d 0/0 -i eth0 -j ACCEPT
```

4. Block those pesky services that are a common security problem or that you just don't want, such as telnet, ftp, http, and imap:

```
ipchains -A input -i eth1 -s 0/0 -d fooall 23 -j DENY
ipchains -A input -i eth1 -s 0/0 -d fooall telnet -j DENY
ipchains -A input -i eth1 -s 0/0 -d fooall 80 -j DENY
ipchains -A input -i eth1 -s 0/0 -d fooall imap -j DENY
```

Note In the previous step, you really don't need to specify eth1 because if it came from eth0, you've already accepted it previously and, therefore, you won't get the chance to deny it.

5. Be sure to accept DNS (on foo1int only), ssh, and returns on most upper ports (and on both networks) as well as smtp and pop-3:

```
ipchains -A input -p all -s 0/0 -d foo1int domain -j ACCEPT
ipchains -A input -p tcp -s 0/0 -d fooall 22 -j ACCEPT
ipchains -A input -p tcp -s 0/0 -d fooall 1024:5999 -j ACCEPT
ipchains -A input -p tcp -s 0/0 -d fooall 6010: -j ACCEPT
ipchains -A input -p tcp -s 0/0 -d fooall 25 -j ACCEPT
ipchains -A input -p tcp -s 0/0 -d fooall pop-3 -j ACCEPT
```

6. Verify that localhost packets are Okay:

```
ipchains -A input -i lo -j ACCEPT
```

7. Block the rest:

```
ipchains -P input DENY
```

8. You want to forward both ways—the input rules are taking care of most of the work:

```
ipchains -P forward ACCEPT
```

9. Make some optimizations:

- Minimum delay for Web, telnet, and ssh traffic:

```
ipchains -A output -p tcp -d 0/0 80 -t 0x01 0x10
ipchains -A output -p tcp -d 0/0 telnet -t 0x01 0x10
ipchains -A output -p tcp -d 0/0 22 -t 0x01 0x10
```

- Maximum throughput for FTP-data:

```
ipchains -A output -p tcp -d 0/0 ftp-data 0x01 0x08
```

- Maximum reliability for `smtp`:

```
ipchains -A output -d tcp -d 0/0 smtp 0x01 0x04
```

- Minimum cost for `pop-3`:

```
ipchains -A output -d tcp -d 0/0 pop-3 0x01 0x02
```

- To finish up (if you got this far, just let it go), enter the following rule:

```
ipchains -P output ACCEPT
```

There's just one more rule that you might want in order to stop IP spoofing (by someone from the outside who is pretending to be you). No one should connect to the external interface, claiming to be from the inside. The following rule enables you to log these attempts and reject them:

```
ipchains -I input 1 -i eth1 -s foo1int -l -j REJECT
```

TESTING THE POLICIES

The easiest way to test the policies is to make up a few cases that you do and don't want to get through and use the `ipchains` check option (`-C`). You'll probably want to use the `-v` option to get a verbose listing of the check. This tells you if the packet is passed. Remember that the `-C` option requires `-s` with address and port, `-d` with address and port, `-p`, and `-i` in addition to the chain name.

Often, enabling logging for some rules can help. This needs to be used judiciously or you will have very large logs, very quickly. One rule at a time is a good idea.

MONITORING

Remember to look through the logs from time to time, particularly if you put in rules that are designed to detect attacks. Furthermore, just in case someone does break in, you might want to have a trusted internal host doing your syslogging for you.

`tcpd`, `tripwire`, `courtney`, and all the other tools don't do any good if they are not properly used and checked. The first thing an attacker does is look for these things. Time is what your firewall is buying you. However, time works *for* the attacker and *against* you. The best time to catch an attack is before the penetration occurs, when your network is being probed. To enter, an attacker must find your weaknesses. This way, you will have warning. It might not be much, though.

UNDER ATTACK

After you've been probed or attacked, you need to have a plan to deal with the situation: Do you allow it to continue in an attempt to track it, or do you stop it cold? Do you alert the authorities? (It *is* a crime.) Do you have the authority to contact the police? If not, who does?

These—and many more—questions are all part of a good network security policy. But it is just as important to practice what you'll do when the time comes. Note that I said *when*, not *if*. Some Internet sites that carry tools for crackers are a constant source of new exploits, so finding out how the attacker entered, if possible, is essential to preventing a recurrence.

NETWORK SECURITY POLICY

Possibly the greatest failing of most companies is the lack of a coherent network security policy. A good policy explains clearly the network policy, penalties for violation of the policies, and enforcement guidelines (what happens to violators). This policy must apply to all—equally. A synthesis of this policy (two or three sentences) needs to be posted on Web and FTP sites to warn guests.

But the document should not focus on the prohibitive/punitive side. Rather, a good policy needs to cover the actions that are to be taken, as well as when and by whom, when your security is at risk. Furthermore, it needs to cover a reasonable timeline for the eventuality that someone, somewhere will at least attempt to penetrate your security. When an attack is discovered, what actions are taken? This includes discovery of the attempt after the fact as well as during an ongoing attack. A number of responses are possible in each situation, but because time is often the key element, those who are involved must know their part. In many larger companies, emergency response teams have been designated. A good reference is RFC-2196, "Site Security Handbook". All current RFCs are available from `http://www.rfc-editor.org/rfc.html`.

CONFIGURING IP MASQUERADING

In a nutshell, IP masquerading enables you to provide access to a TCP/IP network outside your own network through a single server using a single IP address.

The "single IP address" phrase is what makes this statement so significant. With a block of IP addresses, any network can contain multiple machines, each with its own legitimate IP address, and have a gateway machine provide each machine behind it with access to other networks (see Figure 30.1).

One common networking scheme does not follow this recipe, however: home and small business networks, most of which do not have legitimate blocks of IP addresses to work with, and most of which have only dial-up access to other TCP/IP networks, in particular the Internet (see Figure 30.2).

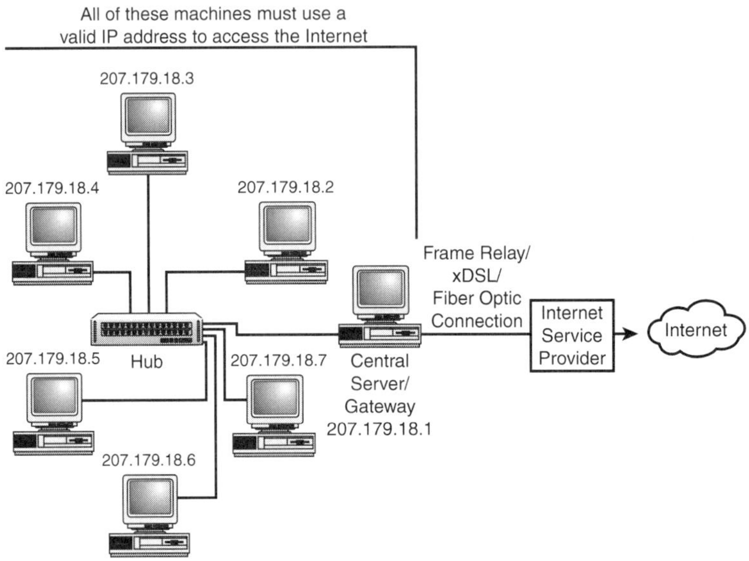

Figure 30.1
This network has a block of IP addresses.

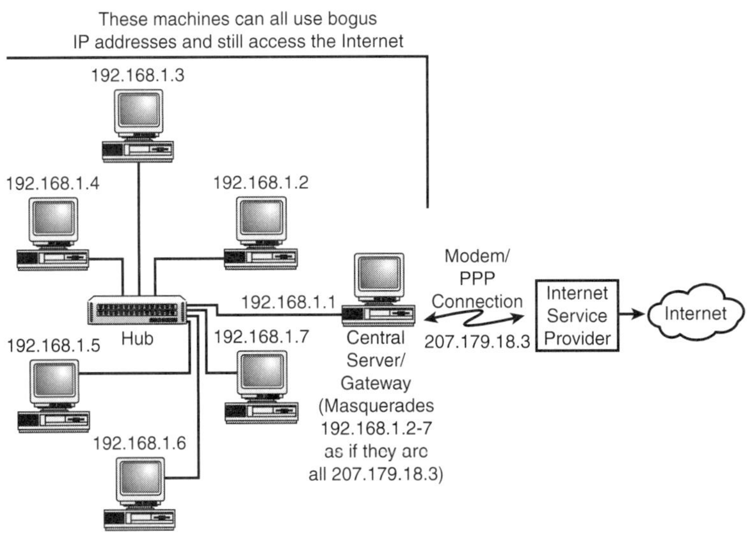

Figure 30.2
This network has one IP address and IP masquerading.

Using IP masquerading, a home or small business network can offer all connected machines access to an outside network such as the Internet using a single IP address on a single server machine. All Internet-bound network packets are masqueraded as if they were being sent from the server that is running IP masquerading. The server maintains the information necessary to route the returning network packets back to the machines that are supposed to receive them.

Note that although IP masquerading is commonly seen on servers connected to the Internet through a modem via PPP, nothing says that you cannot do the same thing using Ethernet connections to the Internet. For example, a company might want to have a training room full of computers networked to the Internet, but it might not want to give up a whole block of IP addresses for the task. If you give the machines bogus IP addresses and masquerade them through one machine, only one IP address is necessary.

Required Kernel Components

The Linux kernel that ships with OpenLinux is precompiled with everything you need to utilize IP masquerading. The kernel for Red Hat does not have support; therefore, it requires you to configure a custom kernel as described in this chapter. Debian 2.1 also requires a new kernel to support IP masquerading and firewalling.

Tip #164 from *Jack*

> **For detailed information on IP masquerading, see the official Web site at** `http://members.home.net/ipmasq/`.

All you need to do to implement it is load some kernel modules and set up some simple firewall rules.

If you want to compile your own kernels, check out the following list of items that need to be compiled into the kernel for IP masquerading to work (the names are listed as they are seen during a `make config`, `make xconfig`, or `make menuconfig` procedure). Figure 30.3 provides a view of the X-based kernel configuration screen.

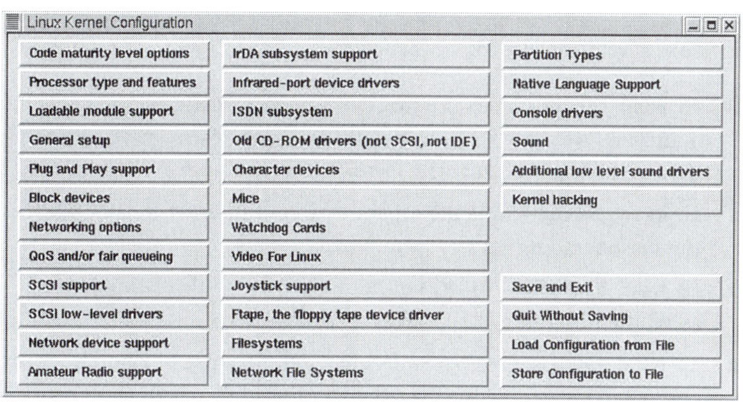

Figure 30.3 Using the `Xconfig` program eases your work load when creating a new kernel.

- Prompt for development and/or incomplete code/drivers
- Loadable module support
- Networking support
- Network firewalls
- TCP/IP networking

- IP: forwarding/gatewaying
- IP: firewalling
- IP: masquerading (experimental)
- IP: ipautofw masquerade support (recommended)
- IP: ICMP masquerading (recommended)
- IP: always defragment (recommended)
- Dummy net driver support (recommended)

Of course, you can compile in other options as either modules or built-in support; the preceding list is just for masquerading features.

SETTING UP

IP masquerading is accomplished through the packet filtering firewall capabilities of modern Linux kernels. When an outgoing network packet hits the firewall machine (the server with IP masquerading set up on it), the firewall rewrites elements of each package to make them look as if they are emanating from the firewall and not the machine behind the firewall. The return packets are modified to go back to the machine that sent the original outgoing packets. The machine on the Internet to which the packets were sent thinks that they were sent from the firewall machine, and the host behind the firewall thinks that the return packets were sent from the machine on the Internet. To both ends of the transaction, nothing odd seems to be going on at all.

Some services cannot be accessed without special handling. The following modules were made for just such services. These modules are all offered on default installations of Linux:

→ See "Working with Kernel Modules," p. 303

- **`ip_masq_ftp.o`**—Gives the machines on your network the capability to use the File Transfer Protocol (FTP) in nonpassive mode through the server that is doing the masquerading.
- **`ip_masq_irc.o`**—Gives the capability to use Internet Relay Chat (IRC) clients through the masquerading server.
- **`ip_masq_quake.o`**—Allows you to participate in three-dimensional Internet gore-fests as typified by the game Quake.
- **`ip_masq_raudio.o`**—Allows masqueraded machines behind your server to receive audio and video streams over the Internet through Real Networks clients.
- **`ip_masq_vdolive.o`**—Permits audio/video streams used by the various VDO-Live clients to pass through the masquerading server.

Your first task is to create a network with bogus IP addresses. The blocks of addresses allocated in RFC1597 as being reserved for private networks are listed here in Table 30.2.

TABLE 30.2 PRIVATE NETWORK ADDRESS BLOCKS

Class	Address Start	Address End	Mask
A	10.0.0.0	10.255.255.255	8
B	172.16.0.0	172.31.255.255	16
C	192.168.0.0	192.168.255.255	24

Unless literally hundreds of computers are to be set up on the network, odds are that the Class C block is the one that is used.

You use the `ipchains` utility to set up the forwarding rules for IP masquerading by using the following syntax:

```
ipchains -P forward DENY
ipchains -A forward -j MASQ -s startIP/mask -d 0.0.0.0/0
```

The first command denies everything from being forwarded through the firewall (a security measure). In the second command, you replace *`startIP`* with the beginning IP address from Table 30.1 for the class of addresses you are using and replace *`mask`* with the corresponding mask value.

For example, if a Class C address block is being used by the computers on the network, you use the following commands:

```
ipchains -P forward DENY
ipchains -A forward -j MASQ -s 192.168.0.0/24 -d 0.0.0.0/0
```

In most cases, this is all that you need to do to set up the firewall rules. Combined with the modules listed earlier, most of the common Internet services are covered by this configuration.

On occasion, you might need to set up special forwarding of specific ports on the masquerading server. One case in particular is when Cu-SeeMe video conferencing is being used. The ports on the masquerading server through which Cu-SeeMe operates need to be forwarded through a specific "control" port; otherwise, its network packets cannot be exchanged with the outside world.

This special form of port forwarding can be implemented using a utility called ipmasqadm. This utility takes general network ports and funnels them through specified control ports. The ipmasqadm utility does not care what it is forwarding; it just takes network packets from a range of ports and sends them out a different port.

For instance, even though ipmasqadm does not care that Cu-SeeMe is running through ports 7648 and 7649, it nonetheless forwards all the traffic that is moving through them to port 7648 if the following command is executed:

```
# Set up Cu-SeeMe firewall hole
ipmasqadm autofw -A -r udp 7648 7649 -c udp 7648 -u
```

This command line tells ipmasqadm to add (`-A`) an autoforward rule (`autofw`) that takes a range (`-r`) of UDP ports, starting at 7648 and ending at 7649, and sends their network traffic to UDP port 7648, which is specified as their new control port (`-c`). It also says not to require that remote hosts connect within 15 seconds of triggering this new control port (`-u`).

If you have this requirement (if you plan on masqueraded machines being able to use Cu-SeeMe through the masquerading server), you need to execute this command with `/etc/rc.d/rc.local` or some other startup script.

→ See "Understanding the Boot Process," p. 234

Caution

The preceding command, which sets up port 7648 as a control port for ports 7648-7649, essentially opens that range of ports to the outside world. The risk in doing so might not be critical, but any access from the outside is a potential risk and needs to be implemented carefully. Do not open ports to the outside world with ipmasqadm unless you have a real need to do so.

One point that is important to note about IP masquerading is that, for the most part, it is a one-way street. You can go from the machines on your network out to the Internet, but without special packet forwarding rules, you cannot get into the systems behind the masquerading server from the Internet.

What does this mean? It means that a machine that has a bogus IP address and is sitting behind a masquerading server cannot serve Web pages out on the Internet, nor can it accept direct FTP connections from the outside, nor Telnet, nor ssh/secure transactions, and so on. Thus services that are to be accessible from outside your network probably need to be set up on the same server machine that is running IP masquerading.

TROUBLESHOOTING IP MASQUERADING

My application doesn't work through IP masquerading!

Make sure your application is supported by IP masquerading. The following programs are known to work: HTTP Web browsers like Netscape and MSIE; ftp, Real Audio, telnet, SSH, POP3 and SMTP (email), NNTP (USENET news), ping, traceroute, IRC, CU-SeeMe (with special modules loaded). Many Internet phone programs either don't work or work only partially.

I don't have a permanent Internet connection, can I still use IP masquerading?

Yes, IP masquerading works just as well with dynamically assigned IPs as with static IPs.

What type of network connection/device do I need?

IP masquerading does not depend on your connection, just so long as you can establish a TCP/IP connection to the net. You can use standard analog modems, cable modems, ISDN modems or routers, bascially anything as long as you can establish TCP/IP.

Does IP maquerading work with just OpenLinux?

No, IP masquerading is not tied to a single Linux distribution, or to Linux in general. See the IP masquerading HOWTO, at `http://www.redhat.com/mirrors/LDP/HOWTO/mini/IP-Masquerade.html`, for more information.

IP masguerading doesn't work.

An open ended question—things to check is to make sure you've updated the kernel to work with IP masquerading. If you've upgraded the kernel recently then check your configurations. Make sure you have enable IP forwarding. Check the HOWTO. Search through the IP Masquerade Mailing list archive at `http://home.indyramp.com/lists/masq/`, for more information.

CHAPTER 31

Connecting to the Internet

In this chapter

by Steve Burnett

Understanding the Requirements for SLIP and PPP

The Linux kernel supports two serial line protocols for transmitting Internet Protocol (IP) traffic: Serial Line Internet Protocol (SLIP) and Point-to-Point Protocol (PPP). These protocols were developed as a poor man's alternative to expensive leased-line setups for getting Internet connectivity. Anyone with a reasonably high-speed modem and a service provider that supports these protocols can get his or her Linux machine IP-connected for a very low cost compared to leased-line systems. SLIP drivers for Linux were available soon after Linux was first released, and PPP support was added shortly thereafter. Although PPP has come to dominate the industry, the SLIP configuration is still helpful for supporting older systems.

You need to make sure that a few features are set up in your Linux kernel or configuration files. TCP/IP networking must be enabled, and the loopback interface should be configured.

→ See "Configuring the Software Loopback Interface," in p. 624

You'll want the IP address of your Domain Name Service (DNS) server to be included in your `/etc/resolv.conf` file to make accessing other machines besides your dial-up host convenient. If your dial-up link is slow or error-prone, you might want to run a name server on your Linux box to cache any DNS lookups and decrease the amount of DNS IP traffic on your dial-up link.

→ See "The `/etc/resolv.conf` File," p. 797

→ See "Using the `named` Daemon to Set Up the Server," p. 798

Using `dip` to Automate SLIP Operations

Linux offers a number of programs to manage your SLIP operations. `dip`, the Dial-Up IP Protocol driver, is one of the most versatile tools. It provides a scripting language for automating control of the modem and automatically sets up the SLIP network interface and kernel routing tables. You can use `dip` to initiate SLIP connections or provide dial-up SLIP service to other machines. The syntax for `dip` is as follows:

```
dip [-tvi] [-m mtu] [scriptfile]
```

Table 31.1 describes `dip`'s most common command-line arguments.

Table 31.1 `dip` Common Command-Line Arguments

Argument	Description
`-a`	Prompts you for username and password.
`-t`	Runs `dip` in command mode. Command mode gives you full access to everything `dip` can do, allowing you to initiate a SLIP connection manually.

TABLE 31.1 dip COMMON COMMAND-LINE ARGUMENTS

Argument	Description
`-v`	Displays the current error level when used with `-t`.
`-i`	Tells `dip` to operate in input mode. This flag is used when `dip` provides SLIP service for others dialing into your machine.
`-m` *mtu*	Forces `dip` to use the specified MTU value.
scriptfile	Specifies the name of the `dip` script to run.

USING dip IN COMMAND MODE

Invoking`dip` with the `-t` option places it in command mode. This mode lets you control `dip` directly and is an excellent tool for developing and debugging `dip` scripts. The following shows you what `dip`'s command mode looks like:

```
$ /sbin/dip -t
DIP: Dialup IP Protocol Driver version 3.3.7i-uri (17 Apr 95)
Written by Fred N. van Kempen, MicroWalt Corporation.

DIP>
```

From the `DIP>` prompt, you can run any `dip` command by typing it and pressing Enter. The `help` command displays a list of the available commands. Invoking a command with incorrect arguments displays a brief usage statement for that command. Table 31.2 describes the commands available for use at the command mode prompt or in `dip` scripts.

TABLE 31.2 COMMANDS AVAILABLE IN dip

Command	Description
`chatkey keyword [code]`	Adds a keyword and error-level code to the set of error codes returned by the `dial` command. You can use the `chatkey` command to detect when your modem returns `BUSY`, `VOICE`, or other specific messages.
`config [arguments]`	Allows you to directly manipulate the SLIP interface `dip` provides. This command normally is disabled because it's a severe security risk. The source code file `command.c` must be modified slightly to enable this command.
`databits bits`	Sets the number of bits that can be used as data in each byte. This command accommodates 6- and 7-bit dial-up connections.
`default`	Causes `dip` to set a default route in the kernel routing table pointed at the remote host.
`dial num`	Dials the specified telephone number.
`echo on¦off`	Turns echo on or off. Echo on makes `dip` display what it's sending to and receiving from the modem.
`flush`	Throws away any responses from the modem that haven't been read yet.

TABLE 31.2 COMMANDS AVAILABLE IN `dip`

Command	Description
`get $var`	Sets the variable `$var` to either the constant `ask` or remote constant specified, prompts you for a value, or takes the next word from the serial line and assigns it to `$var`.
`goto` *`label`*	Jumps to the specified label in the `dip` script.
`help`	Displays a listing of available commands in command mode.
`if $var op` *`number`*	Performs a conditional branch in a `goto label` script. `$var` must be one of `$errlvl`, `$locip`, or `$rmtip`. The number must be an integer, and the following operators are available and have their traditional C language meanings: ==, !=, <<, >>, <<=, and >>=.
`init` *`initstring`*	Sets the initialization string sent to the modem by the reset command to *`initstring`*.
`mode SLIP¦CSLIP`	Sets the protocol mode for the connection and makes `dip` go into daemon mode. This command normally causes `dip` to go into daemon mode and not return control to the script or the `DIP>>` command line.
`modem HAYES`	Sets the modem type. Only the `HAYES` modem type is now supported. (`HAYES` must be capitalized.)
`netmask` *`mask`*	Sets the netmask for the routes `dip` installs to *`mask`*.
`parity E¦O¦N`	Sets the parity of the serial line to even, odd, or none.
`password`	Prompts you for a password and retrieves it in a secure manner. This command doesn't echo the password as you type it.
`print`	Echoes text to the console `dip` started on. Variables included in the text are replaced with their values.
`portdev`	Sets the device `dip` uses.
`quit`	Exits the `dip` program.
`reset`	Sends the init string to the serial line.
`send` *`text`*	Sends the specified text to the serial line. The traditional C-style backslash sequences are properly handled.
`sleep` *`num`*	Delays processing for the specified number of seconds.
`speed` *`num`*	Sets the serial line speed.
`stopbits` *`bits`*	Sets the number of stop bits used by the serial port.
`timeout` *`num`*	Sets the default timeout to the integer value *`num`*. This value is measured in seconds.
`term`	Makes `dip` go into terminal emulation mode. This mode allows you to interface directly with the serial link. Pressing Ctrl+> returns you to the `DIP>>` prompt.
`wait word` *`num`*	Makes `dip` wait for the specified word to arrive on the serial line with a timeout of *`num`* seconds.

dip also provides a number of variables for your use. Some of them, such as the local and remote IP addresses, you can set; others are read-only and are used for diagnostic and informational purposes. Each variable begins with a dollar sign and must be typed in lowercase letters. Table 31.3 lists these variables and their uses.

Table 31.3 Variables Provided by dip

Variable	Description
`$local`	The host name of the local machine.
`$locip`	The IP address assigned to the local machine.
`$remote`	The host name of the remote machine.
`$rmtip`	The IP address of the remote machine.
`$mtu`	The MTU value for the connection.
`$modem`	The modem type being used (read-only).
`$port`	The name of the serial device dip is using (read-only).
`$speed`	The speed setting of the serial device (read-only).
`$errlvl`	The result code of the last command (read-only) executed. Zero indicates success; any other value is an error.

Tip #165 from Steve

Setting the `$local` or `$remote` variable to a host name causes dip to resolve the host name to its IP address and store that in the respective IP address variable. Setting the variable this way saves a step in the scripts you write.

Note

You can't set the read-only variables directly by using the `get` command.

Using dip with Static IP Addresses

Assigning individual IP addresses to each machine that uses a SLIP provider is very common. When your machine initiates a SLIP link to the remote host, dip configures the SLIP interface with this known address. Listing 31.1 shows a dip script using static IP addresses for initiating a SLIP link from notebook.afakecompany.com to server.afakecompany.com.

Listing 31.1 A Sample dip Script for Using Static IP Addresses over SLIP

```
# Connect notebook to server using static IP Addresses
# Configure Communication Parameters
```

LISTING 31.1 CONTINUED

```
port /dev/cua1 # use modem on /dev/cua1 serial line
speed 38400
modem HAYES
reset                          # Send initialization string to modem
flush                          # Throw away modem response

get $local notebook             # Set local IP address
get $remote server             # Set remote IP address

# Dial number for server modem
dial 555-1234
if $errlvl != 0 goto error     # If the dial command fails, error out
wait CONNECT 75
if $errlvl != 0 goto error     # If we don't get a CONNECT string
# from the modem, error out
send \r\n # Wake up login program
wait ogin: 30 # Wait 30 seconds for login prompt
if $errlvl != 0 goto error # Error out if we don't get login prompt
send Snotebook\n # Send SLIP login name for notebook
wait ssword: 5 # Wait 5 seconds for password prompt
if $errlvl != 0 goto error # Error out if we don't get password
send be4me\n # Send password
wait running 30 # Wait for indication that SLIP is up
if $errlvl != 0 goto error # Otherwise error out
# We're in, print out useful information
print Connected to $remote with address $rmtip
default # Make this link our default route
mode SLIP # Turn on SLIP mode on our end
# Error routine in case things don't work
error:
print SLIP to $remote failed.
```

Tip #166 from Steve

Tracking SLIP accounts separately from other types of accounts can be difficult. Traditionally, UNIX user accounts are assigned login names with all lowercase letters. Using the client machine name with a capital *S* added to the front as the login name for that machine's SLIP account makes tracking it easier and avoids login name collisions with normal user accounts.

The script in Listing 31.1 initializes the modem and sets the local and remote IP addresses for the SLIP link. If you use host names here, `dip` resolves them to their IP address equivalents. The script then dials the modem and works its way through the login sequence. When the script is used to log in and ensure that the SLIP link is up on the remote host, it has `dip` configure the routing table and then switch the serial line into SLIP mode.

If an error occurs, the error routine at the end of the script prints a warning message and aborts the script. `dip` is excellent about leaving the serial line in a reasonable state when done with it.

USING dip WITH DYNAMIC IP ADDRESSES

As SLIP became more popular, the task of managing IP addressees for SLIP clients got more and more difficult. This problem got worse when terminal servers supporting SLIP came into use. At that point, you might be assigned any one of a range of IP addresses, depending on which port the terminal server received your call, requiring changes in dip that captured IP address information from the incoming data on the serial line. Listing 31.2 shows a dip script that captures the local and remote IP addresses from the serial line.

LISTING 31.2 A SAMPLE dip SCRIPT FOR DYNAMIC IP ADDRESSES

```
# Connection script for SLIP to server with dynamic IP address
# assignment. The terminal server prints out:
#
# remote address is XXX.XXX.XXX.XXX the local address is YYY.YYY.YYY.YYY

# Set the desired serial port and speed.
port /dev/cua1
speed 38400

# Reset the modem and terminal line.
Reset
flush

# Prepare for dialing.
dial 555-1234
if $errlvl != 0 goto error
wait CONNECT 60
if $errlvl != 0 goto error

# We are connected. Login to the system.
login:
wait name: 10                         # Log in to system
if $errlvl != 0 goto error
send Snotebook\n                      # Send user ID
wait ord: 10
if $errlvl != 0 goto error
send be4me\n                          # Send password
if $errlvl != 0 goto error
get $remote remote 10                 # Get remote IP address
if $errlvl != 0 goto error
get $local remote 10                  # Get local IP address
if $errlvl != 0 goto error
done:
print CONNECTED to $remote with address $rmtip we are $local
default                               # Set routing
mode SLIP                             # Go to SLIP mode
goto exit
error:
print SLIP to $host failed.
exit:
```

The script in Listing 31.2 uses `get $remote remote 10` to watch the serial line and to capture the first thing that looks like an IP address in the `$remote` variable. The command times out in 10 seconds with an error if it doesn't see an IP address.

USING `diplogin` TO PROVIDE SLIP SERVICE

The `dip` program automates starting SLIP links from the client machine. Linux also supports incoming dial-up SLIP links. A few packages are available for doing this job as well. Here, you'll use the `diplogin` program, which is really just another name for `dip`.

Providing SLIP service to others requires that you create a specific account for each person on your Linux box and configure that account correctly. You also need to write an `/etc/diphosts` file with appropriate information for each host you're providing SLIP service for.

CREATING SLIP ACCOUNTS

You can manually create the SLIP account or use the `adduser` script with appropriate responses to each question. The following is a sample `/etc/passwd` entry for `notebook.afakecompany.com` in the `passwd` file on `server.afakecompany.com`:

```
Snotebook:IdR4gDZ7K7D82:505:100:notebook SLIP Account:/tmp:/sbin/diplogin
```

`/tmp` is recommended for use as the home directory for SLIP accounts to minimize security risks by preventing SLIP users from writing files into sensitive areas of your file system by default. Make sure that you use the correct path to the `diplogin` program.

USING THE `/etc/diphosts` FILE

The `/etc/diphosts` file controls access to SLIP on your machine and contains the connection parameters for each account allowed to use SLIP. It contains lines that look similar to the following:

```
Snotebook::notebook.afakecompany.com:notebook SLIP:SLIP,296
```

The fields in this file are the user ID, secondary password, host name or IP address of the calling machine, an informational field not currently used, and the connection parameters for this account. The connection parameters field contains the protocol (SLIP or CSLIP) and the Maximum Transmission Unit (MTU) value for this account.

If the second field isn't empty, `diplogin` prompts for an external security password when the specified account logs in to your machine. If the response from the remote host doesn't match the string in this field, the login attempt is aborted.

Caution

The `diplogin` program requires root privileges to modify the kernel routing table. If you aren't running `dip setuid root`, you can't use a link between `dip` and `diplogin`. You must make a separate copy of `dip` called `diplogin` and have its suid root.

That's all it takes. Setting up SLIP accounts and the `/etc/diphosts` file completely configures your system to support incoming SLIP links.

USING PPP

Point-to-Point Protocol (PPP) is another protocol for sending datagrams across a serial link. Developed after SLIP, PPP contains a number of features SLIP lacks: PPP can automatically negotiate options such as the following:

- IP addresses
- Datagram sizes
- Client authorization

It can also transport packets from protocols other than IP.

AUTOMATING PPP LINKS WITH PPPD AND CHAT

PPP operates in two parts: the PPP driver in the Linux kernel and a program called `pppd` that the user must run. The most basic means of using PPP is to log in manually to the remote host by using a communications program and then manually start `pppd` on the remote and local hosts. It's much more convenient to use a `chat` script with `pppd` that handles the modem, logging in to the remote host, and starting the remote `pppd`. Before you dive into `pppd`, take a quick look at `chat`.

USING THE `chat` PROGRAM

`chat`is a program for automating the interaction between your computer and a modem. It's used mainly to establish the modem connection between the local and remote `pppd` daemon processes. The syntax for `chat` is as follows:

```
chat [options] script
```

Table 31.4 lists the command-line options for the `chat` program.

TABLE 31.4 `chat` COMMAND-LINE OPTIONS

Option	Description
`-f` *`filename`*	Uses the `chat` script in the specified file
`-l` *`lockfile`*	Makes a UUCP-style lock file by using the specified lock file
`-t` *`num`*	Uses the specified number as the timeout in seconds for each expected string
`-v`	Makes a `chat` log of everything it sends and receives to syslog
`script`	Specifies the `chat` script to use

You can't use the `-f` option and specify a `chat` script at the same time; they're mutually exclusive. If you use the `-l` option for `chat`, don't use the `lock` option with `pppd` because the lock file created by `chat` causes `pppd` to fail, thinking that the modem device is already in use.

Tip #167 from *Steve*

When you're debugging `chat` scripts, run `tail -f /var/adm/messages` on one virtual console and use the `-v` option when you run `chat` in another. You can then watch the conversation `chat` is having as it comes up on the first virtual console.

Creating `chat` Scripts

`chat`scripts consist of one or more expect-reply pairs of strings separated by spaces. The `chat` program waits for the expected text and sends the reply text when it receives it. Optional subexpect-subreply pairs can be included in the expect portion, separated by hyphens.

The following is a typical `chat` script for logging in to a Linux machine:

```
ogin:-\r\n-ogin: abbet1 word: costello
```

This script says that `chat` should wait for the string `ogin:` to appear. If `chat` times out before receiving this string, `chat` should send a carriage return and linefeed and wait for the string `ogin:` again. When `chat` sees the `ogin:` string, it sends `abbet1`, waits for the `word:`, and sends `costello` in response.

Tip #168 from *Steve*

Include only the text necessary in expect strings to positively identify what you're looking for. This will minimize the chance of getting a mismatch or having your script blow up because of garbled text. For example, use `ogin:` instead of `login:` and `word:` instead of `password:`.

`chat` normally sends a carriage return after each reply string unless a `\c` character sequence ends the string. Carriage returns aren't looked for in expect strings unless explicitly requested with the `\r` character sequence in the expect string.

Most modems can report why a call failed when they get a busy signal or can't detect a carrier. You can use the `abort` expect string to tell `chat` to fail if it receives the specified strings. Multiple abort pairs are cumulative. The following script is an example of using the `abort` expect string:

```
abort 'NO CARRIER' abort 'BUSY' ogin:-ogin: ppp word: be4me
```

This `chat` script makes `chat` fail if it receives `NO CARRIER` or `BUSY` at any point during the script.

chat recognizes a number of character and escape sequences, as outlined in Table 31.5.

Table 31.5 Character and Escape Sequences Recognized by chat

Sequence	Description
BREAK	Makes chat send a break to the modem when used as a reply string. This special signal normally causes the remote host to change its transmission speed.
''	Sends a null string with a single carriage return.
\b	Indicates the backspace character.
\c	Suppresses the newline character sent after a reply string and must be at the end of the reply string.
\d	Makes chat wait for one second.
\K	Provides another means of specifying a break signal.
\n	Sends a newline character.
\N	Sends a null character.
\p	Pauses for 1/10th of one second.
\q	Prevents the string it's included in from showing in the syslog file.
\r	Sends or expects a carriage return.
\s	Sends or expects a space character.
\t	Sends or expects a tab character.
\\	Sends or expects a backslash character.
\ddd	Specifies an ASCII character in octal.
^C	Specifies the control character represented by C.

Part V Ch 31

Tip #169 from *Steve*

You can use the abort string to prevent low-speed calls on your high-speed modem. To do so, configure your modem to return a CARRIER 28800 string when it makes a connection and add abort CARRIER 14400 to your chat script. This way, chat fails if your modem connects at 14400 bps instead of 28800 bps.

Using PPP with chat

Thepppd program has command-line options that control all aspects of the PPP link. The syntax for the pppd command is as follows:

```
pppd [options] [tty_name] [speed]
```

Table 31.6 describes the most commonly used options.

Table 31.6 Frequently Used pppd Command-Line Options

Option	Description
device	Uses the specified device. pppd adds /dev/ to the string if needed. When no device is given, pppd uses the controlling terminal.
speed	Sets the modem speed.
asyncmap map	Sets the async character map. This map specifies which control characters can't be sent through the connection and need to be escaped. The map is a 32-bit hex number in which each bit represents a character. The 0th bit (00000001) represents character 0 × 00.
auth	Requires the remote host to authenticate itself.
connect program	Uses the program or shell command to set up the connection. chat is used here.
crtscts	Uses hardware flow control.
xonxoff	Uses software flow control.
defaultroute	Makes pppd set a default route to the remote host in your kernel routing table.
disconnect *program*	Runs the specified program after pppd terminates its link.
escape c1,c2,...	Causes the specified characters to be escaped when transmitted. The characters are specified by using the ASCII hex equivalent.
file *filename*	Reads pppd options from the specified file.
lock	Uses UUCP-style locking on the serial device.
mru *num*	Sets the maximum receive unit to the specified number.
netmask *mask*	Sets the PPP network interface netmask.
passive	Makes pppd wait for a valid connection rather than fail when it can't initiate a connection immediately.
silent	Keeps pppd from initiating a connection. pppd waits for a connection attempt from the remote host instead.

More than 40 other command-line arguments control all aspects of PPP at all levels. Refer to the man page for information about them.

Note

The pppd program demands that the file /etc/ppp/options exists, even if it's empty. This file, which is read by pppd, is an excellent place to put options you want pppd to use every time it runs.

You can combine pppd and chat in a number of ways. You can specify all the command-line arguments for both programs on the command line, put the pppd options in a file, or put the chat script in a file. The following is a simple example with everything on the command line:

```
$ pppd connect 'chat '''' ATDT5551234 ogin: notebook word: be4me' \
/dev/cua1 38400 mru 296 lock debug crtscts modem defaultroute
```

This example runs pppd with a simple chat script that dials a phone number and logs the user notebook in to the remote host. The device, speed, MRU, and a number of other options are included.

At the other extreme, you can place most of the options for pppd in a file and have chat read a script file. The following is the call to pppd:

```
pppd /dev/cua1 38400 connect 'chat -f server.chat'
```

The following lines display the contents of the reference file:

```
# Global PPP Options File
mru 296                             # Set MRU value
lock                                # Use UUCP locking
crtscts                             # Use hardware handshaking
modem                               # Use modem control lines
defaultroute                        # Make PPP set up default route
```

pppd reads this file and processes the options it finds within. Any text following a # character is treated as a comment and ignored.

The following chat script sets a number of abort strings, dials the phone number, waits for a login prompt, and logs the ppp user in to the remote host with the password ppp-word:

```
abort 'NO CARRIER'
abort 'BUSY'
abort 'VOICE'
abort 'CARRIER 2400'
"'' ATDT555-1234
CONNECT '\c'
ogin:-BREAK-ogin: ppp
word: ppp-word
```

Providing PPP Service

Configuring your Linux machine to be a PPP server is even easier than setting up a SLIP server. It requires only one new account and a shell script that properly runs the pppd program.

To start, create an account called ppp with an /etc/passwd entry that looks like this:

```
$ ppp:*:501:300:PPP Account:/tmp:/etc/ppp/ppplogin
```

Then set the password appropriately. The UID (501) and GID (300) numbers need not be the same. You can also assign one account to each PPP client you have, if you want. The /etc/ppp/ppplogin file should be an executable script such as the following:

```
#!/bin/sh
# PPP Server Login Script
# Turn off messages to this terminal
mesg n
# Turn off echoing
```

```
stty -echo
# Run pppd on top of this sh process
exec pppd -detach silent modem crtscts
```

This script executes `pppd` with the `-detach` argument to keep `pppd` from detaching itself from the tty it's on. If `pppd` detaches, the script exits, causing the dial-up connection to close. The `silent` option makes `pppd` wait for the remote `pppd` daemon to initiate the link. The `modem` options make `pppd` monitor the modem control lines, and `crtscts` makes `pppd` use hardware flow control.

That's all there is to it. When a user logs in to your machine with the proper user ID and password, the PPP link is established automatically on your box.

KEEPING YOUR PPP LINK SECURE

Keeping your PPP link secure is very important. Allowing anyone to connect your machine to a PPP server or allowing anyone to connect to your PPP server is as bad as letting anyone put a machine directly on your network. PPP provides a direct IP connection, effectively putting the machines on both ends of the link on the same network.

Two authentication protocols have been developed to make PPP more secure: the Password Authentication Protocol (PAP) and the Challenge Handshake Authentication Protocol (CHAP). While a PPP connection is being established, each machine can request the other to authenticate itself. This process allows complete control of who can use your PPP service. CHAP is the more secure protocol and is discussed here.

CHAP uses a set of *secret keys*, which are text strings kept secret by the owners of the machines using CHAP, and an encrypted challenge system to authenticate each other. A useful feature of CHAP is that it periodically issues challenge requests as long as the PPP link is up. This feature, for example, can detect intruders who have replaced the legitimate user by switching phone lines.

The secret keys for CHAP are stored in `/etc/ppp/chap-secrets`. To use authentication on your PPP link, add the `auth` option to the call to `pppd` and add the appropriate information for the host being authenticated into the `chap-secrets` file. The following is a sample `chap-secrets` file for `notebook.afakecompany.com`:

```
# notebook.afakecompany.com CHAP secrets file
# client/server/secret/IP addr
notebook.afakecompany.com server.afakecompany.com ''It's Full of Stars''
➥notebook.afakecompany.com
server.afakecompany.com notebook.afakecompany.com ''three stars''
➥server.afakecompany.com
notebook.afakecompany.com ''three stars'' afakecompany.com
```

Each line contains up to four fields: the client host name, the server host name, the secret key, and an optional list of IP addresses that this client can request be assigned to it. The client and server designations in this file are determined by the host that makes the authentication request (the server). The client has to respond to the request.

This file defines three different CHAP secrets. The first line is used when `server.afakecompany.com` requests CHAP authentication from `notebook.afakecompany.com`; the second is used for the reverse situation. The last line defines a wildcard situation for the client. This situation allows any machine that knows the proper secret key to make a PPP link to `notebook.afakecompany.com`. The wildcard designator (*) can be used in the client or server field.

Careful management of the `chap-secrets` file gives you complete control over the machines that can access your PPP server and the machines that you can access with PPP.

PROJECT: CONFIGURING PPP WITH KDE

KDE is another graphical user interface, presented in Chapter 26, "Working with KDE." Among the tools included as part of KDE is the application, which allows you to use a GUI to set up your dial-up configuration instead of the command line. To use , you need to have the X Windows System running on your Linux system and have KDE installed and running as well. You also need a dial-up PPP account somewhere and the configuration information for that account.

For this project, you're going to define a PPP dial-up for Mike James, an employee of A Fake Company. He'll be calling into his company's network from home. Just follow these steps:

1. To start `kppp`, open a terminal and enter the following at the command prompt:

   ```
   kppp
   ```

   The kppp window appears, as shown in Figure 31.1.

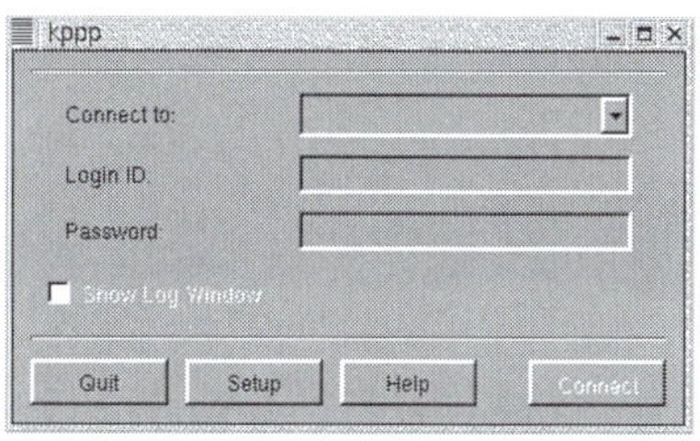

Figure 31.1 In the `kppp` main window, you can choose which PPP configuration to use.

   In the `kppp` main window, you can choose from multiple PPP configurations, such as to an ISP or to an office network. For the two dial-up providers, you are unlikely to have the same name and password, and the modems for the two will be different. For a home system, two users might have separate accounts for the same ISP.

2. Click the Setup button to display the `kppp` Configuration window (see Figure 31.2).
3. Click the New button to display the New Account window (see Figure 31.3).
4. Click the Dial tab to display the Dial pane of the New Account window.
5. For Mike's work configuration, enter the following information:

   Connection Name: `mikework`

   Phone Number: `555-5555`

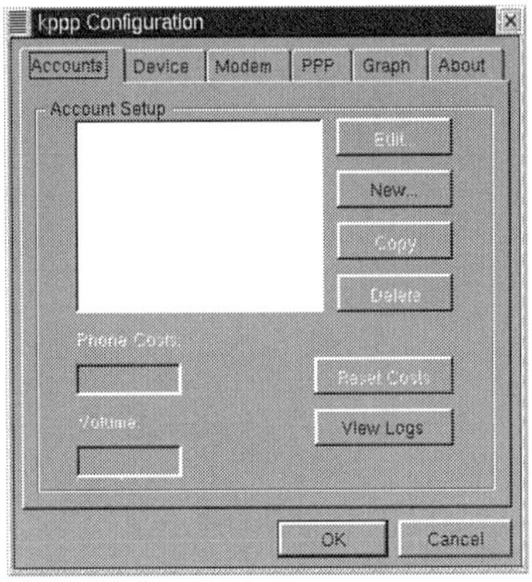

Figure 31.2 In the kppp Configuration window, you can choose your PPP configuration.

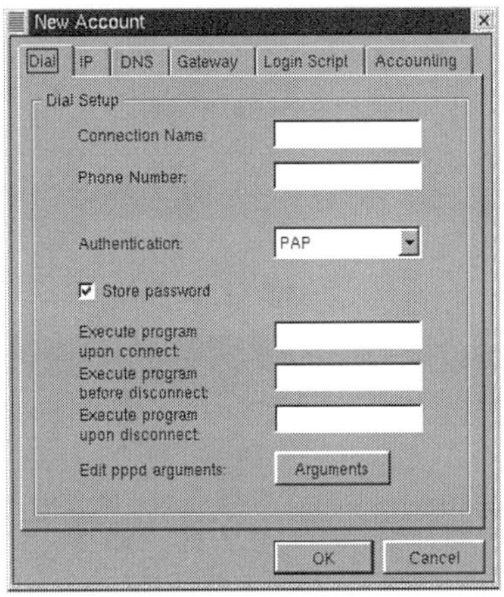

Figure 31.3 In the New Account window of kppp, you can define new accounts.

Authentication: `Terminal-based` (click the downward-pointing arrow and choose Terminal-based from the drop-down menu).

Leave the IP pane alone because A Fake Company uses Dynamic IP Address allocation.

6. Click the DNS tab to display the DNS pane of the New Account window, as shown in Figure 31.4.
7. Enter the following information:

   Domain Name: `afakecompany.com`

   DNS IP Address: `192.168.0.1`
8. Click the Add button to save the IP address and move it to the DNS Address List field.
9. Click OK. The New Account window closes, and the kppp Configuration window displays the name `mikework` (see Figure 31.5).
10. Click OK to close the kppp Configuration window and return to the main kppp window, which now displays the mikework configuration name in the Connect To field, as shown in Figure 31.6.

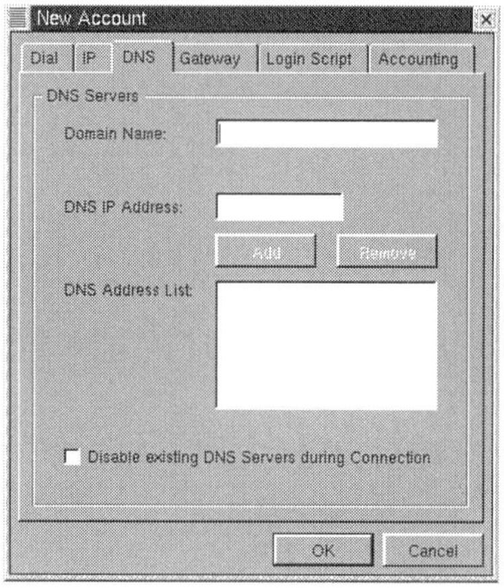

Figure 31.4 In the DNS pane of the New Account window, you can set the DNS server address(es).

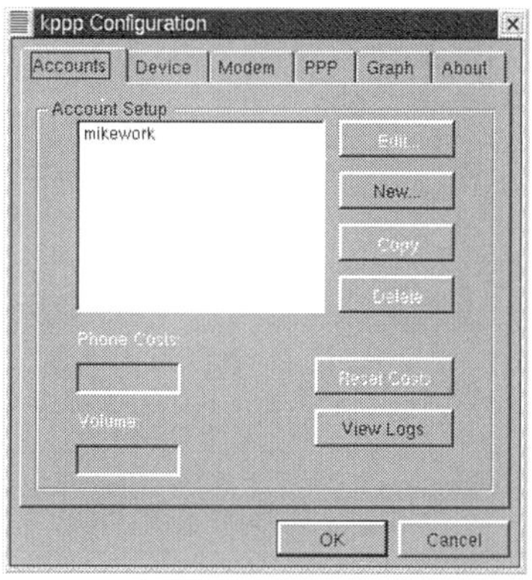

Figure 31.5 The kppp Configuration window displays created accounts.

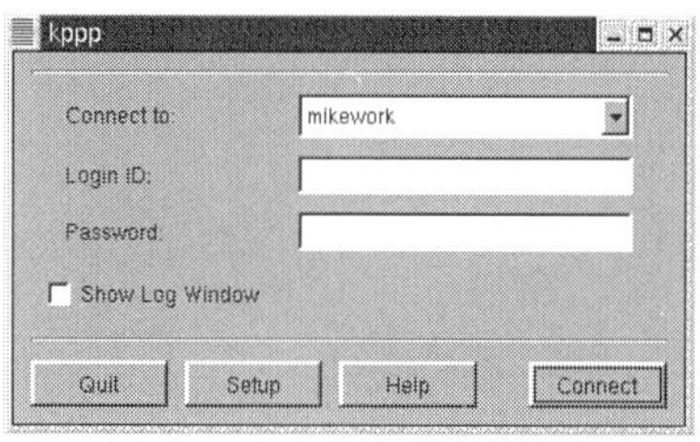

Figure 31.6 You can choose created configurations from the main kppp window.

11. Click the Connect button to have your computer dial the defined number and start a PPP session with the parameters given.

PART VI

Using the Internet

CHAPTER 32

ACCESSING THE NETWORK WITH `telnet`, `ftp`, AND THE `r-` COMMANDS

In this chapter

by Steve Burnett

USING telnet TO ACCESS REMOTE COMPUTERS

The main advantage of computer networking is the capability to share resources and information and to access that information from remote locations. Linux provides a robust set of tools for doing just that. Whereas the World Wide Web lets you access lots of information in a hypertext format, additional tools allow you to log in to remote computers, transfer files, and execute remote commands.

The `telnet` command is a common tool for remote login under most operating systems, including Linux. `telnet` gives you a terminal session on the remote computer that allows you to execute commands as though you were logged in locally.

To log in to a computer via `telnet`, you must know a valid username and password on the remote machine. Although some systems do provide guest login capabilities, such capabilities are very rare due to security concerns. When guest logins are allowed, they almost always place users in a restricted shell or in a menu system. The idea behind these guest environments is to provide computer security and protect the system from malicious or careless unknown users. A restricted shell prevents the users from executing specific commands; a menu system allows choices from only a predefined set of menus, blocking out shell access entirely.

`telnet` also allows users to log in to their own computers from a remote location by entering their usernames and passwords. This way, users can check email, edit files, and run programs on their normal computers as though they were logged in locally. However, you have to make do with a terminal-based environment instead of the X Windows system. `telnet` provides only terminal emulation for common terminals such as the DEC VT-100, which doesn't support graphical environments such as X Windows.

`telnet` is less common than it was even a couple of years ago, especially with the increased availability of Web-based front ends for email and other applications. However, for some situations, `telnet` is still useful. However, telnet is not a secure or safe tool to use in an open network such as the Internet. For more information, see Chapter 13, "Improving System Security."

telnet COMMAND SUMMARY

The basic syntax for `telnet` is as follows:

```
telnet [hostname]
```

`hostname` is the name of a remote computer. If you don't specify a remote host, `telnet` starts in its interactive command mode. If you give a remote host name, `telnet` tries to initiate a session immediately.

`telnet` accepts several command-line arguments, as listed in Table 32.1.

TABLE 32.1 COMMAND-LINE ARGUMENTS FOR THE telnet COMMAND

Argument	Description
`-d`	Turns on debugging.
`-a`	Attempts automatic login.
`-n` *`tracefile`*	Turns on tracing and saves trace data in *`tracefile`*.
`-e` *`escape_char`*	Sets the escape character for the session to be *`escape_char`*. If the *`escape_char`* character is omitted from the argument, this `telnet` session doesn't have an escape character.
`-l` *`user`*	Sends the username *`user`* to the remote system for automatic login. This argument automatically includes the `-a` argument.
`port`	Indicates the port number to connect to on the remote system. This argument is used for specifying different network programs. If it's not specified, `telnet` connects to the default `telnet` port.

SAMPLE telnet SESSION

It's time to take a walk through a sample `telnet` session. You start the `telnet` session by typing `telnet`, followed by the host name of the computer you want to connect to. `telnet` then returns with the message `Trying` *`some IP address`* (where *`some IP address`* is the address of the computer you specified). If `telnet` successfully connects to the computer (that is, the computer is up and running and the network isn't down), Linux reports `Connected to computer name` and then tells you that the escape character is some specific character sequence, almost always Ctrl+]. The escape character specifies the character sequence that you type to drop from your terminal session into the `telnet` command interpreter. You do so if you want to send commands directly to the `telnet` program and not to your remote computer session.

PART VI CH 32

After `telnet` successfully connects to the remote system, the login information is displayed, and the system prompts you for your login ID and password. Assuming that you have a valid username and password for the remote system, you successfully log in and can now work interactively on the remote system.

The following is an example of a `telnet` session from a Linux computer that connects to another Linux computer:

```
$ telnet server.somewhere.com
Trying 127.0.0.1...
Connected to server.somewhere.com.
Escape character is '^]'.
Red Hat Linux release 5.0 (Hurricane)
kernel 2.0.36 on an I686
login:bubba
Password: password
Last login: Mon Nov 15 20:50:43 from localhost
server:~$
server:~$ logout
```

```
Connection closed by foreign host.
$
```

When you're finished with the remote session, be sure to log out. `telnet` then reports that the remote session is closed, and you return to your local shell prompt.

USING `ftp` FOR REMOTE FILE TRANSFER

File Transfer Protocol (FTP) is a simple and effective means of transferring files between computers that are connected on a TCP/IP network. FTP allows users to transfer ASCII and binary files.

During an FTP session, you connect to another computer by using the FTP client program. From this point, you can move up and down through the directory tree, list directory contents, copy files from the remote computer to your computer, and transfer files from your computer to the remote system. Normal file protections apply; you can't get or put a file on the remote system if you don't have the proper permissions for that file.

To use FTP to transfer files, you must know a valid username and password on the remote computer. This username/password combination is used to validate your FTP session and to determine what access you have to files for transfer. Also, you obviously need to know the name of the system the FTP site you want to access is located on.

You should be aware that FTP clients have different command sets, depending on the operating system in question. This chapter covers the Linux FTP client; however, when you start an FTP session with a remote computer, the commands that the remote system expects might be different. It's rare for FTP systems to be completely incompatible with each other. Typically, the commands that you normally use are either slightly different or unavailable.

ANONYMOUS FTP

Due to the explosive growth of the Internet, many organizations have made huge repositories of information available via FTP. These FTP sites have everything from text files to software of every conceivable type available. But how do you access this enormous storehouse of data if you don't have an account on the remote computer? Do you need to get an account on every FTP site to be able to access these files? Not really.

A common convention on the Internet allows guest FTP access to file repositories so that users can transfer files. This guest access is called *anonymous FTP*. To use anonymous FTP, you start an FTP session to the remote system and use `anonymous` as the username and your email address as the password. For example, in the following sample, the user named smith on `linux.somewhere.com` wants to initiate an FTP session with a common FTP site:

```
$ ftp ftp.uu.net
ftp.uu.net (login:smith): anonymous
Password: smith@linux.somewhere.com
```

Note

Many sites don't allow anonymous FTP. Allowing guest users to connect to your computer does involve some risk. In cases in which anonymous FTP isn't allowed, the `ftp` command fails with a message similar to `Login failed - User ''anonymous'' unknown.` Sites that do permit anonymous FTP typically place the users in a restricted directory tree with read-only access. If you're allowed to place files on the remote computer, you usually can put them in only one directory.

Also, several of the Web browsers (Netscape Navigator, for example) support the FTP protocol as well as the HTTP protocol. Because several Web browsers also support email, they can support anonymous FTP connections automatically. Check the user guide for your Web browser for more information.

`ftp` Command Summary

The Linux `ftp` command provides a verbose set of command options in interactive mode. As mentioned earlier, some remote hosts might not support all these commands. However, you might not need to use many of them. Table 32.2 lists the commands available while in FTP.

TABLE 32.2 `ftp` COMMANDS AVAILABLE IN INTERACTIVE MODE

Command	Description
`!`	Escapes to the shell
`$`	Executes a macro
`account`	Sends the `account` command to a remote server
`append`	Appends to a file
`ascii`	Sets the file transfer type to ASCII mode
`bell`	Beeps when a command is completed
`binary`	Sets the file transfer type to binary mode
`bye`	Terminates the FTP session and exits
`case`	Toggles `mget` upper- or lowercase filename mapping
`cd`	Changes the working directory on the remote computer
`cdup`	Changes the remote working directory to the parent directory
`chmod`	Changes file permissions of the remote file
`close`	Terminates the FTP session
`cr`	Toggles carriage return stripping when receiving an ASCII file
`delete`	Deletes the remote file
`debug`	Toggles debugging mode
`dir`	Lists the contents of the remote directory (gives size and permissions)
`disconnect`	Terminates the FTP session (same as `close`)

TABLE 32.2 ftp COMMANDS AVAILABLE IN INTERACTIVE MODE

Command	Description
`exit`	Terminates the FTP session and exits
`form`	Sets the file transfer format
`get`	Gets a file from the remote computer
`glob`	Toggles wildcard expansion of local filenames
`hash`	Toggles printing the # character for each buffer transferred
`help`	Prints local help information
`idle`	Gets or sets the idle timer on the remote computer
`image`	Sets the file transfer type to binary mode (same as `binary`)
`lcd`	Changes the local working directory
`ls`	Lists the contents of the remote directory (gives size and permissions)
`macdef`	Defines a macro
`mdelete`	Deletes multiple files on the remote computer
`mdir`	Lists the contents of multiple remote directories
`mget`	Gets multiple files from the remote computer
`mkdir`	Makes a directory on the remote machine
`mls`	Lists the contents of multiple remote directories
`mode`	Sets the file transfer mode
`modtime`	Shows the last modification time of the remote file
`mput`	Sends multiple files to the remote computer
`newer`	Gets a remote file if the remote file is newer than the corresponding local file
`nmap`	Sets templates for default filename mapping
`nlist`	Lists the contents of the remote directory
`ntrans`	Sets the translation table for default filename mapping
`open`	Connects to the remote FTP site. `op` is a shorter version of the same command
`passive`	Enters passive transfer mode
`prompt`	Forces interactive prompting on multiple commands
`proxy`	Issues the command on an alternate connection
`put`	Sends one file to the remote computer
`pwd`	Prints the working directory on the remote machine
`quit`	Terminates the FTP session and exits
`quote`	Sends an arbitrary `ftp` command
`recv`	Receives a file
`reget`	Gets the file restarting at the end of the local file
`rstatus`	Shows the status of the remote machine

TABLE 32.2 ftp COMMANDS AVAILABLE IN INTERACTIVE MODE

Command	Description
rhelp	Gets help from the remote server
rename	Renames a file
reset	Clears queued command replies
restart	Restarts the file transfer at the specified byte count
rmdir	Removes a directory on the remote machine
runique	Assigns a unique filename to each file received when retrieving multiple files with the same filename to the same directory
send	Sends one file to the remote computer
site	Sends a site-specific command to the remote server, one of `umask`, `idle`, `chmod`, `help`, `group`, `gpass`, `newer`, or `minfo`
size	Shows the size of the remote file
status	Shows the current status
struct	Sets the file transfer structure
system	Shows the remote system type
sunique	Assigns a unique filename to each file sent when sending multiple files with the same filename to the same directory
tenex	Sets the `tenex` file transfer type
tick	Toggles printing byte size counter during transfers
trace	Toggles packet tracing
type	Sets the file transfer type
user	Sends new user information
umask	Gets or sets the `umask` on the remote computer
verbose	Toggles verbose mode
?	Prints local help information

As you can see, `ftp` has quite a few commands. However, you really need to look at only the ones that you use most frequently.

STARTING AN FTP SESSION

You can use the `open` command to open an FTP session with a remote host. Its syntax is as follows:

```
open hostname
```

You usually need this command only if you're going to connect to more than one site during an FTP session. If you want to connect to only one computer during the session, just specify the remote host name on the command line as an argument to the `ftp` command.

ENDING AN FTP SESSION

You can use the `close`, `disconnect`, `quit`, and `bye` commands to end an FTP session with a remote computer. The identical `close` and `disconnect` commands close your connection to the remote computer but leave you in the FTP program on your local computer. If you want to stop what you are doing, but stay connected, the Escape key cancels your last command. The `quit`, `exit`, and `bye` commands close your connection to the remote computer if one is active; then they exit the FTP program on your computer. Pressing Ctrl+c quits the FTP session without waiting for the other system to acknowledge you.

CHANGING DIRECTORIES

You can use the `cd [directory]` command to change directories on the remote computer during your FTP session. The `cdup` command takes you to the parent directory of the current directory. The `lcd` command changes your local directory so that you can specify where to find or put local files.

REMOTE DIRECTORY LISTING

The `ls` command lists the contents of a remote directory, just like `ls` from an interactive shell. The syntax for `ls` is as follows:

```
ls [directory] [local_file]
```

If a directory is specified as an argument, `ls` lists the contents of that directory. If a local filename is given, the directory listing is put into the file you specified on your local computer.

The `dir` and `ls` commands provide a long listing, giving protections, size, owner, and date. The syntax of the `dir` command is as follows:

```
dir [directory] [local_file]
```

The following is an example of a `dir` directory listing:

```
-rw-r—r-      1 root   archive   2928   May   17   1993    README
-rw-r—r-      1 root   archive   1723   Jun   29   1993    README.NFS
dr-xr-xr-x    2 root   wheel     8192   Jun    6   12:16   bind
-rwxr-xr-x    5 root   wheel     8192   Aug    2   06:11   decus
drwxr-xr-x   19 root   archive   8192   Feb    7   1994    doc
drwxr-xr-x    6 root   wheel     8192   Jun   15   15:45   edu
dr-xr-xr-x    7 root   wheel     8192   Sep   28   09:33   etc
```

→ See Chapter 20, "Managing File Systems" p. 439

GETTING FILES FROM A REMOTE SYSTEM

You can use the `get` and `mget` commands to retrieve files from a remote computer. The `get` command retrieves the file that you specify as an argument (*filename*). The following is the `get` command's syntax:

```
get filename [remote_filename]
```

You can also give a local filename, which is the name of the file when it's created on your local computer. If you don't give a local filename, *remote_filename* is used.

The `mget` command retrieves multiple files at once. The syntax for `mget` is as follows:

```
mget filename_list
```

You specify these files by giving a list of filenames separated by spaces or by using a wildcard pattern to `mget`. You're prompted for each file. To turn off prompting, use the `prompt` command before using `mget`. In both cases, the files are transferred as ASCII files, unless you've set the transfer mode to something else.

SENDING FILES TO A REMOTE SYSTEM

You can use the `put` and `mput` commands to send files to a remote computer. The `put` command sends the local file that you specify as an argument. The syntax is as follows:

```
put filename
```

The `mput` command sends a series of local files. The syntax for `mput` is shown here:

```
mput filename_list
```

You specify these files by giving a list of filenames separated by spaces or by using a wildcard pattern to `mput`. When using `mput`, you're prompted for each file. To turn off prompting, use the `prompt` command. In both cases, the files are transferred as ASCII files, unless you've set the transfer mode to something else.

CHANGING THE FILE TRANSFER MODE

FTP transfers files as ASCII files unless you specify something else. Transferring files this way is fine for plain text but renders any binary data useless. The `ascii` and `binary` commands set the transfer mode so that you can prevent damage to your binary files.

Note

Many files that you'll want to transfer are in binary format. Files ending with `.tar` are archives created with the `tar` command. Files ending in `.z` and `.gz` are compressed with either the `compress` command or the GNU `gzip` command, respectively. Files ending in `.zip` are compressed archives created with PKZIP. When in doubt, use binary transfer mode. Using ASCII mode corrupts binary data files.

CHECKING TRANSFER STATUS

When transferring a large file, you might find it useful to have `ftp` give you feedback on how far along the transfer is. The `hash` command causes `ftp` to print a # character onscreen each time the transmission of a data buffer is completed. This command works for sending and receiving files.

LOCAL COMMANDS WHILE IN FTP

You can use the ! character to pass a command to the command shell on your local computer while you're in FTP. This capability can be very useful if you need to do something while you're in the midst of an FTP session. Suppose that you need to create a directory to hold received files. If you enter `!mkdir new_dir`, Linux makes a directory named `new_dir` in your current local directory.

A SAMPLE FTP SESSION

Listing 32.1 shows a short FTP session.

LISTING 32.1 MAKING AN FTP CONNECTION AND GETTING A DIRECTORY LISTING

```
$ ftp opus
Connected to opus.
220 opus FTP server (Linux opus 2.0.6 #4 Mon Nov 15 16:01:33 CDT 1999) ready.
Name (opus:smith): smith
Password (opus:smith): password
331 Password required for smith.
230 User smith logged in.
Remote system type is UNIX.
Using ASCII mode to transfer files.
ftp>> dir
200 PORT command successful.
150 Opening ASCII mode data connection for /bin/ls.
total 8
-rw-r-r-      1 root    daemon     1525 Sep 29 15:37 README
dr-xr-xr-x    2 root    wheel       512 Jun 24 11:35 bin
dr-r-r-       2 root    wheel       512 Jun 24 11:18 dev
dr-r-r-       2 root    wheel       512 Jun 24 11:24 etc
dr-xr-xr-x    4 root    wheel       512 Sep 29 15:37 pub
dr-xr-xr-x    3 root    wheel       512 Jun 24 11:15 usr
-r-r-r-       1 root    daemon      461 Jun 24 13:46 welcome.msg
226 Transfer complete.
433 bytes received in 0.027 seconds (16 Kbytes/s)
ftp>> get README
200 PORT command successful.
150 Opening ASCII mode data connection for README (1525 bytes).
226 Transfer complete.
local: README remote: README
1561 bytes received in 0.0038 seconds (4e+02 Kbytes/s)
ftp>> quit
221 Goodbye.
$
```

In Listing 32.1, a user opens an FTP session to the host opus and logs in as smith. The remote FTP server prompts for the password, which the user types (the password doesn' t appear onscreen). `ftp` then logs smith in to the remote system and displays the `ftp]]` prompt for interactive mode commands. The user tells `ftp` to list the remote directory with the `dir` command and then transfers the file `README` with the `get` command. When finished with the FTP session, the intrepid user then logs out by using the `quit` command and is returned to the local Linux shell prompt.

A SAMPLE ANONYMOUS FTP SESSION

In the preceding section, you saw a user initiate an FTP session with a system and look at some directories. The user had a valid username and password on the remote system. Now look at an anonymous FTP session to a major software archive site on the Internet. Listing 32.2 is similar to Listing 32.1, but it has some interesting differences.

LISTING 32.2 PERFORMING AN ANONYMOUS FTP CONNECTION

```
$ ftp ftp.uu.net
Connected to ftp.uu.net.
220 ftp.UU.NET FTP server
(Version wu-2.4(1) Wed Nov 17 15:45:10 EST 1999) ready.
Name (ftp.uu.net:bubba):  anonymous
331 Guest login ok, send your complete email address as password.
Password: your_email_address
230-
230-                  Welcome to the UUNET archive.
230-   A service of UUNET Technologies Inc, Falls Church, Virginia
230-   For information about UUNET, call +1 703 204 8000,
230-  or see the files in /uunet-info
230-
230-   Access is allowed all day.
230-   Local time is Wed Nov 17 15:53:02 1999.
230-
230-   All transfers are logged with your host name and email address.
230-   If you don't like this policy, disconnect now!
230-
230-   If your FTP client crashes or hangs shortly
230-   after login, try using a
230-   dash (-) as the first character of your password.
230-   This will turn off the informational messages which may
230-    be confusing your ftp client.
230-
230-Please read the file /info/README.ftp
230-  it was last modified on Mon Nov 15 17:39:53 1999 - 2 days ago
230 Guest login ok, access restrictions apply.
ftp>
ftp> dir
200 PORT command successful.
150 Opening ASCII mode data connection for /bin/ls.
total 4149
drwxr-sr-x    2 34    0             512 Jul 26   1992 .forward
-rw-r-r-    1 34     uucp             0 Jul 26   1992 .hushlogin
-rw-r-r-    1 34     archive         59 Jul 31   1992 .kermrc
-rw-r-r-    1 34     archive          0 Jul 26   1992 .notar
drwx-s-x    5 34     archive        512 Jul 23  19:00 admin
lrwxrwxrwx    1 34    archive         1 Jul 26   1992 archive ->
drwxrws-x    4 0     archive        512 Apr 20  16:29 bin
lrwxrwxrwx    1 34    archive        23 Sep 14   1993 by-name.gz ->
➥index/master/by-name.gz
lrwxrwxrwx    1 34    archive        23 Sep 14   1993 by-time.gz ->
➥index/master/by-time.gz
-rw-r-r-    1 34    archive    90112 Apr 26   1991 compress.tar
lrwxrwxrwx    1 0    archive         9 Jul 23 18:50 core -> /dev/null
```

LISTING 32.2 CONTINUED

```
drwxrws-x    2 0    archive      512 Jul 26  1992 dev
drwxrwsr-x  21 34   archive     1024 Sep 29 15:18 doc
drwxrws-x    6 0    archive      512 Apr 14 16:42 etc
lrwxrwxrwx   1 34   archive       31 Dec  8  1993 faces ->
➥/archive/published/usenix/faces
drwxrwsr-x   2 34   archive      512 Jul 26  1992 ftp
drwxrwsr-x   4 34   archive      512 Sep 29 10:34 government
drwxrwsr-x  18 34   archive     1024 Sep 29 10:28 graphics
-rw-rw-r-    1 27   archive   798720 Jul 11 20:54 gzip.tar
lrwxrwxrwx   1 34   archive       17 Jul 26  1992 help -> info/archive-
help
drwxrwsr-x  20 34   archive     1024 Dec  2  1993 index
drwxrwsr-x  19 34   archive      512 Sep 29 10:30 inet
drwxrwsr-x   4 34   archive      512 Sep 29 15:36 info
drwxrwsr-x  25 34   archive      512 Sep 29 10:29 languages
drwxrwsr-x   4 34   archive      512 Sep 29 10:28 library
drwx-s-x     2 0    0           8192 Jul 26  1992 lost+found
lrwxrwxrwx   1 34   archive       20 Aug  2  1992 ls-lR.Z ->
➥index/master/ls-lR.Z
lrwxrwxrwx   1 34   archive       21 Sep 14  1993 ls-lR.gz ->
➥index/master/ls-lR.gz
lrwxrwxrwx   1 34   archive       21 Aug  2  1992 ls-ltR.Z ->
➥index/master/ls-ltR.Z
lrwxrwxrwx   1 34   archive       22 Sep 14  1993 ls-ltR.gz ->
➥index/master/ls-ltR.gz
drwxrwsr-x  24 34   archive     1024 Sep 29 15:10 networking
drwxrwsr-x   2 34   archive      512 Aug 10 09:26 packages
d-xrws-x    17 34   archive      512 Sep 26 12:29 private
drwxrwsr-x  25 34   archive     1536 Sep 29 15:30 pub
drwxrwsr-x  17 34   archive     1024 Sep 29 15:38 published
lrwxrwxrwx   1 34   archive       10 Jul 26  1992 sco-archive -> vendor/sco
drwxrwsr-x  20 34   archive      512 Sep 29 04:18 systems
drwxrwxrwx  14 34   archive     1536 Sep 29 15:36 tmp
lrwxrwxrwx   1 34   archive       17 Jul 26  1992 unix-today ->
➥vendor/unix-today
lrwxrwxrwx   1 34   archive       17 Jul 26  1992 unix-world ->
➥vendor/unix-world
drwxrwsr-x  36 34   archive     1024 Sep 29 15:29 usenet
drwxrws-x    6 0    archive      512 Oct 22  1992 usr
lrwxrwxrwx   1 34   archive       16 Aug  2  1992 uumap -> networking/
uumap
-rw-rw-r-    1 34   archive  3279895 Sep 28 21:05 uumap.tar.Z
drwxrwsr-x   3 210  archive     2560 Sep 29 15:36 uunet-info
drwxrwsr-x  64 34   archive     1536 Sep 29 10:29 vendor
226 Transfer complete.
3257 bytes received in 0.76 seconds (4.2 Kbytes/s)
ftp>
ftp> cd systems/unix/linux
250-Files within this subtree are automatically mirrored from
250-tsx-11.mit.edu:/pub/linux
250-
250 CWD command successful.
ftp>
ftp> binary
200 Type set to I.
```

LISTING 32.2 CONTINUED

```
ftp>> get sum.Z
200 PORT command successful.
150 Opening BINARY mode data connection for sum.Z (80959 bytes).
226 Transfer complete.
local: sum.Z remote: sum.Z
80959 bytes received in 5.6 seconds (14 Kbytes/s)
ftp>> quit
221 Goodbye.
$
```

In Listing 32.2, an FTP session is initiated with `ftp.uu.net`, which is a major FTP archive site on the Internet. The username given at the login prompt is `anonymous` because this is an anonymous FTP. For the password, the full email address is used. `ftp.uu.net` then displays a welcome banner that gives some information about the archive. In this example, you can see that the user changes directories, sets the file mode to binary, gets a compressed binary file, and exits.

USING THE R- COMMANDS

In addition to `ftp` and `telnet`, several other commands allow you to access remote computers and exchange files over a network. These commands are known collectively as the `r-` commands. These commands are generally UNIX-only: The `telnet` and `ssh` applications were developed to provide more generic cross-platform solutions.

The `r-` commands deserve special notice because one of their features can cause a severe security loophole if you aren't careful. When you issue an `r-` command, the remote system checks a file named `/etc/hosts.equiv` to see whether your local host is listed. If it doesn't find your local host, it checks for a file named `.rhosts` in your home directory on the remote machine. The `r-` command then checks to see whether your local host name is in the `.rhosts` file. If your local host is listed in either place, the command is executed without checking for a password.

Although not having to type your password every time you need to access a remote computer can be very convenient, it can obviously cause severe security problems. We recommend that you carefully consider the security implications of using the `r-` commands before setting up `/etc/hosts.equiv` and `.rhosts` files on your local system.

THE `rlogin` COMMAND

The `rlogin` command is similar to the `telnet` command because it allows you to start an interactive command session on a remote system. The syntax of `rlogin` is as follows:

```
rlogin [-8EKLdx] [-e char] [-k realm] [-l user_name] hostname
```

However, the most common usage is simply this:

```
rlogin hostname
```

Table 32.3 explains the various options for `rlogin`.

TABLE 32.3 COMMAND-LINE OPTIONS FOR THE `rlogin` COMMAND

Option	Description
`-8`	Allows an 8-bit input data path at all times, which allows for formatted ANSI characters and other special codes to be sent. If this option isn't used, parity bits are stripped except when the remote stop and start characters are other than Ctrl+s and Ctrl+q.
`-E`	Stops any character from being recognized as an escape character. When this option is used with the `-8` option, it provides a completely transparent connection.
`-K`	Turns off all Kerberos authentication. It's used only when connecting to a host that uses the Kerberos authentication protocol.
`-L`	Allows the `rlogin` session to be run in `litout` mode. Refer to the tty man page for more information.
`-d`	Turns on socket debugging on the TCP sockets used for communication with the remote host. Refer to the `setsockopt` man page for more information.
`-e`	Used to set the escape character for the `rlogin` session. The escape character is ~ by default. You can specify a literal character or an octal value in the form `\nnn`.
`-k`	Requests `rlogin` to obtain Kerberos tickets for the remote host in the specified realm instead of the remote host's realm as determined by `krb_realmofhost(3)`.
`-l`	Allows the remote name to be specified. If available, Kerberos authentication is used.
`-x`	Turns on DES encryption for all data passed via the `rlogin` session. Encryption can affect response time and CPU usage, but it provides increased security.

THE `rsh` COMMAND

The `rsh` command, an abbreviation for *remote shell*, starts a shell on the specified remote host and executes the command, if any, that you specify on the `rsh` command line. If you don't give a command to execute, you're logged in to the remote machine by using `rlogin`.

The syntax of the `rsh` command is as follows:

```
rsh [-Kdnx] [-k realm] [-l user_name] hostname [command]
```

However, the most common usage is this:

```
rsh hostname [command]
```

The *`command`* argument can be virtually any Linux command that you can enter from the shell prompt. Table 32.4 explains the command-line options for `rsh`.

TABLE 32.4 COMMAND-LINE OPTIONS FOR THE rsh COMMAND

Option	Description
`-K`	Turns off all Kerberos authentication. It's used only when connecting to a host that uses Kerberos.
`-d`	Turns on socket debugging on the TCP sockets used for communication with the remote host. See the `setsockopt` man page for more information.
`-k`	Requests `rsh` to obtain Kerberos tickets for the remote host in the specified realm instead of the remote host's realm as determined by `krb_realmofhost(3)`.
`-l`	Allows the remote name to be specified. If available, Kerberos authentication is used, and authorization is determined as with the `rlogin` command.
`-n`	Redirects input from the special device `/dev/null`.
`-x`	Turns on DES encryption for all data passed. Encryption can affect response time and CPU usage, but it provides increased security.

Linux takes the standard input to the `rsh` command and copies it to the standard input of the remotely executed command. It copies the standard output of the remote command to standard output for `rsh`. It also copies the remote standard error to the local standard error file descriptor. Any quit, terminate, and interrupt signals are sent to the remote command. Also, any special shell characters that aren't enclosed within quotation marks, as in >>, are handled locally. If they are enclosed within quotation marks, these characters are handled by the remote command.

THE rcp COMMAND

The `rcp` command, which stands for *remote copy*, is the last of the `r-` commands that you might need to know. It's used to copy files between computers. You can use `rcp` to copy files from one remote computer to another, without either the source or destination being on the local machine.

The `rcp` command has two forms. The first form is used to copy a file to a file. The second form is used when copying files or a directory to a directory. The syntax for the `rcp` command can be either of the following:

```
rcp [-px] [-k realm] filename1filename2
```

```
rcp [-px] [-r] [-k realm] file(s) directory
```

Each file or directory argument is either a remote filename or a local filename. Remote filenames have the form *`rname@rhost:path`*, where *`rname`* is the remote username, *`rhost`* is the remote computer, and *`path`* is the path to the file. The filename must contain a colon.

Table 32.5 explains the arguments for `rcp`.

TABLE 32.5 COMMAND-LINE ARGUMENTS FOR THE rcp COMMAND

Option	Description
`-r`	Recursively copies the source directory tree into the destination directory. For you to be able to use this option, the destination must be a directory.
`-p`	Tries to preserve the modification times and modes of the source files, ignoring the `umask`.
`-k`	Requests `rcp` to obtain Kerberos tickets for the remote host in the specified realm instead of the remote host's realm, as determined by `krb_realmofhost(3)`.
`-x`	Turns on DES encryption for all data passed by `rcp`. Encryption can affect response time and CPU usage, but it provides increased security.

If the path specified in the filename isn't a full pathname, it's interpreted as being relative to the login directory of the specified user on the remote computer. If no remote username is given, the current username is used. If a path on a remote host contains special shell characters, you can quote it by using \, ", or ' as appropriate. Using these special characters causes all the shell metacharacters to be interpreted remotely.

Note `rcp` doesn't prompt for passwords. It performs its copies via the `rsh` command.

THE ssh COMMAND

`ssh` (short for *secure shell*), like the `rsh` command, is a program for logging into a remote machine and executing commands on that remote machine. `ssh` is designed to replace both `rsh` and `rlogin` by providing the capability to define an encrypted session between two untrusted systems over an insecure network. One problem with `telnet` is that, when you log in to the remote system, the password is sent as ASCII over the network. By watching the Ethernet packets, someone could collect your login name and password for the remote system. `ssh` prevents this from happening by using RSA-based authentication for the connection. Because of its security, `ssh` is commonly used by system administrators today. `ssh` clients are available for almost all UNIX-related systems in command-line or GUI forms, and are also available for other operating systems, including Macintosh OS and Microsoft Windows.

The `ssh` command is similar to the `telnet` command because it allows you to start an interactive command session on a remote system. The syntax of `ssh` is as follows:

```
ssh [-a] [-c idea¦blowfish¦des¦3des¦arcfour¦tss¦none] [-e escape_char]
A[-I identity_file] [-l login_name] [-n] [-k] [-V] [=o option] [-p port]
A[-q] [-P] [-t] [-v] [-x] [-C] [-L port"host:hostport] [-R port:host:hostport]
Ahostname [command]
```

However, the most common usage is this:

```
ssh hostname
```

Table 32.6 explains the various options for `ssh`.

TABLE 32.6 COMMAND-LINE OPTIONS FOR THE ssh COMMAND

Option	Description
`-a`	Disables forwarding of the authentication agent.
`-c`	Selects the cipher to use for encrypting the session. `idea` is the default, `arcfour` is the fastest, and `none` is the equivalent of using `rlogin` or `rsh` (no encryption).
`-e`	Sets the escape character for the session.
`-f`	Sets `ssh` in the background after authentication and forwardings are established.
`-i`	Selects the identity file from which the private key for RSA authentication is read.
`-k`	Disables forwarding of Kerberos tickets.
`-l`	Sets the login name for use to the remote machine.
`-n`	Redirects `stdin` from `/dev/nulls` used when `ssh` runs in the background.
`-o`	Used for user-defined options following the format in the configuration file.
`-p`	Sets the port to connect to on the remote host.
`-q`	Activates quiet mode, which suppresses all messages except fatal errors.
`-P`	Uses a nonprivileged port.
`-t`	Forces pseudo-tty allocation.
`-v`	Activates verbose mode (useful for debugging).
`-x`	Disables X11 forwarding.
`-C`	Requests compression of all data.
`-L`	Specifies the local port to forward to the designated remote host and port.
`-R`	Specifies the remote port to be forwarded to the local host and designated port.

For more information on security issues, see Chapter 13, “Improving System Security."

TROUBLESHOOTING

I transferred a binary file, but it doesn't work properly. I can't unzip it, un- `tar` *it, uncompress it, or anything. What should I do?*

Make sure that you set the transfer mode to binary. You can do so by using the `binary` command at the `ftp` prompt.

I'm in the process of transferring a large file and want to check the progress.

Use the hash command. ftp prints the # character onscreen after every data buffer that's processed. The data buffer may vary depending on your version of Linux, but it's typically 1,024, 4,096, or 8,192 bytes.

I was trying to use anonymous FTP, but the site told me that the user anonymous was unknown and that the login failed.

Either you misspelled *anonymous*, or the site doesn't allow anonymous FTP. In the latter case, you must have a valid username and password on the remote computer.

I want to transfer several files, but I don't want FTP to prompt me for each one.

Use the prompt command, which toggles prompting on and off.

I tried to use anonymous FTP, but the site told me that I didn't enter a valid email address as the password.

In the past, the convention during an anonymous FTP connection was to enter guest as the password. Now the convention is to enter your email address. Many FTP sites run special FTP server software that checks the password and makes sure that it's in the form *user@host.somewhere.domain*. Try again and make sure that you enter your full email address correctly.

CHAPTER 33

Surfing the Internet with the World Wide Web

In this chapter

by Steve Burnett

INTRODUCING THE WORLD WIDE WEB

The Internet is a completely distributed network, which means that your computer is connected directly not only with the computer down the hallway, but with thousands of others all over the world. Your computer connects to another computer, which is connected to other computers, and so on.

To make matters more complex, the Internet is international in scope. Virtually every country in the world has some form of access to the Internet. For years, many services were available to get to information (FTP, Gopher, and so on), but none were easy to use. You might want to use FTP, Gopher, Telnet, WAIS, Archie, or another service. To do so, you had to have all the appropriate software. Then you had to know what service to use and when. And so on. Something like the World Wide Web was needed as a form of "information navigator" to make it easier for users to get to information on the Internet.

The Web began as a network and hypertext project at CERN, a European physics research lab, in 1989. Researchers saw a need for people from any location to be able to share and exchange information and documents in real-time from any type of computer. They also wanted a simple and consistent way to handle this information. From this need, the World Wide Web was born.

The Web uses a set ofhypertext links that allow users to easily navigate among documents, graphics, files, audio clips, and so on from sites anywhere on the Internet. When you select a hypertext link in a document, whatever item the link points to is automatically retrieved. One link at a time, Internet users quickly find their way to the various bits of information they want.

UNDERSTANDING THE WEB'S STRUCTURE

The Web is based on a client/server model. The client software package (Web browser software on your computer) contacts a server computer (Web server software) and exchanges messages with that computer through a set of rules that both client and server understand. This set of rules is known as a *protocol*. Web servers and clients communicate through a protocol known as the Hypertext Transfer Protocol (HTTP). When a Web client program retrieves a document from a Web server, the programs are probably communicating by using HTTP. As you'll see later in this chapter, other Internet protocols also may be supported by the Web server.

Of Clients and Servers

The client/server relationship is an important concept in networking and especially in navigation of the Web. A *server* is a computer that offers services for other computers to use. *Services* can be any kind of program, routine, or data provided by the server. For example, a server might return information from a database to which you don't have direct access.

A *client* is a computer that uses services from a server. The client contacts the server and requests some sort of service. Many times, a client computer uses special software designed to interact with a specially designed server program on the server computer.

Under this client/server model, people with different computers in different locations can access information on the same server. You can set up different server computers with different types of data. Because people are using a client software program to communicate with the server, you can develop a different client program for each computer platform that they use. That way, people using Windows or a Macintosh can use client software to access information on a UNIX or Linux server just as easily as UNIX or Linux users can.

To access the Web, you need client software known as a *Web browser*. A Web browser is a program that understands how to communicate to a Web server via the HTTP protocol; it displays information and provides a way to represent hypertext links. Many browsers are available. The most commonly used browsers are Netscape's Navigator and Microsoft's Internet Explorer. You can get a browser in any number of ways: You can get it from your Internet service provider (ISP), buy it in store, download it from the Internet, and so on. After you install the browser and configure the software with your Internet access information, you're ready to go.

Understanding URLs

You get information on the Web by using a descriptive address known as a *uniform resource locator* (*URL*, pronounced *earl*). Think of an URL as a pointer to an object on the Internet that tells you not only where the object is located, but also what it is named and how to access it. Everything you access through the Web has an URL.

The syntax of URLs may look intimidating, but it is really quite straightforward. The following is an example:

```
http://www.ncsa.uiuc.edu/SDG/Software/Mosaic/Docs/whats-new.html
```

Scary? It's really not that bad. The part to the left of the colon (:) specifies the access method to get to the data. This access method defines the protocol used to communicate with the server and also gives a good clue as to the type of interaction that will take place. Table 33.1 lists several valid access methods.

Table 33.1 Valid Access Methods for URLs

Method	Description
`http`	Provides interactive hypermedia links to pages written in Hypertext Markup Language (HTML). This protocol is used to access most Web pages.
`wais`	Accesses a wide area information server (WAIS) site.
`gopher`	Accesses a Gopher server.
`ftp`	Provides an anonymous FTP connection.
`telnet`	Opens a Telnet connection to a site.
`news`	Allows you to read Usenet news.

Before the Web

Many services and sources of information existed before the Web. These services use protocols other than HTTP. However, many Web clients such as Netscape Navigator allow you to access these services from within the browser. For example, you can transfer files to your computer by using FTP, retrieve documents from Gopher servers, perform text searches with WAIS (wide area information server), and read Usenet news.

Following the `://` in the URL is the host name of the server computer you want to contact. After the server name is the directory path to the document you want to view or retrieve. This path depends totally on where the file is located on the remote server. (You might not have a path in some cases, if the file is in a default directory.) Finally, the filename of the document is given. This document can be text, a hypermedia document, a sound file, a graphic, or some other type of file.

So, look again at the example. The URL

```
http://www.ncsa.uiuc.edu/SDG/Software/Mosaic/Docs/whats-new.html
```

uses the HTTP protocol to contact the server computer `www.ncsa.uiuc.edu` and says that you're interested in the document named `whats-new.html` located in the directory `/SDG/Software/Mosaic/Docs`. The `.html` extension on the document name tells your Web client (for example, Netscape Navigator) that this document is written in Hypertext Markup Language (HTML). HTML is a special syntax used to write hypertext pages for the Web.

SEARCHING THE WEB

The Web is huge, and it's getting bigger every day. Rather than click through thousands of pages, you can use search engines to help you find information faster. A *search engine* is a program that looks through its database for information that matches your request. Some search engines, such as AltaVista and Infoseek, search the entire Web and store their information in huge databases. Other search engines search only a specific Web site.

When you see a Search button at a typical Web site, it's usually only for that Web site. When you want to search the entire Web, you need a more general search tool. The following list describes some of the many search engines that scan Web sites across the Internet. Some even let you search other Internet information sources, like those on Usenet or FTP sites.

- **AltaVista** (`http://www.altavista.com`)—For Web and Usenet. You can find anything, anywhere on the Web or Usenet, but you should narrow your search as much as possible; you can easily get too many results back!
- **Yahoo!** (`http://www.yahoo.com`)—For Web, Usenet, email addresses, current news, people searches, city maps, and stocks. Yahoo! isn't really a search engine. It's basically a huge list of Web sites, sorted into categories, that have been submitted by users. It's useful for common information and for getting an idea of just how much—and varied—the information on the Web is. Yahoo! also provides links to search engines.

- **Infoseek** (`http://www.infoseek.com`)—For Web, Usenet, FAQs, current news, email addresses, maps, stocks, and company listings. Infoseek contains a search engine and listing service and is good when you want to search more than the Web or Usenet. Infoseek has a different search language than many of the other search engines.
- **Excite** (`http://www.excite.com`)—For Web, Usenet, and Excite Web site reviews. Excite does conceptual searching of the Web and is good when you're not sure of the exact term you need to search for. Because Excite uses a single-site search engine on many Web sites, it's free.
- **Lycos** (`http://www.lycos.com/`)—For Web, FTP sites, and Gopher sites. Lycos has Yahoo!-like features. It's good for simple searches on common topics. You can search for sounds, graphics, or subjects.
- **Search.Com** (`http:// search.cnet.com/`)—For Web and Usenet. This search engine also lets you search other search engines such as AltaVista, HotBot, or Infoseek. Search.Com provides an A-to-Z listing of other search engines and has a handy utility to suggest which search engines will find what you need.
- **Inference Find!** (`http://www.inference.com/`)—For Web only. Not a search engine itself, Inference Find! groups the results of other search engines and eliminates repeats. As of this writing, it calls WebCrawler, Yahoo!, Lycos, AltaVista, Infoseek, and Excite.
- **HotBot** (`http://www.hotbot.com`)—For Web and Usenet. HotBot is good for finding sites that use a particular technology, such as JavaScript or VRML. You can also narrow your search to a specific geographic location (such as Europe), class of domains (such as `edu`), or a single Web site (such as `www.apple.com`).

Good keywords make your search more effective. You should come up with words that are unique to what you really want to find. Try to avoid heavily used terms, such as *www*, *Internet*, *computer*, and so on. If you do need them, combine them with other more specific terms and Boolean operators to help narrow your search, such as *WWW and Search Engines*.

Note

Most search engines also allow you to use quotation marks ("") to search for phrases. Putting quotation marks around a phrase keeps the words together as a phrase. Without quotation marks, each word in a phrase will be searched for individually. Check your search engine's help for specific details.

You'll probably find that even a search engine lists too many sites to look through. You can reduce the number of sites you find by narrowing your search. Correctly using some simple terms—AND, OR, and NOT—can help you narrow down thousands of sites to just a few.

These terms aren't your everyday AND, OR, and NOT. They come from the symbolic logic system developed by a nineteenth-century mathematician named George Boole. Boolean searches use a basic syntax made up of operators and search terms. Because the terms don't work quite the same as in English grammar, make sure that you get them straight. Table 33.2 shows examples of how to use AND, OR, and NOT.

Table 33.2 Useful Boolean Expressions

Expression	Description
AND or +	Returns pages that contain all your search terms. If all words aren't on the page, the page isn't displayed. Use AND or + when you have dissimilar terms and want to narrow the results to a few precise hits. For example, *BMW AND roadster* or *BMW + roadster* displays only pages that contain both *BMW* and *roadster* on the page.
OR	Returns pages that contain any of your search terms. Use OR to return pages with any of the terms listed in your search. For example, *BMW OR roadster* displays all pages that contain either *BMW*, *roadster*, or both.
NOT	Returns pages that don't contain words specified in your search (not supported by all search engines).

Don't be afraid to experiment. Try several different searches with the same goal in mind so that you can get a better feel for the results that some of these expressions and your search words or phrases return. You'll find that some experimentation with search terms will help you become more adept at narrowing your selections to a manageable size.

Using FTP with a Web Browser

FTP, or File Transfer Protocol, is the method that the Internet uses to exchange files between computers. No matter what you're searching for—software, documentation, FAQ lists, programs, or just about anything else—you probably can get a copy through anonymous FTP.

Anonymous FTP is a service that lets you retrieve data from around the Internet without having an account on that machine. By using anonymous FTP, you can access any files that the system administrators on the remote system have made publicly available.

→ See "Using `ftp` for Remote File Transfer," p. 686

FTP supports ASCII mode transfers for text files and binary mode transfers for other types of files. Fortunately, most Web clients automatically determine the file type for you, so you don't have to worry about it. You usually can determine the type of archive or compression program that was used on the file by looking at the file extension. Table 33.3 lists the most common file extensions you'll encounter.

Table 33.3 Common File Extensions on Binary Files Available Through FTP

Extension	Description
`.Z`	A file compressed with the UNIX `compress` program
`.z`	A file probably compressed with the GNU `gzip` program or the UNIX `compress` program
`.gz`	A file compressed with the GNU `gzip` program
`.tar`	An archive of several files created by the UNIX `tar` program
`.zip`	An archive of several files created by `pkzip`

Sometimes you might find files that have been created by more than one of these methods. For example, the file `programs.tar.Z` is an archive of several files created by the `tar` utility and then compressed with the `compress` utility.

To use a Web client such as Netscape (which has built-in FTP support) to perform anonymous FTP transfers, you replace the protocol portion of the URL with `ftp`. For example, to start an anonymous FTP session to `metalab.unc.edu`, you use the following URL:

```
ftp://metalab.unc.edu
```

This URL causes your Web client to try to make an FTP connection to `metalab.unc.edu` and log you in as an anonymous FTP session. After your FTP session is established, you can navigate through directories and transfer files by clicking the hyperlinks displayed.

Tip #170 from *Steve*

> Most anonymous FTP servers request that you use your email address as your password. If you have problems, check that your email preferences are set correctly in your browser.

To specify a nonanonymous FTP session in Netscape, enter the following:

```
ftp://username@ftp.startup.com
```

`username` is your username, and *`ftp.startup.com`* is the place you want to go. You then are prompted to enter your password.

Note

> When you select a text file to transfer from a remote server in an FTP session, most Web clients display the file onscreen. You need to save the file to disk via a menu selection. Some Web browsers allow you to specify loading a file to disk rather than to the screen.

ON THE WEB

For a listing of FTP sites available via the Web, see the following page:

`http://hoohoo.ncsa.uiuc.edu/ftp/`

USING ARCHIE WITH A WEB BROWSER

Just like with the Web, one major problem you might have with anonymous FTP is figuring out where the files that you're interested in are located on the Internet. To help users locate files, the `archie` system was created. `archie` is basically a search engine for anonymous FTP sites.

Archie is a database query program that contacts anonymous FTP sites around the world and asks each site for a complete list of all its files. `archie` then indexes this information in its own internal database. You can search this database for the location of files on the Internet. Because updating Archie databases is obviously a time-consuming process, the databases are updated usually only about once a month. Thus, it's possible—although unlikely—that the location `archie` gives you is incorrect.

Archie is a popular service. The various Archie servers around the world can get very heavily loaded, and requests can take awhile to complete. Some sites place limits on the number of simultaneous connections to keep the servers from becoming too slow to use. If you try an Archie server and find that it's fully loaded, you can either try a different server or wait a few minutes and try again.

Tip #171 from *Steve*

Many Archie servers now support inquiries via Web forms. To conduct Archie searches, go to the following URL for a list of Archie gateways to the Web. From this page, you can link to many of the mirror sites of the Archie database. Linking to the site closest to you is usually quickest:

`http://archie.emnet.co.uk/`

A list of current Archie servers is maintained at:

`http://archie.emnet.co.uk/services.html`

To connect to one of these servers, telnet to it and log in as `archie`. Each server is slightly different, but most are basically the same. After you log in to a server, you get a prompt such as the following where you can enter your search commands:

```
archie>
```

Different servers have different default search values. To determine what the default setup is for the server that you connect to, use the `show search` command. The `show search` command returns one of the following values:

`regex` — `archie` interprets your search string as a UNIX regular expression.

`exact`	Your search string must exactly match a filename.
`sub`	Your search string matches if a filename contains it as a substring. This search is not case sensitive.
`subcase`	This search is similar to the `sub` search type, except that the case of the letters in the string must match.

You can set the desired search type by using the `set search` command as shown here:

```
archie> set search search-type
```

When you have your search set up the way you want it, you use the `prog` command to search by filename. For example, the following pair of commands

```
archie> set search sub
archie> prog linux
```

performs a search regardless of the case of the Archie database for all files that contain the substring `linux`. For each match that Archie finds, it reports the host computer that has the file, along with the full pathname of the file on that host.

If you get confused or just need some assistance when you're using Archie, type `help` at the `archie>` prompt. You then get information on how to get help in Archie. From the `help>` prompt, type a `?` to see a list of subtopics on which you can get help.

After you find the information you're looking for, you need to exit Archie by typing `exit` or `quit` at the `archie>` prompt.

USING telnet WITH A WEB BROWSER

`telnet` has been around almost as long as the Internet. By using `telnet`, you can connect to databases, library catalogs, and other information resources around the world. Want to see what the weather's like in Vermont? Check on crop conditions in Azerbaijan? Get more information about somebody whose name you've seen online? `Telnet` lets you do this and more. When you telnet to another computer, you're going across the Internet and logging in to that machine. You won't find graphics as you do on the Web; `telnet` is text only.

Note

`gopher` is another early Internet tool, and many Telnet sites are most easily found through Gopher menus. See the following section on Gopher.

To start `telnet` from your browser, enter the URL of the Telnet site you want to go to. For example, the following command starts a `telnet` program and takes you to the location you entered:

```
telnet://pac.carl.org
```

From there, you're out of the browser and have entered "menu land."

→ See "Using telnet to Access Remote Computers," p. 684

Configuring Netscape to Work with `telnet`

`telnet` probably isn't built into your browser. If not, you need to get a `telnet` program, install it on your computer, and then configure the browser to use it. The following is a sample set of instructions for configuring `telnet` for Netscape:

1. From the Netscape Navigator Options menu, choose Preferences.
2. Select Applications and Directories from the available tabs.
3. Select Browse next to the Telnet Application window.
4. Find and select the `telnet` executable.
5. Press Enter. Netscape is now configured.

Most Telnet sites are fairly easy to use and have online help systems. Most also work best—and, in some cases, only—with VT100 emulation. You also might find that many of the resources are now available on the Web.

Tip #172 from *Steve*

`telnet` is no longer quite as common as it once was, because your login name and password are sent unencrypted and are readable by anyone using a packet sniffer. A program called `ssh` is very similar to `telnet`, but is much more secure.

USING gopher WITH A WEB BROWSER

`gopher` is an Internet service that allows you to access information by making selections from a series of menus. `gopher` was one of the first Internet services that made a serious attempt at offering a user-friendly interface.

When you connect to a site that offers Gopher services, you get a menu of available choices. Each menu is either a file or another menu. You can select your choice from the menu without having to know the name or IP address of the destination site or the directory and filenames of the particular information you're asking for. Gopher handles the details for you.

Note

No information resources on the Internet are actually "gopher-specific." Anything you can get through `gopher` can be accessed by other means, such as an HTML Web page, FTP, or `telnet`. In some cases, sites may have chosen to make resources available only via `gopher` for security reasons.

To access a Gopher server with a Web browser, change the protocol part of the URL so that it says `gopher` instead of `http`. For example, the URL for the Gopher server at `metalab.unc.edu` is `gopher://metalab.unc.edu`.

Gopher provides an easy means to navigate the Internet. Unfortunately, the information that Gopher can retrieve may not be well organized, so finding what you want can be a bit of an adventure. Because the items in Gopherspace are presented as a set of menus, you sometimes have to wade through many different menus to get to the file you're searching for. This problem aside, however, a lot of good information is available through `gopher`.

One disadvantage of `gopher` is the lack of a standard subject list for the various `gopher` servers. The administrators for each `gopher` server have organized their information in their own manner. This means that each gopher server you access has different subjects. If `gopher` servers do happen to have some of the same subjects, chances are they aren't named the same way.

ON THE WEB

For a listing of `gopher` sites, see the following:

`http://dir.yahoo.com/Computers_and_Internet/Internet/Gopher/`

ACCESSING USENET NEWS WITH A WEB BROWSER

In the simplest definition, Usenet news (also called *netnews* or simply *news*) is a forum for online discussion. Many computers around the world exchange chunks of information, called *articles*, on almost every subject imaginable. These computers aren't physically connected to the same network; they're logically connected in their capability to exchange data. See Chapter 35, "Surviving Usenet News," for a complete discussion of Usenet news.

News articles on Usenet are divided into newsgroups by subject. These groups are then divided into hierarchies based on very general subject distinctions.

→ See "How Usenet Is Structured," p. 745

Usenet news has discussion on almost any topic that you can think of. It's a great way to find and exchange information.

GETTING ON MAILING LISTS

Another avenue for discussion on the Internet comes from email mailing lists. Mailing lists vary from Usenet news in that the various messages and discussion articles are sent via email rather than via the Usenet news medium.

Why use a mailing list instead of a Usenet newsgroup? Usually, mailing lists are targeted at a smaller group of people. Setting up a new newsgroup on Usenet is fairly difficult because proposal, discussion, and voting periods are required. On the other hand, any system administrator can set up a mailing list. Also, because each mailing list is maintained on one computer, the system administrator has more control over who can be on the list and can deal with problem users more effectively. Some mailing lists, such as those that discuss computer security issues, are restricted to certain people. If you need to be on one of these lists, you have to apply with the list manager to be allowed to subscribe.

FINDING MAILING LISTS

As with Usenet news, mailing lists exist on a wide variety of subjects. A complete list of publicly available mailing lists is posted regularly to the Usenet newsgroup `news.answers`.

ON THE WEB

You can search for mailing lists via the Web at the following site:

`http://www.liszt.com/`

USING MAILING LISTS

Mailing lists are typically set up by using a mail reflector. A *mail reflector* is a special email address that's set up to reflect any mail sent to it back out to a group of people. Usually, two email addresses are associated with a mailing list: that of the list maintainer and that of the list itself.

Suppose that there's an email address for the users of widgets. The email address for the list might be something like `widgets@somewhere.com`. If you send an email message to this list address, it's reflected to all the people who subscribe to the list.

By convention, Internet mailing lists use a special email address for administrative requests, such as subscribing to the list. This address is usually constructed by adding `-request` to the name of the list. So for the imaginary widgets mailing list, the administrative email address would be `widgets-request@somewhere.com`. All mail that addresses administrative topics should be sent to the administrative address.

Each mailing list (and Usenet newsgroup) has its own rules and culture. You should become familiar with the local customs before sending mail out to the list. Usually, you get an introduction message and possibly a list of frequently asked questions (FAQ) when you subscribe to a list. The introduction message contains any special rules that apply to the list. Make sure that you read the FAQ first so that you don't ask the same questions as hundreds of other people.

→ See "Netiquette on Usenet," p. 752

majordomo

One of the most common mailing list programs available is called `majordomo`. `majordomo` is a Perl script that is commonly used on UNIX-based mail servers. The main Web site for `majordomo` is `http://www.greatcircle.com/majordomo/`, where you can download the script and read installation instructions; the FAQ file is located at `http://www.greatcircle.com/majordomo/majordomo-faq.html`.

Tip #173 from Steve

> **Another popular mailing list application is LISTSERV. A FAQ file for the LISTSERV program is available on the Web at `http://www.ou.edu/research/electron/internet/list-faq.htm`.**

`majordomo`, as well as other mailing list managers, does more than simply add and remove names from a subscription list and send mail to everyone on the subscription list: Each has several commands that allow you to query the mailing list manager about the lists. Some of these commands are disabled by the list owner, but they might not be. The best source of information about how a given mailing list is configured is the list owner; many mailing lists maintain a Web site about the list.

Table 33.5 provides a summary of commands `majordomo` responds to. Remember, you should send these commands to the mailing list manager address for a given mailing list, and not the mailing list address itself. Also, if you use a signature file in your email, adding a hyphen on the line just before your signature file, like the example here, prevents the mailing list manager from trying to read your signature file as a set of commands:

```
-
This is my signature file. There are many like it....
```

You can also substitute the word `end` for the hyphen, like this:

```
end
This is my signature file. There are many like it....
```

The commands in Table 35.5 should be in the body of the email you send to the `majordomo` address, not the subject. (If they're in the subject, they don't do anything.) For each command, items contained in brackets (`[]`) are optional; be sure to leave out the brackets around the items when you enter them. An item in angle brackets, such as *<address>*, is a meta-symbol that you should replace with appropriate text (and as with options, without the angle brackets).

Table 33.5 majordomo Command Summary

Command	Meaning
`subscribe` *<list> <address>*	Subscribes you (or your *<address>* if specified) to the named *<list>*.
`unsubscribe` *<list> < address>*	Unsubscribes you (or your *<address>* if specified) from the named *<list>*.

TABLE 33.5 MAJORDOMO COMMAND SUMMARY

Command	Meaning
"unsubscribe *''	Unsubscribes you (or your <*address*>) from all lists. This command might not work if you have subscribed using multiple addresses.
get <*list*> <*filename*>	Gets a file related to <*list*>.
index <*list*>	Returns an index of files you can "get" for <*list*>.
which <*address*>	Finds out which lists you (or your <*address*> if specified) are on.
who <*list*>	Finds out who is on the named <*list*>.
info <*list*>	Retrieves the general introductory information for the named <*list*>.
intro <*list*>	Retrieves the introductory message sent to new users. Nonsubscribers might not be able to retrieve this message.
lists	Shows the lists served by this majordomo server.
help	Retrieves a general message for how to use majordomo.
end	Stops processing commands (useful if your mailer adds a signature).

USING WIDE AREA INFORMATION SERVERS (WAIS)

WAIS (which stands for *wide area information servers*) is a system for searching a large set of databases for information. The term *wide area* implies being able to use a large network, such as the Internet, to conduct searches by using client/server software.

By using WAIS, you can retrieve text or multimedia documents that are stored on databases throughout the Internet. You can think of WAIS as being similar to Gopher, except that WAIS does the searching for you.

Like Gopher, to use WAIS, you need client software or you have to use telnet to connect to a site that provides public access to a WAIS client. You can use an interactive UNIX WAIS client known as *swais*. To use this system, you can telnet to metalab.unc.edu and log in as swais. You then get a menu of databases that you can search. (which stands for wide area information servers) is a system for

CASE STUDY: A MAILING LIST SUBSCRIPTION PROCESS

The most common error for someone new to a mailing list is using the wrong address when attempting to subscribe. Let's look at an example. Brad has an email account through the fictitious company justabody.com. He finds a Web site operated by afakecompany.com focusing on a product he's interested in, so he wants to subscribe to the mailing list and find out more about the product.

The Web site information says the following:

> The address to send information to the mailing list is `coolstuff@afakecompany.com`. If you want to subscribe to the list, send email to `majordomo@afakecompany.com` with "subscribe" in the body of the message, followed by the list's name, like so:
> `subscribe coolstuff`

Brad isn't paying attention, so he sends the following email:

```
From: brad@justabody.com
To coolstuff@afakecompany.com
Subject: subscribe coolstuff
Message content: Please add me to the coolstuff list, thanks.
Brad
```

The coolstuff mailing list is set up to allow only subscribing members to send mail to the list. This decision was made to keep *spam*, or unsolicited commercial email, off the list. So James, the person at A Fake Company who runs the coolstuff mailing list, gets the following email from `majordomo`:

```
Date: Sun, 25 Jul 1999 21:52:57 -0400
From: owner-coolstuff@afakecompany.com
To: owner-coolstuff@afakecompany.com
Subject: BOUNCE coolstuff@afakecompany.com: Non-member submission from [Brad
Davison <brad@justabody.com>]
]]From brad@mail.afakecompany.com Sun Jul 25 21:52:56 1999
Received: from mail.justabody.com (brad@mail.afakecompany.com [348.33.456.112]
(may be forged))
by mail.afakecompany.com (8.8.7/8.8.7) with ESMTP id RWA24521
for <coolstuff@afakecompany.com>; Sun, 25 Jul 1999 21:52:55 -0400
Received: from localhost (brad@localhost)
        by mail.justabody.com (8.8.7/8.8.7) with ESMTP id RWA24521
        for <coolstuff@afakecompany.com>; Sun, 25 Jul 1999 21:51:25 -0400
Date: Sun, 25 Jul 1999 21:51:25 -0400 (EDT)
From: Brad Davison <brad@justabody.com>
To: coolstuff@afakecompany.com
Subject: subscribe
Message-ID: <Pine.LNX.4.04.990345527645530.2264-100000@mail.justabody.com>
Subject: subscribe
Message-ID: <Pine.LNX.4.04.9907252150530.1289-100000@mail.justabody.com>
MIME-Version: 1.0
Content-Type: TEXT/PLAIN; charset=US-ASCII
Please add me to the coolstuff list, thanks.
Brad
```

James sends Brad email suggesting he read the Web site again on how to subscribe to the mailing list. Brad tries again:

```
From: brad@justabody.com
To majordomo@afakecompany.com
Subject: subscribe coolstuff
Message content: subscribe
end
```

Brad receives a Welcome message from `majordomo` welcoming him to the coolstuff list.

CHAPTER 34

USING ELECTRONIC MAIL

In this chapter

by Steve Burnett

UNDERSTANDING EMAIL

Electronic mail, or *email*, has taken over a significant chunk of the technological world. Tens of millions of computer users worldwide have access to electronic mail. A large number of commercial networks or Internet service providers (ISPs) can give you or your organization access to electronic mail around the world.

Email is any program that users on a single computer system or a network of systems use to send and receive electronic messages. At a minimum, you provide the program with the address of the recipient and the message you want to send. The address includes the login name of the person who is to receive the mail. If that user is on another system in a network, the address also includes a means of identifying the target computer system. You either prepare the message while you're using your email program, or you prepare it beforehand by using a text editor such as vi.

→ See "Using vi," p. 207

Using electronic mail has several advantages:

- You can send reports, data, and documents that can reach their destination in a matter of seconds or minutes.
- You don't have to worry about interrupting someone when you send a message, nor are you necessarily interrupted when you receive messages—that's handled by the computer system.
- You don't need to play phone tag or make an appointment to communicate with someone.
- You can send and receive at a convenient time.

When you send email, it's up to the computer system to make the delivery, which can involve putting your message out on a network to be delivered at some other site. At this point, you say that the mail has been sent. Soon after that, the message arrives at the recipient's machine.

If the sender and the receiver are on the same computer system, the sending and receiving take place on one machine. The email system on the target computer verifies that the addressee exists, and the message is added to a file that holds all the email for that user. (If no network is involved, the local computer system verifies the addressee.) The mail-storage file is called the user's *system mailbox* and usually has the same name as the user who's receiving the mail. For example, if your login name is `george`, your system mailbox is the file named `george` in the directory `/var/spool/mail`. When the message has been "delivered" to the mailbox, you say that the mail has been received.

Note

In a common kind of email called Post Office Protocol (POP) mail, email is stored on a remote system and is then retrieved as you read mail. This chapter reflects a full mail system, utilizing the `sendmail` program, which handles the background jobs of sending and receiving email.

Figure 34.1 shows the relationship between sending and receiving email.

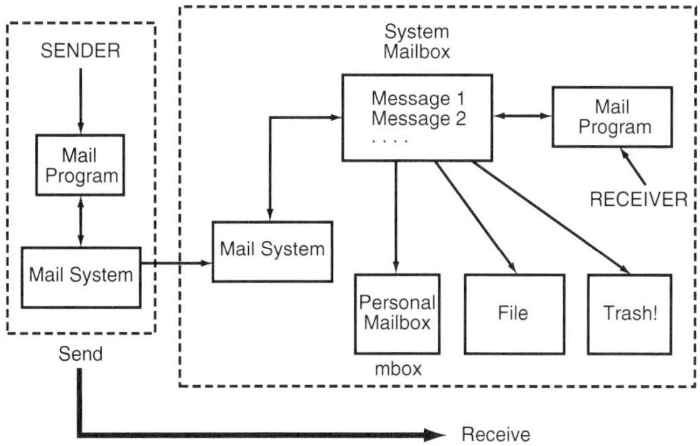

Figure 34.1
Sending and receiving email.

Does the Mail Always Get Through?

When you send email, you might see a message onscreen that says `Mail Sent!` This message means that the mail has been sent—not that it has been received or delivered. Usually, your email system notifies you if your message can't be delivered.

Email messages might not go through for several reasons. If mail is going out to a network, the network address may be correct, but the name of the user on that network may not be correct. Or perhaps the complete address is correct, but because of problems with permissions or quotas, the message cannot be placed in the user's system mailbox. In both cases, the mail is sent but is undeliverable. Another scenario is that the email is delivered but the user's mailbox is corrupted or destroyed. A final possibility is that the recipient ignores email or doesn't log in for several days, weeks, or more.

Your computer system notifies you when you have mail. When you read your email, you can treat it on a message-by-message basis. Some of the things you can do with your mail are the following:

- Delete individual messages after you read them—or without bothering to read them (using email doesn't mean that you won't get junk mail)
- Keep some messages in the system mailbox
- Keep some messages in a personal mailbox
- Keep other messages in individual files or folders
- Reply directly to the sender of a message
- Do a "group reply" to a group of users who all received the same message
- Forward mail to others
- Print your mail

You are responsible for managing your mail so that it doesn't take up any more disk space than necessary. You most certainly don't have to save every piece of email you get. You'll also see that reading your incoming mail is easier if you regularly delete or remove messages from your system mailbox.

Several different email programs are available for Linux, including email programs that are integrated with Web browsers such as Netscape. The most common email interface, available on virtually every UNIX environment, is `mail`. With the `mail` program, you can do the following:

- Manage and view your email
- Include a subject header on email you send
- Include a cc header for sending copies of email to others
- Forward email to others
- Set up mailing lists

The following sections show examples of `mail`. Later in the chapter, you will be introduced to another mail program for Linux—the `elm` mailer.

SENDING EMAIL WITH MAIL

You can send email to an individual, a group of individuals, or a mailing list. Just as when you want to send a paper letter, you must specify the address of the recipient with email. Sometimes you can compose or write a message while you're sending email; at other times, you can send a prepared message; you might even send the output of a command or program with email. When you're using `mail` or `elm`, the message you send has to be a text file—that is, an ASCII file.

> **Note**
>
> The Simple Mail Transport Protocol (SMTP) is used to transfer mail between computers. It now supports only ASCII files. To send a binary file via email, you have to convert the file to ASCII by using the `uuencode` utility. Many more modern GUI-based email clients handle the file conversion and packaging requirements for you.

Regardless of how the message is prepared, you send mail by using a command of the following form:

```
mail address
```

This command starts the `mail` system. You can then compose the mail message and send it to the specified address. In this syntax, *`address`* is the email address of the person who is to receive the message. An address can have several different forms. To send email to someone who has a login ID on the machine you're using, you can use the login ID of that person. For example, to send email to someone on your system whose login name is `george`, you enter the following command:

```
mail george
```

If `george` is on another system that you can access through some network or collection of networks, you must include the name by which that system is known on the network. Suppose that `george` is the name of a user on a computer system whose network name is `apples.startup.com`. You can send email by entering this command:

```
mail george@apples.startup.com
```

The exact form of the address depends on the type of network being used and any local conventions or rules. Ask a local expert or your system administrator about the form of addresses on a network in your company.

To send the same message to several users, you can include each of their addresses on the line with the `mail` command, as in this example:

```
mail fred bill george@quakeserver.afakecompany.com
```

WRITING A MESSAGE WHILE SENDING EMAIL

Many users compose or write messages while they're in the email program rather than compose a message beforehand. This method is usually the quickest—but not the neatest—way to send mail. It's not neat because you have limited editing capabilities while composing your message. Generally, you can deal with only one line at a time. First, you type the command to send email, specify the address(es), and then press Return. Then you type the message, indicating that you're done by typing a period on a line by itself. You can also press Ctrl+d to end the message. For an example of how to send email to a user named `lynn`, enter this command to start the mail system and specify `lynn`'s address on your system:

```
mail lynn
Subject: Congratulations! Lunch Thursday?
```

Now type the message, pressing Return when you want to end a line. The following is a sample message that you might want to send to `lynn` (press Return at the end of each line to space the paragraphs of the message):

```
Lynn,

Just wanted to tell you that I thought you did a great
job at the meeting yesterday! It seems as if we're
finally turning this problem around.

Want to get together for lunch Thursday?
Give me a call.
joe

.
```

You can also end the message with Ctrl+d instead of a period. The computer responds by displaying `EOT`, which means *end of transmission*.

CANCELING A MESSAGE

You can cancel a message while you're writing it, but you can't cancel it after it's sent. To cancel a message while you're writing it, you press whatever key is configured on your system as the interrupt key (usually Ctrl+c or Del). When a message is canceled, it's saved in a file named `dead.letter`, usually in your home directory. You can delete this file or edit it later for another message. When using mail, you must press Ctrl+c twice to cancel (in case you press Ctrl+c or Del by mistake). After canceling your mail message, you see the command-line prompt. The following example shows how the cancel function works:

```
mail lynn
Subject: Congratulations! Lunch Thursday?
Lynn,
Just wanted to tell that I thought you did a great
job<Ctrl-c>
(Interrupt -- one more to kill letter)
```

You now must decide whether you want to continue the letter or kill it. If you decide to continue, you just keep typing the text of the letter as follows:

```
at the meeting yesterday! It seems as if we're finally
turning this problem around.
```

At this point, you decide to cancel the letter again, so you press Ctrl+c or Del. The system responds with (`Interrupt --` one more to kill letter). Because you want to kill the message, press Ctrl+c or Del a second time; `mail` quits, and you see the shell prompt.

Sending a Prepared Message

You might want to use a text editor such as vi to compose a message to be sent by email. If you use a text editor, you have the tools to format the text and check your spelling, for example. What program you use to create the text doesn't matter, as long as you end up with a text or ASCII file.

Suppose that the file you want to send is named `report.txt` and the recipient's address is `tom@kite.fish.com`. Essentially, you can send the file in three ways, as outlined in the following list. In the following examples, the `mail` command uses the option `-s`, and the string that serves as the subject heading is surrounded by quotation marks:

- **Use a pipe**—To send `report.txt` with the `mail` command, you enter the following:

  `cat report.txt ¦ mail -s'' Sales Report'' tom@kite.fish.com`

- **Redirect input**—To send `report.txt` with the `mail` command and the `-s` option, you enter the following:

  `mail -s'' Sales Report'' tom@kite.fish.com < report.txt`

- **Use `~r` to include a file in a message**—To use `mail` to send the file (by using the default `Subject` prompt), you enter these commands:

  ```
  mail tom@kite.fish.com
  Subject: Sales Report
  ~r report.txt
  ~.
  EOT
  ```

You see the system prompt after you complete any of these three methods; the result is the same in any case.

Note

In the third example, you use `~r` to `read`, or include, the file `report.txt` in the email message. This example shows the use of a *tilde command*. To use such commands, you precede a command with the tilde character (~) while you're reading or sending mail. You might find several other tilde commands useful; they're discussed at appropriate points throughout the chapter.

SENDING THE RESULT OF A COMMAND OR PROGRAM BY EMAIL

If you run a command or program that produces results to the screen (known as stdout), you can pipe that output to a `mail` command. Suppose that you have some information in a file called `contrib.lst`, and you want to use the `sort` command to sort the file and then send the results to yourself (login name `bkorn`) and Tom (whom you met earlier in this chapter). To do all that, you enter this command:

```
sort contrib.lst ¦ mail -s ''Sorted Contrib Info'' bkorn tom@kite.fish.com
```

READING YOUR MAIL

Most Linux systems notify you when you log in that you have email. It's up to you to read and act on that email. You can use `mail` or another email program to read any mail you have. As you read your mail, the email program marks each message as read. Depending on what commands you use and how you quit the email program, the messages you've read are kept either in your system mailbox, `/var/spool/mail/$LOGNAME`, or in your login directory in the file named `mbox`.

USING `mail` TO READ MAIL

To read your mail with `mail`, you enter `mail`. If your login name is `bkorn`, for example, you see a display similar to this (what you type is shown in bold):

```
mail
mail     Type ? for help.
"/var/spool/mail/bkorn'': 5 messages 2 new 1 unread
     1 sarah Wed Jan 8 09:17 15/363
     2 tom@kite.fish.com Thu Jan 9 10:18 26/657 Meeting on Friday
U    3 fred_Fri Jan 10 08:09   32/900   New Orders
> N 4 jones Fri Jan 10 13:22   35/1347  Draft Report
N    5 smith@somewhere.com Sat Jan 11 13:21 76/3103 Excerpt from book
?
```

Note the following points about this display:

- The first line identifies the program and says to type a question mark for help.
- The second line indicates that `mail` is reading your system mailbox, `/var/spool/mail/bkorn`, and that you have five messages. Two have arrived since you last checked your mail; one appeared previously, but you haven't yet read it; and two messages have already been read.

- The next five lines give information about your mail. You can ignore the first few characters for now. Each line holds a message number, the address of the sender, the date the message was sent, the number of lines and characters in the message, and the subject (if one was given). Consider the following line:

  ```
  2 tom@kite.fish.com Thu Jan 9 10:18 26/657 Meeting on Friday
  ```

  This line indicates that message number 2 is from `tom@kite.fish.com`—an address that indicates the message came to your machine from another network (mail from a local user is marked with just the user's login ID). The message was sent on Thursday, January 9, at 10:18; it consists of 26 lines and 657 characters. The subject is *Meeting on Friday*.

- A message line starting with `N` indicates new mail—mail received since you last checked your email. A message line starting with `U` indicates unread mail. A message line without `N` or `U` indicates mail you've read and saved in your system mailbox.
- The greater-than character (>) on a message line marks the current message—the message you'll act on next.
- The question mark (?) on the last line is the command prompt from `mail`.

READING THE CURRENT MESSAGE

The current message is marked by the greater-than character (>). To read that message, you can press Return. When you open it, you see something like the following:

```
Message 4:
From jones Fri, Jan 10 13:22 EST 1997
Received: by your.system.com
Date: Fri, 10 Jan 1997 13:22:01 -0500
From: Carol Jones [[jones]]
Return-Path: [[jones]]
To: aborat, lynn, oackerm, bkorn
Subject: Draft Report
Here is a draft of the report I intend to submit next week.
Please take a look at it and let me know your comments.
Thanks.
-----------------------------------Report Starts Here-----------------------------------
Opportunities for Expansion
Prepared by Carol Jones
Over the past 6 months, we've seen an indication of an increase in the
demand for our services. Current market trends indicate that the demand
will continue for at least 18 months and possibly longer. The manager of
our service staff states ''We're up to our necks in new customers and
:
```

The message is displayed one screen at a time. Any time you see a colon, you can press Return to see the next screen or *q* to quit viewing the message. In this case, press Return to see the next screen of the message.

On the last screen, you see `EOF:` (for *end of file*). You can press *q* or Return to get back to the `?` prompt. Notice that the greater-than character still points to the message you've just read. The message that was the current message is still the current message.

Some lines are displayed before the message itself begins. These lines make up the header information, which can be useful. Typically, header information includes the following:

- The message number
- The name of the person who sent the message
- The time the message was sent
- The name of the system that received the message
- The date the message was received
- The "real name" of the sender, as well as his or her login ID
- The return path
- The message recipient(s)
- The subject

All this information is passed on with each email message. The sender is always identified, making forgeries difficult. The real name that appears in the `From` line is taken from a field from the sender's entry in the password file. The mail system uses the `Return-Path` or `Reply-To` information if you generate a reply (as discussed later in this chapter). The `To` line contains the address or list of addresses of the recipients of this message. (This sample message is a group message.) Here, the sender filled in the `Subject` line.

Reading the Next Message

You can read the next message (the message following the current message in your mailbox) in two ways. You can press Return or n to display the next message. It becomes the current message after you read it. You read the next message in the same way you read the current message. After you read the last message in the list, you see the message `'At EOF'`.

Reading Any Message

All the messages in your mailbox are numbered. You can read messages in any order by entering the message number when you see the `?` prompt. For example, to read message number 2, type `2` and press Return. Message number 2 then becomes the current message.

Reading Email from Other Files

When you start `mail`, you read messages kept in your system mailbox, which has the path `/var/spool/mail/$LOGNAME`. Recall from Chapter 16, "Understanding Linux Shells," that `LOGNAME` is the shell variable that holds your login name. If you log in as `bkorn`, your mail is held in `/var/spool/mail/bkorn`. You can read mail from other files that hold complete email messages—that is, messages with the headers and text of the messages. Naturally, you must have read permission for those files.

To read messages from a file, you type the command to start the email program followed by `-f filename` and then press Return. For example, to read the email in the file `mbox`, you enter this command:

```
mail -f mbox¦
```

You can read the mail in that file in the same way you read email from your system mailbox.

Note The `mbox` file is located in your home directory and automatically contains messages you've already read but haven't deleted. These messages are saved to `mbox` when you exit `mail`.

SENDING MAIL WHILE READING

You can send email while you're using the `mail` program to read your messages. To do so, you enter `m address` at the `?` prompt. For an example, follow these steps:

1. Start the `mail` program (type `mail` and press Return).
2. Read some messages or perform other tasks, but at the `?` prompt, enter the following to send email to a user whose login name is `ernie`:

   ```
   m ernie
   ```

3. At the prompt for a subject, type a subject heading, as follows:

   ```
   Subject: Game Time
   ```

4. Type the message, and end it with a period on the last line, as in the following example:

   ```
   Don't forget we're playing V-ball at 6:30
   .
   ```

   The computer responds with the following lines:

   ```
   EOT
   ?
   ```

5. Continue using `mail`.

PRINTING MAIL MESSAGES

When you're using `mail`, you can print the current message to a printer connected to your system. First, you need to make the message you want to print the current message. Then you can enter `¦ lpr` at the `?` prompt. You are, in effect, piping the current message to the `lpr` program.

To print a collection of messages, you can save them in a file and then print the file. See the section "Saving Email to Files with `mail`" later in this chapter for information on effective ways to save messages.

GETTING HELP WITH mail

When you type the command to start your email program, you see a ? prompt. The mail program tells you to type ? for help. To get a list of commands and some information about each command, you type ? and press Return.

After you type ? and press Return, you see a display similar to the following:

```
Mail Commands
t <message list>       type messages
n                  goto and type next message
e <message list>       edit messages
f <message list>       give head lines of messages
d <message list>       delete messages
s <message list>        file append messages to file
u <message list>       undelete messages
R <message list>       reply to message senders
r <message list>       reply to message senders and all recipients
pre <message list>      make messages go back to /usr/spool/mail
p <message list>       print message
m <user list>           mail to specific users
q                      quit, saving unresolved messages in mbox
x                      quit, do not remove system mailbox
h                      print out active message headers
!                      shell escape
cd [directory]            chdir to directory or home if none given
A <message list> consists of integers, ranges of same, or user names
separated by spaces. If omitted, Mail uses the last message typed.
A <user list> consists of user names or aliases separated by spaces.
Aliases are defined in .mailrc in your home directory.
&
```

This listing shows you the commands you can use from the ? prompt. Although some of these commands are explained later in this chapter, the following are some points to note right now:

- In each case, you can use the first letter of the command or type the entire command.
- Items in [] and <> are optional; you don't type the brackets as part of the command.
- You can make the term message list refer to all messages by using *. To save all messages in a file named allmail, for example, type s * allmail and press Enter.
- You can make the term message list refer to a single message number. To save message number 2 to a file named meeting, type s 2 meeting and press Return.
- You can make the term message list refer to a range of message numbers by separating the two message numbers with a hyphen. For example, 2-4 refers to messages numbered 2, 3, and 4. To save messages 2, 3, and 4 in a file named memos, type s 2-4 memos and press Return.
- The term print in the line print message doesn't mean to print messages on a printer. It means to display the messages.
- The edit command is useful for modifying messages before forwarding them to someone else or saving them in a file.

SAVING EMAIL TO FILES WITH MAIL

You'll probably want to save some of the email you receive. Keeping all your mail in your system mailbox is not practical for these reasons:

- You'll have too many messages to wade through when you want to read your mail.
- System administrators often limit the size of your system mailbox. This size limit depends on how your system administrator set up your mailbox. If you reach that limit, you might be prevented from receiving any new mail.
- Your mail won't be organized, and finding important messages or all messages relating to a specific project or topic can be difficult.

Earlier in this chapter, you learned that the messages you've read are saved (unless you say otherwise) in the file `mbox`. You also know that you can read these messages by typing `mail -f mbox` and pressing Return. You can also read messages from other files by using the `mail` command's `-f` option.

You can save the current message in a file in two primary ways (with and without a header) when you use `mail`. With both methods, you can specify a file to hold the message, and the message is added to that file. If you don't specify a file, the message is added to the file `mbox` (your personal mailbox) in your home directory. If you use `q` to quit the `mail` program, the messages are removed from your system mailbox.

When you see the `?` prompt, you can use any of the following methods to save a message:

- Type `s` to add the current message to `mbox` in your home directory.
- Type `s` ***`filename`*** to add the text of the current message to the named file with the headers intact. (This method is useful if you want to use your email program to read the messages later.)
- Type `w` ***`filename`*** to add the text of the current message to the named file without the header information. (This method is useful when you want to use only the text of the messages in a file that may be processed by some other program.)

Tip #174 from
steve

To keep messages in your system mailbox rather than the `mbox` file after you read them, use the preserve command, `pre`. You can use this command with a message list.

You know that messages you've already read are automatically saved to `mbox` unless you use the preserve command.

It's a good idea to get in the habit of specifying a filename when you use the save command, `s`. If you don't specify a filename, the current message is added to the file `mbox`. If you include a message list but don't specify a file, `mail` uses the message list as the name of the file to which it saves the current message. If you use q to quit the email program, the saved messages are removed from your system mailbox.

DELETING AND UNDELETING MESSAGES WITH MAIL

To delete a message from a file of messages you're reading, you use the d command. If you quit the mail program by using q, any messages you deleted with the d command are removed from the file.

You use the d or delete command to mark messages for deletion when you use mail to read your email. If you then quit the program by using q, the marked messages are removed from your mailbox. Unless you've saved them, they're gone for good. For some messages, deleting without saving them is a very good idea.

To delete the current message, type d and press Return. You can also specify a message list.

If you mark a message or a group of messages to be deleted, you can change your mind and undelete the message or messages by using the u command. You must use the u command before you enter q to quit; when you enter q, the messages are gone for good. You use the u or undelete command in the same way you use d or delete.

Tip #175 from *Steve*

To undelete all the messages you marked for deletion, enter u * at the ? prompt.

REPLYING TO EMAIL WITH mail

To reply to email, you use the address specified in the Reply-To header field. If that field isn't present, you use the information in the Return-Path header field. Following are partial headers of two messages; one has both header fields, and the other has only the Return-Path header field. The pertinent fields are in bold in each example.

Message 1:

```
From server@malte.abc.com Mon Nov 8 18:31 EST 1993
Received: from MALTE.ABC.COM by s850.mwc.edu with SMTP
Return-Path: <server@matle.ams.com>
Date: Mon, 9 Nov 98 18:17:15 -0500
Comment: From the DuJour List
Originator: dujour@mathe.abc.com
Errors-To: asap@can.org
Reply-To: <dujour@mathe.abc.com>
Sender: dujour@mathe.abc.com
```

Message 2:

```
From jones Fri, Jan 8 13:22 EST 1999
```

```
Received: by your.system.com
Date: Fri, 8 Jan 1999 13:22:01 -0500
From: Carol Jones <jones>
Return-Path: <jones>
To: aborat, lynn, oackerm, bkorn
Subject: Draft Report
```

To reply to the first message, you use the `Reply-To` address `dujour@mathe.abc.com`. Note that the `Reply-To` and `Return-Path` fields are different. For the second example, you use `jones` to respond to the sender of the message.

Note

You should always use the `Reply-To` address if it's included in the header because it represents the specific address of the sender. When the `Reply-To` address isn't available, the `Return-Path` address usually provides an adequate address back to the sender.

You can let the `mail` program determine the address to use to reply to an electronic mail message. To do so, you can use either of the following commands:

`R`	Addresses a reply to the sender of the message
`r`	Addresses a reply to the sender and all recipients of an email message

With either command, you can specify a message list, as explained earlier in this chapter. Otherwise, the `R` or `r` command applies to the current message.

The following partial header shows how to use these two commands. This header is excerpted from a message from Carol Jones, in which she asks a group to comment on a draft of a report she has prepared:

```
From jones Fri, Jan 8 13:22 EST 1999
Received: by your.system.com
Date: Fri, 8 Jan 1999 13:22:01 -0500
From: Carol Jones <jones>
Return-Path: <jones>
To: aborat, lynn, oackerm, bkorn
Subject: Draft Report
```

To respond to `jones` only, you enter `R` at the `?` prompt. You see the following response:

```
To: jones
Subject: Re: Draft Report
```

The `To` line tells you that the reply is going to one person. The `Subject` header indicates that the message is a reply to the one originally sent.

To make comments for everyone on the distribution list to see, you enter `r` at the `?` prompt. You then see the following response lines:

```
To: jones, aborat, lynn, oackerm, bkorn
Subject: Re: Draft Report
```

The `To` line tells you that the reply is going to everyone on the original distribution list, as well as the author. The `Subject` header indicates that the message is a reply to the one originally sent.

From here on, you enter your message in the manner described earlier in the section "Sending Email with `mail`."

Caution

Be careful about using `r` to reply to a message. Whatever you send is sent to everyone who got a copy of the original message. Because Linux is case sensitive, and most people aren't used to typing capital letters as commands, using `r` is a very common mistake and can sometimes be embarrassing.

Note

Think about what you write and who will read your message before you send a reply. Being sarcastic or scathing doesn't work very well with email; you usually end up sounding like a bully. Using email isn't the same as talking with someone: You don't get a chance to see or hear the person's reactions, and he or she doesn't get a chance to see or hear you either. When you use email, it's a lot easier and more effective to be polite and direct.

You can see how easy it is to forward mail; as soon as you send something to one person, you can never tell where the message will end up or how many people will see it. Think, and be considerate.

→ See "Lack of Visual Reference," p. 748

ROUTING MAIL TO OTHERS

Email is distributed by addresses. Tasks such as forwarding a message, sending copies (cc:) of a message, creating aliases or simpler forms of addresses, and creating mailing lists all involve manipulating addresses. You don't have to do the manipulation directly; the `mail` program has these capabilities built in.

FORWARDING MESSAGES

To forward a message (actually, you're including the message with a message you compose), you must first start `mail` in the same way that you start it to read your messages. Then you use the `m`, `r`, or `R` command to send a message. As you compose your message, you use a tilde command, `~f`, to forward one or several messages. The general form of the `~f` command is `~f` *`msglist`*. The following is a step-by-step example of how to forward a message:

1. Start mail (type mail and press Return). The system responds with something similar to the following:

```
mail Type ? for help.
"/var/spool/mail/bkorn'': 5 messages 2 new 1 unread
     1 sarah Wed Jan 6 09:17 15/363
     2 tom@kite.fish.com Thu Jan  7  10:18  26/657   Meeting on Friday
U    3 fred Fri Jan  8 08:09   32/900   New Orders
> N  4 jones Fri Jan   8 13:22   35/1347   Draft Report
N    5 smith@somewhere.com Sat Jan  9  13:21  76/3103  Excerpt from book
?
```

2. Read message 5 by typing 5 and pressing Return. (The text of that message isn't shown here.) Suppose that you want to forward it to your friends whose addresses are sarah, anglee@hb.com, and lynn@netcong.com.

3. Use the m command to send mail to the addresses listed in step 2, type a subject, and type a beginning for your message, as shown here:

```
? m sarah anglee@hb.com lynn@netcong.com
Subject: Forwarding an excerpt from new Que Linux book
Hi!
I'm forwarding an excerpt I came across from a new book by Que.
It's Special Edition Using Linux, Fifth Edition. I'll be
getting my own copy tomorrow.
Do you want me to pick up a copy for you, too?
```

4. Use the ~f command to forward message number 5 (type ~f 5 and press Return). mail responds with the following message:

```
Interpolating: 5
(continue)
```

5. The cursor is now under the word *continue*. You can continue adding text to your mail message, or you can end it by typing ~. and pressing Return. If you end it, the ? prompt appears.

SENDING A COPY WITH MAIL

You can send a copy of an email message to one or more addresses by putting those addresses on what's known as the *cc: list*. The cc: list works as you expect it to: The mail is sent to the primary address or addresses (those in the To header) and also to the address or addresses in the Cc header. To include addresses in the cc: list, you use the tilde command ~c *address* while you're sending the message.

The following example shows how to send a brief memo to a primary address (wjones) and a copy of it to yourself and another address (your address is bkorn, and the other user's address is ecarlst). You send one to yourself so that you have a copy of the memo. Follow these steps to add a cc: list to the list of recipients:

1. Start mail to send email to the primary address, wjones, and give a subject header. Enter the following commands to achieve this:

```
$ mail fred
Subject: Memo - Sales Agreement with Framistan
```

2. Enter the text of the memo you want to send. For example, type the following:

```
TO:        Fred Jones
Date:     Oct 31, 1999
From:     Henry Charleston
RE:        Sales Agreement With Framistan Motors
On October 27,1999, I held a meeting with the CEO of Framistan Motors.
We concluded and initialed a sales agreement by which Framistan would
purchase 10,000 units of our thermo-embryonic carthurators. The agreement
has been forwarded to the appropriate parties in our organization and
we intend to formally complete the agreement within two weeks.
```

3. Give the `~c` address command to add addresses to the cc: list. For example, type the following to send copies to yourself (`bkorn`) and to `ecarlst`:

```
~c ecarlst bkorn
```

4. To send the message, enter a tilde and period (`~.`) and press Return. The `EOT` message appears, followed by the shell prompt.

Tip #176 from *Steve*

To review and possibly modify the headers on an outgoing message, you can enter `~h` while you're composing the message. You're shown the headers one at a time, and you can modify them.

When a message is sent this way, all the recipients can see the headers `To` and `Cc`. Anyone who replies to the message with the `r` command will send the reply to every address in the `To` and `Cc` lists, as well as to the author.

You can customize `mail` so that it always prompts you for a `Cc` header in the same way that it prompts you for the `Subject` header (this topic is discussed later in the section "Customizing Your `mail` Environment"). Of course, you can keep from entering anything in the `Cc` list by pressing Return.

Using Aliases and Mailing Lists

The`mail` program, like most email programs, allows you to create an alias for an address and a group alias for a list of addresses. You can treat the group alias as a mailing list. Using an alias for an individual address is easier than using the regular address because the alias is typically shorter and easier to remember.

To set an individual or group alias for one mail session, you use the `alias` command at the `?` prompt while you're reading your email. To make the aliases more useful, put the aliases in a file named `.mailrc` in your home directory (as described in the following section).

The following is an example of setting and using aliases with the `mail` program:

1. Start `mail` by entering `mail` at the prompt. After the headers are presented, you see the `?` prompt:

```
mail Type ? for help.
"/var/spool/mail/bkorn'': 5 messages 2 new 1 unread
     1 sarah Wed Jan  5 09:17  15/363
     2 croster@kite.fish.com Thu Jan  6 10:18  26/657    Meeting on Friday
U    3 wjones Fri Jan  7 08:09  32/900    Framistan Order
> N  4 chendric Fri Jan  7 13:22  35/1347   Draft Report
N    5 kackerma@ps.com Sat Jan  8 13:21  76/3103   Excerpt from GREAT new Linux
?
```

2. To set up an individual alias, use the `alias` command followed by the alias for the address. The following example creates the alias `ros` for the address `croster@kite.fish.com`:

   ```
   alias ros croster@kite.fish.com
   ```

3. Use the `ros` alias in an address; `mail` expands it to its complete form. For example, you can enter the command `m ros` to start a message you want to mail to `croster@kite.fish.com`.

To set up a group alias, you use the `alias` command followed by the alias for the addresses. The following creates an alias called `friends` and then forwards some mail to the group:

```
alias friends chendric karlack abc.com!homebase!fran eca@xy.srt.edu
m friends
Subject: Excerpts from new Linux book - get a copy!
~f 5
Interpolating: 5
~.
EOT
?
```

CUSTOMIZING YOUR `mail` ENVIRONMENT

You can customize your `mail` environment by putting commands or set-environment variables in the `.mailrc` file in your home directory. The `mail` program checks that file whenever you use the program. You can set quite a few environment variables and commands in `.mailrc`, and different mail programs use different commands. Check your man page for your mail program for a list of all the `.mailrc` options. Some of the commands `mail` recognizes are given earlier in the section "Getting Help with `mail`"; this section describes a subset of the commands and variables that can be used in the `.mailrc` file. Table 34.1 lists these commands; Table 34.2 lists the environment variables.

TABLE 34.1 `mail` COMMANDS

Command	Definition
`#`	Denotes a comment. No action is taken.
`alias`	Sets an individual or group alias. Used as `alias` *`alias-nameaddress-list`*.
`set`	Sets an environment variable. Used as `set` *`variable-name`* or `set` *`variable-name=string`*.

Tip #177 from *Steve*

You can issue any of the commands in Table 34.1 from the `?` prompt any time you use `mail`; these commands are active only for that session.

TABLE 34.2 mail ENVIRONMENT VARIABLES

Variable	Definition
`askcc`	Prompts for the cc: list after the message is entered. Default is `noaskcc`.
`asksub`	Prompts for the `Subject` list before the message is entered. Enabled by default.
`noheader`	Doesn't print header information on available messages when you start `mail`. Disabled by default.
`ignore`	Ignores interrupt characters when you enter messages. This variable is useful if you have a "noisy" connection over some telephone or other communication lines. Default is `noignore`.
`metoo`	Allows you to receive messages sent to a group alias that contains your address. When you have your name in a group alias, a message normally isn't sent to you. Default is `nometoo`.

Tip #178 from *Steve*

You can set a systemwide environment by putting the commands or set variables in the `/etc/mail.rc` file.

The following example sets up the `.mailrc` file so that you use the commands and environment variables listed in Tables 34.1 and 34.2. The pound sign (#) is used to document the work. You can create this file by using vi or any other editor that can produce a text or ASCII file.

```
# .mailrc file for D. Wayne Love
# make sure interrupts are NOT ignored
set noignore
# set variables so that prompts for Subject and Cc always appear
set asksub
set askcc
# individual aliases
alias billy wcuth
alias ben benjamin@flagstaff.abaced.com
alias me dwlove
# group aliases, mailing list
alias mercs miles@dendarii.net quinn taura
alias research jones brown smith
alias googol djames bkorn cam@googol.org bkorn
```

Place these statements in the .mailrc file. Now whenever you start mail, these command statements are processed.

QUITTING THE mail PROGRAM

As you read email in a mailbox, you can read, skip, or delete messages. (You'll learn about deleting messages later in this chapter.) These actions don't take place in the mailbox itself, but in a temporary copy of the mailbox. You can quit the email program so that your mailbox is changed by your actions (the modified temporary copy replaces the original mailbox), or you can quit so that your mailbox is unchanged regardless of what you did during your email session.

QUITTING AND SAVING CHANGES

To quit the mail program and save the changes that occur, press *q* and then Return at the ? prompt. You see the shell prompt again. When you quit mail this way, messages you read but didn't delete are saved in a file named mbox in your home directory.

Suppose that you use mail to read your mail. Your login name is bkorn, and your home directory is /home/bkorn. When you enter mail to start the mail program, you see the following screen of information:

```
mail Type ? for help.
"/var/spool/mail/bkorn'': 5 messages 2 new 1 unread
     1 sarah Wed Jan   8  09:17    15/363
     2 tom@kite.fish.com Thu Jan   9  10:18 26/657    Meeting on Friday
U    3 fred Fri Jan   10  08:09    32/900    New Order
> N  4 jones Fri Jan   10  13:22    35/1347    Draft Report
N    5 smith@somewhere.com Sat Jan   11  13:21    76/3103    Excerpt from book
?
```

Now suppose that you read the current message by pressing Return, and then you read message 1 by typing 1 and pressing Return at the ? prompt. If you press *q* and then Return to quit, you see the following information:

```
Saved 2 messages in /home/bkorn/mbox
Held 3 messages in /var/spool/mail/bkorn
```

The two messages you read are saved in the file mbox in your home directory; the other three messages are saved in your system mailbox, /var/spool/mail/bkorn.

If you save read messages like this often, mbox can become quite large. You might want to print that file occasionally and delete it. You can also read the mail from that file as though it were your system mailbox, as described later in this chapter.

Note

You can read mail and indicate that the current message is to be kept in your system mailbox, /var/spool/mail/bkorn, and not in the file mbox. To do so after you read a message, you enter pre (for preserve) at the ? prompt.

Quitting and Not Saving Changes

The other way to quit the mail program is to press *x* and then Return at the ? prompt. When you do that, you exit the program with no changes to your system mailbox or any other file—as if you didn't read your mail at all. You then see the shell prompt. You might want to exit the mail program in this way when you want to leave the program but save the mail in your system mailbox.

Using the elm Mailer

As stated earlier in this chapter, several different mail programs are available for Linux. Each has its own advantages and disadvantages.

One mail reader that comes with the Red Hat distribution of Linux is the elm mailer. This mail program is a screen-oriented mailer rather than a line-oriented one. It provides a set of interactive menu prompts and is easy to use. Virtually everything that you can do with mail can be done under elm, and usually much more easily!

Because elm is easy to use, the following sections just touch on the highlights of using it. You can find more in-depth information by using elm's online help or by reading its man page.

Starting elm

To start a mail session with elm, type elm at the command prompt. If this is the first time you've used elm, it prompts you for permission to set up a configuration directory in your account and create an mbox mail file if one doesn't exist. You see the following as you start elm for the first time:

```
$ elm
Notice:
This version of ELM requires the use of a .elm directory in your home
directory to store your elmrc and alias files. Shall I create the
directory .elm for you and set it up (y/n/q)? y
Great! I'll do it now.

Notice:
ELM requires the use of a folders directory to store your mail folders in.
Shall I create the directory /home/gunter/Mail for you (y/n/q)? y
Great! I'll do it now.
```

After elm creates its directory and mbox file, it runs the main mail program. It is a full-screen-oriented mailer. Your screen clears, and you see a display similar to the following:

```
Mailbox is '/var/spool/mail/gunter' with 2 messages [ELM 2.4 PL25]
N  1   Nov 11 Jack Tackett     Linux book
N  2   Nov 11 Jack Tackett     more ideas
You can use any of the following commands
by pressing the first character;
d)elete or u)ndelete mail, m)ail a message,
r)eply or f)orward mail, q)uit
To read a message, press <return>. j = move down, k = move up, ? = help
Command:
```

At the top of the screen, `elm` tells you where your system mailbox is located, how many messages are in it, and what version of `elm` you're running. `elm` then lists one line for each message in your mailbox. It places the letter `N` before each new message, just like the `mail` program. The summary line for each message tells you the message status, the message date, the sender, and the subject. (As always, your display may vary slightly depending on your version of `elm`.) The current message is highlighted in the list (in the preceding listing, the current message appears in boldface).

USING `elm` COMMANDS

At the bottom of the screen is a command summary that tells you what commands you have available for the current screen. As you can see in the preceding example, you can delete or undelete mail, mail a message, reply to a message, forward mail, or quit. Pressing the *j* key moves the message selection to the previous message; the *k* key moves it to the next message. Help is available if you press the *?* key. The `Command:` prompt at the bottom of the screen tells you to press a command key for `elm` to do something.

As you can see, `elm` is very easy to use because of the large number of prompts and onscreen help that's available. Table 34.3 lists all the commands that can be executed from within `elm`.

TABLE 34.3 COMMAND SUMMARY FOR `elm`

Command/Keystroke	Description
Return, Spacebar	Displays the current message
¦	Pipes the current message or tagged messages to a system command
!	Escapes the shell
$	Resynchronizes the folder
?	Displays online help
+, [rpa]	Displays the next index page
-, [lpa]	Displays the previous index page
=	Sets the current message to the first message
*	Sets the current message to the last message
number+Return	Sets the current message to *number*
/	Searches subject lines for a pattern
//	Searches entire message texts for a pattern
]]	Saves the current message or tagged messages to a folder
[[	Scans the current message for calendar entries
a	Changes to "alias" mode
b	Bounces (remails) the current message
C	Copies the current message or tagged messages to a folder
c	Changes to another folder

TABLE 34.3 COMMAND SUMMARY FOR `elm`

Command/Keystroke	Description
`d`	Deletes the current message
Ctrl+d	Deletes messages with a specified pattern
`e`	Edits the current folder
`f`	Forwards the current message
`g`	Sends a group (all recipients) reply to the current message
`h`	Displays the header with a message
`J`	Increments the current message by one
`j, [dpa]`	Advances to the next undeleted message
`K`	Decrements the current message by one
`k, [upa]`	Advances to the previous undeleted message
`l`	Limits messages by specified criteria
Ctrl+l	Redraws the screen
`m`	Mails a message
`n`	Moves to the next message, displaying the current message and then incrementing
`o`	Changes `elm` options
`p`	Prints the current message or tagged messages
`q`	Quits, maybe prompting for deleting, storing, and keeping messages
`Q`	Acts as a quick quit—no prompting
`r`	Replies to the current message
`s`	Saves the current message or tagged messages to a folder
`t`	Tags the current message for further operations
`T`	Tags the current message and goes to the next message
Ctrl+t	Tags messages with a specified pattern
`u`	Undeletes the current message
Ctrl+u	Undeletes messages with a specified pattern
`x`, Ctrl+q	Exits, leaving the folder untouched; asks whether you want to exit if you have changed the folder
`X`	Exits, leaving the folder untouched, unconditionally

PROJECT: USING THE MUTT EMAIL CLIENT

Mutt is a freeware mail client that is rapidly gaining in popularity. Although comparative novices can use it perfectly well (by default, Mutt looks and works much like the `elm` client),

Mutt is especially popular among more knowledgeable users because of its extreme configurability.

Some of the primary features of Mutt include the following:

- Color support
- Support for message threading
- MIME support—including RFC2047 support for encoded headers and PGP/MIME (RFC2015)
- POP3 support
- Support for multiple mailbox formats including `mbox`, MMDF, MH, and maildir
- Key bindings (by default, identical to `elm`)
- Capability to search using regular expression
- Support for Delivery Status Notification (DSN)
- Capability to include attachments from the command line when composing
- Capability to reply to or forward multiple messages at once
- `.mailrc`-style configuration files
- Installation process using GNU `autoconf`

WHERE TO GET MUTT

Mutt is distributed under the GNU public license terms on the Red Hat 6.0 installation CD-ROM, in the Mail directory of the Applications section. An international version of Mutt that contains support for PGP is available from several FTP servers, including `ftp://ftp.gbnet.net/pub/mutt-international/` among others.

FOR MORE INFORMATION ON MUTT

The Mutt home page is at `http://www.mutt.org/index.html`. It contains links to the online Mutt manual by Michael Elkins (at `http://www.mutt.org/doc/manual/`) and the Mutt FAQ by Felix von Leitner (at `http://www.math.fu-berlin.de/~leitner/mutt/faq.html`). The Mutt home page also contains information on several mailing lists devoted to the mail client.

CHAPTER 35

Surviving Usenet News

In this chapter

by Steve Burnett

WHAT IS USENET NEWS?

With the explosive growth of the Internet, Usenet news has attracted lots of attention. Many online services now offer access to Usenet. But what's Usenet? Usenet—short for *user network*—is a proto-network of machines that exchange information grouped into subject hierarchies. The term *proto-network* is used because Usenet isn't a physical network in the normal sense. It's made up of all the computers that exchange Usenet news.

In the simplest definition, *Usenet news*, *netnews*, or simply *news* is a forum for online discussion. Many computers around the world exchange chunks of information, called *articles*, on almost every subject imaginable. These computers aren't physically connected to the same network; they're logically connected in their capability to exchange data. Thus, they form the logical network referred to as Usenet. In this chapter, the terms *Usenet*, *news*, and *netnews* are used interchangeably.

Note

The software that drives Usenet is divided into two parts: newsreaders (the software that users use to read and post news articles) and the software that processes articles and transfers them between systems.

Many people initially think of a PC bulletin board system (BBS) when trying to understand Usenet. Although Usenet news does bear some similarity to a BBS at first glance, some very substantial and important differences are apparent upon closer inspection:

- The various news articles on different subjects don't reside on one computer, as with a BBS. They're sent from computer to computer via a store-and-forward mechanism. Each site that receives news exchanges articles with one or more neighbors in transactions that are known as *news feeds*. As a result, news articles take time to propagate from place to place.
- No one is in charge. Yes, you read that right. Usenet has no overall manager, such as a BBS sysop (system operator). Each site has a good deal of autonomy. Usenet news has been described, very accurately, as "organized anarchy."

In general, Usenet news is divided into two logical parts: the programs and protocols that make up the mechanism for posting articles and transferring news articles between computers, and the user programs for reading and posting news articles. This chapter deals primarily with the user portion.

A USENET GLOSSARY

Usenet news has its own structure and culture, which are discussed later in the section "Usenet Culture." Usenet also has a terminology all its own. These "buzzwords" tend to confuse new users, especially those who use BBS systems. Table 35.1 provides a brief glossary of common terms found on Usenet.

TABLE 35.1 COMMON TERMS ENCOUNTERED ON USENET

Term	Definition
Article	A single message posted to a newsgroup.
AFAIK	Acronym for *As Far As I Know*.
Bandwidth	An engineering term referring to the amount of data a given transmission medium can hold. Commonly used as in the phrase *waste of bandwidth* for articles that contain little useful information.
BTW	Acronym for *By the Way*.
FAQ	An acronym for the *Frequently Asked Questions* list. Many newsgroups post a FAQ on a regular basis. It's usually considered impolite to post a question with the answer already in the FAQ for a group.
Flame	An article that's full of rude, angry, insulting statements directed at another person.
FYI	Acronym for *For Your Information*.
Hierarchy	Usenet's system of grouping newsgroups into a tree structure based on subject.
IMHO	Acronym for *In My Humble Opinion*.
Newsgroup	A logical group of articles that are about one general subject.
Newsreader	A user program, such as `rn`, that's used to read and post articles to Usenet.
net.personality	Someone who's famous within the Usenet or Internet community.
net.police	A mythical organization responsible for enforcing the rules on Usenet. Typically used as sarcasm.
Netiquette	The etiquette of Usenet.
Newbie	Someone who's new to using Usenet news.
Quoting	Including parts of a message to which you're responding. Most news-readers allow you to quote articles. You should quote only relevant portions of an article to save bandwidth. Sometimes also referred to as *quotebacks*.
ROFL	Acronym for *Rolling On the Floor, Laughing*.
RTFM	An acronym for *Read The Forgotten Manual*. Typically used as in "Here's a short answer to your question. RTFM for more info."
Post	To submit an article to a newsgroup.
Signal-to-noise	Engineering term referring to the ratio of the amount of data to the amount of background noise. On Usenet, it refers to how much useful information is in a newsgroup versus the amount of off-topic background chatter. A high signal-to-noise ratio refers to a newsgroup that has lots of useful information and very little off-topic chatter. Signal-to-noise can also be used as a descriptive term for a specific person.

Table 35.1 Common Terms Encountered on Usenet

Term	Definition
Signature	A short file that's included at the end of all your posts. Typically includes your name, email address, and possibly a witty quote of some sort.
Sigfile	See *signature*.
Smileys	Common symbols for denoting emotion in a post or email message. For example, :-) and :-(are a happy face and a sad face. (Tilt your head toward your left shoulder and look at them sideways.)
TIA	Acronym for *Thanks In Advance*.

A Brief History

In late 1979, two graduate students at Duke University began considering how to connect UNIX computers so that they could exchange text messages. Another graduate student at the University of North Carolina became involved in this effort and wrote the first news transfer system, which consisted of a collection of shell scripts. This software was installed on the first two Usenet sites, `unc` and `duke`. In early 1980, another computer at Duke, `phs`, was added. The news software was eventually rewritten in C for public distribution. It became known as the *A News* software.

As the news software grew in popularity, it quickly became obvious that the current news transport software couldn't handle the increasing flow of news. Programmers at the University of California at Berkeley began to rewrite the current A News software to increase its capabilities. This new version, known as *B News*, was released in 1982.

Throughout this time, news articles were being transferred by using the *UNIX-to-UNIX Copy Program* (*UUCP*) protocol. As more sites joined the news network, the network load grew to unmanageable levels. Soon realizing that UUCP no longer worked as the main transport protocol for news, people began looking to the Internet and the TCP/IP protocols for help. In 1986, a software package that implemented the *Network News Transport Protocol* (*NNTP*) was released. This protocol is defined in RFC 977. NNTP allowed news articles to be exchanged by using TCP/IP instead of the slower UUCP protocol. It also allowed users to read and post news from remote machines so that the main news processing software didn't have to be installed on every computer.

When NNTP became available on the Net, the already rapid growth of the Usenet system exploded. The current news-processing software, B News, quickly became too slow to handle the increasing news flow. In 1987, Henry Spencer and Geoff Collyer of the University of Toronto developed a new news-processing software, *C News*. Then Rich Salz developed a news transport system known as *INN*, one of the most widely used news servers on the Internet.

The Usenet news system continues to grow at a rapid pace. Other commercial information service providers are now carrying Usenet news as part of their online services. Several BBS networks, such as FidoNet, also carry Usenet news.

Note

An excellent reference for the history of Usenet news is the news article "Usenet Software: History and Sources," by Dr. Gene Spafford. You can find this article on the World Wide Web at `http://www.faqs.org/faqs/usenet/software/part1/`.

How Usenet Is Structured

Usenet is made up of literally many thousands of newsgroups. How many, exactly? Well, nobody knows for sure—well over 20,000. You can check out thousands of groups on virtually every topic, and that number is growing every day. The topics range from silly or pointless to focused and precisely helpful.

Group Hierarchies

With so many different newsgroups, trying to find information on the subjects that you are interested in would be a nightmare if the newsgroups weren't organized in some way. Usenet newsgroups are organized in a hierarchy based on subject. The names of the newsgroups are made up of subnames, each separated by a period. These names go from a general category to a specific category as you read the name from left to right. At the top of the hierarchy are several standard group categories, plus lots of specialized categories. These standard categories are well established. Table 35.2 lists the top-level group standard categories in the Usenet news system.

Table 35.2 Top-Level Group Standard Categories in the Usenet Hierarchy

Class	Description
`comp`	Many different computer-related topics
`misc`	Miscellaneous topics that don't easily fit into another category
`news`	Various topics that relate to the Usenet news system itself
`rec`	Recreational and hobby subjects
`soc`	Social issues
`sci`	Various scientific topics
`talk`	Subjects designed for ongoing conversations

As with everything else on the Internet, there are exceptions to the rules in Table 35.2. Many other top-level hierarchies exist; most are devoted to different regions of the world. For example, the ba and triangle group hierarchies are concerned with topics of interest to the San Francisco Bay area and the North Carolina Research Triangle Park area, respectively.

One of these additional group hierarchies deserves special discussion. The alt hierarchy has very relaxed rules for newsgroup creation. Virtually anyone can create a group under the alt hierarchy; however, creating a newsgroup under any other top-level group is extremely difficult. The alt hierarchy carries many newsgroups that discuss topics that are out of the mainstream of society. In fact, many people find some of the topics in the alt hierarchy to be objectionable. Many Net debates on censorship have started because sites decided to ban part or all of the newsgroups in the alt hierarchy.

NEWS DISTRIBUTIONS

In addition to grouping articles in hierarchies, Usenet also provides a feature for limiting the spread of an article within the news system. New distributions provide a mechanism for limiting articles to a particular geographic area. If a distribution is set to a particular area, only sites within that distribution area receive the article. The system administrator at each site decides what distributions apply to that site.

Why limit the distribution of an article? Suppose that you live in North Carolina and you're posting a meeting announcement for a local user group meeting. It's unlikely that Usenet readers in Australia are interested in your meeting. By limiting the distribution of your article to the appropriate geographical area, you can save network bandwidth, reduce the cost of sending your message, and reduce the aggravation of users around the world who have to read your message.

You can limit the distribution of your article by including a `Distribution:` line in the header of your article as you post it. Most newsreaders ask you for the distribution when you post an article. After the colon in the `Distribution:` line, enter the appropriate geographical distribution. Table 35.3 lists some commonly used news distribution areas.

TABLE 35.3 COMMONLY USED NEWS DISTRIBUTION VALUES

Value	Explanation
`local`	Typically, articles with a local distribution are limited to a group of local news servers within your organization. This distribution is often used for local organizational newsgroups.
`nc`	Every state has a statewide distribution that's the same as the postal abbreviation for the state. The `Distribution:nc` used in this example limits the article to machines within the state of North Carolina.
`us`	Sends the article to all Usenet sites in the United States.
`na`	Sends the article to all Usenet sites in North America.
`world`	Sends the article to every reachable Usenet site in the world. Typically, this distribution is the default if no other distribution value is specified.

Your site may have some additional distributions that apply. You might be able to use organization-wide or regional distributions to determine the scope of your article. In general, you should try to pick a distribution that sends your article only to the areas where it will be of interest.

NO CENTRAL AUTHORITY

That Usenet has no central authority mystifies many people. Your local system administrator really has authority over only the local system. No central group or organization dictates policy or takes complaints. Despite this glaring lack of regulated structure, Usenet works remarkably well. In fact, many people argue that it works better than if some central authority existed.

How do things keep working in an orderly manner? Usenet is run by cooperation between sites and by customs that have evolved over its life.

Usenet tends to be very good at policing itself. If a user starts to abuse the network, you can rest assured that the user and his or her system administrator will get thousands of email messages and several phone calls about the problem. This response usually results in quick problem resolution.

USENET CULTURE

Usenet has a particular culture all its own. You should take some time to try to become familiar with the facets of this culture before diving in. Life on Usenet will be much easier if you do.

In the past few years, many online communication services have added Usenet news as a feature. As a result, tens of thousands of people who are new to Usenet have started reading and posting Usenet news. Many of these users have complained about Usenet participants being rude or generally unlike the users of their online service. Well, the culture of Usenet is different from almost any other information service that you'll find. It's not better or worse—just different. If you try to make allowances for differences in Net culture, you'll probably find that your experiences on Usenet are a bit easier to handle.

Well over 1 million people—probably several million, though no one knows for sure—read and post Usenet news articles daily. These people are from all occupations, all walks of life, and many different countries around the world. Because Usenet news is carried on computers all over the world, it truly forms an international community. Many of the people that you encounter on Usenet don't speak English as a primary language. You can't assume that the people reading your articles share your cultural background, ethnic group, religion, or social values. The most that you can assume is that whoever reads your article is probably very different from you in several ways.

Tip #179 from *Steve*

One aspect of Usenet culture, the *flame*, is usually an unpleasant experience for new users. A flame is a rude message, usually degrading and filled with insults that someone posts in response to one of your articles. Unfortunately, as you'll see, you can do very little about flames other than ignore them. Usenet is far too large a place for you to try to make everyone happy, and some people really seem to like flaming other people just for the fun of it. Perhaps they find it cheaper than psychotherapy....

Lack of Visual Reference

One problem with electronic communications is that you lack any kind of visual input during the conversation. When you talk to another person face to face, you constantly receive information on a conscious and subconscious level from the other person's body language. Because you can't see the other people who read and post on Usenet, these visual cues are missing. Because you typically use body language and visual cues to determine emotion and feeling, you can easily misunderstand someone's post.

Fortunately, you can use several conventions on Usenet to replace part of the missing visual cues. You can place added emphasis on a particular phrase by surrounding it in asterisks, as in `I *really* mean it!`. Also, the use of all capital letters is considered shouting. If you accidentally post an article with your Caps Lock key on, several people will probably tell you about it.

You can also express emotions by writing them into your message. For example, if you make a sarcastic statement, you can make sure that it's understood as such by adding `<sarcasm>` at the end of the line. *Smileys*, also known as *emoticons*, also work to add emotion to your post. A smiley is an ASCII representation of a face, which you look at sideways to see clearly. For example, :-) is a happy, smiling face, and :-(is a sad face.

ON THE WEB

A canonical list of smileys is available at the following site. Have a look at it if you're really interested; some of them are quite funny and original, but the happy and sad faces are the most commonly used. Using some of the longer or rarer ones will likely result in the same effect as using obscure words in common conversation–you'll just confuse people.

`http://www.eff.org/pub/Net_culture/Folklore/Arts/smiley2.list`

Newsgroup Culture

Just as people are different, each newsgroup on Usenet has a different culture. Each newsgroup has a different subject focus and attracts different types of people. In some groups, you may find large numbers of college students, whereas in others, you may find primarily research scientists.

Some of the more technical hierarchies, such as `comp` and `sci`, tend to be more oriented toward factual discussion, although heated debates do take place. Members of these groups are usually interested in discussing facts and issues related to some technical subject. When you post here, make sure that you take time to carefully compose your article and have references for the various points that you make.

The less technical hierarchies, such as `rec`, tend to be somewhat more opinion-oriented. Remember, you'll probably get replies to your articles that reflect other people's opinions that are quite different from your own. Groups in the `talk` hierarchy, along with some of the `misc` groups, get into some very heated discussions. Many of these groups discuss very sensitive topics such as abortion and gun control. Be careful in these groups if you're new to Usenet. Make sure that you take time to get familiar with the group before posting. Be prepared to receive strongly worded replies and email about your articles. Many of the people here hold very strong beliefs.

Note

When you first start reading a newsgroup, you should take some time to familiarize yourself with the culture of the particular group before posting. Read the group for at least a few days, and try to get a feel for the tone of the articles and the things that are considered to be acceptable and unacceptable behavior. Look for a FAQ to get a feel for the group (if one hasn't been posted recently in the newsgroup, a search using one of the search engines on the Web can help).

In a few newsgroups, posting articles is restricted. These groups are known as *moderated newsgroups*. Moderated newsgroups are managed by a person known as a *moderator*. All articles posted to the group must be approved by the moderator before posting. The moderator decides whether the content of the article is appropriate to the group and, if so, posts the article to the group. Most news software automatically detects whether a newsgroup is moderated, and if so, it emails your article to the moderator instead of posting it directly.

Reading and Posting News

Now that you're familiar with Usenet, you're ready to look at the basic process for reading and posting news articles. The following sections describe reading and posting news in general terms; the exact details depend on the news-reading software that you're using. Many different software packages are available for interacting with news, and each of them is different. Many people use a Web browser with an integrated newsreader, such as Netscape. Others prefer to use a line-oriented tool, such as `rn`. These general concepts should apply across all news reading software.

Subscribing to Newsgroups

The first thing you should do when you start reading news is to decide which newsgroups you want to read. The process of selecting the newsgroups is known as *subscribing*.

Most newsreaders offer you a list of available newsgroups so that you can select the ones in which you're interested. The actual process of subscribing varies among news-reading software packages, but it usually involves selecting a series of newsgroups from a list. From then on, only the groups that you've subscribed to are visible when you read news. You can always subscribe to additional groups anytime you want or unsubscribe from a group in which you're no longer interested.

Remember the earlier mention of over 20,000 newsgroups? If your newsreader is set to download the entire list of all newsgroups carried by your news server, receiving this list may take awhile.

READING NEWS

After you subscribe to your newsgroups, you can begin reading news. You select a newsgroup from a list of your subscribed groups. Your newsreader displays a list of article subjects for the various articles in the newsgroup. These subjects may be sorted in some order, or they may be unsorted, depending on your newsreader. Some newsreaders can sort articles based on subject, showing which articles are replies to other articles. This process is known as *threading*.

When you select an article to read, you see several lines of information at the top of the article. These lines make up the *article header*. The header contains lots of information about the article, including the author, the date it was written, the subject, the newsgroups that the article was posted to, and the path the article took to get to your site. You also might see additional information, such as the organization the author is affiliated with and a set of keywords that identify the content of an article.

Under most newsreaders, an article is marked as read when you look at it. Usually, only new articles are displayed when you select a newsgroup. This means that after you look at an article, it probably won't show up in your article list again. If you want to keep the article, you can save it to disk or print it. You can also usually mark the article as unread so that your newsreader displays it again the next time you go into the newsgroup. Many newsreaders also allow you to list old articles; this way, you have a list of old news articles in a newsgroup that are marked as having been read but haven't yet been deleted by the news system.

REPLYING VIA EMAIL

After you read an article, you might decide that you want to comment on the topic under discussion. If your information isn't of general interest to everyone in the newsgroup, you might want to reply to the article via email, which most newsreaders allow you the option of doing.

If you choose to reply through email, the newsreader software uses the information in the article header to figure out the email address of the author and then invokes an email editor for you to edit your message. You usually also have the option of including the original article in your reply. If you do include the original article, make sure that you edit the original message to include only the relevant portions. After you finish editing your reply, you can send your email message to the article's author.

Because of the common use of email, especially email addresses gleaned from Usenet postings, many Usenet posters *munge*, or modify, their email addresses to stop automated address collectors from being able to send them unsolicited commercial email, known as *spam*. The poster's email address may have an obvious false entry and look something like `mjameson@IHATESPAM.netcrom.com`. Alternatively, the poster may have instructions in his or her sigfile on what to change in the reply-to address to actually reach him or her. For example, a poster with a false address of `sbarnes@sequoia.skytails.org` might have instructions in the sigfile to "Replace *tails* with *wings* to reply."

Posting an Article

The act of creating a news article and sending it out through the Usenet system is known as *posting an article*. When you decide to post an article, you can either post a follow-up article to another article or create a new article on a new subject. Your newsreader typically has different commands for the different types of posts that it can perform.

Posting a Follow-Up

A *follow-up article* is a reply to another article. This article stays in the same subject thread as the original article and is shown as a reply by threaded newsreaders.

When you post a follow-up, you can choose to include the original post. Including parts of the original post is a good way to provide a frame of reference for your reply. Remember that several days may pass between the time some sites see the original article and your reply. If you do choose to include the original article, try to include, or *quote*, only the parts of the article that are relevant to your reply. Trying to wade through several levels of included files and quotes looking for the new information gets tedious. Also, some news servers will reject your reply if the quoted material is more than a certain percentage of your entire message, depending on the policies of the administrators.

You should check the `Subject` line to make sure that the subject still accurately reflects the content of your post, and change it if you're now discussing a new topic. Also, take a look at the `Newsgroup` line to make sure that your follow-up is going to the appropriate newsgroups. In particular, consider whether sending the message to multiple newsgroups is appropriate or whether the topic is relevant to only one or two of the original newsgroups.

Posting a New Article

If you decide to start a thread of discussion on a new subject, you want to post a new article instead of a follow-up. The mechanics of posting the article are very similar to those of posting a follow-up. You give the appropriate command to your newsreader; your newsreader asks for some information, such as the destination newsgroups, subject, and distribution; and you're placed into an editor. The major difference is that you're creating a subject thread instead of replying to one.

Tip #180 from *Steve*

A complete document on Usenet writing style is posted regularly to the newsgroup `news.announce.newusers`.

You should think about several points as you write your article. You can think of them as "Usenet Style Tips" if you want. These tips cover the format of your article and its content.

You should keep your lines fewer than 80 characters long. Many terminals can't display lines that are more than 80 characters. Similarly, you should try to keep the length of your article under 1,000 lines or so. Some sites are still running old versions of the news transport software, and long articles can cause them problems.

Tip #181 from *Steve*

You should not post a file such as a graphic or application to a newsgroup not intended for such files. Most newsgroups that are intended for files are have the word `.binaries` at the end of the newsgroup name.

You probably want to create a signature file that's automatically included at the end of every post. Most newsreaders support signature files, although the exact mechanism varies depending on your software. Most people put their names and email addresses in their signature files, along with their geographical locations. Some people add witty quotes or small ASCII pictures. Try to avoid having a large signature file. It is considered bad netiquette to include your full name, nicknames, an inspirational quote consisting of Whitman's *Leaves of Grass*, and a 20-line ASCII art drawing of your car. A good rule is to limit yourself to four lines. Some news software automatically limits your signature to four lines or so.

You need to give a subject to your article when you post it. Try to pick a subject line that's short yet descriptive. Thousands of people scan the subjects in any particular newsgroup, and you want them to be able to pick out your article if it's of interest to them. Also, carefully consider which newsgroups you're going to post your article to. Most newsreaders allow you to post an article to more than one newsgroup. You should post to only the smallest number of groups that you need. Remember that thousands of people are reading each newsgroup.

NETIQUETTE ON USENET

Throughout this chapter, the importance of being aware of how the tone and content of your message are interpreted has been stressed. This general consideration of behavior on Usenet, and the Internet in general, has its own term—*netiquette*. Netiquette applies to all areas of the Internet, including electronic mail.

The term *netiquette* simply refers to "proper and polite" behavior as it applies to Usenet news. Most of the time, you should have no real problems on Usenet as long as you remember that it's a very big and diverse place. Not everyone on Usenet shares your background, beliefs, or values, and you should try to remember this fact as you post articles.

Make sure that you clearly communicate your ideas in your posts. Because of the lack of body language and the delay between posts and replies, interpreting someone's meaning incorrectly is surprisingly easy. Also, remember that many participants don't speak English as a native language and may be unaware of local idioms and sarcasm.

Blatant commercial advertising is frowned on in Usenet news. Appropriate newsgroups do exist for advertising products and services. Similarly, you should not post chain articles, such as the infamous MAKE.MONEY.FAST or Craig Shergold get-well card article. These articles have been circulating around Usenet for years, and you (and your system administrator) will incur the wrath of thousands of people instantly if you post one of them.

Resist the urge to post flames, especially spelling and grammar flames. Even though flames seem to be a permanent part of the Usenet "landscape," these personal attacks and raving messages accomplish little. If someone should flame you for one of your posts, take time to calm down and carefully consider how to respond; the best solution might be not to respond at all. Sometimes you may receive a flame, but a calm response from you may elicit an apology from the person who flamed you. If you just zip off another flame in anger, you only escalate the problem. Remember that the person on the other end is really a person, not a computer.

Note

If a user is causing a real problem, you can add him or her to your *kill file*, a configuration file for your newsreader that contains a list of users or subjects. Anything that appears in your kill file is automatically not displayed when you read news. Most newsreaders support some version of a kill file. Using this file is a fairly painless way to cut down the noise from really annoying users.

In general, a little common sense and courtesy go a long way in avoiding any problems on Usenet. However, remember that Usenet is a huge place. Simply too many people are out there for you to try to make everyone happy. Eventually, someone will get angry over one of your posts, and you'll probably be flamed.

PROJECT: USING THE RN NEWSREADER

Many different types of news-reading software are available—far too many to describe in this chapter. The `rn` newsreader is a very common news-reading program that can be found on almost every UNIX variant. It was developed by Larry Wall and is widely available. Although `rn` isn't the easiest newsreader to use, nor does it have some of the fanciest features, it's still one of the most popular newsreaders in existence. rn allows you to read news via an ASCII interface that's suitable for local work on a terminal or from a remote network session.

Note

Another newsreader, trn, is quite popular and is distributed with many distributions of Linux. The trn newsreader is almost identical to rn except for the threading support. For compatibility with a wide variety of UNIX systems, only the rn newsreader is discussed in this chapter. For more information on the threading capabilities of trn, refer to its Linux man page.

When you start rn for the first time, you see a message welcoming you to the program, followed by a list of newsgroups. You have the opportunity to subscribe to different groups at this point. If your site carries a large number of groups, setting up your initial subscription information can be quite time-consuming. rn saves your subscription information in your home directory in a file named .newsrc.

After you complete your subscriptions, rn places you in a newsgroup selection mode. The name of each of your subscribed newsgroups is displayed one at a time. You can enter the newsgroup and start reading articles by pressing the *y* key, skip to the next group by pressing the *n* key, or go to the previous newsgroup by pressing the *q* key. You can also get a list of subjects in the newsgroup by pressing the = key at the newsgroup prompt. Most of the commands in rn and trn are one-character commands, and help is available at every command prompt by pressing the *h* key.

After you select a newsgroup to read, you enter article-selection mode. In this mode, several commands can help you navigate the articles in the newsgroup. Table 35.4 lists some of the commands available in article-selection mode.

TABLE 35.4 SOME COMMANDS AVAILABLE IN ARTICLE-SELECTION MODE

Command	Description
n+spacebar	Scans forward for the next unread article. The spacebar does this only at the end of the article, at the article-selection prompt.
spacebar	Shows the next page of the current article if not at the article-selection prompt.
Shift+n	Goes to the next article.
Ctrl+Shift+n	Goes to the next article with the same subject as the current article.
p	Scans backward for the previous unread article; stays at the current article if none is found.
Shift+p	Goes to the previous article.
Ctrl+Shift+r	Goes to the last previous article with the subject that's the same as the current article.
h	Displays help for article-selection mode.

TABLE 35.4 SOME COMMANDS AVAILABLE IN ARTICLE-SELECTION MODE

Command	Description
r	Replies to the article author via email.
Shift+r	Replies to the article author via email and includes the current article.
f	Posts a follow-up article.
Shift+f	Posts a follow-up article and includes the original article in the new article.
`s+filename`	Saves the current article to a file named *`filename`*.
q	Quits the current group and returns to newsgroup selection mode.

Table 35.4 shows only some of the options available within `rn` and `trn`. These feature-rich programs allow lots of user customization. Refer to the man pages and the online help for more information.

PART VII

Setting Up Linux Internet Servers

CHAPTER 36

Getting Started with Apache

In this chapter

by Steve Burnett

Installing Apache

To use a Linux system as a Web server, you must install special server software on your system. Two of the most popular UNIX Web server packages are Apache and NCSA's httpd. In fact, a May 1999 survey showed that Apache and its derivatives accounted for more than 60 percent of all installed Web servers, and it is used on approximately 3 million Web servers. Although this chapter is specific to the Apache server, the vocabulary is certainly applicable to other Web servers. The NCSA family of servers has much in common with Apache with respect to configuration files because Apache was derived originally from the NCSA 1.3 server, and maintaining backward compatibility with existing NCSA servers was originally a mandate with the development team. Such compatibility is less complete now that NCSA and Apache development paths have diverged.

Apache is known to compile on just about every UNIX variant: Solaris 2.x, SunOS 4.1.x, Irix 5.x and 6.x, Linux, FreeBSD/NetBSD/BSDI, HP-UX, AIX, Ultrix, OSF1, NeXT, Sequent, A/UX, SCO, UTS, Apollo Domain/OS, QNX, as well as OS/2; a Windows NT 4.0 port has been completed as of this writing. Portability has been a high priority for the development team.

Apache binaries and their sources are included with most distributions of Linux. The complete source code for Apache is also provided. Because Apache binaries are included on the CD-ROMs, you can skip the compilation process and move on to the next section if you're in a hurry to get Apache up and running. However, if you ever want to add new modules or tweak the functionality provided by Apache, you should know how to compile it. You can find instructions on compiling Apache on the Apache Software Foundation site at `http://www.apache.org/`; the instructions are not covered in this book.

Establishing the File Hierarchy

The next step in the process of setting up a server is to make some fundamental decisions regarding where on the file system different parts of the server will reside. You should write down your decisions for each of these locations; you will need them in the next section, "Basic Configuration":

- Where is the server root? It is the subdirectory in which the server will reside and from which the `conf/` directory, the `logs/` and `cgi-bin/` subdirectories, and other server-related directories lead. The default suggestion is to use `/usr/local/apache`, although the usual server root is `/pub/htdocs`. You can have your configuration files and log files in other locations. The server root was designed to be a convenient place to keep everything server-related together. Also, if the server crashes and leaves a core file, that file will be found in the server root directory.
- Where is the document root? The document root is the directory in which all your HTML and other media reside. A file called `myfile.html` in the document root would be referenced as `http://host.com/index.html`. This directory can be a subdirectory of the server root, or it can be outside the server root and in its own directory. It's

commonly located as a subdirectory of the server root and named `htdocs`. If, for more disk space or other reasons, you choose to move the document root out of the server root directory, you should give it a short name—for example, `/home/www` or `/www/htdocs`. If you're implementing a Web server on top of an FTP server, for example, you might want to point the document root to `/home/ftp/pub`.

- Where will the Web server log files be kept? This space should have a fairly large working area, depending on how busy you estimate your server will be. For a point of reference, a site with 100,000 hits per day (which would fall under moderate traffic, relatively speaking) can expect to generate 15MB of log file information per day. For performance reasons, it's usually best to have the log directory on a separate disk partition, or even a separate disk drive and drive controller altogether, because on even a moderately busy server the access log can be written to several times per second.

Basic Configuration

Apache has three separate configuration files. This model goes back to NCSA, and the reasoning is sound: Administrative configuration falls largely into three main areas, so setting them up as separate files allows Webmasters to give different write permissions to each if they so desire.

You can find the configuration files for Apache in the `conf/` subdirectory of the server root directory. Each has been provided with a `-dist` filename suffix; it's recommended that you make a copy without the `-dist` and edit those new files, keeping the `-dist` versions as backups and reference.

Tip #182 from *Steve*

Although Apache comes with and uses the following three different configuration files, it treats them all identically:

- `httpd.conf`
- `srm.conf`
- `access.conf`

Because `httpd.conf` is the first file read by Apache, you can copy the contents of the other two into `httpd.conf` and delete them if you like. If you delete the two unneeded files, you should add the following directives to `httpd.conf` to prevent Apache from generating error messages about the missing `srm.conf` and `access.conf` files:

```
AccessConfig /dev/null
ResourceConfig /dev/null
```

This chapter presents the three configuration files separately.

The basic format of the configuration files is a combination of a shell-like interface and pseudo-HTML. The elemental unit is the *directive*, which can take a number of arguments, as shown in the following syntax:

```
Directiveargumentargument....
```

For example, the directive might look like one of the following:

```
Port 80
```

```
AddIcon /icons/back.gif ..
```

You can also group directives together inside certain pseudo-HTML tags. Unlike HTML, these tags should be on their own lines, as in the following example of the `Virtualhost` directive:

```
<Virtualhost www.myhost.com>
DocumentRoot /www/htdocs/myhost.com
ServerName www.myhost.com
</Virtualhost>
```

httpd.conf

The default configuration file Apache reads is `httpd.conf`. This file sets the basic system-level information about the server, such as what port it binds to, which users it runs under, and so on. If you aren't the system administrator of the site at which you're installing the server, you might want to ask the administrator to help you with these questions.

The essential items to cover in this file include the following:

- `Port` *number*

  For example:

  ```
  Port 80
  ```

  This number indicates the TCP/IP port number to which the Web server binds. Port 80 is the default port in `http:` URLs. In other words, `http://www.myhost.com/` is equivalent to `http://www.myhost.com:80/`.

Tip #183 from *Steve*

For a number of reasons, however, you might want to run your server on a different port; for example, a server might already be running on port 80 (not secrecy, however; port scanners are too common for security through obscurity to be a valid option here).

- `User #number_or_uid`

  `Group #number_or_uid`

  For example:

  ```
  User nobody
  Group nogroup
  ```

  You need to launch Apache as root to bind to a port lower than 1024. Immediately after grabbing the port, Apache changes its effective user ID to something else, typically as user `nobody`. Apache's changing of its user ID is very important for security reasons.

  This user ID needs to be able to read files in the document root, and it must have read permission on the configuration files. The argument should be the actual username; however, if you want to give a numeric user ID, you can prepend the number with a pound sign (`#`). The `Group` directive follows the same principle: You must decide which group ID you want the server to run with.

Tip #184 from *Steve*

Running your Web server as root means that any hole in the server (be it through the server itself or through a CGI script, which is much more likely) could be exploited by an outside user trying to run a command on your machine. Thus, setting the user to `nobody`, `www`, or some other reasonably innocuous user ID is the safest bet.

- `ServerAdmin email_address`

  You need to set the email address of a user who can receive mail related to the actions of the server. In the case of a server error, the browser visiting your site receives a message to the effect of "please report this problem to `user@myhost.com`." In the future, Apache might send warning email to the ServerAdmin user if it encounters a major systems-related problem.

- `ServerRoot directory`

  For example:

  ```
  ServerRoot /usr/local/apache
  ```

  You can set the server root you decided on earlier. Here, you give the full path and don't end it with a slash.

- `ErrorLog directory/filename`

  `TransferLog directory/filename`

  You can specify exactly where to log errors and Web accesses. If the filename you give doesn't start with a slash, it's presumed to be relative to the server root directory. I suggested earlier that the log files be sent to a separate directory outside the server root; here, you specify the logging directory and the name of the log files within that directory.

- `ServerName` *`DNS_hostname`*

  At times, the Web server needs to know the host name it's being referred to as, which can be different from its real host name. For example, the name `www.myhost.com` might actually be a DNS alias for `gateway.myhost.com`. In this case, you don't want the URLs generated by the server to be `http://gateway.myhost.com/`. `ServerName` allows you to set that name precisely.

srm.conf

The second configuration file to cover before launch is `srm.conf`. The important elements to set in this file include the following:

- `DocumentRoot` *`directory`*

  As described before, this directory is the root level of your tree of documents, which could be either `/usr/local/apache/htdocs` or `/www/htdocs`. This directory must exist and be readable by the user (usually `nobody`) the Web server runs as.

- `ScriptAlias` *`request_path_alias directory`*

  `ScriptAlias` lets you specify that a particular directory *outside* the document root can be aliased to a path in the request *and* that objects in that directory are executed rather than simply read from the file system. For example, the default offering

  ```
  ScriptAlias /cgi-bin/ /usr/local/apache/cgi-bin/
  ```

  means that a request for `http://www.myhost.com/cgi-bin/fortune` executes the program `/usr/local/apache/cgi-bin/fortune`. Apache comes bundled with a number of useful beginner CGI scripts, simple shell scripts that illustrate CGI programming.

  Finally, the directory containing the CGI scripts should *not* be under the document root. Bizarre interactions between the code that handles `ScriptAlias` and the code that handles request/pathname resolution could cause problems.

access.conf

`access.conf` is structured more rigidly than the other configuration files; the content is contained within `<Directory></Directory>`, pseudo-HTML tags that define the scope of the directives listed within.

So, for example, the directives between the following two code lines affect everything located under the `/www/htdocs` directory:

```
<Directory /www/htdocs>

</Directory>
```

Furthermore, wildcards can be used. For example, the following:

```
<Directory /www/htdocs/*/archives/>
....
</Directory>
```

applies to `/www/htdocs/list1/archives/`, `/www/htdocs/list2/archives/`, and so on.

Tip #185 from *Steve*

Although this chapter is still useful, release 1.3.0 and higher of Apache include a GNU Autoconf-style front end, which supports all previous configuration options as well as the enhancements in 1.3.0 and above. Use of that interface for configuration is recommended in general.

User Directories

Sometimes sites with many users enable their users to manage their own parts of the Web tree in their own directories. The users do so by using the URL semantics

```
http://myhost.com/~user/
```

where `~user` is actually an alias to a directory in the users' home directories. This approach is different from using the `Alias` directive, which can map only a particular pseudo-directory into an actual directory. In this case, you want `~user` to map to something like `/home/user/public_html`. Because the number of "users" can be very high, some sort of macro is useful here. That macro is the `UserDir` directive.

With `UserDir`, you specify the subdirectories within the users' home directories where they can put content, and those subdirectories are mapped to the `~user` URL. So, in other words, the default

```
UserDir public_html
```

causes a request for

```
http://myhost.com/~dave/index.html
```

to cause a lookup for the UNIX file

```
/home/dave/public_html/index.html
```

presuming that `/home/dave` is Dave's home directory.

Starting Apache

To start Apache, simply run the binary you compiled earlier (or your precompiled binary) with the `-f` flag pointing to the `httpd.conf` file also created earlier, as in this example:

```
/usr/local/apache/src/httpd -f /usr/local/apache/conf/httpd.conf
```

Several Linux distributions (Red Hat Linux included) include a startup script for the Web server if you install Apache.

At this point, you would be wise to use the ps command to see whether httpd is running. Typically, something like ps -aux ¦ grep will suffice. You might be surprised to see a number of simultaneous httpd processes running. What's going on?

The first Web servers, such as CERN and NCSA, used the model of one main Web server cloning itself with every single request that came in. The clone would respond to the request, while the original server returned to listening to the port for another request. Although this design was certainly simple and robust, the act of *cloning* (or, in UNIX terms, *forking*) was an expensive operation under UNIX, so loads above a couple hits per second were quite punishing even on the nicest hardware. It was also difficult to implement any sort of *throttling*, which reduced the amount of cloning that took place. When the number of clones was very high, it was hard for the original server to know how many clones were still around. Thus, servers had no easy way to refuse or delay connections based on a lack of resources.

Apache, like some of the other UNIX-based Web servers, instead uses the model of a group of persistent children running in parallel. The children are coordinated by a parent process, which can tell how many children are alive, spawn new children (if necessary), and even terminate old children if many are idle, depending on the situation. (*Parent* and *child* are the actual UNIX terms.)

Now, let's get back to the server. At this point, you can start your Web browser and point it to your local server. (You should use the usual http:// format and add the ServerName parameter you defined in the httpd.conf file.) Does it work? If all goes well, you should be able to see a directory index listing of everything in the document root directory, or if an index.html is located in that directory, you see the contents of that file. By default, Apache installs a Web page in the document root telling the Webmaster that the Apache installation was successful.

DEBUGGING SERVER STARTUP

Apache is usually pretty good about giving meaningful error messages, but some are explained in more detail in the following sections.

SERVER STARTUP ERROR MESSAGES

You might see the following messages upon server startup. Note that the descriptions follow the messages.

```
httpd: could not open document config file .....
fopen: No such file or directory
```

These open file error messages are usually the result of giving just a relative path to the -f argument, so Apache looks for the file or files relative to the compiled-in server root (what's set in src/httpd.h) instead of those relative to the directory you're in. You must give the full path or the path relative to the compiled-in server root.

```
httpd: could not bind to port [X]
bind: Operation not permitted
```

The port and bind error messages are most likely caused by attempting to run the server on a port below 1024 without launching it as root. Most UNIX operating systems, including Linux, prevent people without root access from trying to launch any type of server on a port less than 1024. If you launch the server as root, the error message should disappear.

```
httpd: could not bind to port
bind: Address already in use
```

These port and bind error messages mean that something is already running on your machine at the port you've specified. Do you have another Web server running? No standard UNIX mechanism is available for determining what's running on what ports; on most systems, the file `/etc/services` can tell you what the most common daemons are, but it's not a complete list. You could also try using the `netstat` command, with various options such as `-a`.

```
httpd: bad user name ....
httpd: bad group name ....
```

Bad user or group name error messages mean that the user or the group you specified in `httpd.conf` doesn't actually exist on your system. You might see errors telling you that particular files or directories don't exist. If the files appear to be there, make sure that they're readable by the user IDs that the server runs as (that is, both `root` and `nobody`).

Initial Server Startup Error Messages

Suppose that Apache has started up and, according to `ps`, it's actually running. When you go to the site, however, you experience the following problems or error messages:

No connection at all.

First, you should make sure that no firewalls that would filter out packets to the server are between you and the server. Second, you can try using `telnet` to the port you launched the Web server on—for example, `telnet myhost.com 80`. If you don't get a `Connected to myhost.com` message back, your connection isn't even making it to the server in the first place.

`403 Access Forbidden`

Your document root directory may be unreadable, or you might have something in your `access.conf` file that prevents access to your site from the machine where your Web browser is running.

`500 Server Error`

Is your front page a CGI script? The script might be failing.

The errors listed here are the most common errors made in initial server startups. If you can confirm that contact with the server is actually being made, the next best place to look for error information is in the `ErrorLog`.

SECURE TRANSACTIONS WITH SSL

This section takes a slight detour and discusses a variant of the Apache Web server, Apache-SSL, which can conduct secure transactions over the Secure Sockets Layer (SSL) protocol. SSL is an RSA public-key-based encryption protocol developed by Netscape Communications for use in the Netscape Navigator browser and Netscape Web servers.

Eric Young, author of the widely used `libdes` package, with Tim Hudson wrote a library that implements SSL, eponymously named `SSLeay`. The `SSLeay` package has since expanded to become an all-purpose cryptography and certificate-handling library, while retaining the same name, `SSLeay`.

Ben Laurie, a member of the Apache Group, then took the `SSLeay` library and interfaced it with the Apache server, making his patches available to people on the Net. Sameer Parekh of Community ConneXion, Inc. (hereafter referred to as C2) then took Ben Laurie's patches and built a package legal for use within the United States.

Because the RSA technology used by SSL in the United States is covered by patents owned by RSA Data Security, Inc. (RSADSI) (`www.rsa.com`), it isn't legal to use the `SSLeay` package "out-of-the-box" within the United States. C2 licensed the RSA technology to make use of the package legal within the United States by using the RSAREF package, produced by RSADSI and Consensus Development Corporation (`www.consensus.com`).

Due to export restrictions, someone outside the United States cannot legally download and install the C2 Apache-SSL package. In fact, the SSL patches could not be included on the CD-ROM with this book because the book would suddenly have earned the label "munition," and clearance from the U.S. government to export the book would have been required!

To learn more about SSL and Apache, you can go to `http://www.apache-ssl.org`.

As an alternative to Apache-SSL, you can use a module called `mod_ssl`, which is based on Apache-SSL and provides a more supported implementation. You can find the Apache Interface to the `SSLeay` module on the Web at `http://www.engelschall.com/sw/mod_ssl/`.

SPECIAL MODULES

Most of the functionality that distinguishes Apache from the competition has been implemented as modules to the Apache API. The implementation of these modules has been extremely useful in allowing functionality to evolve separately from the rest of the server and for allowing for performance tuning. The following sections cover that extra functionality in detail.

SERVER-SIDE INCLUDES

Server-side includes are best described as a preprocessing language for HTML. The "processing" takes place on the server side. As such, visitors to your site never need to know that you use server-side includes, and thus they require no special client software. The format of these includes looks something like the following:

```
<!--#directiveattribute="value'' -->
```

Sometimes a given "directive" can have more than one attribute at the same time. The funky syntax is due to the desire to hide this functionality within an SGML comment; that way, your regular HTML validation tools work without your having to learn new tags or anything. The syntax is important; leaving off the final `--`, for example, will result in errors.

#include

The `#include` directive is probably the most commonly used. You use it to insert another HTML file into the HTML document. The allowed attributes for `#include` are `virtual` and `file`. The functionality of the `file` attribute is a subset of that provided by the `virtual` attribute, and it exists mostly for backward compatibility, so its use isn't recommended.

The `virtual` attribute tells the server to treat the value of the attribute as a request for a relative link—meaning that you can use `../` to locate objects above the directory and that other transformations, such as `Alias`, will apply. The following is an example of such:

```
<!--#include virtual="quote.txt'' -->
<!--#include virtual="/toolbar/footer.html'' -->
<!--#include virtual=''../footer.html'' -->
```

#exec

The `#exec` directive is used to run a script on the server side and insert its output into the SSI (server-side includes) document being processed. You have two choices: executing a CGI script by using the `cgi` attribute or executing a shell command by using the `cmd` attribute. For example,

```
<!--#exec cgi="counter.cgi'' -->
```

takes the output of the CGI program `counter.cgi` and inserts it into the document.

Note The CGI output still has to include the `"text/html"` content-type header; otherwise, an error occurs.

Likewise,

```
<!--#exec cmd="ls -l'' -->
```

takes the output of a call to `ls -l` in the document's directory and inserts it into the output page as a replacement for the `#exec` command. Like the `file` attribute for the `#include` directive, this type of `#exec` command is mostly for backward compatibility because it's something of a security hole in an untrusted environment.

Note

There are definitely security concerns with allowing users access to CGI functionality and even greater concerns with using `#exec cmd`, such as

```
cmd="cat /etc/passwd''
```

If, as site administrator, you want to let users use server-side includes but not use the `#exec` directive, you can set `IncludesNOEXEC` as an option for the directory in the access configurations.

#echo

The `#echo` directive has one attribute—`var`—whose value is any CGI environment variable as well as a small list of other variables, as shown in Table 36.1.

TABLE 36.1 VALUES FOR THE `var` ATTRIBUTE

Attribute	Definition
`DATE_GMT`	The current date in Greenwich mean time.
`DATE_LOCAL`	The current date in the local time zone.
`DOCUMENT_NAME`	The file system name of the SSI document, not including the directories below it.
`DOCUMENT_URI`	The file system URI of the SSI document. URI stands for *Uniform Resource Identifier*. In a Uniform Resource Locator (URL) of the format `http://host/path/file`, the URI is the `/path/file` part.
`LAST_MODIFIED`	The date the SSI document was modified.

For example, the command

```
<!--#echo var="DATE_LOCAL''-->
```

inserts something along the lines of `Wednesday, 03-Mar-99 10:44:54 GMT` into the document.

#fsize, #flastmod

The `#fsize` and `#flastmod` directives print the size and the last-modified date, respectively, of any object given by the URI listed in the `file` or `virtual` attribute, as in the `#include` directive. For example, the command

```
<!--#fsize file="index.html''-->
```

returns the size of the `index.html` file in that directory.

#config

You can modify the rendering of certain SSI directives by using the `#config` directive. The `sizefmt` attribute controls the rendering of the `#fsize` directive with values of `bytes` or abbrev. The exact number of bytes is printed when bytes is given, whereas an abbreviated version of the size (in KB for kilobytes or MB for megabytes) is given when abbrev (the default) is set. For example, a snippet of SSI HTML like

```
<!--#config sizefmt="bytes''-->
The index.html file is <!--#fsize virtual="index.html'' --> bytes
```

returns The index.html file is 4,522 bytes. Meanwhile,

```
<!--#config sizefmt="abbrev'' -->
```

returns The index.html file is 4K bytes.

The timefmt directive controls the rendering of the date in the DATE_LOCAL, DATE_GMT, and LAST_MODIFIED values for the #echo directive. It uses the same format as the strftime call. (In fact, the server does call strftime, a system call that formats the time in a string of specified length.) The string format consists of variables that begin with %. For example, %H is the hour of the day, in 24-hour format. For directions on how to construct a strftime-format date string, you can consult strftime's man page for a list of variables.

An example might be

```
<!--#config timefmt="%Y/%m/%d-%H:%M:%S'' -->
```

with the resulting date string for January 2, 1999, at 12:30 in the afternoon as

```
1999/01/02-12:30:00
```

Finally, the last attribute the #config directive can take is errmsg, which is simply the error to print if any problems occur parsing the document. For example, the right default is the following:

```
<!--#config errmsg="An error occurred while processing this directive'' -->
```

COOKIES

The use of HTTP *cookies* are a method for maintaining statefulness in a stateless protocol. What does this mean? In HTTP, a session between a client and a server typically spans many separate actual TCP connections, thus making it difficult to tie together accesses into an application that requires state, such as a shopping-cart application. Cookies provide a solution to that problem. As implemented by Netscape in its browser and subsequently by many others, servers can assign clients a cookie, meaning some sort of opaque string whose meaning is significant only to the server itself, and then the client can give that cookie back to the server on subsequent requests.

The mod_cookies module nicely handles the details of assigning unique cookies to every visitor, based on the visitor's host name and a random number. This cookie can be accessed from the CGI environment as the HTTP_COOKIE environment variable, for the same reason that all HTTP headers are accessible to CGI applications. The CGI scripts can use this cookie as a key in a session-tracking database, or cookies can be logged and tallied up to get a good, if undercounted, estimate of the total number of users that visited a site, not just the number of hits or even number of unique domains.

Happily, there are no configuration issues here. You can simply compile with `mod_cookies`, and away you go. The process couldn't be easier.

Tip #186 from *Steve*

For security reasons, some users severely dislike cookie configurations. Think carefully if you need cookies before using them.

CONFIGURABLE LOGGING

For most folks, the default log file format (also known as *CommonLogfileFormat*, or CLF) doesn't provide enough information when it comes to doing a serious analysis of the efficacy of a Web site. It provides basic numbers in terms of raw hits, pages accessed, hosts accessing, timestamps, and so forth, but it fails to capture the "referring" URL, the browser being used, and any cookies being used. So you can get more data for your log files in two ways: by using the NCSA-compatibility directives for logging certain bits of information to separate browsers or by using Apache's own totally configurable log file format.

NCSA COMPATIBILITY

For compatibility with the NCSA 1.4 Web server, two modules were added. These modules log the `User-Agent` and `Referer` headers from the HTTP request stream.

`User-Agent`, which is the header most browsers send, identifies what software the browser is using. Logging of this header can be activated by an `AgentLog` directive in the `srm.conf` file or in a virtual-host-specific section. This directive takes one argument, the name of the file to which the user-agents are logged, as in this example:

```
AgentLog logs/agent_log
```

To use the `AgentLog` directive, you need to ensure that the `mod_log_agent` module has been compiled and linked to the server.

Similarly, the `Referer` header is sent by the browser to indicate the tail end of a link. In other words, when you're on a page with an URL of "A," and a link on that page has an URL of "B," and you follow that link, the request for page "B" includes a `Referer` header with the URL of "A." This header is very useful for finding what sites link to your site and what proportion of traffic they account for.

The logging of the `Referer` header is activated by a `RefererLog` directive, which points to the file to which the referers get logged:

```
RefererLog logs/referer_log
```

One other option the `Referer` logging module provides is `RefererIgnore`, a directive that allows you to ignore `Referer` headers. `RefererIgnore`is useful for weeding out the referers from your own site, if all you're interested in is links to you from other sites. For example, if your site is `www.myhost.com`, you might want to use the following:

```
RefererIgnore www.myhost.com
```

Remember that logging of the `Referer` header requires compiling and linking in `mod_log_referer`.

TOTALLY CONFIGURABLE LOGGING

The previous modules were provided, like many Apache features, for backward compatibility. They have some problems, though. Because they don't contain any other information about the request they're logging from, telling which `Referer` fields went to which specific objects on your site is nearly impossible. Ideally, all the information about a transaction with the server can be logged into one file, extending the Common Logfile Format or replacing it altogether. Well, such a beast exists in the `mod_log_config` module.

The `mod_log_config` module implements the `LogFormat` directive, which takes as its argument a string, with variables beginning with `%` to indicate different pieces of data from the request. Table 36.2 lists the variables.

TABLE 36.2 VARIABLES FOR THE `LogFormat` DIRECTIVE

Variable	Definition
`%h`	Remote host.
`%l`	Remote identification via `identd`.
`%u`	Remote user, as determined by any user authentication that may take place. If the user wasn't authenticated and the status of the request is a 401 (authorization error), this field may be bogus.
`%t`	Common Logfile Format for time.
`%r`	First line of request.
`%s`	Status. For requests that are internally redirected, this is the status of the original request; `%>s` gives the last request.
`%b`	Bytes sent.
`%{STUFF}i`	Contents of `STUFF:` header line(s) in the request from the client to the server.
`%{STUFF}o`	Contents of `STUFF:` header line(s) in the response from the server to the client.

For example, if you want to capture in your log just the remote host name, the object requested, and the timestamp, you would use the following:

```
LogFormat ''%h \"%r\'' %t''
```

This command logs things that look like the following:

```
host.outsider.com ''GET / HTTP/1.0'' [06/Mar/1996:10:15:17]
```

You Can Quote Me on This

You really have to use quotation marks around the request variable. The configurable logging module automatically interprets the values of the variables rather than just reads the variable name. You use a slash-quote, `\"`, to indicate that you want an actual quotation mark character rather than the end of the string. For example, if you want to add logging of the `User-Agent` string, your log format becomes

```
LogFormat ''%h \"%r\'' %t \"%{User-Agent}i\"''
```

Because the `User-Agent` field typically has spaces in it, it too should be quoted. Suppose that you want to capture the `Referer` field:

```
LogFormat ''%h \"%r\'' %t %{Referer}i''
```

You don't need the escaping quotation marks because `Referer` headers, as URLs, don't have spaces in them. However, if you're building a mission-critical application, you might as well quote it also, because the `Referer` header is supplied by the client and, thus, you have no guarantees about its format.

The default log file format is the Common Logfile Format (CLF), which is expressed as follows:

```
LogFormat ''%h %l %u %t \"%r\'' %s %b''
```

In fact, most existing log file analysis tools for CLF ignore extra fields tacked onto the end. To capture the most important extra information and yet have that information still be parsable by those tools, you might want to use this format:

```
LogFormat ''%h %l %u %t \"%r\'' %s %b %{Referer}i \"%{User-Agent}i\"''
```

Tip #187 from Steve

If you want even more control over what gets logged, you can use the configurable logging module to implement a simple conditional test for variables. This way, you can configure it to log variables only when a particular status code is—or isn't—returned. The format for trapping a status code is to insert a comma-separated list of those codes between the `%` and the letter of the variable:

```
%404,403{Referer}i
```

This example means that the `Referer` header is logged only if the status returned by the server is `404 Not Found` or `403 Access Denied`. All other times, just a `-` is logged. Having only 403 or 404 errors logged might be useful if you care about using `Referer` only to find old links that point to resources no longer available.

To negate the `Referer` status code, you put an exclamation point (`!`) at the beginning of the list of status codes. For example,

```
%!401u
```

logs the user in any user authentication transaction, unless the authentication failed, in which case you probably don't want to see the name of the bogus user anyway.

Remember that, like many functions, logging functions can be configured per virtual host. Thus, if you want all logs from all virtual hosts on the same server to go to the same log, you might want to do something like

```
LogFormat ''hosta ....''
```

in the <VirtualHost> sections for hosta and

```
LogFormat ''hostb ....''
```

in the <VirtualHost> sections for hostb. More details about virtual hosts appear later in the section "Virtual Hosts."

Note You have to compile in mod_log_config to configure logging on a "per-virtual-host" basis. You must also make sure that the default logging module, mod_log_common, isn't compiled in; otherwise, the server gets confused.

Host-Based Access Control

You can control access to the server, or even a subdirectory of the server, based on the host name, domain, or IP number of the client's machine. You do so by using the directives allow and deny, which can be used together with order. allow and denycan take multiple hosts:

```
deny from badguys.com otherbadguys.com
```

Typically, you want to do one of two things: You want to deny access to your server from everyone but a few other machines, or you want to grant access to everyone except a few hosts. You deny access from all but a few machines by using these commands:

```
order deny,allow
allow from mydomain.com
deny from all
```

This directive means "Grant access only to hosts in the domain mydomain.com." This domain could include host1.mydomain.com, ppp.mydomain.com, and the-boss.mydomain.com.

The preceding directive tells the server to evaluate the deny conditions before the allow conditions when determining whether to grant access. Likewise, you can handle the "exclude only a couple of sites" case described earlier by using the following:

```
order allow,deny
allow from all
deny from badguys.com
```

order is needed because—again—the server needs to know which rule to apply first. The default for order is deny,allow.

In a third argument to order, called mutual-failure, a condition has to pass the allow and deny rules to succeed. In other words, it has to appear in the allow list, and it must not appear in the deny list, as in the following example:

```
order mutual-failure
allow from mydomain.com
deny from the-boss.mydomain.com
```

In this example, `the-boss.mydomain.com` is prevented from accessing this resource, but every other machine at `mydomain.com` can access it.

Caution

Protecting resources by host name is dangerous. A determined person who controls the reverse-DNS mapping for his or her IP number can relatively easily spoof any host name he or she wants. Thus, it's strongly recommended that you use IP numbers to protect anything sensitive. In the same way, you can simply list the domain name to refer to any machine in that domain. You also can give fragments of IP numbers, as shown here:

```
allow from 204.62.129
```

This example allows only hosts whose IP numbers match, such as 204.62.129.1 or 204.62.129.130.

Typically, these directives are used within a `<Limit>` container, and even that within a `<Directory>` container, usually in an `access.conf` configuration file. The following example is a good template for most protections; it protects the `/www/htdocs/private` directory from any host except those in the 204.62.129 IP space:

```
<Directory /www/htdocs/private>
Options Includes
AllowOverride None
<Limit GET POST>
order allow,deny
deny from all
allow from 204.62.129
</Limit>
</Directory>
```

USING .HTACCESS FILES

Apache uses special files, known as `.htaccess` files, for controlling access to directories. Searching directories for `.htaccess` files is fairly painful. Because `.htaccess` files work hierarchically, when a request is made for `/path/path2/dir1/dir2/foo`, Apache looks for an `.htaccess` file in *every* subdirectory. In the example of `/path/path2/dir1/dir2/foo`, it looks through at least five subdirectories—a significant disk access load that's best to avoid if possible.

To solve the problem of too many disk hits, you should put anything controlled via your `.htaccess` files into the `access.conf` configuration file or even the `srm.conf` file. If you have to look for `.htaccess` files in subdirectories and can narrow it down to a specific subdirectory, you can have the server look only for .htaccess files in that subdirectory by using AllowOverride.

Suppose that your document root is in /www/htdocs, and you want to turn off the searching for all .htaccess files except those in /www/htdocs/dir1/dir2 and everywhere below. To do so, you would put something like the following into your access.conf configuration file:

```
<Directory /www/htdocs>
Options All
AllowOverride None
</Directory>
<Directory /www/htdocs/dir1/dir2>
Options All
AllowOverride All
</Directory>
```

Listing the directories in that order is important so that the second <Directory> doesn't take precedence over the first.

Understanding Security Issues

The security of your server is, no doubt, one of your biggest concerns as a Web site administrator. Running a Web server is, by nature, a security risk. For that matter, so is plugging your machine into a network at all. However, you can do a lot to make your Web server more secure from external forces (people trying to break into your site) and internal forces (your own Web site users mistakenly or willingly opening up holes).

CGI Issues

The biggest cause for concern about protecting your site from external threats is CGI scripts. Most CGI scripts are shell-based, using Perl or C-shell interpreted programs rather than compiled programs. Thus, many attacks have occurred by exploiting "features" in those shells. This section doesn't go into too much detail about how to make CGI scripts themselves safe. As an administrator, you should know a couple of important points, however.

A CGI script runs with the user ID of the server child process. In the default case, this is nobody. To adequately protect yourself, you might want to consider the nobody user an untrustworthy user on your site, making sure that this user doesn't have read permission to files you want to keep private and doesn't have write permission anywhere sensitive. Certain CGI scripts—for example, a guestbook application that allows users to record comments about your Web site—demand write access to certain files. So if you want to enable those types of applications, it's best to specify a directory to which CGI scripts can write without worrying about a malicious or misdirected script overwriting data that it shouldn't.

Furthermore, as a site administrator, you can limit the use of CGI to specific directories by using the ScriptAlias directive. Alternatively, if you have turned on .cgi as a file extension for CGI scripts, you can use the Options ExecCGI directive in access.conf to further control the use of CGI files.

Let me give you an example of controlling access with `ExecCGI`: If you want to allow for CGI to be used everywhere on the site (with a document root of `/home/htdocs`) except for the "users" subdirectory because you don't trust your users with CGI scripts, your `access.conf` should look something like Listing 36.1.

LISTING 36.1 A SAMPLE `access.conf` FILE SHOWING DIRECTORY CONFIGURATION INFORMATION

```
<Directory /home/htdocs/>
Options Indexes FollowSymLinks Includes Multiviews ExecCGI
AllowOverride None
</Directory>
<Directory /home/htdocs/users/>
Options Indexes SymLinksIfOwnerMatch IncludesNOEXEC Multiviews
AllowOverride None
</Directory>
```

Because `ExecCGI` isn't in the `Options` list for the second directory, no one can use CGI scripts there.

Unfortunately, there really is no middle ground between allowing CGI scripts and disallowing them. Now, most languages used for CGI programs don't have security concepts built into them, so you need to deal with rules such as "don't touch the hard disk" or "don't send the `/etc/passwd` file in email to an outside user" as though you had actual Linux users who needed the same restrictions applied to them. Maybe this will change when Sun's Java language gets more use on the server side, or when people use raw interpreted languages less and higher-level programming tools more often.

TRUST ISSUES WITH SERVER-SIDE INCLUDES

As you can see from Listing 36.1, another change was made between the *trusted* part of the server and the *untrusted* part: the `Includes` argument to `Options` was changed to `IncludesNOEXEC`. `IncludesNOEXEC` allows your untrusted users to use server-side includes without allowing the `#include` of CGI scripts or the `#exec` command to be run. The `#exec` command is particularly troublesome in an untrusted environment because it basically gives shell-level access to an HTML author.

SYMBOLIC LINKS

In an untrusted environment, UNIX *symbolic links* (which enable linking across file system boundaries) also are a concern for Web site administrators. Malicious users could very easily create symbolic links from directories where they have write permission to an object or resource, even outside the document root, to which all they need is read permission. For example, a user could create a link to the `/etc/passwd` file and then release it onto the Web, exposing your site to potential crack attempts—particularly if your operating system doesn't use shadow passwords.

Note In a recent incident involving the AltaVista search engine (`www.altavista.com`), a search for words common to password files (`bin`, `root`, `ftp`, and so on) turned up references to actual password files that had, intentionally or not, been left public. These password files included a few with encrypted passwords, which were easy enough to break with a few hours of CPU time on most workstations.

To protect against symbolic link security breaches, you have two options as the site administrator: to allow only symbolic linking if the owner of the link and the owner of the linked-to resource are the same by using `SymLinksIfOwnerMatch`, or to disallow symbolic links altogether by not specifying `FollowSymLinks` or `SymLinksIfOwnerMatch`.

Also note that both `<Directory>` segments in Listing 36.1 included `AllowOverride None`. Not allowing symbolic links is the most conservative setting; if you want to allow certain elements in those directories to be tuned by using `.htaccess` files, you can specify them by using the `AllowOverride` directive. However, stating `None` is the safest policy.

Publicly Writable Spaces

The last security threat that's specific to Web servers is that of allowing publicly writable spaces to be served up via HTTP. For example, many sites allow their FTP "incoming" directory to be accessed via the Web directly. This can be a security hole if someone were to place there a malicious CGI script or a server-side include file that calls `#exec` to do some damage. If you decide you need to take the risk of providing public writable spaces, you can take some steps to protect yourself:

- The most conservative setting you should set for the `Options` directive is this:

  ```
  Options Indexes
  ```

  You could use `None`, but `Indexes` really doesn't introduce any additional security problems, as long as you're comfortable with others being able to download anything that has been submitted. In the light of recent legislation by the U.S. government regarding "indecent" materials, you might not want to take this risk either.
- Make sure that you set `AllowOverride None` so that people can't upload an `.htaccess` file into your directory and modify all your settings and security policies.
- Make sure that the FTP daemon you're using doesn't allow the execute bit to be set. By preventing the execute bit to be set, you prevent the execution of uploaded CGI scripts. If you're using `XBitHack` to activate your server-side includes, you can prevent those includes from being run as well. This approach is mainly a backup for setting the `Options`, as in Listing 36.1, which should protect you against these threats anyway.

These same rules apply if you have CGI scripts that generate their own uniquely addressable HTML or CGI files. For example, if the `guestbook.cgi` program constantly appends the submitted personal information to a `guestbook.html` file, all the same rules apply; the contents of that HTML file must be considered unsafe. This possible security breach can be plugged if the CGI script double-checks what's getting written and removes "dangerous" code, such as server-side includes.

PROJECT: ADDING CUSTOMIZED ERROR MESSAGES

Apache can give customized responses in the event of an error. You can control these responses by using the `ErrorDocument` directive in the configuration files. The syntax is as follows:

```
ErrorDocument HTTP_response_codeaction
```

`HTTP_response_code` is the event that triggers the *`action`*. The *`action`* can be any of the following

- A local URI to which the server is internally redirected
- An external URL to which the client is redirected
- A text string that starts with a `"` character and where the `%s` variable contains any extra information, if available

The following is an example:

```
ErrorDocument 500 ''Ack! We have a problem here: %s.
ErrorDocument 500 /errors/500.cgi
ErrorDocument 500 http://backup.myhost.com/
ErrorDocument 401 /subscribe.html
ErrorDocument 404 /debug/record-broken-links.cgi
```

Two extra CGI variables are passed to any redirected resource: `REDIRECT_URL` contains the original URL requested, and `REDIRECT_STATUS` gives the original status that caused the redirection. This information will help the script if its job is to try to figure out what caused the error response.

CHAPTER 37

Configuring FTP Servers

In this chapter

by Steve Burnett

INSTALLING WU-FTP

File Transfer Protocol (FTP) is a simple and effective means of transferring files between computers that are connected on a TCP/IP network. FTP allows users to transfer both ASCII and binary files and is documented in RFC 959 and RFC 1759.

During an FTP session, you connect to another computer by using the FTP client program. From this point, you can move up and down through the directory tree, list directory contents, copy files from the remote computer to your computer, and transfer files from your computer to the remote system. Normal file protections apply; you can't get or put a file on the remote system if you don't have the proper permissions for that file.

wu-ftpd is the common name for wuarchive-ftpd. Developed by Bryan D. O'Connor, wu-ftpd is a replacement FTP service. Its name is derived from its origin: wu-ftpd was originally developed at Washington University (`*.wustl.edu`). Immensely popular, wu-ftpd is used on many FTP sites across the globe. This chapter will present how to install and configure wu-ftpd.

wu-ftpd is included with Red Hat Linux, so you should be able to select it during installation. You should know that many Linux distributions make a service operable when it is installed as part of the system setup. You should review the chapter on system security and disable services you do not want until you have time to configure those services. The following are good sources of information for WU-FTP:

- `http://www.landfield.com/wu-ftpd/`—A resource center
- `http://www.cetis.hvu.nl/~koos/wu-ftpd-faq.html`—The WU-FTP Frequently Asked Questions file
- `http://sunsite.doc.ic.ac.uk/sun/sunsite-sun-info/sun-faq/FAQs/SettingUpSecureFTP.faq`—Some advice for securing an FTP site

You can always find the latest version of wu-ftpd 9 with the latest security patches, bug fixes, and so on at `ftp.wu-ftpd.org` in `ftp://ftp.wu-ftpd.org/pub/wu-ftpd/` (please use FTP to access this directory). You can access this system via anonymous FTP.

ANONYMOUS FTP

Many organizations have made huge repositories of information available via FTP. These FTP sites hold everything from text files to software of every conceivable type available. But how do you access this enormous storehouse of data if you don't have an account on the remote computer? Do you need to get an account on every FTP site to be able to access these files? Not really.

A common convention on the Internet allows guest FTP access to file repositories so that users can transfer files. This guest access is called *anonymous FTP*. To use anonymous FTP, you start an FTP session to the remote system and use `anonymous` as your username and your email address as the password. For example, in the following sample, the user named smith on `linux.somewhere.com` wants to initiate an FTP session with a common FTP site:

```
$ ftp ftp.uu.net
ftp.uu.net (login:smith): anonymous
Password: smith@linux.somewhere.com
```


Note

Many sites don't allow anonymous FTP. Allowing guest users to connect to your computer does involve some risk. In cases in which anonymous FTP isn't allowed, the `ftp` command fails with a message similar to `Login failed - User ''anonymous'' unknown`. Sites that do permit anonymous FTP typically place the users in a restricted directory tree with read-only access. If you're allowed to place files on the remote computer, you usually can put them in only one directory.

Also, several of the Web browsers (Netscape Navigator, for example) support the FTP protocol as well as the HTTP protocol. Because several Web browsers also support email, they can support anonymous FTP connections automatically. Check the user guide for your Web browser for more information.

To begin an anonymous FTP session, follow these steps:

1. Open a terminal window and enter the following at the command prompt:

   ```
   [burnett@ns burnett]$ ftp
   ```

   The terminal prompt changes to the following, indicating that the FTP program is running:

   ```
   ftp>
   ```

2. Enter the following command:

   ```
   ftp> open ftp.wu-ftpd.org
   Connected to ftp.wu-ftpd.org.
   220 ftp.wu-ftpd.org FTP server ready.
   Name (ftp.wu-ftpd.org:burnett):
   ```

3. Enter the name `anonymous`. The system responds with the following

   ```
   331 Guest login ok, send your complete e-mail address as password.
   Password:
   ```

4. Enter your complete email address as the password. The FTP server uses this password to track how many unique users are logging into the server over a given time period.

Note

If you don't want to give your email address, and instead you simply type a random string of garbage, such as `rgjlrlk`, the system might reject your anonymous login. Some servers are configured to test the anonymous passwords for proper email construction, so they reject passwords that are not formed like email addresses.

After you've entered your email address as your password, the server responds with the following message:

```
230-Welcome to the FTP server for the WU-FTPD Development Group
230-
230-This server is the primary distribution site for the WU-FTPD daemon.
230-
230-The pub directory contains the distribution and supporting files.
230-
230-If you are uploading contributions, please place them in the incoming
230-directory and email wuftpd-members@wu-ftpd.org announcing your upload.
230-
230 Guest login ok, access restrictions apply.
Remote system type is UNIX.
Using binary mode to transfer files.
ftp>
```

5. Enter `pwd`, as shown here, and press Enter to see the current directory:

```
ftp> pwd
257 ''/'' is current directory.
```

6. Enter `ls`, as shown here, to list the files in the current directory:

```
ftp> ls
200 PORT command successful.
150 Opening ASCII mode data connection for directory listing.
total 16
d--x--x--x    2 root    root              1024 Jul  19 12:19 bin
d--x--x--x    2 root    root              1024 Jan  12  1999 dev
d--x--x--x    2 root    root              1024 May  25 10:30 etc
drwxrwx-wx    2 root    wuftpd            1024 Jul  19 20:15 incoming
drwxrwx--x    3 root    wuftpd            2048 Jul 28 19:46 private
drwxrwxr-x    6 root    wuftpd            2048 Jul   9 07:43 pub
226 Transfer complete.
ftp>
```

7. Use `cd` to change to the `/pub` directory, as shown here, and you see the following response:

```
ftp> cd pub
250-This directory contains the following:
250-
250-ANNOUNCE-WUFTPD
250-   The original email announcing the formation of the WU-FTPD Development
250-   Group.
250-
250-BeroFTPD
250-   Directory containing the current versions of BeroFTPD. The Development
250-   Group has determined a primary goal for future releases is to merge many
250-   of the features of BeroFTPD back into the base release of the daemon.
250-   Until that work is completed, the most-current version of BeroFTPD will
250-   remain available here.
250-
250-README-MIRRORS
250-   The original email announcing the currently-known mirrors of the WU-FTPD
250-   Development Group's FTP site.
250-
250-README
```

```
250-   This file.
250-
250-support
250-   Directory containing many of the support packages either needed to
250-   create a working FTP server, or to assist in the operation of existing
250-   sites. The WU-FTPD Development Group has stated the goal of including
250-   many of these support facilities into future releases of the daemon.
250-   Until that work is completed, these supporting packages will remain
250-   available here.
250-
250-wu-ftpd
250-   Directory containing the base distribution of the WU-FTPD daemon and
250-   supporting documentation.
250-
250-
250-Other sources of information
250-
250-wu-ftpd Resource Center:    http://www.landfield.com/wu-ftpd/
250-wu-ftpd FAQ:                http://www.cetis.hvu.nl/~koos/wu-ftpd-faq.html
250-wu-ftpd list archive:       http://www.landfield.com/wu-ftpd/mail-archive/
250-
250-Please read the file README
250-   it was last modified on Fri May 21 23:30:39 1999 - 70 days ago
250-Please read the file README-MIRRORS
250-   it was last modified on Thu Jul 22 02:36:57 1999 - 8 days ago
250 CWD command successful.
ftp>
```

Notice that the README file in the /pub directory is piped to the terminal when you change directories to that directory.

8. Use cd to change to the wu-ftpd directory, as follows:

```
ftp> cd wu-ftpd
250-This directory contains the base distribution of the WU-FTPD daemon and
250-supporting documentation.
250-
250-ANNOUNCE-RELEASE
250-   The original email announcing the public release of the current version
250-   of the daemon.
250-
250-FIXES
250-   Directory containing the FIXES-* files documenting the changes the daemon
250-   has gone through since the release of version 2 by the Washington
250-   University at St. Louis. These may be incomplete, inaccurate or down-
250-   right misleading, but they're all we have for now.
250-
250-   This directory is available for on-the-fly tar and compression. If you
250-   want to read all the FIXES, please retrieve FIXES.tar.gz or FIXES.tar.Z
250-   rather than each individual file.
250-
250-README
250-   This file.
250-
250-attic
250-   Directory containing historical versions of the daemon, patches or other
250-   historical information. You don't want to run anything you find here;
250-   it's only for research purposes.
```

```
250-
250-binaries
250-   Directory containing by-machine pre-compiled binary distributions of the
250-   daemon. These are kept as current as possible. Browse arround to see
250-   if there's a binary for your system; it could save you a lot of time
250-   and trouble.
250-
250-examples
250-   Directory containing an example of a fully-functional, minimal-install
250-   FTP site. Many of your questions can be answered by the examples you'll
250-   see in here.
250-
250-quickfixes
250-   Directory containing by-version patches released to fix problems between
250-   releases.
250-
250-rfc0959.txt
250-   The definition of the current FTP protocol implemented by the WU-FTPD
250-   daemon. Not for the faint-of-heart.
250-
250-telnet.testing.HOWTO
250-   A short document explaining how to test the operation of your daemon
250-   using the telnet command. Often times problems are masked by the
250-   operation of your ftp client (command); this procedure allows you to see
250-   the inner-workings of the protocol.
250-
250-unsupported
250-   Patches to the daemon which are too old or too crufty to be included in
250-   the base release of the daemon. These are here because the WU-FTPD
250-   Development Group likes the ideas and may, at some time, include the
250-   features in a future version of the daemon.
250-
250-upload.configuration.HOWTO
250-   A longish document describing how to safely configure your FTP site to
250-   allow remote users to upload files. This is one of the thorniest issues
250-   for running a secure site; the document attempts to make the
250-   considerations more clear. This document is included in the base release.
250-   The version here may be more up-to-date that what you received, so check
250-   the date.
250-
250-wu-ftpd-current.tar.Z
250-wu-ftpd-current.tar.gz
250-   The current public-release version of the daemon. These are symbolic
250-   links to the actual files. Both GNU Zip (gz) and UNIX compress (Z)
250-   versions are available. Download the GNU format unless your system only
250-   supports UNIX compress.
250-
250-wu-ftpd-faq.txt
250-   Koos van den Hout's WU-FTPD Frequently Asked Questions (FAQ) .. if you
250-   have a problem, the answer is almost always here .. honest. Please read
250-   this document completely before posting your questions to the support
250-   mailing lists. This copy may be out-of-date; check the URL given inside
250-   for the most-current version.
250-
250-Please read the file README
250-   it was last modified on Wed May 26 09:01:36 1999 - 65 days ago
250-Please read the file README-MIRRORS
```

```
250-   it was last modified on Thu Jul 22 02:36:57 1999 - 8 days ago
250 CWD command successful.
ftp>
```

9. Use `cd` to change to the `binaries/intel/linux/redhat` directory:

```
ftp> cd binaries/intel/linux/redhat
250-Offical Redhat RPMs
250-------------------------------------
250-
250-   Binaries
250- -------------
250-   RH 4.2: wu-ftpd-2.5.0-0.4.2.i386.rpm
250-   RH 5.2: wu-ftpd-2.5.0-0.5.2.i386.rpm
250-   RH 6.0: wu-ftpd-2.5.0-2.i386.rpm
250-
250-   Source
250- -------------
250-   RH 4.2: wu-ftpd-2.5.0-0.4.2.src.rpm
250-   RH 5.2: wu-ftpd-2.5.0-0.5.2.src.rpm
250-   RH 6.0: wu-ftpd-2.5.0-2.src.rpm
250-
250-WU-FTPD Development Group
250-------------------------------------
250-The source RPMs should be usable on any system supporting RPM.
250-
250-This first group uses the default Redhat SPEC file and is built using all
250-defaults.
250-
250-   For Redhat 4.2 or later
250-   ----------------------------------------
250-   wu-ftpd-2.5.0-1.RH4-2.i386.rpm
250-   wu-ftpd-2.5.0-1.RH4-2.src.rpm
250-
250-   For Redhat 5.1 or later
250-   ----------------------------------------
250-   wu-ftpd-2.5.0-1.RH5-1.i386.rpm
250-   wu-ftpd-2.5.0-1.RH5-1.src.rpm
250-
250-   For Redhat 6.0 or later
250-   ----------------------------------------
250-   wu-ftpd-2.5.0-1.RH6-0.i386.rpm
250-   wu-ftpd-2.5.0-1.RH6-0.src.rpm
250-
250-The second group uses experimental SPEC files developed by a member of the
250-WU-FTPD Development Group. Installation should be quite a bit easier as
250-more conditions are checked for. The binaries are built for Redhat 4.2
250-using statically linked binaries so they should work on all Redhat systems.
250-
250-   For classical operation (using inetd)
250-   ----------------------------------------
250-   wu-ftpd-2.5.0-inet-1.i386.rpm
250-   wu-ftpd-2.5.0-inet-1.src.rpm
250-
250-   For operation as a standalone daemon
250-   ----------------------------------------
250-   wu-ftpd-2.5.0-standalone-1.i386.rpm
250-   wu-ftpd-2.5.0-standalone-1.src.rpm
```

```
250-
250-Please read the file README
250-   it was last modified on Fri Jun 11 10:13:26 1999 - 49 days ago
250 CWD command successful.
ftp>
Ls the current directory:
ftp> ls
200 PORT command successful.
150 Opening ASCII mode data connection for directory listing.
total 8212
-r--r--r-- 1 wuftpd wuftpd 1500 Jun 11 10:13 README
-r--r--r-- 1 wuftpd wuftpd 163730 Jun 10 16:41 wu-ftpd-2.5.0-0.4.2.i386.rpm
-r--r--r-- 1 wuftpd wuftpd 278405 Jun 10 16:42 wu-ftpd-2.5.0-0.4.2.src.rpm
-r--r--r-- 1 wuftpd wuftpd 164117 Jun 10 16:42 wu-ftpd-2.5.0-0.5.2.i386.rpm
-r--r--r-- 1 wuftpd wuftpd 278099 Jun 10 16:43 wu-ftpd-2.5.0-0.5.2.src.rpm
-r--r--r-- 1 wuftpd wuftpd 161701 May 21 23:39 wu-ftpd-2.5.0-1.RH4-2.i386.rpm
-r--r--r-- 1 wuftpd wuftpd 270140 May 21 23:39 wu-ftpd-2.5.0-1.RH4-2.src.rpm
-r--r--r-- 1 wuftpd wuftpd 161940 May 21 23:39 wu-ftpd-2.5.0-1.RH5-1.i386.rpm
-r--r--r-- 1 wuftpd wuftpd 269939 May 21 23:39 wu-ftpd-2.5.0-1.RH5-1.src.rpm
-r--r--r-- 1 wuftpd wuftpd 165732 May 21 23:39 wu-ftpd-2.5.0-1.RH6-0.i386.rpm
-r--r--r-- 1 wuftpd wuftpd 270340 May 21 23:39 wu-ftpd-2.5.0-1.RH6-0.src.rpm
-r--r--r-- 1 wuftpd wuftpd 168048 Jun 10 16:44 wu-ftpd-2.5.0-2.i386.rpm
-r--r--r-- 1 wuftpd wuftpd 278093 Jun 10 16:46 wu-ftpd-2.5.0-2.src.rpm
-r--r--r-- 1 wuftpd wuftpd 493153 May 25 14:25 wu-ftpd-2.5.0-inet-1.i386.rpm
-r--r--r-- 1 wuftpd wuftpd 272183 May 25 14:25 wu-ftpd-2.5.0-inet-1.src.rpm
-r--r--r-- 1 wuftpd wuftpd 498847 May 25 14:25 wu-ftpd-2.5.0-standalone-1.i386.rpm
-r--r--r-- 1 wuftpd wuftpd 273546 May 25 14:25 wu-ftpd-2.5.0-standalone-1.src.rpm
226 Transfer complete.
ftp>
```

Assuming you're installing for Red Hat Linux 6.0 on an Intel processor, three options are present in this directory as of this writing:

- `wu-ftpd-2.5.0-2.i386.rpm`—Built using the default Red Hat SPEC file.
- `wu-ftpd-2.5.0-inet-1.i386.rpm`—Built using experimental and enhanced SPEC files. The binaries are built for Red Hat 4.2 using statically linked binaries, so they should work on all Red Hat systems. This file was built for classical operation, using the inetd service.
- `wu-ftpd-2.5.0-standalone-1.i386.rpm`—Built using experimental and enhanced SPEC files. Installation should be quite a bit easier as more conditions are checked for. The binaries are built for Red Hat 4.2 using statically linked binaries, so they should work on all Red Hat systems. This file was built for operation as a standalone daemon.

In this case, you should choose the first file.

10. Enter the `get` command for the file you want to retrieve, as shown here:

```
ftp> get wu-ftpd-2.5.0-1.RH6-0.src.rpm
local: wu-ftpd-2.5.0-1.RH6-0.src.rpm remote: wu-ftpd-2.5.0-1.RH6-0.src.rpm
200 PORT command successful.
150 Opening BINARY mode data connection for wu-ftpd-2.5.0-1.RH6-0.src.rpm (270340
bytes).
226 Transfer complete.
270340 bytes received in 157 secs (1.7 Kbytes/sec)
ftp>
```

11. Enter `quit`, as shown here, to quit FTP and return to your terminal window. The remote FTP server gives a summary report of your activity in this session:

```
ftp> quit
221-You have transferred 270340 bytes in 1 files.
221-Total traffic for this session was 276748 bytes in 1 transfers.
221-Thank you for using the FTP service on ftp.wu-ftpd.org.
221 Goodbye.
You have new mail in /var/spool/mail/burnett
[burnett@ns burnett]$
```

12. Do an extended `ls` to ensure the file is present:

```
[burnett@ns burnett]$ ls -al wu-ftpd-2.5.0-1.RH6-0.src.rpm
-rw-rw-r--   1  burnett  burnett   270340 Jul 30 21:22 wu-ftpd-2.5.0-1.

RH6-0.src.rpm
```

You can then use the Red Hat Package Manager (RPM) to install the WU-FTP package. Use of the Red Hat Package Management system is presented in Chapter 7, "Upgrading and Installing Software."

CONFIGURING WU-FTPD

Before you start configuring wu-ftpd, you should read the man page for it. Carefully review the possible startup options, such as `-a` and `-L`. Table 37.1 shows some options for invoking wu-ftpd.

TABLE 37.1 EXAMPLES OF WU-FTPD COMMAND-LINE OPTIONS

Field	Description
`-l`	Provides additional logging information
`-i`	Logs uploads
`-o`	Logs downloads

To start the configuration, you need to find the existing FTP entry in the `/etc/inetd.conf` file and edit it to refer to wu-ftpd, as shown in the following example:

```
ftp stream tcp nowait root /usr/sbin/ftpd ftpd -lio
```

If you want to install wu-ftpd on a nonstandard port, you need to edit both the `/etc/services` and `/etc/inetd.conf` files. This technique can be useful for debugging wu-ftpd without interrupting the existing FTP service.

Next, add a line to `/etc/services` indicating the service name, port number, and protocol, as shown here:

```
wuftp 3010/tcp # command port to test wu-ftpd
```

You also might want to add a second line like this to `/etc/services`:

```
wuftp-data 3009/tcp # data port to test wu-ftpd
```

Now you can add or edit the appropriate FTP line to the `/etc/inetd.conf` file, the key part being to reference the same service name as is in the `/etc/services` file:

```
wuftp stream tcp nowait root /usr/sbin/ftpd ftpd -lio
```

Your next step is to make sure that the name of the service wu-ftpd matches in both the `/etc/inetd.conf` and the `/etc/services` files.

Finally, you can run `bin/ckconfig` from the distribution to verify your setup at this point and then try logging in to your FTP server as a real user.

Project: Setting Up an Anonymous FTP Server

If you want to set up an anonymous FTP server, you should use only the most recent version of the preferred FTP service. Older versions may contain exploits that can be used by the unscrupulous to gain access to your server or its contents.

Setting Permissions

When you're ready to set permissions for your anonymous FTP server, the permissions system of Linux can be helpful. For example, the anonymous FTP root directory (`~ftp`) and its subdirectories should not be owned by the FTP account or be in the same group as the FTP account. If any of these directories are owned by FTP or are in the same group as the FTP account and are not write-protected, an intruder can add files or modify other files. One way to secure the FTP service is to make the directories owned by the root account; after all, if the intruder has root access, he or she can do anything. Making the FTP root directory and its subdirectories owned by root, part of the system group, and protected so that only root has write permission helps to secure the anonymous FTP service.

The following is an example of an anonymous FTP directory setup:

```
drwxr-xr-x  7   root   system  512 Apr 7     12:33 ./
drwxr-xr-x 25   root   system  512 Jan 18     10:40 ../
drwxr-xr-x  2   root   system  512 Mar 21    11:46 bin/
drwxr-xr-x  2   root   system  512 May 23    18:49 etc/
drwxr-xr-x 10   root   system  512 Oct 16     11:34 pub/
```

All files and libraries involved, specifically those used by the FTP daemon as well as those in `~ftp/bin` and `~ftp/etc`, should have the same protections as these directories.

Password and Group Files

When you're setting up your anonymous FTP server, do *not* use the system's `/etc/passwd` file as the password file or use the system's `/etc/group` as the group file in the `~ftp/etc` directory. Placing these system files in the `~ftp/etc` directory allows intruders access to the files in question.

A more safe method is to use a dummy version of both the `~ftp/etc/passwd` and `~ftp/etc/group` files. These files should be owned by root. The `dir` command uses these dummy versions to show owner and group names of the files and directories instead of displaying arbitrary numbers. The following are some other tips to consider:

- The `~/ftp/etc/passwd` file should contain no account names that are the same as those in the system's `/etc/passwd` file. These files should include only those entries that are relevant to the FTP hierarchy or needed to show owner and group names.
- Make sure that the password field has been cleared. The following examples show the use of asterisks (*) to clear the password field.

  The following is an example of entries in a `~ftp/etc/passwd` file from an anonymous FTP area on `afakecompany.com`:

  ```
  toys:*:3822:20:Software Toys::
  ftp:*:3823:90:Anonymous FTP::
  doc:*:3824:90:User Documentation::
  ```

  The following is an example group file from the anonymous FTP area on `cert.org`:

  ```
  toys:*:20: ftp:*:90:
  ```

CHAPTER 38

Configuring Domain Name Service (DNS)

In this chapter

by Steve Burnett

HOW THE NET BEGAN

When the Internet was first formed, the number of hosts on the Net was very small. Maintaining the name/address mapping was fairly easy: Each host simply kept a complete list of all host names and addresses in a local file. As the growth of the Internet accelerated, this system quickly became unwieldy. When a new host was added, it was necessary to update every host file on every computer. Also, because each new computer resulted in a new line in every host file, the size of the host files began to grow to quite a large size. Clearly, a new solution was needed.

Mapping Internet system names to IP addresses is a task that requires a good degree of consideration. With the explosive growth of the Internet over the past few years, the original system of maintaining host name to IP address mappings in a local flat ASCII file quickly proved impractical. With thousands of computers on the Net and more being added daily, a new system was needed. That new system was a network-wide distributed database known as BIND, the Berkeley Internet Domain server. Also referred to variously as the Domain Name Service, the Domain Name System, or DNS, this system provides an effective, relatively transparent host name to the IP address mapping mechanism.

DNS is notoriously hard to configure, but when you're successful, maintaining it is fairly easy.

INTRODUCING DNS

DNS provides a mechanism for converting IP addresses into mnemonic names that represent \hosts, networks, and mail aliases. It does so by dividing the entire Internet IP and name space into different logical groups. Each group has authority for its own computers and other information.

Because DNS is a complicated topic, it has its own specialized set of terms. Table 38.1 lists the definitions of some commonly used DNS terms.

TABLE 38.1 COMMONLY USED DNS TERMS

Term	Definition
Domain	The logical entity or organization that represents a part of a network. For example, `afakecompany.com` is the name of the primary domain for the fictitious business A Fake Company.
Domain name	The name portion of a host name that represents the domain that contains the host. For example, in the address `quakeserver.afake-company.com`, the domain name is `afakecompany.com`. This term is also used interchangeably with *domain*.
Host	A computer on a network.
Node	A computer on a network.

TABLE 38.1 COMMONLY USED DNS TERMS

Term	Definition
Name server	A computer that provides DNS services to map DNS names to IP addresses.
Resolve	The act of translating a DNS name into its corresponding IP address.
Resolver	A program or library routine that extracts DNS information from a name server.
Reverse resolution	The act of matching a given IP address to its DNS name. This process is also called reverse DNS.
Spoof	The act of appearing to the network as having a different IP address or domain name.

DNS can be conceptually divided into the following three parts:

- **Domain name space**—This part is a specification for a tree structure that identifies a set of hosts and provides information about them. Conceptually, each node in the tree has a database of information about the hosts under its authority. Queries attempt to extract the appropriate information from this database. In simple terms, the domain name space is just the listing of all different types of information, names, IP addresses, mail aliases, and such that are available for lookup in the DNS system.
- **Name servers**—These programs hold and maintain the data located in the domain name space. Each name server has complete information about a subset of the domain name space and cached information about other portions.

  A name server has complete information for its area of authority. This authoritative information is divided into areas known as *zones*, which can be divided among different name servers to provide redundant service for a zone. Each name server knows about other name servers that are responsible for different zones. If a request comes in for information from the zone that a given name server is responsible for, the name server simply returns the information. However, if a request comes in for information from a different zone, the name server contacts the appropriate server with authority for that zone.
- **Resolvers**—These programs or library routines extract information from the name servers in response to a query about a host in the domain name space.

CONFIGURING THE RESOLVER

The first step in using DNS is to configure the resolver library on your computer. You must configure your local resolver if you intend to use DNS name resolution, even if you're not going to run a local domain name server.

THE /etc/host.conf FILE

The local resolver libraries are configured via a file named host.conf that is located in the /etc directory. This file tells the resolver what services to use and in what order. This file is a plain ASCII file that lists resolver options, one per line. Fields can be separated by either spaces or tabs. The # character indicates the start of a comment.

You can specify several options in the host.conf file, as shown in Table 38.2.

TABLE 38.2 CONFIGURATION OPTIONS FOR THE /etc/host.conf FILE

Option	Description
order	Specifies in what order different name resolution mechanisms are tried. The specified resolving services are tried in the order listed. The following name resolution mechanisms are supported: hosts (attempts to resolve the name by looking in the local /etc/host file), bind (queries a DNS name server to resolve the name), and nis (uses the Network Information Service [NIS] protocol to try to resolve the host name).
alert	Takes off or on as arguments. If this option is turned on, any attempt to spoof an IP address is logged via the syslog facility.
nospoof	If reverse resolution is used to match a host name to a specified address, nospoofresolves the host name that's returned to verify that it does match the address that you queried. This option prevents spoofing of IP addresses. You enable it by specifying nospoof on. Caution: Using this option can cause a noticeably additional load on the server.
trim	Takes a domain name as an argument. trim removes the domain name before performing an /etc/hosts lookup on the name. This way, you can put just the base host name in /etc/hosts without specifying the domain name.
multi	Takes off or on as arguments. It is used only with host queries to determine whether a host is allowed to have more than one IP address specified in /etc/hosts. This option has no effect on NIS or DNS queries.

The following is an example of an /etc/host.conf configuration file that uses these options:

```
# Sample /etc/host.conf file
#
# Lookup names via DNS first then fall back to /etc/hosts
order bind hosts
# We don't have machines with multiple addresses
multi off
# check for IP address spoofing
nospoof on
# and warn us if someone attempts to spoof
alert on
# Trim the afakecompany.com domain name for host lookups
trim afakecompany.com
```

This example shows a general resolver configuration for the domain afakecompany.com. The resolver looks up the host names by using DNS first and then tries the local /etc/hosts file.

Note Specifying the local /etc/hosts file in the resolution search is a good idea. If, for some reason, your name servers should be unavailable, you can still resolve the names for hosts listed in your local hosts file. You should also keep a list of all your local hosts in your /etc/hosts files on each of your local computers.

Multiple IP addresses for a single machine are disabled. This host checks for IP address spoofing by re-resolving the host name that a reverse IP address lookup returns. This procedure is a bit of a performance hit, but it helps make sure that no host is pretending to be a different host than it really is. Also, you've set up the resolver to warn you if an attempt to spoof is detected. Finally, the resolver trims the domain afakecompany.com from any host names that are looked up in the local /etc/hosts file.

THE /etc/resolv.conf FILE

Now that you've configured the basic behavior of the resolver library, you need to set up some information for the DNS portion of the resolver. You need to do so only if you're using DNS for host name resolution—that is, by specifying bind in the order statement of the /etc/host.conf file. But then you wouldn't be reading this chapter if you weren't going to use DNS, would you?

The /etc/resolv.conf file controls the way the resolver uses DNS to resolve host names. It specifies the DNS name servers to contact when resolving a host name and in what order to contact them. It also provides the local domain name and some clues as to how to guess at the domain name of hosts that are specified without a domain name.

Table 38.3 lists the valid options for the /etc/resolv.conf file.

TABLE 38.3 CONFIGURATION OPTIONS FOR THE /etc/resolv.conf FILE

Option	Description
domain	Specifies the local domain name of this host. If it's not given, the resolver tries to get the local domain name from the getdomainname() system call.
nameserver	Specifies the IP address of a DNS name server to contact for name resolution. You can list up to three name servers by using the nameserver option multiple times. The name servers are tried in the order listed. You should put your most reliable name server first so that queries don't time out on a server that's likely to be down.
search	Lists domains to try if no domain name is specified as part of a query host name. If no search option is given, the list of domains is created by using the local domain plus each parent domain of the local domain.

The following is a sample /etc/resolv.conf file for afakecompany.com:

```
# /etc/resolv.conf for afakecompany.com
#
```

```
# Set our local domain name
domain afakecompany.com
# Specify our primary name server
nameserver 166.82.1.3
```

In this example, you specify the local domain via the `domain` option and list one name server to use for resolving host names.

Note

You need to specify the IP address of the DNS name server as an argument to the `nameserver` option—not the host name. If you specify the host name, DNS doesn't know which host to contact to look up the host name of the name server.

The preceding example doesn't use the `search` option to specify the search order. This means that if you try to query the address of a machine—for example, `skippy`—the resolver tries to look up `skippy` first. If this lookup fails, the resolver looks up `skippy.afakecompany.com` and then `skippy.com`.

DNS servers can and do go down unexpectedly. If you rely solely on a DNS server for name resolution, you might find yourself unable to work if it crashes. Make sure that you specify multiple servers and keep a good list of hosts in your local `/etc/hosts` file, just in case.

USING THE NAMED DAEMON TO SET UP THE SERVER

Now the real magic starts. You've seen how to set up the basics of resolver configuration and how to tell your resolver which name servers to contact. In the following sections, you'll learn the mechanics of setting up a name server.

The DNS name server under Linux is provided by the `named` (pronounced *name-de*) daemon. This daemon is typically started at boot time and reads its configuration information from a set of configuration files. `named` typically runs until the machine is shut down. After `named` starts and is initialized with its configuration information, it writes its process ID to the `/etc/named.pid` ASCII file. It then starts listening for DNS requests on the default network port specified in `/etc/services`.

THE `named.boot` FILE

The first file that `named` reads when it starts is typically `/etc/named.boot`. This very small file is the key to all the other configuration files used by `named`; it contains pointers to the various configuration files and to other name servers. In the `named.boot` file, comments start with a semicolon and continue to the end of the line. Several options can be listed in the `named.boot` file; Table 38.4 lists these options.

TABLE 38.4 CONFIGURATION OPTIONS FOR THE named.boot FILE

Option	Description
`directory`	Specifies the directory where the DNS zone files are located. You can specify several different directories by using the `directory` option repeatedly. You can give file pathnames as being relative to these directories.
`primary`	Takes a domain name and filename as arguments. The `primary` option declares `named` to be authoritative for the specified domain and causes `named` to load the zone information from the specified file.
`secondary`	Tells `named` to act as a secondary server for the specified domain. It takes a domain name, a list of addresses, and a filename as arguments. `named` tries to transfer the zone information from the hosts specified in the address list and then stores the zone information in the file specified on the option line. If `named` can't contact any of the hosts, it tries to retrieve the information from the secondary zone file.
`cache`	Sets up caching information for `named`. The `cache` option takes a domain name and a filename as arguments. The domain name is typically specified as . (dot). The file contains a set of records, known as *server hints*, which list information about the root name servers.
`forwarders`	Takes a list of name servers as arguments. This option tells the local name server to try to contact the servers in this list if it can't resolve an address from its local information.
`slave`	Turns the local name server into a slave server. If the `slave` option is given, the local server tries to resolve DNS names via recursive queries. It simply forwards the request to one of the servers listed in the `forwarders` option line.

In addition to the options listed here, a few additional options aren't commonly used. Refer to the `named` man page for more information on these options.

Note Because `afakecompany.com` isn't attached to the Internet, many of the IP host and network addresses in these examples are fake. When you're setting up your own name server, make sure that you use the correct addresses assigned to you.

The following is a sample `named.boot` file:

```
; named.boot file
; A sample named.boot for afakecompany.com
;
directory /var/named
;
cache . named.ca
primary afakecompany.com named.hosts
primary 197.198.199.in-addr.arpa named.rev
```

This example sets up the primary name server for `afakecompany.com`. As you can see, comments start with the ; character. The `directory` statement in the file tells `named` that all its working files are located in the `/var/named` directory. Because none of the other files listed in the `named.boot` file have directory paths associated with them, they're located in `/var/named`.

Tip #188 from *Steve*

`/var/named` is the default directory. The name server can be installed anywhere, and the configuration files may be located anywhere, as long as you define the directory path in `named.boot`.

The next line sets up the caching information for this name server. This option should be present on almost every machine running as a name server. It tells `named` to enable caching and load the root server information from the file `named.ca`.

Tip #189 from *Steve*

The `cache` entry is very important. Without it, no caching is enabled on the local name server, which can cause severe performance problems for name lookups. Also, the local server can't contact any root name servers and, as a result, can't resolve any non-local host names unless it's set up as a forwarding name server.

The next line in the `named.boot` file tells `named` that this server has primary authority for the domain `afakecompany.com`. The zone and host information records are in the file `named.hosts`. You'll learn about these zone authority records in detail in the following section.

A second `primary` line in the `named.hosts` file shows that you also have primary zone authority for the zone `197.198.199.in-addr.arpa` with zone information in the `named.rev` file. This strange syntax is `named`'s way of getting information to match IP addresses to DNS names. Because DNS was originally set up to match DNS names to IP addresses, a different `primary` line is needed to do reverse resolution.

Note

The `in-addr.arpa` domain is used to specify reverse, or IP address, to DNS name resolution.

DATABASE FILES AND RESOURCE RECORDS

All information in the various `named` database files is stored in a format known as a *resource record*. Each resource record has a type associated with it, which tells the record's function. A resource record is the smallest piece of information that `named` uses.

Most people find the syntax for resource records and master database files in general to be a bit arcane and obscure. It doesn't help matters that some resource records have to appear in certain places in certain files. Most DNS configuration problems can be traced to errors in these master configuration files. All this said, it's time to dive in and look at the resource record syntax and the various master files.

Note

Within the master configuration files, you have the option of specifying absolute host names or host names relative to this domain. Host names are considered absolute if they end in a dot character (`.`), as in `foo.`, `afakecompany.`, or `com.`. Host names that don't end with a dot are considered relative to the local domain, also known as the *origin*. You can refer to the origin itself by using the `@` character.

Resource records use a general syntax that's consistent across all types of resource records. To add to the confusion, however, several parts of the record are optional depending on the record type and may assume a default value if not specified. The basic format of a resource record is the following:

```
[owner] [ttl] [class] typedata
```

Fields are separated by whitespace such as spaces or tabs. Table 38.5 describes what the various fields mean.

TABLE 38.5 FIELDS IN THE RESOURCE RECORD DATA FORMAT

Field	Description
`owner`	Identifies the domain or host name that the record applies to. If no name is given, the domain name of the previous resource record is assumed.
`ttl`	Identifies the time-to-live field, which tells how long, in seconds, the information in this record is valid after it's retrieved from a DNS server. If no `ttl` value is given, the minimum `ttl` of the last Start of Authority (SOA) record is used.
`class`	Specifies a networking address class. For TCP/IP networks, you use the value `IN`. If the class isn't given, the class of the previous resource record is used.
`type`	Lists the type of the resource record. This value is required. The various resource record types are listed in the next section.
`data`	Specifies the data associated with this resource record. This value is required. The format of the data field depends on the content of the type field.

As you can see, the format of a resource record can get quite confusing. Several fields are optional, and the `data` field depends on the type of the resource record. To make matters worse, resource records come in several different types. Table 38.6 lists the most common resource record types; a few additional types are rarely used. If you're interested in the additional types, refer to the appropriate RFCs and the man pages for `named`.

TABLE 38.6 COMMONLY USED RESOURCE RECORD TYPES

Type	Description
A	Associates a host name with an address. The data field holds the address in dotted decimal format. Any given host can have only one A record, which is an address record, because this record is considered authoritative information. Any additional host name or address mappings for this host must be given by using the CNAME type.
CNAME	Associates an alias for a host with its canonical name, the name specified in the A record for this host.
HINFO	Provides information about a host. The data field holds the hardware and software information for a particular host. It's just a free-format text string, so you can put in whatever makes sense for your hardware.
MX	Sets up a mail exchanger record. The data field holds an integer preference value followed by a host name. MX records tell a mail transport to send mail to another system that knows how to deliver it to its final destination.
NS	Points to a name server for another zone. The data field of the NS resource record contains the DNS name of the name server. You need to specify an A record as well to match the host name with the address of the name server.
PTR	Maps addresses to names, as in the in-addr.arpa domain. The host name must be the canonical host name.
SOA	Tells the name server that all the resource records following it are authoritative for this domain. (SOA stands for *Start of Authority*.) The data field is enclosed by parentheses and is typically a multiline field. The data field of the SOA record contains the following entries: origin—The canonical name of the primary name server for this domain. It's usually given as an absolute domain name ending with a . (dot), so it's not modified by the named daemon. contact—The email contact of the person who's responsible for maintaining this domain. Because the @ character has special meaning in resource records, it's replaced by a . (dot). If the person responsible for maintaining zone information about afakecompany.com is Mike, the contact address is listed in the file as mike.afakecompany.com. serial—The version number of the zone information file, which is given as an integer. It's used by secondary name servers to determine when the zone information file has changed. You should increment this number by one every time you change the information file so that the name server will notice the changes. refresh—The length of time in seconds that a secondary server should wait before trying to check the SOA record of the primary name server. The SOA records don't change very often, so you can usually set this value to be on the order of one day or so. retry—The time in seconds that a secondary server waits to retry a request to a primary server if the primary server isn't available. Typically, it should be set to a few minutes or so. expire—The time in seconds that the secondary server should wait before throwing away the zone information if it has been unable to contact the primary server. This number should typically be very large, on the order of 30 days or so. minimum—The default ttl value for resource records that don't specify a ttl. If your network doesn't change very much, this number can be set to a fairly large value, such as a couple of weeks. You can always override it by specifying a ttl value in your resource records.

Tip #190 from *Steve*

The MX record does not have to be another local system, but can be another system entirely. The name server `name.afakecompany.com` can host the Web site for the domain `nothinghere.com`, but an MX record can forward all mail addressed to `nothinghere.com` to another server not associated with `afakecompany.com`.

As you can see, the format of the resource records gets complicated in a hurry. Things should get clearer as you look at a few of the master configuration files used by `named`.

Tip #191 from *Steve*

Some of the options for the `nslookup` command can redefine the default settings for the command, such as the *root* option. If you consistently find yourself specifying custom settings for `nslookup`, you can put the custom settings in a file in your home directory named `.nslookup` (note the `.` at the beginning of the file name).

The `named.hosts` File

In the `named.boot` file you created earlier in this chapter, you listed `named.hosts` as being the file that contains information about your local domain, `afakecompany.com`. You could have named the file anything you wanted by listing the name on the `primary` line of `named.boot`. The `named.hosts` file contains authoritative information about the hosts in the zone of authority—`afakecompany.com`. Listing 38.1 shows a sample `named.hosts` file that uses several of the resource record types.

Listing 38.1 A Sample `named.hosts` File

```
; named.hosts file for afakecompany.com
;
@          IN      SOA     ns.afakecompany.com. mike.afakecompany.com. (
6 ; serial number
86400 ;refresh 24 hrs
300 ; retry 5 minutes
2592000 ; expire 30 days
86400 ; minimum 24 hrs
)
IN         NS   ns.afakecompany.com.
;
; your domain itself afakecompany.com
;
@          IN          A          184.122.110.1
IN         MX          100        mailhost.afakecompany.com
IN         HINFO       PC-486     Linux
```

LISTING 38.1 CONTINUED

```
;
; your primary nameserver
;
ns              IN     A          184.122.110.1
nameserver      IN     CNAME      ns.afakecompany.com.
;
; other hosts
;
mailhost        IN    A      184.122.110.2
jarre           IN    A      184.122.110.3
IN              MX    100     mailhost.afakecompany.com
skippy          IN    A      184.122.110.4
IN              MX    100     mailhost.afakecompany.com
;
; the localhost
;
localhost       IN    A       127.0.0.1
```

Note

Host names in resource records that end with a `.` (dot) aren't translated any further. If the dot isn't the last character in the host name, `named` assumes that the host name you gave is relative to the origin domain name referred to by `@` and appends the domain name to the host name.

Look at the `named.hosts` file in Listing 38.1 in detail. The first record that you come to in this file is the `SOA` (Start of Authority) record for the sample domain. The first line of this record starts with the `@` character, which indicates the current origin or domain (`afakecompany.com`). The definition of the origin comes from the domain listed on the corresponding `primary` line in `named.boot`. After that, you see the codes `IN` and `SOA`, which tell `named` that this resource record uses Internet (TCP/IP) addressing and is a start-of-authority record.

The next two entries on the line are the canonical name of the primary name server for this domain (`ns.afakecompany.com`) and the email contact with the `@` replaced by a dot (`mike.afakecompany.com`). You then list the various fields of the data required by an SOA record, one per line. (Refer to Table 38.6 for a complete explanation of each of these entries.)

After the `SOA` record, the next line is a name-server resource record, which lists `ns.afakecompany.com` as being a name server for the domain. Because no domain is listed in the domain field, it's assumed to be the last domain specified, which was `@`, listed in the `SOA` record. And, of course, the `@` character really expands to be the local domain, `afakecompany.com`. What could possibly be easier to understand?

The next three lines set up some information about the `afakecompany.com` domain itself. Although you've listed the domain name as `@` for clarity because it was the last domain name listed in the file, these resource records would still apply to it by default if you had left the domain field blank. The following line allows users to refer to afakecompany.com as though it were a real machine:

```
@      IN      A      184.122.110.1
```

It has been assigned the IP address of 184.122.110.1, which, as you'll see, is really the IP address of ns.afakecompany.com. The next line sets up a mail exchanger MX record for afakecompany.com so that all mail going to it gets forwarded to mailhost.afakecompany.com instead. The last line in this group sets up a host information HINFO record for afakecompany.com, which tells the world that it's a PC-486 running Linux.

A few lines earlier in the file, you listed ns.afakecompany.com as being your name server via an NS resource record. For named to work correctly, you must provide an address or A record that gives the address of ns.afakecompany.com. The next line in your file does just that. Following the "glue record" that gives the address of the name server, you have a CNAME resource record. This record tells you that nameserver.afakecompany.com is an alias for ns.afakecompany.com.

You then proceed to set up address records for three other hosts in your domain: mailhost, jarre, and skippy. Notice that after the A records for jarre and skippy are MX records that route any mail received by jarre or skippy to mailhost.afakecompany.com. Because no name was specified in the first field of these MX records, they apply to the previous name—jarre or skippy.

Note Because the owner field of a resource record defaults to the last one specified if it's left blank, you can easily group records that apply to one host. However, you must be careful if you add new records for new hosts to a file. If you add them to the middle of a file, you might cause the default host to change for some of the existing resource records. Look carefully before you add resource records to an existing file.

Finally, the last host in this named.hosts file is the localhost, which is mapped to address 127.0.0.1. As you can see, the syntax for these files gets quite complicated and gives you lots of room for errors.

The named.rev File

Thenamed.rev file is very similar to the named.hosts file, except that it essentially works in reverse; it maps addresses to host names. Listing 38.2 shows a sample named.rev file for afakecompany.com.

Listing 38.2 A Sample named.rev File

```
; named.rev file for afakecompany.com
;
@         IN      SOA     ns.afakecompany.com. mike.afakecompany.com. (
6 ; serial number
```

LISTING 38.2 CONTINUED

```
86400 ;refresh 24 hrs
300 ; retry 5 minutes
2592000 ; expire 30 days
86400 ; minimum 24 hrs
)
IN     NS      ns.afakecompany.com.
;
; reverse map your IP addresses
;
1           IN      PTR     ns.afakecompany.com.
2           IN      PTR     mailhost.afakecompany.com.
3           IN      PTR     jarre.afakecompany.com.
4           IN      PTR     skippy.afakecompany.com.
```

In this example, you have the same SOA record that you saw in the `named.hosts` file. This record just sets up the authority information for the domain. In this case, `@`, the value of the origin, is set to `197.198.199.in-addr.arpa` from the `primary` line in the `named.boot` file. Recall that the `in-addr.arpa` domain refers to reverse mapping of addresses to names.

Note

The address listed as part of your `in-addr.arpa` line is your network address backward. Your sample network for this chapter has the address 184.122.110.0. When you list it in the reverse mapping data files, you list it as the following:

```
197.198.199.in-addr.arpa
```

You have the `NS` record that lists the name server for your domain. Following that are the records that make up the reverse address resolution records. They are `PTR` records and give the host number (the part of the IP address not listed in the `in-addr.arpa` value) and the canonical host name that matches it. You must use the canonical host name here instead of a relative host name. For example, the following line tells `named` to map the host address `184.122.110.2` to the host name `mailhost.afakecompany.com`:

```
2   IN    PTR     mailhost.afakecompany.com.
```

THE `named.ca` FILE

As stated earlier in this chapter, the caching operation of `named` is very important. Fortunately, the `named.ca` file that sets up caching is also usually the simplest of the `named` configuration files. It just lists the root name servers for the various domains with their IP addresses. It contains a couple of special field indicators that tell `named` that they are root servers.

You can probably just copy the format of the sample `named.ca` file in Listing 38.3. To get a complete current list of the root name servers, use the `nslookup` utility.

Listing 38.3 A Sample named.ca File

```
; named.ca file
;
. 99999999      IN     NS         NS.NIC.DDN.MIL.
99999999    IN      NS       NS.NASA.GOV.
99999999    IN      NS       KAVA.NISC.SRI.COM.
99999999    IN      NS       TERP.UMD.EDU.
99999999    IN      NS       C.NYSER.NET.
99999999    IN      NS       NS.INTERNIC.NET.
;
NS.NIC.DDN.MIL.     99999999      IN      A      192.112.36.4
NS.NASA.GOV.        99999999      IN      A      128.102.16.10
KAVA.NISC.SRI.COM.  99999999      IN      A      192.33.33.24
TERP.UMD.EDU.       99999999      IN      A      128.8.10.90
C.NYSER.NET.        99999999      IN      A      192.33.4.12
NS.INTERNIC.NET.    99999999      IN      A      198.41.0.4
```

As you can see, the `named.ca` file simply maps `NS` name server records to the appropriate addresses for them.

Note Another way to assign addresses to systems in a network is to use the Dynamic Host Configuration Protocol (DHCP), which is very popular for systems that may not be attached to a given network at all times, such as notebook computers. You can find the ISC's (the Internet Software Consortium) Web site for the DHCP service on the Web at `http://www.isc.org/view.cgi?/products/DHCP/index.phtml`.

Troubleshooting

DNS is a very complex system. You can do many things wrong that will cause your system not to behave properly. Many of the problems that occur with a DNS setup may appear to be identical but come from different causes. However, most of the problems result from syntax errors in your configuration files. The following are a few troubleshooting tips:

- Make sure that you specify the host names correctly in your DNS configuration files. If you're using an absolute host name, be sure to end it with a dot.
- Be especially careful with the names used in `SOA` and `CNAME` records. If you make errors here, these resource records can redirect host name queries to computers that don't exist.
- Be sure to increment the serial number in your configuration files when making changes. If you forget, DNS will not reread the file.

- Be sure to enter the correct IP address for `A` records and check to see that it matches your `/etc/hosts` file (if you have one). Also, make sure that the DNS name and IP address match the corresponding reverse resolution information in `named.rev`.
- Your best tool for figuring out errors is the `nslookup` command. Use `nslookup` to test your DNS server thoroughly. Do regular and reverse resolution for every address in your DNS database to make sure that all the names and addresses are correct.

CHAPTER 39

CONFIGURING EMAIL

In this chapter

by Steve Burnett

AN OVERVIEW OF ELECTRONIC MAIL 822

The following sections present a broad overview of electronic messaging. First is a discussion of some of the general concepts of electronic mail, including two basic kinds of mail software and where sendmail belongs in that division. Next, you'll find a description of the RFCs (Requests for Comment), where the protocols used to communicate within and across networks are defined. Finally, you'll find explanations of some of the protocols used to define electronic messages.

HISTORY AND GENERAL CONCEPTS

One of the first widely used office mail systems was IBM's PROFS. A mainframe-based system, PROFS had features similar to modern email systems such as Microsoft Exchange and Lotus Notes. Such features included the following:

- Strong administration and management tools
- Security customization
- Scheduling capabilities

PROFS and other messaging systems of the time shared several similarities. Whether mainframe- or UNIX-based, they were text-based and were considered host-based centralized messaging systems. Because PROFS was scalable and adaptable, IBM only recently switched away from it for its enterprise mail use.

As personal computers grew in acceptance and became widely used throughout corporations, people started to take advantage of the shift in computing power from the mainframe to the desktop. An early application of personal computer networks was file sharing, which made use of a central file server and a shared universally accessible network drive. Shortly thereafter, messaging systems began to take advantage of the new power on users' desktops. So host-based messaging shifted (in some cases) to LAN-based messaging.

THE SHARED-FILE MESSAGING MODEL

cc:Mail is an example of *LAN-based messaging*, which is also called *shared-file messaging*. In the shared-file messaging model, the desktop client has all the power and all the control. A client sends messages to a mailbox on a server and *polls* the server to retrieve mail from its specified mailbox directory. The server is passive, only storing messages. It performs no processing or sorting and has no provisions for setting rules to control message flow. Shared-file messaging provided the following gains over host-based messaging:

- Added attachments to text-only messages
- Required lower-cost servers
- Simplified setup
- Improved performance for some client actions

However, shared-file messaging systems introduced new problems. Because each user needed full access to the file system, including other users' mailboxes, security was an issue. Also, because each client had to poll a server to get new mail, network traffic increased. Network bandwidth is a bottleneck more often than server or client bandwidths are.

The Client/Server Messaging Model

The client/server messaging system divided the tasks of message processing between the desktop workstations and the servers. Using a push model for messages, mail clients no longer clogged the network by constantly polling for new messages. Client/server messaging also improved on shared-file messaging by improving security so that users would have more difficulty reading others' mail. With the more intelligent server, the sorting and processing of messages could be performed before messages were transferred across the network to a client.

MUAs, MTAs, and MDAs

An electronic mail system can be broken down into three elements: the Mail User Agent (MUA), the Mail Transport Agent (MTA), and the Mail Delivery Agent (MDA).

The MUA is the user interface—the software with which the user reads mail, organizes mail into directories or folders, and sends mail. People prefer different features in their MUAs, and not all MUAs are available on all platforms. Many MUAs can coexist on the same machine. For example, a UNIX workstation can have any or all of the following MUAs available for use: mailx, elm, pine, mutt, mailtool, and dtmail. A given user can use any MUA present on his or her system because the MUAs are simply local applications. In addition, MUA functionality is often included in multipurpose software such as Lotus Notes and Netscape Mail.

The MTA isn't used to write a mail message; it's used to route the mail from a local MUA to another MTA on another system. (sendmail is an example of an MTA that is not used to read or write mail directly. sendmail is intended only to deliver preformatted messages.) Mail routing may occur either locally or remotely. In a local mail transfer in which both the sender and destination have accounts on the same machine, the MTA is responsible for transporting mail from itself to a local MDA. In the process, the MTA may possibly edit the protocols, addresses, and routing of the mail message. A message created on a UNIX-to-UNIX Copy Protocol (UUCP) network requires some transformation before that message can be received by a person on a Transmission Control Protocol/Internet Protocol (TCP/IP) network. The MTA acts as a gateway for mail to get a message from one network to another network that uses different protocols. In the vast majority of situations, a given machine has only a single MTA.

The MDA is the third component of the mail-handling routine. Although sendmail handles SMTP mail transfer between MTAs directly, sendmail relies on Mail Delivery Agents (MDAs) to handle local delivery from the sendmail queue to a queue used by an MUA. Two common MDAs that sendmail is often configured to use are `/bin/mail` and `procmail`. `/bin/mail` is almost universally available on UNIX systems; `procmail` is widely available and is both faster and much more capable than the standard `/bin/mail`, providing strong capabilities for the presorting and preprocessing of mail.

Tip #192 from *Steve*

> To better understand the MUA/MTA/MDA relationship, consider a real-world example of a person sending a letter. The MUA represents the person sending the letter: That person writes a letter, places it in an envelope, puts an address and stamp on it, and then delivers it to a post office. The MTA is like the post office staff: They accept the letter, examine the address, reformat the address if necessary, and route the letter either to a mailbox in the same post office (if the letter is local) or to another post office (for a remote destination). The MDA corresponds to the postal worker who delivers the mail from the post office to the intended location. If a gateway is used, this analogy can be extended: An MTA that receives a letter for a destination in another state has to transfer that message to another MTA that knows how to deliver letters in the target state.

THE IETF REQUESTS FOR COMMENT

A *Request for Comment*, or *RFC*, is a formal description of protocol formats used on the Internet. These protocols are also adhered to by many non-Internet systems. The RFCs are issued by the Internet Engineering Task Force (IETF). RFCs are identified and referred to by numbers for clarity; it's easier to refer to RFC822 than to refer to the "Standard for the Format of ARPA Internet Text Messages." As of this writing, more than 2,000 RFCs have been published, some of which have been made obsolete by later RFCs. To find a given RFC, look for the IETF on the World Wide Web at `http://www.ietf.org/`.

Because mail is such a commonly used function of the Internet, many of the RFCs set standards for mail exchange. sendmail and other MTAs address the needs and definitions of many of these protocols. However, attempting to describe in detail all the RFCs relevant to mail transport and format could take years of time and thousands of pages.

Table 39.1 presents, in chronological order, the RFCs relevant to sendmail.

TABLE 39.1 RFCS DEALING WITH ELECTRONIC MAIL MESSAGING

Number	Title	Comment
RFC819	Domain Naming	Contains convention for Internet user applications.
RFC821	Simple Mail Transfer Protocol	Defines SMTP.

Table 39.1 RFCs Dealing with Electronic Mail Messaging

Number	Title	Comment
RFC822	Standard for the Format of ARPA Internet Text Messages	Defines the format (headers, body, and how to separate the two) for Internet text mail messages.
RFC976	UUCP Mail Interchange	
Format Standard	Defines the UNIX-to-UNIX Copy Protocol (UUCP) format of mail messages between two systems.	
RFC1123	Requirements for Internet Hosts—Application and Support	Extends and updates RFC822,mostly by clarifying ambiguous issues in the original document.
RFC1327	Mapping between X.400 (1988)/ISO 10021 and RFC822	Updates RFC822.
RFC1521 and RFC1522	MIME (Multipurpose Internet Mail Extensions) Parts One and Two	Provides another extension to the mail format defined in RFC822 by defining Multipurpose Internet Mail Extensions (MIME), which, among other things, allows insertion of binary files such as graphics and sound to mail messages. These two were made obsolete by RFC2045_2049.
RFC1651	SMTP Service Extensions	Introduces ESMTP (Extended Simple Mail Transfer Protocol).
RFC1652	SMTP Service Extension for 8-bit MIME Transport	
RFC1653	MTP Service Extension for Message	
RFC1869	SMTP Service Extensions	Makes RFC1651 obsolete.
RFC1870	SMTP Service Extension for Message Size Declaration	Makes RFC1653 obsolete.

TABLE 39.1 RFCS DEALING WITH ELECTRONIC MAIL MESSAGING

Number	Title	Comment
RFC1891	SMTP Service Extension for Delivery Status Notifications	
RFC1892	The Multipart/Report Content Type for the Reporting of Mail System Administrative Messages	
RFC1893	Enhanced Mail System Status Codes	
RFC1894	An Extensible Message Format for Delivery Status Notifications	
RFC2045_2049	Multipurpose Internet Mail Extensions (MIME) Parts One through Five	Make RFC1521 and RFC1522 obsolete.

INTERNET PROTOCOLS

sendmail uses the *Simple Mail Transfer Protocol* (*SMTP*) to move messages between two mail servers. Acting as a server-to-server protocol, SMTP requires another protocol such as POP3 to collect and process messages locally and deliver the messages to specific users. SMTP is the communications protocol generally used in UNIX-based networks for mail over TCP/IP connections. Unlike the UUCP protocol, which must have a "map" of which machines exist between the sender and the destination, TCP/IP allows one system on a network to talk "directly" to another by passing packets of information back and forth between the two. SMTP, which is a TCP-based client/server protocol, is defined in the IETF's RFC821, titled "Simple Mail Transfer Protocol."

SMTP is complex in details but is fundamentally simple. After a reliable connection is established, the mail client (MUA) initiates a brief handshaking sequence with the mail server (MTA). The client then sends one or more messages to the MTA for delivery. Before each message is sent, the mail client sends a list of the message's local recipients and the sender's address. In an obvious paper mail parallel, this information is referred to as the message's *envelope*.

The handshaking sequence and message content exchange take place in a formal language made up of four-character commands and three-digit reply codes. For example, an Extended Simple Mail Transport Protocol (ESMTP) mail exchange log might look like this:

```
$ /usr/sbin/sendmail -v david@mail.fake.com < message
david@mail.fake.com... Connecting to localmail.mail.fake.com. via smtp...
220 localmail.mail.fake.com ESMTP Sendmail 8.9/8.9/; Sat, 22 May 1999 08:06:22
230_0700
>>> EHLO gateway.oppositemail.com
250 localmail.mail.fake.com Hello michael@gateway.oppositemail.com [192.168.0.5],
250 pleased to meet you
```

```
>>> MAIL From:michael@gateway.oppositemail.com
250 <michael@gateway.oppositemail.com>... Sender ok
>>> RCPT To:david@mail.fake.com
250 Recipient ok
>>> DATA
354 Enter mail, end with ''.'' on a line by itself
>>> .
250 WAA11745 Message accepted for delivery
david@mail.fake.com... Sent (WAA11745 Message accepted for delivery)
Closing connection to localmail.mail.fake.com.
>>> QUIT
221 localmail.mail.fake.com closing connection
```

A framework for additional features in electronic mail is called *Extended Simple Mail Transport Protocol (ESMTP)*. ESMTP is a mechanism by which any extensions used with traditional SMTP can be negotiated between the client and server. The mechanism, as described in RFC1651, is open ended: Two possible extensions were defined in RFC1652 and RFC1653.

RFC1652 defines 8-bit MIME encoding, which enables a user to send 8-bit data in mail messages without having to recode the data using base64, quoted-printable, or some other encoding method. This type of encoding also eliminates the breakage that can result from sending 8-bit data to an RFC821-compliant SMTP server that doesn't know what to do with the components it receives.

Message size declaration (defined in RFC1653) offers a method for a server to limit the size of a message it is prepared to accept. With RFC821 SMTP, the only possibility is for the server to discard the message after it has been sent in its entirety and after the message has crossed the network onto the server. Unfortunately, deleting the message after the message has arrived is a waste of bandwidth, and the mail client has no way of knowing that the message was discarded because of its size.

Other extensions possible with ESMTP include requesting a delivery status notification on outgoing messages (so that senders can be notified when messages arrive at their destination) and negotiating encryption between secure mail servers for more secure mail.

MAIL MESSAGE FORMATTING

SMTP defined how to transfer a mail message across the Internet but did not define how to recognize a mail message. RFC822 defines the format of Internet electronic mail messages. The format is simple, as befits a standard:

- A header containing various required and optional message attributes
- A blank line
- The message contents

The header fields are much longer than the content in the sample message given here:

```
Return-Path: david@mail.fake.com
Received: from localmail.mail.fake.com (localmail.mail.fake.com [168.9.100.10])
by gateway.oppositemail.com (8.9/8.9) with ESMTP id WAA01322 for
<robert@oppositemail.com>; Sat, 22 May 1999 18:17:06 _0500
```

```
Received: from beta.mail.fake.com (beta.mail.fake.com [207.266.47.2]) by
localmail.mail.fake.com (8.9/8.9) with SMTP id WAA13732 for
<robert@oppositemail.com> Sat, 22 May 1999 18:22:06 _0500
Message-Id: 199802180506.WAA13732@localmail.mail.fake.com
X-Sender: pete@localmail.mail.fake.com
X-Mailer: Amiga Eudora Lite Version 2.1.2
Mime-Version: 1.0
Content-Type: text/plain; charset="us-ascii''
Date: Sat, 22 May 1999 18:22:08 _0500
To: robert@oppositemail.com
From: David Wylie david@mail.fake.com
Subject: Test message

This is a test message.
David
```

The blank line after the `Subject` line divides the header from the message body that follows. Any subsequent blank line is part of the message body and has no structural significance. Most header fields are brief and have a fairly obvious meaning (such as `Subject`), whereas some others are lengthy and not readily understood (such as `Received`). For a detailed explanation of the many standard and less-standard header fields, see Chapter 35 of Bryan Costales's and Eric Allman's *sendmail, 2nd Edition* (O'Reilly & Associates).

Each header line consists of a "keyword-value" pair that defines a characteristic of that message. For example, a required characteristic of a mail message is a message recipient. This characteristic is defined by the keyword `To:`, one or more spaces or tabs, and then the value that specifies the mailing address of the recipient. In the preceding message, this characteristic is defined by the following line:

```
To: robert@oppositemail.com
```

SENDMAIL

sendmail is generally considered one of the few true nightmares of UNIX system administration. sendmail is difficult to configure and can be approached in much the same way that novices approach UNIX. When someone once complained to Eric Allman (the creator of sendmail) that sendmail administration was complicated, he replied, "Configuring sendmail is complex because the world is complex." Although sendmail can do just about anything you can think of, instructing it how to do what you want it to can be a chore.

However, although sendmail is difficult to work with, recent versions have improved the tasks of configuring and administering sendmail substantially. The addition of a large set of M4 macros and the ability to use intelligible names for options plus the single-character switches in the configuration file has made sendmail configuration an easier task. sendmail has also become a reasonably mature product. Although flaws are still found almost monthly, sendmail is used in enterprise networks for mail delivery across a wide set of networks and in high-volume environments.

sendmail's History

In the late 1970s, Eric Allman was at the University of California at Berkeley. He wrote the predecessor to sendmail, called delivermail, which was released in 1979 to solve the problem of transferring mail among the three networks on campus at that time. Those three networks were ARPAnet (which was using NCP, or Network Control Protocol), a UUCP mail system, and an internal network called BerkNet.

The next year, ARPAnet started to convert from NCP to TCP (Transmission Control Protocol). Previously, mail was delivered using FTP (File Transfer Protocol), but SMTP was developed to plan for the possible growth of the network's mail traffic by several orders of magnitude.

In response to these changes, Allman adopted an inclusive approach to formats of electronic mail messages. If a message didn't match the preferred format, sendmail attempted to fix the message format instead of immediately rejecting the message. Allman also chose to limit the functional goal of sendmail to be a router of mail, instead of including the functionality of an end-user mail application. The 4.1c version of BSD (Berkeley Software Distribution) UNIX included the first public release of sendmail.

Meanwhile, others were busy extending sendmail's capabilities separately from Allman. In addition to various private efforts, several commercial vendors such as Sun and Hewlett-Packard developed their own versions of sendmail as they saw needs for improvements not included in the current versions. Out of these parallel developments came several versions of sendmail with varying levels of compatibility. In 1998, Allman took sendmail to commercial status as of version 8.9, leaving the 8.8.x version the freeware it always was.

Tip #193 from *Steve*

A reference to "V5," "V7," "V8," or something similar is referring to the version number of sendmail. V5 is version 5.x, V7 is version 7.x, V8 is version 8.x, and so on.

sendmail's Architecture

In general, compilation and installation of the sendmail distribution are often simpler than they first appear. The source package includes make-description files tailored for many different systems and a "build" script that chooses the correct one for the local environment. At times, administrators might need to make minor changes to the make-description file that's most similar to their particular environment in order to match the specific local system.

sendmail the Daemon

sendmail itself is normally configured to run on a UNIX system as a *daemon* to listen for incoming mail.

Note A *daemon* is a UNIX system program that runs in the background without a controlling terminal window.

When sendmail is run as a daemon, unless it's instructed not to on startup, it forks and runs in the background, listening on socket 25 for incoming SMTP connections. The command to run sendmail as a daemon on a Berkeley UNIX-based system might look something like this:

```
/usr/lib/sendmail -bd -q30m
```

This command can be defined as one of the startup commands executed when the UNIX system boots. The following sample command is taken from a startup script named `sendmail.init` found in the `/etc/rc.d/init.d` directory on a Linux system:

```
# Start daemons.
echo -n ''Starting sendmail: ''
daemon sendmail -bd -q1h
echo
touch /var/lock/subsys/sendmail
;;
```

The `-bd` flag launches sendmail as a daemon, and the `-q1h` switch instructs sendmail to check the queue once every hour. In contrast, the sample command preceding this one has the `-q` switch instructing sendmail to check the queue every 30 minutes.

The first action sendmail takes when it's started is to read the `/etc/sendmail.cf` configuration file.

sendmail Configuration and Control Using the `sendmail.cf` File

Part of sendmail's power is derived from the access provided to sendmail's underlying configuration files. As mail messages are funneled through sendmail's configuration files, sendmail performs all message routing functions, including parsing, forwarding, delivering, returning, and queuing.

The core of sendmail's configuration is the `sendmail.cf` file. A complex configuration file read only once at sendmail's initial runtime, `sendmail.cf` contains three important types of information:

- Options such as operational control switches, mailer definitions, and the locations of other sendmail subconfiguration files
- Rulesets for rewriting addresses on incoming and outgoing messages
- Macros for use in rulesets

Tip #194 from *Steve*

No one bothers to write a `sendmail.cf` file starting with a blank page in a text editor. If you are configuring sendmail for a new network, you can almost certainly find a sendmail.cf file that requires minimal changes. Of course, after you have a functioning mail server, you should make a backup of the working configuration and put it somewhere safe.

Version 8 and above of sendmail added the use of the m4 macro preprocessor, which is used to generate sendmail.cf files containing the features you select. A sendmail m4 creation file typically should be given an .mc (macro configuration) file suffix, but it is not required for the process to work. Many sample .mc scripts are supplied with the standard sendmail distributions.

For example, a minimum .mc file for a Linux workstation (without appropriate comments) could be something like this:

```
OSTYPE(linux)dnl
MAILER(local)dnl
```

The preceding are the only two required macros in an .mc file. You are likely to want more features, but this file—named smallest_linux.mc—could be run with the following command (assuming you are in the /usr/lib/sendmail/cf/cf directory, where the standard sendmail distribution places m4 files):


```
m4 ../m4/cf.m4 smallest_linux.mc > sendmail.cf
```

The following list provides a breakdown of the elements in the preceding command:

m4	Calls the m4 preprocessor
../m4/cf.m4	Identifies m4's default configuration file
smallest_linux.mc	Is the two-line macro configuration file
> sendmail.cf	Specifies that output is to be placed in the sendmail.cf file

Now that you have used m4 to generate a sendmail.cf file containing exactly the features you requested, you still need to customize the sendmail.cf file for use at your site. Using m4 for sendmail.cf generation, however, is fast and accurate. In addition to using the many m4 macros that ship with the sendmail distribution, you can also write your own as you feel necessary and include them for use.

Tip #195 from *Steve*

For a quick sendmail configuration file, you can fill out the World Wide Web form interface to the m4 configuration tool (for version 8 sendmail) at http://www.completeis.com/sendmail/sendmail.cgi. Select your desired options with the Web form, and a sendmail.cf file with the chosen options will be returned to you.

sendmail Configuration Files and Their Locations

`sendmail.cf` is the first file that sendmail reads on startup. The `sendmail.cf` file contains the locations of all other subconfiguration files used by sendmail, which are listed in Table 39.2.

Table 39.2 sendmail Configuration Files

Filename and Location	Description
`/etc/aliases`	ASCII text list of defined aliases to names
`/etc/aliases.db`	Database of aliases compiled from `/etc/aliases`
`/etc/sendmail.hf`	Help file
`/var/log/sendmail.st`	Collected statistics
`/var/spool/mqueue/*`	Temporary files for mail queue
`/var/run/sendmail.pid`	The process ID of the daemon

The locations listed in Table 39.2 are only the default locations of the files. Because their locations are defined within `sendmail.cf`, you can set them to whatever name and directory path you like.

sendmail contains far too many configuration options to list in this book. The syntax for options comes in two types: very cryptic and a bit less cryptic. In the cryptic version of option syntax, the `O` (capital *o*, not zero) command starts an option command in the `sendmail.cf` file. So the following two sample commands from a `sendmail.cf` file perform the same function:

```
O8pass8
```

```
O EightBitMode=pass8
```

These commands tell sendmail to pass 8-bit formatted data as 8 bits, and not to truncate it to 7 bits. Notice the syntax change: The single-character version (`O8`) does not contain a space between the `O` and the number signifying which option is being set, whereas the name version (`O EightBitMode`) must contain a space between the `O` command and the name of the option. As with all other sendmail commands, the `O` must be in the leftmost position on the line, which is also column 1.

This restriction prevents misinterpretation of commands, such as this next line that also can be found in a `sendmail.cf` file:

```
DMMONGO
```

This command defines , a macro (`M`), to have the value `MONGO` so that you can use `$M` when rewriting rules instead of typing `MONGO`. Without the restriction that a command is identified by an `O` in the leftmost column, the `O` in `MONGO` might be interpreted as a command.

The options just presented illustrate the form of the option command for use within a configuration file. However, you can define options either in an m4 macro file or on the command line. The command-line versions of the preceding options use a dash before the option, a lowercase *o* to indicate a single-character option command, and an uppercase *O* to indicate a named option command, as shown in these examples:

```
-o8pass8
-O EightBitMode=pass8
-O EightBitMode=pass8
```

SENDMAIL RULESETS

sendmail uses rules to rewrite addresses on incoming and outgoing mail. These rules are the center of sendmail's capability, as well as its complexity: sendmail's rewriting rules are a specialized text-oriented programming language. Eric Allman designed sendmail so that the ruleset performs two core tasks:

- Examines each recipient's address to determine which MDA should be used to send the message to (or nearer to) the recipient
- Transforms addresses in both the envelope and the message header to facilitate delivery or reply

Rewriting rules are organized into rulesets. A *ruleset* is a subroutine or module consisting of a sequence of rules. When an address is passed to a ruleset, the subroutine passes the address to each of its rules in order. If the matching clause matches the investigated address, the rule is applied, the address is transformed, and the result is passed to the next rule. If the address does not match the current rule, the address is not transformed, and the next rule in the set is tried.

SENDMAIL RULESET SYNTAX

Each ruleset is identified by a number, and each new ruleset begins with an *S* in the leftmost column, followed by its identifying number. Rules begin with the letter *R* and are not numbered. A non -R command ends the ruleset, for example:

```
########################################
###    Ruleset 0 -- Parse Address   ###
########################################
S0
R$*              $: $>98 $1       handle local hacks
```

Rule syntax is cryptic but fairly simple. Each rule has a left-hand side and a right-hand side. A comment portion is optional. The two sides and the optional comment are separated by tabs. The left-hand side is compared to the address as a string pattern. If the pattern matches the left-hand side, the address is transformed by the rule's right-hand side and is passed on to the next rule.

In `sendmail.cf`, an octothorp (#) begins a comment line. Empty lines are ignored. The `S0` defines the beginning of Ruleset 0. The `R` on the next line defines the beginning of a rule. The `$*` accepts every address that is passed to it, and the `$: $>98 $1` passes the address to Ruleset 98 for further processing. The text `handle local hacks` is a comment. Because rules are tab-delimited, the comment portion does not require a comment marker (#)at the beginning.

THE CORE SENDMAIL RULESETS

Several standard rulesets exist, and they may appear in any order in `sendmail.cf`. When sendmail reads the configuration file, it sorts the rules appropriately. A ruleset that is expected but is not present is treated as if it were present but empty. The following are the main rulesets:

- Ruleset 0 resolves an MDA by reading the address.
- Ruleset 1 processes the sender's address.
- Ruleset 2 processes the recipient's address.
- Ruleset 3 preprocesses all addresses.
- Ruleset 4 post-processes all addresses.
- Ruleset 5 rewrites unaliased local users.

ALIASING IN SENDMAIL

An *alias* is an abbreviation for one or more full mailing addresses. Although an alias may be merely a nickname for a longer address you don't want to type every time (such as `john` for `john.dagenhamster@someothercompany.com`), an alias can also be the name of a list of several recipients.

Many MUAs maintain their own alias lists, but these alias lists are normally in formats that cannot be shared with other MUAs. If you typically use pine on a Linux workstation, its alias file is not available to your Lotus Notes client on your Windows 95 or 98 workstation when you write a letter with that tool. In contrast, the many possible alias lists contained in aliases maintained in sendmail's alias file are recognized and expanded when a message is processed by sendmail, regardless of the MUA used to create that message. sendmail allows for multiple alias files—up to 12 by default.

You can learn more details about sendmail from the Web at `http://www.sendmail.org/` or from Bryan Costales's and Eric Allman's book *sendmail, 2nd Edition* (O'Reilly & Associates).

PROJECT: CREATING A MAILING LIST WITH SENDMAIL AND MAJORDOMO

majordomo is one of the most common mailing list programs on the Internet. It allows you to create and manage mailing lists. After the mailing list is created, the list can be maintained entirely through email, without root access to the mail server.

Before you can create a mailing list, you need the following:

- A Linux (or other UNIX) system
- sendmail or another mail transport agent installed
- Perl (because majordomo is a Perl script)

Go to `http://www.greatcircle.com/majordomo/` and download and install majordomo. After you have majordomo installed, you can make a mailing list by following these steps:

1. Make sure you have a secure connection (either local or over ssh).
2. Log in.
3. Change to root by entering `su root` and the root password (unless you were already root).
4. Enter the following to move to the `/etc/` directory:
   ```
   cd /etc/
   ```
5. Enter the following to edit the aliases file:
   ```
   vi aliases
   ```
6. Write a block that looks like this:
   ```
   # my friends
   friends: ''¦/usr/local/majordomo/wrapper resend -l friends friends-list''
   friends-list: :include:/usr/local/majordomo/lists/friends
   owner-friends: yourusername
   friends-owner: yourusername
   friends-approval: yourusername
   friends-request: ''¦/usr/local/majordomo/wrapper request-answer friends''
   ```
7. When you're done, remember to save and exit vi:
   ```
   Esc :wq
   ```
8. Enter the following command to compile the aliases:
   ```
   newaliases
   ```
   You should see a reply that looks like this:
   ```
   /etc/aliases: 25 aliases, longest 39 bytes, 528 bytes total
   /etc/aliases.majordomo: 63 aliases, longest 94 bytes, 2966 bytes total
   ```
9. Enter the following:
   ```
   cd /usr/local/majordomo/lists
   ```
10. Enter the following to create a new file that will contain the email addresses of the subscribers:
    ```
    vi friends
    ```
11. Type your email address; then save and quit vi.
12. Enter the following to change the file's ownership from root to `majordom`:
    ```
    chown majordom friends
    ```
13. Enter the following to change the file's group membership from root to `daemon`:
    ```
    chgrp daemon friends
    ```
14. Enter the following to get out of root:
    ```
    exit
    ```

15. In your mail program, send mail to the listname. In this example, it's `friends@afakecompany.com`. majordomo then creates a configuration file named `friends.config` in `/usr/local/majordomo/lists`.

16. Customize the `config` settings. Some suggested changes to the default settings for a new list would be the following:

```
From:   admin_passwd     = friends.admin
To:     admin_passwd     to [whatever you want]

From:   description      =
To:     description      = The mailing list for my friends

From:   mungedomain      =  no
To:     mungedomain      =  yes

From:   reply_to         =
To:     reply_to         = friends-list

From:   subscribe_policy =  closed
To:     subscribe_policy =  open

From:   subject_prefix   =
To:     subject_prefix   = [FRIENDS]
```

17. Enjoy the list!

CHAPTER 40

Configuring a Usenet News Service

In this chapter

by Steve Burnett

A Usenet Primer

Usenet is often confused with the Internet, but Usenet isn't the Internet. Usenet is not a network, but instead is a service carried over the Internet, as well as many computers not directly part of the Internet. The best way I've found to describe Usenet is to say that it is 20,000 (or so) bulletin boards, each with a different title describing what the topic for that board is supposed to be. You can look for a bulletin board with a topic you think you might be interested in and read some or all of the messages on the board that day. If you want to, you can put a message up to either reply publicly to someone else's message or to start a new discussion. You can also copy a person's address and send him or her a private letter that doesn't appear on the board. Later, you can come back and see whether the board has any new and interesting messages from other people.

Usenet is unlike a party telephone line because you don't deal with other people in real-time. You can't interrupt someone while he or she is thinking of what to write on the board. (You could, however, repeat that person's message afterward and quote it out of context; but besides being rude, that's not the same as interrupting the person and preventing others from hearing his or her words.) Usenet is very like a party, though, because very little control is placed on who can say something. If a person insists, for example, that squirrels are the only warm-blooded animals that cannot carry rabies, he or she can post that message. Of course, people who know this statement is false can reply with the correct information. Then, while the first person can continue to insist that he or she is right, the rest of the readers of that board are likely to start ignoring messages from the first person.

Note

For information on the history of Usenet, you can use Netscape to go to `http://www.yahoo.com/Reference/FAQs/` for several FAQs (Frequently Asked Questions) concerning Usenet.

History and Origins of Usenet

Back in the dark ages of computing (circa late 1970s), a version of UNIX labeled V7 was released. One of the applications included was UUCP, which stands for UNIX-to-UNIX-Copy. In 1979, two graduate students at Duke University started using UUCP to exchange messages between two systems at the university. Next, a set of shell scripts was developed to exchange messages between Duke and the network at the University of North Carolina at Chapel Hill. Later, the shell scripts were rewritten in C, and they have been rewritten and extended many times since then. In general, Usenet works by news servers connecting to each other and asking "Do you have this posting #37590576 to newsgroup `alt.binaries.misc`? No? Okay, here it is." Or alternatively, "Do you have this posting #37590576 to newsgroup `alt.binaries.misc`? Yes? Okay, how about this one?" until the first server has passed every message on topics the second server will accept. The server software was first called A News, then B News, then C News, and then INN (Internet News). Other news server software includes Netscape's Collabra and Backplane's Diablo.

Usenet Structure

To quote Douglas Adams in *The Hitchhikers' Guide to the Galaxy*, "Space is BIG. Really BIG." Usenet (as of this writing) is approximately 20,000 different newsgroups, with several million total participants. Some of these newsgroups are dead, and no one ever posts to them. Some newsgroups are highly active and are likely to split into multiple newsgroups soon (either because no one can keep up with the sheer volume or because a large segment of that newsgroup is interested in a narrower subset of topics than the other readers of the newsgroup).

An example of newsgroup spawning happened in `comp.sys.powerpc`, a newsgroup devoted to discussions of the PowerPC RISC processor. When Be, Inc. announced the BeBox, a dual-processor workstation running a new operating system, a substantial fraction of the newsgroup focused exclusively on Be's hardware and software. To accommodate both the interests of the people who wanted to discuss the BeOS and the wishes of the people with no interest in the BeOS, a newsgroup called `comp.sys.be` was formed. Alternatively, a topic discussion such as "undocumented features of the PowerPC processor family" would be of interest to the entire newsgroup, and the information generated from this discussion might become a large section of the newsgroup's FAQ or a separate FAQ altogether.

Tip #196 from *Steve*

If you are new to Usenet, you should make sure the newsgroup `news.announce.newusers` is on your subscription list. Basic informational guides about aspects of Usenet are periodically reposted to this newsgroup every two weeks.

Although the sheer volume of Usenet can appear overwhelming, its structure is based on some logic. Table 40.1 presents some of the first-level divisions of Usenet. A first-level identifier appears as the leftmost part of every Usenet name.

Table 40.1 Usenet Hierarchy Names

Hierarchy Name	Description
`biz`	Business
`comp`	Anything to do with computers
`misc`	Miscellaneous
`news`	Usenet issues, general information
`rec`	Recreational (sports, crafts, hobbies)
`sci`	Scientific

Table 40.1 Usenet Hierarchy Names

Hierarchy Name	Description
soc	Social (personal, cultural)
talk	Conversation on anything
alt	Everything else

Other first-level identifiers for newsgroups tend to be regional. For example, a newsgroup with a name starting with `de.*` is generally populated by speakers of the German language, and most of the `de.*` hierarchy deals with German and European issues.

The `alt.*` hierarchy of newsgroups is an enormous part of Usenet. The requirements for creating an `alt.*` newsgroup are easier than the requirements for creating a major hierarchy newsgroup. In addition, the `alt.*` newsgroups are not always carried by every Internet access provider, for two reasons. The first reason is bandwidth: The `alt.*` newsgroups are a substantial portion of all Usenet newsgroups, and some of them—especially the newsgroups devoted to binary files of either applications or images—can take up enormous amounts of bandwidth. The second reason for restricting distribution of the `alt.*` newsgroups is offensiveness: The `alt.*` newsgroups tend to tolerate more extreme or obnoxious language and topics than the mainstream newsgroups, and people are more likely to be offended by their content.

Note

Some Internet access providers have a "user-defined" policy for Usenet access: They provide groups from the full Usenet newsgroups list, but they carry only newsgroups the users of that network have asked for. This "a la carte" policy substantially reduces the actual bandwidth of the Usenet feed required for the network, but the users' interests are not restricted or censored. Other Internet access providers have a mixed policy: They carry only groups that they approve of *and* that their users ask for.

→ See Chapter 35, "Surviving Usenet News," p. 741

Usenet Servers

Many Usenet news server programs have been written. A few of them are described here:

- INN is one of the most common news server applications. The cornerstone of the package is `innd`, an NNTP server service daemon that is descended from C News. INN was maintained by Rich Salz until he turned over ongoing development and maintenance to the Internet Software Consortium (ISC) in 1996. If you're familiar with older news servers, `innd` can be characterized as a C News relaying news service that can read multiple NNTP streams. Access to the news posts in the news server's database is handled by a separate server named `nnrpd`. A new `nnrpd` is started or spawned for each client newsreader accessing the local database. The latest version is INN 2.2 available from servers as indicated on `http://www.isc.org/inn.html`. Dave Barr maintains an excellent informational INN Web page at `http://www.visi.com/~barr/INN.html`.

- Diablo, available from Matt Dillon's Backplane Systems, is a backbone news feed *transit* server. Diablo is designed to accept news feeds from other news hosts and route them to other news servers quickly and efficiently. You cannot run the transit server portion of Diablo on a machine that needs to accept `nntp` post commands or newsreading-related `nntp` commands. It's a router for news feeds only.
- Leafnode is a news server package designed for small sites only. It's intended to serve tens of clients and to operate over a slow link to the Internet. Leafnode uses very little space on disk and comparatively little bandwidth, and it tends to recover rapidly from errors. Unfortunately, its recovery strategy is generally to delete a news post if it's corrupted or otherwise malformed, so you might lose a news post you're reading if a problem occurs. You can find the software and more information at `http://wpxx02.toxi.uni-wuerzburg.de/~krasel/leafnode.html`.

CONFIGURING USENET CLIENTS

Usenet operates on the familiar client/server relationship: A server exchanges messages with another server and stores the messages on the local system. To read a Usenet newsgroup, you need to contact your network or Internet service provider (ISP) and ask for the name of an NNTP server. When you have a server name (which normally looks something like either `test.fake.com` or `192.168.2.221`), you can start.

TIN AND NN

TIN and NN are two very similar newsreaders with similar configuration requirements, and both are included in many common Linux distributions.

If you're using a version of TIN compiled with the NNTP options from a UNIX shell account, you can try one of these commands:

- If you are using the ksh or bash shell, use the following:
  ```
  $ NNTPSERVER= test.fake.com tin -r -f .fakenewsrc I .newsnet/.index
  ```
- If you are using the C shell or tcsh shell, use the following:
  ```
  % setenv NNTPSERVER test.fake.com; tin -r -f .fakenewsrc I .newsnet/.index
  ```

For NN, the configuration is similar:

- If you are using the ksh or bash shell, use the following:
  ```
  $ NNTPSERVER=test.fake.com nn newsrc=~ .fakenewsrc
  ```
- If you're using the C shell or tcsh shell, use the following:
  ```
  % setenv NNTPSERVER test.fake.com nn newsrc=~/.fakenewsrc
  ```

At some point while reading newsgroups, you either might want to contribute to a current discussion or start a new conversational topic. Before you start actively participating in Usenet, you need to understand the rules of the Usenet subculture. Follow this general advice when you start posting messages to a newsgroup:

- Don't post until you've read the group for at least a week and have a feel for the tone of the newsgroup. Do you consider the average discussion too rude and brutal, or would the newsgroup's current residents consider you an irritant?
- Look for and read the FAQ (if one exists). Many of the Usenet's FAQs are archived at `ftp://rtfm.mit.edu/pub/usenet/`.
- Post only to newsgroups in which your message is relevant. If you are trying to sell a waterbed in California, you should probably advertise only in `.forsale` newsgroups in the immediate area. Readers of the `triangle.forsale` newsgroup serving the eastern North Carolina area are unlikely to want to ship your waterbed across the country. Similarly, if you have a question about Amiga computers, don't post your query to a Macintosh-oriented newsgroup.

You might post a message to a newsgroup but look at that newsgroup later and not see your message. Some newsgroups are moderated, which means that all posts to that newsgroup are read by a person or group of persons who weed out inappropriate messages and don't send them to the newsgroup. You can find out whether a newsgroup is moderated by reading the FAQ for that newsgroup, by reading the charter for that newsgroup, or by reading messages on that newsgroup for a week or two before posting, and noticing whether anyone describes himself or herself as a moderator of that newsgroup.

Note

If you don't see a FAQ immediately visible on the newsgroup when you first log in, try using one of the Usenet-capable search engines such as `http://www.dejanews.com` or `http://www.altavista.digital.com` and searching for the newsgroup name and *FAQ* as keywords. Alternatively, you might ask "Is there a FAQ for this group?" in your first message to save you a world of angst.

In general, if you use common sense, you'll probably be fine. For more advice on the sometimes tricky topic of Netiquette, you can use your Web browser to go to `http://www.fau.edu/netiquette/netiquette.html`, a Web site with many good resources for newcomers to the Internet in general.

PROJECT: CONFIGURING PINE AS A NEWSREADER

Pine is most commonly used as a mail reader, but it can also be used as a newsreader. To set up your pine mail client for accessing Usenet, press S (Setup) and then C (Config). Then edit the line *news collections* to read as follows:

```
*{test.fake.com/NNTP}[]
```

Next, press E to exit pine and restart it. Then press L (List Folders), go down to the news folders, and select A (Add) to subscribe to the newsgroups you want.

The resulting screen might look similar to this:

```
PINE 3.96    FOLDER LIST                          Folder: INBOX 313 Messages
--------------------------------------------------------------------------
Folder-collection <mail/[]>   ** Default for Saves **    (Local)
--------------------------------------------------------------------------
                 [ Select Here to See Expanded List ]
--------------------------------------------------------------------------
News-collection <News on test.fake,com>                   (Remote)
--------------------------------------------------------------------------
[ Select Here to See Expanded List ]
```

Although reading news can be fun and informative, only reading (and not posting) messages in newsgroups is a behavior pattern called *lurking*, which may be frowned upon by long-time Usenet people. If you want to post new Usenet messages to newsgroups or to send replies by electronic mail, you must typically also fill out the following fields:

- Your name (first and last name)
- Your email address (`userid@hostname.domain`)
- The computer that forwards your mail (ask your system administrator for the SMTP mail server's name)

This information is typically already set up for your mail reader software. You should be able to use the same entries. Check with a system administrator to make sure, though.

PART VII CH 40

Note Most system administrators have an information sheet already prepared with this information. If they don't, keep this information summary where you can get to it so that the next person to ask can benefit from your research.

With pine and other newsreaders, as well as most email applications, you can define a *signature file*. A signature file is a block of information you want included with every posting you make to a newsgroup. Typically, people include their names, email addresses, and (if a work-related account) their titles or ranks. Sometimes people might also include a short quote they consider witty.

Tip #197 from
Steve

Information you would rarely want to put in a signature file are your home address and telephone number. Without even considering the possibility of malicious or prankish behavior, there is always the possibility that the person making a legitimate business call from Singapore to you (in New York City) can forget the time zone difference. Remember that if a person can read your email or news post over the Internet, he or she can almost always reply the same way.

Another caution if you set up a signature file is to remember that you have your signature file defined. Manually pasting your signature file onto the end of your outgoing message or attaching the signature file as an attached file when the signature file is automatically included will make you look silly.

PART VIII

APPENDIXES

APPENDIX A

SOURCES OF INFORMATION

In this appendix

LINUX WEB SITES

Because Linux is a child of the Internet, you can find a great many Web sites related to Linux. In fact, Linux is a pretty popular subject on the Web. Table A.1 lists the URLs that contain most of the Linux information on the Web.

TABLE A.1 MAJOR LINUX WEB SITES

URL	Description
`http://metalab.unc.edu/mdw`	*The* site for Linux information; the home of the Linux Documentation Project (LDP)
`http://metalab.unc.edu/linux/links.html`	Home to a plethora of links to many Linux related sites; one of the best on the Net
`http://www.Linux.org.uk`	The Web site for European Linux users
`http://www.li.org`	The Linux International Web site
`http://www.linuxworld.com`	The Linux World Web site
`http://freshmeat.net`	A site that provides recent announcements for a wide variety of Linux projects (Not for newbies)
`http://slashdot.org`	The place to get all the news a geek could ever want; not 100 percent Linux but great nonetheless
`http://www.redhat.com`	The Red Hat Linux Web site
`http://www.caldera.com`	Caldera's Web site
`http://www.linuxgames.com`	A site-tracking development of games for the Linux platform
`http://www.linux.org`	The Linux Organization Web site
`http://www.debian.org`	The Official Debian Linux Organization Web site
`http://linuxtoday.com`	A site dedicated to providing relevant news about Linux and the open source industry to the business community
`http://www.corel.com`	Corel's Web site with links to all their Linux related products, including WordPerfect for Linux
`http://www.stardivision.com`	The official Web site for StarDivision—whose products include StarOffice
`http://www.slackware.org`	The official Web site for Slackware

TABLE A.1 MAJOR LINUX WEB SITES

URL	Description
`http://sunsite.unc.edu/linux-source`	The Linux Source Navigator, which allows you to view Linux source code in hypertext
`http://www.yahoo.com/Computers_and_Internet/Operating_Systems/Unix/Linux`	The Yahoo! site pointing to many current sites

USENET NEWSGROUPS

If you have access to Usenet newsgroups, you might enjoy the following newsgroups, which provide a variety of information about Linux. Only two, `comp.os.linux.announce` and `comp.os.linux.answers`, are moderated.

→ See "Usenet Culture," p. 747

- `comp.os.linux.announce`—This moderated newsgroup is used for important announcements, such as bug fixes.
- `comp.os.linux.answers`—This moderated newsgroup provides answers to any of your Linux questions, especially about setting up Linux. Please read the appropriate Linux documentation and FAQs before posting a question to this group.
- `comp.os.linux.development.system`—This newsgroup is devoted to the many programmers around the world who are developing the Linux system.
- `comp.os.linux.development.apps`—This newsgroup is devoted to the many programmers around the world who are developing applications for Linux.
- `comp.os.linux.hardware`—This newsgroup provides answers to hardware compatibility questions.
- `comp.os.linux.setup`—This newsgroup provides help with Linux setup and installation problems.
- `comp.os.linux.advocacy`—This newsgroup provides a medium to discuss why Linux is the greatest operating system.
- `comp.os.linux.networking`—This newsgroup provides answers to networking Linux with the rest of the world.
- `comp.os.linux.x`—This newsgroup provides answers to installing and running X under Linux.
- `comp.os.linux.m68k`—The purpose of this newsgroup is to promote interest and development of the port of Linux to Motorola's 680x0 architecture.

A newsgroup named `comp.os.linux.misc` serves as a catchall for any Linux topic not suited to the other newsgroups. Also, more than 170 other Usenet newsgroups contain the word *Linux*. A sample of the more common Linux newsgroups are listed as follows. Go exploring!

alt.linux.sux
alt.uu.comp.os.linux.questions
aus.computers.linux
de.comp.os.linux.hardware
de.comp.os.linux.networking
de.alt.sources.linux.patches
fj.os.linux
han.sys.linux
linux.apps.linux-bbs
linux.apps.seyon.development
linux.debian
linux.debian.user
linux.dev.680x0
linux.dev.apps
linux.dev.c-programming
linux.dev.debian
linux.dev.fido
linux.dev.fsstnd
linux.dev.hams
linux.dev.interviews
linux.dev.laptop
linux.dev.linuxnews
linux.dev.localbus
linux.dev.mca
linux.dev.msdos
linux.dev.new-lists
linux.dev.normal
linux.dev.oasg
linux.dev.pkg
Linux.dev.qag
linux.dev.serial
linux.dev.sound
linux.dev.svgalib
linux.dev.term
linux.dev.wabi
alt.os.linux
alt.os.linux.slackware
dc.org.linux-users
de.comp.os.linux.misc
de.comp.os.linux.x
uk.comp.os.linux
fr.comp.os.linux
linux.apps.bbsdev
linux.apps.seyon
linux.apps.flexfax
linux.debian.announce
linux.dev.gcc
linux.dev.admin
linux.dev.bbs
linux.dev.config
linux.dev.doc
linux.dev.fsf
linux.dev.ftp
linux.dev.ibcs2
linux.dev.japanese
linux.dev.linuxbsd
linux.dev.linuxss
linux.dev.lugnuts
linux.dev.mgr
linux.dev.net
linux.dev.newbie
linux.dev.nys
linux.dev.oi
linux.dev.ppp
linux.dev.scsi
linux.dev.seyon
linux.dev.standards
linux.dev.tape
linux.dev.uucp
linux.dev.word

linux.dev.kernel

linux.dev.x11

linux.fido.ifmail

linux.free-widgets.announce

linux.free-widgets.bugs

linux.free-widgets.development

linux.local.chicago

linux.local.nova-scotia

linux.local.silicon-valley

linux.motif.clone

linux.new-tty

linux.news.groups

linux.ports.alpha

linux.samba

linux.samba.announce

linux.sdk

linux.wine.users

linux.test

DejaNews, now located at www.deja.com, archives most, if not all, of the Linux newsgroups. LinuxWorld also provides an open news server for its site located at forum.linuxworld.com.

ONLINE DOCUMENTS

Matt Welsh spearheads a dedicated group of Linux enthusiasts who are systematically writing a complete set of Linux manuals that are made available on the Internet. You can find the latest versions of the documentation at sunsite.unc.edu in the /pub/Linux/docs directory. You can also find earlier versions of these documents in your version of Linux's /docs directory. The current home for the LDP is located at this address:

http://sunsite.unc.edu/mdw

Available documents include the following:

- "Linux Installation and Getting Started," by Matt Welsh.
- "The Linux System Administrators' Guide," by Lars Wirzenius.
- "The Linux Network Administrators' Guide," by Olaf Kirch.
- "The Linux Kernel Hackers' Guide," by Michael K. Johnson.
- "The Linux Frequently Asked Questions (FAQ) List," maintained by Ian Jackson. It's composed of questions and answers on myriad Linux topics.
- "The Linux META-FAQ," maintained by Michael K. Johnson.
- "The Linux INFO-SHEET," maintained by Michael K. Johnson.
- "The Linux Software Map," maintained by Aaron Schab. This document contains information about each of the software packages available for Linux via FTP.

LINUX HOW-TOS

Appendix B, "The Linux How-To Index," provides an index to all the available How-To documents. These How-To documents provide detailed explanations of their topics. Some of the titles include the following:

- "The Linux Installation How-To"
- "The Linux Hardware How-To"
- "The Linux Printing How-To"

See Appendix B for a complete list of Linux How-To and mini-How-To site addresses. These files are located in the `/usr/doc/HOWTO` directory on your local drive. Most are archived with `gzip` to save disk space. To read these or other compressed files, you can use the `zless` command.

Many FAQs about Linux topics and GNU programs are shipped with Linux and can be found in the `/usr/info` directory.

MAN PAGES

The Linux operating system itself provides plenty of online help via the `man` command. To access online help, you can enter `man` followed by the topic for which you want information.

MAGAZINES

Linux Journal is the leading U.S. periodical devoted explicitly to Linux. You can request more information about this publication from the following address:

Linux Journal
P.O. Box 85867
Seattle, WA 98145
206-527-3385
`http://www.linuxjournal.com`

Linux Magazine—The Chronicle of the Revolution
Linux Magazine
(510) 665-7847
`adamgood@linux-mag.com`
`http://www.linux-mag.com/index.html`

LINUX FTP SITES

You can find a great deal of up-to-date information regarding Linux on the Internet. Table A.2 lists the FTP sites that maintain Linux archives. The main archive site, located at the University of North Carolina-Chapel Hill, is named `sunsite.unc.edu`.

Table A.2 FTP Sites with Linux Archives

Site Name	Directory
tsx-11.mit.edu	/pub/linux
sunsite.unc.edu	/pub/Linux
nic.funet.fi	/pub/Linux
ftp.mcc.ac.uk	/pub/linux
ftp.dfv.rwth-aachen.de	/pub/linux
ftp.informatik.rwth-aachen.de	/pub/Linux
ftp.ibp.fr	/pub/linux
kirk.bond.edu.au	/pub/OS/Linux
ftp.uu.net	/systems/unix/linux
wuarchive.wustl.edu	/systems/linux
ftp.win.tue.nl	/pub/linux
ftp.stack.nl	/pub/Linux
ftp.ibr.cs.tu-bs.de	/pub/os/linux
ftp.denet.dk	/pub/OS/Linux

→ See "Using ftp for Remote File Transfer," p. 686

For Linux Developers

So you think that Linux is the greatest thing to come along in quite some time, and you want to help develop future releases? Well, you're in luck. An active set of mailing lists on the Internet is devoted to various topics and issues surrounding Linux development. This set is a multichannel mailing list, meaning that messages on different topics are sent to different groups of people. You must subscribe to each channel that you're interested in. If you think you want to get involved in a Linux development project, you can get more information by sending an email message to

`majordomo@vger.rutgers.edu`

with `lists` in the body to get a list of the lists there. You can add a line with `help` in the body to get the standard `Majordomo` help file, which has instructions for subscribing and unsubscribing.

APPENDIX B

The Linux How-To Index

In this appendix

WHAT ARE LINUX HOW-TOS?

This appendix contains an index to the Linux How-Tos and mini-How-Tos, as well as other information about the How-To project. Linux How-Tos are documents that describe in detail certain aspects of configuring or using Linux. For example, the "Installation How-To" gives instructions on installing Linux, and the "Mail How-To" describes how to set up and configure mail under Linux. Other examples include the "NET-3 How-To" and the "Printing How-To."

How-Tos are comprehensive documents, much like a FAQ, but generally not in question-and-answer format. However, many How-Tos contain a FAQ section at the end.

Several How-To formats are available: plain text, PostScript, DVI, and HTML.

In addition to the How-Tos, you can find a multitude of mini-How-Tos on short, specific subjects. They are available only in plain text and HTML format.

WHERE CAN I GET LINUX HOW-TOS?

You can retrieve How-Tos via anonymous FTP from the following sites:

`ftp://metalab.unc.edu/pub/Linux/docs/HOWTO`

`ftp://tsx-11.mit.edu/pub/linux/docs/HOWTO`

You also can retrieve them from many mirror sites, such as the following:

`ftp://metalab.unc.edu/pub/Linux/MIRRORS.html`

You can browse How-Tos in HTML format from `http://metalab.unc.edu/LDP/HOWTO/` on the World Wide Web. Many mirror sites, such as `http://metalab.unc.edu/LDP/mirrors.html`, also mirror the HTML files. Because `metalab.unc.edu` is heavily used, try to use a mirror site if possible.

Near the beginning of the month, How-Tos are also posted to the Usenet newsgroup `comp.os.linux.answers`. A tool called NewstoHOWTO assembles the postings.

HOW-TO TRANSLATIONS

How-To translations are available on `metalab.unc.edu` and mirrors around the world. So far, the following are available:

Chinese (`zh`)	Croatian (`hr`)
French (`fr`)	German (`de`)
Hellenic (`el`)	Indonesian (`id`)
Italian (`it`)	Japanese (`ja`)
Korean (`ko`)	Polish (`pl`)

Slovenian (`sl`)	Spanish (`es`)
Swedish (`sv`)	Turkish (`tr`)

If you know of any other translation projects, please let me know, and I will add them to this list. If you are interested in getting your translations archived on `metalab.unc.edu`, please read the directory structure specification at the following Web site and get in touch with me:

`http://metalab.unc.edu/pub/Linux/docs/HOWTO/translations/Directory-Structure`

HOW-TO INDEX

The following Linux How-Tos are currently available:

"3Dfx How-To," by Bernd Kreimeier, `bk@gamers.org`. How to use 3Dfx graphics accelerator chip support. Updated 6 February 1998.

"AX25 How-To," by Terry Dawson, `terry@perf.no.itg.telecom.com.au`. How to configure AX25 networking for Linux. Updated 17 October 1997.

"Access How-To," by Michael De La Rue, `access-howto@ed.ac.uk`. How to use adaptive technology with Linux. Updated 28 March 1997.

"Alpha How-To," by David Mosberger, `davidm@azstarnet.com`. Overview of Alpha systems and processors. Updated 6 June 1997.

"Assembly How-To," by Francois-Ren Rideau, `fare@tunes.org`. Information on programming in x86 assembly. Updated 6 June 1999.

"Bash Prompt How-To," by Giles Orr, `giles@interlog.com`. How to create and control terminal and xterm prompts. Updated 7 January 1999.

"Benchmarking How-To," by Andre D. Balsa, `andrewbalsa@usa.net`. How to do basic benchmarking. Updated 15 August 1997.

"Beowulf How-To," by Jacek Radajewski, `jacek@usq.edu.au`, and Douglas Eadline, `plogic.com`. Introduces the Beowulf Supercomputer architecture and provides background information on parallel programming. Updated 22 November 1998.

"BootPrompt How-To," by Paul Gortmaker, `gpg109@rsphy1.anu.edu.au`. List of boot time arguments and overview of booting software. Updated 15 May 1999.

"Bootdisk How-To," by Tom Fawcett, `fawcett@croftj.net`. How to create a boot/root maintenance disk for Linux. Updated 15 May 1999.

"Busmouse How-To," by Chris Bagwell, `cbagwell@sprynet.com`. Information on bus mouse compatibility with Linux. Updated 4 May 1998.

"CD Writing How-To," by Winfried Trumper, `winni@xpilot.org`. How to write CDs. Updated 11 April 1999.

"CDROM How-To," by Jeff Tranter, `jeff_tranter@pobox.com`. Information on CD-ROM drive compatibility for Linux. Updated 24 March 1999.

"Chinese How-To," by Chih-Wei Huang, `cwhuang@phys.ntu.edu.tw`. How to configure Linux for use with the Chinese character set. Updated June 1998.

"Commercial How-To," by Mr.Poet, `poet@linuxports.com`. Listing of commercial software products for Linux. Updated 7 March 1999.

"Config How-To," by Guido Gonzato, `guido@ibogfs.cineca.it`. How to fine-tune and customize your Linux system. Updated 19 January 1999.

"Consultants How-To," by Mr. Poet, `poet@linuxports.com`. Listing of Linux consultants. Updated 19 May 1999.

"Cyrillic How-To," by Alexander L. Belikoff, `abel@bfr.co.il`. How to configure Linux for use with the Cyrillic character set. Updated 23 January 1998.

"DNS How-To," by Nicolai Langfeldt, `janl@math.uio.no`. How to set up DNS. Updated 11 February 1999.

"DOS/Win to Linux How-To," by Guido Gonzato, `guido@ibogfs.cineca.it`. How to move from DOS/Windows to Linux. Updated 22 February 1999.

"DOSEMU How-To," by Uwe Bonnes, `bon@elektron.ikp.physik.th-darm-stadt.de`. How-To about the Linux MS-DOS Emulator, DOSEMU. Updated 24 April 1999.

"Danish How-To," by Niels Kristian Bech Jensen, `nkbj@image.dk`. How to configure Linux for use with the Danish character set. Updated 20 February 1999.

"Diskless How-To," by Robert Nemkin, `buci@math.klte.hu`. How to set up a diskless Linux box. Updated 13 May 1999.

"Distribution How-To," by Eric S. Raymond, `esr@snark.thyrsus.com`. A list of Linux distributions. Updated 8 May 1999.

"Emacspeak How-To," by Jim Van Zandt, `jrv@vanzandt.mv.com`. How to use "emacspeak" with Linux. Updated 10 April 1999.

"Esparanto How-To," by Wolfram Diestel, `diestel@rzaix340.rz.uni-leipzig.de`. How to use Esperanto in general and ISO-8859-3 in particular with Linux. Updated June 1998.

"Ethernet How-To," by Paul Gortmaker, `gpg109@rsphy1.anu.edu.au`. Information on Ethernet hardware compatibility for Linux. Updated 5 May 1999.

"Finnish How-To," by Pekka Taipale, `pjt@iki.fi`. How to configure Linux for use with the Finnish character set. Updated 14 February 1996.

"Firewall How-To," by Mark Grennan, `markg@netplus.net`. How to set up a firewall using Linux. Updated 8 November 1996.

"French How-To," by Guylhem Aznar, `guylhem@danmark.linux.eu.org`. How to configure Linux for use with the French character set.

"Ftape How-To," by Kevin Johnson, `kjj@pobox.com`. Information on ftape drive compatibility with Linux. Updated August 1998.

"GCC How-To," by Daniel Barlow, `daniel.barlow@linux.org`. How to set up the GNU C compiler and development libraries. Updated 28 February 1996.

"German How-To," by Winfried Trmper, winni@xpilot.org. Information on using Linux with German-specific features. Updated 19 March 1997.

"Glibc2 How-To," by Eric Green, ejg3@cornell.edu. How to install and migrate to the glibc2 library. Updated 8 February 1998.

"HAM How-To," by Terry Dawson, terry@perf.no.itg.telecom.com.au. How to configure amateur radio software for Linux. Updated 1 April 1997.

"How-To Index," by Tim Bynum, linux-howto@metalab.unc.edu. Index of How-To documents about Linux. Updated 19 June 1999.

"Hardware Compatibility How-To," by Patrick Reijnen, antispam.patrickr@antispam.bart.nl. A list of hardware known to work with Linux. Updated 20 March 1999.

"Hebrew How-To," by Yair G. Rajwan, yair@hobbes.jct.ac.il. How to configure Linux for use with the Hebrew character set. Updated 12 September 1995.

"INFO-SHEET," by Michael K. Johnson, johnsonm@redhat.com. Generic introduction to the Linux operating system. Updated 1 September 1998.

"IPCHAINS How-To," by Paul Russell, Paul.Russell@rustcorp.com.au. How to install and configure the enhanced IP firewalling chains software. Updated 12 March 1999.

"IPX How-To," by Terry Dawson, terry@perf.no.itg.telecom.com.au. How to install and configure IPX networking. Updated 6 May 1998.

"IR How-To," by Werner Heuser, r2d2c3po@zedat.fu-berlin.de. An introduction to the software provided by the Linux/IR project. Updated 9 February 1999.

"ISP Hookup How-To," by Egil Kvaleberg, egil@kvaleberg.no. Basic introduction to hooking up to an ISP. Updated 5 March 1998.

"Installation How-To," by Eric S. Raymond, esr@snark.thyrsus.com. How to obtain and install Linux. Updated 20 November 1998.

"Intranet Server How-To," by Pramod Karnad, karnad@indiamail.com. How to set up a Linux Intranet server. Updated 7 August 1997.

"Italian How-To," by Marco "Gaio" Gaiarin, gaio@dei.unipd.it. How to configure Linux for use with the Italian character set. Updated 3 November 1998.

"Java-CGI How-To," by David H. Silber, dhs@orbits.com. How to set up Java-capable CGI bin. Updated 1 December 1998.

"Kernel How-To," by Brian Ward, ward@blah.math.tu-graz.ac.at. How to upgrade and compile the Linux kernel. Updated 5 June 1999.

"Keyboard and Console How-To," by Andries Brouwer, aeb@cwi.nl. Information about the Linux keyboard, console, and non-ASCII characters. Updated 25 February 1998.

"KickStart How-To," by Martin Hamilton, martinh@gnu.org. Briefly describes how to use the Red Hat Linux KickStart system to rapidly install large numbers of identical Linux boxes. Updated 11 January 1999.

"LinuxDoc+Emacs+Ispell How-To," by Philippe Martin, feloy@wanadoo.fr. Assists writers and translators of Linux How-Tos or any other paper for the Linux Documentation Project. Updated 27 February 1998.

"META-FAQ," by Michael K. Johnson, johnsonm@redhat.com. A listing of Linux sources of information. Updated 25 October 1997.

"MGR How-To," by Vincent Broman, broman@nosc.mil. Information on the MGR graphics interface for Linux. Updated 30 May 1996.

"MILO How-To," by David A. Rusling, david.rusling@reo.mts.dec.com. How to use the Alpha Linux Miniloader (MILO). Updated 6 December 1996.

"MIPS How-To," by Ralf Baechle, ralf@gnu.org. Describes the MIPS port of the Linux operating system, common problems and their solutions, availability, and more. Updated 31 March 1999.

"Mail How-To," by Guylhem Aznar, guylhem@danmark.linux.eu.org. Information on electronic mail servers and clients. Updated January 1999.

"Modem How-To," by David S. Lawyer, bf347@lafn.org. Help with selecting, connecting, configuring, troubleshooting, and understanding modems for a PC. Updated May 1999.

"Multi-Disk How-To," by Stein Gjoen, sgjoen@nyx.net. How to set up multiple hard disk drives. Updated 27 May 1999.

"Multicast How-To," by Juan-Mariano de Goyeneche, jmseyas@dit.upm.es. Tries to cover most aspects related to multicast over TCP/IP networks. Updated 20 March 1998.

"NET-3 How-To," by Terry Dawson, terry@perf.no.itg.telecom.com.au. How to configure TCP/IP networking under Linux. Updated August 1998.

"NFS How-To," by Nicolai Langfeldt, janl@math.uio.no. How to set up NFS clients and servers. Updated 3 November 1997.

"NIS How-To," by Thorsten Kukuk, kukuk@suse.de. Information on using NIS/YP on Linux systems. Updated 9 March 1999.

"Networking Overview How-To," by Daniel Lpez Ridruejo, ridruejo@esi.us.es. Gives an overview of the networking capabilities of the Linux operating system, providing pointers for further information and implementation details. Updated 10 July 1998.

"Optical Disk How-To," by Skip Rye, Skip_Rye@faneuil.com. How to use optical disk drives with Linux. Updated 11 December 1998.

"Oracle How-To," by Paul Haigh, paul@nailed.demon.co.uk. How to set up Oracle as a database server. Updated 4 August 1998.

"PCI How-To," by Michael Will, Michael.Will@student.uni-tuebingen.de. Information on PCI-architecture compatibility with Linux. Updated 30 March 1997.

"PCMCIA How-To," by Dave Hinds, dhinds@allegro.stanford.edu. How to install and use PCMCIA Card Services. Updated 15 May 1999.

"PPP How-To," by Robert Hart, hartr@interweft.com.au. Information on using PPP networking with Linux. Updated 31 March 1997.

"PalmOS How-To," by David H. Silber, pilot@orbits.com. How to use your Palm OS device with a Linux system. Updated 20 September 1998.

"Parallel Processing How-To," by Hank Dietz, pplinux@ecn.purdue.edu. Discussion of parallel processing approaches for Linux. Updated 5 January 1998.

"Plug and Play How-To," by David Lawyer, bf347@lafn.org. How to get your Linux system to support Plug-and-Play. Updated June 1999.

"Polish How-To," by Sergiusz Pawlowicz, ser@arch.pwr.wroc.pl. Information on using Linux with Polish-specific features. Updated 8 February 1999.

"Portuguese-How-To," by Carlos Augusto Moreira dos Santos, casantos@cpmet.ufpel.tche.br. Este documento pretende ser um guia de referncia de configuraao do Linux e seus programas.... Updated 24 May 1999.

"PostgreSQL How-To," by Al Dev (Alavoor Vasudevan), aldev@hotmail.com. How to set up PostgreSQL as a database server. Updated 8 January 1999.

"Printing How-To," by Grant Taylor, gtaylor+pht@picante.com. How-To on printing software for Linux. Updated 9 March 1999.

"Printing Usage How-To," by Mark Komarinski, markk@auratek.com. How to use the printing system for a variety of file types and options. Updated 6 February 1998.

"Quake How-To," by Bob Zimbinski, bobz@mr.net, and Thomas Mike Hallock, medina.net. This document explains how to install, run, and troubleshoot Quake, QuakeWorld, and Quake II on an Intel Linux system. Updated 30 August 1998.

"RPM How-To," by Donnie Barnes, djb@redhat.com. How to use the Red Hat Package Manager (.rpm). Updated 8 April 1997.

"Reading List How-To," by Eric S. Raymond, esr@snark.thyrsus.com. Interesting books pertaining to Linux subjects. Updated 20 April 1999.

"Root RAID How-To," by Michael A. Robinton, michael@bzs.org. How to create a root-mounted RAID file system. Updated 25 March 1998.

"SCSI Programming How-To," by Heiko Eissfeldt, heiko@colossus.escape.de. Information on programming the generic Linux SCSI interface. Updated 7 May 1996.

"SMB How-To," by David Wood, dwood@plugged.net.au. How to use the Session Message Block (SMB) protocol with Linux. Updated 25 March 1999.

"SRM How-To," by David Mosberger, davidm@azstarnet.com. How to boot Linux/Alpha using the SRM firmware. Updated 17 August 1996.

"Security How-To," by Kevin Fenzi, kevin@scrye.com. General overview of security issues. Updated 25 April 1999.

"Serial How-To," by David Lawyer, bf347@lafn.org. How to use serial devices (modems, terminals, and so on) with Linux. Updated May 1999.

"Serial Programming How-To," by Peter H. Baumann, Peter.Baumann@dlr.de. How to use serial ports in programs. Updated 22 January 1998.

"Shadow Password How-To," by Michael H. Jackson, mhjack@tscnet.com. How to obtain, install, and configure shadow passwords. Updated 3 April 1996.

"Slovenian How-To," by Primoz Peterlin, primoz.peterlin@biofiz.mf.uni-lj.si. Information on using Linux with Slovenian-specific features. Updated 15 February 1999.

"Software Building-How-To," by Mendel Leo Cooper, thegrendel@theriver.com. How to build software packages. Updated 16 May 1999.

"Software Release Practice How-To," by Eric S. Raymond, esr@snark.thyrsus.com. Describes good release practices for Linux open-source projects. Updated 18 June 1999.

"Sound How-To," by Jeff Tranter, jeff_tranter@pobox.com. Sound hardware and software for the Linux operating system. Updated 24 March 1999.

"Sound Playing How-To," by Yoo C. Chung, wacko@laplace.snu.ac.kr. How to play various sound formats under Linux. Updated 11 August 1998.

"Spanish How-To," by Gonzalo Garcia Agullo, Gonzalo.Garcia-Agullo@jrc.es. Information on using Linux with Spanish-specific features. Updated 20 August 1996.

"TclTk How-To," by Luca Rossetti, lukaros@tin.it. Describes the Linux approach to Tcl, a scripting language. Updated 7 November 1998.

"teTeX How-To," by Robert Kiesling, kiesling@terracom.net. How to install the teTeX package (TeX and LaTeX) under Linux. Updated 9 November 1998.

"Text-Terminal How-To," by David S. Lawyer, bf347@lafn.org. Explains what text terminals are, how they work, and how to install and configure them. Updated June 1999.

"Thai How-To," by Poonlap Veeratanabutr, poon-v@fedu.uec.ac.jp. How to configure Linux for use with the Thai character set. Updated 4 August 1998.

"Tips How-To," by Paul Anderson, paul@geeky1.ebtech.net. How-To on miscellaneous tips and tricks for Linux. Updated June 1998.

"UMSDOS How-To," by Jacques Gelinas, jacques@solucorp.qc.ca. How to install and use the UMSDOS file system. Updated 13 November 1995.

"UPS How-To," by Harvey J. Stein, abel@netvision.net.il. Information on using a UPS power supply with Linux. Updated 18 November 1997.

"UUCP How-To," by Guylhem Aznar, guylhem@danmark.linux.eu.org. Information on UUCP software for Linux. Updated 6 February 1998.

"Unix and Internet Fundamentals How-To," by Eric S. Raymond, esr@snark.thyrsus.com. Describes the working basics of PC-class computers, UNIX-like operating systems, and the Internet in nontechnical language. Updated 3 December 1998.

"User Group How-To," by Kendall Grant Clark, kclark@ntlug.org. Tips on founding, maintaining, and growing a Linux user group. Updated 24 April 1998.

"VAR How-To," by Mr. Poet, poet@linuxports.com. Listing of Linux value-added resellers. Updated 7 March 1999.

"VME How-To," by John Huggins and Michael Wyrick, vmelinux@va.net. How to run Linux on your VMEbus Pentium and other PCI local bus-based VMEbus processor designs. Updated 30 July 1998.

"VMS to Linux How-To," by Guido Gonzato, guido@ibogfs.cineca.it. How to move from VMS to Linux. Updated 20 April 1998.

"Virtual Services How-To," by Brian Ackerman, brian@nycrc.net. How to set up virtual hosting services. Updated 15 August 1998.

"WWW How-To," by Wayne Leister, n3mtr@qis.net. How to set up WWW clients and servers. Updated 19 November 1997.

"WWW mSQL How-To," by Oliver Corff, corff@zedat.fu-berlin.de. How to set up a Web server database with mSQL. Updated 17 September 1997.

"XFree86 How-To," by Eric S. Raymond, esr@snark.thyrsus.com. How to obtain, install, and configure XFree86 3.2 (X11R6). Updated 12 May 1999.

"XFree86 Video Timings How-To," by Eric S. Raymond, esr@snark.thyrsus.com. How to compose a mode line for XFree86. Updated 13 June 1999.

"X Window User How-To," by Ray Brigleb, ray@croftj.net. Information on configuring the X Window environment for the Linux user. Updated 22 January 1999.

Mini-How-To Index

The following mini-How-Tos are available:

"3 Button Mouse mini-How-To," by Geoff Short, geoff@kipper.york.ac.uk. How to configure your mouse to use three buttons. Updated 31 May 1998.

"ADSM Backup mini-How-To," by Thomas Koenig, Thomas.Koenig@ciw.uni-karlsruhe.de. How to install and use the ADSM backup program. Updated 15 January 1997.

"Asymmetric Digital Subscriber Loop (ADSL) mini-How-To," by David Fannin, dfannin@dnai.com. Addresses ordering, installation, and configuration. Updated 10 April 1999.

"AI-Alife mini-How-To," by John A. Eikenberry, jae@ai.uga.edu. Information about AI software for Linux. Updated 13 January 1998.

"Advocacy mini-How-To," by Paul L. Rogers, Paul.L.Rogers@li.org. Suggestions on how to advocate the use of Linux. Updated 7 May 1998.

"Alsa Sound mini-How-To," by Valentijn Sessink. Describes the installation of the Alsa sound drivers for Linux. Updated 18 May 1999.

"Apache SSL PHP/FI frontpage mini-How-To," by Marcus Faure, marcus@faure.de. How to build a multipurpose Web server. Updated July 1998.

"Automount mini-How-To," by Don, don@sabotage.org. Describes the autofs automounter, explains how to configure it, and points out some problems to avoid. Updated 17 April 1999.

"Backup with MSDOS mini-How-To," by Christopher Neufeld, neufeld@physics.utoronto.ca. How to back up Linux machines with MS-DOS. Updated 5 August 1997.

"Battery Powered mini-How-To," by Hanno Mueller, hanno@lava.de. How to reduce a Linux system's power consumption. Updated 21 December 1997.

"Boca mini-How-To," by David H Dennis, david@freelink.net. How to install a Boca 16-port serial card (Boca 2016). Updated 1 August 1997.

"BogoMips mini-How-To," by Wim C.A. van Dorst, baron@clifton.hobby.nl. Information about BogoMips. Updated 8 February 1999.

"Bridge mini-How-To," by Chris Cole, cole@lynkmedia.com. How to set up an Ethernet bridge. Updated 7 September 1998.

"Bridge+Firewall mini-How-To," by Peter Breuer, ptb@it.uc3m.es. How to set up an Ethernet bridge and firewall. Updated 19 December 1997.

"Bzip2 mini-How-To," by David Fetter, dfetter@best.com. How to use the new bzip2 compression program. Updated 29 June 1998.

"Cable Modem mini-How-To," by Vladimir Vuksan, vuksan@veus.hr. How to use a cable modem with a cable ISP. Updated 9 June 1999.

"Cipe+Masquerading mini-How-To," by Anthony Ciaravalo, acj@home.com. How to set up a Virtual Private Network between your LAN and other LANs using cipe through Linux-masquerading firewall machines. Updated 28 October 1998.

"Clock mini-How-To," by Ron Bean, rbean@execpc.com. How to set and keep your clock on time. Updated December 1996.

"Coffee mini-How-To," by Georgatos Photis, gef@ceid.upatras.gr. Thoughts about making coffee with Linux (humorous). Updated 15 January 1998.

"Colour ls mini-How-To," by Thorbjoern Ravn Andersen, ravn@dit.ou.dk. How to set up colors with `ls`. Updated 7 August 1997.

"Cyrus IMAP mini-How-To," by Kevin Mitchell, kevin@iserv.net. How to install the Cyrus IMAP server. Updated 21 January 1998.

"DHCP mini-How-To," by Vladimir Vuksan, vuksan@veus.hr. How to set up a DHCP server and client. Updated 11 June 1999.

"DPT Hardware RAID mini-How-To," by Ram Samudrala, `me@ram.org`. How to configure hardware RAID. Updated 9 April 1999.

"Diald mini-How-To," by Harish Pillay, `h.pillay@ieee.org`. How to use diald to dial an ISP. Updated 3 June 1996.

"Ext2fs Undeletion mini-How-To," by Aaron Crane, `aaronc@pobox.com`. How to retrieve deleted files from an ext2 file system. Updated 2 February 1999.

"Fax Server mini-How-To," by Erez Strauss, `erez@newplaces.com`. How to set up a fax server. Updated 8 November 1997.

"Firewall Piercing mini-How-To," by Franois-Ren Rideau, `rideau@ens.fr`. How to use PPP over Telnet transparently through an Internet firewall. Updated 27 November 1998.

"GIS-GRASS mini-How-To," by David A. Hastings, `dah@ngdc.noaa.gov`. How to install Geographic Information System (GIS) software. Updated 13 November 1997.

"GTEK BBS-550 mini-How-To," by Wajihuddin Ahmed, `wahmed@sdnpk.undp.org`. How to set up the GTEK BBS-550 multiport board with Linux. Updated 20 August 1997.

"Hard Disk Upgrade mini-How-To," by Yves Bellefeuille, `yan@ottawa.com`. How to copy a Linux system from one hard disk to another. Updated 31 January 1998.

"IO Port Programming mini-How-To," by Riku Saikkonen, `Riku.Saikkonen@hut.fi`. How to use I/O ports in C programs. Updated 28 December 1997.

"IP Alias mini-How-To," by Harish Pillay, `h.pillay@ieee.org`. How to use IP aliasing. Updated 13 January 1997.

"IP Masquerade mini-How-To," by Ambrose Au, `ambrose@writeme.com`. How to use IP masquerading. Updated 7 February 1999.

"IP Subnetworking mini-How-To," by Robert Hart, `hartr@interweft.com.au`. Why and how to subnetwork an IP network. Updated 31 March 1997.

"ISP Connectivity mini-How-To," by Michael Strates, `mstrates@croftj.net`. How to get mail and news over a dial-up connection. Updated 6 November 1997.

"Install from ZIP mini-How-To," by Kevin Snively, `k.snively@seaslug.org`. How to install Linux from a parallel port zip drive. Updated 29 April 1998.

"Kerneld mini-How-To," by Henrik Storner, `storner@osiris.ping.dk`. How to use kerneld (dynamic module loading). Updated 19 July 1997.

"LBX mini-How-To," by Paul D. Smith, `psmith@baynetworks.com`. How to use Low-Bandwidth X (LBX). Updated 11 December 1997.

"LILO mini-How-To," by Alessandro Rubini, `rubini@linux.it`. Examples of typical LILO installations. Updated 16 August 1998.

"Large Disk mini-How-To," by Andries Brouwer, `aeb@cwi.nl`. How to use disks with more than 1,024 cylinders. Updated 26 April 1999.

"Leased Line mini-How-To," by Rob van der Putten, `rob@sput.webster.nl`. How to set up leased-line modems. Updated July 1998.

"Linux+DOS+Win95+OS2 mini-How-To," by Mike Harlan, `r3mdh@raex.com`. How to use Linux, DOS, OS/2, and Windows 95 together. Updated 11 November 1997.

"Linux+FreeBSD mini-How-To," by Niels Kristian Bech Jensen, `nkbj@image.dk` How to use Linux and FreeBSD together. Updated 15 January 1999.

"Linux+NT-Loader mini-How-To," by Bernd Reichert, `reichert@dial.eunet.ch`. How to use Linux and the Windows NT boot loader together. Updated 2 September 1997.

"Linux+Win95 mini-How-To," by Jonathan Katz, `jkatz@in.net`. How to use Linux and Windows 95 together. Updated 26 October 1996.

"Loadlin+Win95 mini-How-To," by Chris Fischer, `protek@brigadoon.com`. How to use Linux and Windows 95 together, using `loadlin`. Updated 13 March 1999.

"Mac Terminal mini-How-To," by Robert Kiesling, `kiesling@terracom.net`. How to use an Apple Macintosh as a serial terminal. Updated 9 November 1997.

"Mail Queue mini-How-To," by Leif Erlingsson, `leif@lege.com`. How to queue remote mail and deliver local mail. Updated 3 September 1997.

"Mail2News mini-How-To," by Robert Hart, `iweft@ipax.com.au`. How to set up a mail-to-news gateway. Updated 4 November 1996.

"Man Page mini-How-To," by Jens Schweikhardt, `schweikh@noc.dfn.de`. How to write man pages. Updated July 1998.

"Modules mini-How-To," by Riley H. Williams, `rhw@bigfoot.com`. How to set up and configure kernel modules. Updated 14 November 1997.

"Multiboot using LILO mini-How-To," by Renzo Zanelli, `rzanelli@southeast.net`. How to multiboot between Windows 95, Windows NT, and Linux. Updated 26 March 1998.

"NCD X Terminal mini-How-To," by Ian Hodge, `ihodge@nortel.ca`. Describes how to connect an NCD X terminal to a UNIX host. Updated 3 April 1998.

"NFS-Root mini-How-To," by Andreas Kostyrka, `andreas@ag.or.at`. How to set up diskless Linux machines. Updated 8 August 1997.

"NFS-Root-Client mini-How-To," by Ofer Maor, `ofer@hadar.co.il`. How to set up diskless Linux machines using NFS. Updated 2 February 1999.

"Netrom-Node mini-How-To," by Karl Larsen, `k5di@yahoo.com`. How to set up the ax25-utilities package for Amateur Radio such as making Netrom Nodes. Updated 19 October 1998.

"Netscape+Proxy mini-How-To," by Sarma Seetamraju, `sarma@usa.net`. How to set up a proxy server for Netscape. Updated 15 August 1997.

"Netstation mini-How-To," by Kris Buytaert, Kris.Buytaert@advalvas.be. How to hook up an IBM Netstation to your local network using a Linux box as a server. Updated 22 February 1998.

"News Leafsite mini-How-To," by Florian Kuehnert, sutok@gmx.de. How to set up a leaf news site. Updated 4 January 1998.

"Offline Mailing mini-How-To," by Gunther Voet, freaker@tuc.ml.org. How to set up email addresses without a dedicated Internet connection. Updated 4 June 1998.

"PLIP mini-How-To," by Andrea Controzzi, controzz@cli.di.unipi.it. How to set up PLIP (Parallel Line Interface Protocol). Updated 12 March 1998.

"Partition mini-How-To," by Kristian Koehntopp, kris@koehntopp.de. How to choose disk partitions. Updated 3 November 1997.

"Partition Rescue mini-How-To," by Rolf Klausen, rolfk@romsdal.vgs.no. How to rescue deleted Linux partitions. Updated 22 October 1997.

"Path mini-How-To," by Esa Turtiainen, etu@dna.fi. How to use the PATH environment variable. Updated 15 November 1997.

"Pre-installation Checklist mini-How-To," by S. Parthasarathy, algo-log@hd1.vsnl.net.in. Preinstallation checklist and questionnaire. Updated 29 August 1998.

"Process Accounting mini-How-To," by Albert M.C. Tam, bertie@scn.org. How to set up process accounting. Updated 8 August 1997.

"Proxy ARP Subnet mini-How-To," by Bob Edwards, bob@faceng.anu.edu.au. How to use proxy ARP with subnetting. Updated August 1997.

"Public Web Browser mini-How-To," by Donald B. Marti Jr., dmarti@best.com. How to set up a guest account to use a WWW browser. Updated 5 January 1998.

"Qmail+MH mini-How-To," by Christopher Richardson, rdn@tara.n.eunet.de. How to install qmail and MH. Updated 5 March 1998.

"Quota mini-How-To," by Albert M.C. Tam, bertie@scn.org. How to set up disk quotas. Updated 8 August 1997.

"RCS mini-How-To," by Robert Kiesling, kiesling@terracom.net. How to use RCS (Revision Control System). Updated 14 August 1997.

"RPM+Slackware mini-How-To," by Dave Whitinger, dave@whitinger.net. How to install the Red Hat Package Manager (RPM) under Slackware. Updated 13 April 1998.

"RedHat CD mini-How-To," by Morten Kjeldgaard, mok@imsb.au.dk, and Peter von der Ah, pahe+rhcd@daimi.au.dk. How to make your own CDs from the Red Hat Linux distribution equivalent to the ones commercially available from Red Hat. Updated 9 September 1998.

"Remote Boot mini-How-To," by Marc Vuilleumier Stckelberg, Marc.Vuilleu-mierStuckelberg@cui.unige.ch. How to set up a server-based boot selector. Updated February 1999.

"Remote X Apps mini-How-To," by Vincent Zweije, zweije@xs4all.nl. How to run remote X applications. Updated 14 July 1998.

"SLIP-PPP Emulator mini-How-To," by Irish, irish@eskimo.com. How to use SLIP-PPP emulators with Linux. Updated 7 August 1997.

"Sendmail Address Rewrite mini-How-To," by Thomas Roessler, roessler@guug.de. How to set up sendmail's configuration file for the home user's dial-up access. Updated 6 May 1998.

"Sendmail+UUCP mini-How-To," by Jamal Hadi Salim, jamal@glcom.com. How to use sendmail and UUCP together. Updated August 1998.

"Secure POP via SSH mini-How-To," by Manish Singh, yosh@gimp.org. How to set up secure POP connections using ssh. Updated 30 September 1998.

"Small Memory mini-How-To," by Todd Burgess, tburgess@uoguelph.ca. How to run Linux on a system with a small amount of memory. Update 29 October 1997.

"Software RAID mini-How-To," by Linas Vepstas, linas@fc.net. How to configure software RAID. Updated 21 November 1998.

"Soundblaster AWE mini-How-To," by Marcus Brinkmann, Marcus.Brinkmann@-ruhr-uni-bochum.de. How to install the Sound Blaster AWE 32/64. Updated 11 January 1998.

"StarOffice mini-How-To," by Matthew Borowski, mkb@poboxes.com. Information on installing the StarOffice suite. Updated 2 June 1998.

"Term Firewall mini-How-To," by Barak Pearlmutter, bap@cs.unm.edu. How to use term over a firewall. Updated 15 July 1997.

"TkRat mini-How-To," by Dave Whitinger, dave@whitinger.net. How to install and use the TkRat mail program. Updated 2 February 1998.

"Token Ring mini-How-To," by Mike Eckhoff, mike.e@emissary.aus-etc.com. How to use token ring cards. Updated 7 January 1998.

"Ultra-DMA mini-How-To," by Brion Vibber, brion@pobox.com. How to use Ultra-DMA drives and controllers. Updated 27 May 1999.

"Update mini-How-To," by Stein Gjoen, sgjoen@nyx.net. How to stay updated about Linux development. Updated 3 February 1998.

"Upgrade mini-How-To," by Greg Louis, glouis@dynamicro.on.ca. How to upgrade your Linux distribution. Updated 6 June 1996.

"VAIO mini-How-To," by Hideki Saito, hideki@chatlink.com. Explains installation of Linux on Sony VAIO computers. Updated 16 September 1998.

"Vesafb mini-How-To," by Alex Buell, alex.buell@tahallah.demon.co.uk. How to use the vesafb device. Updated 2 August 1998.

"VPN mini-How-To," by rpd Magosnyi, mag@bunuel.tii.matav.hu. How to set up a VPN (Virtual Private Network). Updated 7 August 1997.

"Visual Bell mini-How-To," by Alessandro Rubini, `rubini@linux.it`. How to disable audible bells and enable visual bells. Updated 11 November 1997.

"Windows Modem Sharing mini-How-To," by Friedemann Baitinger, `baiti@toplink.net`. How to set up Windows to use a shared modem on a Linux machine. Updated 2 November 1997.

"WordPerfect mini-How-To," by Wade Hampton, `whampton@staffnet.com`. How to set up WordPerfect for Linux. Updated 13 August 1997.

"X Big Cursor mini-How-To," by Joerg Schneider, `schneid@ira.uka.de`. How to use enlarged cursors with X Windows. Updated 11 August 1997.

"XFree86-XInside mini-How-To," by Marco Melgazzi, `marco@techie.com`. How to convert XFree86 to XInside modelines. Updated September 1997.

"xterm Title mini-How-To," by Ric Lister, `ric@giccs.georgetown.edu`. How to put strings into the title bar of an xterm. Updated 7 January 1998.

"ZIP Install mini-How-To," by John Wiggins, `jwiggins@comp.uark.edu`. How to install Linux onto a zip drive. Updated 10 January 1999.

"ZIP Drive mini-How-To," by Kyle Dansie, `dansie@ibm.net`. Provides a quick reference guide on setting up and using the Iomega zip drive with Linux. Updated 10 January 1999.

Special How-To Index

"The High Availability How-To," by Harald Milz (`hm@seneca.muc.de`) is available at the following site:

`http://metalab.unc.edu/pub/Linux/ALPHA/linux-ha/High-Availability-HOWTO.html`

It is not included with the How-To collection because it relies on figures and cannot be distributed in all supported formats.

"The Graphics mini-How-To," by Michael J. Hammel, (`mjhammel@graphics-muse.org`) is available at the following Web site:

`http://www.graphics-muse.org/linux/lgh.html`

It is not included with the How-To collection because it needs to use a lot of images that don't translate to other output formats.

Unmaintained How-Tos and Mini-How-Tos

You can find a number of unmaintained documents at `http://metalab.unc.edu/pub/Linux/docs/HOWTO/unmaintained`.

They are kept around because old documentation is sometimes better than none. However, you should be aware that you are reading old documentation.

WRITING AND SUBMITTING A HOW-TO

If you are interested in writing a How-To or mini-How-To, please get in touch with me first at `linux-howto@metalab.unc.edu`.

The following are a few guidelines that you should follow when writing a How-To or mini-How-To:

- Try to use meaningful structure and organization, and write clearly. Remember that many of the people reading How-Tos do not speak English as their first language.
- If you are writing a How-To, you must use the SGML-Tools package, available from `http://www.pobox.com/~cg/sgmltools`, to format the How-To. This package enables you to produce LaTeX (for DVI and PostScript), plain text, and HTML from a single source document, and was designed specifically for the How-Tos. Using this package also gives all the How-Tos a uniform look. It is very important that you format and review the output of the formatting in PostScript, plain text, and HTML.
- If you are writing a mini-How-To, use either SGML (as described earlier) or HTML. If you use SGML for your mini-How-To, it will be published along with the How-Tos in Linux Documentation Project (LDP) books.
- Make sure that all the information is correct. I can't stress this point enough. When in doubt, speculate but make it clear that you're only guessing.
- Make sure that you are covering the most recent version of the available software. Also, be sure to include full instructions on where software can be downloaded from (FTP site name, full pathname), and the current version number and release date of the software.
- Include a FAQ section at the end, if appropriate. Many How-To documents need a "FAQ" or "Common Problems" section to cover information that can't be covered in the regular text.
- Use other How-Tos or mini-How-Tos as models. The SGML source to the How-Tos is available on Linux FTP sites. In addition, take a look at the LDP Style Guide for some guidelines. Make sure that your name, email address, date, and a version number appear near the beginning of the document. You also can include WWW addresses and a snail mail address if you want. The standard header is

  Title
  Author's name and email address
  Version number and date

  For example:

  The Linux How-To Index
  by Tim Bynum
  v2.10.29, 31 July 1997
- Be prepared to receive questions and comments about your writing. Several hundred people access the How-To collection every day from around the world.

After you have written the How-To, you can mail it to Tim Bynum at `linux-howto@metalab.unc.edu`. If you used SGML-Tools, simply mail Tim the SGML source; he'll take care of formatting the documents. He'll also take care of archiving the How-Tos on `metalab.unc.edu` and posting them to the various newsgroups.

It is important that you go through Tim when submitting a How-To because he maintains the archives and needs to keep track of what How-Tos are being written and who is doing what.

All you have to do is send him periodic updates whenever appropriate.

COPYRIGHT

Copyright ©1995–1998 by Tim Bynum.

Unless otherwise stated, Linux How-To documents are copyrighted by their respective authors. Linux How-To documents may be reproduced and distributed in whole or in part, in any medium physical or electronic, as long as this copyright notice is retained on all copies. Commercial redistribution is allowed and encouraged; however, the author would like to be notified of any such distributions.

All translations, derivative works, or aggregate works incorporating any Linux How-To documents must be covered under this copyright notice. That is, you may not produce a derivative work from a How-To and impose additional restrictions on its distribution. Exceptions to these rules may be granted under certain conditions; please contact the Linux How-To coordinator at the address given below.

In short, we wish to promote dissemination of this information through as many channels as possible. However, we do wish to retain copyright on the How-To documents and would like to be notified of any plans to redistribute the How-Tos.

If you have questions, please contact Tim Bynum, the Linux How-To coordinator, at `linux-howto@metalab.unc.edu` via email.

APPENDIX C

THE GNU GENERAL PUBLIC LICENSE

What exactly is GNU? Many believe GNU software is public domain, and some believe GNU software is shareware. Neither is true. Basically, GNU software is scopyrighted software that authors have granted the permission to distribute under certain conditions. Those conditions include the provision to provide source code and that no part of the software may be placed under a copyright that restricts the further distribution of the software; that is, you can't use source code copyrighted under the GNU License within your program without making your source code freely available.

Although the GNU copyright specifies that you must make your source code available, it doesn't mean you have to give your program away for free; you can charge a fee for your program, but that fee *must* include the source code for both the GNU portions and your portion. You can't charge a fee for the executable part of the program and then another fee for the source code; you must charge one price for both. Thus, you can't withhold or charge extra for what you might consider proprietary source code. This is the main objection many software executives have with using GNU software within their programs; they don't want to make their source code available to their competitors.

But the concept of GNU goes further, and perhaps the best source to explain this concept is Richard Stallman, the patriarch of the GNU philosophy. Stallman is a founder and proponent of the Free Software Foundation (FSF). He believes very strongly that all software should be free and that computer systems should be open for use by anyone. The fact that programs such as Linux and Emacs are freely available matches his philosophy. Anyone can take them for his or her own use. Users are also encouraged to make modifications and share those changes with others.

Note

The GNU License is sometimes referred to as the *GNU copyleft*, as a play on the word *copyright*. GNU is also a play on words–*GNU's Not UNIX*. For more information on the GNU copyleft, see `http://www.fsf.org/copyleft/copyleft.html`.

What does all this information have to do with Linux? Well, the various components of Linux are distributed under GNU's General Public License. Thus, Linux is neither in the public domain, nor is it shareware; Linus Torvalds and the others retain copyright to their work under the GPL. The rest of this appendix is the GPL as published by the Free Software Foundation.

ON THE WEB

The Web site for the Free Software Foundation is

`http://www.fsf.org`

THE GNU LICENSE

Version 2, June 1991

PREAMBLE

The licenses for most software are designed to take away your freedom to share and change it. By contrast, the GNU General Public License is intended to guarantee your freedom to share and change free software—to make sure the software is free for all its users. This General Public License applies to most of the Free Software Foundation's software and to any other program whose authors commit to using it. (Some other Free Software Foundation software is covered by the GNU Library General Public License instead.) You can apply it to your programs, too.

When we speak of free software, we are referring to freedom, not price. Our General Public Licenses are designed to make sure that you have the freedom to distribute copies of free software (and charge for this service if you wish), that you receive source code or can get it if you want it, that you can change the software or use pieces of it in new free programs; and that you know you can do these things.

To protect your rights, we need to make restrictions that forbid anyone to deny you these rights or to ask you to surrender the rights. These restrictions translate to certain responsibilities for you if you distribute copies of the software, or if you modify it.

For example, if you distribute copies of such a program, whether gratis or for a fee, you must give the recipients all the rights that you have. You must make sure that they, too, receive or can get the source code. And you must show them these terms so they know their rights.

We protect your rights with two steps: (1) copyright the software, and (2) offer you this license which gives you legal permission to copy, distribute and/or modify the software.

Also, for each author's protection and ours, we want to make certain that everyone understands that there is no warranty for this free software. If the software is modified by someone else and passed on, we want its recipients to know that what they have is not the original, so that any problems introduced by others will not reflect on the original authors' reputations.

Finally, any free program is threatened constantly by software patents. We wish to avoid the danger that redistributors of a free program will individually obtain patent licenses, in effect making the program proprietary. To prevent this, we have made it clear that any patent must be licensed for everyone's free use or not licensed at all.

The precise terms and conditions for copying, distribution and modification follow.

GNU General Public License Terms and Conditions for Copying, Distribution, and Modification

This license applies to any program or other work which contains a notice placed by the copyright holder saying it may be distributed under the terms of this General Public License. The "Program," below, refers to any such program or work, and a "work based on the Program" means either the Program or any derivative work under copyright law: that is to say, a work containing the Program or a portion of it, either verbatim or with modifications and/or translated into another language. (Hereinafter, translation is included without limitation in the term "modification.") Each licensee is addressed as "you."

Activities other than copying, distribution and modification are not covered by this License; they are outside its scope. The act of running the Program is not restricted, and the output from the Program is covered only if its contents constitute a work based on the Program (independent of having been made by running the Program). Whether that is true depends on what the Program does.

1. You may copy and distribute verbatim copies of the Program's source code as you receive it, in any medium, provided that you conspicuously and appropriately publish on each copy an appropriate copyright notice and disclaimer of warranty; keep intact all the notices that refer to this License and to the absence of any warranty; and give any other recipients of the Program a copy of this License along with the Program.
2. You may charge a fee for the physical act of transferring a copy, and you may at your option offer warranty protection in exchange for a fee.

   You may modify your copy or copies of the Program or any portion of it, thus forming a work based on the Program, and copy and distribute such modifications or work under the terms of Section 1 above, provided that you also meet all of these conditions:

   - You must cause the modified files to carry prominent notices stating that you changed the files and the date of any change.
   - You must cause any work that you distribute or publish, that in whole or in part contains or is derived from the Program or any part thereof, to be licensed as a whole at no charge to all third parties under the terms of this License.
   - If the modified program normally reads commands interactively when run, you must cause it, when started running for such interactive use in the most ordinary way, to print or display an announcement including an appropriate copyright notice and a notice that there is no warranty (or else, saying that you provide a warranty) and that users may redistribute the program under

these conditions, and telling the user how to view a copy of this License. (Exception: if the Program itself is interactive but does not normally print such an announcement, your work based on the Program is not required to print an announcement.)

These requirements apply to the modified work as a whole. If identifiable sections of that work are not derived from the Program, and can be reasonably considered independent and separate works in themselves, then this License, and its terms, do not apply to those sections when you distribute them as separate works. But when you distribute the same sections as part of a whole which is a work based on the Program, the distribution of the whole must be on the terms of this License, whose permissions for other licensees extend to the entire whole, and thus to each and every part regardless of who wrote it.

Thus, it is not the intent of this section to claim rights or contest your rights to work written entirely by you; rather, the intent is to exercise the right to control the distribution of derivative or collective works based on the Program.

In addition, mere aggregation of another work not based on the Program with the Program (or with a work based on the Program) on a volume of a storage or distribution medium does not bring the other work under the scope of this License.

3. You may copy and distribute the Program (or a work based on it, under Section 2) in object code or executable form under the terms of Sections 1 and 2 above, provided that you also do one of the following:

   - Accompany it with the complete corresponding machine-readable source code, which must be distributed under the terms of Sections 1 and 2 above on a medium customarily used for software interchange; or,
   - Accompany it with a written offer, valid for at least three years, to give any third party, for a charge no more than your cost of physically performing source distribution, a complete machine-readable copy of the corresponding source code, to be distributed under the terms of Sections 1 and 2 above on a medium customarily used for software interchange; or,
   - Accompany it with the information you received as to the offer to distribute corresponding source code. (This alternative is allowed only for noncommercial distribution and only if you received the program in object code or executable form with such an offer, in accord with Subsection b above.)

   The source code for a work means the preferred form of the work for making modifications to it. For an executable work, complete source code means all the source code for all modules it contains, plus any associated interface definition files, plus the scripts used to control compilation and installation of the executable. However, as a special exception, the source code distributed need not include anything that is normally distributed (in either source or binary form) with the major components (compiler, kernel, and so on) of the operating system on which the executable runs, unless that component itself accompanies the executable.

If distribution of executable or object code is made by offering access to copy from a designated place, then offering equivalent access to copy the source code from the same place counts as distribution of the source code, even though third parties are not compelled to copy the source along with the object code.[/nl_list]

4. You may not copy, modify, sublicense, or distribute the Program except as expressly provided under this License. Any attempt otherwise to copy, modify, sublicense or distribute the Program is void, and will automatically terminate your rights under this License. However, parties who have received copies, or rights, from you under this License will not have their licenses terminated so long as such parties remain in full compliance.
5. You are not required to accept this License, since you have not signed it. However, nothing else grants you permission to modify or distribute the Program or its derivative works. These actions are prohibited by law if you do not accept this License. Therefore, by modifying or distributing the Program (or any work based on the Program), you indicate your acceptance of this License to do so, and all its terms and conditions for copying, distributing or modifying the Program or works based on it.
6. Each time you redistribute the Program (or any work based on the Program), the recipient automatically receives a license from the original licensor to copy, distribute or modify the Program subject to these terms and conditions. You may not impose any further restrictions on the recipients' exercise of the rights granted herein. You are not responsible for enforcing compliance by third parties to this License.
7. If, as a consequence of a court judgment or allegation of patent infringement or for any other reason (not limited to patent issues), conditions are imposed on you (whether by court order, agreement or otherwise) that contradict the conditions of this License, they do not excuse you from the conditions of this License. If you cannot distribute so as to satisfy simultaneously your obligations under this License and any other pertinent obligations, then as a consequence you may not distribute the Program at all. For example, if a patent license would not permit royalty-free redistribution of the Program by all those who receive copies directly or indirectly through you, then the only way you could satisfy both it and this License would be to refrain entirely from distribution of the Program.

   If any portion of this section is held invalid or unenforceable under any particular circumstance, the balance of the section is intended to apply and the section as a whole is intended to apply in other circumstances.

   It is not the purpose of this section to induce you to infringe any patents or other property right claims or to contest validity of any such claims; this section has the sole purpose of protecting the integrity of the free software distribution system, which is implemented by public license practices. Many people have made generous contributions to the wide range of software distributed through that system in reliance on consistent application of that system; it is up to the author/donor to decide if he or she is willing to distribute software through any other system, and a licensee cannot impose that choice.

This section is intended to make thoroughly clear what is believed to be a consequence of the rest of this License.

8. If the distribution and/or use of the Program is restricted in certain countries either by patents or by copyrighted interfaces, the original copyright holder who places the Program under this License may add an explicit geographical distribution limitation excluding those countries, so that distribution is permitted only in or among countries not thus excluded. In such case, this License incorporates the limitation as if written in the body of this License.

9. The Free Software Foundation may publish revised and/or new versions of the General Public License from time to time. Such new versions will be similar in spirit to the present version, but may differ in detail to address new problems or concerns.

   Each version is given a distinguishing version number. If the Program specifies a version number of this License which applies to it and "any later version," you have the option of following the terms and conditions either of that version or of any later version published by the Free Software Foundation. If the Program does not specify a version number of this License, you may choose any version ever published by the Free Software Foundation.

10. If you wish to incorporate parts of the Program into other free programs whose distribution conditions are different, write to the author to ask for permission. For software which is copyrighted by the Free Software Foundation, write to the Free Software Foundation; we sometimes make exceptions for this. Our decision will be guided by the two goals of preserving the free status of all derivatives of our free software and of promoting the sharing and reuse of software generally.

    NO WARRANTY

11. BECAUSE THE PROGRAM IS LICENSED FREE OF CHARGE, THERE IS NO WARRANTY FOR THE PROGRAM, TO THE EXTENT PERMITTED BY APPLICABLE LAW. EXCEPT WHEN OTHERWISE STATED IN WRITING THE COPYRIGHT HOLDERS AND/OR OTHER PARTIES PROVIDE THE PROGRAM "AS IS" WITHOUT WARRANTY OF ANY KIND, EITHER EXPRESSED OR IMPLIED, INCLUDING, BUT NOT LIMITED TO, THE IMPLIED WARRANTIES OF MERCHANTABILITY AND FITNESS FOR A PARTICULAR PURPOSE. THE ENTIRE RISK AS TO THE QUALITY AND PERFORMANCE OF THE PROGRAM IS WITH YOU. SHOULD THE PROGRAM PROVE DEFECTIVE, YOU ASSUME THE COST OF ALL NECESSARY SERVICING, REPAIR OR CORRECTION.

12. IN NO EVENT UNLESS REQUIRED BY APPLICABLE LAW OR AGREED TO IN WRITING WILL ANY COPYRIGHT HOLDER, OR ANY OTHER PARTY WHO MAY MODIFY AND/OR REDISTRIBUTE THE PROGRAM AS PERMITTED ABOVE, BE LIABLE TO YOU FOR DAMAGES, INCLUDING ANY GENERAL, SPECIAL, INCIDENTAL OR CONSEQUENTIAL DA-

MAGES ARISING OUT OF THE USE OR INABILITY TO USE THE PROGRAM (INCLUDING BUT NOT LIMITED TO LOSS OF DATA OR DATA BEING RENDERED INACCURATE OR LOSSES SUSTAINED BY YOU OR THIRD PARTIES OR A FAILURE OF THE PROGRAM TO OPERATE WITH ANY OTHER PROGRAMS), EVEN IF SUCH HOLDER OR OTHER PARTY HAS BEEN ADVISED OF THE POSSIBILITY OF SUCH DAMAGES.

END OF TERMS AND CONDITIONS

How to Apply These Terms to Your New Programs

If you develop a new program, and you want it to be of the greatest possible use to the public, the best way to achieve this is to make it free software which everyone can redistribute and change under these terms.

To do so, attach the following notices to the program. It is safest to attach them to the start of each source file to most effectively convey the exclusion of warranty; and each file should have at least the "copyright" line and a pointer to where the full notice is found:

```
<one line to give the program's name and a brief idea of what it does.>
Copyright © 3519yy <name of author>

This program is free software; you can redistribute it and/or modify it under
the terms of the GNU General Public License as published by the Free Software
Foundation; either version 2 of the License, or (at your option) any later
version.

This program is distributed in the hope that it will be useful, but WITHOUT
ANY WARRANTY; without even the implied warranty of MERCHANTABILITY or FITNESS
FOR A PARTICULAR PURPOSE. See the GNU General Public License for more details.

You should have received a copy of the GNU General Public License along with
this program; if not, write to the Free Software Foundation, Inc.,
675 Mass. Ave, Cambridge MA 02139 USA.
```

Also add information on how to contact you by electronic and paper mail.

If the program is interactive, make it output a short notice like this when it starts in an interactive mode:

```
Gnomovision version 69, Copyright 19yy name of author
Gnomovision comes with ABSOLUTELY NO WARRANTY; for details type ''show w''.
This is free software, and you are welcome to redistribute it
under certain conditions; type ''show c'' for details.
```

The hypothetical commands `show w` and `show c` should show the appropriate parts of the General Public License. Of course, the commands you use may be called something other than `show w` and `show c`; they could even be mouse-clicks or menu items—whatever suits your program.

You should also get your employer (if you work as a programmer) or your school, if any, to sign a "copyright disclaimer" for the program, if necessary. Here is a sample; however, you need to alter the names:

```
Yoyodyne, Inc., hereby disclaims all copyright interest in the program
'Gnomovision' (which makes passes at compilers) written by James Hacker.

<signature of Ty Coon> 1 April 1989
Ty Coon, President of Vice
```

This General Public License does not permit incorporating your program into proprietary programs. If your program is a subroutine library, you may consider it more useful to permit linking proprietary applications with the library. If this is what you want to do, use the GNU Library General Public License instead of this license.

APPENDIX D

THE OPEN SOURCE DEFINITION

The Open Source movement exploded into public awareness during 1998 with the popularity of Linux. This appendix provides the text of the Open Source definition, originally written as part of the Debian distribution. Again this definition, like the GPL, emphasizes the right of individual access to the source code for any program released into the Open, but also provides criteria for releasing a program into the Open Source universe.

ON THE WEB

For more information on the Open Source Movement, check out its Web site:

`http://www.opensource.org`

And for the complete text of this definition, check out the following:

`http://www.opensource.org/osd.html`

THE OPEN SOURCE DEFINITION

(Version 1.4)

Open source doesn't just mean access to the source code. The distribution terms of an open-source program must comply with the following criteria:

1. Free Redistribution

   The license may not restrict any party from selling or giving away the software as a component of an aggregate software distribution containing programs from several different sources. The license may not require a royalty or other fee for such sale. (rationale)

2. Source Code

   The program must include source code, and must allow distribution in source code as well as compiled form. Where some form of a product is not distributed with source code, there must be a well-publicized means of obtaining the source code for no more than a reasonable reproduction cost—preferably, downloading via the Internet without charge. The source code must be the preferred form in which a programmer would modify the program. Deliberately obfuscated source code is not allowed. Intermediate forms such as the output of a preprocessor or translator are not allowed. (rationale)

3. Derived Works

   The license must allow modifications and derived works, and must allow them to be distributed under the same terms as the license of the original software. (rationale)

4. Integrity of The Author's Source Code

   The license may restrict source code from being distributed in modified form only if the license allows the distribution of "patch files" with the source code for the purpose of modifying the program at build time. The license must explicitly permit distribution of software built from modified source code. The license may require derived works to carry a different name or version number from the original software. (rationale)

5. No Discrimination Against Persons or Groups

   The license must not discriminate against any person or group of persons. (rationale)

6. No Discrimination Against Fields of Endeavor

   The license must not restrict anyone from making use of the program in a specific field of endeavor. For example, it may not restrict the program from being used in a business, or from being used for genetic research. (rationale)

7. Distribution of License

   The rights attached to the program must apply to all to whom the program is redistributed without the need for execution of an additional license by those parties. (rationale)

8. License Must Not Be Specific to a Product

   The rights attached to the program must not depend on the program's being part of a particular software distribution. If the program is extracted from that distribution and used or distributed within the terms of the program's license, all parties to whom the program is redistributed should have the same rights as those that are granted in conjunction with the original software distribution. (rationale)

9. License Must Not Contaminate Other Software

   The license must not place restrictions on other software that is distributed along with the licensed software. For example, the license must not insist that all other programs distributed on the same medium must be open-source software. (rationale)

10. Conforming Licenses and Certification

    Any software that uses licenses that are certified conformant to the Open Source Definition may use the Open Source trademark, as may source code explicitly placed in the public domain. No other license or software is certified to use the Open Source trademark.

(The following information is not part of the Open Source Definition, and it may change from time to time.)

The GNU GPL, the LGPL, the BSD license, the X Consortium license, the Artistic, the MPL, the QPL, the libpng license, the zlib license, and the IJG JPEG library license are examples of licenses that we consider conformant to the Open Source Definition.

To have a license reviewed for certification, write `certification@opensource.org`. We strongly encourage use of already-certified licenses from the above list, since this allows use of the Open Source mark without the need for review. Please report misuse of the Open Source mark to `mark-misuse@opensource.org`.

Change history:

> 1.0—identical to DFSG, except for addition of MPL and QPL to clause 10.
>
> 1.1—added LGPL to clause 10.
>
> 1.2—added public-domain to clause 10.
>
> 1.3—retitled clause 10 and split off the license list, adding material on procedures.
>
> 1.4—now explicit about source code requirement for PD software.
>
> 1.5—allow "reasonable reproduction cost" to meet GPL terms.

Bruce Perens wrote the first draft of this document as The Debian Free Software Guidelines, and refined it using the comments of the Debian developers in a month-long e-mail conference in June, 1997. He removed the Debian-specific references from the document to create the Open Source Definition.

Send questions or suggestions about this page to `webmaster@opensource.org`.

INDEX

SYMBOLS

A

D

G

H

J

K

L

N

O

P

S

U

V

X

Y

Z

Installing Debian GNU/Linux 2.1

Installing Debian GNU/Linux 2.1 For Intel x86

The first step of booting the Debian installation system can be accomplished with one of the following media:

- A bootable CD-ROM
- A boot loader running in another operating system
- A boot floppy

After you've booted into Linux, the dbootstrap program will launch and guide you through the second step, the initial system configuration.

Choosing Your Installation Media

First, choose the media to use to boot the installation system. Next, choose the method you will use to install the base system.

Installing from a CD-ROM

If you have a CD which is bootable, and if your system supports booting from a CD-ROM, you don't need any floppies.

1. Reboot your system. When your system starts up, you should see a message that indicates a setup program. Usually, you can access this by pressing the Delete or F2 key. In your boot device options, you should be able to choose which device should be booted from first.
2. Put Disc 1 into the drive and exit the BIOS setup program. The install program will start automatically.

If your hardware does not support bootable CD-ROMs, you should boot into DOS and execute the `boot.bat` file, which is located in the `\boot` directory on Disc 1.

Even if you cannot boot from the CD-ROM, you can install the base Debian system from the CD-ROM. Simply boot using one of the other installation techniques; when it is time to install the base system and any additional packages, just point your installation system to the CD-ROM drive.

Installing from a DOS Partition

It is possible to install Debian from an already installed DOS partition on the same machine. To do so, follow these instructions:

1. Copy the following files into a directory on your DOS partition: `resc1440.bin`, `drv1440.bin`, `base2_1.tgz`, `root.bin`, `linux`, `install.bat` and `loadlin.exe`.
2. Boot into DOS (not Windows) without any drivers being loaded. To do this, you have to press `F8` at exactly the right moment.
3. Execute `install.bat` from your chosen directory in DOS.

Writing Disk Images From DOS, Windows, or OS/2

You'll find the `rawrite2.exe` program file in the same directory as the floppy disk images. There's also a `rawrite2.txt` file containing instructions for using rawrite2.

To write the floppy disk image files to the floppy disks, first make sure that you are booted into DOS. Many problems have been reported when trying to use rawrite2 from within a DOS box in Windows. Double-clicking on rawrite2 from within the Windows Explorer is also reported not to work. If you don't know how to boot into DOS, press `F8` while booting.

1. After you've booted into DOS, use the command

   ```
   rawrite2 -f file -d drive
   ```

   where *`file`* is one of the floppy disk image files, and *`drive`* is either A: or B:, depending on which floppy drive you are writing to. You will be using the `resc1440.bin` and the `root.bin` images to set up your boot floppies.
2. Reboot your computer with the boot disk in the A: drive. The install program will start automatically.

Installing Caldera OpenLinux 2.3

Installing Caldera OpenLinux 2.3 from the CD-ROM

1. Insert the CD-ROM into the CD drive.
2. Restart your computer.
3. You may need to change your BIOS settings to boot from the CD-ROM. Typically, you enter your BIOS setup program with the F2 or Del key.
4. Make your changes (if any) and exit the BIOS setup utility.
5. If your CD drive is capable of booting from CD-ROMs, you will boot into the Caldera setup program.
6. Follow the onscreen prompts to complete the installation.

Installing Caldera OpenLinux 2.3 from DOS or Windows 95/98

1. If you are in Windows 95 or Windows 98, choose Start, Restart the computer in MS-DOS mode.
2. Navigate to your CD drive and go to the directory `\COL\LAUNCH\DOS`.
3. Type `INSTALL` and press Enter.
4. Your computer will start the Caldera setup program.
5. Follow the onscreen prompts to finish the installation.

Installing Caldera OpenLinux 2.3 from Boot Floppies

1. While in DOS or Windows, format two 1.44MB floppies or one 2.88MB floppy.
2. Navigate to your CD drive and go to the directory `\COL\LAUNCH\FLOPPY`.
3. Type `RAWRITE3` and press Enter.
4. When prompted to do so, `INSTALL.144` if you are using 1.44MB floppies, or `INSTALL.288` if you are using a 2.88MB floppy, and press Enter.
5. When prompted to do so, type in the drive letter of the disk(s) you are going to prepare and press Enter. Because you are going to be booting from this disk, it's typically A:.
6. If you are creating a 1.44MB boot disk, you need to create a second disk. Repeat step 3. When prompted to do so, type `MODULES.144` and press Enter.
7. Repeat step 5.
8. If you don't already have the boot floppy in your disk drive, insert it now.
9. Restart your computer.
10. You may need to change your BIOS settings to boot from the floppy drive. Typically, you enter your BIOS setup program with the F2 or Del key.
11. Make your changes (if any) and exit the BIOS setup utility.
12. If your computer is set up properly, you will boot into the Caldera setup program.
13. Follow the onscreen prompts to complete the installation.